GALATIANS
AND
CHRISTIAN THEOLOGY

GALATIANS AND CHRISTIAN THEOLOGY

Justification, the Gospel, and Ethics
in Paul's Letter

Edited by
MARK W. ELLIOTT
SCOTT J. HAFEMANN
N. T. WRIGHT
AND JOHN FREDERICK

Baker Academic
a division of Baker Publishing Group
Grand Rapids, Michigan

© 2014 by Mark W. Elliott, Scott J. Hafemann, N. T. Wright, and John Frederick

Published by Baker Academic
a division of Baker Publishing Group
P.O. Box 6287, Grand Rapids, MI 49516-6287
www.bakeracademic.com

Printed in the United States of America

All rights reserved. No part of this publication may be reproduced, stored in a retrieval system, or transmitted in any form or by any means—for example, electronic, photocopy, recording—without the prior written permission of the publisher. The only exception is brief quotations in printed reviews.

Library of Congress Cataloging-in-Publication Data
Galatians and Christian theology : justification, the gospel, and ethics in Paul's letter / edited by Mark W. Elliott, Scott J. Hafemann, N. T. Wright, and John Frederick.
    pages cm
Includes bibliographical references and index.
ISBN 978-0-8010-4951-4 (pbk.)
1. Bible. Galatians—Criticism, interpretation, etc. I. Elliott, M. W. (Mark W.), editor of compilation.
BS2685.52.G33 2014
227'.406—dc23   2014010592

Unless otherwise indicated, Scripture quotations are the authors' translations.

Scripture quotations labeled ESV are from The Holy Bible, English Standard Version® (ESV®), copyright © 2001 by Crossway, a publishing ministry of Good News Publishers. Used by permission. All rights reserved. ESV Text Edition: 2007

Scripture quotations labeled KJV are from the King James Version of the Bible.

Scripture quotations labeled NIV are from the Holy Bible, New International Version®. NIV®. Copyright © 1973, 1978, 1984, 2011 by Biblica, Inc.™ Used by permission of Zondervan. All rights reserved worldwide. www.zondervan.com

Scripture quotations labeled NRSV are from the New Revised Standard Version of the Bible, copyright © 1989, by the Division of Christian Education of the National Council of the Churches of Christ in the United States of America. Used by permission. All rights reserved.

Scripture quotations labeled RSV are from the Revised Standard Version of the Bible, copyright 1952 [2nd ed., 1971] by the Division of Christian Education of the National Council of the Churches of Christ in the United States of America. Used by permission. All rights reserved.

14 15 16 17 18 19 20   7 6 5 4 3 2 1

In keeping with biblical principles of creation stewardship, Baker Publishing Group advocates the responsible use of our natural resources. As a member of the Green Press Initiative, our company uses recycled paper when possible. The text paper of this book is composed in part of post-consumer waste.

Contents

Preface: Galatians and Christian Theology   ix
Abbreviations   xiv

Part 1   Justification

1. Messiahship in Galatians?   3
   N. T. Wright
2. Paul's Former Occupation in *Ioudaismos*   24
   Matthew V. Novenson
3. Galatians in the Early Church: Five Case Studies   40
   Karla Pollmann and Mark W. Elliott
4. Justification and Participation: Ecumenical Dimensions of Galatians   62
   Thomas Söding
5. Arguing with Scripture in Galatia: Galatians 3:10–14 as a Series of Ad Hoc Arguments   82
   Timothy G. Gombis
6. Martin Luther on Galatians 3:6–14: Justification by Curses and Blessings   91
   Timothy Wengert
7. Yaein: Yes and No to Luther's Reading of Galatians 3:6–14   117
   Scott Hafemann

8. "Not an Idle Quality or an Empty Husk in the Heart": A Critique of Tuomo Mannermaa on Luther and Galatians   132
    Javier A. Garcia

9. Judaism, Reformation Theology, and Justification   143
    Mark W. Elliott

10. Can We Still Speak of "Justification by Faith"? An In-House Debate with Apocalyptic Readings of Paul   159
    Bruce McCormack

Part 2 Gospel

11. The Singularity of the Gospel Revisited   187
    Beverly Roberts Gaventa

12. Apocalyptic *Poiēsis* in Galatians: Paternity, Passion, and Participation   200
    Richard B. Hays

13. "Now and Above; Then and Now" (Gal. 4:21–31): Platonizing and Apocalyptic Polarities in Paul's Eschatology   220
    Michael B. Cover

14. Christ in Paul's Narrative: Salvation History, Apocalyptic Invasion, and Supralapsarian Theology   230
    Edwin Chr. van Driel

15. "In the Fullness of Time" (Gal. 4:4): Chronology and Theology in Galatians   239
    Todd D. Still

16. Karl Barth and "The Fullness of Time": Eternity and Divine Intent in the Epistle to the Galatians   249
    Darren O. Sumner

17. "Heirs through God": Galatians 4:4–7 and the Doctrine of the Trinity   258
    Scott R. Swain

Part 3 Ethics

18. Flesh and Spirit   271
    Oliver O'Donovan

19. "Indicative and Imperative" as the Substructure of Paul's Theology-and-Ethics in Galatians? A Discussion of Divine and Human Agency in Paul   285
    Volker Rabens

20. Grace and the Countercultural Reckoning of Worth: Community Construction in Galatians 5–6   306
    John M. G. Barclay

21. Paul's Exhortations in Galatians 5:16–25: From the Apostle's Techniques to His Theology   318
    Jean-Noël Aletti

22. The Drama of Agency: Affective Augustinianism and Galatians   335
    Simeon Zahl

23. Life in the Spirit and Life in Wisdom: Reading Galatians and James as a Dialogue   353
    Mariam J. Kamell

List of Contributors   365
Subject Index   366
Scripture Index   371
Author Index   377

Preface

Galatians and Christian Theology

Reason for Being

This volume, from the St Andrews Galatians and Christian Theology Conference (2012), is the fruit of the fourth of our series of triennial Scripture and Theology conferences at the University of St Andrews. From the inception of this series back in 2003 (with a conference on the Gospel of John), the idea was to bring Scripture scholars and theologians together to try to get them to talk to one another, even if to begin with it seemed that too much of the talking was "talking past" one another. During the Genesis and Christian Theology conference (2009), the vision seemed to be realized during many of the sessions: a real attempt was made and satisfaction was experienced in the meeting of minds and even conceptualities across the biblical-theological studies divide. Yet perhaps even then we did not see as much of that interaction either in the preparation of the main papers or in what was finally produced in print as we had hoped would happen.

So it seemed to the organizers—and to the editors of this volume writing this now—delightful and significant when in July 2012 many of the biblical scholars and theologians giving the main papers had clearly taken the initiative, not only in discussion but also in the talks they prepared, to begin to occupy themselves with the writings of those on the other side of this divide. They had taken a look "to see how the other half lives." Thus discussions that followed the paper presentations began at a point further down the line than had been the case at previous conferences. McCormack, O'Donovan, and Söding struck us as those who had deliberately wandered quite some way from their home subject in order to see their own subdiscipline more clearly. (As Tom Waits sang, "I never saw the east coast until I moved to the west.") But also there were papers by biblical scholars who wanted to approach the *res*, the matter, with which the Pauline text dealt via a consideration of contextual philosophical and ethical thinking—Barclay, Rabens, and Cover in particular. The several papers by Pollmann and Elliott, Wengert, and Hafemann that looked at Galatians from the history of its interpretation, which has been by nature integrative, helped to frame the context for these cross-disciplinary discussions. That this happened with a minimum of prompting from conference organizers and editors does not mean that this volume is necessarily better than its predecessors (on John, Hebrews, and Genesis), but it is at least more integrated. In responding to Baker Academic's helpful encouragement to include several shorter papers as well as the main addresses, we are able to show that uninvited papers reinforced and enhanced the main concerns we had. This does not mean that the range of topics was censored: when we came to select the short papers, what did matter was that they attempted to "do" Scripture and theology and managed to do it in a way that we felt was promising and encouraging.

It was perhaps salutary to have a few papers that seemed unmistakably one thing or the other, but even then (in the case of papers by Wright, Gaventa, Novenson, Still, and Gombis) the question of Paul's Messiah, Paul's gospel, and Paul's Judaism are hardly nontheological questions, especially since these questions are also being asked by extracanonical texts. There were occasional moments where the theological atmosphere felt too much for the average exegete, and where perhaps theologians felt overly constrained by the need to stay close to the six chapters of Galatians. Such moments of discomfort are salutary. The last thing we wanted was a collection of essays that were of no use to the study of either Scripture or theology, just for the sake of intradisciplinarity within divinity studies. One might add that at St Andrews we are proud that the historical-exegetical and the conceptual-applicative tasks have stood together under the one heading: divinity. There might not be much of a future for such an old-fashioned sounding term, but it does the job for us. Still, the intradisciplinary process is one of attraction and repulsion, and it keeps things more honest.

Structure and Content

In terms of what is covered and the volume's structure, it was pleasing when our biblically-theologically eagle-eyed commissioning editor at Baker Academic,

Jim Kinney, saw that the material fell gracefully into three parts: Justification, Gospel, and Ethics.

When it comes to Galatians, whatever one's feeling about the amount of coverage this topic has received in recent years since E. P. Sanders on the one hand for Scripture studies (1977), and since the Roman Catholic–Lutheran *Joint Declaration on Justification* on the other hand for theology (1999), there is no escaping "Justification." But perhaps there is a going through it and beyond, even while never leaving it behind. There is a fair amount in this volume not only about Luther and Lutherans (Wengert, Zahl) but also about the patristic (Pollmann and Elliott) debates. One accusation leveled against those promoting the new perspective on Paul (NPP) was that they did not really know the Reformers. The NPP rejoinder might have been and might be that those resisting the NPP knew the Reformers all too well. These essays (esp. Wengert and Hafemann, but also Garcia and Elliott) do not stick with the Reformers for their own sake.

The NPP not only has come of age but it also now has a look of seniority. The direction that the impact of the New Yale School in theology and biblical studies and concurrent forces regarding narrative readings, biblical intertextuality, and the role of the faith community as an interpretative community would take us is to move beyond justification to something that is not reducible to that conceptuality: whether it be the Messiah and all that can be unpacked there, or "the gospel" as the heralding of an inbreaking new thing, something that transformed both Paul's thinking and the very language and style used to articulate it. In the conference and in this volume, the notions and interrelationships of eschatology, apocalyptic, covenant, and the expectation of a transformed "reading" and living community were never far from view and, when not expressed, were always just below the surface. Considering all of this involves weighing the debt to Judaism(s) and to Hellenism(s) if one is to grasp the gospel in Galatians more fully; yet it leads one as well to the meaty matters of the *ordo salutis*, as well as to issues of time, eternity, election, and God's very being as Trinity. The perceptive reader will be called to reflect on such things by the essays in this volume, even when these issues are more implicit than explicit—and this is the real strength of such integrative ventures. One might add that the question of "the faith of Jesus Christ" was never wholly absent from the discourse during the conference.

Ethics, of course, is not just a logical outworking of previous realities of the past; it is also an organic part and expression of that spiritual new thing itself, the gospel, expressed in the presence and work of the Holy Spirit as part of the dawning of the gospel in action. If one might excuse the bathos, they belong together like British fish and chips as one meal. Ethics is part of the main dish of the meal; it is not dessert or *Nachtisch*. Paul and James would have rejoiced together on this point, whatever differences they might have had (Kamell). Erasmus's instinctive insistence that the medium is the message—in other words, that the style and the content of the text are intertwined—is given more than a hearing in these later papers (e.g., Aletti). In terms of Galatians itself, those in attendance remarked about the way in which Galatians 5–6 played such an important role in the conference, in contrast to how these chapters are so often left out of the discussion as secondary.

One other observation by our colleagues at Baker Academic was that the Christian history of theology and biblical interpretation ran through so much of the gathered material that it did not need to be given a section all to itself. In other words, a strong awareness of the hermeneutical dimension is there in nearly all the papers included in this volume, and this is something that also helps to integrate the contributions.

Cross-Cultural Contribution

Bringing together Europe and America, or more accurately English-speaking and non-English-speaking worlds of scholarship, and surviving to see a successful outcome is no light task. One of the great successes was that this did not seem artificial like some blind date, but was embraced naturally by those who felt that their worlds already overlapped. The conference language was English, but we are pleased that six of our essays were written by those for whom English is not their mother tongue. Once more, thanks to all those in that category who attended, and more widely to those, wherever they were from, who concurred that the conference "seemed to run itself." That had less to do with the organization (although Beth Tracy's unflappable guiding presence should be mentioned) than with what Germans would call the *Stimmung*.

It strikes one that systematic theology (ST), if not quite having an identity crisis, is at least going through a phase of redefinition. There are a number of fine theologians working on refocusing the discipline for the future, but that a few sparkling contributions stand out on the contemporary landscape is perhaps a reflection of their paucity as well as their clarity. It could be argued that ST has done best when it has been informed by the best thinking on contemporary worldviews wedded together with the best scholarship on historical texts, beginning with the Scriptures. Nor can biblical studies rest on its laurels. At some conferences there can be an embarrassment of exegetical riches, but due to their historical isolation, they too often remain bland and unimaginative, or at best quirky, and make no contribution to how Christians ought to think and live today. When taken together, the essays in this volume attempt to offer some help on both fronts. We send these collected essays forth in the hope that they will both advance the study of their respective areas and also contribute toward the ongoing dialogue between disciplines that these conferences have attempted to foster.

M. W. Elliott
S. J. Hafemann
N. T. Wright
J. Frederick
St Andrews, August 2013

Abbreviations

General

AD	anno Domini	mg.	marginal (note)
alt.	altered	n	note
BC	before Christ	NAB	New American Bible
BCE	before the Common Era	NASB	New American Standard Version
ca.	circa, about/around		
CE	in the Common Era	NIV	New International Version
cent.	century	NJB	New Jerusalem Bible
cf.	*confer*, compare	NPP	New Perspective on Paul
chap(s).	chapter(s)	NRSV	New Revised Standard Version
ed.	edited by/editor		
e.g.	for example	NT	New Testament
Ep.	*Epistle(s)*	OT	Old Testament
esp.	especially	par.	and parallel/s
ESV	English Standard Version	rev.	revised
ET	English translation	RSV	Revised Standard Version
et al.	and others	s.v.	*sub verbo*, under the word
KJV	King James Version	trans.	translation, translated by
lit.	literally	v(v).	verse(s)
LXX	Septuagint (the Greek Old Testament)	vol./vols.	volume(s)

Old Testament

Gen.	Genesis	Num.	Numbers
Exod.	Exodus	Deut.	Deuteronomy
Lev.	Leviticus	Josh.	Joshua

Judg.	Judges	Lam.	Lamentations
Ruth	Ruth	Ezek.	Ezekiel
1–2 Sam.	1–2 Samuel	Dan.	Daniel
1–2 Kings	1–2 Kings	Hosea	Hosea
1–2 Chron.	1–2 Chronicles	Joel	Joel
Ezra	Ezra	Amos	Amos
Neh.	Nehemiah	Obad.	Obadiah
Esther	Esther	Jon.	Jonah
Job	Job	Mic.	Micah
Ps./Pss.	Psalm/Psalms	Nah.	Nahum
Prov.	Proverbs	Hab.	Habakkuk
Eccles.	Ecclesiastes	Zeph.	Zephaniah
Song	Song of Songs	Hag.	Haggai
Isa.	Isaiah	Zech.	Zechariah
Jer.	Jeremiah	Mal.	Malachi

New Testament

Matt.	Matthew	1–2 Thess.	1–2 Thessalonians
Mark	Mark	1–2 Tim.	1–2 Timothy
Luke	Luke	Titus	Titus
John	John	Philem.	Philemon
Acts	Acts	Heb.	Hebrews
Rom.	Romans	James	James
1–2 Cor.	1–2 Corinthians	1–2 Pet.	1–2 Peter
Gal.	Galatians	1–3 John	1–3 John
Eph.	Ephesians	Jude	Jude
Phil.	Philippians	Rev.	Revelation
Col.	Colossians		

Old Testament Apocrypha and Pseudepigrapha

2 Bar.	*2 Baruch*	*1–4 Macc.*	*1–4 Maccabees*
Jub.	*Jubilees*	*Sir.*	*Sirach (Ecclesiasticus)*
Let. Aris.	*Letter of Aristeas*		

Apostolic Fathers

Barn.	*Epistle of Barnabas*	Ign. *Phil.*	Ignatius, *To the Philadelphians*
Ign. *Magn.*	Ignatius, *To the Magnesians*		

Greek and Latin Works

Augustine

C. Jul.	Contra Julianum
Doctr. chr.	Christian Instruction
Enarrat. Ps.	Enarrations on the Psalms
Exp. Gal.	Exposition on the Epistle to the Galatians
Gen. lit.	Genesis Literally Interpreted
Serm.	Sermons

Cicero

Tusc.	Tusculanae disputationes

Clement of Alexandria

Strom.	Stromata [Miscellanies]

Eusebius

Hist. eccl.	Ecclesiastical History
Praep. ev.	Preparation for the Gospel

Herodotus

Hist.	Histories

Josephus

Ant.	Jewish Antiquities
J.W.	Jewish War

Libanius

Or.	Orations

Philo

Alleg. Interp.	Allegorical Interpretation
Cher.	The Cherubim
Confusion	Confusion of Tongues
Gig.	De gigantibus [The Giants]
Rewards	Rewards and Punishments

Plutarch

Cic.	Cicero

Sallust

Bell. Jug.	Bellum Jurgurthinum

Sextus Empiricus

Math.	Against the Mathematicians

Tertullian

Marc.	Against Marcion

Other Sources

AB	Anchor Bible
ABR	Australian Biblical Review
ACT	Ancient Christian Texts
AnBib	Analecta biblica
ANTC	Abingdon New Testament Commentaries
ASE	Annali di storia dell'esegesi
AugStud	Augustinian Studies
BBC	Blackwell Bible Commentaries

BDAG	W. Bauer, F. W. Danker, W. F. Arndt, and F. W. Gingrich. *Greek-English Lexicon of the New Testament and Other Early Christian Literature*. 3rd ed. Chicago: University of Chicago Press, 2000.
BETL	Bibliotheca ephemeridum theologicarum lovaniensium
BFCT	Beiträge zur Förderung christlicher Theologie
Bib	*Biblica*
BNTC	Black's New Testament Commentaries
BSac	*Bibliotheca sacra*
BSLK	*Bekenntnisschriften der evangelisch-lutherischen Kirche*. 11th ed. Göttingen: Vandenhoeck & Ruprecht, 1992.
BT	*The Bible Translator*
BWA	*The Basic Writings of Saint Augustine*. Edited by Whitney J. Oates. Vol. 1. New York: Random House, 1948.
BWANT	Beiträge zur Wissenschaft vom Alten und Neuen Testament
BZNW	Beihefte zur Zeitschrift für die neutestamentliche Wissenschaft
CBET	Contributions to Biblical Exegesis and Theology
CBQ	*Catholic Biblical Quarterly*
CBR	*Currents in Biblical Research*
CCSL	Corpus Christianorum: Series latina. Turnhout: Brepols, 1953–.
CD	Cairo Genizah copy of the *Damascus Document*
CD	*Church Dogmatics*, by Karl Barth. Translation of *Kirchliche Dogmatik* by G. W. Bromiley, T. F. Torrance et al. 4 vols. in 14. London: T&T Clark, 1932–67; and later editions, such as 1956–75.
CIJ	*Corpus inscriptionum iudaicarum*. Edited by Jean-Baptiste Frey. 2 vols. Rome: Pontifical Institute of Christian Archaeology, 1936–52.
CPF	*Christ Present in Faith: Luther's View of Justification*, by Tuomo Mannermaa. Edited by Kirsi Stjerna. Minneapolis: Fortress, 2005.
CR	Corpus reformatorum
CSEL	Corpus scriptorum ecclesiasticorum latinorum
CTQ	*Concordia Theological Quarterly*
CTR	*Criswell Theological Review*
DH	*Dignitatis Humanae*. Declaration of the Second Vatican Council, promulgated by Pope Paul VI on December 7, 1965. http://www.vatican.va/archive/hist_councils/ii_vatican_council.
DHR	Dynamics in the History of Religions
DiKi	Dialog der Kirchen
DS	Heinrich Denzinger and Adolf Schönmetzer, eds. *Enchiridion symbolorum*. 1854. 32nd ed. Freiburg im Breisgau: Herder, 1963. http://archive.org/details/enchiridionsymb00creegoog.
ECC	Early Christianity in Context
EMSP	European Monographs in Social Psychology
EQ	*Evangelical Quarterly*
ExpTim	*Expository Times*
FC	Fathers of the Church. Washington, DC: Catholic University of America Press, 1947–.
GNT	Grundrisse zum Neuen Testament
HBT	*Horizons in Biblical Theology*

HST	Handbuch systematischer Theologie
HTKNT	Herders theologischer Kommentar zum Neuen Testament
HTR	*Harvard Theological Review*
ICC	International Critical Commentary
Int	*Interpretation*
JAC	*Jahrbuch für Antike und Christentum*
JAJ	*Journal of Ancient Judaism*
JBL	*Journal of Biblical Literature*
JDDJ	*Joint Declaration on the Doctrine of Justification*, by the Lutheran World Federation and the Roman Catholic Church. Grand Rapids and Cambridge, UK: Eerdmans, 2000.
JECS	*Journal of Early Christian Studies*
JETS	*Journal of the Evangelical Theological Society*
JQR	*Jewish Quarterly Review*
JSJ	*Journal for the Study of Judaism in the Persian, Hellenistic, and Roman Periods*
JSJSup	Journal for the Study of Judaism in the Persian, Hellenistic, and Roman Periods: Supplement Series
JSNT	*Journal for the Study of the New Testament*
JSNTSup	Journal for the Study of the New Testament: Supplement Series
JTI	*Journal of Theological Interpretation*
JTS	*Journal of Theological Studies*
Judaica	*Judaica: Beiträge zum Verständnis des jüdischen Schicksals in Vergangenheit und Gegenwart*
KD	*Kerygma und Dogma*
Lampe	G. W. H. Lampe, ed. *Patristic Greek Lexicon*. Oxford: Oxford University Press, 1968.
LC 1521	*Loci communes rerum theologicarum seu Hypotyposes theologicae, 1521*, by Philipp Melanchthon. In *Melanchthons Werke*. Vol. 2.1. Edited by Hans Engelland. Gütersloh: C. Bertelsmann, 1952.
LCC	Library of Christian Classics
LCL	Loeb Classical Library
LNTS	Library of New Testament Studies
LQ	*Lutheran Quarterly*
LSJ	H. G. Liddell, R. Scott, and H. S. Jones. *A Greek-English Lexicon*. 9th ed. with revised supplement. Oxford: Oxford University Press, 1996.
LW	Luther's Works. Edited by J. Pelikan, H. T. Lehmann et al. Multivolume. Philadelphia: Fortress; Saint Louis: Concordia Pub. House, 1955–.
MB	*Melanchthon and Bucer*. Edited by Wilhelm Pauck. Library of Christian Classics. Philadelphia: Fortress, 1969.
MM	Moulton, J. H., and G. Milligan. *The Vocabulary of the Greek Testament*. London, 1930. Reprint, Peabody, MA: Hendrickson, 1997.
MT	Masoretic Text
MTS	Marburger theologische Studien
Neot	*Neotestamentica*
NICNT	New International Commentary on the New Testament

NIGTC	New International Greek Testament Commentary
NTAbh	Neutestamentliche Abhandlungen
NTD	Das Neue Testament Deutsch
NTL	New Testament Library
NTOA	Novum Testamentum et Orbis Antiquus
NTP	Novum Testamentum patristicum
NTS	*New Testament Studies*
OECS	Oxford Early Christian Studies
OSHT	Oxford Studies in Historical Theology
OTP	*The Old Testament Pseudepigrapha*. Edited by J. H. Charlesworth. 2 vols. Garden City, NY: Doubleday, 1983–85.
PG	Patrologia graeca. Edited by J.-P. Migne. 161 vols. in 165, plus index. Paris: J.-P. Migne, 1857–66. Index, 1912. http://graeca.patristica.net/#t161
ProEccl	*Pro ecclesia*
QD	Quaestiones disputatae
1QS	*Rule of the Community*, among the Dead Sea Scrolls
RevExp	*Review and Expositor*
SacEr	*Sacris erudiri: Jaarboek voor Godsdienstwetenschappen*
SC	Sources chrétiennes. Paris: Cerf, 1941–.
ScrTh	*Scripta theologica*
SEAug	Studia ephemeridis Augustinianum
SJLA	Studies in Judaism in Late Antiquity
SJT	*Scottish Journal of Theology*
SNTW	Studies of the New Testament and Its World
SP	Sacra pagina
SPhilo	*Studia philonica*
ST	See note 1 in chap. 16.
SUNT	Studien zur Umwelt des Neuen Testaments
TANZ	Texte und Arbeiten zum neutestamentlichen Zeitalter
TEH	Theologische Existenz heute
THKNT	Theologischer Handkommentar zum Neuen Testament
ThTo	*Theology Today*
TLZ	*Theologische Literaturzeitung*
TNTC	Tyndale New Testament Commentaries
TynBul	*Tyndale Bulletin*
VC	*Vigiliae christianae*
WA	Weimarer Ausgabe. D. *Martin Luthers Werke: Kritische Gesammtausgabe*. Multivolume. Weimar: H. Böhlau, 1883–2009. http://www.lutherdansk.dk/WA/D.%20Martin%20Luthers%20Werke,%20Weimarer%20Ausgabe%20-%20WA.htm.
WA BI	*Die deutsche Bibel*, in WA
WA BR	*Briefe* (Correspondence), in WA
Walch	Johann Georg Walch, ed. *Dr. Martin Luthers sämtliche Schriften*. 25 vols. St. Louis: Concordia, 1880–1910.
WBC	Word Biblical Commentary
WCC	World Council of Churches

WMANT	Wissenschaftliche Monographien zum Alten und Neuen Testament
WTJ	*Westminster Theological Journal*
WUNT	Wissenschaftliche Untersuchungen zum Neuen Testament
ZEE	*Zeitschrift für evangelische Ethik*
ZNW	*Zeitschrift für die neutestamentliche Wissenschaft und die Kunde der älteren Kirche*
ZPE	*Zeitschrift für Papyrologie und Epigraphik*
ZTK	*Zeitschrift für Theologie und Kirche*

PART 1

Justification

1

Messiahship in Galatians?

N. T. Wright

Introduction

Question and Method

My question in this essay brings together an unusual combination. Most scholars who write about Galatians pay no attention to messiahship; most who write about messiahship spend little time on Galatians. A long tradition of Pauline scholarship has assumed that Paul used the word *Christos* simply as a proper name, and even those who have allowed Paul some residual messianic meaning have not usually seen such meaning in this letter. Why, people might ask, would this letter, warning Paul's gentile converts against the attractions of Judaism, make use of such an obviously Jewish notion as messiahship? I nevertheless want to propose that Jesus's messiahship is central and vital in Galatians. For reasons of space, I shall concentrate on chapter 3 in particular.

In my proposal I am encouraged by Matthew Novenson's recent book *Christ among the Messiahs*.[1] Novenson has made a strong case for seeing *Christos* in Paul neither as a name, nor exactly as a "title," but as an "honorific," somewhat like *Augustus* in the triple phrase *Imperator Caesar Augustus*, where

---

1. Matthew V. Novenson, *Christ among the Messiahs: Christ Language in Paul and Messiah Language in Ancient Judaism* (New York: Oxford University Press, 2012).

Imperator is a title, *Caesar* the personal name,[2] and *Augustus* an honorific, adding an extra halo of meaning. Novenson wisely restricts himself to certain key texts, and though he naturally mentions Galatians (particularly 3:16), he does not venture far into its complexities.

There are problems of method and historical background in approaching a question like this, but there is no space here to set them out. In particular, I regard it as a red herring to discuss *Christos* as the possible carrier of Paul's incarnational Christology. First-century meanings of "Messiah" were varied and complex, but incarnation was not among them.[3] When we look not only at key texts but also at actual first-century men and movements who grabbed at vague royal expectations and bent them to their own purposes,[4] we see that expectation was focused primarily on the nation, not on an individual;[5] that a variety of scriptural texts was available to back up messianic claims;[6] and particularly, that though we must assume that messianic or similar movements were inevitably "political," looking for a radical change in their society, this too does not make them monochrome. A movement that beats its plowshares into swords and marches on Jerusalem is "political"; so is a movement that symbolically reenacts Joshua's entry into the land by plunging people into the Jordan.

How then can one make the case for messianism in Galatians? I begin with two preliminary points concerning large-scale features of the first-century landscape.

The Landscape

First, as I have argued before, the idea of Jesus as Messiah was alive and well, actively not merely presuppositionally, in every other form of Christianity we know in the first century, including the Gospels, Acts, Hebrews,

---

2. Which, admittedly, was already carrying an important connotation (heir to the divine Julius Caesar) as well as its denotation by the time Augustus was putting it on coins.

3. Cf. Jacob Neusner, W. S. Green, and E. Frerichs, eds., *Judaisms and Their Messiahs at the Turn of the Christian Era* (Cambridge: Cambridge University Press, 1987), a sustained polemic against uniform notions of "messiahship."

4. Cf. N. T. Wright, *The New Testament and the People of God* (London: SPCK; Minneapolis: Fortress, 1992), chap. 7.

5. "The main task of a Messiah, over and over again, is the liberation of Israel, and her reinstatement as the true people of the creator God" (ibid., 320); how this happens varies considerably: so 307-20, esp. the conclusions on 319-20. I therefore resist Novenson's suggestion (*Christ among the Messiahs*, 3n6) that I have simply picked up from earlier scholarship a monochrome messianic portrait and applied it to Paul.

6. E.g., Gen. 49:10 (the "scepter"); Num. 24:17 (the star and the scepter); 2 Sam. 7:4-17; Pss. 2; 8; 110; Isa. 11:1-10.

Revelation, and also the apostolic fathers.[7] Some who suggest that Paul must have abandoned messianic belief as irrelevant or even repellent to the wider gentile world do not seem to notice that the same should then be true for Luke, or John, or Ignatius of Antioch, and it obviously is not.[8] We recall the emperor Domitian's investigating Jesus's blood relatives on the assumption that they were part of a royal family,[9] and Josephus's referring to James as "the brother of the so-called Messiah" (had *Christos* been a mere name, one would not write "so-called").[10] The earliest church was firmly rooted in Jesus-based messianism.[11] If, therefore, Paul made no use of the messianic significance of the word *Christos*, he would be the sole exception in an otherwise universally messianic movement,[12] making it all the more peculiar that he should distinguish the word *Christos* so carefully from both *Iēsous* and *Kyrios*.[13]

Second, we must remind ourselves of the widespread and diverse Jewish practice of retelling the single ancient biblical story. The Bible itself contains such retellings, such as those in Deuteronomy, both the "wandering Aramaean" speech (in chap. 26) and the great prophetic covenant narrative

---

7. I assume that the *Gospel of Thomas* and similar texts come from the second century at the earliest; see N. T. Wright, *Judas and the Gospel of Jesus: Have We Missed the Truth about Christianity?* (London: SPCK; Grand Rapids: Baker Books, 2006).

8. This theme has been repeated with monotonous regularity, from Adolf Deissmann a century ago in *Paul: A Study in Social and Religious History* (London: Hodder & Stoughton, 1912), 133: "The dogmatic Messiah of the Jews is fettered to his native country. The spiritual Christ could move from place to place"; to several in our own day, e.g., M. Zetterholm, ed., *The Messiah in Early Judaism and Christianity* (Minneapolis: Fortress, 2007), 40.

9. See N. T. Wright, *The Climax of the Covenant: Christ and the Law in Pauline Theology* (Edinburgh: T&T Clark; Minneapolis: Fortress, 1992), 41–43. The Domitian story is in Eusebius, *Hist. eccl.* 3.19–20.

10. Josephus, *Ant.* 20.200; cf. Wright, *New Testament and the People of God*, 353–54; here we leave out of the account the famous but controversial passage about Jesus in *Ant.* 18.63–64; cf. N. T. Wright, *Jesus and the Victory of God* (London: SPCK; Minneapolis: Fortress, 1996), 439–40.

11. One can also cite the use in Antioch of *Christianoi* (Acts 11:26), which, *pace* Martin Hengel, *Between Jesus and Paul: Studies in the Earliest History of Christianity*, trans. J. Bowden (London: SCM, 1983), 72, does not mean that the word had been "firmly established . . . as a 'proper name' over a fairly long period of time."

12. Cf. John J. Collins, *The Scepter and the Star: The Messiahs of the Dead Sea Scrolls and Other Ancient Literature* (1995; New York: Doubleday, 2010), 2, describing as "astonishing" the claim of John G. Gager in *The Origins of Anti-Semitism* (Oxford: Oxford University Press, 1983) and Lloyd Gaston in *Paul and the Torah* (Vancouver: University of British Columbia Press, 1987) "that Paul did not regard Jesus as the messiah." Collins cites Rom. 1:3–4, but it is precisely the obviously messianic meaning of that passage that has led many to discount it as a statement of Paul's own position; cf. A. Chester, *Messiah and Exaltation: Jewish Messianic and Visionary Traditions and New Testament Christology* (Tübingen: Mohr Siebeck, 2007), 111n16.

13. On the distinction, see Wright, *Climax of the Covenant*, 44; and, e.g., "Romans 8:9–11" in *The New Interpreter's Bible*, ed. L. E. Keck et al., 12 vols. [Nashville: Abingdon, 1994–2004], 583–85.

in chapters 27–30. There are the psalms, particularly 105 and 106, and the Davidic psalms, which indicate the transfer of the Abrahamic promises to the royal house.[14] The prophets tell the same story, looking back to Abraham from the time of exile and looking onward to redemption. The narrative prayers of Ezra 9, Nehemiah 9, and Daniel 9 do the same, with the Daniel narrative linking up with chapters 2 and 7 to provide a long-range story of successive world kingdoms that will be overthrown by the coming kingdom of God. We know from Josephus that Daniel was being read in the first century in terms of a world ruler who would arise from Judaea.[15] The same point emerges from many Second Temple texts, both the complacent list of heroes in Sirach and the history of revolutionary zeal in 1 Maccabees 2. Works such as the Animal Apocalypse in *1 Enoch* and the historical visions of *4 Ezra* and *2 Baruch* tell the same story from different angles, as do some of the Qumran documents. We might also compare, of course, *Jubilees*, Pseudo-Philo, and many others.[16]

Six things about these narratives need to be noticed. First, they are of many types, shapes, sizes, and emphases. There is no standard model. Second, they always get the historical order right: whichever heroes or villains they choose, they know and use the full implicit narrative. Third, however they tell this story, they always perceive it not merely as an ancient story from which one might cull types and patterns, examples and warnings, but as a *single continuous story* in which they themselves are now living.

Fourth and most important, almost all these retellings of Israel's story are more about Israel's rebellion and sin, and God's judgment upon them, particularly in the exile, than they are about a smooth upward journey toward the light. (Obvious exceptions might be Psalm 105 and Sirach.) The nineteenth-century idea of immanent development has no foothold in these texts. Ancient Judaism regularly told its story in terms of persistent failure and God's fresh redemptive actions; the Abrahamic covenant was invoked not as the start of a triumphalist progression, but as the ultimate hope for grace when otherwise the story had become a nightmare. The "apocalyptic" message of most of these extremely varied Jewish texts nests within the solid and unbroken covenant theology they all evince.

Fifth, we see the same tradition of Jewish-style storytellings continuing through the first two generations of the Christian movement, not least in the

---

14. Pss. 2; 72; cf. Ps. 89.

15. Cf. Josephus, *J.W.* 6.312–15; see discussion in Wright, *New Testament and the People of God*, 312–13.

16. On all these now see N. Calduch-Benages and J. Liesen, eds., *History and Identity: How Israel's Later Authors Viewed Its Earlier History* (Berlin: de Gruyter, 2006).

Gospels, Acts, and Hebrews. The New Testament as a whole, however varied its sociocultural context, does not abandon the Jewish tradition of fresh tellings of the biblical story as a covenantal narrative that had passed through many dark and catastrophic times but was now emerging into clarity and focus because of Jesus.[17] Paul does the same in Romans 9 and 10.

Sixth, and most obviously relevant to our topic, these stories frequently point forward to a coming climactic figure, and that figure is often, admittedly not always, messianic: the warrior king in the *Psalms of Solomon*, the lion in *4 Ezra*, the fountain and vine in *2 Baruch*, arguably also the large white bull in the Animal Apocalypse, and not least the world ruler who, in first-century readings of Daniel, would arise from Judaea. One could indeed turn the point around. Not all Israel stories climax with a Messiah. Not all Messiahs, when they are there, look alike. But all Messiah narratives come at the point where an implicit Israel narrative is being resolved. They come in fulfillment of the ancient promises, especially those to Abraham, and they concern the rescue of the nation from the appalling mess into which its many rebellions have landed it.

You will see where this is going. But before we move to exegesis, let me introduce you to some statistics.

Vital Statistics

We have all learned to beware of word statistics. They can lead to mere concordance worship, or the left-brain attempt to turn theology into mathematics. Nevertheless, the word usage in Galatians does, I think, offer a straw in the wind.

If you were to ask someone reasonably biblically literate what Galatians is about, they might say "salvation from sin," "Paul's gospel," or "justification by faith." They might perhaps say "Paul's theology of the cross" or "Paul's critique of the law." Those have all been major themes in the tradition of interpreting this letter. Conversely, Galatians has regularly been invoked in discussions of soteriology, where those ideas cluster together. But the sheer numbers raise a question mark. Paul never uses *sōzein*, *sōtēr*, or *sōtēria* in Galatians. He mentions *hamartia* only three times.[18] The *dikaios* root, likewise, is comparatively

---

17. See Matt. 1; Luke 1; 24:25–27, 44–46; Acts 7; Heb. 11 (further in N. T. Wright, *Paul and the Faithfulness of God*, vol. 2 [London: SPCK; Minneapolis: Fortress, 2013]). Some have suggested that there are "embedded" scriptural narratives in James (e.g., 5:10–11, 17–18; and the mention of Abraham and Rahab in 2:21–25). This seems to be far-fetched.

18. Gal. 1:4; 2:17; 3:22; of those, 1:4 is in an opening formula, and 2:17 goes closely with the two occurrences of *hamartōlos* (2:15, 17), suggesting that the concern is there with the status of gentiles rather than with actual sin.

infrequent, as is *stauros* and *stauroō*.¹⁹ The gospel, *euangelion*, is found seven times, as is the verb *euangelizomai*, almost all in the first two chapters.²⁰

A higher strike rate occurs for *pistis*, "faith" or "faithfulness," which occurs twenty-two times, and for the law, *nomos*, which is found thirty-two times, almost as many as *ou, ouk,* and *ouch* (36x altogether), or Paul's vital connective *gar* (37x).²¹ Even *theos* is found only thirty-one times, and *pneuma* a mere eighteen. Out beyond them all is *Christos*, forty times or more (depending on variant readings), and backed up with a couple of key messianic references to Jesus as "Son of God."²² By contrast, the title *kyrios* is found only five times: twice in the opening and closing greetings, and once in the reference to James, "the Lord's brother."²³ Even the proper name "Jesus" is found only eighteen times, again allowing for variant readings. *Christos*, in other words, is far and away the most frequent term in Paul's theological vocabulary in this letter. We might contrast Romans, where we find 155 uses of *theos* and 68 of *Christos*; similar proportions occur in the two Corinthian Letters.²⁴ To find words in Galatians that occur more frequently than *Christos*, we have to look to *hymeis* in all its cases (47x) and, inevitably, *kai* and *de* (58x each).²⁵ *Christos* is not far behind even these.

Now perhaps this means nothing at all. Perhaps Paul uses *Iēsous* or *Christos* interchangeably, and here just happens more often to call him *Christos*, as a mere proper name.²⁶ But there are enough scholars who have insisted, against the trend, that Paul does use *Christos* with *active and not merely residual*

---

19. One use of *dikaios* itself (Gal. 3:11), 4 of *dikaiosynē* (2:21; 3:6, 21; 5:5), 8 of *dikaioō* (2:16 [3x], 17; 3:8, 11, 24; 5:4). We find *stauros* in 5:11; 6:12, 14; and *stauroō* in 3:1; 5:24; 6:14. The resurrection is mentioned only in the opening greeting (1:1), though it is arguably present just below the surface of the argument in many passages in the letter: see N. T. Wright, *The Resurrection of the Son of God* (London: SPCK; Minneapolis: Fortress, 2003), 219–25.

20. We find *euangelion* in Gal. 1:6, 7, 11; 2:2, 5, 7, 14; *euangelizomai* in 1:8 (2x), 9, 11, 16, 23; 4:13. The important word *epangelia*, "promise," is found 10x, with one use of the cognate verb, almost all in the second half of chap. 3: *epangelia* in 3:14, 16, 17, 18 (2x), 21, 22, 29; 4:23, 28; *epangellomai* in 3:19.

21. Two other regular connectives, *ara* and *oun*, appear only 6x each; *alla*, "but," is found 23x; the preposition *dia* occurs 19x.

22. For "Son of God," see 2:20; 4:4, 6 (and cf. 1:16).

23. See 1:3, 19; 5:10; 6:14, 18. The reference in 4:1 is part of the illustration of the young "master" of the household, which could count as an oblique advance hint for the arrival of the "Son of God" in 4:4.

24. Thus, e.g., in 1 Corinthians: *theos*, 106x, and *Christos*, 65x; in 2 Corinthians, *theos*, 79x, and *Christos* 47x; in 1 Thessalonians, *theos*, 36x, and *Christos*, 10x.

25. Counting the contracted form *kagō* for *kai egō*.

26. Thus Chester, *Messiah and Exaltation*, 114 (cf. 111), representing the majority of scholars: "The sheer quantity of usage of *Christos* in itself proves nothing." His next sentence, however, is a challenge: "What matters is the way (and contexts) in which it is used, and these suggest hardly anything specifically messianic." That depends. When a scholar resolutely puts the telescope to a blind eye, there is no knowing what signals may go unnoticed. The master at this is W. G.

messianic significance here, that his arguments do turn on this, and that we should be encouraged to look afresh at the way, and the contexts, in which the word is used.[27] That is the task to which I now turn. I shall argue, first, that *Christos* does indeed mean "Messiah" in Galatians and that this meaning is active within the argument, not merely as a residual memory; second, that the word *Christos* seems to be at the heart of Paul's incorporative ecclesiology in Galatians; and third, rather obviously granted the first two but not granted the history of scholarship, that the first of these explains the second.

Christos as "Messiah" in Galatians

My first and most important move has to do with the *narrative* that dominates Galatians. The very idea of such a narrative has often been ruled out or ascribed to Paul's opponents rather than to him. But I persist.[28] Throughout the letter, Paul regularly sees Jesus as the one in whom Israel's long, strange, and often dark narrative has come to surprising but appropriate fulfillment. The point is obvious, in the light of our earlier quick survey of biblical, Second Temple, and early Christian retellings of the story of Israel: if we discover a narrative, starting with Abraham and continuing with Moses and the law, finding itself in deep trouble but then finding a God-sent deliverer through whom promises are fulfilled after all, the trouble is resolved, and God's new age is ushered in—then, almost whatever words might be used for such a figure, the natural assumption would be that this person is Israel's Messiah. When we find, in a letter that frequently tells or alludes to that story, that the person whose arrival has brought this narrative to its appointed goal and has accomplished the promised deliverance is referred to as *Christos*, we ought to say "game over." This is the Messiah. And his messiahship means what it means within that narrative.

Kramer, *Christ, Lord, Son of God* (London: SCM, 1966), e.g., 209 on *Christos* preceded by the article: "In no case can we discover an appropriate reason for the determination."

27. Cf. N. A. Dahl, *Jesus the Christ: The Historical Origins of Christological Doctrine*, ed. D. H. Juel (Minneapolis: Fortress, 1991), chap. 1, though he seems almost to give away the farm with his first sentence: "Paul's Christology can be stated almost without referring to the messiahship of Jesus." By the end of the essay, however, he is clear that "Jesus' messiahship actually had a fundamental significance for the total structure of Paul's Christology" (22). Among Germans, interestingly, cf. Günther Bornkamm, *Early Christian Experience*, trans. P. L. Hammer (London: SCM, 1969), 76; Oscar Cullmann, *The Christology of the New Testament*, rev. ed. (1957; repr., London: SCM; Philadelphia: Westminster, 1963), 134 (though neither develops the idea in the way that I am doing); Albrecht Oepke, *Der Brief des Paulus an die Galater*, 3rd ed. THKNT (1937; Berlin: Evangelische Verlagsanstalt, 1973), 159.

28. See Wright, *Paul and the Faithfulness of God*, chap. 7.

The narrative in Galatians particularly comes in chapters 3 and 4 and is alluded to at many other points. The attempt of some to say that Paul is referring to the story of Abraham only because his opponents have forced him onto their preferred territory, and that he gives no positive sense to Israel's long history, is demonstrably flawed.[29] That is not—to use the category regularly invoked in support of such a position—how apocalyptic works. Apocalyptic writing frequently retells Israel's story, taking it through dark and gloomy pathways but pointing onward to a sudden, surprising, yet appropriate and (not least) *covenantal* resolution. So it is here: Paul is indeed an apocalyptic theologian, but "apocalyptic" does not mean "nonhistorical" or "noncovenantal."

Paul's narratival world can run back to Adam, but in Galatians he takes it back to Abraham. Galatians 3 engages with Genesis 15, where God makes the covenant with Abraham, which brings into fresh focus the original promise in Genesis 12 that in Abraham all the nations would be blessed. The question of how this can come about, granted all the barriers that appear to be in the way, is precisely the question with which Paul wrestles throughout chapter 3, until the eventual resolution in verse 29: if you are Christ's, you are Abraham's seed, heirs according to the promise. In terms both of Paul's argument and of the underlying biblical narrative, this is the QED moment. We have a miniature version of the story of Israel, working forward from Abraham, through the puzzles and problems of the law, and ending with *Christos*. How can this not be the Messiah?

The same is true of the further fresh telling of the story, this time echoing the exodus traditions, in 4:1–7. This story nests within the earlier one, a link made explicit in Genesis 15, where the "exodus" promise is part of the covenant with Abraham. Here the resolution to the problem of slavery is the sending of God's Son and then the sending of the Spirit of the Son. The obvious parallel in Romans shows that this too is clearly messianic: in Romans 8, another retelling of the exodus story, Paul draws on Psalm 2, where the Son's promised inheritance consists of the whole world.[30] Paul does not use Psalm 2 in Galatians, but its theme of *klēronomia*, "inheritance," is correlated in Galatians 3:18 with the promise to Abraham. This theme then comes at what we might call the messianic moment in the narrative in 3:29, being reaffirmed at the "inheritance" moment in the miniature exodus narrative of 4:1–7: if a son, then an heir through God (4:7).

By itself, an exodus narrative would not generate a messianic fulfillment. It was Moses who brought the people out of Egypt, under the ultimate leadership

---

29. Cf., e.g., Christopher D. Stanley, *Arguing with Scripture: The Rhetoric of Quotations in the Letters of Paul* (New York: T&T Clark, 2004), 120.

30. See Rom. 8:17–25.

of the pillar of cloud and fire. However, given the way in which, in Second Temple Judaism, the ultimate redemption was seen as a new exodus, an echo of the exodus might well point to messianic fulfillment, as in Isaiah 40–55 and indeed Daniel 9. In Second Temple literature, whether "apocalyptic" or not, if we found a passage promising a new exodus and highlighting the role of one man as instrumental in bringing it about, this would probably be the Messiah. If Paul is saying that those hopes are realized and that destiny is fulfilled, and speaks of *Christos* and/or God's Son as the one through whom this has come about, it is ridiculous to say that he did not mean the word to carry this meaning, or that this meaning was merely residual but theologically irrelevant.

A more detailed survey of Galatians 3 and 4 fills out the point. The single argument of 3:6–4:7 divides into four parts, each telling the same story in miniature.[31] In each case the story begins with the earlier history of Israel, faces the problem into which that history has run, and postulates *Christos* as the one through whom the problem has been resolved and the original purpose fulfilled. In each case there are much stronger echoes of Genesis 15 than are usually brought out. Of course, the passage is regularly regarded as a tour de force on Paul's part, making texts and words dance about in a manner we find fanciful and unhistorical. This is normally explained in terms of Paul's rabbinic methods of exegesis; yet even if this were the right way to approach the passage, the result would still stand. The more rabbinic we make Paul, the more we would know that when he wrote *Christos* he meant "Messiah."[32]

The context in Genesis offers many clues to a different and less apparently arbitrary way of reading the chapter, to which we shall return. For the moment we look at the three stages of Galatians 3.

Starting in 3:6, Paul states the promise and then poses the problem: God's purpose is to bless the world through Abraham, but the curse of the Torah has intervened to block this intention. For our purpose we simply note that in 3:10–14 it is *Christos* who has come to set it all right, to enable the original divine purpose to be fulfilled despite the blockage.[33]

---

31. There is no space here to explore the structural balance of the segments, but it is noticeable that Gal. 3:6–14 has 150 words; 3:15–22 has 156; 3:23–29 with 87 is much shorter; and 4:1–7 has an additional 100 words. Did Paul perhaps think of 3:23–4:7 as a unit, making three similar units (150; 156; 187 words), flanked by an introduction (3:1–5, with 62 words) and conclusion (4:8–11, with 51 words)? Or four units (150; 156; 87; 100 words), with that introduction and conclusion?

32. See, e.g., Deissmann, *Paul*, 105; Philip F. Esler, *Galatians* (London and New York: Routledge, 1998), 193. Even James Dunn in *A Commentary on the Epistle to the Galatians*, BNTC (London: A&C Black, 1993), 184, who wants to rescue Paul from the charge of arbitrary or fanciful exegesis, explains the argument as "thoroughly rabbinical."

33. See Wright, *Climax of the Covenant*, chap. 7.

The same is true in the more complicated passage 3:15–22,[34] for which we need a firm grasp on Genesis 15, which Paul is expounding. God promises Abraham a reward, understood in terms of his inheritance (*klēronomia*), both human and geographical. The promise is then spelled out and repeated (15:4): Abraham's own physical offspring will inherit. God then invites Abraham to contemplate the stars and declares, "so shall your seed be," *houtōs estai to sperma sou*—in other words, your family will be uncountable (Gen. 15:5 LXX). This is the promise that Abraham believed, with the consequence that "it was reckoned to him as righteousness" (Gen. 15:5, quoted already in Gal. 3:6). The theme of *klēronomia* is repeated again and again (many translations fail to bring this out), and this is the point of the covenant that is then made. Abraham's *sperma* will be slaves for four hundred years, but then they will be rescued and will finally gain their *klēronomia*. Thus when Paul speaks of a *diathēkē* in Galatians 3:15, continues to speak of the *sperma* and the *klēronomia* in the following verses, and mentions the length of time between the promise and the Torah, it seems perverse to deny that he is expounding the themes of covenant, seed, and inheritance as we find them in Genesis 15. This is especially so when we glance ahead to Galatians 3:29 and see that those are the terms in which he sums up the whole chapter.

We should then interpret Galatians 3:15–22 in parallel to 3:6–14: God makes promises, the Torah gets in the way, but God's initial purpose will be realized. And the point of all this for our present argument is verse 16: the terms of the covenant do not specify a plurality of families, but a single family, "who is Christ," *hos estin Christos*.[35] Postponing again the particular puzzles here, we merely note that once again *Christos* is the final moment in the implicit narrative. This is then picked up at the conclusion of the paragraph in 3:22, where the *Christos* that inherits the promise is further defined in terms of *pistis*, picking up the *pistis* of Abraham in 3:6–9. Again we should be clear that we are looking at a narrative, from Abraham to the present time, which (like so many of the Second Temple retellings of the story) passes through a dark and puzzling phase but arrives at resolution. For Paul, the marker of that resolution is *Christos*. In terms of the implicit Jewish narrative, there is every reason why this should mean "Messiah" and no reason why it should not. The absence of messiahship in scholarship on Galatians is directly related to the screening out of Paul's retelling of the scriptural story.[36]

---

34. See ibid., chap. 8.
35. This is the point, not least, of the much-puzzled-over 3:19–20, on which see ibid., chap. 8.
36. What is more, the argument of 3:16–22 has drawn attention to a double feature of Gen. 15 that becomes prominent in Gal. 4:1–7 as slavery and freedom: (1) Abraham's slave may have looked as though he was to inherit, but in fact Abraham's own son will do so. (2) Abraham's

What about the promise of the land? Paul has not spiritualized this promise, as so many have assumed.[37] The clue is in Romans 4 and 8, and in their retrieval of the messianic promises in Psalms 2 and 72: the whole world is now God's holy land, subject to the rule of the Messiah. Thus, despite the blockages put in its way, the Abrahamic promise on the one hand has come through the new exodus and on the other hand has come through the messianic figure whose presence demands the extension of the promise from land to world. The figure so designated in Scripture is the son of David, who is the Son of God; in Galatians, it is the *Christos*, who is the Son of God. It becomes increasingly clear not only that when Paul writes *Christos* here he means "Messiah" but also that this meaning is more than a mere background acknowledgment of a now irrelevant reality. Paul's argument makes the sense it does only on the basis that this *Christos* really is Israel's Messiah, the anointed Davidic king. Take that away and we are left with somewhat problematic proof texts for an argument about something else.

All this comes to a head in 3:23–29. Paul does not now begin with Abraham, but with the blockage that has stood in the way both of the promises and of their *pistis* fulfillment, as in 3:22. The Torah kept Israel under lock and key (3:22), under the close supervision one might give to a young and unruly child (3:25), until the eschatological moment. And the arrival at the eschatological moment is described as *eis Christon* (3:24). Again, faced with an implicit Jewish narrative that arrives at an eschaton and finds a particular character there, we might expect that character to be either the Messiah or someone approximating thereto, and when the word used to designate this figure is *Christos*, we should look for no other alternatives. It makes no sense to deny that for Paul this word here means "Messiah," or to suggest that messiahship plays no significant role in Paul's argument.

The final step in this part of our own argument is provided by 4:1–7. Here Paul tells the new version of the exodus narrative in order (among other things) to work toward his designed conclusion in 4:8–11, where, as in the exodus itself, the redemptive action unveils the full and true character of God himself, over against all pagan idols.[38] And for a fourth and final time,

---

descendants, his *sperma*, will be slaves in a foreign land and will then be brought out and given their inheritance at last.

37. E.g., W. D. Davies, *The Gospel and the Land: Early Christianity and Jewish Territorial Doctrine* (Berkeley: University of California Press, 1974), 161–220. Cf. the critique in Walter Brueggemann, *The Land: Place as Gift, Promise, and Challenge in Biblical Faith* (Philadelphia: Fortress, 1977), 170–83.

38. Cf. Exod. 3:6, 13–15. Note that Exod. 3:16–22 harks back to Gen. 15: the promise of the land of the Canaanites, the rescue from the enslaving nation, the coming out with great possessions, etc.

the narrative comes to its climax with a particular figure. This time, however, the figure is not called *Christos*; he is called *huios theou*, Son of God; and he bestows "sonship," *huiothesia*, on those who receive "the Spirit of the Son," so that they are no longer slaves, but sons. And in case we might forget, "if sons, then heirs," *klēronomoi*. Like the Abrahamic promise that would come true when the sins of the Amorite were at last full,[39] so this promise came true "when the fullness of time had come," *hote de ēlthen to plērōma tou chronou* (4:4). Paul is not embarrassed, as some of his readers have been, at a chronological sequence that ends with a final fulfillment. Indeed, he has been developing the idea, in line with Genesis and Exodus, on and off throughout the chapter. The chronological sequence of Israel's history, starting with Abraham and surmounting all the problems and challenges on the way, has reached its fullness. Any Second Temple Jew would know that the figure who then emerges as the agent of that fulfillment might well be the Messiah. When Paul calls this figure *Christos*, we should take him seriously.

Our preliminary conclusion, then, is that *Christos* in Galatians 3 and 4 really does refer to Jesus as Israel's Messiah, through whom the One God has accomplished the long-awaited liberation. The word cannot be reduced to the status of a name, or even of a name with residual (but theologically irrelevant) memory of an earlier titular meaning.

This leads to my second basic point: that *Christos* in Galatians, whether or not it carries positive messianic meaning, is the vehicle for Paul's *incorporative* or *participatory* vision of the people of God.

Christos and Incorporation or Participation

Galatians contains some of the best-known statements of Paul's theology of incorporation or participation. This category, increasingly recognized as central, has nevertheless proved difficult to understand. My own proposal on that front follows from my central argument here, but for the moment we simply note the way in which, within the argument of Galatians 3 and 4, this incorporation or participation focuses on *Christos*.

Galatians 3:24-29 offers a whole range of *Christos*-based incorporative language. Beginning with verse 24, we noted earlier that the long-awaited fulfillment of the Abrahamic promises has arrived through a historical sequence that leads *eis Christon*. This results in justification on the basis of

---

39. Gen. 15:16 LXX, *anapeplērōntai*.

pistis, in being no longer under the *paidagōgos* of Torah (3:25).[40] But this is explained, not in terms of a forensic scheme as in Romans 3, but in terms of *incorporation into Christos*, as a result of which believers are said to be "sons of God" (3:26).[41] This in turn is further explained (*gar*) by the fact that they have *entered this incorporative reality* by being baptized *eis Christon* and by *putting on Christos* (3:27), also presumably at the time of baptism. *Christos* seems to be, for Paul, a kind of flexible receptacle into which people come, whether by plunging into the water, which (as in Rom. 6) symbolizes his death, or by putting him on like a suit of clothes. Once that has happened, they are then "in him." Some have made heavy weather of the different prepositions and cases, but so far this seems straightforward to me.

This complex statement of believers' eschatological identity (3:24–27) then leads to the real crunch of Paul's argument. It is stated in two points, one negative and the other positive, both vital for the whole argument of the letter, both again incorporative, and both again having *Christos* as the focus of that incorporation. Negatively (3:28), the distinctions of Jew and Greek or slave and free have become irrelevant, and even the two-sided creation of male and female is beside the point; Paul, obviously, is referring both to the divided table fellowship in Antioch and the threatened imposition of the male-only rite of circumcision in Galatia.[42] These divisions have been left behind, he says, because "you are all one in *Christos*" (3:28b). Then comes the positive point in 3:29, building on that explanatory clause of 3:28b: "If you are *Christou*, you are Abraham's *sperma*, and in accordance with the promise you are *klēronomoi*." This obviously picks up the key points of 3:16–22, and with it the meaning of Genesis 15: the promise of the single *sperma*, which is not to be thwarted by Torah's divisive work, and the resulting Abrahamic and, indeed, messianic inheritance. The fulcrum of this dense final statement, too, remains *Christos*: the *ei de* at the start of verse 29 indicates that Paul intends the genitive *Christou* to carry the same meaning as *en Christō* at the end of 3:28. Paul's whole argument has been that the Galatian Christians are already part of the family of Abraham. He has made the point by telling the story from Abraham to the present, from one angle after another, always bringing that great biblical narrative to its goal in terms of *Christos*.

---

40. This move from a kind of slavery to implicit freedom is the same move that we note in 4:1–7 and again in 4:21–5:1.

41. I use the surely not gender-specific "sons," rather than, say, "children," to resonate with Paul's exposition esp. as it arrives in 4:1–7 and with, e.g., Exod. 4:22.

42. Might it also have been the case that several of the gentile converts were slaves, while the Jewish believers were free?

Standing back from this tightly packed argument, we see preliminarily what has happened. The narrative sequence of the Abrahamic promises and their fulfillment has expressed that fulfillment in terms of *Christos*, not simply in the sense of an individual Messiah whose arrival and achievement mark the goal of the story and the accomplishment of redemption and liberation, but in the sense of an incorporated body, a whole in whose identity believers participate. The single family, the *klēronomia* promised to Abraham, was the goal toward which the promises had always been aiming. Paul has given that single Abrahamic family a name: *Christos*. How does this work?

As we saw, Paul is here expounding Genesis 15 in its entirety. He is reading it in the light of other passages such as 12:3[43] and the various repetitions of the promise concerning the "seed" that will inherit the land.[44] The "seed," indeed, carries much of the load both in Genesis 15 and in Galatians 3, and it is here, particularly in Galatians 3:16–22, that my proposal solves the double problem of 3:16.[45]

First, it is routinely forgotten that throughout the Genesis passages the collective noun *sperma* means not simply "descendants," as though the *sperma* were simply a collocation of individuals, but more specifically "family." That is the perfectly good English collective noun corresponding to *sperma*.[46] Ironically, commentators often point out the collective meaning of *sperma* in order to criticize Paul for apparently ignoring it in 3:16, failing to see that it is precisely the collective or corporate meaning that Paul intends in the chapter as a whole. People regularly take Paul to task for his apparently individualizing exegesis of *sperma*, and then continue to read the passage as being about something else, as though *hos estin Christos* is simply a fancy and perhaps fanciful way of getting from the distant patriarch to the all-important Savior. Perhaps it is we who have individualized Paul's meaning.

Second, commentators on 3:16 have also usually ignored the fact that here Paul is building toward the chapter's climax, in which the word *Christos* is used incorporatively six times in the final six verses. The meaning of *Christos* here really does seem to be "the people of God," "the people promised to Abraham," and tellingly in the final verse, "the promised *sperma*." These two problems—ignoring the meaning of "family" for *sperma*, and ignoring the obvious incorporative meaning of *Christos* at the end of the chapter—cancel

---

43. Quoted in Gal. 3:8; cf. too Gen. 18:18.
44. Gen. 13:15; 17:8; 24:7.
45. For what follows, see Wright, *Climax of the Covenant*, chap. 8.
46. One might speculate on why this has been avoided; perhaps it is because of the assumption that Galatians as a whole is talking only about the salvation of individuals, not the identity of the church.

each other out and provide an excellent, if striking, exegesis of 3:16. Paul is well aware of, and intends, the collective meaning of *sperma* and lines it up precisely with the incorporative meaning of *Christos*. But if that collective meaning is "family," it can also have its own plural, "families." This offers a straightforward reading of 3:16: the promises did not say "to your families," as though referring to two or more families, but to one, "to your family"—*hos estin Christos*, which is *Christos*. The end of the chapter should leave us in no doubt that this does not mean "which is the single person Jesus," but rather, "which is the single *Christos* in whom the people are now incorporated."[47]

I submit that if it had not been for that final phrase *hos estin Christos*—and for the useful role it has played in enabling scholars to laugh up their sleeves at Paul's apparently bizarre exegetical habits![48]—there need have been little controversy about 3:16, or about Paul's whole sequence of thought. God made the promises to Abraham and his family, singular, not his "families," plural. This is of obvious and immediate relevance both to the Antioch incident in chapter 2, where the action of Peter and Barnabas implied that there were, after all, two families, and to the specifically Galatian situation, where the actions of the agitators likewise implied that uncircumcised gentile Christians were part of a family separate from Jewish Christians. We must therefore suppose that Paul is happy to use the word *Christos* to refer to *a collective, an incorporative whole*. That is what God promised Abraham, and nothing can stand in its way. Hence 3:19–20: Torah, given by God through the hand of Moses the mediator, could not by itself create the single seed, but "he is not the mediator of the one," of the singular *sperma*. God is one, however, and as in Romans 3:29, he therefore promised and will produce a single family of Jews and gentiles together. God will therefore deal with the blockage that Torah places between the Abrahamic promises and their fulfillment. The result is that now, as in 3:22, the promise is given *to believers* on the basis of the *pistis Iēsou Christou*. This explanation of the incorporative or participatory sense of *Christos* is confirmed elsewhere in the letter.[49]

---

47. Paul seems to assume that his hearers know already, without the later explanation, that *Christos* carries this incorporative meaning. He is, to be sure, capable of teasing people by saying something cryptic and explaining it only later, but since 3:17–22 depends on this point being grasped (hence the confusion among commentators who misunderstand 3:16 when they then get to 3:19–20!), we must assume that he thinks the point will be clear.
48. Cf. Stanley, *Arguing with Scripture*, 183: "Did Paul really expect the Galatians to be impressed by his argument from the singular form of the Greek noun 'seed' in Galatians 3:16?"
49. There are the typical uses of *en Christō*, as in 1:22 (the *ekklēsiai* of Judaea that are "in Christ," differentiated presumably from the ordinary non-Christian Jewish synagogues in the region). There are the sharp warnings of 5:1–6, where Paul speaks of the benefits that *Christos* gives, which would be lost if one were to be separated *apo Christou*, and where he repeats in

We must conclude that the incorporative or participatory sense of *Christos* has come to be used as a shorthand for "the church" or "the people of God"—though, of course, the people of God have been radically redefined by Paul, not least here in Galatians. The fulfillment of the Abrahamic promises has been no smooth crescendo, no easy ascent into the light, no straight path leading to glory. It has been a matter of shocking, startling, world-changing divine action—as the promises had always foretold. The only way the covenant can be fulfilled is through apocalypse, though the converse of this is that the One God, when unveiling the new reality, makes it clear that this had been in mind from the start.

So how does this notion of "incorporation" or "participation" actually work? And what must we say about the relationship between the two points we have now established, on the one hand that Paul says *Christos* because he is thinking of Jesus as Israel's promised Messiah, and on the other hand that when he says *Christos* he is thinking of this figure as the one in whom God's single family, promised to Abraham, is now summed up? The obvious answer has long been resisted but now, I suggest, should be obvious: for Paul, the Messiah represents his people. They are summed up "in him." When God looks at the *Christos*, he sees all those who belong to him, who have come "into him" in baptism, who are "clothed with him," who are "one in him"—and who, in particular, have died and risen with him, as in 2:19–20. To risk an overused word, he constitutes their *identity*. They are, in other words, "Israel," Abraham's family.[50] Incorporation and participation are central Pauline ways of speaking about the church; for him, the church is Israel, and that identity is focused on Israel's Messiah. To expound this we need a new section.

Messiah and Israel: The Heart of Paul's Participatory Soteriology

These themes have been largely ignored for two reasons. First, the subject of Galatians has been assumed to be soteriology, whereas it is in fact ecclesiology, the definition of God's single family and the struggle to maintain that identity in the face of sharp pressure. (Soteriology is, of course, presupposed.) Second, Pauline soteriology, especially here, has been identified in terms of

---

a different form the point of 3:29: *en Christō Iēsou* neither circumcision nor uncircumcision matters, but rather "faith working through love" (5:2, 6). And the genitive in 3:29a is repeated in 5:24: *hoi tou Christou*, those who belong to *Christos*, have crucified the flesh with its passions and desires.

50. See Dahl, *Jesus the Christ*, 21: "Because Jesus is the Messiah, the ones who believe in him are the 'saints' of the end of time, the *ekklēsia* of God, the true children of Abraham, and part of the 'Israel of God.'" See further Wright, *Paul and the Faithfulness of God*, chaps. 11 and 15.

"justification by faith," and so it has been defined as the polar opposite of a Jewish scheme of thought identified in terms of "justification by works," with the result that "Paulinism" itself has been seen as the polar opposite of "Judaism." In consequence, Jewish categories of thought—messiahship, patriarchs, covenants, "Israel" itself—have been seen as part of "the problem," the thing Paul is reacting against. To the contrary, what we have here is a radically redefined Jewish ecclesiology—something that, on both counts, Protestant exegesis has neither wanted nor recognized.

What then is the connection between *Christos* as "Messiah" and *Christos* as "the one in whom God's people are incorporated, the one in whom they participate"? Here again, what seems obvious to some of us has been resisted or simply ignored. On the evidence of this letter alone, it looks as though the Messiah *represents* Israel, represents Abraham's family. As we noted before, in first-century movements various leaders shaped their *individual* profiles and propaganda to the *national* aspirations. Messiahship varied according to the type of national hope of which it was a function. There is then fluidity of thought between king and nation, the one and the many. If we had no other evidence for this, Galatians 3:16 in the light of 3:24–29 should have provided enough to clinch the point.

Part of the problem, I think, is that after earlier attempts to understand something that was called "corporate personality," associated with writers such as H. Wheeler Robinson, a reaction has set in, especially within an individualist and Protestant mind-set. The long-running investigations of Paul's "in Christ" language have not produced any startling successes, though the promise to Abraham ("*in you* all the nations will be blessed"), echoed in the promises to Isaac and Jacob, has been plausibly suggested as a possible source, especially when "in your seed" is added to "in you."[51] Some might suggest that because Paul saw the *Christos* as the true *sperma Abraam*, he was then able to develop his distinctive *en Christō* and related language from that Abrahamic beginning.

This seems to me less likely than the other way around. I suspect that the line of derivation may have gone from (1) an awareness of God's purposes for his people being summed up in the Messiah to (2) a way of highlighting their original basis in the Abrahamic promises. In Paul's mind the most obvious link between the Messiah and the people of God is the resurrection. God has done for Jesus in the middle of history—the Jesus who has been crucified as a messianic pretender!—what Paul had expected God to do for all Israel at the

---

51. Alexander J. M. Wedderburn, "Some Observations on Paul's Use of the Phrases 'in Christ' and 'with Christ,'" *JSNT* 25 (1985): 83–97. See Gen. 12:2–3, "in you"; 18:18, "in him"; 22:18, "in your seed"; 26:4 (to Isaac), "in your seed"; 28:14 (to Jacob), "in you and in your seed."

end.[52] The demonstration at Easter that Jesus really was and is Messiah is thus simultaneously the demonstration that he really was and is Israel in person. It is this realization, I suggest, that sparked Paul's view of Jesus as both Messiah and the incorporative representative of Israel. I would be happy to see indications of fluidity between king and people anywhere in ancient Judaism, but with such evidence either absent or controversial, I would settle for the hypothesis that the resurrection itself generated this link in Paul's mind. We should not be afraid of postulating radical innovation, especially since belief in Jesus's messiahship is so clearly bound up with belief in his resurrection, which itself provided the unanticipated shock of a partially inaugurated eschatology. If Israel's God has done for Jesus what he was to have done for the people as a whole, that might well generate a new manner of incorporative speech, with a long-range analogy to Abraham and a more specific analogy to David. That implicit narrative has a lot going for it, not only in Paul. When, therefore, in Galatians we meet at the same moment (1) a *Christos* in and through whom God's eschatological rescuing purposes are effected and (2) a *Christos* in whom God's people participate and are summed up, one who is the *sperma Abraam*, in whom his people become "inheritors" of the promise, we are entitled to declare our own QED. It is *because* Jesus is the anointed king of Israel that he thus represents and incorporates the single family of Abraham. Messiahship is central, and theologically load bearing, for the entire argument.

We are therefore in a position, on the basis of Galatians alone, to answer the question posed by Ed Sanders toward the end of *Paul and Palestinian Judaism*.[53] Paul's thought hinges, he says, on "participation in Christ," but he has no theory to propose as to how this concept works. The answer lies partly in Paul's Israel-shaped ecclesiology, partly in the incorporative meaning that Paul gives to *Christos*, and wholly in the combination of the two. To belong to the Messiah is to belong to Israel, and vice versa. That is more or less exactly what Paul says in Galatians 3:29.

All this would enable us, but for the constraints of space, to move back at last to 2:15–21, where Paul states in a dense, allusive, but rhetorically charged summary what has happened in and through the Messiah. If the Messiah represents Israel, to belong to this "Israel" one must follow the Messiah, specifically in his *pistis*, which is the one and only badge of membership in the single family. Because the Messiah has died and been raised, to belong to "Israel" one

---

52. On the "messianic" charge against Jesus, see, e.g., Martin Hengel, *Studies in Early Christology* (Edinburgh: T&T Clark, 1995), 41–58; Wright, *Jesus and the Victory of God*, chap. 11; idem, *Resurrection of the Son of God*, 559–63.

53. E. P. Sanders, *Paul and Palestinian Judaism: A Comparison of Patterns of Religion* (London: SCM, 1977), 522–23.

must die and rise with him. This incorporative death and resurrection mean that the Messiah's people die to the "flesh," where circumcision is the marker, and come "alive to God," to the One God, who desires the single family. The continuous narrative from Abraham to the Messiah is anything but smooth and easy. It is marked, all through, by the cross.[54] But it is a narrative nonetheless.

At the climax of chapter 2, however, Paul brings in two apparently quite different meanings, or at least implications, of *Christos*. First, the new life that the believer possesses is not a return to the previous identity: "Nevertheless I live; yet not I, but *the Messiah lives in me.*" This is not the same thing as "being in the Messiah." To be "in the Messiah" is a matter of *status*, of who one is in God's eyes. To have the Messiah living within one is a matter of actual, personal, inner transformation.[55] The Galatian believers are already *en Christō*. That is the basis of Paul's argument. But he can still speak of himself as a mother being in labor with them once more, not until they come right *into the Messiah*, but until the Messiah is fully formed *in them* (4:19).[56] Elsewhere Paul says the same thing by talking of the Spirit, or the Spirit of the Son.[57] This transformation ("*theōsis*," indeed, if you will) is vital for Paul, and it is effected through the Messiah's transformative indwelling. It is not the same thing either as "being in Christ" or as the "justification" that takes place through that new status.[58]

There remains a fourth and final messianic meaning, which emerges at last in 2:20: "The life I do still live in the flesh, I live within the faithfulness of the Son of God, who loved me and gave himself for me." Here, as in 4:4, there should be no doubt that "Son of God" means "Messiah."[59] Equally, again as in 4:4 and Romans 8:3, the Son is the one who, sent from the Father, embodies and enacts the Father's own love.[60] Sometimes Paul can speak, as here, about the Messiah's love, and sometimes about God's love expressed in the sending and death of the Messiah.[61] This makes sense only with an implicit but very

---

54. This is exactly borne out by the equally cutting remarks, and their christological content in particular, in Gal. 5:2-7 and 6:11-16.

55. A long line, going back at least to Deissmann, *Paul*, 123-28, has seen the expressions as interchangeable; but this, in line with Deissmann's overall project, collapses "theology" into "religion."

56. See Beverly R. Gaventa, *Our Mother Saint Paul* (Louisville: Westminster John Knox, 2007), 29-39.

57. In this letter, Gal. 4:6; elsewhere, e.g., Rom. 8:9-11.

58. Against, e.g., Michael J. Gorman, *Inhabiting the Cruciform God: Kenosis, Justification, and Theosis in Paul's Narrative Soteriology* (Grand Rapids: Eerdmans, 2009).

59. As in Ps. 2 and elsewhere.

60. This is central to the very similar argument in Rom. 5:6-9, esp. 5:8: God demonstrates his own love for us in that the Messiah died for us while we were still sinners.

61. Cf. Rom. 8:31-32, 35, 37, 39.

high Christology. It is nonsense to say that God loved people so much that he sent someone else to do the difficult job.[62] None of this, in Galatians 2 or elsewhere, is said simply for the sake of defining who Jesus really was and is, vital though it is to get that clear. It is said in order to ground the new messianic reality—the Israel reality, the reality of Abraham's single family—in the action and the very life of Israel's God.[63]

Certain scholars have attempted to explain the rise of incarnational Christology on the basis of sundry figures in Jewish writings who seem to have occupied a suprahuman status: angels, other mediator figures, maybe even messiahs.[64] I do not find this helpful. The Jewish texts in question are not so clear. There is no indication in the New Testament that anyone was saying, in effect, "Ah, well, if Jesus was or is Messiah, then perhaps that means he is God incarnate." The evidence points in the other direction. The forgotten element in New Testament Christology is the forgotten element in Second Temple eschatology: Israel's God himself had promised that he would come back in person, to deal with Israel's exile and the world's injustice. The "second coming" of Jesus borrows biblical and Jewish language about the coming of Israel's God; so too, I suggest, does the "first coming." I do not see in pre-Christian Judaism any indication that people were anticipating a divine Messiah. I see two things: (1) a longing for Israel's God to return in rescuing power and judgment; and (2) a hope, expressed in some circles though not others, for a Messiah who would, at the most, be the specially accredited agent of this God at that moment. Paul, I believe, creatively combined these two strands; the title "Son of God," up to this point indicating either Israel or the Messiah, is the place where we can watch this combination happening. It is not a matter of earlier figures who might conceivably stretch upward toward some kind of divinity. It is a matter of Israel's God's "sending forth his Son," revealing—as part of the shocking apocalypse!—that messiahship, like image-bearing humanness itself, was all along a category designed, as it were, for God's own use. I see no indication that anyone had thought like this in pre-Christian Judaism. I see every sign that Paul grasped this point and wove it into the very heart of his highly charged and passionate letters.

Thus the multiple interlocking meanings of *Christos* in Galatians, all held within the basic meaning of messiahship in terms of bringing Israel's narrative

62. As in Rom. 9–11, Jesus is Israel's Messiah according to the flesh and also "God over all, blessed forever," and in that dual but still totally messianic identity, he is both the *telos nomou* and the *kyrios pantōn*: Rom. 9:5 (with echoes of 1:3–4); 10:4, 12.

63. See esp. Gal. 4:9: "now that you have come to know God, or rather be known by God."

64. See particularly W. Horbury, *Jewish Messianism and the Cult of Christ* (London: SCM, 1998).

to its God-ordained climax and summing up God's people in himself, hold together what later theology would see as the objective and subjective poles of God's saving action. Those categories, though, like "divinity" and "humanity," are far too abstract and bloodless to do justice to Paul's passionate prose. Once we recognize that throughout Galatians Paul really does mean "Messiah" when he calls Jesus *Christos*, and with that meaning he has specifically in mind *both* the Messiah's bringing of Israel's long story to its strange, revolutionary, and indeed "apocalyptic" climax *and* his representative summing up of his people in himself, we see how a great many otherwise puzzling features of his theology fit together in mutually supporting sense.

For that, however, we need a final concluding section.

Conclusion: Messiahship and Pauline Theology

Out of many possible concluding points, I here highlight only two. First, there is after all no distinction in Paul's mind between two types of thinking, "juridical" on the one hand, and "participationist" on the other. Just as those other false polarizations, "covenant" and "apocalyptic," belong firmly together, so when Paul speaks of being "justified in Christ," we should take him at his word. "Participation," for Paul, is ecclesiological, containing within it the juridical soteriology that Paul develops elsewhere. And all is messianic.

Second, if Jesus really was Israel's Messiah, we are bound to raise the question of Messiah in a political sense. Galatians does not emphasize Jesus as *kyrios*. But it does warn against "another gospel" (1:6). The only "other gospel" for which we have any evidence in the world of first-century Anatolia was the gospel of Caesar and Rome. Whether it was Ancyra or Pisidian Antioch that was the center of Paul's "Galatia," the title of the most recent archaeological survey of Pisidian Antioch says it all: "Building a New Rome."[65] Once we have "justification" and "participation" properly related to each other, perhaps it is time to ask once more about "gospel" and "empire."[66]

---

65. E. K. Gazda and D. Y. Ng, *Building a New Rome: The Imperial Colony of Pisidian Antioch (25 BC–AD 700)* (Ann Arbor, MI: Kelsey Museum of Archaeology, 2011).

66. See, e.g., Justin K. Hardin, *Galatians and the Imperial Cult* (Tübingen: Mohr Siebeck, 2008); Brigitte Kahl, *Galatians Re-Imagined: Reading with the Eyes of the Vanquished* (Minneapolis: Fortress, 2010); and an increasing number of others, though not without some strong protests, e.g., J. M. G. Barclay, *Pauline Churches and Diaspora Jews* (Tübingen: Mohr Siebeck, 2011), chap. 19 (discussed in Wright, *Paul and the Faithfulness of God*, chap. 12).

2

Paul's Former Occupation in *Ioudaismos*

MATTHEW V. NOVENSON

Paul and Judaism

Modern New Testament studies is positively littered with treatments of the topic "Paul and Judaism."¹ Arguably the most important book in Pauline studies in the last half century was one titled *Paul and Palestinian Judaism*, which was itself in part a response to another influential volume titled *Paul and Rabbinic Judaism*.² As I write these words, we have just seen the release of Thomas G. Casey and Justin Taylor's edited volume *Paul's Jewish Matrix* and Reimund Bieringer and Didier Pollefeyt's edited volume *Paul and Judaism*.³ Lest one think that this is merely a preoccupation of Anglophone scholarship, from the European continent we have, for instance, Gerd Lüdemann's *Paulus*

---

1. To which the present essay is now an addition. I received valuable feedback on an earlier draft from John Barclay, Mark Elliott, Beverly Gaventa, and N. T. Wright. The essay is much improved thanks to their careful attention, and any remaining deficiencies are my own responsibility.
2. E. P. Sanders, *Paul and Palestinian Judaism: A Comparison of Patterns of Religion* (Philadelphia: Fortress, 1977); W. D. Davies, *Paul and Rabbinic Judaism: Some Rabbinic Elements in Pauline Theology* (London: SPCK, 1948).
3. Thomas G. Casey and Justin Taylor, eds., *Paul's Jewish Matrix* (Rome: Gregorian & Biblical Press, 2011); Reimund Bieringer and Didier Pollefeyt, eds., *Paul and Judaism: Crosscurrents in Pauline Exegesis and the Study of Jewish-Christian Relations*, LNTS 463 (London: T&T Clark, 2012).

und das Judentum,⁴ Timo Laato's *Paulus und das Judentum*,⁵ Martin Hengel and Ulrich Heckel's edited volume *Paulus und das antike Judentum*,⁶ and (to cite another very recent contribution) Ines Pollmann's *Gesetzeskritische Motive im Judentum und die Gesetzeskritik des Paulus*.⁷ In the interest of full disclosure, even I have a monograph whose subtitle, at least, takes the form "*x* in Paul and *y* in ancient Judaism."⁸

For all that, however, the word "Judaism" itself (or rather, its putative Greek equivalency Ἰουδαϊσμός) occurs only twice in the Pauline corpus—the only two instances in the entire New Testament. Paul refers to Ἰουδαϊσμός (which I will leave untranslated for now so as not to beg the question) twice in a single sentence in Galatians 1, in which he relates a brief bit of autobiography. The pertinent passage reads:⁹

Ἠκούσατε γὰρ τὴν ἐμὴν ἀναστροφήν ποτε ἐν τῷ Ἰουδαϊσμῷ, ὅτι καθ' ὑπερβολὴν ἐδίωκον τὴν ἐκκλησίαν τοῦ θεοῦ καὶ ἐπόρθουν αὐτήν, καὶ προέκοπτον ἐν τῷ Ἰουδαϊσμῷ ὑπὲρ πολλοὺς συνηλικιώτας ἐν τῷ γένει μου, περισσοτέρως ζηλωτὴς ὑπάρχων τῶν πατρικῶν μου παραδόσεων.

For you heard of my former occupation in Ἰουδαϊσμός, that I was persecuting the church of God severely, and was destroying it, and was excelling in Ἰουδαϊσμός beyond many of my peers among my people, being exceedingly zealous for my ancestral traditions. (Gal. 1:13–14)

In this passage, Paul uses the term Ἰουδαϊσμός to signify an aspect of his own pattern of activity (ἀναστροφή, "occupation") in the time before the divine revelation that he mentions elliptically in Galatians 1:15–16: εὐδόκησεν . . . ἀποκαλύψαι τὸν υἱὸν αὐτοῦ ἐν ἐμοί, ἵνα εὐαγγελίζωμαι αὐτὸν ἐν τοῖς ἔθνεσιν; "He [God] was pleased to reveal his son in me so that I might preach him among the gentiles."¹⁰ But what is Ἰουδαϊσμός? From the plain etymological

---

4. Gerd Lüdemann, *Paulus und das Judentum*, TEH 215 (Munich: Kaiser, 1983).

5. Timo Laato, *Paulus und das Judentum: Anthropologische Erwägungen* (Åbo: Åbo Academy Press, 1991).

6. Martin Hengel and Ulrich Heckel, eds., *Paulus und das antike Judentum*, WUNT 58 (Tübingen: Mohr Siebeck, 1991).

7. Ines Pollmann, *Gesetzeskritische Motive im Judentum und die Gesetzeskritik des Paulus*, NTOA/SUNT 98 (Göttingen: Vandenhoeck & Ruprecht, 2012).

8. Matthew V. Novenson, *Christ among the Messiahs: Christ Language in Paul and Messiah Language in Ancient Judaism* (New York: Oxford University Press, 2012).

9. For this and all subsequent NT references, I follow the Greek text of Nestle-Aland, *Novum Testamentum Graece*, 28th ed. (Stuttgart: Deutsche Bibelgesellschaft, 2012). Translations of all primary texts are my own unless otherwise noted.

10. On this event, see in particular Alan F. Segal, *Paul the Convert: The Apostolate and Apostasy of Paul the Pharisee* (New Haven: Yale University Press, 1990), 58–71.

analogy, most modern English versions render it with "Judaism" (so RSV, NRSV, NASB, NIV; cf. KJV: "the Jews' religion"; Luther Bibel: *Judentum*).[11] This identification of Paul's word Ἰουδαϊσμός with our word for the religion of the synagogue, together with the polemical program of an epistle in which Paul opposes those who would "compel gentiles to judaize" (Gal. 2:14), has given us the traditional trope of Galatians as a manifesto against Judaism.[12] Many modern exegetes, however, have questioned whether Paul actually addresses Judaism as a religion in Galatians, and recently some have raised the question whether the word Ἰουδαϊσμός even means "Judaism." It is this latter question, as it pertains to Galatians, that is the burden of this essay.

Paul and *Ioudaismos*

There has been diversity in the particulars of the interpretation of Ἰουδαϊσμός in Galatians 1, but a leitmotif in most interpretation since late antiquity is the notion that Ἰουδαϊσμός signifies "Judaism," the religion of the synagogue, and that this epistle comprises in part Paul's criticism of that religion. It is not Paul but Ignatius of Antioch who introduces the terminological distinction between Ἰουδαϊσμός and Χριστιανισμός, the latter word possibly an Ignatian coinage.[13] Infamously, Marcion of Sinope also reads Galatians as the story of a conflict between two opposing religions, but he takes the further step of inferring a conflict between two opposing gods.[14] Tertullian, anticipating the emerging catholic position, denies Marcion's ditheism but concedes his

---

11. Similarly Martin Hengel, *Judaism and Hellenism*, 2 vols., trans. John Bowden (London: SCM, 1974), 1:2: "The word ['Ἰουδαϊσμός] means both political and genetic association with the Jewish nation and exclusive belief in the one God of Israel, together with observance of the Torah given by him."

12. On which see John Riches, *Galatians through the Centuries* (Oxford: Blackwell, 2008), 84–87.

13. See Ign. *Magn.* 10.3: Ἄτοπόν ἐστιν, Ἰησοῦν Χριστὸν λαλεῖν καὶ ἰουδαΐζειν. Ὁ γὰρ Χριστιανισμὸς οὐκ εἰς Ἰουδαϊσμὸν ἐπίστευσεν, ἀλλ' Ἰουδαϊσμὸς εἰς Χριστιανισμόν, εἰς ὃν πᾶσα γλῶσσα πιστεύσασα εἰς θεὸν συνήχθη, "It is absurd to profess Jesus Christ and to judaize. For Christianity did not trust in Judaism, but Judaism in Christianity, in which every tongue that trusts in God has been gathered together." Ign. *Phil.* 6:1: Ἐὰν δέ τις Ἰουδαϊσμὸν ἑρμηνεύῃ ὑμῖν, μὴ ἀκούετε αὐτοῦ. Ἄμεινον γάρ ἐστιν παρὰ ἀνδρὸς περιτομὴν ἔχοντος Χριστιανισμὸν ἀκούειν, ἢ παρὰ ἀκροβύστου Ἰουδαϊσμόν; "If someone interprets Judaism to you, do not listen to him. For it is better to listen to Christianity from a circumcised person than Judaism from someone with a foreskin" (Greek text ed. P. T. Camelot, *Ignace d'Antioche. Polycarpe de Smyrne: Lettres. Martyre de Polycarpe*, 4th ed., SC 10 [Paris: Cerf, 1969]). On these passages, see in particular Shaye J. D. Cohen, "Judaism without Circumcision and 'Judaism' without 'Circumcision' in Ignatius," *HTR* 95 (2002): 395–415.

14. See Marcion, *Antitheses*, as reconstructed by Adolf von Harnack, *Marcion: The Gospel of the Alien God*, trans. John E. Steely and Lyle D. Bierma (Durham, NC: Labyrinth, 1990),

exegetical point: "The epistle which we also allow to be the most decisive against Judaism [*Iudaismus*] is that wherein the apostle instructs the Galatians" (Tertullian, *Marc.* 5.2).[15] Augustine's reading of our passage is similar to Tertullian's, albeit subtler in certain respects: "If by persecuting the church of God and trying to destroy it, Paul advanced in Judaism [*Iudaismus*], it is clear that Judaism is opposed to the church of God, not because of the spiritual law that the Jews [*Iudaei*] received but because of their own carnal and slavish way of life" (Augustine, *Exp. Gal.* 7.2).[16]

This interpretive tradition, according to which Galatians is Paul's own treatise *adversus Iudaeos*, persists in the modern period. Martin Luther reads Paul's "former occupation in Judaism" as a cipher for the vain religious hopes of "the pope, the Turks, the Jews, and all such as trust in their own merits."[17] In this Lutheran vein, Rudolf Bultmann comments that in Galatians 1:13–14 Paul realizes "God's judgment upon his [Paul's] self-understanding up to that time—i.e., God's condemnation of his Jewish striving after righteousness [*jüdischen Strebens nach der Gerechtigkeit*] by fulfilling the works of the law."[18] Karl Barth's comment on our passage in *Church Dogmatics* IV.3 does not impugn Jewish religiousness as Bultmann's does, but Barth too sees in Galatians a criticism of Judaism as such: "There can be no doubt that his attitude and conduct (ἀναστροφή, Gal. 1:13) accorded with the mode of Jewish life [*jüdischer Art*] (ἐν Ἰουδαϊσμῷ) as then expected. . . . What he did not know was the necessity of radical conversion thus laid upon Israel, its obligation to accept the divine decision which actually precludes all seeking of its own righteousness."[19] Among the last generation of interpreters, Hans Dieter Betz writes, "According to Galatians, Judaism is excluded from salvation altogether."[20] And, playing Barth to Betz's Bultmann, J. Louis Martyn

---

53–63; and cf. the fragments in Tertullian, *Adversus Marcionem*, book 4. See further Sebastian Moll, *The Arch-heretic Marcion*, WUNT 250 (Tübingen: Mohr Siebeck, 2010), 84–89, 107–15.

15. Trans. Peter Holmes in *Ante-Nicene Fathers*, ed. Alexander Roberts and James Donaldson, vol. 3 (Grand Rapids: Eerdmans, 1986). See further John M. G. Barclay, "Tertullian, Paul, and the Nation of Israel: A Response to Geoffrey D. Dunn," in *Tertullian and Paul*, ed. Todd D. Still and David E. Wilhite (London: T&T Clark, 2013), 98–103.

16. Eric Plumer, trans., *Augustine's Commentary on Galatians*, OECS (Oxford: Oxford University Press, 2003). See further Paula Fredriksen, *Augustine and the Jews: A Christian Defense of Jews and Judaism* (New Haven: Yale University Press, 2010), esp. 213–34.

17. Martin Luther, *A Commentary on St. Paul's Epistle to the Galatians* (Philadelphia: Smith, English, 1860), 151.

18. Rudolf Bultmann, *Theology of the New Testament*, trans. Kendrick Grobel, 2 vols. (New York: Scribner, 1951–55), 1:187.

19. Karl Barth, *Church Dogmatics* [*CD*], IV/3 (1961): 199–200.

20. Hans Dieter Betz, *Galatians: A Commentary on Paul's Letter to the Churches in Galatia*, Hermeneia (Philadelphia: Fortress, 1979), 251.

cautions, "The ruling polarity [in Galatians] is not that of Christianity versus Judaism, church versus synagogue, . . . [but] rather the cosmic antinomy of God's apocalyptic act in Christ versus religion."²¹ Like Barth, however, Martyn concedes that by the logic of Galatians, Judaism finally falls on the "religion" side of this antinomy.²²

Ioudaismos and Judaizing

This whole interpretive tradition, of course, is predicated on the notion that Paul refers to or at least assumes the existence of something called "Judaism." But is that the case? In a provocative 2007 journal article, Steve Mason proposed a radical revision of the prevailing understanding of the word Ἰουδαϊσμός and its cognates.²³ Mason argues that "there was no category of 'Judaism' in the Greco-Roman world, no 'religion' too, and that the *Ioudaioi* were understood until late antiquity as an ethnic group comparable to other ethnic groups."²⁴ This article has attracted a great deal of attention in the several years since, especially regarding Mason's claim that the substantive adjective Ἰουδαῖος always has the ethnic-regional sense "Judean," never the religious sense "Jew."²⁵ In this essay I am concerned only with the word Ἰουδαϊσμός, so I set aside the Judean-versus-Jew issue altogether. In what follows, I render Ἰουδαῖος as "Jew" throughout, since doing so is conventional and will not distract from my central point.²⁶

One of the main points of Mason's article is the morphological observation that the abstract noun Ἰουδαϊσμός is directly related to the verb ἰουδαΐζω, "to judaize," which means "to act like a Jew" or "to adopt Jewish customs" (see

---

21. J. Louis Martyn, *Galatians: A New Translation with Introduction and Commentary*, AB 33A (New York: Doubleday, 1997), 37.
22. Ibid., 38.
23. Steve Mason, "Jews, Judaeans, Judaizing, Judaism: Problems of Categorization in Ancient History," *JSJ* 38 (2007): 457–512.
24. Ibid., 457.
25. Among the numerous responses to Mason, see in particular Daniel Boyarin, "Rethinking Jewish Christianity: An Argument for Dismantling a Dubious Category," *JQR* 99 (2009): 7–36; David M. Miller, "The Meaning of *Ioudaios* and Its Relationship to Other Group Labels in Ancient 'Judaism,'" *CBR* 9 (2010): 98–126; idem, "Ethnicity Comes of Age: An Overview of Twentieth-Century Terms for *Ioudaios*," *CBR* 10 (2012): 293–311; Seth Schwartz, "How Many Judaisms Were There?," *JAJ* 2 (2011): 208–38; Beth A. Berkowitz, *Defining Jewish Different: From Antiquity to the Present* (New York: Cambridge University Press, 2012), 112–15; Adiel Schremer, "Thinking about Belonging in Early Rabbinic Literature: Proselytes, Apostates, and 'Children of Israel,'" *JSJ* 43 (2012): 249–75.
26. As with Schartz, "How Many Judaisms?," I think that there are good reasons for retaining the translation "Jew," but I will not make that argument here.

LSJ; BDAG; Lampe: s.v. ἰουδαΐζω).²⁷ Of course, all the various Ἰουδαι- cognates derive finally from the geographic root Ἰουδαία, the Greek name for the region of the southern Levant. But, Mason points out, the word Ἰουδαϊσμός does not signify just the religion practiced in Ἰουδαία or by Ἰουδαῖοι. Rather, it is a nominal form of the verb "to judaize," and—this is the crucial point—judaizing is something that only non-Jews can do. The verb ἰουδαΐζω, like virtually all Greek -ιζω verbs built on ethnic roots (ἀττικίζω, λακωνίζω, μηδίζω, ἑλληνίζω, etc.), signifies the adoption of native practices by nonnative persons. As Shaye Cohen puts it, "*Medizein* means neither 'to be a Mede' nor 'to become a Mede,' but 'to act like a Mede.'"²⁸ And again, "Jews do not judaize, any more than Medes medize or Greeks hellenize."²⁹

If so, then Ἰουδαϊσμός ought to mean not "the customs of the Jewish people," as we generally use it to mean, but rather "the adoption of Jewish customs by non-Jewish people." Perhaps, then, Ἰουδαϊσμός should not be translated "Judaism" at all, but rather something like "judaizing" or "judaization," and this is precisely what Mason proposes.³⁰ On his account, Ἰουδαϊσμός emphatically does not correspond to our word "Judaism"; in fact, Mason reckons that no ancient word corresponds to our word "Judaism."³¹ Ancient writers, for their part, had the concept "indigenous ancestral traditions," which pertained to any given ethnic group (the πάτρια or ἔθη or νόμοι of the Medes or the Greeks or the Jews), but they did not have ethnos-specific words for these traditions. They also had the word Ἰουδαϊσμός (and its counterparts Μηδισμός, Ἑλληνισμός, etc.), but these words referred to the act of transethnic sympathizing or imitating, not to the indigenous traditions themselves.³²

When Mason, therefore, reads Paul as speaking of his own former occupation in Ἰουδαϊσμός, he takes this to mean that Paul claims to have been involved in the judaizing industry, so to speak.³³ Not as a judaizer himself, of course, because that would be impossible by definition—Paul is a Jew, and only non-Jews can judaize. Perhaps, however, Paul means that before his apostolic

---

27. Mason, "Problems of Categorization," 460–70.
28. Shaye J. D. Cohen, *The Beginnings of Jewishness: Boundaries, Varieties, Uncertainties* (Berkeley: University of California Press, 1999), 178.
29. Cohen, "Judaism without Circumcision," 398.
30. Mason, "Problems of Categorization," 463–64.
31. Ibid., 460–80.
32. Mason further claims that ancient writers had no such concept as "religion" (ibid., 480–88), but this is a metalevel claim that does not necessarily follow from his lexical observations. For a fuller treatment of this problem, see Brent Nongbri, *Before Religion: A History of a Modern Concept* (New Haven: Yale University Press, 2013).
33. Mason, "Problems of Categorization," 469: "It is not as though the Judaizers [i.e., Paul's opponents in Galatians] are doing something he has neglected, for the same mind-set was part of his background."

call, he was involved in efforts to encourage non-Jews to judaize in some way. Mason concedes that Paul tells us little about the details of his preapostolic work, but on his revisionist account of Ἰουδαϊσμός some such reading of Galatians 1:13–14 follows.[34] If correct, this would materially affect both our understanding of Paul's biography (perhaps he was a Jewish missionary to gentiles before his apostolic call)[35] and our understanding of the situation in the Galatian churches (perhaps Paul opposes not the religion Judaism but the ethnos-bending practice of judaizing).[36] But is this proposal correct? Is there really no such thing as Judaism in Galatians, or indeed anywhere in antiquity?

Who Does *Ioudaismos*?

I propose that Mason's incisive proposal is partly right and partly wrong, that the verbal noun Ἰουδαϊσμός does indeed designate a sectarian activity rather than a whole religious system, but that, contrary to etymology, it is an activity undertaken by Jews. So, first of all, it is indeed the case that the verb "to judaize" means for a non-Jew to adopt Jewish customs. To put the same point differently, the grammatical subject of the verb "to judaize" is always a gentile, never a Jew. So in Galatians 2, when Paul rebukes Peter for withdrawing from table fellowship with the gentile believers at Antioch, he says, εἰ σὺ Ἰουδαῖος ὑπάρχων ἐθνικῶς καὶ οὐχὶ Ἰουδαϊκῶς ζῇς, πῶς τὰ ἔθνη ἀναγκάζεις ἰουδαΐζειν; "If you, being a Jew, live gentilishly and not Jewishly, how can you compel the gentiles to judaize?" (Gal. 2:14). Here, significantly, Peter is not judaizing; rather, he is compelling gentiles to judaize. The scholarly convention that calls Paul's opponents "judaizers" is therefore the wrong way around. "Judaizing" is not what Paul's opponents are doing; it is what the Galatian believers are contemplating doing.[37] In grammatical terms, ἰουδαΐζω is an

---

34. Ibid.: "We do not know whether Paul ever 'compelled gentiles to judaize' in his pre-Christian life, as he now charges Peter with doing."
35. As suggested, in different forms, by Hans Hübner, "Gal 3,10 und die Herkunft des Paulus," *KD* 19 (1973): 215–31; Martin Hengel, *The Pre-Christian Paul*, trans. John Bowden (London: SCM, 1991), 57–61; and Terence L. Donaldson, *Paul and the Gentiles: Remapping the Apostle's Convictional World* (Minneapolis: Fortress, 1997), 273–84; among others.
36. As suggested by Stanley K. Stowers, *A Rereading of Romans: Justice, Jews, and Gentiles* (New Haven: Yale University Press, 1994), whose argument is related to but distinguishable from the treatments of Lloyd Gaston, *Paul and the Torah* (Vancouver: University of British Columbia Press, 1987); John G. Gager, *Reinventing Paul* (New York: Oxford University Press, 2000); and Pamela Eisenbaum, *Paul Was Not a Christian: The Original Message of a Misunderstood Apostle* (New York: HarperCollins, 2009).
37. A point well made by John M. G. Barclay, *Obeying the Truth: A Study of Paul's Ethics in Galatians* (Edinburgh: T&T Clark, 1988), 36n1.

intransitive, not a transitive verb.[38] Paul's usage reflects the standard sense of the word. At the end of the Greek version of the book of Esther, when the Jews arm themselves against their would-be executioners, the narrator reports that πολλοὶ τῶν ἐθνῶν περιετέμοντο καὶ ἰουδάιζον διὰ τὸν φόβον τῶν Ἰουδαίων; "Many of the gentiles underwent circumcision and judaized for fear of the Jews" (Esther 8:17 LXX).[39] Likewise, in classical usage, Plutarch relates the story of Cicero's prosecuting a former praetor named Verres, one of whose accusers was a freedman named Caecilius, who himself had been "accused of judaizing" (ἔνοχος τῷ ἰουδαΐζειν), that is, of improperly following Jewish customs rather than his own (Plutarch, *Cic.* 7.6).[40] In short, when Jews follow their own ancestral customs, there is no special word for that, but when gentiles follow Jews' ancestral customs, it is called "judaizing."[41]

Second, again in agreement with Mason, the form Ἰουδαϊσμός is the nominalization of the verb ἰουδαΐζω, so that by the normal rules of etymology Ἰουδαϊσμός ought to mean "the observance of Jewish customs by non-Jewish persons."[42] This is the normal pattern for verbs ending in -ιζω and their respective nominalized forms ending in -ισμός.[43] So βαπτίζω means to perform a water ritual, and a βαπτισμός is the ritual washing itself. Καθαρίζω means to purify, and a καθαρισμός is a purification or cleansing. Θερίζω means to reap or harvest, and a θερισμός is a reaping or a harvest. The same is true, albeit with some variation, of ethnic -ισμός nouns. The verb ἑλληνίζω means "for a non-Greek to adopt Greek ways,"[44] and the noun Ἑλληνισμός means "the adoption

---

38. As are all ethnic -ιζω verbs in the vast majority of instances. There are a few exceptions, e.g., the late (fourth-century CE) use of ἑλληνίζω in Libanius, *Or.* 11.103: καὶ ὅλως οὐδένα τόπον ἐπιτήδειον δέξασθαι πόλιν ἀφῆκε γυμνόν, ἀλλ' ἑλληνίζων διετέλεσε τὴν βάρβαρον, "In sum, no place that was suitable for receiving a city did he [Seleucus] leave bare, but in his hellenizing he finished the barbarian world."

39. For the text of Greek Esther, I follow A. Rahlfs, *Septuaginta*, 9th ed., vol. 1 (Stuttgart: Württemberg Bible Society, 1935). On this episode, see Cohen, *Beginnings of Jewishness*, 181–82.

40. On this episode, see Louis H. Feldman, *Jew and Gentile in the Ancient World: Attitudes and Interactions from Alexander to Justinian* (Princeton: Princeton University Press, 1993), 345; and Brian A. Krostenko, *Cicero, Catullus, and the Language of Social Performance* (Chicago: University of Chicago Press, 2001), 160–61.

41. So also in Josephus, *J.W.* 2.454, 463; Ign. *Magn.* 10.3; Alexander Polyhistor (citing Theodotus, *On the Jews*) apud Eusebius, *Praep. ev.* 9.22.5.

42. In a different context, Cohen recommends glossing Ἰουδαϊσμός with "Jewishness" (Cohen, *Beginnings of Jewishness*, 1–10). Relative to the particular issues with which Cohen is here concerned (in particular, the modern categories of ethnicity and religion), his translation is apt, but it does not account for the features of ancient usage that are the subject of the present essay.

43. So rightly Mason, "Problems of Categorization," 461–62.

44. Or a more specific variation on this meaning, esp. "to speak the Greek language" (e.g., Sextus Empiricus, *Math.* 1.246, where it is a contrast term for βαρβαρίζω). Cf. the old political use of μηδίζω in the sense "to take the side of the Medes" in, e.g., Herodotus, *Hist.* 4.144; Thucydides 3.62.

by non-Greeks of Greek ways."[45] Since Ἰουδαϊσμός is the nominalization of the verb ἰουδαΐζω, "to behave like a Jew," then it should simply mean "the act of behaving like a Jew," and like its parent verb it should signify something that only non-Jews can do.

Third and finally, however—and here I part ways with Mason—that is not what Ἰουδαϊσμός means in actual use. In all the (admittedly few) pre-Christian instances of the word up to and including Paul, the noun Ἰουδαϊσμός is something that Jews do, even though sometimes in the very same texts, including Galatians, the verb ἰουδαΐζω is something that non-Jews do.[46] In this instance, use belies etymology. If we consider Mason's reading of Galatians 1:13–14 ("my former occupation in the judaizing industry"), the fly in the ointment is that there is no mention of gentiles in the passage. Paul does not say that he used to compel gentiles to judaize, as he accuses Peter of doing in 2:14.[47] Rather, Paul identifies his own former activity as Ἰουδαϊσμός; he himself is the implied subject of the verbal idea.

In this respect, Paul's usage actually conforms to convention. In 2 Maccabees and its literary imitator 4 Maccabees, Ἰουδαϊσμός is the name of the cause championed by Judah Maccabee and his Jewish partisans (2 Macc. 2:21; 8:1; 14:38; 4 Macc. 4:26), on which I will have more to say below.[48] In the Roman period, the word Ἰουδαϊσμός is attested twice in the epigraphic record, once in a third- or fourth-century-CE funerary inscription for a woman from Porto near Rome, and once in a third-century-CE synagogue benefaction inscription from Stobi in Macedonia. The relevant bit of the epitaph of Cattia Ammias (*CIJ* 537) reads:[49]

Καττία Ἀμμιὰς θυγάτηρ Μηνοφίλου πατ(ρὸς) συναγωγῆς τῶν Καρκαρησίων καλῶς βιώσασα ἐν τῷ ἰουδαϊσμῷ ἔτη ζήσασα τριάκοντα καὶ τέσσαρα μετὰ τοῦ συμβίου.

---

45. So LSJ, s.v. Ἑλληνισμός: "imitation of the Greeks," as in 2 Macc. 4:13: ἦν δ᾽ οὕτως ἀκμή τις Ἑλληνισμοῦ καὶ πρόσβασις ἀλλοφυλισμοῦ διὰ τὴν τοῦ ἀσεβοῦς καὶ οὐκ ἀρχιερέως Ἰάσωνος ὑπερβάλλουσαν ἀναγνείαν, "Thus there was such an extreme of hellenization and increase of foreignization on account of the exceeding impurity of Jason, who was impious and no high priest" (Greek text, ed. Rahlfs, *Septuaginta*). Well into late antiquity, Ἑλληνισμός sometimes signifies "paganism" in contrast to Christianity (as in Julian, *Ep.* 84), but this usage is a world away from Paul's social context in the Julio-Claudian period.

46. I say "pre-Christian" because in patristic usage from Ignatius onward, Ἰουδαϊσμός takes on a new, stereotyped sense, which is beyond the scope of this essay. On this development, see Cohen, *Beginnings of Jewishness*, 185–92; Mason, "Problems of Categorization," 470–76; Boyarin, "Rethinking Jewish Christianity," 8–12.

47. As Mason himself concedes in "Problems of Categorization," 469.

48. On this usage, see Jan Willem van Henten, *The Maccabean Martyrs as Saviours of the Jewish People: A Study of 2 and 4 Maccabees*, JSJSup 57 (Leiden: Brill, 1997), 201–4.

49. For the Greek text of both inscriptions, I follow *CIJ*.

Cattia Ammias, daughter of Menophilus the father of the synagogue of the Karkaresians, lived virtuously in Ἰουδαϊσμός, having dwelt thirty-four years with her spouse.

And the relevant bit of the Stobi synagogue inscription (*CIJ* 694) reads:

[Κλ.] Τιβέριος Πολύχαρμος ὃ καὶ Ἀχύριος, ὁ πατὴρ τῆς ἐν Στόβοις συναγωγῆς ὃς πολειτευσάμενος πᾶσαν πολειτείαν κατὰ τὸν ἰουδαϊσμὸν εὐχῆς ἕνεκεν τοὺς μὲν οἴκους τῷ ἁγίῳ τόπῳ.

Claudius Tiberius Polycharmus, also called Achyrius, father of the synagogue at Stobi, who, having administered every policy in accordance with Ἰουδαϊσμός, has in fulfillment of a vow [given] the buildings for the holy place.

Scholars have generally taken Ἰουδαϊσμός in both inscriptions to mean simply "Judaism" in the sense of the religion practiced by the presumably Jewish honorees.[50] In favor of this majority opinion, there is no positive evidence that either Cattia Ammias or Polycharmus was a gentile proselyte unless we allow the word Ἰουδαϊσμός to count as evidence to that effect, as Mason cautiously does.[51] There is more to say about this, but for now it is enough to note that both inscriptions make very good sense if we take them to use the word Ἰουδαϊσμός (as 2 Maccabees, 4 Maccabees, and Galatians use it) to signify something that Jews themselves do.

To summarize the argument to this point: the verb ἰουδαΐζω means for non-Jews to observe Jewish customs, whereas the cognate noun Ἰουδαϊσμός means the defense and promotion of Jewish customs by Jewish people. This phenomenon runs contrary to the rules of etymology, but it is the case. In this instance, as sometimes happens, etymology is not a trustworthy guide. The vicissitudes of language use here result in an anomaly, and that anomaly becomes fixed as a new pattern of speech.

50. Thus, e.g., A. Marmorstein, "The Synagogue of Claudius Tiberius Polycharmus at Stobi," *JQR* 27 (1937): 373–84; Martin Hengel, "Die Synagogeninschrift von Stobi," *ZNW* 57 (1966): 145–83; Yehoshua Amir, "The Term *Ioudaismos*: A Study in Jewish-Hellenistic Self-Identification," *Immanuel* 14 (1982): 34–41 (in Hebrew); Margaret H. Williams, "The Meaning and Function of *Ioudaios* in Graeco-Roman Inscriptions," *ZPE* 116 (1997): 249–62; Lee I. Levine, *The Ancient Synagogue: The First Thousand Years* (New Haven: Yale University Press, 2005), 270–73.

51. Mason, "Problems of Categorization," 479: "A scenario in which Polycharmus was either a wealthy gentile sympathizer or a convert, who donated his private property for the sacred use of the *Ioudaioi*, seems at least as good an explanation . . . as the assumption that he was a *Ioudaios* born and raised." Hans Lietzmann made the same suggestion about Polycharmus of Stobi already in 1933 (Hans Lietzmann, "Die Synagogeninschrift in Stobi/Ausgrabungen in Doura-Europos," *ZNW* 32 [1933]: 93–95).

Maccabean Invention of *Ioudaismos*

How did this particular anomaly emerge? The answer, I propose, lies in the second-century-BCE Maccabean Revolt, and especially in the literary account of the revolt related in 2 Maccabees. It is well known that the word Ἰουδαϊσμός is first attested in and was perhaps coined by 2 Maccabees, either by Jason of Cyrene or by the anonymous redactor whose condensed version of Jason's account has come down to us.[52] More to the point, 2 Maccabees introduces the word Ἰουδαϊσμός as a contrast term for Ἑλληνισμός, the adoption of Greek customs by non-Greeks. In a programmatic statement, the author laments how in the period just prior to the revolt, ἦν δ' οὕτως ἀκμή τις Ἑλληνισμοῦ καὶ πρόσβασις ἀλλοφυλισμοῦ διὰ τὴν τοῦ ἀσεβοῦς καὶ οὐκ ἀρχιερέως Ἰάσωνος ὑπερβάλλουσαν ἀναγνείαν; "there was such an extreme of hellenization and increase of foreignization on account of the exceeding impurity of Jason, who was impious and no high priest" (2 Macc. 4:13).

The heroes of the book, by contrast, are those stouthearted Jews who reject the siren song of Ἑλληνισμός and devote themselves to the cause that 2 Maccabees names Ἰουδαϊσμός. The author tells of the heavenly visions that were given to τοῖς ὑπὲρ τοῦ Ἰουδαϊσμοῦ φιλοτίμως ἀνδραγαθήσασιν; "Those who with honor acted manfully for the sake of Ἰουδαϊσμός" (2:21). During the persecutions under Antiochus IV, Judah Maccabee and his band secretly canvass the villages of Judaea, προσεκαλοῦντο τοὺς συγγενεῖς καὶ τοὺς μεμενηκότας ἐν τῷ Ἰουδαϊσμῷ προσλαμβανόμενοι; "summoning their kinfolk and enlisting those who had persevered in Ἰουδαϊσμός" (8:1). The martyr Razis, called an elder of Jerusalem and a patriarch of the Jews, κρίσιν εἰσενηνεγμένος Ἰουδαϊσμοῦ, καὶ σῶμα καὶ ψυχὴν ὑπὲρ τοῦ Ἰουδαϊσμοῦ παραβεβλημένος; "was indicted for Ἰουδαϊσμός and risked life and limb for the sake of Ἰουδαϊσμός" (14:38).[53]

In all these instances, the neologism Ἰουδαϊσμός signifies the defense under duress of Jewish ancestral traditions by certain Jews. Unlike our word "Judaism," Ἰουδαϊσμός in 2 Maccabees does not simply mean "what Jews do." It means, rather, "what Jews who reject hellenization do," "what zealous Jews do," or—in 2 Maccabees's quaint idiom—"what manly Jews do."[54] In 2 Maccabees—and this is very important—not all Jews practice Ἰουδαϊσμός, because Ἰουδαϊσμός is the name not of an ancestral religion but of a cause, a political movement, a program of activism. It is not the ancestral religion itself; it is

---

52. See Amir, "The Term *Ioudaismos*"; Cohen, *Beginnings of Jewishness*, 105–6; van Henten, *Maccabean Martyrs*, 201–4.

53. On these passages, see Martha Himmelfarb, "Judaism and Hellenism in 2 Maccabees," *Poetics Today* 19 (1998): 19–40.

54. On the theme of manliness in 2 Maccabees, see ibid., 34–37.

one party's program for defending the ancestral religion.⁵⁵ To put it another way: before the persecutions under Antiochus IV, there was no such thing as Ἰουδαϊσμός. There was a set of Jewish ancestral traditions, of course, but those traditions did not have a name because they did not have to be chosen, maintained, or defended. Before the Antiochene persecutions, they were just "what we Jews do." In the course of the Antiochene persecutions, however, the decision to persevere publicly in certain ancestral traditions (abstaining from eating pork, circumcising male infants, etc.) became an incendiary political statement. To reappropriate a famous phrase from the sociologist Peter Berger, Jewish religion in the Hellenistic period came under "the heretical imperative."⁵⁶ To practice it at all meant to choose it, which had not been the case for Jews before, and this choice warranted a name. Of course, there was already a name for gentiles who chose to observe Jewish customs: the verb ἰουδαΐζω, "judaizing." The neologism Ἰουδαϊσμός, "judaization," is a morphological twist on that existing term, a new word used to signify the suddenly radical choice by Jews to follow their own ancestral ways.

The Silence of Galatians on Judaism

Let us, then, find our way back to Galatians. The extant literary and documentary evidence suggests that even after the tumultuous events that gave rise to the term, this activist connotation remained part of the sense of the noun Ἰουδαϊσμός. As in the Hellenistic period, so also in the Roman period, when ancient writers refer to Jewish religion and culture, they use the standard terms νόμοι ("laws"), ἔθη ("customs"), παραδόσεις ("traditions"), πάτρια ("ancestral ways"), and so on.⁵⁷ When they very infrequently use the word Ἰουδαϊσμός, they mean not the ancestral customs themselves but a sectarian program for the

---

55. On this point, see the famously provocative treatment of Elias Bickerman, *The God of the Maccabees: Studies on the Origin and Meaning of the Maccabean Revolt*, SJLA 32 (Leiden: Brill, 1979).

56. See Peter L. Berger, *The Heretical Imperative: Contemporary Possibilities of Religious Affirmation* (New York: Doubleday, 1979). For Berger, the heretical imperative refers to the characteristic situation of religions in modernity, whereas my concern here is Judaism in the Hellenistic period. In both historical contexts, as distant as they are from each other, it is the encounter with religious pluralism that brings about the necessity of choice.

57. Examples of this convention are myriad. To cite just a few by way of illustration: ἀλλάξει τὰ ἔθη ἃ παρέδωκεν ἡμῖν Μωϋσῆς; "He will change the customs which Moses handed down to us" (Acts 6:14); οὐδὲν ἐναντίον ποιήσας τῷ λαῷ ἢ τοῖς ἔθεσι τοῖς πατρῴοις; "I did nothing hostile to the people or the ancestral customs" (Acts 28:17); παρέβησαν τὰ πάτρια ... ἐπὶ τοὐναντίον οἷς ὁ νόμος αὐτῶν ἐκέλευε ποιοῦντες; "They transgressed the ancestral ways, . . . doing contrary to what their law commanded" (Josephus, *Ant.* 4.139; Greek text ed. Benedict Niese, *Flavii Iosephi opera*, 4 vols. [Berlin: Weidmann, 1887–90]).

defense and promotion of those customs. This proposal makes good sense of the two late ancient Ἰουδαϊσμός inscriptions discussed earlier. On my reading, Cattia Ammias and Polycharmus were not just good Jews (*pace* Hengel and Levine) or proselytes (*pace* Lietzmann and Mason) but rather Jewish activists, advocates for the cause of Ἰουδαϊσμός in their respective Diaspora contexts. As Mason rightly points out, the Stobi inscription says of Polycharmus that he πολειτευσάμενος πᾶσαν πολειτείαν κατὰ τὸν ἰουδαϊσμὸν; "administered every policy in accordance with Ἰουδαϊσμός."[58] This πολειτεία language becomes much more intelligible if Ἰουδαϊσμός signifies a political cause rather than a lifestyle. Indeed, perhaps the word Ἰουδαϊσμός is as rare as it is, in inscriptions as in literary texts, precisely because it pertains not to Jews in general but to activist Jews in particular.

This brings us back to Galatians 1. Interpreters ancient and modern have noted, of course, that Paul portrays himself in Galatians 1:13–14 as an exceptionally zealous Jew: περισσοτέρως ζηλωτὴς ὑπάρχων τῶν πατρικῶν μου παραδόσεων; "being exceedingly zealous for my ancestral traditions." Most have thought, however, that the word Ἰουδαϊσμός in these verses refers to Jewish religion in general and that Paul's zeal was something added to it, so to speak.[59] On this conventional reading, all ancient Jews practice Ἰουδαϊσμός, but Paul practiced it more earnestly than most. But this is not quite right. Paul writes about Jewish religious practice, both his own and others', in a number of passages. He speaks, for instance, of infant circumcision, the people Israel, the Hebrew race, tribal ancestry, halakic schools of thought, ritual purity, the covenants, the law of Moses, the temple service, the divine promises, and the ancestors (Rom. 9:4–5; Phil. 3:5–6). In none of these contexts, however, does Paul ever use the word Ἰουδαϊσμός.[60]

Galatians 1:13–14 is different, however, because the subject at hand is not Jewish religion as such but Paul's own past involvement in anti-Jesus-movement agitation. The point of the passage is not that Paul used to be a Jew but now is a Christian.[61] The point is that Paul's gospel can have come from only God himself, because up to the time of his revelation Paul had been a leader in an aggressively traditionalist party. The point becomes clearer if we gloss Ἰουδαϊσμός not with "Judaism" but with something like "the judaization movement":

58. See Mason, "Problems of Categorization," 478.
59. See, e.g., Arland J. Hultgren, "On Translating and Interpreting Galatians 1:13," *BT* 26 (1975): 146–48; idem, "Paul's Pre-Christian Persecutions of the Church: Their Purpose, Locale, and Nature," *JBL* 95 (1976): 97–111.
60. A point well made by Mason, "Problems of Categorization," 469–70.
61. So rightly and famously Krister Stendahl, *Paul among Jews and Gentiles* (Philadelphia: Fortress, 1976), 7–23.

"For you heard of my former occupation in the judaization movement, that I was persecuting the church of God severely, advancing in the movement on account of my exceeding zeal," and so on. For Paul as for 2 Maccabees, not all Jews practice Ἰουδαϊσμός. Virtually all Jews follow the ancestral traditions, but only a subset fight for the cause of judaization, defending the traditions even to the point of harassing other Jews whom they suspect of endangering those traditions, as both Judah Maccabee and Paul did. It is this kind of political activism that goes by the name Ἰουδαϊσμός in ancient sources.

What, then, does Galatians say about "Judaism" in our sense, that is, the religion of Paul's non-Christian Jewish contemporaries? In truth, very little. Galatians does not view Jewish religion as such as a rival means of justification.[62] Indeed, Galatians 2:15–16 arguably suggests the contrary:

Ἡμεῖς φύσει Ἰουδαῖοι καὶ οὐκ ἐξ ἐθνῶν ἁμαρτωλοί εἰδότες ὅτι οὐ δικαιοῦται ἄνθρωπος ἐξ ἔργων νόμου ἐὰν μὴ διὰ πίστεως Ἰησοῦ Χριστοῦ, καὶ ἡμεῖς εἰς Χριστὸν Ἰησοῦν ἐπιστεύσαμεν.

We who are Jews by nature (not sinners from among the gentiles), because we know that a person is not justified from works of the law except through the faith of Jesus Christ, we have also trusted in Christ Jesus.[63]

In other words, pagan sinners (like the gentiles in the Galatian churches) might mistakenly think that the law is a mechanism for being justified, but Jews know better than to make that category mistake.[64] In Galatians, Paul's expectation concerning his Jewish kinfolk is that Peter's apostolate to the circumcision (2:8) will bring them into the messianic fold in due course. Their religion as such is not in view in Galatians, because it does not present a problem. It will eventually present a problem in Romans 9–11, because there Paul reckons with the realization that Peter's apostolate to the circumcision has been less than entirely successful. In Galatians, however, Paul seems to expect that the messianic ingathering of Israel will take care of itself.

This suggests an interpretation of the curious benediction upon "the Israel of God" in Galatians 6:16: ὅσοι τῷ κανόνι τούτῳ στοιχήσουσιν, εἰρήνη ἐπ'

---

62. This is, of course, a controversial claim, but for the purposes of this essay it is only possible to make it and to sketch some main lines of the argument.

63. The adverbial participle εἰδότες is frequently taken as a concession (e.g., RSV: "yet who know") on the assumption that Paul expects his fellow Jews to aspire to be justified by the law, but this assumption is by no means obvious, and it is arguably wrong.

64. Indeed, this might further suggest that the agitators themselves are judaizing gentile Christians rather than Jewish Christians, which, if true, would resolve some of the difficulties surrounding Paul's description of them in Gal. 6:12–13, but that is a topic for another essay.

αὐτοὺς καὶ ἔλεος καὶ ἐπὶ τὸν Ἰσραὴλ τοῦ θεοῦ; "As many as follow this rule, peace be upon them, and mercy also upon the Israel of God."[65] "This rule" is the notion that new creation has rendered obsolete both circumcision and uncircumcision (6:15), and "those who follow it" are the receptive among Paul's Galatian audience, those who take his view over against his opponents' view (cf. 5:10). In the immediate context, this pertains to the circumcision controversy in the letter, which is, of course, a matter of concern for the gentile churches in Galatia. As for "the Israel of God," everywhere else that Paul uses the word Ἰσραήλ and cognates (Rom. 9:6, 27, 31; 10:19, 21; 11:2, 7, 25, 26; 1 Cor. 10:18; 2 Cor. 3:7, 13; Phil. 3:5), the word refers to the Jewish ethnos.[66] As Susan Eastman has shown, there is very good reason to think that the same is true here.[67] This second clause wishes mercy upon God's people Israel (cf. "mercy" and "Israel" in Rom. 9:14–29; 11:25–32), whom Paul expects will soon trust the messiah through Peter's apostolate to the circumcision (Gal. 2:7–8). It parallels the first clause, which wishes peace upon all who heed Paul's plea to be justified not by judaizing but by trusting Christ.[68]

Conclusion

In Galatians Paul is simply not concerned with what we call Judaism, that is, the religion of non-Christian Jews. He is incensed at the prospect of his gentile believers judaizing (Gal. 2:14; 5:2–12), but that is an altogether different thing: a particular kind of ethnos-bending activity. He recalls his own former advocacy for "judaization" (Gal. 1:13–14), but that too is an altogether different thing: a traditionalist political cause. It is true, of course, that Paul was very much involved in his ancestral religion before his apostolic call, but then, Paul was very much involved in his ancestral religion after his apostolic call as

---

65. The syntax of the benediction is difficult but not impenetrable. An excellent recent treatment is Susan Grove Eastman, "Israel and the Mercy of God: A Re-reading of Galatians 6:16 and Romans 9–11," *NTS* 56 (2010): 367–95, with whom my argument here has close affinities.

66. So rightly E. P. Sanders, *Paul, the Law, and the Jewish People* (Philadelphia: Fortress, 1983), 176, who unnecessarily concludes that Gal. 6:16 is an exception to this rule.

67. See Eastman, "Israel and the Mercy of God," 385–90, against the tide of majority opinion. The main alternatives are that Paul uses "the Israel of God" to signify Jewish Christians (thus classically Gottlob Schrenk, "Was bedeutet 'Israel Gottes'?," *Judaica* 5 [1949]: 81–94) or the church as a whole (thus classically Nils A. Dahl, "Der Name Israel," *Judaica* 6 [1950]: 161–70).

68. Paula Fredriksen, "Judaizing the Nations: The Ritual Demands of Paul's Gospel," *NTS* 56 (2010): 232–52, rightly notes that technically Paul does expect his gentiles to judaize inasmuch as they must reject their own ancestral gods and worship the Jewish God (e.g., 1 Thess. 1:9). In this respect Paul's gospel is not "law-free." Judaizing comes in degrees, however, and in comparison to his rival teachers in Galatia, Paul demands very little in the way of judaizing, so little that, as Paul himself sees it, he does not demand judaizing at all (Gal. 2:14).

well, indeed, to the very end of his life. But that is not what he is discussing in Galatians 1:13–14. He is talking about his former occupation in a movement for the defense of Jewish ancestral ways, a sectarian political program that Paul, like other Hellenistic- and Roman-period writers, calls Ἰουδαϊσμός. For Paul's reflections on what we call Judaism—that is, the observance of Jewish customs by Jewish people—one must look to Romans: "Israel has pursued a law of righteousness as if by works" (Rom. 9:31–32), "They undertook to establish a righteousness of their own" (Rom. 10:3), and so on. And ultimately, not even Romans can provide all that the Christian tradition needs for a theological account of Judaism, because even at the end of his epistolary career, Paul did not yet imagine Judaism as we know it.[69]

---

69. So rightly Sanders, *Paul, the Law, and the Jewish People*, 197.

3

Galatians in the Early Church

Five Case Studies

KARLA POLLMANN AND MARK W. ELLIOTT

Preliminary Remarks

In recent scholarship it has been repeatedly noted that the second half of the fourth century saw an unprecedented rise of interest in Paul's Letters. This interest is expressed in the work of no less than six authors who produced commentaries on his letters within this period of time in the Latin West, although the East also saw the production of such commentaries.[1] Reasons mentioned for the increase in attention to this body of New Testament writings in the second half of the fourth century include the progress in sophisticated dogmatic thinking and the ever more differentiated controversies with various

---

1. Eric Plumer, trans., *Augustine's Commentary on Galatians*, OECS (Oxford: Oxford University Press, 2003), 5, with further literature; Thomas Martin, "Pauline Commentaries in Augustine's Time," in *Augustine through the Ages*, ed. Allan Fitzgerald (Grand Rapids: Eerdmans, 1999), 625–28, lists Greek commentaries on Paul and summarizes reasons for their large number. Origen is the first who wrote a commentary on Galatians, although it is lost for the most part; see Martin Meiser, *Galater* (Göttingen: Vandenhoeck & Ruprecht, 2007), 25–29; for commentaries on Galatians after 325 CE, see Meiser, *Galater*, 36–41.

pagan and heretical groups. Moreover, it could also be related to the simultaneous increase in popular veneration of Paul as a saint. This latter explanation is less convincing than Meiser's observation[2] that at the same time (i.e., the second half of the fourth century) we can also observe a significant increase in the production of commentaries on pagan authors like Plato, Aristotle, and Virgil. *Thus, this rich commentary production also on Christian writings has to be seen in the context of a cultural fight for intellectual hegemony.* In the following we will predominantly concentrate on the Latin tradition and on commentaries on Galatians in particular. As Wilhelm Geerlings explains, in this short period the "gospel of grace" came to form the center of the church's proclamation, and issues of theodicy that preoccupied the Manichaeans were pushed to the side.[3] Complete commentaries on Galatians have been written in Latin chronologically by the following:[4]

- The Christian Neoplatonist Marius Victorinus wrote shortly after 362.
- The otherwise unknown so-called Ambrosiaster (temporarily and mistakenly identified with Ambrose of Milan) wrote between 366 and 384 in Italy.
- The great scholar and biblical exegete Jerome wrote in 386.
- The young and exegetically still inexperienced Augustine (354–430) wrote in 394–395, before he was ordained bishop. Left unfinished, his work was planned as part of a large project to comprise complete separate commentaries on each of Paul's Epistles.
- The so-called Budapest Anonymous presumably wrote in Rome in 396–405; he follows in particular the Antiochene tradition of exegesis.
- The philologically open-minded Pelagius wrote in 405–410. In his circle we find the first testimonies for reading and using the "modern" translation of the Bible by Jerome, the so-called Vulgate.

In this essay we shall deal with the first four of these, as well as consider a work of verse: the anonymous fifth-century *Carmen adversus Marcionitas*. Especially from a modern perspective of professional exegetes, it is important to note that in late antiquity these commentaries were not written by scholars

2. Meiser, *Galater*, 37.
3. "Das Evangelium der Gnade bildet nun das Zentrum der kirchlichen Verkündigung" (W. Geerlings, "Hiob und Paulus, Theodizee und Paulinismus in der lateinischen Theologie am Ausgang des vierten Jahrhunderts," *JAC* 24 [1981]: 56–66, esp. 65); Geerlings concludes that "die Theodizeefrage nur als Randproblem dieser exegetischen Tradition angesehen werden kann."
4. Karla Pollmann, "Non est masculus et femina—Gal 3:28 in Kommentarauslegungen des 4./5. und des 20. Jahrhunderts: Ein nicht eingelöstes Vermächtnis?," in *Spiritus et Littera: Beiträge zur Augustinus-Forschung*, ed. G. Förster et al. (Würzburg: Augustinus bei Echter, 2009), 683–90.

who specialized in this "discipline." Instead of being the result of several years of concentrated research, such commentaries served rather as tools in the daily struggle to communicate a theological position or defend a certain interpretation against "heresies."[5] Therefore it is somewhat questionable whether a categorization of these commentaries into "doctrinal" or "philological" makes much sense since all these commentaries had the important function to prevent the Bible from becoming a "book of heresies."[6]

Marius Victorinus: Philosophy and Exegesis

The first commentator in order of chronology is Marius Victorinus: a rhetor, a public figure, and a man who was widely read in Platonic and Neoplatonic philosophy, and a late convert to Christianity. He was hardly an obvious candidate for illuminating the mysteries of Paul's writings, but it seems that after having staked out his theological position in his *Dialogues of the Trinity*, he lost his job as a paid Christian master when the Arianizing and then paganizing emperor Julian stopped Christians from teaching. During that enforced sabbatical, toward the end of his life, he wrote these commentaries as a way to reinforce his Nicene, trinitarian beliefs. These are on view in his Galatians commentary, which fortunately is extant, such that Pierre Hadot is justified in describing Marius's view of faith as intellectual in the sense that he insists that Christians needed to believe the right doctrine about God:[7] after all, his philosophical models are Plotinus and Porphyry. Yet, in his philosophical theology there is also a primacy of will in God: the Son is called the Father's will in its determining. There is scant place for any human will in salvation.[8]

With a use of clarifying paraphrase and a sprinkling of rhetorical terms, the structure of the work suggests that Galatians 3:20 is possibly the highlight of Galatians for Victorinus: "Now a mediator involves more than one party; but God is one." Christ is God even while being the go-between. This trinitarian focus might seem like reading Galatians against the grain, but Victorinus would not be ashamed of this example of his actualizing of the message for

---

5. Meiser, *Galater*, 37–41.
6. Andrew Cain, *St. Jerome: Commentary on Galatians, a Translation* (Washington, DC: Catholic University of America Press, 2010), 41.
7. P. Hadot, *Marius Victorinus: Recherches sur sa vie et son œuvre* (Paris: Études augustiniennes, 1971), 247: "La vie chrétienne est pour lui une vie philosophique, une vie 'selon l'Esprit.'" Hadot equates *sola fideism* with intellectualism: "Ipsa enim fides sola justificationem dat et sanctificationem"; ibid., 247n81: "In Gal 2,15 [1164C] la foi est conçue par Victorinus comme une adhésion intellectuelle."
8. See Ernst Benz, *Marius Victorinus und die Entwicklung der abendländischen Willensmetaphysik* (Stuttgart: Kohlhammer, 1932).

his own situation. This is just as much theology as his trinitarian speculations, arguably more so. The commentary also includes a dismissal of Jewish claims about the law's mediation and a quick march to secure the point of justification by faith. Victorinus's confessed innovation is to interpret the "two sons," allegorized by Paul in Galatians 4 to mean "two covenants," as the two peoples or "churches" of Jews and gentiles. Here Victorinus is hardly dismissive of the Jews themselves. Eva Schulz-Flügel is right to say that it would be better to call his "antijudaism" an "anti-legalism,"[9] and nowhere else is there any polemic against Jews.

Unlike most patristic commentators, he does not quote wider Scripture to explain Scripture, but interprets Paul only by Paul and ignores other commentators. Jerome was possibly quite right to charge that Victorinus was ignorant of the Old Testament Scriptures. Thomas Scheck seconds Jerome's criticism: "Moreover, even a cursory reading of Victorinus's exegesis of St. Paul shows that he simply does not consult the Old Testament or even the Gospels for clarification of Paul's meaning. He interprets Paul solely from Paul in the manner in which the Greeks explained Homer solely from Homer."[10] Victorinus was atypical among early Christian writers, as one who made little attempt to be panbiblical.

Stephen Cooper (in the notes to his fine translation of this commentary) observes that the Pauline commentaries were written after trinitarian treatises, hence in about 364–366. Yet "the question of the nature of Christ . . . was for Victorinus precisely a soteriological matter,"[11] even though Raspanti argues that both works come out of the same moment; for example, on Galatians 1:11 there is an attack on those who think that *secundum hominem* ("according to humanity") implies a low Christology.[12] Or, on Galatians 4:4 the text has "made under the law," and *not* "made, under the law." However, these instances are exceptional, and there is no place for the sophisticated arguments of the (trinitarian) *Dialogues*. So was Victorinus's mind made up philosophico-theologically before he approached Scripture? This requires us to look at his trinitarian treatises: just how "biblical" were those? One detail suggesting that biblical usage re-formed his philosophical terminology can be seen in his understanding of "spirit." For Stoics and Neoplatonists, *pneuma* was

---

9. Eva Schulz-Flügel, "Paulusexegese: Victorinus, Ambrosiaster," in *Augustin Handbuch*, ed. Volker Drecoll (Tübingen: Mohr Siebeck, 2007), 115–19.

10. T. Scheck, *St. Jerome's Commentary on Galatians, Titus, and Philemon* (Notre Dame, IN: University of Notre Dame Press, 2010), 16.

11. S. A. Cooper, *Marius Victorinus: Commentary on Galatians* (Oxford: Oxford University Press, 2005), 138–39.

12. G. Raspanti, *Mario Vittorino esegeta di S. Paolo* (Palermo: L'Epos, 1996).

a material reality and hence was not to be used as a synonym for "intellect," *nous*. Yet for the Christian Victorinus, "the terms *nous* and *spiritus* became synonyms,"[13] a clear case of his adaptation to biblical language.[14] Thus *pneumatikos* (as in 1 Cor. 2:14) just means "with higher, better understanding." It is no coincidence that he does not use the verse "The letter kills" (2 Cor. 3:6), for the letter is not opposed to the spiritual sense. Likewise, Raspanti is probably right to suppose that Christology and soteriology are conjoint issues, and Victorinus has already made appeal to Pauline texts where Christocentric soteriology can be used to refute Arianism: the radical *sola fide* soteriology is a corollary of that Nicene conviction.[15]

Yet the surprise or the novelty is that he goes on to write of Christ as source and agent of justification, and presents a "sola fideism" of which most Reformers would have been proud. Referring to 3:1–4, Victorinus illustrates how in the case of the Galatians, God has provided grace in response to faith, for instance on Galatians 3:22, "*ut fides sola Iesu Christi sufficiat ad iustificationem liberationemque nostram.*" "Sola fides" is not found in Origen, yet it possibly is there in Hilary on Matthew 9:6;[16] yet Hilary is not any earlier than Victorinus, and it is not a big theme for him. Perhaps our Roman rhetor was quite the creative theologian. Schulz-Flügel has noted his preference to use *liberare*, with its legal associations of transfer from slavery, to translate σώζειν.[17]

Ambrosiaster: Morality and Spirit

The second commentator is Ambrosiaster. This name, given by the eighteenth-century Benedictine editors, designates him as an ersatz Ambrose, once it was agreed, as Erasmus had suspected, that these Pauline commentaries were not by Ambrose of Milan. For a long time the North African church (Augustine included) and the Irish believed they were written by Hilary of Poitiers.[18] Souter

---

13. Massimo Stefani, "Sull'antropologia di Mario Vittorino," *ScrTh* 19 (1987): 63–111, 86n132.

14. Cooper, *Marius Victorinus*, 123.

15. See the arguments in Werner Erdt, *Marius Victorinus Afer, der erste lateinische Pauluskommentator* (Frankfurt: Peter Lang, 1980), 245–59.

16. Hilaire de Poitiers, *Sur Matthieu*, vol. 1, in SC 254:200: "Et remissum ab eo quod lex laxare non poterat; fides enim sola iustificat." On Marius's *sola fideism*, Benz, *Marius Victorinus*, 156–60, has associated it with an initiation experience not unlike that of Roman mystery cults, and experienced as a quietistic liberation from the former way of life. Salvation likewise does not hinge on serving the poor (on Gal. 2:10).

17. Schulz-Flügel, "Paulusexegese," 115.

18. Alexander Souter, *A Study of Ambrosiaster* (Cambridge: Cambridge University Press, 1905), 165.

thinks the references to persecution and paganism suggest the 370s as a likely date. Ambrosiaster, whoever he was, drew illustrations from other countries, especially Egypt: "It was perhaps in Egypt that he acquired his remarkable interest in the Jews."[19] He is nonhostile toward Judaism and quotes from all the Old Testament books except Ruth and Nahum, although he had little respect for original languages, as his run-in with Jerome bears out.[20] His other main work, the *Quaestiones*, identified by Souter just over a century ago to be by the writer of these Pauline commentaries, was long thought to be by Augustine. A number of scholars think his true identity was the convert "Isaac the Jew," with whom Pope Damasus fell out in the middle of the 380s. In recent times others, such as Sophie Lunn-Rockliffe, have reasons to doubt this.[21] Judging by his terminology, he had legal training, and it seems he was a careful scholar, reediting at least his Romans and Corinthians commentaries. What comes to the fore in his Galatians commentary are the themes of law and gospel, but also that of church order, to the extent that Gerald Bray doubts he could have been a layman.[22] Bussières supports this clerical status by arguing that his other work (the *Questiones*) served a catechetical purpose.[23]

Perhaps Ambrosiaster is best known for his interpretation of Romans 5:12 as teaching the doctrine of original sin, for Augustine would come to read this and, thinking it was Hilary, would pay this interpretation much respect (see *Contra duas epistulas Pelagianorum* 4.7).[24] But Ambrosiaster also embraced anthropological positions with which the bishop of Hippo would become less happy; for example, God creates each soul anew as good, and it is only the body that is procreated and fallen. Moreover, he thought that the law existed to encourage faithful overcoming.[25]

Writing about the Pauline commentaries as a whole, Souter observes:

---

19. Ibid., 180.
20. See *Ep.* 27 to Marcella, where Jerome defends himself for working with the Greek text. According to Damasus (*Ep.* 35.2), they disagreed on issues of *pascha*, the LXX, and whether Melchizedek was a type of Christ or of the Holy Spirit. Also Ambrosiaster on Gal. 1 saw no reason why the brothers of Jesus could not be his true brothers. (This was also Helvidius's position, which Jerome had opposed at length.)
21. Sophie Lunn-Rockliffe, *Ambrosiaster's Political Theology*, OECS (Oxford: Oxford University Press, 2009), 35–40.
22. Gerald Bray, *Ambrosiaster: Commentaries on Galatians—Philemon*, ACT (Downers Grove, IL: IVP Academic, 2009), xv.
23. Marie-Pierre Bussières, ed., *Ambrosiaster: Contre les païens et Sur le destin*, with translation and notes, SC 512 (Paris: Cerf, 2007), 40.
24. See Karla Pollmann, *Saint Augustine the Algerian*, 2nd ed. (Göttingen: Ruprecht, 2007), 32–33.
25. Ibid., 56: "Etant disposé à prendre une vue optimistique sur les possibilités morales de la nature humaine."

The work is throughout Roman and practical in tone. Common-sense explanations are the rule. The tone is rather that of the calm dispassionate searcher for truth than that of the mystic visionary who seeks to soar to the heights of the Apostle's thought. We have here none of the spiritual insight of an Augustine or a Bengel, but the work of a conscientious writer who seeks in Scripture for plain useful lessons which may serve to elevate the daily lives of his Roman fellow citizens.[26]

Ambrosiaster was original in the sense of not obviously drawing on anybody else, a frequency of reference to Roman law and its terms, displaying a dislike of superstitious ceremonies and a great interest in the last things.[27]

The punchy introduction to the Galatians commentary shows his penchant for being decisive: "Anyone who believes in Christ and simultaneously follows the law of deeds [*lex factorum*], poorly understands Christ." One might think he is opposed to the law in all its forms, but far from it. As Geerlings explains, Ambrosiaster had a threefold concept of law:[28] first, the *lex divina*, set out in the first four commandments of the Decalogue; second, the *lex moralis* (or *naturalis*), displayed in the following six commandments, and third, the *lex factorum*, meaning ritual laws and new moon and Sabbath observances. But Ambrosiaster's point is that the one who now serves Christ the Lawgiver cannot be judged by the law. Through this faith the Spirit is given in order to make spiritual people stand over the law. Yet he appreciates the old law (*vetus lex*) as the moral, nonceremonial law that brings people to Christ, and this not just by means of condemnation, as was the case with the ceremonial law. Hence the Ten Commandments can be viewed positively, even as part of the gospel. For instance, on Galatians 3:12 he observes: "The law is beneficial, . . . but this refers to the Ten Commandments." On Galatians 3:15, picking up on Paul's analogy *secundum hominem*, Ambrosiaster (and also Augustine) sees by the legal analogy that God's promise to Abraham is a *testamentum* and thus inviolable—whereas Jerome wanted to treat it as "*pactum*," hence variable, revocable, or time bound.[29] There is a spiritual law that should help versus the flesh—see his comments on 5:17—but we can all know such a law in its form as natural law, although believers do need the Spirit's help. The general assumption is that the Old Testament is binding in its ethos but not

---

26. Souter, *A Study of Ambrosiaster*, 6.

27. Ibid., 155.

28. W. Geerlings, "Das Verständnis von Gesetz im Galaterbriefkommentar des Ambrosiaster," in *Die Weltlichkeit des Glaubens in der Alten Kirche: Festschrift für Ulrich Wickert*, BZNW 85 (Berlin: de Gruyter, 1997), 101–13.

29. Marie-Pierre Bussières, "L'influence du synode tenu à Rome en 382 sur l'exégèse de l'Ambrosiaster," *SacEr* 45 (2006): 107–24, esp. 123.

in ceremonial law, not least circumcision—which is what is meant by "works of the law."

Faith is a matter of will (as per his commentary on Rom. 4:4). Ambrosiaster was indeed interested in the question of the will, but in the sense of allowing a place for human cooperation and wondering as to the possibilities for humans as moral agents. Hence one might conclude that *sola fide* is less frequently employed by Ambrosiaster (and in a decidedly weakened and guarded sense), yet its appearance in his commentary on Galatians (in the preface and at 3:22 and 5:5) is nevertheless significant in its positive use of the term, as on Galatians 4:22–31.[30] One of the key themes is that of the mutual alternatives, slavery or freedom: "The Jerusalem, which Paul calls our mother, is the rule of the Lord's mystery by which we are born into freedom. . . . This life and light is the mother of believers" (on Gal. 4:26). Certainly those of the synagogue have become slaves of sin, whereas Christians have the familial inheritance of sons, evidenced by the receiving of the Spirit, not of the now obsolete circumcision.

Finally, his comment on Galatians 2:21 is useful: "His death is the justification of sinners." Then on 3:6 he writes: "Righteousness is not imputed by the works of the law, but by faith . . . receiving the Spirit." His interpretations of 4:6 especially and 5:5 emphasize the Spirit's work and presence. Bussières has argued that "revisions of some of Ambrosiaster's *Questiones* show an increased preoccupation with the divinity of the Holy Spirit," and has plausibly suggested that both the Council of Constantinople in 381 and the synod held at Rome in 382 led Ambrosiaster to articulate more explicitly the divinity and, specifically, the consubstantiality of the Holy Spirit with the Father and the Son.[31] Bussières informs us that not all the questions underwent revision in light of the Council of Constantinople, but certain ones (esp. 109 and 125) did articulate the consubstantiality of the Spirit.[32]

Jerome: Theology and Philology

Jerome wrote the most extensive extant commentary on Galatians in late antiquity.[33] In the preface to book 1 of his commentary, he claims to be the first to do this in Latin. He passes over his immediate predecessor Ambrosiaster (with whom he overlapped in Rome at the same time from 382 to 385, although

---

30. See Hilaire de Poitiers, SC 512:229.
31. David Hunter, "The Significance of Ambrosiaster," *JECS* 17 (2009): 1–26, esp. 1, 11. According to Raspanti, Ambrosiaster's approach was much more christological and historical; see G. Raspanti, "Aspetti formali dell'esegesi paolina dell'Ambrosiaster," *ASE* 16 (1999): 525–36.
32. Bussières, "L'influence du synode enu à Rome en 382," 107–24, esp. 124.
33. Cain, *Jerome: Galatians*, 49: two-thirds longer than the other five.

it is not clear whether they ever met) in a hostile *damnatio memoriae*, and he accuses Marius Victorinus of not knowing Scripture while writing his commentaries on Paul. Jerome himself confesses to relying heavily on Origen, whose commentary on Galatians is lost except for a few fragments,[34] and on several other Greek commentaries. It is very difficult for us to determine how many sources were used and how accurately Jerome used them. Careful comparisons between his commentary and the scant remains of Origen's commentary suggest both a relative closeness of their approaches and that Jerome borrowed generously from Origen. However, it is clear from the beginning that Jerome nevertheless attempted to assert or build his own authority as *the* Latin biblical exegete. Indeed, by dislocating his Latin predecessors, Jerome stylizes himself as the true inaugurator of a Latin commentary tradition on Paul and at the same time as an ambassador of the older Greek exegetical tradition into the Latin West.[35]

Moreover, after his *Commentary on Philemon*, this on Galatians was his second New Testament commentary and one of his very earliest works; hence Jerome uses it *programmatically* to develop his attitude toward the Bible as a scholar.[36] Among all the other Latin commentaries, his stands out as a "variorum commentary that presents alternative interpretations of given passages rather than the author's alone."[37] Presumably Jerome adopted the method of accumulating learned opinions under a textual lemma from his pagan grammar teacher Donatus. Jerome is nevertheless keen to promote what are, in his opinion, more adequate readings of Scripture within the range of available options. As he considers the exegetical effort in principle open-ended, he sometimes arrives at no final conclusion.

Raspanti has identified the following central issues that Jerome deals with in his commentary on Galatians:[38]

- Jerome sees the end of Judaism expressed in particular in the incident at Antioch (2:11–14).

---

34. M. A. Schatkin, "The Influence of Origen upon St. Jerome's Commentary on Galatians," VC 24 (1970): 55; Roger Gryson, *Répertoire général des auteurs ecclésiastiques latins de l'antiquité et du haut moyen âge* (Freiburg im Breisgau: Herder, 2007), 534.

35. Cain, *Jerome: Galatians*, 19–34, esp. 30–34.

36. Giacomo Raspanti, "The Significance of Jerome's *Commentary on Galatians* in His Exegetical Production," in *Jerome of Stridon: His Life, Writings and Legacy*, ed. Andrew Cain and Josef Lössl (Aldershot, UK; Burlington, VT: Ashgate, 2009), passim.

37. Cain, *Jerome: Galatians*, 34–35, which I modify somewhat since Jerome is not as open as Cain seems to suggest.

38. Giacomo Raspanti, *Commento alla epistola ai Galati: Introduzione, traduzione e note* (Turnhout: Brepols, 2010), 44–66.

- He emphasizes the importance of the *hebraica veritas*, the unity of the entire Bible, and the refutation of circumcision and of literalism (3:1–18, 3:19–5:12).
- Jerome's anthropology (5:13–26, esp. 5:17) specifies soul, flesh, spirit—with no dualism but with freedom to change, repent, and improve one's ways.
- He promotes an ascetic ideal (5:13–26, esp. 22–23).
- Jerome gives exegetical arguments against heresies (esp. Marcionism).

As characteristic of the early church in general, philological and hermeneutical decisions are closely linked to theology.

Jerome (*On Galatians* 3 preface; CCSL 77A:158.48–49) formulates the tasks of a commentator as the following: "Explain obscure things, summarize obvious things, spend time over doubtful things" (*obscura disserere, manifesta perstringere, in dubiis immorari*). While he is happy to offer figural readings of books of the Old Testament and of Matthew in his respective later commentaries, Jerome's explanations of Galatians are straightforward and literal, which could include comments on grammar, style, realia, and—most remarkably—textual criticism.[39] Sometimes a precise translation is needed against heretics. In his early *Commentary on Galatians*, Jerome emphasizes points against docetic positions, which deny the human side of Jesus and the factual truth of the incarnation; thus he writes that 4:4 (CCSL 77A:108) refers to the Son of God and should therefore be translated as *factum ex muliere* (γενόμενον ἐκ γυναικός), not *per mulierem*.[40] Jerome's principle *ad fontes* is expressed in *On Galatians* 2.3.10: "I have the habit, every time the apostles quote the Old Testament, of having recourse to the original texts and of looking carefully to see how the quotations were written in the original text." While all this sounds perfectly straightforward and sensible to us, Raspanti has identified five problems this could cause for Jerome in his own historical context:[41]

1. By having recourse to the Hebrew version, Jerome risked a devaluation of the LXX, which tradition had come to accept as divinely inspired and authoritative.
2. By deviating from the biblical text as it was shared by the majority of the church, Jerome risked the accusation of heresy, since it was seen as one of the markers of heresy to deviate from the biblical text that the majority of churches accepted.

---

39. Cain, *Jerome: Galatians*, 35–36.
40. Meiser, *Galater*, 39 and 180n693.
41. Raspanti, "Significance," 166.

3. By potentially challenging the correctness of Old Testament quotations in the New Testament, Jerome also broached the sensitive issue of the unity of the Old Testament and the New Testament, which again was a battle fought against heresies.
4. His "new" approach to the Old Testament forced Jerome to engage fully in the hermeneutic debate about the right interpretative method to be applied to the Old Testament, at a time of increasing hostility toward excessive allegorization and toward Origen in particular.
5. Finally, a new Latin translation of the Old Testament intensified the polemic between Jewish and Christian communities. Jerome was intensely interested in textual matters of the Old Testament in order to be able to produce the best Latin translation, which the Jewish community had never produced.

In this minefield where philological and theological issues were inextricably intertwined, Galatians was for Jerome a "star witness" to justify his philological program, with "Paul as a model of philology and biblical exegesis."[42] To defend his novel translation enterprise, Jerome needed to back it up with extensive activity as a commentator, which at the same time aimed at reconciling Christian exegesis with pagan literary standards. Paul's Letter to the Galatians, with its ample quotes predominantly from the LXX text of the Old Testament, at the same time advocated the literal and the allegorical interpretation of the Old Testament. Thus Galatians endorsed Jerome's philological program and allowed him to kill two birds with one stone: first, the recovery of the *hebraica veritas*; and second, the valorization in the West of the rich hermeneutic tradition extant in Greek.[43]

Jerome also considers Hebrew (i.e., rabbinic) exegesis as an important source to clarify Hebrew (or Old Testament) *realia* like the significance of Jewish festivals. But Jerome did not rely on rabbinic scholarship for philological assistance with the Hebrew Bible text, nor did the rabbis influence his Vulgate translations other than rarely, and he did not rely on them to provide a Christian exegesis. His careful distinction between philological and exegetical approaches enables him to utilize some aspects of Jewish expertise while rejecting others.[44]

All in all, the severe criticism of his new translation, which was based on the Hebrew text rather than the divinely inspired LXX, made Jerome adopt

---

42. Ibid.
43. Ibid., 171.
44. John Cameron, "The Rabbinic Vulgate?," in *Jerome of Stridon: His Life, Writings and Legacy*, ed. Andrew Cain and Josef Lössl (Aldershot, UK; Burlington, VT: Ashgate, 2009), 117–30.

an ambivalent position: on the one hand he defended his novel philology *ad fontes*, while on the other he also accepted the divinely inspired renderings of the LXX. This sometimes led to inconsistent remarks about the LXX in Jerome, as in the prologue to his *Commentary on Ecclesiastes* (CCSL 72:249), *Apology* 2.24 (CCSL 79:60–61), and *Epistle 106*, to the Goths Sunnia and Fretula.[45] But in the end his penchant for the *hebraica veritas* gains the upper hand.[46] For instance, in Galatians 3:10, Paul quotes Deuteronomy 27:26, "Cursed is everyone who does not remain *in all* that is written." Only the LXX supports the repeated *omnis* (πᾶς) in "everyone" and "in all that is written," which is contained neither in the Hebrew version nor in any of the Greek recensions, like those of Aquila, Symmachus, and Theodotion. Yet the presence of "in all that is written" was central to later Christian use of Paul's text in order to support both the Christian rejection of the law and the Christian condemnation of Jewish observance. At this place in his commentary, Jerome must therefore ask whether it was the LXX that added "everyone" and "in all that is written," or whether this had actually been contained in the original Hebrew version of the text. Jerome opts for the latter alternative and claims that the Jews had deliberately corrupted the Hebrew text at a later stage, as Paul must surely have been aware of the importance of "everyone" and "in all that is written." Therefore he could give appropriate weight to his statement only if he quoted correctly from the Hebrew original. Here Jerome subjugates Paul to his own philological program: LXX is good, Hebrew version is better. The alternative would be that one could ask: why should Christians bother about the *Hebraica veritas* if even for Paul in many instances the LXX was good enough?

Similarly, in Galatians 3:13–14 Paul quotes Deuteronomy 21:23 ("Cursed is everyone who is hung on a tree") and gives it a christological interpretation.[47] True to his philological program, Jerome checks the various Old Testament versions and comments:

> I cannot ascertain why the Apostle either added to or took away from the statement, "Everyone who hangs on a tree is cursed by God." For if he was exclusively following the authority of the Septuagint translators, he was obliged to insert the phrase "by God," just as they had done. But if, as a Jew among Jews, he thought that what he had read in his own language was the closest to the truth,

---

45. Stefan Rebenich, *Jerome* (London and New York: Routledge, 2002), 58; Cain, *Jerome: Galatians*, 37–38.
46. For the following, cf. Megan Hale Williams, *The Monk and the Book: Jerome and the Making of Christian Scholarship* (Chicago and London: University of Chicago Press, 2006), 76, slightly modified.
47. Marcion used this passage to prove the discrepancy between the God of the OT and the God of the NT, see Meiser, *Galater*, 19.

he had to omit both "everyone" and "on a tree," which are not found in the Hebrew original. This leads me to believe either that the ancient manuscripts of the Jews contained a different reading than they do now, or that the Apostle (as I said above) captured the sense rather than [the] literal meaning of Scripture.[48]

Jerome then insinuates that Paul's text differs from the Hebrew because later Jews tampered with the text in order to defame Christians. He concludes that if Christians knew Hebrew themselves, they could reclaim the Old Testament.[49] One has to bear in mind that Jerome did not retranslate Galatians into Latin but used the Old Latin version in his commentary, which he occasionally corrected by comparing it against the Greek.[50] A further goal of his *Commentary on Galatians* (as in his other works) is the refutation and eradication of heresies, of enemies of the church, in this case in particular Marcion.[51]

Jerome on Galatians 2:11–14

Occasionally Paul is found to obey Jewish law, so why does he rebuke Peter? According to Jerome, both Peter and Paul only *seemingly* obey Jewish law in order not to alienate Jewish Christians, and Paul feels obliged to rebuke Peter since he is concerned that otherwise the Christians from a pagan background might gather the wrong impression, that Jewish law is essential for being a proper Christian (*On Galatians* 1, on 2:11–13; CCSL 77A:53.29–30, *reus simulationis*; 53.45, *correptionis hypocrisi*; 54.52, *utilem vero simulationem*). Even Christ indulged in temporary guises for salutary purposes, in what was later called his *pia fraus* (54.60–63, *simulationem peccatricis carnis adsumpserit*). Peter and Paul are like good cop and bad cop, offering something to Jewish and to pagan-background Christians alike. Jerome compares this to a public trial where the lawyers on both sides engage in a "serious" argument with each other, so that both parties they represent, as well as the public audience at the trial, get the impression this is not a sham (*praevaricatio*). Likewise, will not Peter and Paul, the vessels of wisdom, engage in a holy controversy (*sanctum iurgium*) in a simulated dispute (*simulata contentio*; see also CCSL 77A:57) in order to generate peace and faith within the church (CCSL 77A:55.77–89)?

Then follows a critical discussion of those who suggest that Cephas is not identical with Peter, something that Jerome carefully refutes. Cephas

---

48. Cain, *Jerome: Galatians*, 38.
49. Ibid., 39.
50. Ibid.
51. Ibid., 41–46: e.g., Gal. 2:16 ("No one is justified by the law but by faith in Jesus Christ"). Marcion therefore sees patriarchs excluded from salvation, whereas Jerome sees them saved because of their faith in the promise of the Messiah, who had not yet come.

means in Syriac and Hebrew what Peter means in Greek ("rock"). Luke does not mention the incident in Antioch in Acts, but he does not mention other events either. Another problem was that the pagan Neoplatonist Porphyry used this story to undermine the authority of the two main apostles. But to deny that it was Peter who was rebuked is not a solution, for, as Jerome states, "If because of the blasphemy of Porphyry we have to invent another Cephas, lest Peter is believed to have erred, then we will have to erase infinite passages in the divine Scriptures which this man incriminates because he does not understand them." Jerome promises to give a more extensive refutation of Porphyry elsewhere (CCSL 77A:56–57), which unfortunately he never did. Finally, Jerome defends his explanation of a simulated trial-like dispute between Peter and Paul: "But if there is someone who is not pleased by this explanation based on which the exegetical result is that neither did Peter sin nor is Paul cheekily exposed as having rebuked someone senior, then that person must expound: based on which logic (*consequentia*) did Paul rebuke in someone else something which he did himself as well?" (e.g., circumcision of Timothy; CCSL 77A:57.11–15).[52]

Jerome also defends this explanation of Galatians 2:11–14 against that of Augustine in a virulent exchange of letters (*Epistles 28–82*, predominantly written between 402 and 405, a few earlier ones between 395 and 399). The controversial points are the biblical canon (whether it should be based on the Hebrew Bible or on the LXX), the trustworthiness of Scripture as evident from Galatians 2:11–14, and, as a consequence, the validity of ceremonial law in general. Again noticing the close interdependence between hermeneutics, theology, and practical lifestyle consequences, one can summarize thus:[53] Augustine, depending on the Latin exegetical tradition (esp. Cyprian and Ambrose), pleads for the factual truth of the controversy between Peter and Paul. Paul rightly rebukes Peter because he wanted to force pagan-background Christians to adopt Jewish ceremonial law; the incident is not a simulation, since Scripture's *auctoritas* (authority) does not allow that Paul reports an incident as true if it was faked.[54] Consequently, Augustine allows for a transitional generation of Christians whose parents had been Jews to continue to follow Jewish law, but denies this for all other Christians. Augustine emphasizes the dogmatic

---

52. For the reception of this and other passages from Jerome's *Commentary on Galatians*, see Cain, *Jerome: Galatians*, 49–50.

53. Ralph Hennings, *Der Briefwechsel zwischen Augustinus und Hieronymus und ihr Streit um den Kanon des Alten Testaments und die Auslegung von Gal. 2,11–14* (Leiden: Brill, 1994), 121–30.

54. Hennings, ibid., 123, emphasizes that Augustine is the first exegete to interpret Gal. 2:11–14 in connection with the issue of the general *auctoritas* of Scripture (*Ep.* 28.3, in CSEL 34/1:109.9–10), which would be endangered if this story were accepted as a *simulatio*.

reliability of his interpretation, which is an important criterion for accepting the authority of exegetes.

Jerome, following the Greek theologico-exegetical tradition from Origen up to John Chrysostom, which was from the early fourth century onward influenced by Porphyry(!),[55] advocates to interpret the controversy between Peter and Paul as a consciously staged verbal complot between the two apostles, which had the intention to avoid a split between pagan-background and Jewish Christians. Peter willingly accepts Paul's rebuke as the latter's care for the pagan-background Christians. In this context, Jerome is not interested in the hermeneutical issue of the truth of Scripture. Instead, Jerome concentrates on the importance of the meaning of the Jewish law for Christians. According to him, Jewish law has been put in abeyance after Jesus's passion. This does not mean that the rules of the Old Testament have no relevance anymore for Christians, but they must be understood spiritually (Jerome, *Epistle* 112 14; CSEL 55:384.10–12 = Augustine, *Epistle* 75 14; CSEL 34/II:308.1–3, *haec dicimus, non quo legem iuxta Manichaeum et Marcionem destruamus, quam et sanctam et spiritalem iuxta apostolum novimus*). Thus, for Jerome there is a clear separation between Jews and Christians, and he does not allow a period of transition. Likewise, it does not depend on the decision of the apostles whether they want to keep the Jewish law, depending on the circumstances. If they seem to keep it, they either do it under pressure or they pretend (Jerome, *Epistle* 112 15; CSEL 55: 386.22 *fallaci simulation*). To secure this position, Jerome refers to the large number of Greek exegetes who represent it and hides behind their responsibility for this position. He does not insist on this interpretation as the only true one, but against Augustine he defends his method of translating and collecting various authorities and different opinions (Jerome, *Epistle* 112 13; CSEL 55:382.5–8; *neque enim eiusdem est criminis in explanatione scripturarum diversas maiorum sententias ponere et heresim sceleratissimam rursum in ecclesiam introducere*).

In these letters Jerome in principle is congruent with his commentary on Galatians, written twenty years earlier. But within this commentary (on Gal. 2:6) as well as in other places, he contradicts himself when he at some points seems to accept, like Augustine, the factual truth of the incident in Galatians 2:11–14. Alfons Fürst is helpful in emphasizing both the nonlinearity of the contradictions in Jerome's exegesis at this point and the context in which the relevant statements were made.[56] As far as I know, however, scholarship

---

55. Hennings, *Briefwechsel zwischen Augustinus und Hieronymus*, 225–28: using Gal. 2:11–14, Porphyry sought to undermine the credibility of the archapostles Peter and Paul.

56. Alfons Fürst, *Augustins Briefwechsel mit Hieronymus* (Münster: Aschendorff, 1999), 80–87, partly correcting Hennings, *Briefwechsel zwischen Augustinus und Hieronymus*, 28–45.

has not yet attempted to explain why these contradictions occur in the first place, other than accusing Jerome of inconsistency. I suggest that different directions of exegesis are triggered by the opponent or reader one intends to target predominantly. Where Jerome argues against a position put forward by the educated pagan Porphyry, an allusion to pagan legal trial practice makes perfect sense: in this context, the notion of "lie" will be meaningful and accepted cultural practice, and effective in refuting pagan criticism of the Bible. In other instances, where Jerome accepts Galatians 2:11–14 as true, he argues against the Pelagians. While Jerome is not entirely friendly with them, he still regards them, at least in principle, as fellow Christians, with other cultural references that count. Here the truth of Scripture can and should be maintained, especially since the Pelagians were not hostile toward the literal sense of this passage but raised other issues. This raises the interesting question as to how far exegesis can vary and even contradict itself at times in order to serve a certain argumentative goal in differing contexts—in what one might call *Gelegenheitsexegese*.

A Brief Glance at Jerome's Comments on Galatians 4:21–31

On Galatians 4:24a, Jerome remarks that its term *allegoria* is an indication that Paul knew secular literature to a moderate degree (Jerome quotes all the instances: Epimenides, Aratus, and Menander) and that allegory can be found not only in secular orators and poets but also in Holy Writ (CCSL 77A:139). Following the pagan grammatical definition, *allegoria* refers to the sense of several words, word groups, or sentences, not to single words (CCSL 77A:139.1–4), which in other places Paul calls *intellegentia spiritalis* (CCSL 77A:140). Jerome is aware of potential problems with Paul's inconsistent terminology.

In Galatians 4:27 Paul quotes Isaiah 54:1 LXX, but Jerome does not comment on that. In the following he separates Jews from Christians (CCSL 77A:145) and defines Christian liberty as ethical freedom from all vices, concupiscence, and error (CCSL 77A:146). This is different from Augustine's interpretation in *The City of God*, which inserts this passage into his gigantic vision of salvation history through the ages;[57] and it is different from Philo of Alexandria (20 BCE–50 CE), a Hellenistic Jewish biblical philosopher writing around the time of Paul. In his *Preliminary Studies*, he offers an allegorical explanation of Genesis 16 that is meant to emphasize the superiority of philosophy over propaedeutic (worldly!) encyclical instruction: Hagar is the intellectual handmaid, representing the liberal arts, whereas Sarah represents philosophy,

---

57. See p. 60 below.

which is the true goal of education. Moreover, virtue (Sarah) is superior to education (Hagar), although the acquisition of all the preliminary branches of education is wholly necessary (25). But it is a mistake to dally too long with the encyclical handmaidens rather than to return to one's true wife, philosophy (77–78). Jerome finds this a complicated passage, as Ishmael had also been the object of promises—in Genesis 16:10–12 through an angel of the Lord and in 17:20 through God himself (16:10–12). As it is done by an angel, this could, according to Jerome, be regarded as to be of *minor auctoritas* than the promise by God, which went to Sarah on behalf of Isaac (Gen. 17), who declares Isaac to be *heir*. But the issue of how to solve this tension exegetically *is open-ended*, and better explanations can perhaps still be found as Jerome declares by quoting Philippians 3:15 (CCSL 77A:138.49–53).

Despite this, Jerome insists that Genesis 16 must be interpreted in a spiritual way in order to liberate us for the promise. *Again there is a connection between hermeneutics and soteriology.* The allegorical interpretation of Hagar and Sarah as mothers of two different communities must not be understood in a genealogical fashion: it must not be that Moses and all the prophets are defined as children of Hagar, and all the pagan-background Christians as children of Sarah. Rather, those who understand Scripture allegorically are Sarah's children, and its literal interpreters are Hagar's children. Sarah, the free one, is the mother of the church as gathered from the heathens, and thus she is the mother of the saints (CCSL 77A:148–49).[58] But within the church itself, there are also free ones and "slaves" (to sin), and even within one person there can be a change from slave existence to freedom when the person converts (CCSL 77A:142). Jerome then reinforces this point through taking up an argument by Marcion and the Manichaean heresy: they use this passage in Paul as proof *against* the unity of Old Testament and New Testament. However, this allegory preserves it, since it was put there *non pro voluntate legentis, sed pro scribentis auctoritate* (CCSL 77A:142.53–54).

Augustine: Ecclesiology and Personal Faith

And then there is Augustine. Writing his Galatians commentary in about 394–395, Augustine had a model in church history that not for the first or the last time would influence his exegesis or at least confirm it, for the North African bishop Cyprian of a century and more earlier was eventually humble enough to be rebuked only on the question of rebaptism, having promoted the

---

58. For this motif, see also below, the *Carmen adversus Marcionitas*.

truth of reason over tradition, as he believed Paul had done to Peter.[59] Reason ruled against accepting the rebaptism of heretics, no matter that there was a tradition of it. Peter had been persuaded, and bishops like Quintus should be too! Moreover, even the present pope should act as Peter did and come to realize that custom and institution are no match for the truth. In his work on *Baptism*, Augustine takes this to justify asking: what right did Cyprian have to play the role of Peter and refuse the validity of heretical baptism?

In a sense, then, Cyprian as a model is actually a main source for Augustine's treatment of Galatians 2:11–14, as a less-than-humble interpreter who had to learn humility. Also, for Augustine, the Scripture had no truck with lying: it was the apostolic words, not the apostolic lives, that needed to be flawless (as Maurice Wiles put it). And Augustine was a rigorist when it came to speaking the truth. The authority of Scripture might have partly been the issue, as Plumer[60] thinks. Unlike in a Manichaean scheme, there is no place for "heroes" and villains, but instead a Christian understanding of weakness is displayed alongside a doctrine of rebuke and forgiveness. Augustine speaks of Peter's "error" rather than "sin": "So while Augustine does not judge Peter's action as severely as Victorinus does, he does not trivialize it either."[61] But Peter is the hero of the incident at Antioch: "Peter had learned from the Lord to be gentle and humble in heart."[62] In Plumer's assessment, "Augustine adds a characteristic, Catholic emphasis: even though Paul's gospel was true, it still needed to be confirmed by the other apostles in order to demonstrate that Paul's efforts were not in vain."[63] The lesson is that an interpreter needs to be gentle of heart as interpreter as well as knowledgeable: "The Commentary furnishes a practical example of the theory of interpretation set forth in the *De doctrina christiana* and indeed paves the way for that theory."[64] If one would not dare to claim influence, one can at least surmise some kind of "family resemblance" between Victorinus and Augustine.

In Augustine are reflections of Marius Victorinus: they both agree that Jesus as "proscribed" means losing his inheritance.[65] Cooper has presented the case

---

59. "Non est autem de consuetudine praescribendum, sed ratione vincendum" (Cyprian, *Ep.* 71.3); see Gerd Haendler, "Cyprians Auslegung zu Galater 2,11ff.," *TLZ* 97 (1972): 561–66.

60. Eric Plumer, trans., *Augustine's Commentary on Galatians*, OECS (Oxford: Oxford University Press, 2003), 50; following R. S. Cole-Turner, "Anti-heretical Issues and the Debate over Galatians 2:1–14 in the Letters of St. Augustine to St. Jerome," *AugStud* 11 (1980): 156–66.

61. Plumer, *Augustine's Commentary on Galatians*, 145n49.

62. Ibid., 147.

63. Ibid., 107.

64. Ibid., 120.

65. On Gal. 3:1: "*Ante quorum oculos Christus Iesus proscriptus est, crucifixus*, hoc est, quibus videntibus Christus Iesus hereditatem suam possessionemque suam amisit."

that Augustine knew Victorinus's commentary, and that on Galatians 2:19 they both present two alternative interpretations for "dead to law."[66] There is perhaps stronger evidence that Augustine also knew Ambrosiaster in that they both confuse the James who was witness of the transfiguration with James the brother of Jesus and pillar of the Jerusalem church. Also, Ambrosiaster and Augustine equate the two *testamenta* with the two *populi*. A possible reflection of *Christian* Neoplatonic influence (i.e., that of Victorinus) on Augustine's exegesis is the latter's account of Galatians 2:20 as a refusal of any attempt to establish one's own righteousness, even in the Christian asceticism of overcoming self-will. So he could not accept the position that the mortification of one's own will was the result of a good use of the will's freedom.[67] Behind this lies a curious anthropology—the inner man as intellect that can understand divine things: "That now I live, in the flesh since he cannot say that Christ still lives in a mortal manner, for life in the flesh is mortal, he says 'in faith of the son of God I live' that also Christ might live in the believer by dwelling in the inner man through faith, so that he would later satisfy him by sight, when the mortal will have been absorbed by life."[68] When Augustine repeats "In faith I live of the Son of God," in the context it sounds very much like faith as the *fides quae*, "faith about the Son of God," attained by the intellectual part of himself.

The *Carmen adversus Marcionitas*: Theology and Literature

Of course, writing commentaries was not the only way in which theologians in the early church and beyond engaged with biblical texts, including Paul's Letters. An area understudied in this respect is early Christian poetry, a genre that goes back to late antiquity.[69] Regarding Galatians, the so-called *Carmen adversus Marcionitas* has an intriguing poetical exegesis to offer. This poem

---

66. Cooper, *Marius Victorinus*, 8–9.

67. M. Meiser, *Galaterbrief*, NTP 9 (Göttingen: Vandenhoeck & Ruprecht, 2007), 116: "AUGUSTINUS aktualisiert Gal 2,20a als Absage an jeden Versuch, die eigene Gerechtigkeit aufzurichten. So kann er auch der Inanspruchnahme der Stelle durch PELAGIUS nichts abgewinnen, der behauptet hatte, die Abtötung der eigenen *voluntas* sei das Ergebnis einer guten Nützung der *arbitrii libertas*."

68. Plumer, *Augustine's Commentary on Galatians*, 148: "Quod autem nunc vivo, inquit, in carne, quia non posset dicere Christum adhuc mortaliter vivere, vita autem in carne mortalis est, *in fide*, inquit, *vivo filii dei*, ut etiam Christus sic vivat in credente habitando in interiore homine per fidem, ut postea per speciem impleat eum, cum absorptum fuerit mortale a vita."

69. Culminating in John Milton's *Paradise Lost*, on whose theology see Trevor Hart, "Poetry and Theology in Milton's *Paradise Lost*," in *Genesis and Christian Theology*, ed. Nathan MacDonald, Mark W. Elliott, and Grant Macaskill (Grand Rapids: Eerdmans, 2012), 129–39.

comprises 1,302 hexameters in five books, its author is not known, and it is directed against the followers of Marcion, the so-called Marcionites. Therefore it was mistakenly regarded as a work by the second-/third-century Christian writer Tertullian, who produced a lengthy prose work titled *Against Marcion* (*Adversus Marcionem*), also in five books. However, since we have no evidence that Tertullian ever wrote poetry, and since other literary-historical reasons such an early date for this poem are highly unlikely, the author can only be called Pseudo-Tertullian. I have dated the poem into the first half of the fifth century at the earliest; as a *terminus post quem* I have suggested Augustine's first half of *The City of God*, thus around 420.[70] The *terminus ante quem* is not so certain and could be much later.

The poem's aim is to refute the venomous heresy of the Marcionites. The author considers the Marcionites' main vice to be, first, their claim that contradictions between the Old Testament and the New Testament make it clear that they proclaim two different Gods, and that Jesus cannot be the Son of the God of the Old Testament; second, their serious reduction of the biblical canon; and third, their denial of Jesus's factual incarnation, meaning their adherence to so-called docetism.[71] Characteristic of this type of elitist poetry is a very advanced rephrasing of relevant biblical passages. In a poetically seamless manner, the poets are normally keen to integrate doctrinal aspects and exegetical positions as they were familiar to them from exegetical prose treatises. Moreover, sometimes the integration of a biblical passage in a sophisticated narrative can generate original exegetical results. One example for the latter is the paraphrase of Galatians 4:21–31 in book 3 of the *Carmen adversus Marcionitas*. The argumentative goal of this book is to demonstrate the continuity of the Christian people from its beginnings in the Old Testament (*ecclesia ab Abel*)[72] up to the time of Marcion. The book begins with a methodological reflection, claiming that the presupposition for this proof is the allegorical interpretation of Genesis 16:21 according to Galatians 4:21–31, in

---

70. Karla Pollmann, *Das Carmen adversus Marcionitas: Einleitung, Übersetzung, Text und Kommentar* (Göttingen: Vandenhoeck & Ruprecht, 1991), 28–33. Sebastian Moll, *The Arch-Heretic Marcion* (Tübingen: Mohr Siebeck, 2010), 21–23, wants to date the poem again into the third century, which is not sensible from a literary-historical perspective. Metrical, stylistic, and motivic reasons are also against it. Moll, 21–23, considers the "passion" of the poet as the only important argument for dating it into the third century. This is naive, as, e.g., Jerome, in his *Commentary on Galatians* from 386, also argues passionately against Marcion. Nor is a theologically "pure" rendering of Marcion's doctrine a sufficient reason for an early date of the poem. Much more worthy of attention is the review of Pollmann by Isabella Gualandri, *Gnomon* 69 (1997): 160–62, who wants to date the poem into the sixth century, mainly for metrical reasons.

71. Pollmann, *Das Carmen adversus Marcionitas*, 33.

72. Ibid., 161–62.

particular with Sarah as the mother of the promised people (*Carmen* 3.1–13). Verses 14–241 list biblical figures from Abel up to John the Baptist as *typoi* whose virtuous and faithful attitude prefigured and adumbrated the glory of the coming Messiah (14–224), who himself was then in turn a role model for his disciples and others willing to suffer for their faith (225–241). Verses 242–271 frame this section by referring to the methodological reflection at the beginning of this book, emphasizing that Sarah took part in the mechanism of "first suffering then glory" as true testimony for God in the same way as her descendants. In the concluding section (272–302), these descendants are specified as the bishops of Rome from Peter until Anicetus (ca. 154–166, the time of Marcion), who managed to defend the true faith successfully against Marcion.

Particularly striking is the transition from *Carmen* 3.1–13 to what follows: Sarah, once barren, bore a new and promised people; "she bore one single people from many nations, a people whose pious members from its beginning always had to suffer" ([12] *haec genuit gentem multis ex gentibus unam*/[13] *cuius principio semper pia membra laborant*). Then verse 14 ensues with the explanation that Abel, and others after him, belonged to this people. This is an interesting transition because of its chronological discontinuity: Sarah is a good deal later than Abel, and although the soteriological-exegetical logic is explained and coherent, the narrative proceeds in a rather abrupt fashion. This abruptness is not so striking in Augustine's *City of God* 15.1–5. There, in chapter 1, Augustine explains that he wants to talk about the progress (*procursus*) of the two *civitates*: the *terrena civitas* and the *civitas dei*. As scriptural support for this method, in chapter 2 he inserts the allegorical interpretation of Genesis 16 in Galatians 4:21–31, thereby extending to world history the schema of letter and spirit.[73] In chapter 3 he deals with the barren Sarah, who was made fruitful by God's grace; in chapter 4 he briefly discusses strife and peace in the earthly city. In chapter 5 he starts his narrative beginning with Abel as the first member (not founder!) of the city of God, and Cain as the founder (!) and first member of the earthly city. Our poem does not have all that space, and indeed does not want such space. Its narrative-didactic theological technique can best be explained by arguing that it uses the onset of book 15 of *The City of God* and condenses it poetically, with the aim of using Augustine's argument, interwoven with an ensuing Old Testament/New Testament paraphrase, in order to prove against Marcion the continuity of the people of promise through history from its very beginning.

---

73. James McEvoy, "The Patristic Hermeneutic of Spiritual Freedom and Its Biblical Origins," in *Scriptural Interpretation in the Fathers: Letter and Spirit*, ed. Thomas Finan and Vincent Twomey (Dublin and Portland, OR: Four Courts Press, 1995), 17.

Conclusion

These exegetes of late antiquity do not only offer their readers insight into the formation of a Christian intellectual culture to rival that of pagan antiquity, while making use of it as it seemed fit; they also provide insights into the *meaning* of Galatians that modern readers would do well to give the benefit of the doubt, thus not regarding the epistle as merely naive and tendentious, but especially as living, pastoral, and also theologically and philosophically sophisticated.

4

Justification and Participation

Ecumenical Dimensions of Galatians

THOMAS SÖDING

The Letter to the Galatians is a document of ecumenism in the New Testament. It has, however, become a document of confessional conflicts. Today, thank God, it is rediscovered as a document of ecumenical understanding. Paul wrote the letter to clarify the identity of believers, to motivate the mission, and to deepen the unity of the church. Since ancient times the letter was used as an instrument for shaping different answers to the question of how a human being can find a merciful God. Today the letter is interpreted as a basis for a differentiated consensus in the doctrine of justification. The history of its reception[1] reflects the substance, the dynamic, and the rhetoric of Galatians, but it needs an exegetical and hermeneutical clarification. What is the Pauline stimulus? What are the presuppositions, the perspectives, and the problems of his controversial theology? What is the ecumenical potential of the letter today?

---

1. Cf. John Riches, *Galatians through the Centuries* (New York: Wiley Blackwell, 2007); Martin Meiser, *Galater*, NTP 9 (Göttingen: Vandenhoeck & Ruprecht, 2008).

Pauline Ecumenism in the Mirror of Galatians

In the last sentence of the letter's *paraklēsis*, Paul writes: "Whenever we have time [καιρός], let us work for the good of all, and especially for those of the household of faith [τοὺς οἰκείους τῆς πίστεως]" (Gal. 6:10). Here the key word οἰκουμένη (Rom. 10:18; Ps. 19:5 LXX) finds a specific variation: in the house of the world there is the house of God, the house of faith, the Christian church. Its members are not isolated; they are interested in the life of others; they should try to support them. But they have to concentrate their energy on the comembers of the church; in the community of faith they find the neighbors whom they are called to love first (Lev. 19:18; Gal. 5:14).

Limits

The dialectic between openness for others and the deepness of the ecclesial fellowship is essential for the Pauline concept of ecumenism over all, not only in Galatians. But it is not evident that this epistle should be read as an ecumenical *consensus* document.

In its prooemion the letter starts with a double anathema (Gal. 1:8, 9). Paul criticizes the propagandists[2] of "another gospel" (1:6), which in his eyes is not a real gospel but a perversion (1:7). In Galatians there is no initiative for reconciliation, as in 2 Corinthians. Paul, fighting for the faith of his readers in the local churches that he founded, stresses the "either–or." The antithetical structure of the justification thesis "not by the works of the law but through faith of Jesus Christ" (2:16) brings the necessity of a decision into focus. In his report on the apostolic council (2:1–10), Paul blames the opponents he has faced in Jerusalem as "false brothers, who slipped in to spy on the freedom we have in Christ Jesus, so that they might enslave us" (2:4). Therefore, if Galatians is an ecumenical document, ecumenism is not a radical openness for whatever might be said by the baptized, but a process of theological discourse within a wide field of predication, meditation, and practice, searching for the freedom of the faith (2:4), the truth of the gospel (2:5), and the community of the church (2:9). Whether Paul was right to exclude his opponents in Galatia and the "false brothers" in Jerusalem from the apostolic community is a matter of discussion. But his introduction makes clear that for him his letter marks the outer limits of the church in order to include a huge number of members with their traditions, especially to invite into the church as many of the gentiles as

---

2. Cf. John C. Hurd, "Reflections concerning Paul's 'Opponents' in Galatia," in *Paul and His Opponents*, ed. Stanley E. Porter, Pauline Studies 2 (Leiden: Brill, 2005), 129–48.

possible, but also to exclude those who claim circumcision and Pharisaic purity as requirements for all believers,[3] so that ecumenical openness is restricted.[4]

Dimensions

Although there are problems with reading Galatians as a letter of ecumenism, as much as he can Paul is engaged in order not only to unite the church but also to profile the real plurality of Christian lifestyles. This plurality is an essential aspect of the ecclesial unity that constitutes spiritual community. In Galatians, Paul opens the personal, missionary, and ecclesial dimensions of justification theology on two levels: a threefold remembering and a threefold actualization.

Remembrance

Remembrance is the essence of the letter's *narratio* (Gal. 1:13–2:16; cf. 1:21). A first dimension of remembrance refers to Paul's vocation as an apostle.[5] In Galatians 1:13–16 he represents himself as a former enemy of the church (cf. 1 Cor. 15:9) who was called by God to become a missionary of Christ, the risen Crucified One. His aggression against the church before reaching Damascus (cf. Acts 9:1–22) was targeted against a new sect of Judaism with (what he regarded as) a stupid message and a dangerous enthusiasm. As an apostle of Jesus Christ, however, he has a mission of peace. Paul ends the Letter to the Galatians with a handwritten notice: "As many as follow this rule [κανών]—peace be upon them, and mercy, and upon the Israel of God" (Gal. 6:16).[6] The "rule" seems to be the theocentric Christology, soteriologically interpreted by the doctrine of justification. How does this interpretation of the "rule" in 6:16 relate to the statement in 6:15? In the vision of Paul, the *ekklēsia* is constructed by God (cf. 1 Cor. 3:9–17) as a house of life for both Jews and Greeks. In Romans, he discusses the problem that the great majority of the Jews will not become members of the church, so that he has to set forth what the special role of the Jews may be in God's salvation plan; but in Galatians, Paul concentrates on the proclamation of the gospel and the

---

3. Cf. Donald A. Carson, Peter T. O'Brien, Mark A. Seifrid, eds., *Justification and Variegated Nomism*, vol. 1, *The Complexities of Second Temple Judaism*, WUNT 2/140 (Tübingen: Mohr Siebeck, 2001); idem, vol. 2, *The Paradoxes of Paul*, WUNT 2/181 (Tübingen: Mohr Siebeck, 2004).
4. Another problem in Galatians is the image of Judaism. But in Romans, Paul was able to integrate the justification of believers and the salvation of Israel.
5. Cf. Robert Vorholt, *Der Dienst der Versöhnung: Studien zur Apostolatstheologie bei Paulus*, WMANT 118 (Neukirchen-Vluyn: Neukirchener, 2008).
6. There is a discussion whether "Israel of God" refers to the Jews or to the church members; cf. Susan Grove Eastman, "Israel and the Mercy of God. A Re-reading of Galatians 6.16 and Romans 9–11," *NTS* 56 (2010): 367–95.

invitation into the church. His own mission to the gentiles is part of the mission of the whole church, which is addressed first to the Jews (cf. Rom. 1:16–17). Though expressed later in Ephesians, already in Galatians the peace for which Paul works is the peace between humans and God (cf. Rom. 5:1) received in the ecclesial family, including the relation between Jews and Greeks. But Paul could not have been an apostle of peace if he had not found peace himself. In Philippians, Paul describes as "knowledge of Christ Jesus" (3:8) what in Galatians 1:16 he interprets as "revelation." This revelation and knowledge do not entail a liberation from a strong system of religious duties to a liberal religion, as viewed by many nineteenth- and twentieth-century researchers, especially in Germany;[7] nor are they a liberation from an existential uncertainty rooted in an excessive demand by Pharisaic perfectionism, as viewed in some recent psychological approaches.[8] The vocation is rather repentance from violence to peace, from zeal without recognition to dynamic faith, and from rejection of the Crucified to the recognition of the Son of God. Paul reflects this personal dimension in Galatians, presenting himself as a model of salvation (2:19–20). By faith Paul is discovering himself to be beloved by God, although he earlier was God's enemy. Paul thus reflects the theology of justification not as part of the revelation he received, but as a consequence of his vocation: justifying faith allows him, as well as every believer, to find the peace of God in his own heart (Rom. 5:1); justifying faith allows him as well to convey to the gentiles the invitation into the "kingdom of God," the reign "of righteousness and peace and joy in the Holy Spirit" (Rom. 14:17), and to be engaged not only as founder but also as pastor of his communities.

A second dimension of remembrance refers to the apostolic council (Gal. 2:1–10).[9] For Paul, the essential agreement between Jerusalem and Antioch was the recognition of a community of faith in a variety of missions: "When James and Cephas and John, who were acknowledged pillars, recognized the grace that had been given to me, they gave to Barnabas and me the right hand

---

7. Cf. Ferdinand Christian Baur, *Paulus, der Apostel Jesu Christi: Sein Leben und Wirken, seine Briefe und seine Lehre; Ein Beitrag zu einer kritische Geschichte des Urchristenthums*, ed. Eduard Zeller after Baur's death, 2nd ed. (1866–67; reprint, Osnabrück: Zeller, 1968); Rudolf Bultmann, *Theologie des Neuen Testaments (1948–1953)*, ed. O. Merk (Tübingen: J. C. B. Mohr, 1984).

8. Cf. Gerd Lüdemann, *Die Auferstehung Jesu: Historie—Erfahrungen—Theologie* (Stuttgart: Radius, 1994).

9. Cf. Karl-Wilhelm Niebuhr, "Gemeinschaft der Apostel. Das 'Apostelkonzil' als Bezugspunkt und Modell konziliarer Gemeinschaft in der Kirche," in *Die Ökumenischen Konzilien und die Katholizität der Kirche: Das elfte Gespräch im bilateralen theologischen Dialog zwischen der Rumänischen Orthodoxen Kirche und der Evangelischen Kirche in Deutschland* [April 1–7, 2006, in Eisenach], ed. Dagmar Heller and Johann Schneider, Beiheft zur Ökumenische Rundschau 83 (Frankfurt: Lembeck, 2009), 46–69.

of fellowship [κοινωνίας], agreeing that we should go to the gentiles and they to the circumcised" (2:9). The grace that Paul was given is the vocation as apostle; his genuine apostleship, the apostleship for gentiles, was recognized and accepted by the Jerusalem church (2:6–7). Titus is the living argumentum ad hominem, representing the personal dimension of the discussion about mission strategies (2:3). In the eyes of Paul, it was therefore necessary to resist the opponents, who probably were arguing on the basis of Genesis 17 to establish circumcision—not only as an identity marker of religious affiliation[10] but also as, one might say, a sacrament of the covenant: as a visible sign with an invisible effect, making one a member of the people of God and thus situated within the horizon of the promise of salvation. As described in Galatians, the reason for Paul's resistance is not the expectation of having better chances for successful mission without circumcision (which was also true). The real reason for Paul is that the demand for circumcision darkens the salvific sufficiency of faith and draws the sense of the law in a wrong way; in Galatians 3:19–25 Paul claims that it was not given as an instrument of salvation but as a mirror of sin, as a guard for sinners, and as a "schoolmaster to bring us unto Christ" (3:24 KJV). For Paul, the apostolic council was an indispensable consequence of God's universal saving will revealed and realized in Jesus Christ. The theology of justification makes clear the logic of that promise.

A third dimension of remembrance refers to Paul's conflict with Peter, Barnabas, and "all" the other Jewish Christians at Antioch (Gal. 2:11–14).[11] Paul connects the narration of that event with the first explication of the justification antithesis between the works of the law and the faith of Christ (2:15–16). While the Jerusalem decision was structured to open the church for gentiles, the Antioch conflict exposes the intraecclesial relations between Jews and Greeks. Under the pressure "of the circumcision faction" (2:12), the Christian Jews separate from the common meals with the other Christians (2:11). It is plausible that the Eucharist was also impacted. Therefore it was a crucial point of ecclesial communion. Paul argues in favor of freedom. The Christians from among the gentiles have their own standing in the church with their own rights. The Jewish Christians need to respect them as brothers and sisters, without any conditions. The only necessary and sufficient ground to be a church member is baptism. So Paul is sure that he must criticize Cephas and the others, including Barnabas. Although it does not need to represent his

---

10. Cf. James D. G. Dunn, "The New Perspective on Paul (1983)," in *Jesus, Paul, and the Law: Studies in Mark and Galatians* (London: SCM, 1990), 183–206, plus "Additional Note" on 206–14.

11. Cf. Th. Söding, "Apostel gegen Apostel: Ein Unfall im antiochenischen Großstadtverkehr (Gal 2,11–14)," in *Das frühe Christentum und die Stadt*, ed. Reinhard von Bendemann and Markus Tiwald, BWANT 198 (Stuttgart: Kohlhammer, 2012), 92–113.

historic position, the justification antithesis works against the separation of Jewish and gentile believers and for their unification in the spirit of freedom. Whether Paul was successful is a real question, but the rhetoric of Galatians 2 gives the impression that it was a real conflict, that Paul gave a convincing argument, and that the justification theology is able to join the Jews with faithful gentiles in the church. Paul appeals to Cephas's personal experience and insight as a Jew as he calls him to remember their common conviction of justification by faith.

Looking back in anger, Paul marks three characteristic places where justification theology is rooted and works: it is a theology of conversion in order to show the way a sinner finds a place "in Christ" and therefore in the church; it is a theology of mission in order to understand God's saving will *secundum scripturas*; and it is a theology of ecclesial unity in order to deepen the community between Jews and gentiles inside and outside the church. These three aspects—the personal, the missionary, and the ecclesial—belong together because of the freedom God gives: to be newly created (Gal. 6:15; cf. 2 Cor. 5:17) as "Hörer des Wortes" (Karl Rahner), in which the faithful finds identity in the love of Christ; to be convinced that the gospel is such a joy that it has to be told to others; and to share this love with others who share it, thereby establishing the church as *koinōnia*. The vocation of the apostle, the experiences of the gentile mission, and the work of building up the church are genuine places to discover the meaning and to sharpen the sense of justification.

The common category of these three aspects is participation: participation in faith, participation in mission, and participation in the church, the body of Christ (Rom. 12:3-8; 1 Cor. 12:12-27; cf. Gal. 3:26-29). In all three dimensions it is God the Father who fulfills his righteousness, Jesus the Son "in" whom the justification fits, and the Holy Spirit who (1) opens individual believers for the community and mission of the church, (2) opens the apostolic mission for the religious desire of humans, and (3) opens the ecclesial community for the plurality of the believers' biographies and the invitation to others.[12]

ACTUALIZATION

Actualization is the essence of the letter's *argumentatio* (Gal. 2:15 [3:1]–5:12). In writing Galatians, Paul is arguing against the ecumenical idea of his opponents: community with Jerusalem and with Israel would be possible only

---

12. On the essential connection between soteriology, spirituality, and ethics, cf. Volker Rabens, "Power from in Between: The Relational Experience of the Holy Spirit and Spiritual Gifts in Paul's Churches," in *The Spirit and Christ in the New Testament and Christian Theology: Essays in Honor of Max Turner*, ed. I. Howard Marshall, Volker Rabens, and Cornelis Bennema (Grand Rapids: Eerdmans, 2012), 138-55.

by practicing circumcision. His *narratio* is intended to clarify that he is in full communion with the church of Jerusalem and with all the other apostles (cf. 1 Cor. 15:1–11). His *argumentatio* is intended to clarify that he is in full accordance with the Scriptures when he stresses justifying faith because it is the authentic answer of the gospel. With his *narratio* and his *argumentatio*, Paul wishes to reintegrate the Galatians into the church, which they are tempted to leave; he wishes that they would continue to belong within the framework of his apostolic service, and hence he tries to convince them by teaching the truth of the gospel.

In Paul's address to the Galatians, the three aspects of the justification event are worked out from the side of the believer. The personal aspect takes shape in the field of praying and imitating. The "I" of the letter writer is not only the individual "I" of Paul the apostle, but in some essential aspects it also is the "I" of every believer, who is welcome to identify him- or herself with Paul (Gal. 4:12). The apostle imitates Christ so that the believers can imitate him (cf. 1 Cor. 4:16; 11:1; also Gal. 4:14). As an apostle he is their mother (cf. 1 Cor. 4:14–15; Phil. 2:22; 1 Thess. 2:7; 2:11; Philem. 10):[13] "My little children, for whom I am again in the pain of childbirth until Christ is formed [μορφωθῇ] in you" (Gal. 4:19 NRSV).[14] The pain is the work Paul has to do because of the Galatian troubles. His teaching via his epistle aims at a rebirth of the Galatians as children of God. It is in every believer as a member of the church and in the whole community of individual believers where this formation has to take place. The new life that the Galatians must rediscover is the reality of justification by faith. Christ is the subject. He characterizes those who believe in him. According to the Philippian hymn (2:7), Christ took on the "form of a slave" (μορφὴν δούλου); according to Romans, the believers are "predestined to be conformed to the image [συμμόρφους τῆς εἰκόνος] of his Son" (Rom. 8:29 NRSV). Galatians 4:19 identifies this synapse between soteriology and ethics. The believers have to fill out the form of the life that Christ designs. To live the faith means to imitate Christ (cf. 1 Cor. 11:1; 1 Thess. 1:6–7) and, more, to let Jesus be the "I" in the life of every believer, as Paul describes it in Galatians 2:19–20. It is the theology of faith that reflects what happened in history and what happens in the presence of the church, as well as in the biography of every Christian. To be a Christian is a lifelong process of identity building, of belonging to Christ and his church. An essential expression of this

---

13. Cf. Beverly Roberts Gaventa, "The Maternity of Paul: An Exegetical Study of Galatians iv.19," in *The Conversation Continues: Studies in Paul and John in Honor of J. L. Martyn*, ed. Robert T. Fortna and Beverly Roberts Gaventa (Nashville: Abingdon, 1990), 191–94.

14. A parallel is 1 Cor. 2:16; cf. Christof Strüder, *Paulus und die Gesinnung Christi: Identität und Entscheidungsfindung aus der Mitte von 1 Kor 1–4*, BETL 190 (Leuven: Peeters, 2006).

identity is praying. To cry "Abba!" (Gal. 4:6), guided by the Spirit, expresses the privileged status of every believer: "So you are no longer a slave but a son, a daughter, and if a child then also an heir, through God" (4:7). Everybody who is justified participates in this prayer; every "Abba!" prayer deepens the participation of the believer in the love of God, the heavenly Father.

The missionary aspect of justification takes shape in the Pauline report about his former service in Galatia. It seemed to be a mission impossible because of the difficulties he had to contend against: problems of health, reputation, and oppression (Gal. 4:13–14). But the existence of the Galatian communities is a fruit of Paul's apostleship and of his concept of the gentile mission. Although the anti-Pauline missionaries say that mission without circumcision is a wooden iron, Paul counters with evidence from the effect of his work. He asks them: "Did you receive the Spirit by doing the works of the law or by believing what you heard?" (Gal. 3:2 NRSV). This is the Spirit of God, working in the prayers of the faithful and in the friendship between Paul and the Galatians. The faith of the Galatians consists in knowing God (4:9), just as it does for Paul (cf. Phil. 3:8). The apostolic mission aimed at the understanding of faith (cf. Gal. 6:6), the personal acceptance of the gospel (cf. 3:1), and the convinced practice of spiritual freedom (6:9).

Because of the local troubles, the Letter to the Galatians focuses the mission the Christians have received. But Romans and Philippians, as well as the Corinthian correspondence, show that Paul wants to enable the communities to participate actively in the mission of the church—not so much as wandering preachers but by attractive worship, social care, and understandable teaching. The justification theology reflects what happened in the Galatian churches because of the Pauline mission—and what can happen when faith is working "through love" (Gal. 5:6).

The ecclesial aspect of justification takes shape in the community because apostolic service is essential for the church. The opponents of Paul see a gap between Galatia and Jerusalem because of the freedom of the Pauline mission. Therefore Paul needs to argue in both directions: that he was fully accepted as an apostle and that his justification theology, highlighted in the antithesis of Galatians 2:16, is not his own special theory but is a common tradition.[15] So the Galatians would be separated not only "from Christ" (5:4) but also from the church if they want to be justified by the law. For Paul, "faith" in itself is not only personal but also ecclesial: "We believe" (Gal. 2:16) and "I" believe

---

15. Cf. Christoph Burchard, "Nicht aus Werken des Gesetzes gerecht, sondern aus Glauben an Jesus Christus—seit wann?," in *Geschichte—Tradition—Reflexion: Festschrift für Martin Hengel*, vol. 3, *Frühes Christentum*, ed. Hermann Lichtenberger (Tübingen: Mohr Siebeck, 1996), 405–15.

(cf. 2:19–20). The "I" is essential because of the freedom of faith; the "we" is essential because of the communion of faith. God liberates every believer to become a believer, and God brings together all believers in order that they might share their understanding of the gospel, celebrate their liturgy, and build up their house of faith. Justification theology reflects the fundamental role of personal and ecclesial faith for the church as well as the role of the church's mission for the freedom and communion of the believers.

The actualization of the personal, the missionary, and the common dimensions of justification theology in the situation addressed by the letter follows the logic of faith and connects the believers in Galatia with the other Christian churches. Therefore, Galatians is an ecumenical letter because of its justification theology, and its justification theology is developed as ecumenical theology.

Structures

The threefold remembrance and threefold actualization of justification theology in Galatians are characteristic for Pauline theology as a whole. Taking a glance at Romans confirms and differentiates Paul's approach.

The personal dimension is expressed, in extreme emotion, by the "I" of Romans 7: "Wretched man that I am! Who shall deliver me from the body of this death?" (7:24 KJV). There is the sin of Adam in the sins of other humans, which Paul is analyzing; there is no possibility of self-rescue because of the deepness of sin as reflected in the greatness of promise. There is the word of reconciliation proclaimed by the apostle and received by faith (5:1–11): "Thanks be to God through Jesus Christ our Lord!" (Rom. 7:25a NRSV). In Romans as well as in Galatians, Paul concretizes this personal dimension as freedom. Justification is liberation from sin and death; it is liberation to share the love of God in love for one's neighbors.

The missionary dimension is expressed from the very beginning: "For I am not ashamed of the gospel; it is the power of God for salvation to everyone who has faith, to the Jew first and also to the Greek. For in it the righteousness of God is revealed from faith to faith" (Rom. 1:16–17). The whole argument of Romans is an explication of that introduction. The necessity of mission comes from the power of sin over Jews and Greeks and from the promise of God for Jews and Greeks (1:18–3:20). The aim of mission is faith, because faith, like the faith of Abraham, is the authentic answer of the whole person to the word of God, trusting and recognizing, confessing and converting, confirmed by and connected with the faith of other believers (3:21–8:38). The mission of the church is dialectically connected with the "No" to the gospel of most of the Jews—a mystery of faith that invites the Christians to search for the special mission of the Jews in the salvific plan of God, as Joseph Ratzinger argues.[16]

The ecclesial mission is not only expressed in the understanding of faith as such but also concretized in three aspects: first, the sacramental aspect in the theology of baptism (Rom. 6:1–11); second, the spiritual aspect in common prayer (8:14–30); and third, the moral aspect in the reconciliation created between members with Jewish roots and members from the gentiles (11:20–31), as well as between those who are "weak" and those who are "strong" (14:1–15:13).

The Pauline theology of justification reflects these three aspects because it connects God's grace with human freedom, personal experience with ecclesial community, and God's righteousness, or justice, with human righteousness and justice (6:13, 16, 18–19). Therefore it is ecumenical theology in itself.

Pauline Justification Theology Mirrored in Ecumenical Controversies

It may be that there was a dark space in the first centuries of Christianity where Paul with his justification theology was more or less an undercover agent of liberation theology.[17] But since late antiquity, the justification topic has become of great importance in the Latin church. Hence, Pauline theology was the crucial point in the controversies between Protestant and Catholic theology, although there were many political and social factors involved in the division of the church in the European continent, as well as in England, Wales, and Scotland.

Backgrounds

Augustine discovers Paul[18] in the challenge of Pelagianism (*The Spirit and the Letter* 29–50; CSEL 60). His theology of grace, at least in some polemic expressions, seems to lose the Pauline dialectic between God's sovereignty and human freedom; it is in danger of blaming sexuality as being the grimace of evil. But it was an ingenious transformation of Paul's anthropology: a rediscovery of the "I" in the stream of time, in the horizon of eternity, and in the world of temptations and conversions; the *Confessions* (CSEL 33)

---

16. Joseph Ratzinger, *Kirche—Zeichen unter den Völkern: Studien zur Ekklesiologie und Ökumene*, 2 vols. (Freiburg im Breisgau: Herder, 2010), 2:1130.

17. Cf. Ernst Dassmann, *Der Stachel im Fleisch: Paulus in der frühchristlichen Literatur bis Irenäus* (Münster: Aschendorff, 1979).

18. Cf. Settimana Agostiniana Pavese, *Agostino lettore e interprete di Paolo*, SEAug 107 (Rome: Institutum patristicum Augustinianum, 2007); Ludwig Fladerer, *Augustinus als Exeget: Zu seinen Kommentaren des Galaterbriefes und der Genesis*, Sitzungsberichte Österreichische Akademie der Wissenschaften: Philosophisch-historische Klasse 795 (Wien: Österr. Akad. der Wiss., 2010).

belong to the eminent *Wirkungsgeschichte* of Paul's justification theology. As a result, the Augustinian interpretation stresses the anthropological reading of Galatians and other Pauline Letters. The question of personal salvation, now and then, is on the screen in a historical situation in which the *Imperium Romanum* came to its end—and the symbiosis of Christian church and Christianized state with it.

Consequently, Augustine highlighted not only the personal but also the ecclesial dimension of faith. Catholicity is necessary[19]—against Donatism.[20] The unity of the church has to be made sure not only with a Pauline *anathema* but also with legal discipline and political support. It is this combination that lacks the missionary dimension and turns the church's understanding of faith into an antisectarian dogmatism. Ironically, this dogmatism is a tribute to the success of Christian mission, but unfortunately it is also a tribute to an understanding of religious truth that tends to identify true theology with true philosophy, while Paul's relation between faith and reason is more of a dialectic.

The Augustinian reading of Paul was of great influence in Western theology. Aquinas's soteriology is the best example.[21] His scholastic distinctions allowed him to overcome Augustine's unbalanced predestination theory by a theology of grace that enables all the faithful, not only church ministers, to participate in the process of redemption. But his intellectualistic understanding of *fides* has difficulties interpreting the Pauline antithesis between faith and the works or the law. Therefore, Aquinas's contribution to mission is his *Summa contra gentiles*, which is more or less an apology for Christianity rather than a theory of proclaiming the gospel in the style of Paul.

Another problem is the shape of Augustine's juristic thinking. On the one side, law and justice are a great gift of Roman culture to world civilization; the peoples of the north were hungry to get this delicious dish. Anselm of Canterbury was engaged in reframing the New Testament gospel in the language of law. On the other side, justification theology now appears as an *analogia* of human law systems, with courts and judges, penitents and penalties, expiation and satisfaction. This has the danger of creating a bureaucratic system. An exegetical theology of the law is needed to overcome this ambiguity.

---

19. Cf. Joseph Ratzinger, *Volk und Haus Gottes in Augustins Lehre von der Kirche: Die Dissertation und weitere Studien zu Augustinus und zur Theologie der Kirchenväter*, Gesammelte Schriften 1 (Freiburg im Breisgau: Herder, 2011).

20. Cf. Settimana Agostiniana Pavese, *Agostino e il Donatismo*, SEAug 100 (Rome: Institutum patristicum Augustinianum, 2007).

21. Cf. Otto Hermann Pesch, *Theologie der Rechtfertigung bei Martin Luther und Thomas von Aquin: Versuch eines systematisch-theologischen Dialogs*, Walberberger Studien der Albertus-Magnus-Akademie 4 (Mainz: Grunewald, 1967).

Highlights

A new situation came into being with Luther and the Roman Catholic answer at the Council of Trent. On both sides Augustine was hermeneutically dominant.[22]

LUTHER AND TRENT

Luther (1483–1546), the Augustinian who was deeply rooted in monastic movements of his time, renewed the theological energy of Paul's justification theology not only for personal conversion but also for church reform. Both belong together. In his tract *Von der Freiheit eines Christenmenschen*, he reconstructs this connection and applies it in a political statement.[23] In a religious system of commandments and achievements, debits and merits, doubts and atonements, the baptized believer is in existential fear of losing the love of God and of being condemned in the last judgment. The believer's only hope is Jesus Christ, the redeemer. As an exegete of Galatians[24] and Romans,[25] Luther responds by radicalizing the problem of sin and by strengthening the promise of salvation. He adopts the cry for salvation in Romans 7:24 as his own, the cry of the Christian sinner. Luther actualizes Paul's critique of the "works of the law" as a critique of the religious acts commanded by the church as necessary steps on the way of salvation, focused not only on indulgences but also on eucharistic sacrifice, on conditions for reconciliation, and on the devotional praxis regarding Holy Mary and the canonized saints. He interprets justifying "faith" as pure trust in God and as a certitude of being saved by God only because of his love, without claiming any religious achievements. Luther affirmed and accented the ecclesial dimension of justification theology as a matter of principle, with the intention of strengthening the unity of the church by means of reformation. The missionary impetus was reinforced because of a strict understanding of *sola fide*, but contaminated by Luther's anti-Jewish and anti-Islamic polemic.

The Council of Trent (1545–1463) answered the challenge of Protestantism[26] by redesigning the Augustinian reading of Paul within a framework other than

---

22. Cf. Arnoud S. Q. Visser, *Reading Augustine in the Reformation: The Flexibility of Intellectual Authority in Europe, 1500–1620*, OSHT (Oxford: Oxford University Press, 2011).

23. Cf. Reinhold Rieger, *Von der Freiheit eines Christenmenschen = De libertate Christiana*, Kommentare zu Schriften Luthers 1 (Tübingen: Mohr Siebeck, 2007).

24. Cf. Gerhard Ebeling, *Evangelische Evangelienauslegung: Eine Untersuchung zu Luthers Hermeneutik* (1942; Tübingen: Mohr Siebeck, 1991).

25. Cf. Hans Hübner, *Rechtfertigung und Heiligung in Luthers Römerbriefvorlesung: Ein systematischer Entwurf*, Glaube und Lehre 7 (Witten: Luther Verlag, 1967).

26. Cf. Roberto Del Riccio, *Die rechtfertigende Kraft des Evangeliums: Eine Untersuchung zum heilsgeschichtlich-personalen Verständnis des Rechtfertigungsgeschehens im Konzil von Trient*, Europäische Hochschulschriften 791 (Frankfurt: Peter Lang, 2004).

the Lutheran one.[27] It tells the story of a mature man who searches for the way of redemption. He is able and willing to recognize and to confess his sins. He asks what he, with the help of God, has to do to be well prepared for the grace of baptism (cf. DS 1524). He recognizes that he will never have a chance to blaze his trail to heaven by doing enough good works to compensate for his sins and to establish his own position in Christ. Nevertheless, he is called and thus he is able to convert to the faith because of God's preceding grace (DH 1525–27). In the water of baptism he has received the promise to be born again; he is liberated from sin and sanctified by the Holy Spirit (DH 1528–31). As a result, he is admonished to live his life as a member of the Catholic Church, guided by their pastors. His faith has to be formed by love, because faith is understood as a mental assent to the truth, while love is conceptualized as a holistic answer to the word of God, unifying the love of God with the love of neighbor. The ecclesial dimension of justification theology is dominant because the church has both the message and the instruments of reconciliation. Mission, which will become the future of the church in the century of discovery, becomes merely an integration into and formation within the Catholic Church. What happens with the Tridentine system of soteriology when the genuine Pauline concept of faith reshapes a Catholic justification theology is now an open question.

In any case, the Lutheran as well as the Catholic reformulation of justification theology has the possibility of opening up the Pauline anthropology to the experiences of men and women in modernity. Yet both concepts are problematic since their justification theologies lose their function of uniting the church and motivating its mission.

MODERN AUTHORS

The critique against religious achievement, however, became the most influential application of these developments within the Western hemisphere in the nineteenth and twentieth centuries. Adolf von Harnack portrayed Paul, especially in his Letter to the Galatians, as a liberator from the Jewish casuistic.[28] But his neo-Marcionism was not so much anti-Jewish as anti-Catholic. He tries to conciliate Pauline and modern concepts of freedom against the supposed paternalism of the Catholic hierarchy. But Harnack tends to reduce

---

27. Cf. Albrecht Peters and Otto Hermann Pesch, *Einführung in die Lehre von Gnade und Rechtfertigung* (Darmstadt: Wissenschaftliche Buchgesellschaft, 1987).

28. Adolf von Harnack, *Das Wesen des Christentums: Neuauflage zum 50. Jahrestag des ersten Erscheinens mit einem Geleitwort von Rudolf Bultmann* (Stuttgart: Klotz, 1950); idem, *Marcion: Das Evangelium vom fremden Gott* (Darmstadt: Wissenschaftliche Buchgesellschaft, 1985).

theology to morality, so that his concept of faith is weak; for him, mission seems to be the worldwide marketing of Protestant culture, and unity seems to be an attribute only of the invisible church, while the plurality of confessions mirrors the necessity of cultural progress.

It is this problem of liberal theology that Rudolf Bultmann wishes to solve with a renewed understanding of justifying faith.[29] For half a century his interpretation was a leading one in scientific exegesis. On the one hand, he formed an existential understanding of faith, the new self-understanding of believers who are not worthy or justified by their own deeds, but by the grace of God. On the other hand, he critiqued liberal theology's fixation on achievements in religious and social affairs. So his theory seems to be a modern concretization of mercy: a pastoral help for losers, for weak and handicapped persons who are not able to make up the balance with great efforts, while the original Reformation critique was focused on the impossibility of anyone's claiming achievements before God. Is that existential approach a theological sublimation of the German political disasters of the first half of the twentieth century? Is it a protest against industrialism, colonialism, and functionalism? Whatever its source, Erik Peterson[30] and Heinrich Schlier,[31] two converts and two defenders of the Pauline authorship of Ephesians, did sharpen the critique that in Bultmann's concept the ecclesial and missionary dimension of justification is missed.

But this critique did not avoid the success of the Bultmannian interpretation in modern Catholicism. The Second Vatican Council was the time to criticize the formation of the Catholic Church under the Pius popes. The freedom of Christian faith should be respected and maintained against the strict regulation of sexuality, the legislation of sacraments, and the centralization of the hierarchy. Paul was invoked as the patron of this liberation.[32]

This interpretive consensus between Lutheran and Catholic exegetes in America[33] and Germany[34] was a pillar of the ecumenical consensus in justifica-

---

29. Bultmann, *Theologie des Neuen Testaments*.

30. Erik Peterson, *Der Brief an die Römer*, ed. Barbara Nichtweiß, Ausgewählte Schriften 6 (Würzburg: Echter, 1997); idem, *Der erste Brief an die Korinther und Paulus-Studien*, ed. Hans-Ulrich Weidemann, Ausgewählte Schriften 7 (Würzburg: Echter, 2006).

31. Heinrich Schlier, *Grundzüge einer paulinischen Theologie* (Freiburg im Breisgau: Herder, 1978).

32. Cf. *pars pro toto*, Josef Blank, "Warum sagt Paulus: 'Aus Werken des Gesetzes wird niemand gerecht'?" (1969), in *Paulus: Von Jesus zum Urchristentum* (Munich: Kosel, 1982), 42–68.

33. Cf. Hugh G. Anderson et al., *Justification by Faith*, Lutherans and Catholics in Dialogue 7 (Minneapolis: Fortress, 1985).

34. Cf. Karl Lehmann, ed., *Lehrverurteilungen—kirchentrennend?*, vol. 2, *Materialien zu den Lehrverurteilungen und zur Theologie der Rechtfertigung*, DiKi 5 (Freiburg im Breisgau: Herder; Göttingen: Vandenhoeck & Ruprecht, 1989).

tion theology. Prepared in different national[35] and international conferences,[36] proclaimed in the Joint Declaration,[37] and discussed in many contexts, the ecumenical movement tries to overcome the traditional controversies in anthropology and ecclesiology by a common discussion of the sixteenth-century problems, including a common reading of Paul. The subsequent signing of the *Declaration* by the World Methodist Council is an indication of an ongoing process of ecumenical understanding. The influence of Augustinian anthropocentrism is strong, although the effectiveness of God's grace, the asymmetry between *justus et peccator*, the necessity of good works not as a condition but as a consequence of justification, the differentiation between gospel and law, and the assurance of salvation have all been clarified in a new way. Thus, although without explicit ecclesial consequences, essential aspects of Pauline justification theology have been received and reintegrated into a modern reception history.

Reflections

At the same time as this ecumenical progress was taking place, a new approach began, reading Paul and his justification theology from a new perspective. It was in Scandinavia,[38] the United States,[39] and the United Kingdom[40] that this project was beginning to dominate exegetical research. A new interest in Jewish-Christian dialogue, a new method of religious sociology, and a new influence of Reformed covenant theology, Methodist sanctification theology, and Anglican peace theology inspired a critique of anthropocentrism, the achievement paradigm of religious boasting, and the presentation of the law not as part of the problem but as part of the solution of salvation.

This paradigm helps us to see some dimensions of Paul's justification theology much clearer than in the anthropocentric focus: the social function of circumcision and purity laws, the new partnership between men and women, slaves and free, Jews and Greek, and the difference and coherence between conversion and living the faith. The study of Second Temple Judaism

---

35. Cf. Karl Lehmann and Wolfhart Pannenberg, eds., *Lehrverurteilungen—kirchentrennend?*, vol. 1, *Rechtfertigung, Sakramente und Amt im Zeitalter der Reformation und heute*, DiKi 4 (Freiburg im Breisgau: Herder; Göttingen: Vandenhoeck & Ruprecht, 1986).

36. Cf. *Lutheran–Roman Catholic Joint Commission, Church and Justification: Understanding the Church in the Light of the Doctrine of Justification* (Geneva: WCC, 1994).

37. Lutheran World Federation and the Roman Catholic Church, *Joint Declaration on the Doctrine of Justification* (Grand Rapids: Eerdmans, 2001).

38. Cf. Krister Stendahl, *Paul among Jews and Gentiles* (Philadelphia: Fortress, 1978).

39. Cf. Ed P. Sanders, *Paul* (Oxford: Oxford University Press, 1991).

40. Cf. James D. G. Dunn, *The Theology of Paul the Apostle* (Edinburgh: T&T Clark, 1998); N. T. Wright, *Paul in Fresh Perspective* (Minneapolis: Fortress, 2009).

promoted by the Qumran texts presents a picture of a religious plurality that provides great insight into the destruction of sin and the construction of God's grace. The new approach is more plausible historically because it reflects the *Sitz im Leben* of Paul's theology and the mission of the church. It is more theologically profound because it connects the so-called Old Testament and New Testament witness. It is of more ecclesial substance because the point is not separation from Judaism but participation in the people of God.

But there are problems, too.[41] Paul's theology echoes the cry for salvation; it opens the ear for spoken and unspoken prayers; it opens the eyes for the "whole creation," which "has been groaning in pain until now" (Rom. 8:22). The aim of the mission is not the triumph of the church, but the freedom of humans, who find peace for their souls and bodies in the community of believers. The church is not only a social phenomenon but also the people of God "in Christ." The "works of the law" are identity markers not only in a horizontal but also in a vertical dimension. The mission is addressed not only to the gentiles but also to the Jews, although the apostolic council decided that the Jewish Christians should go to the Jews (Gal. 2:9). However, the antithesis between faith and works of law is addressed not only to gentiles but also to Jews. There likewise is the problem of "boasting," not so much *coram Deo* but in relation to others who do not belong to Israel (Rom. 2:17, 23; 3:27) and in the eyes of others who admire religious achievements (Rom. 4:2).[42]

Whether the critique leveled by this new perspective is correct or not, it was a problem in the ecumenical dialogue of the twentieth century that this new perspective was not integrated within ecumenical conversation. Indeed, it is now an established position that one must distinguish between the Pauline and the Lutheran profile of justification theology.[43] But this differentiation has not yet become a key position in ecumenical discourse because the discussion has been dominated by the controversies of the sixteenth century and the Lutheran or Tridentine reading of Paul, rather than by Paul himself and his presentation of justification theology in the life of the young church and by the christological hermeneutic of Scripture. This is a problem for the established ecumenical discussions, yet it presents a good chance for a new dialogue.

41. Cf. Peter Stuhlmacher, *Revisiting Paul's Doctrine of Justification: A Challenge to the New Perspective; With an Essay by Donald A. Hagner* (Downers Grove, IL: IVP Academic, 2001).
42. Cf. Florian Wilk, "Ruhm coram Deo bei Paulus?," ZNW 101 (2010): 55-77.
43. Cf. Paul Althaus, *Paulus und Luther über den Menschen: Ein Vergleich* (Gütersloh: Gütersloher Verlagshaus, 1963); Volker Stolle, *Luther und Paulus: Die exegetischen und hermeneutischen Grundlagen der lutherischen Rechtfertigungslehre im Paulinismus Luthers*, Arbeiten zur Bibel und ihrer Geschichte 10 (Leipzig: Evangelische Verlagsanstalt, 2002).

Recent Ecumenism in the Mirror of Paul

The main question is whether an orientation toward Paul in his biblical setting and the integration of new perspectives would weaken or strengthen the ecumenical consensus in justification theology. Would it be possible to deepen it, together with deepening Jewish-Christian relations? Would it be possible to integrate not only the New Testament but also the Old Testament into a common understanding of justification? Would it be possible to build up ecclesial unity and to redefine the original mission of the church? Would it be possible to argue that the personal dimension of faith is essentially connected with the ecclesial and missionary dimensions?

New Attempts

In 2006 the Lutheran World Federation and the Pontifical Council for Promoting Christian Unity, together with the Methodist World Conference and the World Communion of Reformed Churches, started a new exegetical-ecumenical study project in justification theology.[44] It was a result of the self-commitment of the Official Common Statement from 1999 "to continued and deepened study of biblical foundations of the doctrine of justification" (n. 3). The paper was presented on July 11, 2006. It was accompanied by a German ecumenical study document from a multilateral perspective.[45]

In both studies the aim is to respect the plurality of the Reformation movement and the Catholic reaction, the developments of theology in Catholicism as well as in Protestantism in the past five hundred years, the canonical function of the Bible, and the NPP. Therefore, both studies endeavor in fuller form to present the Old Testament witness as fundamental for a Christian theology of justification. In their treatment of the New Testament, both studies attempt to present not only Paul and his explicit justification theology but also James, Peter, and John, and, as a matter of first priority, the gospel of the kingdom of God, the kingdom of heaven, as it is handed down in the Synoptic Gospels. Both studies are concerned to present Paul not as a single character in the world of the church but as a Jew who believes in Jesus Christ,

---

44. *The Biblical Foundations of the Doctrine of Justification: An Ecumenical Follow-Up to the Joint Declaration on the Doctrine of Justification*, presented by a task force of biblical scholars and systematic theologians from the Lutheran World Federation, the Pontifical Council for Promoting Christian Unity, the World Communion of Reformed Churches, and the World Methodist Council (Geneva: WCC, 2011).

45. ET of the common declaration: *Accepted by God, Transformed by Christ: The Doctrine of Justification in Multilateral Ecumenical Dialogue; A Study on the Doctrine of Justification by the German Ecumenical Study Commission* (DÖSTA) (Geneva: WCC, 2008).

as an exegete who gives an inspired interpretation of the Holy Scripture, and as an apostle who is not the first but the last among his peers (1 Cor. 15:8) and who therefore is embedded with his theology in the faith of the early church. But both studies are concerned as well to sharpen the profile of the explicit and reflected theology of justification, with its critical power and constructive dynamic, so that the charisma of Paul and his Letter to the Galatians, as well as his Letters to the Philippians and Romans, can be discovered anew. Both studies agree that an ecumenical understanding among Christians also must create peace with the Jews; it must maintain the unity of the Scriptures with its variety of texts and positions; it must motivate the mission and the communion of the church today; it must hear—and, if possible, answer—the questions of contemporary persons regarding how to search for God, how to be happy, and how to find a good way to live and to die.

Pauline Stimulus

In going forward, it now seems possible to widen the ecumenical dialogues in the three dimensions that Paul opens up, above all in his Letter to Galatians. In view of Paul's own ecumenical theology of justification, the personal, the missionary, and the ecclesial dimensions of the ecumenical justification theology need a theological reflection that is able not only to analyze the biblical and historical challenges but also to deal with today's challenges.

Today the question of faith is discussed under the suspicion that it is an illusion to trust in God. This may not be a new challenge, but it is important. The Pauline response is to be found in his concept of faith. To trust in God, to be sure of his promises, to be convinced by his word, and to be obedient to his will—these form the very essence of faith; otherwise faith would not be faith. But there are arguments for trusting in God. One argument is the existence of a *consensus fidei*: there is a community of believers who express their faith in common words of confession. The faithful are able to express in very clear, essential, and positive words whom they do trust and what they do believe. This public nature of faith is a clarification of confidence; it gives us the chance to speak about the faith, to engage in apologetics, and to exchange with others a witness about why Christians do trust in God and how they live their lives. In Galatians, Paul directly or indirectly quotes many formulas or motifs from common Christian creeds, beginning with the *praescriptum* (1:4). The heart of his justification thesis is a common confession: "We . . . believe in Christ Jesus" (2:16).

A second argument is that of Scripture. Paul argues as an exegete. His quotations from the Bible of Israel are not ornaments but arguments. Galatians

2:16 ends with a free and hidden quotation from Psalm 143:2: "because 'no one will be justified'—by the works of the law." The passages on Moses and the mediation of the law and on the timing of God's acting in Galatians 3:19–25 and on Sarah and Hagar, Jerusalem and Sinai, in Galatians 4:21–31 are major pillars in the construction of Paul's discourse.

A third argument is that of reason. In Galatians there is no parallel to the so-called *theologia naturalis* in Romans 1:18–25, but Paul does argue on the basis of the experiences of the Galatians: their knowledge is "to be known by God" and their decision was to convert from the "weak and beggarly elemental spirits" to the one and only God (Gal. 4:9). It is the freedom of faith to confess God, but there would be no freedom of faith without this knowledge, and there would be no faith without the roots of Scripture. Moreover, the Galatians have experienced that it is the love of Jesus Christ that makes the dead alive and the sinner justified by faith. The theology of justification first expressed in Galatians is the Pauline concept of that reality because it reflects faith as the soul of life as a whole.

The question of mission is discussed under the suspicion that to proclaim one gospel to all nations is an imperialistic ideology.[46] Indeed, there are such big shadows hanging over the history of Christian mission that it is not easy to overcome this suspicion. But going back to Paul opens up the possibility of understanding the true sense of mission. In Romans 3:29–30 the apostle expresses the theological reason for mission: "Or is God the God of Jews only? Is he not the God of Gentiles also? Yes, of Gentiles also, since God is one" (NRSV). In Galatians 5:1 Paul formulates the christological reason for mission: "For freedom Christ has set us free" (NRSV). Therefore the Pauline mission is a process of invitation and liberation. It is monotheism in its christological concretization that opens the global horizon for mission and allows all people to become citizens of heaven (Phil. 3:20) by belonging to the church on the earth. Not only Jews but also gentiles have the right to the gospel—and the freedom of decision. Therefore mission is *diakonia* (2 Cor. 5:18). Thus, in describing his first visit in Galatia, Paul emphasizes his program of nonviolence (Gal. 4:13–14): the combination of bodily infirmity and spiritual power convinced the Galatians, and the "truth" to which Paul witnesses won them for the faith. Religious enlightenment is an essential aspect of Paul's mission. Justification theology is the Pauline concept of that mission of peace because it centers the whole life on faith in God.

---

46. The central argument comes from David Hume, *The Natural History of Religion* (London: A. Millar, 1757).

The question of unity is discussed under the suspicion of a *Gleichschaltung*. But in Pauline theology the concept of *koinōnia* is dominant:[47] a community of many through their participation in one. The genuine plurality of the church is that of men and women, slaves and free, Jews and Greeks (Gal. 3:28). But this plurality makes sense only as the other side of unity: a common belonging to the one God, the one Christ, and the one Spirit. Paul is working as a missionary of Christ in order to widen the horizon of Christianity; he is also working as an apostle of Christ to bring together the different communities in the one church of God. Justification theology is the Pauline concept of that communion.

Justification is directed to participation because it is liberation. Participation is directed to justification because it is the result of the love of God, which all believers share.

---

47. Cf. Th. Söding, *Einheit der Heiligen Schrift? Zur biblischen Theologie des Kanons*, QD 211 (Freiburg im Breisgau: Herder, 2008), 204–13.

5

Arguing with Scripture in Galatia

Galatians 3:10–14 as a Series of Ad Hoc Arguments

TIMOTHY G. GOMBIS

In Galatians 3:10–14, Paul makes a series of assertions followed by scriptural citations. Various Christian traditions regard Paul as leveling a theological critique about the character of the Mosaic law, opposing the Mosaic law to the Christian gospel, contrasting passive faith versus active obedience, or perhaps pitting Christianity against Judaism.

I argue that Paul is not making abstract theological claims about the Mosaic law or Judaism in opposition to Christian faith. He is, rather, making a series of strategically ad hoc arguments, very specifically addressing the local crisis in Galatia as he understands it. His singular rhetorical aim is to dissuade his non-Jewish readers from judaizing—being circumcised and adopting the rituals and patterns of life that constitute a Jewish identity.

On my proposed reading, "works of law" (v. 10) and "the law" (vv. 11–12) are oblique references to the influencers' teaching—what he calls "this persuasion" in Galatians 5:8. Thus what Paul says about "the law" and "whoever is of works of law" in this passage are *not* claims he would make in other, less polemical contexts. This is not how Paul would express himself if he were describing the character of the Mosaic law to some other audience, or if he were addressing Jew-gentile relations in the abstract. His statements have exclusive relevance to the local crisis in Galatia. Paul uses Scripture to argue against *the specific gospel perversion in Galatia*, not to critique Judaism, the Mosaic law, or Jewish identity. Theologians and biblical scholars, therefore, must draw upon Galatians 3:10–14 with great sensitivity to this specific, local crisis when they reflect on Paul's view of Judaism, the Mosaic law, the relationship of faith to obedience, and the character of Jewish Christianity.

My treatment of this passage is necessarily cursory. I will sketch my proposed reading and engage other viewpoints minimally. First I will treat Paul's statements in 3:10 and 13–14, and then his assertions in 3:11–12.

The Curse of the Law and Redemption in Christ (Gal. 3:10, 13–14)

Paul speaks of two groups in Galatians 3:7–10. He refers to "those who are of faith, . . . who are blessed, along with faithful Abraham" in verses 7 and 9. Paul is hopeful that a contingent in the Galatian churches has remained faithful to his gospel. Of the other group he says, "As many as are of works of law are under a curse" (v. 10). He is referring to the influencers in Galatia and anyone persuaded by them that to be numbered among the people of God, it is necessary to believe in Christ Jesus *and* to convert to Judaism through circumcision.[1]

But what does Paul mean in declaring that "those who are of works of law" are under a curse? Two factors interpret Paul's claim: his argument about "sinners" and "transgressors" in Galatians 2:15–21; and the text Paul cites in verse 10, Deuteronomy 27:26, interpreted within its context of 27:15–26.[2]

Transgressors and Sinners (Gal. 2:15–21)

In Galatians 2:15–21, Paul presents an argument to Jewish Christians like Peter that Jews must embrace non-Jewish Christians as fellow and equal members of the people of God. Jewish identity is not sufficient for justification before God, and justification is not limited to Jewish Christians. Paul begins in 2:15–16 by stating that even though he and Peter are "Jews by nature" and

---

1. In Gal. 2:15–16, Paul equates being "of works of law" with being Jewish, but in 3:10 it is unlikely that he is referring to all Jewish people everywhere with the phrase "whoever is of works of law." He does not believe that he and other Jewish Christians are cursed by the law. He has in mind only those who subscribe to the influencers' teaching.

2. Timothy G. Gombis, "The 'Transgressor' and the 'Curse of the Law': The Logic of Paul's Argument in Galatians 2–3," *NTS* 53 (2007): 81–93.

not "sinners from among the gentiles," they still must join with non-Jews in believing in Christ for justification, since the ground of justification is not ἐξ ἔργων νόμου, but ἐκ πίστεως Χριστοῦ.

In 2:17 he asks, if it is so that "while seeking to be justified in Christ, we ourselves have also been found sinners, is Christ then a minister of sin?" Paul is forcing on his fellow Jewish Christians the implication of their need to seek justification before God on the same basis as non-Jews; their own need sets them in fellowship with gentile "sinners" in the newly constituted people of God. Paul then puts the question: if God's way of justifying forces Jews to fellowship with gentile "sinners," is Christ leading them into sin? The answer is obviously negative (2:17).

This is precisely the problem, however, for Jews like Peter and the Jewish Christians who came to Antioch (Gal. 2:11–14). And this was likely the problem driving the influencers to come to Galatia and try to compel Paul's fledgling community "to judaize." The assumption was widespread among Jews in the first century that table fellowship with gentiles was disobedience to the law.[3] For Paul, however, Christ Jesus himself is leading them into fellowship with gentiles, so loyalty to Christ demands fellowship with gentiles qua gentiles.

Paul then offers two crucial arguments, each beginning with γάρ—the first in 2:18 and the second in 2:19–21. First, he states, "If I rebuild what I have once destroyed, I prove myself to be a transgressor." In speaking of himself, Paul still has in mind Jewish Christians like Peter and the Jewish missionaries in Galatia. Paul's "rebuilding" refers to a reaffirmation of the law's supposed prohibition of table fellowship with non-Jews. If, after disregarding the law's distinctions between Jew and non-Jew, Paul goes back and reaffirms the law and its distinctions, he becomes a transgressor of it.[4] How is this so?

Paul is putting Peter's behavior in Antioch (and that of the Jewish missionaries in Galatia) in theological and covenantal perspective. When Peter came to Antioch, he had table fellowship with gentiles, recognizing that the barrier

---

3. Eating with gentiles was not prohibited by the law, but the assumption that it was sinful to associate with gentiles was widespread among Jews in the first century. Peter tells those gathered in Cornelius's house, "You yourselves know that it is unlawful for a Jew to associate with or to visit a Gentile" (Acts 10:28 NRSV). In addition to this text, Richard Hays cites the *Let. Aris.* 142 ("To prevent our being perverted by contact with others or by mixing with bad influences, [Moses] hedged us in on all sides with strict observances connected with meat and drink and touch and hearing and sight, after the manner of the Law") and *Jub.* 22.16 ("Eat not with them, . . . for their works are unclean") ("Galatians," in *The New Interpreter's Bible*, ed. L. E. Keck et al., 12 vols. [Nashville: Abingdon, 1994–2004], 11:233). Rather than overturning their teaching based on an appeal to what the law actually says on this matter, Paul shapes his argument by assuming their misunderstanding that the law prohibits fellowship and eating with gentiles.

4. J. L. Martyn, *Galatians: A New Translation with Introduction and Commentary*, AB 33A (New York: Doubleday, 1997), 256.

to Jewish Christian fellowship with non-Jewish Christians had been eliminated in the death and resurrection of Jesus ("what I have once destroyed"). By subsequently separating himself from the gentiles (2:12), Peter reaffirmed that the distinction was still binding ("if I rebuild") and that such fellowship was still disobedience to the law and to God. Paul is saying that if he were to do now what Peter did in Antioch, he would be a "transgressor." He would be embodying two mutually exclusive confessions. On the one hand, by confessing faith in Christ, he affirms the unity of the people of God, Jew and non-Jew, in Christ. On the other, he holds to the law's supposed prohibition of fellowship with non-Jews.

In the same moment that Peter is being unfaithful to the law of Moses, he is confessing that one *must* remain faithful to the law. He is both transgressing the covenant stipulations *and* claiming that one must observe them. Paul is exposing the internally incoherent logic of Jewish Christians who are flinching from the full implications of an inclusive gospel. Peter and his fellow Jewish Christians are concerned to avoid becoming sinners by fellowshipping with gentiles, *but in so doing, they do something far worse: they themselves become transgressors of the law.*[5]

Those in the Antioch and Galatian churches who maintain that the law's distinctions are still in force and that table fellowship with gentiles is forbidden are transgressors. They affirm two mutually exclusive convictions—that neither circumcision nor uncircumcision is anything (5:6; 6:15), *and* that the distinction between circumcision and uncircumcision means *everything*. Paul's covenantal reasoning in 2:15–21, then, helps to explain Paul's logic regarding the curse of the law in 3:10.

The Curse of Deuteronomy 27:26

Let us now consider Galatians 3:10, with Paul's citation of Deuteronomy 27:26. Deuteronomy 27:15–26 enumerates twelve curses on individuals who commit especially heinous sins. Because anyone who does these things is especially perverse, they must be put out of the community of Israel so that they may bear God's curse alone. The final curse in verse 26 is a summary statement issuing a curse on anyone who "does not confirm the words of

---

5. As Paul's argument unfolds, being a "transgressor" is not an actual problem for those in Christ. In Gal. 2:19–21 Paul claims that he, along with all Jewish Christians, have died with Christ and are no longer bound to "remain within" its circumscribing boundaries. He is now free to participate fully in the life of Christ, embodied through fellowship with all others who are in Christ, regardless of their ethnicity. By his participation in the death of Christ, therefore, Paul dies to the requirement to avoid table fellowship with non-Jews, and through his participation in the resurrection of Christ, Paul may now "live to God."

this law by doing them." Such a person is an intentional covenant breaker and must be cut off from the people of God, lest God's curse fall upon the entire nation.[6]

In Galatians 3:10a, Paul's assertion that the group in view is accursed should be interpreted by the text from Deuteronomy and within his broader sustained argument. Paul's claim is that those who hold to the influencers' teaching are in the same position as the "transgressor" (Peter) he has described earlier in Galatians 2 and the one who is cursed in Deuteronomy 27:26. How so?

Deuteronomy 27:26 pronounces a curse on anyone who does not "remain within" the boundaries marked out by the law. For Paul, anyone who affirms the "rule" that "neither circumcision nor uncircumcision is anything" (Gal. 6:15–16) is outside those boundaries, having "destroyed" the distinctions between Jew and non-Jew among God's people (cf. Gal. 2:18). Any such persons who affirm the necessity for non-Jews to be circumcised immediately become transgressors. Their prior affirmation of the unity of Jew and non-Jew in Christ demonstrates their failure "to remain within" the law. These are two mutually exclusive convictions: requiring the observance of distinctions, and no longer observing distinctions. Anyone with this covenantally inconsistent posture incurs the sanction ("the curse") of the law. Paul's argument, then, is that the teaching of Jewish Christians like Peter and the influencers in Galatia is internally incoherent, is impossible, and must be abandoned.

Yet Paul is advancing a purely rhetorical argument to demonstrate the impossibility of the influencers' position. He is not claiming that the law can actually curse anyone. In his death Christ has already absorbed its power to curse. Those who participate in the death and resurrection of Christ are freed from the law's circumscribing function. This is Paul's point in 2:19, to which he returns in 3:13. Christ redeemed Christian Jews from "under

---

6. An increasingly popular interpretation regards Paul as drawing on the larger narrative movement of Deut. 27–30, making reference to the curse of exile. That is, those who are "of works of law" in Galatia are joining a people who are in exile, abiding under the curses of covenantal failure (N. T. Wright, *The Climax of the Covenant: Christ and the Law in Pauline Theology* [Minneapolis: Fortress, 1992], 141–47; James M. Scott, "'For as Many as Are of Works of the Law Are under a Curse' (Galatians 3.10)," in *Paul and the Scriptures of Israel*, ed. C. A. Evans and J. A. Sanders [Sheffield: JSOT Press, 1993], 213). While I find the narrative movement of exile and restoration quite compelling as a larger interpretive matrix for reading much of the NT, I do not think it is helpful here. I am not convinced that because Paul includes a word or phrase from the section of national curses in Deut. 28–30 that he intends to override the force of the individual curse. Paul cites Deut. 27:26 as part of the curses on individuals in Deut. 27:15–26. These are individuals whose behavior embodies rejection of the law and are therefore cursed by God. They must be put out of the nation so that they bear God's judgment alone, lest God's curse fall upon the entire nation. Deut. 27:15–26 is indeed closely related to the national curses in chaps. 28–30, but Paul does not combine them.

law" so that all who identify with him are freed from its circumscribing limitations—its requirement to "remain within" the boundaries marked out by its practices.

The force of Paul's argument in 3:10, then, is that the influencers' teaching is internally incoherent. Because of their Christian confession, they must embrace gentiles as their siblings in God's new family. But they claim that gentiles cannot be saved unless they judaize through circumcision. Paul shows that their attempts to uphold the law make them unfaithful to it and subject to its sanctions. Their teaching cannot stand on its own grounds, and it must be jettisoned.

This Persuasion Is Not from Faith (Gal. 3:11–12)

Paul's statements in Galatians 3:11–12 pick up on earlier elements in the letter and press their full implications. In verse 11, Paul states that "now because no one is justified by law [ἐν νόμῳ] before God, it is obvious that the righteous will live by faith [ἐκ πίστεως]."[7] The phrase ἐν νόμῳ in verse 11 does not refer to the Mosaic law in the abstract: instead, it is theological shorthand for the influencers' persuasion that the Galatians must respond to the gospel by judaizing. As H. D. Betz has noted, Galatians is filled with theological abbreviations, expressions Paul uses as theological or rhetorical shorthand.[8] Here Paul uses the phrase ἐν νόμῳ as an expression synonymous to ἐξ ἔργων νόμου in verse 10.

At this point in his argument, Paul assumes that he has already established that no one is justified before God on the basis of "works of law." That is, one's ethnic identity has no bearing on justification before God.

Paul then quotes Habakkuk 2:4 in Galatians 3:11b, a text that has rich implications for his overall argument. Habukkuk is paradigmatic of a faithful response to an unpredictable and upsetting word from God. This prophet was greatly troubled to hear that the God of Israel was going to judge the nation through the Babylonians. How can God judge Israel by those idolatrous pagans? God's response is that, in contrast to the proud and wicked one, God's approved person (ὁ δίκαιος) will be preserved by a faithful response to what God has said—that is, ἐκ πίστεως.

Paul appeals to Habakkuk because the prophet's situation is an instance of the revelation of God subverting human expectation, much like the revelation

---

7. For this reading of 3:11, see Wright, *Climax of the Covenant*, 149–50; Bruce W. Longenecker, *The Triumph of Abraham's God: The Transformation of Identity in Galatians* (Nashville: Abingdon, 1998), 164.

8. Hans D. Betz, *Galatians: A Commentary on Paul's Letter to the Churches in Galatia*, Hermeneia (Philadelphia: Fortress, 1979), 27.

of the gospel of Christ. Just as it was inconceivable to the prophet that the God of Israel would use the pagan hordes as an instrument of judgment against God's people, it is equally confounding that the salvation provided by the God of Israel would involve the human response of participation in an identity shaped exclusively by πίστις without any reference to circumcision.

Paul quotes Habakkuk, then, to demonstrate that being set right with God comes only by the response of πίστις and *not by any other kind of response*. In this case, the response that Paul rules out is the one being advocated by the influencers to judaize—to receive circumcision as the rite of conversion to a fully Jewish way of life.

Paul goes on to claim in 3:12a that ὁ δὲ νόμος οὐκ ἔστιν ἐκ πίστεως ("the law is not from faith/faithfulness"). According to a traditional Protestant reading, Paul is opposing the character of the Mosaic law to the character of faith commended in the gospel. Whereas the law demands "doing," faith calls only for "believing."

Paul is not, however, speaking of the character of the law in the abstract when he refers to ὁ νόμος. He is referring obliquely to the persuasion of the influencers that judaizing is the appropriate response to the gospel on the part of non-Jews. Paul is claiming that judaizing is most definitely not the kind of response God commends; it is *not ἐκ πίστεως*. Their response to the gospel should look very much like Paul's own transformation as a result of the "revelation of God's Son in" him (Gal. 1:16). Paul speaks of his life in Galatians 1–2 as a living embodiment of gospel transformation. After being claimed by Jesus, who loved and gave himself up for Paul, the rest of Paul's life is lived "from the faithfulness of the Son of God" (2:20).

What does such a life look like? Tracing Paul's movements in 1:16–2:14 indicates that his posttransformation life was determined by revelation and no longer by the centrality of Jerusalem and adherence to human authorities.

In Galatians 3:11–12, Paul is *not* contrasting "doing" as a mode of life with "believing." Indeed, he claims that his opponents and their disciples in Galatia *actually are disobeying God by requiring conversion to Judaism*. In 4:21 he asks why they refuse to listen to the law and states flatly in 6:13 that they do not keep the law themselves.

In 3:12b Paul quotes Leviticus 18:5, which promises the blessing of life if Israel obeys the law, for the revelation of the God of Israel is the way of life. This text is quoted three times in Ezekiel 20 (vv. 11, 13, 21), in a context that speaks of the coming judgment in light of Israel's unfaithfulness.[9] While

---

9. Joel Willitts, "Context Matters: Paul's Use of Leviticus 18:5 in Galatians 3:12," *TynBul* 54 (2003): 113.

Ezekiel laments Israel's failure, the text still points to the promise that those who walk in obedience to Torah will enjoy the blessing of life from God: "I gave them my statutes and informed them of my ordinances, by which, if a man does them, he will live" (Ezek. 20:11). In his confession of national sin, Nehemiah also quotes Leviticus 18:5, noting that the nation has sinned against the ordinances of God, "by which if a man observes them he will live" (Neh. 9:29). Again, while admitting the covenantal failure of Israel, this passage cites Leviticus 18:5 to uphold the faithfulness of God to bless those who are obedient to God's word.

The citations of Leviticus 18:5 all make the same point: the God of Israel blesses obedience to his word and brings punishment against those who disobey. This is precisely how Leviticus 18:5 is used in the *Damascus Document* (CD 3.15–16), indicating that the community producing these texts thought of itself as the faithful remnant, rendering to God the kind of obedience that brings the blessing of life.[10]

Paul quotes Leviticus 18:5, then, as God's promise to bless those who are obedient. For the Galatians, the specific obedience that brings the blessing of God is to affirm the "rule of faith" that neither circumcision nor uncircumcision is anything (Gal. 6:16), but that πίστις working through love is everything (5:6). Paul expects their obedience to take the form of resisting the influencers' persuasion to judaize.[11]

Conclusion

According to my proposal, then, Paul's claim regarding the law's curse is a rhetorical argument whereby he exposes the internal incoherence of the influencers' persuasion. From Paul's perspective, they regard fellowship with uncircumcised, non-Jewish, professing Christians as disobedience to the law, but their Christian confession puts them in the same family and at the same table with them. Seeing Peter confused in this way, Paul called him a "transgressor." He employs this same rhetoric against those in Galatia, claiming that they are under the law's curse.

---

10. As Wright notes, this is the thrust of Paul's citation of Lev. 18:5 in Rom. 10:5. A true obedience to the Mosaic law would have led one to receive the revelation of God in Christ (Wright, *Climax of the Covenant*, 149).

11. The thrust of Paul's argument here is similar to that which he deploys in Romans, esp. Rom. 2:12–29, where he argues that Jewish identity is irrelevant for justification. It is not the hearers of the law who are justified, but those who do it. Further, Paul uses Lev. 18:5 in just this way in Rom. 10:5, indicating that those who truly were obedient to the law would recognize the truth of the new revelation in Christ and would respond with πίστις.

This is an ad hoc argument on Paul's part, one that, I contend, he would not employ in some other nonpolemical situation. He does not refer to the law's curse in any other context, nor is it found in Luke's record of Paul's preaching in Acts. Paul is not condemning all humanity under the law's curse in Galatians 3:10, nor is this a notion that Paul might use in gospel proclamation. It has exclusive reference to the Galatian crisis.

Paul's second argument is that the move the influencers are commending to the Galatians is not the way of πίστις for non-Jews. Paul does not denigrate the Mosaic law here or claim that its deficiency is that it demands works while the gospel calls for faith.

By way of theological appropriation, Galatians 3:10–14 is one of a few Pauline passages cited by theological traditions that set Judaism in opposition to Christianity. The recent post–new perspective reevaluation of the relationship between Judaism and Christianity is long past due and salutary. Much more can and should be said about this, especially since these discussions are just hitting their stride, but space limitations preclude elaboration here.

6

Martin Luther on Galatians 3:6–14

Justification by Curses and Blessings

TIMOTHY WENGERT

The history of biblical interpretation—which, as Gerhard Ebeling once proclaimed, defines the history of the church[1]—is as much art as science: to assess properly the work of any Christian exegete, one must first suspend disbelief and view the particular theologian's biblical interpretation as sui generis,

---

A condensed version of this essay has also appeared in Timothy J. Wengert, *Reading the Bible with Martin Luther* (Grand Rapids: Baker Academic, 2013).

1. Gerhard Ebeling, *Kirchengeschichte als Geschichte der Auslegung der Heiligen Schrift* (Tübingen: Mohr, 1947). For studies of Luther's interpretation of Galatians, see most recently Juha Mikkonen, *Luther and Calvin on Paul's Epistle to the Galatians: Analysis and Comparison of Substantial Concepts in Luther's 1531/35 and Calvin's 1546/48 Commentaries on Galatians* (Åbo: Åbo Akademi University Press, 2007; http://www.doria.fi/bitstream/handle/10024/29221/MikkonenJuha.pdf?sequence=3), and esp. the bibliography (252–58) for earlier works. Among these works, see Karin Bornkamm, *Luthers Auslegungen des Galaterbriefs von 1519 und 1531: Ein Vergleich* (Berlin: de Gruyter, 1963); and Juhani Forsberg, *Das Abrahambild in der Theologie Luthers: Pater fidei sanctissimus* (Wiesbaden: Steiner, 1984). A recent, more theologically focused study is by Volker Stolle, *Luther und Paulus: Die exegetischen und hermeneutischen Grundlagen der lutherischen Rechtfertigungslehre im Paulinismus Luthers* (Leipzig: Evangelische Verlagsanstalt, 2002).

unique within its own setting, and one must take care not to impose one's own biased judgments about the text on some deceased saint of the church who, after all, is dead and cannot offer self-defense. In the case of Martin Luther, practicing this art is all the more necessary, given that his radical theology and hermeneutic are very much foreign to present-day Protestant and Roman Catholic approaches to Scripture.

Regarding Paul's Letter to the Galatians, Luther left posterity with four sources of interpretation:[2] an initial set of lectures from 1516 to 1517; a first-published commentary of 1519 (revised in 1523); and a second set of lectures in 1531, which were then polished and published in 1535.[3] This essay's concentration on Luther's published commentaries on Galatians does not gainsay the fact that his work in the classroom also provides helpful clues to his overall approach to Paul's letter.

The *Argumentum*

To appreciate fully the distinctive qualities of sixteenth-century biblical interpretation in general and the Wittenberg contributions of Martin Luther and Philipp Melanchthon in particular, the unique shape of Reformation commentaries demands attention. Unlike medieval commentaries, where the *divisio* and the *quaestio* took center stage, Luther's published works and those of others from the Wittenberg school of biblical interpretation always begin with an *argumentum*, a detailed outline of the biblical author's main argument.[4] This approach even contrasts to Luther's much more scholastic first lectures on Galatians of 1516–1517, which were still divided into glosses and scholia, and where only a single marginal gloss introduced the main theme of Paul's letter.[5]

---

2. This is unlike Romans, on which an early set of lectures (never meant for publication) and a widely popular preface to the book written initially for his 1522 German translation of the NT are all we have from him. For the standard Lutheran view of Romans, one must study the work of Philipp Melanchthon, who produced no less than five commentaries on that book (1522, 1529, 1532, 1540, 1556).

3. They are found, respectively, in WA 57/2:iii–xxvi, 5–108; WA 2:436–618 (ET of the commentary: LW 27:153–410); and WA 40/1-2 (combining lectures and commentary [ET of the commentary: LW 26 and LW 27:3–149]).

4. For Melanchthon's unique contributions to "rhetorical criticism," see Timothy J. Wengert, "Philip Melanchthon's 1522 Annotations on Romans and the Lutheran Origins of Rhetorical Criticism," in *Biblical Interpretation in the Era of the Reformation*, ed. Richard A. Muller and John L. Thompson (Grand Rapids: Eerdmans, 1996), 118–40. Other Renaissance figures, such as Erasmus or John Calvin, also included such devices.

5. WA 57/2:5, 11–16: "In nulla epistola tanto studio tantoque verborum ductu suum apostolatum commendat ut in hac, quam et solam propria manu se scripsisse testatur. Hec autem

On the one hand, this approach to biblical interpretation may seem surprisingly modern since Renaissance exegetes predicated the *argumentum* on the belief that authors actually had a point to make when they wrote and that a later reader could best understand what they had written by paying attention to the author's central themes. At the same time, it also implies that one cannot reduce what Wittenberg's theologians were writing about biblical texts to mere whim or to an overly aggressive commitment to justification by faith alone. Whether they succeeded in unlocking Paul's intent or not, they clearly began with the premise that, working with the best tools that grammar, rhetoric, and dialectics—the so-called trivium of university training—had to offer and concentrating on the author's main point, an interpreter could best divine what that author was trying to say.

On the other hand, for Wittenberg's exegetes Paul's *argumentum* was never trivial but had broad implications for Christian life and thought. Some biblical texts (e.g., the command to practice the Jubilee) were truly God's word, Luther would argue, but not God's word for him or his immediate hearers. In the case of Paul, this is where the argument raged. When Erasmus of Rotterdam, that mercurial humanist and supporter of Rome, argued on Jerome's behalf that the first eleven chapters of Romans were *only* about Jewish law and had very little direct application to the sixteenth-century reader, the battle was joined by Wittenberg's exegetes who, as is well known, struggled against such irrelevancy by insisting that the terms "law," "gospel," "faith," and "grace" had far wider application than simply to a struggle over circumcision or other Jewish ceremonies.

Indeed, the battle for Luther was joined not so much over Romans—he did not have ready access to Erasmus's arguments when he began lecturing on that book in 1515—but over Galatians. Luther's approach to Galatians and its *argumentum* can be understood only in the light of his dismissal of the Erasmian argument to the contrary. This is not to say that Luther did not use Erasmus's annotations on and paraphrase of this book. Indeed, the 1519 commentary is filled with praise for the Dutch humanist. But all these positive assessments revolved around the meaning of Greek texts. Moreover, in the second edition (1523), almost every reference to Erasmus disappeared. In the wake of the Leipzig debates, it was already clear that Erasmus would not commit to the Evangelical cause, and in 1524, with the publication of *De libero arbitrio*, Erasmus completed his public retreat back to the safety of Rome.

---

omnia nulla facit superbia, sed magna necessitate, ne sc. Evangelium subverterretur ab illis, qui ex Iudeis crediderant et legem servandam docebant ac sic in opera [pocius] quam in gratiam confidere faciebant."

But we already know from Luther's much earlier correspondence just how disappointed Luther was with Erasmus and the patristic source (Jerome) on which he relied for his interpretation. Just as he was beginning his lectures on Galatians, on October 19, 1516, Luther wrote to Georg Spalatin, director of higher education for Electorate of Saxony: "What disturbs me about that most erudite man, Erasmus, are these things, my dear Spalatin: that in his interpretation of the apostle [Paul] he understands the righteousness of works or of the law or one's own righteousness (for so the Apostle calls it [in Rom. 10:3]) as those ceremonial and figurative observations. Moreover, he does not want the apostle to speak plainly in Romans 5 about original sin (which at least he admits [exists])."[6] After praising Augustine's contrasting approach and pointing out that many other church fathers agreed with Augustine, Luther then returns to a comparison of his approach to that of Erasmus. "I do not at all doubt that in this I disagree with Erasmus, because in interpreting the Scriptures I simply esteem Jerome less than Augustine, while he esteems Augustine less than Jerome in everything."[7] Then, returning to the question of the law, he writes:

> Therefore the righteousness of the law or of deeds is in no way only in ceremonies but more correctly also in the deeds of the entire Decalogue. When things are done outside of faith in Christ, although they make Doers, Rulers and clearly upright men from a human perspective, nevertheless they do not taste more righteous than sour figs. For we do not, as Aristotle thinks, become righteous by doing righteous deeds—except in a counterfeit way—but righteous people (as I would say), by being made and being [righteous], do righteous deeds. First it is necessary for the person to be changed, then [come] works. Abel was pleasing [to God] before his offerings.[8]

Reading Luther's *Argumenta* to Galatians in this light, we discover two things. First, interpreting Paul's writings in the light of Jewish ceremonial law was not new. Second, Luther was fully aware of this alternative and rejected it not simply on theological grounds but also on exegetical ones. Indeed, the alternatives of a moralistic or legalistic interpretation of Paul, on the one hand, and an interpretation grounded in the unconditional mercy of God in Christ, on the other, have faced the church and its exegetes from the patristic period to the present. In present-day struggles to interpret Galatians or Romans, one dare not forget these ancient debates.

6. WA BR 1:70.4–8 (no. 27).
7. WA BR 1:70.17–19.
8. WA BR 1:70.25–32.

How, then, did this rift between Erasmus and Luther reflect itself in Luther's commentaries? Here is the first sentence of Luther's *Argumentum* from 1519. "Although the Galatians had first been taught a sound faith by the apostle, that is, taught to trust in Jesus Christ alone, not in their own righteous [deeds] or in those of the Law, later on they were again misled by the false apostles into trusting works of legal righteousness; for they were very easily deceived by the fact that the name and the example of the great and true apostles were falsely appealed to as commending this."[9] Luther cuts short any attempt to reduce Paul's argument to one over Jewish ceremonies and insists on contrasting human righteousness of law to the righteousness of faith in Christ. In 1535, Luther states it this way in his *Argumentum*: "First of all, we must speak about the *argumentum*, that is, about the issue with which Paul deals in this epistle. This is the *argumentum*: Paul wants to establish the teaching of faith, grace, and the forgiveness of sins, or Christian righteousness, so that we may have perfect knowledge of and grasp the difference between Christian righteousness and all other kinds of righteousness. For righteousness is of many kinds."[10] Luther then defines political righteousness, the ceremonial righteousness found in papal and other traditions—all of which parents and teachers may pass down to the next generation, as long as they do not teach that they can forgive sin or placate God or merit grace. To this he adds the legal righteousness of the Decalogue, which "we teach after teaching about faith." He then contrasts these forms with Christian righteousness:

> Over and above all these there is the righteousness of faith or Christian righteousness, which is to be distinguished most carefully from all the others. For they are all contrary to this righteousness, both because they proceed from the laws of emperors, the traditions of the pope, and the commands of God and because they consist in our works and can be done by us either "from our own natural powers," as the sophists call it, or even from God's gift (for these kinds of righteousness of works are also God's gift, as are all of our possessions). But this most excellent righteousness, namely of faith, which God imputes to us through Christ apart from our works, is neither political, nor ceremonial, nor the righteousness of the divine law, nor does it rest in our works, but is quite the opposite. That is, this righteousness is a completely passive righteousness, just as those listed above are active. For here we do nothing and render nothing to God, but we only receive and suffer another, namely God, to work in us. Therefore it is legitimate to call this righteousness of faith or Christian righteousness passive. And this righteousness, which the world does not understand,

---

9. WA 2:451.2–5 (LW 27:161; corrections have been applied to some LW quotations).
10. WA 40/1:40.15–19 (LW 26:4).

is hidden in mystery—indeed, Christians themselves do not sufficiently understand it and only with difficulty grasp it in the midst of assaults [*tentationes*; the Latin equivalent for Luther of *Anfechtungen*]. Therefore, it must always be hammered home and cultivated by continuous practice, and whoever does not grasp or take hold of it in afflictions and terrors of conscience cannot stand fast. For there is no other firm and certain consolation for consciences than this passive righteousness.[11]

Thus, nearly twenty years after complaining about Erasmus's approach to Paul and the law, Luther continues to view Galatians in light of the unconditional grace and mercy of God in Christ alone and not simply as a discussion of Jewish ceremonies.

Galatians 3:6–14 in 1519

Only in the context of Luther's definition of Paul's basic argument can one understand his specific comments on Galatians 3:6–14, which is the focus of this analysis. In 1519, Luther's commentary still reflects the style and approach of late-medieval interpretation of Scripture. As a result, he does not as fully discuss the shape of Paul's argument but instead approaches the verses individually, commenting extensively on the patristic and later interpretations of the text.

On Galatians 3, Luther begins by examining Jerome's two solutions to Paul's apparent harshness (in talking about being bewitched). He rejects the first, where Jerome argued that this reflects the characteristics of their nationality as easily bewitched, but accepts the second, which has Paul's treating the Galatians as children, given how they have moved from greater things of faith to lesser things by trusting the law again.

In 3:3 Luther takes issue with Jerome's interpretation and his distinction between works of the (ceremonial) law and good works. Far from arguing that one receives the Holy Spirit through good works, as Jerome imagined, Luther insists instead that the Holy Spirit comes through preaching heard with faith. "The apostle is referring not only to ceremonial law but also to absolutely every law; for since faith alone justifies and does good works, it follows that absolutely no works of any law whatsoever justify, nor are the works of any law good, only those of faith."[12] He then discusses at length the necessity of hearing God's word with faith.

---

11. WA 40/1:40.28–30 and 41.12–26 (LW 26:4–5).
12. WA 2:508.12–15 (LW 27:248).

Through 3:5, then, Luther understands Paul as discussing the experience of the Galatians. With verse 6 he then notes that Paul introduces the example of Abraham. Here Luther realizes that the discussion is somewhat truncated and assumes that the Galatians already were familiar with the fuller arguments, which they had heard directly from Paul and which are explicated extensively in Romans 4. What jumps out at the reader in this part of his exposition is Luther's deep concern for what the Danish scholar Leif Grane discovered already in Luther's interpretation of Romans from 1515 to 1516, namely, the *modus loquendi theologicus*, the theological mode of speaking.[13] Here Luther addresses this issue from two angles. On the one hand, Luther notices that Paul reads Scripture in a peculiar way. On the other hand, Luther points out that Paul does not follow "the rules of logical arguments."[14]

On the first point Luther states, "From this passage you see how intently and observantly Paul wants Scripture to be read. For who would have drawn these proofs from the text of Genesis?"[15] Paul's approach to Scripture defies both Paul's own interlocutors, the pseudo-apostles, but also Luther himself, who is equally dumbfounded by Paul's arguments that Abraham's faith preceded the work of circumcision and that he did not earn the right to have Isaac as an heir but received him as a result of a "counterpromise" (*repromissio*) and thus through faith, which created all of Abraham's offspring.

If in Luther's eyes Paul focuses Scripture only on God's promise and faith, thus not on works or the claims of the flesh, Paul also is, secondly, a poor logician. Luther seems to have viewed Paul's argument in verses 5–7 as an enthymeme, that is, an abbreviated logical argument in which the minor is missing. The major is simply "Abraham's faith was reputed [or reckoned] as righteousness [v. 6]," and the conclusion "therefore receiving the Spirit and doing virtuous deeds is from the hearing of faith [v. 5]."[16] The missing middle term of the Pauline syllogism is therefore that the faith being reckoned for righteousness is identical to receiving the Spirit (v. 5). But Luther recognizes a

---

13. See Leif Grane, *Modus loquendi theologicus: Luthers Kampf um die Erneuerung der Theologie (1515–1518)* (Leiden: Brill, 1975).

14. WA 2:511.11 (cf. LW 27:252): "Sed non servat Apostolus regulas dialecticae consequentiae." A *consequentia dialectica* is a technical term for logical syllogisms employed in dialectics, the bread and butter of late medieval scholasticism.

15. WA 2:511.1–2 (LW 27:252).

16. WA 2:511.12 (cf. LW 27:252). The tight logic of the Latin original makes translation extremely difficult. In this passage, Luther first states the conclusion (indicated by the words that follow: "And this he [Paul] proves") and follows it with the major premise ("and this he proves because thus the faith of Abraham was reckoned for righteousness"). The following "therefore" [*ergo*] was Luther's own conclusion in his search for the middle term in the syllogism. ("Therefore is not 'faith is reckoned for righteousness' 'to receive the Spirit'?")

possible tautology: "Therefore, either [Paul] proves nothing or 'to receive the Spirit' and 'to be reckoned for righteousness' are the same thing."[17]

In what follows, however, Luther obliquely questions Erasmus's suggestion that the words *charis Theou* in Greek ought better to be translated as *favor Dei* than as *gratia Dei*. Here is how Luther argues.

> Because [the preceding] is also true, therefore it is also repeated, lest divine reckoning be thought to be nothing outside God, considering that there are [those] for whom the word of the Apostle, *gratia*, is thought to mean favor rather than gift. For when God favors and reckons, the Spirit truly is received—gift and grace. Otherwise, if grace only signifies favor as favor is practiced among human beings, it was and remains in God from eternity. For as God loves in reality and not only in word, so also he favors in the present reality and not only in word.[18]

By 1521, in *Against Latomus*, Luther supports Erasmus's arguments fully, probably as a result of conversations with Philipp Melanchthon. There he argues that *charis* is best translated *favor Dei*.[19] With the second edition of the commentary in 1523, he simply deletes this section, a further indication of his change of mind.

In 1519, however, Luther still is using a medieval understanding of *gratia gratum faciens* (the grace that makes [us] acceptable [to God]), a concept thought to provide some sort of ontological infusion of a *habitus caritatis* into the soul. But Luther's concern is more a matter of avoiding a division of words from reality (as in Augustine's distinction between *signum* and *res*).[20] Whenever God promises (*verbum*), God delivers (*res*). Thus what Luther worries about here is an understanding of God's grace that simply defines a characteristic of God verbally (something "in God"), without any connection to the real life of faith ("the present reality").

But Luther also notices a second poor syllogism in Paul, this time in 3:6–7. The text, "Abraham believed, therefore those who are from faith are Abraham's sons," is illogical, since Paul's Jewish opponents could as easily say, "Abraham

---

17. WA 2:511.14–15 (cf. LW 27:252). Thus the entire syllogism reads: Major: (Abraham's) faith was reckoned for righteousness (v. 6); minor: Faith to be reckoned as righteousness is the same as to receive the Spirit; conclusion: Therefore faith receives the Spirit (v. 6).

18. WA 2:511.15–21 (cf. LW 27:252 and the German translation in Walch 8:1472).

19. WA 8:106.1–28. See Rolf Schäfer, "Melanchthon's Interpretation of Romans 5:15: His Departure from the Augustinian Concept of Grace Compared to Luther's," in *Philip Melanchthon (1497–1560) and the Commentary*, ed. Timothy J. Wengert and M. Patrick Graham (Sheffield: Sheffield Academic Press, 1997), 79–104. For a comparison of Luther and Melanchthon's theologies, see Martin Greschat, *Melanchthon neben Luther: Studien zur Gestalt der Rechtfertigungslehre zwischen 1528 und 1537* (Witten: Luther Verlag, 1965), esp. 80–109.

20. See Augustine, *Doctr. chr.* 1.2.2.

was circumcised; therefore the circumcised are his sons." Here, Luther argues, the missing term is the begetting of Isaac, which takes place in the flesh but from faith in God's promise (given that Abraham was incapable of begetting a child from the flesh on his own). "Thus [Isaac] is the son not so much of Abraham but of the one believing the God who promises."[21]

Luther's rigorous analysis of Paul's weaknesses continues with verse 8. First, and this solves a problem that vexed Jerome, Luther glosses the phrase "Scripture foreseeing" with the words "That is, the Spirit in Scripture."[22] He then can dismiss Jerome's worry that the apostle quotes Scripture according to the sense and not the words. Instead, Luther wonders how Paul can use this verse as a proof text at all, since it refers to Genesis 12, while the promise of an offspring does not occur until Genesis 15. Jerome solves the problem by referring the text to Genesis 22, and although Luther grants that this might be the case (so that Paul's use of "you" simply is an abbreviated form of "your offspring"), he concludes the discussion with a surprising dismissal of the entire issue: "It makes no difference which he said here."[23] Why? "Because these things were said to Abraham, not to any old person or to the flesh but to one who believes, obeys, is spiritual and another person altogether—in short, to one who holds the promise—therefore it follows that Scripture wants to teach us that there are no sons of Abraham except such who would be sons and seed of this [believing] Abraham."[24]

So far, Luther has reconstructed Paul's argument something like this: Abraham had a son according to faith in the promise alone; I am a son according to faith in the promise; therefore I am a son of Abraham from faith. However, he even realizes that this argument could be attacked. Thus, in commenting on verse 9, he reconstructs an objection to Paul's argument: "But some quibbler will still object, 'Such a line of argumentation does not stand up: "Abraham believes, therefore those who believe are his sons," because Abraham indeed merited son and seed through faith, but it does not hence follow that his sons ought to believe.'"[25] Otherwise, Luther goes on to say, anything that Abraham possessed, including Canaan, would have to believe.

In the first instance Luther solves this logical flaw by referring to the simple-mindedness of the Galatians, who (unlike the Romans) simply needed to know that "they cannot be children of Abraham unless they are like him."[26] But

21. WA 2:511.32–33 (cf. LW 27:253).
22. WA 2:512.4–5 (LW 27:253).
23. WA 2:512.17 (LW 27:254).
24. WA 2:512.18–21 (LW 27:254).
25. WA 2:512.33–36 (LW 27:254).
26. WA 2:513.3–4 (LW 27:254–55).

Luther also knows that a deeper mystery lurks here: the truth of the premises in this argument rests in God's reliability. "Since, however, the divine promise and predestination cannot be false, with no difficulty the conclusion [of the syllogism] will also be infallible that all who have been promised are among the faithful, so that the faith of those promised stands not on the necessity of works and their faith but on the reliability of divine election."[27] Indeed, divine election for Luther is nothing other than God's unconditional promise—the only trustworthy thing upon which one might build, since neither works nor even faith are that reliable.

At the heart of Luther's understanding of the *modus loquendi* of both Scripture and Paul's logic, then, beats his discovery of God's completely unconditional, trustworthy, and foolish promise. Without this promise, Paul seems to misquote and misunderstand Scripture, proffers only weak arguments to make his case, and forces the reader to interpret everything according to human standards—whether of works or of faith. On the contrary, if Scripture simply reveals the divine decision to have mercy, then only Paul's illogic truly comprehends what is at stake: the Spirit's understanding of God's heart.

But Luther is not yet done. By quoting Deuteronomy 27:26 in Galatians 3:10, Paul turns Moses on his head and again speaks absurdly. "Look at the Apostle's astounding syllogism!"[28] Moses cursed those who did *not* do what was in the law; Paul curses those who perform works of the law. Some (such as Festus Porcius: Acts 26:24) could well call Paul insane! Luther's solution? "Whoever are outside faith may indeed perform the works of the law, but they do not fulfill the law."[29] If the one circumcised does not fulfill the whole law, neither does anyone else doing any other work of the law. Thus Moses placed all people under a curse because no one fulfills any part of the law, and thus everyone needs a redeemer, Christ. Those who seem to fulfill the law are merely pretending.

Luther then pauses to go after "my neutralists," as he calls them, that is, those who distinguish good works from meritorious works and argue that sinners can do good works that fulfill the law.[30] Paul, these opponents argue,

27. WA 2:513.6–9 (LW 27:255).
28. WA 2:513.23–24 (cf. LW 27:255).
29. WA 2:513.32–33 (cf. LW 27:256).
30. WA 2:514.7 (cf. 503.7 and WA 5:408.22). This involved most of the medieval tradition, including Thomas Aquinas, but Luther probably had Gabriel Biel and Luther's own modernist opponents in mind. Biel argued that in a state of sin a sinner can bring forth an act of true love of God *quoad substantiam actuum* ("according to the substance of the act") although not according to the intention of the Lawgiver, God, who intends for persons doing such work to be infused with a *habitus caritatis*. For Luther, who often cited 1 Tim. 1:9, all that was done outside of faith was sin.

is speaking only of ceremonial works, which bring death and a curse. Luther instead argues that the ceremonial law is not evil unless one trusts it; Paul, on the contrary, is speaking of all law. Then Luther takes on Jerome by name. Jerome cleaned up Paul's logic by adding the words "every" and "all" to the text. Yet this ceremonial narrowing contradicts Galatians 3:13–14, since Christ did not simply redeem from the curse of the ceremonial law, given that the gentiles were never under that law in any case. "For, as I have said before, Christ accomplishes too little, if he only freed us from circumcision, Sabbaths, clothing, foods, and ablutions and not from the far more serious sins against the law: lust, greed, wrath, ungodliness."[31] Jerome's argument turns Christ into a savior of bodies, not souls. Luther concludes: "But therefore the work of any law whatsoever is a sin and curse, if it is done outside of faith, that is, outside the purity of heart, innocence, and righteousness."[32] For Luther, what is written in the law is faith, and "this [faith] alone performs all things of the law."[33]

Following this line of argument, Luther then interprets 3:11 as the underlying assumption (*subsumptio*) for Paul's citation of Deuteronomy. He paraphrases Paul to say, "You hear from Moses that that one is cursed who does not do what has been written [in the law], and I at the same time have assumed that such are those who live from works."[34] Performing works of the law and keeping the law are, in Luther's view of Paul, two separate things. The keeping of the law occurs only by faith, as Paul's citation of Habakkuk 2:4 proves. Without faith the works of the law are death and unrighteous and thus do not "fulfill what is written" (Deut. 27:26).

Luther then turns to Galatians 3:12, which he views as again reiterating Paul's main point that the law and faith are not the same. "Neither [the law] itself nor its works are from faith or with faith."[35] For Luther, Paul's citation of Leviticus 18:5 shows that the doer of law lives in those deeds that evade punishment and acquires the law's rewards, yet does not live in God or as a son of Abraham, but rather is dead toward God. With this Luther can then introduce one of his favorite themes from this period of his life: the distinction between outward appearances (where a human being seems in the eyes of others to fulfill the law) and inward unrighteousness (living without faith). He again attacks Jerome's interpretation, blaming it on his false understanding

31. WA 2:514.18–21 (LW 27:257).
32. WA 2:514.22–24 (LW 27:257).
33. WA 2:514.36 (cf. LW 27:257).
34. WA 2:514.39–40 and 515.1 (cf. LW 27:258, translating "sunt" as "rely on"; and Walch 8:1475, translating "sunt" as "umgehen").
35. WA 2:515.13–14 (cf. LW 27:258).

of law and excessive allegorizing of the law learned from Origen. Far from the persons of the Old Testament being mere shadows and thus placing them under Moses's curse, Luther insists that this "is altogether false, for they lived before God justified and sanctified by faith, even before the law and the works of the law were commanded."[36]

This brings us, finally, to Luther's 1519 interpretation of Galatians 3:13–14. In the first place, Luther insists on placing everyone under the curse of the law. As a result, from the outset he attacks Gabriel Biel, who defines the person in a state of sin as one who can fulfill the law "according to the substance of the act" but, because the sinner has not been infused with the habit of love (*habitus caritatis*) received only in a state of grace, that person still does not fulfill the law "according to the intention of the Lawgiver" (namely, God, who insists that one must have this very *habitus*). Luther dismisses such an approach. "I find fault with those who are neither under the curse of the law nor require Christ, the Redeemer."[37] Here the spark igniting the Reformation—namely, the attack on indulgences in the 95 Theses—and Luther's interpretation of Paul converge. By trying to find a way out from under the curse through "doing what is in you" (*facere quod in te est*), Luther's contemporaries had in his view eliminated Christ as Redeemer. "Who can endure this poison?" he wonders.[38]

In contradistinction to the scholastic argument, Luther insists that those outside grace are not sinning by not committing adultery or murder but by inward sins of lust, hatred, and the like. "For this hidden uncleanness of heart and flesh is not removed except by faith through Christ's grace."[39] The law's intent, he continues, was not that it be kept by earning grace, understood as yet another requirement of divine legislation; rather, the law's intent was that it be kept but only with grace. Thus the point of the law was to force a person to seek grace outside the self. "Therefore we who are without faith's grace are all under the law's curse."[40] This insight—that the law was supposed to drive a person to Christ and to grace, so that each one could be stripped of works and merit and have only faith—drives Luther's entire approach to the law in Paul. "For since 'the righteous lives' only 'by faith,' the curse of the law is clearly on unbelievers, lest we make Christ's redemption worthless or only refer it to ceremonial things, from which even a human being could redeem us."[41]

---

36. WA 2:515.31–33 (LW 27:259). In the same section, Luther tries to rescue Jerome's approach, since later in the commentary Jerome admits that all are also sinners according to the moral law.
37. WA 2:516.9–10 (LW 27:259).
38. WA 2:516.12 (LW 27:260).
39. WA 2:516.18–19 (LW 27:260).
40. WA 2:516.21–22 (LW 27:260).
41. WA 2:516.22–25 (LW 27:260).

In the same section, Luther links this text to Paul's comment in 2 Corinthians 5:21 ("God made Christ to be sin for us"). Then, building on Paul's paradoxes in these two texts, Luther invents more of his own. "In an entirely similar turn of phrase, 'he died so that we may be life in him'; 'he was ashamed so that we might be made a boast in him'; 'he was made all things for us so that we might become all things in him.' That is, if we believe in him, then the law is already fulfilled, and we are freed from the curse of the law."[42] For Luther, then, Paul's paradoxes of blessing and curse or of sin and righteousness are not texts to be explained away but manners of speaking to be applied in every possible situation for the sake of faith.

Luther then mocks Jerome for trying to avoid admitting that Christ was cursed by God. For Luther, Jerome's objections miss Paul's point, which Jesus also affirmed by applying Isaiah 53:12 ("He was numbered with the transgressors") to himself. As he develops his criticism of Jerome further, Luther again defines humans inwardly and outwardly and argues that there is thus a twofold blessing and a twofold curse. The inner blessing is grace and righteousness in the Holy Spirit, and its concomitant curse is sin; the outer blessing is material abundance, and the curse is poverty. Christ, then, was cursed with an outward curse and blessed inwardly at the same time.

Luther links the other half of Paul's argument (that the blessing comes to the gentiles) to one of his key insights into Christian life: good works do not make people good, but good people do good works. Or here, he opined, "the gentiles will be Abraham's sons, not because they imitate him but because they were given a promise. Therefore they will also imitate him because they have become sons as a result of God's promising and fulfilling, not as a result of their doing and imitating. For imitation does not make sons, but sonship makes imitators."[43]

Galatians 3:6–14 in 1535

In his book on Luther's second commentary on Galatians, Kenneth Hagen argues that Luther's exegetical method has more in common with monastic reading of texts than with either scholastic or humanist approaches.[44] While this certainly helps to explain the length of Luther's comments and the meditative

---

42. WA 2:516.33–36 (LW 27:260).
43. WA 2:518.13–16 (LW 27:260). See Klaus Petzold, *Die Grundlagen der Erziehungslehre im Spätmittelalter und bei Luther* (Heidelberg: Quelle & Meyer, 1969).
44. Kenneth Hagen, *Luther's Approach to Scripture as Seen in His "Commentaries" on Galatians, 1519–1538* (Tübingen: Mohr Siebeck, 1993).

form they take, Hagen's theory is simply too narrow. At this point in his career, Luther employs all the methods and approaches available to him. Thus, as we have already seen, his lectures and commentary feature a detailed *argumentum*, characteristic of humanist approaches to Scripture of all stripes. He also refers to the Greek text, ancient commentaries, and the rhetorical turns in Paul's argument, which also has little to do with monastic readings of texts but much to do with the peculiar brand of Wittenberg humanism that marks all biblical exegesis emanating from that place. His expansive commentary, while certainly having much in common with a form of monastic *lectio divina*, does not finally fit into any one category cleanly, since Luther employs not only meditation per se (which is marked by conversation between the soul [or exegete] and God) but also paraphrase (a beloved humanist exegetical technique) and direct application of the text to Luther's own situation.[45] It might be better to identify Luther's method more broadly with a homiletical style that assumes the interpretation of an individual verse reaches its goal only when strengthening the hearers' faith.

In the 1535 commentary, Luther divides up Paul's arguments more clearly, noting that the apostle begins with an argument from experience (3:1–5) before moving on to an argument from Scripture, specifically Abraham (3:6–14), and finally to one based upon a human analogy (3:15–18). Whereas in the first section of this chapter, Luther again explicitly rejects reducing Paul's understanding of law to ceremonies, in the middle section, which is the topic for this paper, he also has other, bigger fish to fry.

To appreciate Luther's approach, however, we must begin by identifying some of the most obvious and prevalent exegetical techniques. In addition to the *argumentum*, described above, Luther especially uses paraphrase and what we might call direct application to his current situation. These arose out of his central theological commitment to the *modus loquendi* described above, or in the context of this commentary, better described as the *viva vox evangelii*—the living voice of the gospel. Yet we would be premature in labeling such an approach to Galatians purely eisegesis. On the contrary, it represents a fierce struggle with the text of Paul as authority, that is, as a text that (to play on the original meaning of the Latin *auctoritas*) produces something in the reader. For Luther, this production is always law that condemns and puts to death, and gospel that forgives and brings to life.

Moreover, Luther employs paraphrase as an especially adept form of such

---

45. See Mark U. Edwards, *Luther and the False Brethren* (Stanford, CA: Stanford University Press, 1975); and Timothy J. Wengert, "Luther and Melanchthon—Melanchthon and Luther," *Luther-Jahrbuch* 66 (1999): 55–88.

"authorization," since it allows Paul to speak the very words he wrote but directly to the hearer or reader and with a fullness that brings his words into (in this case) the sixteenth century.[46] Luther's goal in this process is to bring lively meaning to Paul's words. Of the many examples in this section of the commentary, consider Luther's remarks on Galatians 3:9 ("Therefore, those who are from faith will be blessed with faithful Abraham"):[47]

> Here the emphasis and entire force is in the word, "with *faithful* Abraham." For Paul obviously distinguishes Abraham from Abraham, making one and the same person into two persons. It is as if he were saying: "There is an Abraham who works and an Abraham who believes. Our concern is not with the Abraham who works. For 'if he is justified by works, he has something to boast about, but not in the sight of God' [Rom. 4:2]. Let that begetting Abraham, who is a worker, who is circumcised, and who observes the law, properly pertain to the Jews. But to us the other Abraham, namely, the faithful one, applies, about whom Scripture declares that through his faith he obtains the blessing of righteousness and that he obtains the promise of the same blessing for all those who believe as he did. Thereupon, the world is promised to Abraham, but as a believing one. Therefore the whole world ought to be blessed, that is, ought to receive the imputation of righteousness, if it believed as Abraham."[48]

What Luther does here is simply explain the centrality of the word (in the Vulgate) "faithful." He then uses Paul's parallel discussion of Abraham in Romans 4 to prove that the distinction of the two Abrahams comes from Paul. (Indeed, throughout this section he refers to Paul's broader arguments in Romans.)

Because of his final comment, Luther then proceeds to investigate the meaning of the words "to bless." "The blessing is nothing other than the promise of the gospel," he begins.[49] Being blessed means to hear this very promise. "This promise is preached and dispersed through the gospel to all nations."[50] The prophets derived all of their prophecies by understanding this text spiritually. "In sum, all prophecies about Christ's reign and the spreading of the gospel into the entire world flow from this text."[51] Luther views Paul's argument as a

---

46. It is no accident that Erasmus too produced complicated paraphrases of the entire NT.
47. This represented the Vulgate. On the basis of the Greek, Erasmus translated "are blessed." The German Bible followed the Greek as well: "werden . . . gesegnet."
48. WA 40/1:386.15–25 (LW 26:244–45), emphasis added.
49. WA 40/1:386.26 (cf. LW 26:245).
50. WA 40/1:386.28–29 (cf. LW 26:245).
51. WA 40/1:387.13–14 (cf. LW 26:245). Luther did not derive all prophecies from this but only those having to do specifically with the *reign* of the Messiah and the spread of the gospel *everywhere*.

kind of analogy. Thus he writes: "Therefore, as the imputation of righteousness reached Abraham through the hearing of faith, so also it reached and still reaches all nations." Why can Paul say this? "For it is the speech of the same God, which was first made known to Abraham and afterward to all nations."[52]

In making this shift from Abraham to all nations, Luther can then apply the text to his own hearers and readers. "Therefore, 'to bless' is to preach and teach the word of the gospel, to confess Christ, and to spread knowledge of him to others." This was the priestly office continued in the New Testament "by preaching, administering the sacraments, by absolving, by consoling and explaining the word of grace that Abraham had and that was his blessing. When he believed it, he received the blessing, so also we who believe it are blessed."[53]

What Luther sees Paul doing in interpreting Abraham's promise is what he also observes in the prophets—and what Luther thinks he himself is doing: a dynamic reorientation of the original promise to a new set of hearers. "[The prophets] did not view the promises made to the fathers lifelessly [*frigide*], as the impious Jews did and as the sophists and sectarians do today, but they read and sharpened them with the greatest diligence, and whatever they prophesied concerning Christ and his reign they drew from this source."[54] Here Luther grounds how he reads Paul in how Paul and the prophets read Genesis: not "lifelessly," that is, literally (as if the only point is to promise some land to Abraham), but spiritually, which is the only kind of blessing that can be received by faith.

If Luther hinted at the connection between Paul's description of Abraham's faith and his own day in the preceding, he comes right out and says so in the next lines. Here Luther uses what I have identified elsewhere as a *sicut . . . ita* (just as . . . so also) construction to make his point.[55] "However, just as [*quemadmodum*] the Jews boast only in the Abraham who works, so also [*ita*] the pope only proposes a Christ who works or is an example."[56] Note that Luther's quarrel is not simply with an interpretation of Abraham but especially with the analogous ways people misinterpret both Abraham and Christ. In his further description of the pope's message, we actually catch a glimpse of the ongoing discussions between the so-called Reformed Catholics and the Wittenbergers. In 1534, Philipp Melanchthon journeyed to Leipzig

52. WA 40/1:387.17–20 (cf. LW 26:245).
53. WA 40/1:387.24–27 (cf. LW 26:245).
54. WA 40/1:387.31–32 and 388.12–13 (cf. LW 26:246).
55. Timothy J. Wengert, *Philip Melanchthon's* Annotationes in Johannem *in Relation to Its Predecessors and Contemporaries* (Geneva: Droz, 1987), 198–201.
56. WA 40/1:389.12–13 (cf. LW 26:246).

(whose duke, Georg of Saxony, was a sworn enemy of Luther) for conversations about the differences between Roman Catholics and Lutherans. One of the sticking points revolved around the interpretation of John 13:15. The Catholic side insisted that this new commandment was part of the gospel, so that the gospel was not simply free forgiveness in Christ but also included the law of love. Melanchthon's solution, as I have written elsewhere, was to develop a third use of the law—hence even the command to love was not gospel but remained law, lest the unconditional promise of forgiveness be overwhelmed by another form of works-righteousness.[57] Luther's similar solution is recorded here in the 1535 Galatians commentary:

> [The pope] says, "Whoever wants to live in a godly way ought to walk as Christ walked, as it says in John 13[:15], 'I give an example to you, so that as I did, you may also do.'" We do not deny that Christ's example is to be imitated by the godly and must be done well, but in this they do not become righteous before God. Paul here is introducing a discussion not about what we ought to do but on what grounds we are justified. Here Christ alone, dying for our sins and rising for our righteousness, must be set forth as our righteousness. Moreover, he must be apprehended by faith as gift, not as example.[58]

With this, Luther returns to the distinction between the Abraham who worked and the Abraham who believed. "Thus the believing Abraham must be separated from the working Abraham as far as heaven is distant from earth. The believing one is a completely divine human being, a son of God, the inheritor of the entire world, victor over the world, sin, death, the devil, etc., and thus is one who cannot be praised enough."[59] Thus faith suffices before God, while works and examples are for this world and the neighbor.

Luther introduces the next section (Gal. 3:10–14) by pointing out that from the words "They will be blessed" Paul constructs an argument from contraries. This exegetical insight is crucial for Luther. "For the Scripture is filled with antitheses. Only a very talented person perceives the antitheses in the Scriptures and can interpret the Scriptures through them."[60] Indeed, unlike his colleague Melanchthon, Luther finds the key to interpreting Scripture precisely here,

---

57. Timothy J. Wengert, *Law and Gospel: Philip Melanchthon's Debate with John Agricola of Eisleben over* Poenitentia (Grand Rapids: Baker, 1997), 177–210.
58. WA 40/1:389.13–20 (cf. LW 26:246–47). He immediately repeated his original point, using again the "ut Iudaei . . . ita Papistae et omnes Iustitiarii" construction. Already Augustine had distinguished between Christ as gift or sacrament and as example, a comparison Luther introduced as early as 1520 in his tract *The Freedom of a Christian*.
59. WA 40/1:390.21–24 (cf. LW 26:247).
60. WA 40/1:391.17–19 (cf. LW 26:248).

because such antitheses overturn reason and drive the reader to faith in Christ. In this way, Luther formalizes his remarks in 1519 regarding Paul's illogic.

Both Paul and Luther move effortlessly then from blessing to curse. Since the blessing is found only in the promise to Abraham as revealed in the gospel, anything outside that blessing is under a curse. To get out from under the curse of the law—both the divine law given to Moses and any other human laws and traditions—a person has only the promise of blessing or the faith of Abraham. In light of this, Luther introduces yet another wrinkle into his exegetical method, one that marks all Wittenberg exegetes: he insists that part of the meaning of text is wrapped up in its effect on the hearer. "It is extremely valuable to know this, because it has the power for consoling consciences."[61]

Luther then picks up another important thread in Wittenberg exegesis, the distinction between faith's righteousness and civil or fleshly righteousness. He complains that Jerome and others have ignored this distinction and thus take what Paul is saying about the law spiritually and confuse that with civil righteousness. Thus, although civil righteousness is outside of Christ and faith, it is not ipso facto under a curse but simply does not serve divine righteousness. Only when one confuses the two forms of righteousness does one come under the law's curse. Why does Luther make this distinction? His Roman opponents have consistently argued that his position foments rebellion:

> The pope and the bishops cannot bear this, but it is not appropriate for us to keep silence. For we ought to confess the truth and say that the papacy is cursed, the laws and courts of the emperor are cursed, because according to Paul whatever is outside the promise and faith of Abraham is cursed. When the opposition hears this, they interpret our words unfavorably, as if we were teaching that the government is not to be accorded with respect but rather as if we were condemning all laws and were dissolving and destroying the Empire.[62]

Against these charges, Luther insists on distinguishing physical and spiritual blessings. Here we can see how the challenges of his theological opponents, whose views he takes very seriously, influence what he says in his commentary. He heightens what he sees as Paul's paradoxical, blanket statement in order to answer his accusers. "In sum, we say that all things are God's good creatures, . . . that is, they are temporal blessings that pertain to this life. But the self-righteous [*iustitiarii*] of all ages—Jews, papists, sectarians, etc.—confuse and mix together these things, because they do not distinguish between corporal

---

61. WA 40/1:392.19 (cf. LW 26:249). This phrase was not as clearly expressed in Luther's lectures (WA 40/1:392.6).
62. WA 40/1:394.17–22 (cf. LW 26:250).

and spiritual blessings. Thus they say, 'We have the law; it is good, holy and just. Therefore we are justified through it.'"[63]

Other things in Luther also did not change between 1519 and 1535. Just as in 1519 he saw the scandal of Paul's argument in verse 10—proving an affirmative statement from a negative one—so here, too, he calls this "an amazing [*mirabilis*] proof,"[64] rather like proving from Jesus's statement in Matthew 19:17 ("If you observe the commandments of God, you will enter life") the opposite ("If you do not observe the commandments, you will enter life"). "No one understands this text except by properly holding the article of justification. Jerome sweats over this enough but leaves it unexplained."[65] Luther, of course, never sees a contradiction in Scripture he does not like. So he here creates a delightful absurdity: "If you have fulfilled the law, you have not fulfilled it; if you have not fulfilled it, you have fulfilled it."[66] For Luther, it all comes down to the words "to do" (as in the one who "does" the law). Keeping the law, he argues, is not simply a matter of doing what is commanded but instead is a matter of the heart and thus keeping it *completely*. The very claim to be keeping the law means relying on one's own works and hence, by that very reliance, trusting in one's self and not in God, thus breaking the first commandments about God and hence all of the commandments. For him the verb "to do" includes faith. "Therefore, when clearly and properly defined, the term 'to do' simply means to believe in Jesus Christ and, given that the Holy Spirit is received through faith in Christ, to do the things that are in the law."[67] He then reverts to a favorite image for the relation between works and faith, one that attacks the Aristotelian ethics with which he grew up, which claimed that a person becomes good by doing good. "Faith grasps the very 'maker' [of works] and makes a tree, by which fruits may be 'made.' First there must be a tree, then the fruit. For apples do not make a tree, but a tree makes apples. So faith first makes the person who afterward 'makes' works."[68]

For Luther, the paradoxical nature of Paul's writing and, hence, of the Word of God is never far from his mind. Already in Galatians 3:6, he finds an impossible juxtaposition of "faith" and "righteousness." Luther's "theology of the cross," which is not a theory about the atonement but a methodological key to understanding God's way of acting with sinners, states that God is

---

63. WA 40/1:395.15–21 (LW 26:250–51).
64. WA 40/1:396.31 (cf. LW 26:252).
65. WA 40/1:397.18–20 (cf. LW 26:252).
66. WA 40/1:397.31 (cf. LW 26:252).
67. WA 40/1:401.20–22 (cf. LW 26:255).
68. WA 40/1:402.13–17 (= LW 26:255). Throughout this passage Luther uses a single verb, *facere*, which can be rendered either "to do" or "to make."

revealed in the last place one would reasonably look. In the case of Paul's use of Abraham, it is patently absurd to reason that Abraham could be justified by faith and not by works. Luther begins by defining faith as radically as possible:

> Here Paul fashions out of faith in God the supreme worship, the supreme submission, the supreme obedience and sacrifice. . . . But to attribute glory to God is to believe in him, regard him as truthful, wise, righteous, merciful, and almighty, in short, to acknowledge him as the Author and Lavisher of every good thing. Reason does not do this, only faith does. It consummates the Deity; and, if I may put it this way, it is the creator of the Deity, not in God's substance but in us.[69]

He mentions reason as the counterpoint to faith and, to set up his argument, defines faith in terms of *iustitia*. Here Luther, who in other instances can reject "reason's" definition of *iustitia*, uses it for his own purposes. Aristotle, Cicero, Justinian's *Institutes*, and a host of other ancient authors defined *iustitia* as "giving to each their own." So Luther then defines faith as justifying "because it renders to God what is due to him," which (he points out) is the legal definition.[70] In this case specifically, however, it is to admit that what God speaks is true. The trouble, Luther explains, is that according to reason God speaks "impossible, mendacious, foolish, weak, absurd, abominable, heretical, and diabolical things."[71] Whether one is talking about Christ's presence in the Supper, or about baptism as regenerative, or about the incarnation and crucifixion, it is completely absurd to reason, which, on the contrary, imagines that its own choices and works are God-pleasing, rather than hearing and believing God's voice.

As a result, reason must die. "But faith slaughters reason and kills the beast that the whole world and all creatures cannot kill."[72] The notion that reason has to die relates directly to Luther's understanding of the function of the law à la Paul ("I through the law died to the law" [Gal. 2:19]). Here the scandal of faith that "lets God be God"[73] itself destroys the very claims of reason to

---

69. WA 40/1:360.17–18, 20–25 (cf. LW 26:226–27). For more on Luther's theology of the cross in Galatians, see Gerhard Ebeling, "*Fides occidit rationem*: Ein Aspekt der theologia crucis in Luthers Auslegung von Gal 3,6," in *Lutherstudien*, vol. 3, *Begriffsuntersuchungen—Textinterpretationen: Wirkungsgeschichtliches* (Tübingen: Mohr [Siebeck], 1985), 181–222.

70. WA 40/1:361.12–14 (cf. LW 26:227). He makes a similar move in his preface to Romans (WA BI 7:10.28–33 and 11.28–34).

71. WA 40/1:361.15–16 (cf. LW 26:227). In the lectures, Luther specifically mentions the Erasmians. In the mid-1530s, Luther had again crossed swords with Erasmus. See Martin Brecht, *Martin Luther: The Preservation of the Church, 1532–1546*, trans. James L. Schaaf (Minneapolis: Fortress, 1993), 78–84.

72. WA 40/1:362.15–16 (= LW 26:228).

73. Philip Watson, *Let God Be God! An Interpretation of the Theology of Martin Luther* (Philadelphia: Muhlenberg, 1950).

freedom of choice and the power of its own works. "Thus all upright people, entering with Abraham into the darkness of faith, put reason to death, saying: 'Reason, you are foolish. You do not understand what belongs to God. . . . Do not judge; but listen to the Word of God and believe.'"[74]

As a further result of this line of thinking, Luther then defines faith and imputation: "For Christian righteousness consists in two things, namely, faith in the heart, and the imputation of God." Here, using scholastic terminology borrowed from Aristotle, he defines faith as *iustitia formalis* (formal righteousness). Rather than importing medieval scholastic ontology into justification at this point, however, Luther is actually doing the opposite. For medieval theology, the "form" of righteousness (where "form" always bears the Aristotelian insistence that everything is composed of matter and form) is always faith *formed* by love. Faith itself can be only the material component—giving what we might call the building blocks of faith (the *fides quae*) rather than complete faith, which demands the "form" of love.[75] Luther, on the contrary, insists that faith itself is one's "formal" righteousness. There is no need of works of love or a habit of charity to complete it. Instead, whatever is lacking in faith—now understood as trust in God (giving God his own)—is made up for in the divine imputation of Christ's righteousness, where both are gifts from God, not human works.

For Luther, then, proper interpretation of Paul revolves around proper definition of the words, which happens only in the midst of a struggle against reason, which "reasonably" imagines that Paul cannot mean what he says but has to allow room for works. Luther's summary of Galatians 3:6 further confirms that faithful interpretation revolves around definition. "I have said these things to interpret the verse, 'And it was reckoned to him as righteousness,' in order that the students of Sacred Scriptures may understand that Christian righteousness is to be defined properly and accurately in this way, namely as trust in God's Son. . . . Here these specifics must [now] be added as *differentia*."[76] Luther uses a term from Aristotle's *Analytics* to continue his definition by looking at *differentia*, that is, the genus and species of a thing.[77] In this case, Luther insists that *iustitia* is composed of two parts: faith in the heart, and God's reckoning of faith as perfect righteousness, the very mixture he finds in

---

74. WA 40/1:362.23–26 (cf. LW 26:228).
75. See, e.g., Luther's criticism of this term in WA 40/1:325.23–230.28. For him (229.18–21): "Est ergo formalis nostra iustitia non charitas informans fidem, sed ipsa fides et nebula cordis, hoc est, fiducia in rem quam non videmus, hoc est, in Christum qui, ut maxime non videatur, tamen praesens est."
76. WA 40/1:366.22–27 (cf. LW 26:231).
77. Cf. CR 13:521.

Paul's text, which combines faith and imputation. For Luther, only preserving this distinction leads to understanding Paul properly.[78] Faith weakly attributes glory to God; God shores up this God-given faith with Christ's righteousness.

Precisely in this situation "is the Christian person at the same time [*simul*] righteous and sinner, holy and profane, an enemy and son of God." "The sophists," as Luther calls them, do not believe this, and so their teaching on justification only drives people to despair. "We, on the contrary, teach in the way described above, and we console the afflicted sinner."[79] This *simul* means for Luther that the Christian, as the high priest, offers sacrifices morning and evening: in the evening slaying reason, and in the morning glorifying God. It also implies that the point of proper exegesis is consolation of the afflicted.

Martin Luther's exposition of this section of Galatians culminates in a lengthy interpretation of 3:13–14. Here all of the criticisms of past exegesis and of his contemporary opponents come to a head. The text comprises the very kind of outrageous, paradoxical language that Luther so relished and that his opponents and even later followers insisted on domesticating in favor of their blending of human capacities, merit, and an inhering disposition toward the good. First, Jerome followed by Erasmus could not imagine how Christ could be cursed. Paul, of course, had quoted the Hebrew text incorrectly, and Jerome went about correcting Paul on that basis. But in such tinkering with Paul, Luther finds a remarkable irony: that Jerome and his opponents were willing to argue against the clear text of Paul in order to accommodate their own theological tastes, even if their motive was to shield pious souls from hearing that Christ was cursed. Rather than harmonize Paul with Deuteronomy, Luther prefers to leave each text to stand on its own. For Luther, that Christ became a curse *for us* is the highest doctrine and comfort Scripture can give the sinner, the dying, and those oppressed.

To prosecute his case and heighten the paradox, Luther employs a host of remarkable rhetorical ploys, quite foreign to modern expectations of good commentary. But then, if Luther is correct that this text from Paul claims so central a place for the believer, then anything less challenging and personal would result in not taking Paul seriously at all. That is, precritical exegesis such as Luther's challenges our present academic predilections precisely in the directness of its claims to meaning.[80] One way Luther accomplishes this is through what might be termed exegetical fantasy. The various concepts in the text—law, curse, Christ—receive voice as Luther, literally, reenacts the meaning of the text for his hearers and readers. Here his imaginative, homiletical method

---

78. WA 40/1:368.15–25 (LW 26:232).
79. WA 40/1:369.13 (cf. LW 26:233).
80. David C. Steinmetz, "The Superiority of Pre-Critical Exegesis," *ThTo* 27 (1980): 27–38.

of interpretation takes full flight, fueled by Paul's own powerful language. As a first attempt at explaining this verse, Luther simply states:

> And all the prophets saw this, that Christ was to become the greatest thief, murderer, adulterer, robber, desecrator, blasphemer, etc., there has ever been anywhere in the world, because he is not acting in his own person now. Now he is not the Son of God, born of the Virgin, but he is a sinner, who has and bears the sin of Paul, who was a blasphemer, persecutor, and assaulter; of Peter, who denied Christ; of David, who was an adulterer and a murderer. . . . In short, he has and bears all the sins of all people in his body.[81]

Here Luther already uses several of his favorite rhetorical techniques—congeries and examples—to interpret the text. A bit later, he emphasizes both the text's comfort and the "sophists'" betrayal of sinners by their interpretations. "The sophists, when they separate Christ from sins and sinners and set him forth only as an example for us to imitate, deprive us of this knowledge of Christ and most delightful comfort, namely, that Christ became a curse for us to set us free from the curse of the law."[82]

For Luther, Christ's becoming a curse for us equates to his incarnate existence. Suddenly the readers' own reasonable objections find a voice. "But it is completely absurd and insulting to call the Son of God a sinner and a curse!" he states, but then continues, "If you want to deny that He is a sinner and a curse, then deny also that he suffered, was crucified, and died."[83] By insisting on "faith formed by love" as the way to remove sin, the "Papists" have taken all power from the incarnation itself. "This is clearly to unwrap and extricate Christ from our sins, to make him innocent, to burden and overwhelm ourselves with our own sins, and to look at them, not in Christ but in ourselves. This is to abolish Christ and make him useless."[84]

With this, Luther sets the stage for a dramatic approach to interpreting this text.

> This is the most joyous of all teachings and the one most filled with comfort. It teaches that we have the indescribable and inestimable mercy and love of God. For when the merciful Father saw that we were being oppressed and held under a curse

---

81. WA 40/1:433.26–32 (= LW 26:277).
82. WA 40/1:434.21–24 (cf. LW 26:278). Luther equated the text to 2 Cor. 5:21 and John 1:29.
83. WA 40/1:434.29–36 (= LW 26:278).
84. WA 40/1:436.27–31 (= LW 26:279). See also WA 40/1:441.15–16 (= LW 26:282), where Luther linked his opponents ("sophists and fanatics") to Arius: "When Arius denied this [Christ's divinity], it was necessary also for him to deny the doctrine of redemption." A similar, modern interpretation of Arius is in Dennis Groh and Robert Gregg, *Early Arianism—a View of Salvation* (Philadelphia: Fortress, 1981).

through the law and that we could not be liberated from it by anything, then he sent into the world his Son, upon whom he heaped all the sins of all people, and said to him: "Be Peter the denier; Paul the persecutor, blasphemer, and assaulter; David the adulterer; the sinner who ate the apple in paradise; that thief on the cross. In short, be the person of all human beings, the one who has committed the sins of all people. Therefore, see to it that you pay and make satisfaction for them." Then the law comes and says: "I find him a sinner, who takes upon himself the sins of all people. I do not see any other sin than those in him. Therefore let him die on the cross!" And so it attacks him and kills him. By this deed the whole world is purged and expiated from all sins and thus also set free from death and from all evil. But when sin and death have been abolished by this one man, God could not see anything else in the whole world than sheer cleansing and righteousness, particularly if the world believed it. And if any remnants of sin remain, still for the sake of Christ, the shining Sun, God would not notice them.[85]

Of course, here we find not only drama but also remnants of what might be called a satisfaction metaphor for the atonement. Yet scarcely a page later, Luther employs a very different, battle-like picture for the effect of Christ's taking the curse upon himself:

Now let us see how two such extremely contrary things come together in this person. Not only my sins and yours, but also the sins of the entire world, past, present, and future, attack him, try to condemn him, and even do condemn him. But because in that same person, who is the highest, the greatest, and the only sinner, there is also eternal and invincible righteousness, therefore these two clash: the highest, the greatest, and the only sin; and the highest, the greatest, and the only righteousness. Here one of them of necessity must yield and be conquered, since they come together and collide with tremendous force. Thus the sin of the entire world attacks righteousness with the greatest possible force and fury. What happens? Righteousness is eternal, immortal, and invincible. Sin is also a most powerful and cruel tyrant, dominating and ruling over the whole world, capturing and placing all people in slavery. In short, sin is the greatest and most powerful god who devours the whole human race. . . . It, I say, attacks Christ and wants to devour him as it had devoured all the others. But it does not see that he is a person of invincible and eternal righteousness. In this duel, therefore, it is necessary for sin to be conquered and killed, and for righteousness to prevail and live. Thus in Christ absolutely all sin is conquered, killed, and buried; and righteousness remains the victor and the ruler eternally. Thus also death, which is the almighty empress of the entire world, . . . clashes against life with full force and would conquer and swallow it; and certainly what [death] attempts, it accomplishes. But because life was immortal, even when it

---

85. WA 40/1:437.18–27 and 238.12–18 (cf. LW 26:280).

conquered it escaped victorious, conquering and killing death. . . . Thus there is the same conflict between the curse, which is divine wrath against the whole world, and the blessing, that is, the eternal grace and mercy of God in Christ.[86]

Finally, Luther's interpretation of Galatians 3:13, and hence this entire portion of Galatians, links its meaning to comfort and consolation. This is the hallmark of Wittenberg's interpretation of Scripture: that the meaning of a text consists of two parts, doctrine (definition) and its effect. When the effect of a doctrine leads to despair, then no matter how reasonable the interpretation might seem, it still is false. If the person assaulted by sin, death, terror, wrath, the devil, and evil finds no consolation in a particular view of Scripture or Christ, then there is only hell to pay, and the interpretation must be false. So Luther concludes this section of his work on Galatians with these words, "With thanksgiving and with a sure confidence, therefore, let us receive this teaching, so sweet and so full of comfort, which teaches that Christ became a curse for us (that is, a sinner worthy of the wrath of God), that he clothed himself in our person, that he laid our sins upon his own shoulders, and that he said: 'I have committed the sins that all people have committed.'"[87] It all comes down to Paul's ὑπὲρ ὑμῶν (for us [3:13]). Once again, Luther interprets the text with a dramatic monologue:

> By this favorable exchange with us, he took upon himself our sinful person and granted us his innocent and victorious person. Clothed and dressed in this, we are freed from the curse of the law, because Christ himself voluntarily was made a curse for us, saying, "For my own person of humanity and divinity I am blessed, and I am in need of nothing whatever. But I shall empty myself [Phil. 2:7]; I shall take on your clothing and mask; and in this I shall walk about and suffer death, so that I may free you from death."[88]

From this Luther then derives personal comfort, addressing the reader and hearer directly:

> Therefore if sin makes you anxious, and if death terrifies you, just think that this is an empty specter and an illusion of the devil—as it certainly is. For in fact there is no sin, no curse, no death, and no devil any longer, because Christ has conquered and destroyed all of these things. Therefore, the victory of Christ is

---

86. WA 40/1:438.32–35; 439.13–31; and 440.15–16 (= LW 26:281). Luther noted the "amazing and outstanding" power of the phrase "in himself," which showed that this battle took place in Christ. See WA 40/1:440.30–33 (= LW 26:282): "If you look at this Person, therefore, you see sin, death, the wrath of God, hell, the devil and all evils conquered and put to death. To the extent that Christ rules by His grace in the hearts of the faithful, there is no sin or death or curse."

87. WA 40/1:442.31–34 and 443.14–15 (cf. LW 26:283–84).

88. WA 40/1:443.23–29 (= LW 26:284).

completely certain without any defect in the reality itself, which is completely true, but it lies rather instead in our incredulity, for it is difficult for reason to believe such immeasurable good things.[89]

Luther sums up his insights into this text as follows: "Undoubtedly Paul explained these things more fully in the presence of the Galatians. For this is the proper office of the apostles: to make clear the work and glory of Christ and to strengthen and comfort troubled consciences."[90] This twofold project—illumining Christ's work and giving comfort (*doctrina et usus*)—was at the heart of Wittenberg's interpretation of Scripture and stood in direct conflict not only with Jerome and Erasmus, with scholastics and Romanists, but also with our own rather tame, law-centered approaches to texts that show we cannot believe Paul's own radical words and prefer the safety of interpretation that leaves people to their own devices as they stare into the modern or postmodern abyss.

---

89. WA 40/1:444.19–24 (LW 26:284–85).
90. WA 40/1:451.25–27 (= LW 26:290).

7

Yaein

Yes and No to Luther's Reading of Galatians 3:6–14

SCOTT HAFEMANN

Scripture is filled with antitheses. It belongs to a clever person to discern the antitheses in the Scriptures and through them to be enabled to interpret the Scriptures.

Luther, *Lectures and Commentary on Galatians 1531/1535*[1]

Luther was indeed a very "clever person." Tim Wengert's essay (chap. 6 above) reminds us, therefore, that if our goal is to understand a sacred text from the past, we must suspend *disbelief* in order not to impose our own critical judgments on a deceased saint who cannot offer self-defense (p. 91 above). Facing the Gadamerian "melting of the horizons of understanding" (*Horizontverschmelzung*), the opposite is true as well: we must also strive to suspend our *belief* in order not to be unduly swayed by the power of our heritage or by

---

1. Martin Luther, *Lectures and Commentary on Galatians 1531/1535*, in WA 40/1:391.17–19. Other quotations from Wengert's chapter are identified in the text or in the notes. "Yaein" is a phonetic contraction of the German *ja und nein*, "yes and no."

the peer pressure of our contemporary communities, which often lionize the deceased saint.[2] For many, the sustained critique of the "Lutheran" paradigm since 1977 has rendered "Luther" merely an unreflected, exegetical-theological foil, the contemporary equivalent of Marcion.[3] For others, quoting Luther, our Protestant church father, is on a par with quoting Scripture.

Luther's Reading of Galatians 3:6–14

Faced with having to navigate between this hermeneutical rock and a hard place, Wengert's essay in the present volume helps us once again to hear Luther himself: from Luther's 1519 *Argumenta* to Galatians, with its blend of university-trained exegetical skills and a new "theological mode of speaking" (*modus loquendi theologicus*), to the monastery-like "homiletical style" of the Galatians commentary of 1535, in which the exposition of a text reaches its goal only when it directly impacts its readers through "the living voice of the gospel" (*viva vox evangelii*) (pp. 92, 97, 104 above). In doing so, Wengert's analysis underscores afresh that the interpretive key to Luther's 1519 exegetical-theological reading of Galatians 3:6–14, as well as to its later meditative applications in 1535, is his antithetical and anthropological understanding of Paul's law/gospel contrasts. Luther's legacy is to be found in his theological construction of these contrasts, which are determinative for his exposition and for his understanding of its theological significance in the life of the Christian.

The "law," for Luther, is a metonymy for any and all attempts to secure one's righteousness through a reliance on one's own works, which by definition are done "from our own natural powers" apart from God's grace and forgiveness. In contrast, the "gospel" represents the "completely passive righteousness of faith," "which God imputes to us through Christ apart from our works" (WA 40/1:40.28–30; 41.12–26) (pp. 95–96 above). This view of

---

2. Hans-Georg Gadamer, *Wahrheit und Methode*, 4th ed. (Tübingen: Mohr Siebeck, 1975), 290. In his words, "Die Stellung zwischen Fremdheit und Vertrautheit, die die Überlieferung für uns hat, ist das Zwischen zwischen der historisch gemeinten, abständigen Gegenständlichkeit und der Zugehörigkeit zu einer Tradition. *In diesem Zwischen ist der wahre Ort der Hermeneutik*" (279, emphasis in original).

3. Taking its impetus from the sustained critique by the Lutheran bishop Krister Stendahl, *Paul among Jews and Gentiles and Other Essays* (Philadelphia: Fortress, 1976 [part of which is based on lectures delivered in 1963–64]), esp. 12–13, 79–80, 85–88, and brought to the fore in a way impossible to ignore by the now-programmatic work of E. P. Sanders, *Paul and Palestinian Judaism* (Philadelphia: Fortress, 1977), though Sanders prefers to speak of Reformation-influenced, Christian misunderstandings of both Judaism and Paul and mentions Luther only five times (according to the index).

the passive righteousness of faith, in antithesis to the active righteousness of human works, is the key to understanding the many contrasting statements of Galatians 3:6–14 (p. 96 above).[4] In Luther's 1535 application of this text to universal human experience, the Pauline law/gospel contrast between active works and passive faith is to produce in the reader a "law that condemns and puts to death and [a] gospel that forgives and brings to life" (p. 104).

At the heart of Luther's reading of Galatians 3:10–14, therefore, is his corresponding rejection of the attempt, from Jerome to Erasmus, to reduce the "works of the law" in Paul's writings to a Jewish or ceremonial subset of the law peculiar to the ancient world. To do so would domesticate Paul's argument, separate it from all subsequent generations, and open the door to a moralistic view of the rest of the law, which could then be considered Paul's own understanding of the pathway to righteousness (p. 96). Instead, "works of the law" refers to "the deeds/works of the entire Decalogue"; moreover, Luther takes these works to be merely one expression of righteous works in general, so that Paul's rejection of "works of the law" is a rejection of any righteousness based on deeds. Paul's polemic against the law as a basis for righteousness before God consequently remains relevant to every age (WA BR 1:70.25–32, quoted on p. 94 above). When placed in antithesis to the gospel, the active demands of the law are intended to force a person to rely passively on a grace outside of the self, since to be without faith's grace is to be under the law's curse (WA 2:516.21–22, quoted on p. 102). In a stark

---

4. In response to Gal. 3:3, e.g., Luther declares that "since faith alone justifies and does good works, it follows that absolutely no works of any law whatever justify, nor are the works of any law good, only those of faith" (WA 2:508.12–15, quoted above, p. 96). Luther took Deut. 27:26 to teach works-righteousness: "You hear from Moses that that one is cursed who does not do what has been written [in the law], and I at the same time have assumed that such are those who live from works" (WA 2:514.39–40) (*Galatians*, 1519; quoted above, p. 101). Regarding Gal. 3:10–11, Wengert says, "Performing works of the law and keeping the law are, in Luther's view of Paul, two separate things. The keeping of the law occurs only by faith, as Paul's citation of Hab. 2:4 proves. Without faith the works of the law are death and unrighteous and thus do not 'fulfill what is written' (Deut. 27:26)" (p. 101 above). So Gal. 3:12 teaches that the law and faith are not the same: "Neither [the law] itself nor its works are from faith or with faith" (WA 2:515.13–14, quoted above, p. 101). Thus Lev. 18:5, quoted in Gal. 3:12, refers to living in the law in order to avoid punishment by outward appearances that seem to fulfill the law, while in reality the person is dead toward God, lacking true righteousness by faith (p. 101 above). Luther: "If we believe in [Christ], then the law is already fulfilled, and we are freed from the curse of the law" (WA 2:516.33–36, quoted above, p. 103). For Luther, therefore, the ultimate issue is existential, located in the human heart before God. This could lead him to what Wengert calls Luther's "delightful absurdity," much like later existentialism's internal battles over meaning itself: "If you have fulfilled the law, you have not fulfilled it; if you have not fulfilled it, you have fulfilled it" (WA 40/1:397.31, p. 109 above). The very claim to keep the law means that one is breaking it, since it is an expression of relying on one's own works, trusting in one's self and not in God (p. 109 above).

departure from the tradition, "This insight—that the law was supposed to drive a person to Christ and to grace, so that each one could be stripped of works and merit and have only faith—drives Luther's entire approach to the law in Paul" (p. 102).

Luther's law/gospel antithesis also makes clear that he rejects the medieval, scholastic understanding of faith, in which faith is separated from the obedience of good works, so that faith, the material component of righteousness, must be subsequently formed by love in order to be genuine (*fides caritate formata*). For Luther, faith itself is already a "formal righteousness" (*iustitia formalis*), so that there is no need for the works of love to complete it (p. 111). "Instead, whatever is lacking in faith—now understood as trust in God (giving God his own)—is made up for in the divine imputation of Christ's righteousness, where both are gifts from God, not human works" (p. 111). Proper interpretation of Paul thus requires a proper definition of Paul's words: *iustitia* is composed of two parts, faith in the heart, and God's reckoning of faith as perfect righteousness, that is, faith and imputation (pp. 111–12). "Faith weakly attributes glory to God; God shores up this God-given faith with Christ's righteousness" (p. 112).

Finally, and surprisingly, Luther's equation of works of the law with the law as a whole does not lead him to reject the latter, as often assumed, though for Luther the law is no longer needed as the sole or primary arbiter of good works. Rather, Luther's law/gospel contrast leads to the conclusion that "righteous people, . . . by being made and being [righteous], do righteous deeds. First it is necessary for the person to be changed, then [come] works" (p. 94).[5] Hence, regarding Galatians 3:10: "But therefore the work of any law whatsoever is a sin and curse, if it is done outside of faith, that is, outside the purity of heart, innocence, and righteousness" (WA 2:514.22–24) (quoted on p. 101). "For Luther, what is written in the law is faith, and 'this [faith] alone performs all things of the law'" (WA 2:514.36) (p. 101 above). Or again, in *Lectures on Galatians*, Luther maintains that deeds are the fruit of a tree made good by faith: "First there must be a tree, then the fruit. For apples do not make a tree, but a tree makes apples. So faith first makes the person who afterward 'makes' works" (WA 40/1:402.13–17) (p. 109 above). Thus Luther too teaches the legal righteousness of the Decalogue, but only "after teaching about faith" (WA 40/1:40).

---

5. Cf. pp. 100 and 103 above: good works do not make people good, but good people do good works; gentiles will be Abraham's children not because they imitate him but because they were given a promise and are elect; yet they will also imitate him because they have become sons as a result of God's promising: "For imitation does not make sons, but sonship makes imitators (*Galatians*, 1519; WA 2:518.13–16).

"Yes" to Luther

Hearing Luther again reminds us that most of the exegetical and theological issues being raised in this volume find their genesis in a series of well-known interpretive questions regarding Paul's argument in Galatians 2–3 that are brought to the fore by Luther's readings. In this sense, our questions about Galatians become, at the same time, questions concerning Luther's reading of Galatians.

First, the history of interpretation has proved Luther right that the meaning and significance of the phrase ἔργα νόμου are decisive for understanding much of Paul, both exegetically and theologically, since in Galatians and Romans the "works of the law" are the negative counterpole to Paul's positive formulation of his gospel. What is the referent of ἔργα νόμου? And what, for Paul, is wrong with them? Are the "works of the law," as Luther argues, to be equated with what the law itself teaches in its entirety as part of a larger divine, dialectical strategy designed to drive us to its antithesis? If so, do they perform this function (1) because they are impossible to keep, and/or (2) because they teach a different way of securing righteousness altogether, so that the very attempt to keep them is *itself* sin, as Bultmann concludes based on Galatians 2:16; 3:10; and 5:4?[6]

Wengert has pointed out that Luther seems to teach both. In Luther's reading of Deuteronomy 27:26 in Galatians 3:10, Moses cursed those who did not do what was in the law, while Paul curses those who perform works of the law (p. 101). For Luther, works done outside faith do not fulfill the law (WA 2:513.32–33). Indeed, "Those who seem to fulfill the law are merely pretending" (p. 100). At the same time, Luther argues that Moses placed all people under a curse because no one fulfills any part of the law, so that everyone needs a redeemer, namely, Christ.

But if, as most scholars now argue, Paul does not hold that the Torah itself teaches an ill-fated, moralistic works-righteousness whose goal is to drive one to faith, can the Pauline expression "works of the law" nevertheless still be a reference to "legalism," but now to a *Jewish perversion* of the Torah into a legalistic works-righteousness?[7] Or do the "works of the law" refer to the very thing that Luther rejects, namely, an ethnically determined, myopic view

---

6. Rudolf Bultmann, *Theologie des Neuen Testaments*, 8th. ed. expanded by Otto Merk (Tübingen: Mohr Siebeck, 1980), 263–65. In his words, the way of the works of the law and the way of grace and of faith are opposites, "weil *das Bemühen des Menschen, durch Erfüllung des Gesetzes sein Heil zu gewinnen*, ihn nur in die Sünde hineinführt, ja im Grunde selber *schon die Sünde ist*" (264–65, emphasis in original).

7. See the now-programmatic article of C. E. B. Cranfield, "St. Paul and the Law," *SJT* 17 (1964): 43–68.

of the Torah as perceived through the first-century *Jewish lens* of identity-preserving, ceremonial "boundary markers"?[8]

As for my own reading of Galatians, I agree with Luther that ἔργα νόμου refers not to a perversion of the law into legalism or to an overemphasis on some subset of the law, but rather to what the Torah itself commands, taken as a whole. This is the most natural reading of νόμου as a genitive of source or possession, which is supported by the mutually interpreting parallels between ἔργα νόμου in 2:16; 3:2, 5, 10a, on the one hand, and by the absolute use of νόμος in 2:19, 21 and 3:10b, 11–13, on the other. The corresponding reference from Deuteronomy 27:26 in Galatians 3:10 to "doing all things written in the book of the law" simply decodes ἔργα νόμου in Paul's argument.[9]

Second, Luther is right in regarding Paul's contrasts to be a metonymy for a larger set of realities. Indeed, contemporary "participationist" and/or "apocalyptic" readings of Paul, despite their protests to the contrary, have followed Luther's lead in taking the law/gospel contrast to be a metonymy for a larger set of anthropological realities centered on sharing in Christ's own cruciform life of faithfulness over against the enslaved and enslaving law.[10] For Luther, the law/gospel contrast represents a personal and perhaps even private antithesis between two materially different ways of relating to God, an active way of righteous deeds versus a passive way of receiving grace. Though recent participationist-apocalyptic readings of Paul's "in Christ" language are often presented as an alternative to the traditional Lutheran paradigm, are they not simply another version of this same existential reading of the law/gospel contrast, albeit with a different referent for the "gospel"?[11] The more

---

8. Summarized now in James D. G. Dunn, "The New Perspective on Paul: Whence, What, Whither?," in *The New Perspective on Paul: Collected Essays* (Tübingen: Mohr Siebeck, 2005), 1–88, esp. 17–33.

9. For a summary of the ways in which Torah is used in the majority of its instances to designate its commands, both in the OT and NT, see Tom Schreiner, "The Commands of God," in *Central Themes in Biblical Theology: Mapping Unity in Diversity*, ed. Scott Hafemann and Paul R. House (Grand Rapids: Baker Academic, 2007), 66–101.

10. See, e.g., the programmatic works of J. Louis Martyn, *Theological Issues in the Letters of Paul* (Edinburgh: T&T Clark, 1997), esp. 64, 75, 77–84, 119–21, 134–35, 143–55, for whom the law can be equated with "religion" per se and the gospel with an apocalyptic "revelation"; and Michael J. Gorman, *Cruciformity: Paul's Narrative Spirituality of the Cross* (Grand Rapids: Eerdmans, 2001), esp. his treatment of the meaning of "faith" as "co-crucifixion," i.e., as a Spirit-enabled participation in the faithfulness of Christ maintained to the point of death and in his cruciform resurrection, which is a "faithfulness that expresses itself in love" (Gal. 5:6; see 95–154). For its application to justification, see idem, *Inhabiting the Cruciform God: Kenosis, Justification, and Theosis in Paul's Narrative Soteriology* (Grand Rapids: Eerdmans, 2009), esp. the thesis statement on 79–86.

11. For this same move regarding Luther himself, see Carl E. Braaten and Robert W. Jenson, eds., *Union with Christ: The New Finnish Interpretation of Luther* (Grand Rapids: Eerdmans,

fundamental question, therefore, is whether such an existential understanding, whether Lutheran or participationist-apocalyptic, maps the larger significance of Paul's concept of the gospel in the first place.

In my own reading of Galatians, the introduction in 1:1–4 leads not to a new, "vertical" understanding of humanity's relationship *coram deo* but to a scripturally anticipated, "horizontal" understanding of Paul's gospel as the eschatological inbreaking of God's rule and reign in time and space through the crucifixion and resurrection of the Messiah.[12] As a result, rather than reading Paul's law/gospel contrast *anthropologically*, as Luther advocates, it should be read *historically* against the backdrop of God's covenant with Israel on the one hand, and within the context of the current culture of the Greco-Roman Empire on the other. In Paul's own words, the metonymy Luther frames in terms of a law/gospel antithesis is more precisely expressed in the contrast in Galatians 2:16 between ἔργα νόμου and πίστις Ἰησοῦ Χριστοῦ, which is then repeated in the absolute contrasts in 2:21 between νόμος and Χριστός, and in 3:12 between νόμος and πίστις (for the contrast in 3:2 and 5 between ἔργα νόμου and ἀκοὴ πίστεως, see below). Finally, in Galatians 3:21–22 νόμος alone, as "Scripture," can be contrasted with the full expression, πίστις Ἰησοῦ Χριστοῦ.

The fact that Paul can contrast the covenant *entity* νόμος (Torah) with the *person* of the Messiah indicates that this antithesis is not a reference to opposing theological principles or to materially different ways of relating to God, not to a "works way" versus a "faith way."[13] Rather, Paul's contrast is between

---

1998); and Tuomo Mannermaa, *Christ Present in Faith: Luther's View of Justification* (Minneapolis: Fortress, 2005).

12. See now the essay in this volume by N. T. Wright, (chap. 1, p. 23), who argues, now supported by the work of Novenson, that "throughout Galatians, Paul really does mean 'Messiah' when he calls Jesus *Christos*, and with that meaning he has specifically in mind . . . the Messiah's bringing of Israel's long story to its strange, revolutionary and indeed 'apocalyptic' climax." However, the second half of Wright's conclusion regarding the accompanying incorporative and participatory meaning of Jesus as the Messiah—arguing that *Christos* for Paul also refers to "a collective, an incorporative whole" (p. 17), so that in Gal. 3:16 *Christos* means "the people of God" (p. 16)—remains unconvincing to me.

13. So too Ardel B. Caneday, "The Faithfulness of Jesus Christ as a Theme in Paul's Theology in Galatians," in *The Faith of Jesus Christ: Exegetical, Biblical, and Theological Studies*, ed. Michael F. Bird and Preston M. Sprinkle (Milton Keynes, UK: Paternoster, 2009), 185–205, who argues that the meaning of being justified διὰ πίστεως Ἰησοῦ Χριστοῦ and ἐκ πίστεως Χριστοῦ in Gal. 2:16 must be interpreted in contrast to ἐξ ἔργων νόμου as this latter phrase is used throughout Gal. 3. This explains why it does not fit to say that "works of the law" refers to "human activity" versus the "faithfulness of Christ" and why we cannot argue that ἐκ πίστεως Χριστοῦ is to be determined by Paul's quote of Hab. 2:4 (Rom. 1:17; Gal. 3:12). Nor can we follow those who argue that the ἐκ πίστεως Χριστοῦ construction derives from ἐξ ἔργων νόμου, since, as Ardel points out, πίστις Χριστοῦ occurs in Phil. 3:9, but "works of the law" does not

the old epoch of the old covenant, represented by the Sinai Torah, and the new epoch of the new covenant, represented by the Messiah, who through his faithfulness has fulfilled God's promises originally made to Abraham (3:15–20). These same promises are now granted to those who, through their own life of faith, belong to Christ (taking the nondesignated use of πίστις in 3:7–9 to refer to the faith of the Christian in parallel to the faith of Abraham in v. 9). Within the context of Paul's argument throughout 2:15–3:29, the use of πίστις in 2:16 and 3:2, 5, 12 clearly signals that "faith(fulness)" is the characteristic feature of the new covenant age. For Paul, πίστις becomes a metonymy for the new age of the new covenant because it characterizes both the Messiah who has brought it about and the life of those who belong to him (see esp. 3:29 as the climactic main point of 3:25–29).

This historical and eschatological two-covenant reading of the law/gospel contrast is confirmed by 3:17, where the Abrahamic promise is identified with a covenant (διαθήκη) that came 430 years before the law. In 3:14 this same promise is said to be fulfilled in Christ Jesus and appropriated διὰ τῆς πίστεως. Just as "law" comes to stand for the covenant and the period of time before Christ, so too "faith" stands for the covenant and the messianic period of time after the law. In 3:21–25 πίστις can consequently be personified as the signature of the new covenant epoch: in 3:23 and 25 "faith" came and was revealed as the culmination of the law's role in history, even though Paul emphasizes that Abraham believed God beforehand (quoting Gen. 15:6 in Gal. 3:6 and referring to the πίστις Ἀβραάμ in 3:9) and that those "in Christ" believe in him afterward (cf. πιστεύω in 2:16; 3:22). Given this periodization of history into two epochs, with "faith" personified as a metonymy for the new age of the new creation (cf. Gal. 5:6 with 6:15), the coming of *faith* after the period of the law in 3:23, 25 corresponds to the coming of *Christ* as the goal of the law's pedagogy in 3:24. Read in this way, the reference to οἱ ἐκ πίστεως ("those from the new covenant epoch of faith") in 3:7 and 9 (cf. 5:24, οἱ τοῦ Χριστοῦ) becomes the counterpart to 2:16's ἄνθρωπος ἐξ ἔργων νόμου ("a man from the old covenant epoch of the Torah's works"), construing ἐξ ἔργων νόμου adjectively in line with its customary syntactical position rather than adverbially with δικαιοῦται (cf. 2:12, τοὺς ἐκ περιτομῆς; 2:15, ἐξ ἐθνῶν ἁμαρτωλοί; and the related contrast in 4:23 between ὁ ἐκ τῆς παιδίσκης and ὁ ἐκ τῆς ἐλευθέρας).[14]

---

occur in Philippians, while in Rom. 3:21–22 it occurs opposite "apart from law" and in Gal. 2:20 opposite simply "the law."

14. Caneday's insight, "Faithfulness of Jesus Christ," 194–95, that ἐξ ἔργων νόμου (2:16) used adjectivally, οἱ ἐκ περιτομῆς (2:12), and ἐξ ἐθνῶν ἁμαρτωλοί (2:15) all function idiomatically to denote origin or pedigree, not an attempt at "works-righteousness clarifies the argument of so

"No" to Luther

Over against Luther's reading, an eschatological construal of the law/gospel contrast supports the subjective rendering of πίστις Χριστοῦ as a reference to the faithfulness of Christ throughout 2:16–21 and 3:22–29.[15] In particular, it refers to his faithfulness in going to the cross as the sole ground of justification, since the Messiah's death on the cross is the basis on which the eschatological life of faith under the new covenant is established (cf. Jer. 31:34; Gal. 1:4; 2:19–20; 3:13). In Paul's words, the promises were spoken to Abraham, who believed (πιστεύω; cf. Gen. 15:6 in Gal. 3:6), and to his seed, the Messiah, who is therefore also characterized by his faith (πίστις Χριστοῦ; cf. Gen. 22:17–18 in Gal. 3:16). Thus, those of faith (οἱ ἐκ πίστεως, 3:7), who themselves believe in the Messiah as the fulfillment of God's covenant promises to Abraham (2:16, πιστεύω εἰς Χριστὸν Ἰησοῦν; cf. 3:22), are being blessed together with the faith of Abraham (πίστις Ἀβραάμ, 3:9). Such an eschatological reading of the subjective genitive, πίστις Χριστοῦ, best explains its ten uses throughout Paul's Letters.

The subjective reading of πίστις Χριστοῦ does not lessen Luther's decisive emphasis on the need for faith in Christ, but it does further support transposing Luther's reading of the law/gospel contrast into a new, eschatological key. When Paul declares in 3:12, ὁ δὲ νόμος οὐκ ἔστιν ἐκ πίστεως, he is declaring the eschatological divide that separates the old and new covenant epochs.[16]

---

much of Gal. 2–4. Hence, in 3:10, ὅσοι ἐξ ἔργων νόμου does not mean "as many as *rely* on works of the law," but "as many as are *identified* with the old covenant Law expressed in its commands" (my interpretation, following Caneday, 195n39, emphasis added). "Those from the circumcision" and "those from the works of the law" are not pejorative descriptions but descriptions of a Jew whose life is defined by the law as a reference to the Old Covenant (194n38). According to 2:16, the great danger is that tracing descent from "the eclipsed covenant instead of from Christ, *now that Messiah has come*, leaves one exposed before God" (195, emphasis added). To do so is an "inherent repudiation of Christ, through whom alone the Torah's curse is removed and the blessing of Abraham comes" (195). Conversely, in 3:7 and 9, οἱ ἐκ πίστεως [Χριστοῦ] is again "an idiom of origin" that grounds the conclusion "that Christ is the exceptional one whose πίστις defines those who truly are Abraham's sons" (3:7). The focus of the argument is not "one's *act of believing* but one's *spiritual origin*, one's spiritual lineage," as seen in 3:7 (199, emphasis in original). "The question of spiritual lineage is the central cord that runs through Paul's entire argument (cf. 4:28–29)" (199). Caneday thus construes 2:15–16: "We by nature are Jews and *not sinners from the Gentiles*, but knowing that *a human from the deeds required by the Law* is not justified *except through* πίστεως Ἰησοῦ Χριστοῦ, even we believed in Christ Jesus in order to be justified from πίστεως Χριστοῦ and not from the deeds required by the Law, because no flesh shall be justified from the deeds required by the Law" (194; emphasis in original).

15. Caneday, "Faithfulness of Jesus Christ," 187, is again helpful. As he queries, if 3:22 is subjective, why not also translate the subsequent five uses of "faith" in 3:23–26, which are anaphoric (four have the article), as references to the faithfulness of Christ?

16. So again Caneday, "Faithfulness of Jesus Christ," 196, therefore the forefront of the polarity is not "works" versus "faith" but "Torah" versus "Christ," which represent two distinct

Contrary to the agitators in Galatia, the old covenant must not be equated with or brought over into the new. To insist on the continuing validity of the old-covenant works of the law by requiring that gentiles live like Jews, even though the new has arrived (2:14; 4:21), is tantamount to rejecting the sole sufficiency of the cross for justification (2:21). It is also to misunderstand the nature of the old covenant epoch itself. Under the old covenant, Israel was granted the Torah, but the majority of the people were not granted the promise that has been made to Abraham—that is, the Spirit, by whose presence and power they would be able to keep it (cf. 3:14 with 5:4–5). Despite their deliverance from slavery in Egypt, they remained "slave-like children" rather than "sons" and "heirs" (4:1–7). In other words, they were children of Hagar rather than of Sarah, who again represent two covenants (δύο διαθῆκαι, 4:24), this time as those associated with the "flesh-" and "Spirit-character" of their respective "children" (4:21–31). To add the old to the new, Hagar to Sarah, would mean bringing over into the new-covenant era *historically* that epoch of "slavery" *spiritually* in which Israel, as slave-children born "after the flesh" (4:23, 29), suffered the curses of Torah as a result of not having kept the covenant (Deut. 27:26 in Gal. 3:10). Yet it is only the children of Sarah who receive with Isaac the inheritance of Abraham as free children of the promise, born according to the Spirit (cf. 3:14, 18, 29; with 4:23, 28–29). And again, this promised inheritance reaches its fulfillment and is made possible by the *eschaton*-creating "faithfulness of Jesus as the Messiah," who is also the seed of Abraham (3:16).

Luther is right, therefore, that there is an anthropological corollary to Paul's eschatological law/gospel contrast. In this regard Luther rightly stresses that there is a missing minor premise in the argument of Galatians 3:5–6, namely, that exercising faith, which is reckoned as righteousness, is the result of having received the Spirit. Contra Luther, however, Paul's logic is not poor. Paul makes his premise clear in 3:14, where he identifies the promise to Abraham with the Spirit; thus, the life-creating power of the Spirit in the lives of the gentiles makes them fellow heirs of Abraham. The anthropological corollary of the law/gospel contrast is not an existentially different way of relating to God but the eschatological gift of the Spirit that has been given to the true descendants of Abraham. The problem with the "works of the law" is not that they are impossible to keep or wrongheaded. Rather, Israel was intended to keep the covenant stipulations, but apart from an Isaac-like remnant, Israel failed to do so (4:28). This history-of-redemption fact is displayed tragically in

---

covenants: the one bounded by the law, the other by Christ. "ἡ πίστις Χριστοῦ has ended Torah's jurisdiction" (196).

the divine curse of the exile. But now, in fulfillment of God's promise of the Spirit to Abraham (3:14), made possible by the reality of the Christ's cross-shaped sovereignty in their lives (2:20), God's people, Jew and gentile alike, will live by fulfilling the law, just as Leviticus 18:5 promises (Gal. 3:12b; cf. 5:5–6, 14, 24–25).[17] This law keeping, characterized by faith working in love, cannot be conceived as a return to a legalistic works-righteousness, since the believers' keeping of the law is the direct consequence not of their own initiative or strength, or of their being circumcised or uncircumcised, but of the Spirit-established and Spirit-led life of the new creation (cf. Gal. 5:6 and 14–16 with 6:14–15).

This is why in Galatians 3:2 and 3:5 Paul can interpret the eschatological contrast between the works of the law and the faith of Christ in terms of a experiential contrast between ἔργα νόμου and ἀκοὴ πίστεως, in which the latter is used to encompass both the faithfulness of Christ (πίστεως) and the Christian's new life of faithful obedience (ἀκοή) that Christ brings about as part of the new creation.[18] In 3:3, Paul identifies this experiential contrast with his characteristic antithesis between the Spirit and the flesh,

17. Despite his strong arguments for the subjective reading of πίστις Χριστοῦ, Caneday fails to follow his eschatological reading to its corresponding conclusion: why should "Torah" as referenced in 3:6, 8 be read as "a designed impediment to the fulfillment of God's promise to Abraham" ("Faithfulness of Jesus Christ," 199–200), which leads once again to a deeds/faith dichotomy in the end? Thus, for Caneday, Jesus accomplishes what Torah could not, since "Torah requires deeds; Christ's faithfulness elicits faith in him. Life is not within Torah's power to give; life comes through death to Torah, which entails being crucified with Christ. Works required by the Law condemn; Christ's faithfulness justifies. Torah curses; Christ blesses" (203–4). If read eschatologically, however, the contrast is between the Torah unfulfilled by Israel and the Torah fulfilled by those who are a new creation of the new age (Gal. 6:15).

18. For a helpful survey of the various proposed understandings of the phrase ἐξ ἀκοῆς πίστεως, see now Martinus C. de Boer, *Galatians: A Commentary* (Louisville: Westminster John Knox, 2011), 173–77, who takes it to mean "on the basis of what was heard of faith." The debate is over whether ἀκοή refers to the "act of hearing" or the "proclamation/message that is heard," and whether πίστις refers to "the human act of faith" or "the faith/gospel message that is believed," as well as how one construes the force of the genitive. My view follows that of Lightfoot, who took it to mean "a hearing that comes of faith" (see de Boer, 174), in which ἀκοή is taken to be a verbal noun referring to the act of hearing. Against its OT backdrop, it thus connotes obedience. In turn, πίστις is a subjective genitive referring to the faithfulness of Jesus from 2:16–21, which, against its new-covenant backdrop, is the source of this hearing as obedience. In this way, ἐξ ἀκοῆς πίστεως provides an exact counterpart to ἐξ ἔργων νόμου in 3:2 and 5: the "hearing" of faithful obedience parallels "works," while "faith" as a metonym for the new covenant parallels "law" as a metonym for the old. The strongest argument usually adduced against this reading is the use of ἀκοή in 1 Thess. 2:13 (λόγον ἀκοῆς) and Rom. 10:16–17 (τίς ἐπίστευσεν τῇ ἀκοῇ ἡμῶν; ἄρα ἡ πίστις ἐξ ἀκοῆς, ἡ δὲ ἀκοὴ διὰ ῥήματος Χριστοῦ), where it is said to refer clearly to the message/proclamation of the gospel (cf. de Boer, 175). In both cases, however, the expression is not the same; moreover, in the case of 1 Thess. 2:13 ἀκοή may also refer to the act of hearing/obedience brought about by the word of God.

to which he will return at length in 5:16–26. The experiential parallels in 3:1–6 reflect that, for Paul, a divide runs through the human heart that characterizes the two covenant epochs, a divide that is just as eschatological as that which divides history. On the one side are "the works of the law," an epoch characterized by Israel's failure as a whole to keep the covenant because Israel remained in the "flesh." On the other side is the "hearing [= obedience] of faith," an epoch characterized by Jew and gentile alike keeping the great command of Deuteronomy 6:4–5 because they have received the Spirit (cf. 4:4–6).[19]

Picking up his argument from 3:1–5 and 4:6, Paul describes this Spirit-created hearing of faith as a "walking by the Spirit" (5:16), against whose fruit in the life of the believer there is no (curse of the) law (5:23); those fulfilling the law (cf. 5:14) are not "under the law" (ὑπὸ νόμον, 5:18), meaning not "under its curse" (ὑπὸ κατάραν, 3:10; cf. 3:13).[20] In contrast, those who do "the works of the flesh" (5:19) "will not inherit the kingdom of God" (5:21). So it becomes clear that neither circumcision nor uncircumcision pulls any weight when it comes to being justified before God, but what does avail is both the faith of and faith in Christ that works outwardly in love as the fulfillment of the law (5:6, 14). For this reason (note the γάρ in 5:6a), Paul concludes in 5:5 that, rather than falling from the grace of God in Christ by returning to the law (= old covenant; cf. 5:4), believers "are awaiting the hope of righteousness by the Spirit [πνεύματι] from faith [ἐκ πίστεως]" (5:5), most likely an inclusive use of πνεῦμα and πίστις to refer to the new-covenant reality as a whole.

The key to the historical and anthropological antitheses in Paul's theology is not material or existential (two different ways of relating to God) but eschatological (two different epochs, with two contrasting consequences). Paul's theology is built on the eschatological divide between the two ages, a divide that has been brought about by God's act in the Son (2:20; 4:5) and the Spirit (3:1–5; 4:6), built on the two covenants constitutive of them (4:21–31), and characterized by the distinct ways of life they bring about (5:16–26). This raises the question of the relationship between Paul's apocalyptic and covenantal categories, which, as several of the essays in this volume illustrate, is now on the front burner of Pauline scholarship.

---

19. In Deut. 6:4–5 LXX the laws to be written on the heart are construed as τὰ δικαιώματα (καὶ τὰ κρίματα), which Paul picks up in Rom. 1:32; 2:26; 5:16, 18; 8:4; in 2:26 and 8:4 the δικαίωμα is kept by the believer who lives according to the Spirit.

20. That Paul's use of "under the Law" (ὑπὸ νόμον) is "rhetorical shorthand" for being "under the curse of the Law" (ὑπὸ κατάραν τοῦ νόμου; see Gal 3:10, 13) has been argued by T. A. Wilson, "'Under Law' in Galatians: A Pauline Theological Abbreviation," *JTS* 56 (2006): 362–92; for its incorporation into the argument of Galatians, see idem, *The Curse of the Law and the Crisis in Galatia*, WUNT 2/225 (Tübingen: Mohr Siebeck, 2007).

"Yes" and "No" to Luther

Luther was right that any full-orbed exegetical and theological treatment of Paul will have to explicate the relationship between faith and good works in the light of the Pauline distinction between faith and works of the law. The focus on Galatians 5 that emerged in the conference reflects a renewed interest in grappling with the age-old, purported Pauline bifurcations between indicative and imperative, imputed and imparted, justification and sanctification, salvation by grace and judgment by works. The importance of this discussion is highlighted by Campbell's observation that the NPP has often simply shifted the location of "legalism" from "getting in" to "staying in," so that it is still faced with a synergistic view of Paul's theology that comes down to a justifying-faith-plus-sanctifying-works, two-step approach to life before God.[21] Yet for Paul, do "believers" ever start with faith and then progress on to something *else* in their relationship with God?

Here we can do no better than return to Luther. In his magisterial work on Luther's theology, Oswald Bayer insists that Luther's rejection of a dualistic contrast between theory-contemplation and practice-action led him to a unique "third way" of describing faith as the *vita passiva* (the "passive" nature of faith): "*Faith is not knowledge and not action, neither metaphysical nor moral, neither* vita activa *nor* vita contemplativa, *but vita passiva.*"[22] For Luther, "the decisive aspect of the *vita passiva* is that it is linked to a specific experience: to an experience for which I am not the prime initiator, but which instead I suffer."[23] As Luther put it in his *Treatise on Good Works*, the righteousness of faith is passive "in that we allow God alone to work in us and we ourselves, with all our powers, do not do anything."[24] Moreover, since for

---

21. Douglas Campbell, *The Deliverance of God: An Apocalyptic Rereading of Justification in Paul* (Grand Rapids: Eerdmans, 2009), 103. Theologically, then, "in strictly theoretical terms," there is not a great deal that separates covenantal nomism from legalism. As Campbell points out, for E. P. Sanders the giving of the covenant in the *past* establishes only the "possibility of salvation," i.e., establishing the covenant is "a moment of divine, if contractually limited generosity" (Campbell, *Deliverance of God*, 103). With covenantal nomism, legalism still exists in the *present and future*, in which salvation remains dependent on evaluating the individual performance of the covenant conditions. "In short, it seems that the essential theoretical differences between covenantal nomism and legalism have effectively collapsed," since both are contractual (i.e., conditional) (104).

22. Oswald Bayer, *Martin Luther's Theology: A Contemporary Interpretation* (Grand Rapids: Eerdmans, 2008), 43. In what follows I am simply expounding Bayer's reading of Luther.

23. Ibid., 42.

24. Ibid., 43, quoting WA 6:244.3–6. As Bayer puts it, "That which alone is passive, the righteousness of faith (*iustitia passiva*), which can only be suffered, . . . happens when all thinking that one can justify oneself, in a metaphysical sense, as well as when all acting, in a moral sense, together with the desire to unite the two efforts, are radically destroyed" (43).

Luther faith was already a "formal righteousness" (*iustitia formalis*), there was no need for a separately conceived "works of love" to complete it (contra the scholastic articulation of *fides caritate formata*) or for a third use of the law (contra Melanchthon), inasmuch as faith itself acts *according to its own nature* in love (Wengert, p. 111 above; and p. 101 on Gal 3:10).

Hence, although for Luther "the righteousness of faith" is passive in the sense of being given solely as a gift by God, nevertheless faith *itself* is active and always acts according to its own nature in love. This is why Luther does not arrange faith and love in a hierarchy: as Luther put it, love is "there at the same time with faith" (Luther's *Treatise on Good Works*, WA 6:210.5–9).[25] In Bayer's words, "Love does not get added to faith at a later time, in order to make it complete. Much rather—which is how the Greek phraseology of Galatians 5:6 can be translated—the faith goes forth in love with the energy that is *its own* and that is *within itself*; as *faith* it is active in love."[26] For Luther, faith, by its very nature as trust in God's promises of provision for oneself, reaches out to meet the needs of others.

Bayer drives home the point that for Luther, since faith is the "mover" of action, faith as trust in God's promise is "the *opus operum* (the 'work of all works')," in other words, "that work *of God (opus Dei)* that makes *human* works (*opera hominum*) good; as Luther says, it is the 'master worker and the chief in charge.'"[27] Luther illustrates this from the Ten Commandments: faith was the fulfillment of the first commandment in that the people trusted God's promise, "I am the LORD your God!," which declared that God is committed to meet his people's needs as an expression of his goodness and mercy.[28] Furthermore, the fulfillment of the first commandment as a call for faith must be given priority over all other commandments as their foundation and as the matrix for their interpretation.[29] Viewed from the perspective of the first commandment, all of God's commandments are calls to trust God to meet one's own needs, the manifestation of which is seen in meeting the needs of others: "To conceptualize faith now as fulfilling the first commandment, as 'faithfulness,'" apart from which no other commandments can be fulfilled, "is absolutely one of the most important theological insights of Luther, the foundational significance of which can hardly be valued too highly."[30]

---

25. Bayer, *Luther's Theology*, 286, quoting Luther's *Treatise on Good Works*, WA 6:210.5–9.

26. Bayer, *Luther's Theology*, 287 (first two emphases are added), referring to *On the Freedom of a Christian*, WA 7:34.32–33; 7:64.35–37; *De veste nuptial*, WA 39/1:265–333; and his commentary on Gal. 5:6, LW 27:28–31.

27. Bayer, *Luther's Theology*, 283, quoting Luther, "*Treatise on Good Works*," WA 6:213.14.

28. Bayer, *Luther's Theology*, 283, pointing to Luther's *Large Catechism*, in BSLK 560.40–41.

29. Bayer, *Luther's Theology*, 283, 285.

30. Bayer, *Luther's Theology*, 285, quoting Luther's *Treatise on Good Works*, WA 6:209.33–35.

Using the fifth commandment as an example, Luther says, "We should fear and love God *so that* we . . . do not hurt or harm our neighbor in his body, but help him and care [for him] in all bodily needs."[31] Note that Luther uses a result clause, indicating an automatic consequence to bind together loving God and loving neighbor. Bayer comments that this is intentional for Luther, who explains each of the subsequent commandments as a direct result of keeping the first.[32] For Luther, love as the fulfillment of the law is not a moral obligation of faith; that is, it is not a purpose clause to be fulfilled later. "Faith—with an inner necessity—cannot help but be active in love; all good works spring from and 'flow' from faith. Thus the fulfilling of the faith in works is not a temporal or psychological consequence, but is a consequence that proceeds logically from the nature of faith."[33]

Luther's understanding of the organic link between faith and works is one more example of the way in which he relentlessly drives home the central reality of God's grace- and mercy-determined relationship with his people. Luther's uncompromising focus on God's sovereignty and its implications for understanding the life of faith remains vitally important both in the history of interpretation and for the formulation of our biblical theology. For as Wengert points out, Luther's theological speech in the voice of the gospel made it clear that faith justifies because it is faith that glorifies God by giving God his due (p. 110 above). Wengert also reminds us that Luther presents a "radical theology and hermeneutic" that are "very much foreign to present-day Protestant and Roman Catholic approaches to Scripture" (p. 92). I suspect that he may think they are foreign to my own reading of Paul. But Paul's theology, based on his two-epoch, two-covenant hermeneutic, becomes even more radical once his law/gospel contrast is understood eschatologically, rather than materially or existentially. An eschatological reading of Pauline polarities makes it possible to reconceptualize the relationship between faith and obedience as part of a single, organic, indivisible whole that is made possible by the redeeming cross of Christ and brought about by the transforming presence of the Spirit.

---

31. Bayer, *Luther's Theology*, 286, quoting Luther in *BSLK* 508.31–34, emphasis added.
32. Bayer, *Luther's Theology*, 286.
33. Ibid.

8

"Not an Idle Quality or an Empty Husk in the Heart"

A Critique of Tuomo Mannermaa on Luther and Galatians

JAVIER A. GARCIA

Introduction

In 1979 the Finnish Luther scholar Tuomo Mannermaa published the monograph later translated as *Christ Present in Faith: Luther's View of Justification*,[1] which became the catalyst for what is now known as the Finnish School in Luther studies. This interpretation arose out of ecumenical dialogues between the Lutheran Church of Finland and the Russian Orthodox Church in the early 1970s.[2] In 1998 *Union with Christ: The New Finnish Interpretation of Luther*,[3]

For the original and longer version of this article, see Javier Garcia, "A Critique of Mannermaa on Luther and Galatians," *Lutheran Quarterly* 27.1 (2013): 33–55. Reprinted with permission from *Lutheran Quarterly*.

    1. Tuomo Mannermaa, *Christ Present in Faith: Luther's View of Justification*, ed. Kirsi Stjerna (Minneapolis: Fortress, 2005), cited in this volume as *CPF*.

    2. Tuomo Mannermaa, "Why Is Luther So Fascinating? Modern Finnish Research," in *Union with Christ: The New Finnish Interpretation of Luther*, ed. Carl E. Braaten and Robert E. Jenson (Grand Rapids: Eerdmans, 1998).

    3. For this work, see the preceding note.

edited by Carl Braaten and Robert Jenson, marked the full-scale introduction of this theological trend to the English-speaking world. Mannermaa's own foundational work was then made available in English in 2005. While still representing a minority position among Luther scholars, the Finnish School has gained a following. The most recent installment, *Engaging Luther: A New Theological Assessment*, was published in 2010.[4]

Mannermaa's interpretation replaces the traditional forensic reading of justification in Luther's theology with an emphasis on participation and theosis. For Mannermaa, the traditional view that God (merely) declares sinners righteous ignores the centrality of the believer's union with Christ through faith in justification, a union that entails participation in the divine life and deification. Against what he perceives as the negative influence of neo-Kantianism in German Luther studies, Mannermaa stresses the *inhabitatio Dei* as equal to and inseparable from forensic justification.[5] Justification is not a "legal fiction" whereby God declares sinners righteous while they remain in reality sinners, but instead confers the status of righteousness according to the ontological reality that results from Christ's *real* (or *real-ontic*) presence in the believer.[6] In Mannermaa's reading, therefore, justification by faith is synonymous with participation and deification, as the indwelling righteous Christ brings believers to participate in the divine life and makes believers ontologically divine.

Mannermaa's position touches on every major Lutheran doctrine and has far-reaching academic and confessional implications. Given the interconnectedness of Luther's thought, to alter justification—the "article by which the church stands or falls"—would completely change the understanding of the reformer's theology. Mannermaa also condemns the Formula of Concord, the classic 1580 Lutheran confessional statement, as contradicting the doctrine of justification presented in Luther's texts. It is no surprise that Mannermaa and the Finnish School remain deeply controversial in Luther studies. Recent criticisms of Mannermaa's reading include the following: a disregard for modern Luther historiography, decontextualized readings of *theōsis* in Luther's texts, faulty metaphysical analysis,[7] an incorrect priority of the gift over grace,[8] and compromise of Lutheran doctrines for ecumenical purposes.[9] Nevertheless, the

4. Olli-Pekka Vainio, ed., *Engaging Luther: A (New) Theological Assessment* (Eugene, OR: Cascade, 2010).
5. *CPF*, 1–2.
6. Ibid., xii.
7. Carl R. Trueman, "Is the Finnish Line a New Beginning? A Critical Assessment of the Reading of Luther Offered by the Helsinki Circle," *WTJ* 62 (2003): 242–43.
8. Timo Laato, "Justification: The Stumbling Block of the Finnish Luther School," *CTQ* 72 (2008): 327–46, http://media.ctsfw.edu/2477.
9. Mark C. Mattes, "A Future for Lutheran Theology?," *LQ* 19 (2005): 444–45.

Finnish School's approach has gained acceptance in many parts of Lutheranism, not least in Finland, and in the wider academy. Often this acceptance has come with extensive accolades.[10]

This essay analyzes *Christ Present in Faith* in relation to Luther's *Lectures on Galatians 1535*.[11] If, as is widely recognized, the Finnish School arose from this book by Mannermaa, and if it in turn claims to depend on Luther's *Lectures on Galatians*, then a particularly useful way to interrogate Mannermaa and the Finnish School is through a close examination of these texts. Luther's *Lectures on Galatians* is a pivotal text in his theology. Luther worked on Galatians several times in his career,[12] but the final version, published in 1535, represents the mature Luther and contains the decisive formulations of some of his most important doctrines. In agreement with the Formula of Concord that "Luther's *Lectures on Galatians* has the final authority concerning the doctrine of justification," Mannermaa relies on the commentary for his interpretation of Luther's theology.[13] A proper understanding and appraisal of Mannermaa's argument, then, requires a return to Luther's commentary. For reasons of space, this essay does not consider the question of neo-Kantianism, the underlying metaphysics of Mannermaa's thought, or Luther's compatibility with the Formula of Concord. The primary interest of this study is the overall argument of *Christ Present in Faith*, its loyalty to Luther's commentary, and the implications this has for the theology represented by the Finnish School.

There are two further reasons why this study may make a contribution to this debate. First, it is curious that, despite the Finnish School's spreading fame and its dependence on Mannermaa's *Christ Present in Faith*, there are very few studies that consider the work's major arguments. As Mark Mattes remarks, "If [Mannermaa's] work is that influential in world Lutheranism, it is surprising that the work has not undergone greater critique."[14] Second, the discussion surrounding the Finnish School responds to a rising phenomenon in Protestantism. More and more, forensic justification has fallen under criticism, and the "Old Luther" has been undermined as dated.[15] Instead, in academic theology as well as confessional Christianity, Eastern concepts such as participation and deification are gaining popularity. Whatever the causes, a

---

10. Robert E. Jenson, "Response to Tuomo Mannermaa, 'Why Is Luther So Fascinating?,'" in Braaten and Jenson, *Union with Christ*, 21. See also *CPF*, xi.

11. Martin Luther, *Lectures on Galatians 1535*, in LW 26 and 27; WA 40/1 and 40/2.

12. LW 27:ix; WA 40/1:6.

13. *CPF*, 6.

14. Mattes, "Future for Lutheran Theology?," 445.

15. Gerhard O. Forde, "Forensic Justification and the Christian Life: Triumph or Tragedy?," in *A More Radical Gospel: Essays on Eschatology, Authority, Atonement, and Ecumenism*, ed. Steven D. Paulson and Mark C. Mattes (Grand Rapids: Eerdmans, 2004), 114-15.

great many theologians are veering away from traditional Western Protestantism and toward the East.[16]

Justification and Christology

In part 1, "The Doctrine of Justification and Christology," Mannermaa interprets Luther's doctrine of justification in *Lectures on Galatians* as one that completely depends on Christology. Mannermaa's solution to the "legal fiction" of forensic justification is to render justification ontological in nature. By starting with a "patristic" Christology that emphasizes participation in the divine life, Mannermaa interprets Luther as seeing justification as *theōsis*, or "a human being becoming one with God through a real exchange of attributes between the sinner and Christ."[17] Christology is crucial for Mannermaa because it determines that Christ himself—both his person and work—"*is* identical with the righteousness of faith."[18] Thus Mannermaa understands justification in Luther's commentary as the believer's ontological participation in Christ through his indwelling, which makes the believer *really* righteous before God.

There is, however, one basic exegetical problem. Instead of beginning with Luther's preface, which clearly lays out his priority of defining and distinguishing between law and gospel in Galatians, Mannermaa begins his analysis later in Luther's text by focusing on what he perceives to be both Luther's basis for justification and his shared emphasis with patristic Christology, namely, the incarnation. For Mannermaa, the most important aspect of the incarnation in *Lectures on Galatians* is that Christ took on humanity's sin in his person, a fact that makes the incarnation immediately relevant to Luther's understanding of atonement. Mannermaa argues that in the incarnation Christ "*really* . . . bears the sins of all human beings in the human nature he has assumed."[19] Christ atones for sin within himself (in his person) through the incarnational triumph of his divine attributes over the human attributes of his flesh.[20] Mannermaa gives no indication that the cross is the apex of this inner drama of the incarnation; instead, the cross is strangely absent from his opening chapter,

---

16. See Bruce McCormack, "Participation in God, Yes; Deification, No: Two Modern Protestant Responses to an Ancient Question," in *Denkwürdiges Geheimnis: Beiträge zur Gotteslehre: Festschrift für Eberhard Jüngel zum 70. Geburtstag*, ed. Ingolf U. Dalfeth, Johannes Fischer, and Hans-Peter Großhans (Tübingen: Mohr Siebeck 2004), 347.
17. *CPF*, xv.
18. Ibid., 5 (emphasis in original).
19. Ibid., 13 (emphasis in original).
20. Ibid., 16.

"The Basis for Justifying Faith." In Mannermaa's reading of Luther, then, it is the incarnation that atones for sins, not Christ's death on the cross.

It follows for Mannermaa that participation in the person of Christ characterizes the benefits of faith. Salvation comes from participating in Christ's person.[21] Faith, in uniting believers ontologically to Christ, brings them victory because Christ in his person *is* their victory over sin, death, and the curse.[22] This ontological communication of attributes through participation is, for Mannermaa, Luther's "happy exchange."[23] Therefore, according to Mannermaa, Luther understands faith and justification primarily through the believer's real union with Christ's person.

Contrary to Mannermaa, however, it is not the incarnation but rather the distinction between law and gospel that is the actual starting point for Luther's *Lectures on Galatians*, as is clearly set forth in his preface. Mannermaa actually depends on sections where Luther treats Christology more than 250 pages into his commentary. Carl Trueman gives a fair criticism: "It is, to say the least, extremely surprising that Mannermaa makes no attempt to set the teaching he finds on righteousness in the main text of the *Commentary on Galatians* within the larger framework laid out in the preface."[24] The main project of Luther's preface is to introduce the distinction between law and gospel, a theme that dominates the rest of the commentary. Mattes rightly puzzles over Mannermaa's choice of Luther's *Lectures on Galatians* for his "alternative theory of divinization," since its overarching theme is "the proper distinction between law and gospel."[25]

Luther speaks of law and gospel in the preface under the rubric of active and passive righteousness. He presents "the difference between Christian righteousness and all other kinds of righteousness" as the focus of his commentary.[26] Christian righteousness distinguishes itself from other kinds of righteousness as "merely a passive righteousness."[27] Of the different kinds of active righteousness, Luther sharply contrasts Christian righteousness to the righteousness of the law: while the righteousness of the law is impossible to fulfill, passive righteousness comes through faith in Christ.[28] To distinguish between passive and active righteousness, and to receive the former instead of seeking the latter—this, in Luther's estimation, is to understand Christian

21. Ibid., 16.
22. Ibid., 15.
23. Ibid., 17.
24. Trueman, "Is the Finnish Line a New Beginning?," 238.
25. Mattes, "Future for Lutheran Theology?," 445.
26. LW 26:4; WA 40/1:40.28–29.
27. LW 26:4; WA 40/1:41.3–5.
28. LW 26:8; WA 40/1:46.7–18.

righteousness, justification, and the whole of Christian doctrine.[29] Hence, introducing the distinction between law and gospel, and teaching readers to distinguish between them in order to be able to accept the gospel, is the aim of Luther's preface and commentary.

The contrast of law and gospel, however, is more than just a doctrine for Luther. They produce a dynamic that is unique to their internal relation. Quoting from Luther's *Lectures on Galatians* and echoing the work of Gerhard Ebeling and others, Simeon Zahl argues that in Luther's theology the word is an "event" or "encounter" with God, which "is determined by the irreducibly twofold nature of the Word as it encounters us: as Law, and as Gospel."[30] The word first encounters sinners in the law that accuses, convicts, and demands by violently revealing all they lack before God's perfect law.[31] Once the law terrifies their consciences, the gospel encounters them as God's unrelenting promise in Christ Jesus that he is *pro me*.[32] The law and the gospel, then, as constituent aspects of the word, profoundly affect the believer's experience of justification. As Zahl specifies from *Lectures on Galatians*, although law and gospel are "innately opposed to one another, calling the hearer to mutually exclusive standards of righteousness," they "are closely related in the Word, each serving a unique and necessary function in producing justifying faith."[33] Luther himself establishes the overarching importance of this distinction in *Lectures on Galatians:* "The distinction between the Law and the Gospel is necessary to the highest degree; for it contains a summary of all Christian doctrine."[34] Only by grasping this distinction can believers accept the gospel and understand justification by faith as it applies to their lives. A most serious indictment of Mannermaa's argument, then, is the total absence of this defining distinction not only in his reading of the Galatians commentary but also generally in his understanding of Luther's doctrine of justification.

Furthermore, against Mannermaa, Luther's Christology in *Lectures on Galatians* revolves around the death of Christ in particular much more than the incarnation in general. Following the preface, Luther attributes the believer's victory over sin not to the incarnational victory in Christ's person,

---

29. LW 26:9; WA 40/1:48.25–29.

30. Simeon Zahl, *Pneumatology and Theology of the Cross in the Preaching of Christoph Friedrich Blumhardt: The Holy Spirit between Wittenberg and Azusa Street* (London: T&T Clark, 2010), 172.

31. Oswald Bayer, *Martin Luther's Theology: A Contemporary Interpretation* (Grand Rapids: Eerdmans, 2008), 61.

32. Ibid.; see WA 40/1: 295–96.

33. Zahl, *Pneumatology and Theology*, 173.

34. LW 26:117; WA 40/1:209.16–17.

but instead to Christ's death: "He is heartened by the victory that comes from the death of Christ. In his conscience the assurance of this victory begins to prevail over sin and death, for he has the guarantee of the forgiveness of sins."[35] What transfers this victory to the believer and comforts the conscience is not participation, but faith in the gospel: "Therefore your bones and mine will know no rest until we hear the Word of grace and cling to it firmly and faithfully."[36] As Luther stresses continually, God's favorable disposition toward humanity, *pro nobis* as set forth in the gospel, provides the pastoral comfort of the doctrine of justification.[37]

In the passage Mannermaa relies on most for his defense of participation, he fails to understand how Luther is using a Christology of the incarnation to advance the distinction between the law and the gospel. Mannermaa's Christology rests on quotations taken from Luther's commentary on Galatians 3:13: "Christ redeemed us from the curse of the Law, having become a curse for us."[38] Evidently this verse concerns Christ's relation to the law. From the beginning of this section, Luther's main thrust is that Christ was not a sinner in his own person (and thus not deserving of death), but he bore "the person of a sinner" (that is, every sinner) so that he could be cursed "for us" at the cross: "In short, He has and bears all the sins of all men in His body—*not in the sense* that He has committed them *but in the sense* that He took these sins, committed by us, upon His own body, *in order to* make satisfaction for them with His own blood."[39] This is incompatible with Mannermaa's view that somehow there is an incarnational atoning victory in Christ's person *before* the cross. Mannermaa regularly omits the surrounding context of Luther's quotations, which plainly demonstrate that the reformer is leveraging the incarnation as grounds for the crucifixion.[40] Moreover, William W. Schumacher rightly draws attention to the importance of imputation for Luther in this section, against Mannermaa's ontological description. Schumacher remarks, "The conflict or struggle carried out in Christ is thus the battle between the sin of the whole world, *imputed* to him, and the righteousness of Christ who

---

35. LW 26:27; WA 40/1:75.19–22.
36. LW 26:27; WA 40/1:74.24–26.
37. LW 26:37–39, 172–79, 231–36, 276–91, 430–31, etc.; WA 40/1:89–91, 290–98, 365–74, 431–32, 648–51, etc.
38. LW 26:276; WA 40/1:432.17–20.
39. LW 26:277, emphasis added; WA 40/1:433.32–434.12.
40. "In short, be the person of all men, the one who has committed the sins of all men. *And see to it that you pay and make satisfaction for them*" and "*By this deed* [Christ's death on the cross] the whole world is purged and expiated from all sins, and thus it is set free from death and from every evil." From LW 26:280; WA 40/1.437.25–438.15 (the added emphases are where Mannermaa omits text in *CPF*, 15).

is both true God and true man."⁴¹ Mannermaa thus fails to realize that this short section of the commentary serves to advance the law/gospel theme by assuring believers of their freedom from the law through Christ rather than describing a radical new atonement theory based on ontological participation.

Timo Laato has also provided noteworthy insights into the foundations of Mannermaa's interpretation in *Christ Present in Faith*. According to Laato, the root of the problem lies in Mannermaa's reading of favor (*favor*) and gift (*donum*). Mannermaa defines the former as God's forgiveness and removal of his wrath and the latter as God's really giving himself with all his attributes to the believer in faith.⁴² Curiously, while Mannermaa claims that Luther develops this concept in *Against Latomus*, he "does not deal with that work in detail; he does not even quote from it," choosing instead to focus on *Lectures on Galatians*, although this text, in Mannermaa's own admission, "does not deal thematically with the difference between 'gift' and 'favor.'"⁴³ Mannermaa then reverses the traditional priority of grace (*favor*) over the gift (*donum*), thereby rendering the gift the "'basis and prerequisite' of grace."⁴⁴ To insist on Luther's prioritization of grace over the gift, Laato uses extended passages from *Against Latomus*, where Mannermaa abridges the text to support his interpretation.⁴⁵ Laato concludes:

> By looking at the entire section, we see that Luther says just the opposite of what Mannermaa claims. Union (*unio*) with Christ is not enough to calm the heart. Not the gift (*donum*) but grace (*favor*) "really produces true peace of heart." Grace is "a greater good than the healing brought about by righteousness, which we have said comes from faith." A Christian would "rather—if it were possible—want to be without the healing brought about by righteousness than without God's grace." The reason is that the gift is only an inner good whereas grace is an external good.⁴⁶

This pertains to salvation history. Christ can be received only as a gift because he has first achieved favor for sinners at the cross. Mannermaa's mistake is that "he does not confess that salvation depends on Christ as *favor*, not as *donum*. . . . The center of gravity moves from the historical event of the cross to the here and now, where the believer is united with the divine person through

---

41. William W. Schumacher, *Who Do I Say That You Are? Anthropology and the Theology of Theosis in the Finnish School of Tuomo Mannermaa* (Eugene, OR: Wipf & Stock, 2010), 41.
42. Mannermaa, quoted in Laato, "Justification: The Stumbling Block," 329.
43. Ibid.
44. Ibid., 330.
45. Ibid.
46. Ibid., 331.

faith."⁴⁷ Laato rightly links Mannermaa's "special christological emphasis" regarding Christ's person and his pushing aside salvation history: when the focus shifts to Christ's triumph of attributes in his person, the cross is inevitably lost from view.⁴⁸

Another accusation against Mannermaa is his likeness to Andreas Osiander. Laato stops short of completely identifying Mannermaa's thesis with Osiander's, but their interpretations of Luther are practically identical. Relying on Bengt Hägglund, Laato enumerates the key points for which the Formula of Concord rejected Osiander. Osiander claimed that a righteousness acceptable before God is (1) not based on Christ's vicarious satisfaction on the cross, (2) thereby requires Christ's divine nature to dwell in the sinner, and (3) therefore views righteousness as "inner renewal or the ability to do good."⁴⁹ The Formula of Concord protected against these errors by safeguarding *favor* as prior to *donum*, and rejecting "the equating of *inhabitatio Dei* (which belongs to *sanctification*) and *iustitia Dei* (which belongs to *justification*)."⁵⁰ From various angles, Laato argues that the common stress of Osiander and Mannermaa on the indwelling of Christ's divine nature in the sinner through faith rather than vicarious atonement is antithetical to the orthodox Lutheran understanding of justification.⁵¹ Perhaps Mannermaa would object that his "Luther" has theosis in the person of Christ rather than in the divine nature, thus distinguishing him from Osiander. However, Mannermaa's concept of the incarnational triumph in Christ's person amounts to the same thing: since Christ's divine attributes conquer the human attributes he absorbs in assuming sinful flesh, so in uniting themselves to Christ through faith, believers primarily participate in Christ's victorious divine nature, a fact that characterizes the main event of their justification. The happy exchange thus becomes the communication of divine attributes from Christ's divine essence through believers' union with his incarnate person. While some may deem such similarities between Mannermaa's and Osiander's readings of Luther as merely a historical curiosity, it is important to keep in mind the colossal efforts of sixteenth-century Lutherans to repudiate Osiander. Timothy J. Wengert, who also recognizes the parallels between the Finnish School and Osiander, remarks:

> By insisting on the centrality of the equivalent of *theōsis* in Luther's thought, the Finnish school has constructed a curious historical conundrum. How can

---

47. Ibid., 337.
48. Ibid., 337–38n48.
49. Bengt Hägglund, quoted in Laato, "Justification: The Stumbling Block," 338.
50. Laato, "Justification: The Stumbling Block," 339.
51. Ibid., 342.

one properly construe Luther's influence in the sixteenth century, given the rejection of Osiander's reading of Luther by an overwhelming majority of his contemporaries in favor of a forensic understanding of justification? How can one argue that Luther was such a brilliant teacher if nearly all of his closest students completely misunderstood his teaching on justification by faith and if the only person to understand his position never sat in his classroom and was universally vilified by the very students who did? . . . When it came to justification by faith, *all* of the important Evangelical theologians of the 1550s rejected Osiander's position in favor of forensic justification in one form or another. If Luther employed *theōsis* in his theology (itself a questionable thesis), then at least it was not in relation to the doctrine of justification as nearly all of his theological heirs understood it.[52]

Indeed, the resounding call to condemn Osiander was such that it united various otherwise divided factions against this common enemy throughout the 1550s.[53] It is no small detail that Mannermaa's interpretation strongly resembles Osiander's and thus provides serious grounds for caution.

Mannermaa's Christology has major ties with and implications for theological anthropology. Schumacher, who echoes many of Laato's critiques,[54] holds that Mannermaa collapses Christology into anthropology, thereby eliminating the uniqueness of Christ. He explains: "Basing justification on the 'real' presence of Christ in faith, as Mannermaa does, means that the believer's human essence and existence must be understood in specifically 'Christological' categories, rather than in terms of creation. The incarnation of God in Christ becomes the pattern of the believer's own nature."[55] Specifically, the struggle between the human and divine natures in Christ's person are mirrored in humanity's struggle between the Spirit and the flesh, thereby establishing the incarnation as "the paradigm to which humanity will now conform, as the divine and the human are united."[56] Mannermaa's imposition of Christology and anthropology is deeply problematic, however, since it "fails to recognize the uniqueness of the person of Christ, and the unrepeatable union of the divine and human natures in him," a failure that was

52. Timothy J. Wengert, *Defending Faith: Lutheran Responses to Andreas Osiander's Doctrine of Justification, 1551–1559*, (Tübingen: Mohr Siebeck, 2012), 3–4.
53. Ibid., 10.
54. Cf. Schumacher, *Who Do I Say That You Are?*, 19–61. For another recent study on Mannermaa that interacts with Laato and Schumacher closely, see Mark J. McInroy, "Rechtfertigung als Theosis: Zur neueren Diskussion über die Lutherdeutung der Finnischen Schule," *Catholica* (Münster) 66 (2012): 1–18.
55. Schumacher, *Who Do I Say That You Are?*, 49.
56. Ibid., 51.

explicitly rejected by the Formula of Concord.[57] Although Mannermaa objects that this confessional document is unfaithful to Luther's original intentions, it still poses a substantial challenge to his overemphasis on the so-called real consequences of union with Christ for believers. Rebutting Mannermaa's interpretation, Schumacher supports the classic Lutheran interpretation that for Luther all of reality (anthropology included) is determined by the creative and dynamic word of God, thus making the life of faith "real-verbal" rather than "real-ontic."[58] Clearly, then, Mannermaa's Christology encounters problems on various levels, not least of which is anthropology.

Conclusion

Mannermaa places the weight of Luther's Christology and his subsequent understanding of Luther's doctrine of justification on one isolated passage well into Luther's commentary. Luther details his priorities for the commentary in the preface, however, and subsequently discusses Christology almost exclusively in terms of the atonement achieved at the cross, which frees sinners from the law. This ultimately relates to Luther's principal theme of passive and active righteousness as well as the distinction between the law and the gospel. Moreover, there are wider issues at stake in Mannermaa's reworking of justification tied to salvation history, the necessary priority of *favor* over *donum*, the shadow of Osiander, and theological anthropology.

---

57. Ibid., 50.
58. Ibid., 48–49.

9

Judaism, Reformation Theology, and Justification

Mark W. Elliott

This essay will attempt to show how a new perspective on the Jewish religion of Paul's time, and hence of Paul himself, need not imply a total revision of Reformation theology, or more precisely, the doctrine of justification by faith, if "faith" is understood as that which makes room for a perception of the Messiah Jesus.

The [New Perspective on the] Messiah and the Law in Galatians

According to the new perspective on Paul (NPP), Paul in Galatians does not view Jewish religion as such as a rival means of justification. Indeed, Galatians 2:15–16 suggests the contrary: "We who are Jews by birth [φύσει Ἰουδαῖοι] [i.e., not former sinners from among the gentiles] . . . know that a person is not justified from works of the law except through the faith/trust of Christ, and so we have trusted in Christ." So, in this allegedly most apocalyptic of all letters, the following words prove to be interesting: "works of the law do not justify except through the trust of Christ": ἐὰν μὴ διὰ πίστεως Ἰησοῦ Χριστοῦ. "Except" is a concession, and ἐὰν μή always works that way for

Paul.[1] Therefore, with faith in the Messiah in place, works of the law will justify. In other words, pagan sinners might mistakenly think that the Torah is a mechanism for justification, but Jews know better than to make that category mistake. Jews have been looking for Messiah all along for justification, in which works of the law can find their proper place, as the means of laying hold of that gift of righteousness. As Wright, Novenson, and others in this volume argue, the Messiah is the center of justification.

So, as Gathercole has it in his criticism of Dunn's case, these "works of the law" are markers that symbolize the whole synecdochically. They stand for the Jewish way of living, which will justify if done, as the verse of Leviticus (3:12) quoted here indicates: ὁ ποιήσας αὐτὰ ζήσεται ἐν αὐτοῖς ("He who did these will live/be made alive by/in them" [Gal. 3:12])—so long as the Messiah is also trusted, not least to help when one has not lived by the laws.[2] However, when Gathercole writes, "There is no reason why one can *assume* that the formula would function not only as Paul's *magna carta*, but also as the basis of a law-observant mission to the gentiles,"[3] this seems to miss the point, which is that *even* Jews (Paul, Peter, whoever) know that *faith* is all-important for justification. And it is precisely this decisive exercise of faith as primary that many Jewish Christians are presently not doing, although they should know better as the ones who have waited for the Messiah. Instead, they are advocating a justification by works, when it should be by faith, then by works.

If, as it seems, Paul as a Christian did not become suddenly less Jewish, then from where did he get the categories of presence and participation—on which Sanders toward the end of *Paul and Palestinian Judaism* and some of the newer brands of the NPP insist—if, as Martin Hengel argued, his schooling was not Platonic? If it has to do with participating in the presence of God in the temple, that might explain it, with this participation now being ecclesially mediated. Yet there is evidence in Paul's theology of an individual's being indwelt by God's Spirit too, which Schweitzer and in our day a number have seen as being at the heart of Paul's gospel.[4] Also, ideas of corporate personality—again

---

1. A. A. Das, "Another Look at ἐὰν μή in Galatians 2:16," *JBL* 119 (2000): 529–39. On 530: "Since ἐὰν μή occurs only twelve times in the undisputed Pauline corpus, a brief overview will demonstrate that Paul always uses ἐὰν μή to express exception."

2. As against those, such as Francis Watson in *Paul and the Hermeneutics of Faith* (London and New York: T&T Clark, 2004), who thinks that Paul ultimately discards Leviticus in favor of Deuteronomy.

3. Simon J. Gathercole, "The Petrine and Pauline Sola Fide in Galatians 2," in *Lutherische und neue Paulusperspektive: Beiträge zu einem Schlüsselproblem der gegenwärtigen exegetischen Diskussion*, ed. Michael Bachmann, WUNT 1/182 (Tübingen: Mohr Siebeck, 2005), 309–27.

4. Albert Schweitzer, *Die Mystik des Apostels Paulus* (Tübingen: Mohr, 1930).

hellenized, but essentially Jewish and hence possibly revealed to Paul through Scripture—could also be a notion that contributed toward Paul's understanding. Nevertheless, driving it all is still a messianism, such that Hengel could write: "On the Damascus Road the one who according to Deuteronomy 21:22f was 'accursed,' who had been put to death on the tree of shame encountered him in divine glory. Exalted to the right hand of God, i.e., to share God's throne on the Merkaba, he revealed himself to Paul as Son of God, as messiah of Israel *and* redeemer of all who believe."[5] The key here is revelation, since the difference it makes is epistemological, that is, something to behold and believe. The upshot is a strong identification with Christ the hero, who *is* the onlooking believer's righteousness. I suggest that the mode of participation remains typically "Jewish"; in shorthand, it is "moral," as pertaining to the will. One can participate in something by a willed relationship to that Other. In this one can learn something from the Reformers and their interpretation of Paul and Galatians.

The New Perspective on the Reformers

If in recent years, going back to Krister Stendhal in the 1960s, there has been a tendency to deliver Paul from his captivity to the interpretive concept of a "forensic" grace passively received by faith, it is worth noting that simultaneously something similar has been done to Luther (notably by the Finnish school, led by Tuomo Mannermaa) and Calvin (mostly by neo-Barthian systematic theologians).[6] In the recent *Luther Handbuch*, Dietrich Korsch in his article on faith and justification concludes that for Luther, faith allows God in—to be "present"—hence faith creates "God among us."[7] Or take George Hunsinger, who writes in "Fides Christo Formata: Luther, Barth and the Joint Declaration" that faith as this true participation means we can be declared righteous. "Faith as participation is the real heartbeat of the Reformation. . . . The proper sequence, logically speaking, runs from participation to declaration, not the reverse. . . . In Luther we can arguably detect a certain priority for wedding metaphors over courtroom metaphors."[8] Moreover, these courtroom metaphors, if they are to be kept at all, must be allowed to be flexible. For

---

5. Martin Hengel, *The Pre-Christian Paul* (London: SCM, 1991), 84.
6. E.g., J. Todd Billings, *Calvin, Participation, and the Gift: The Activity of Believers in Union with Christ* (New York: Oxford University Press, 2007).
7. A. Beutel, ed., "Glaube und Rechtfertigung," in *Luther Handbuch* (Tübingen: Mohr Siebeck, 2005), 372–81.
8. Wayne Stumme, ed., *Gospel of Justification in Christ* (Grand Rapids: Eerdmans, 2006), 69–84, 75.

example, *simul iustus et peccator* is allowed, so long as it is explained that the believer is continuously well on the way to reaching the state of *iustus*.

In a similar way, the Calvinist *unio cum Christo* must be steered in a certain direction.[9] Now Calvin is clear, as the end of *Institutes* II (17.2) has it, that justification is that which is achieved for "us" the elect, meaning those who will have faith in Christ on the cross: "For in some ineffable way, God loved us and yet was angry towards us at the same time, until he became reconciled to us in Christ. . . . We, . . . estranged from him by sin, have, by Christ's sacrifice, acquired free justification in order to appease God." Here justification has to do with the judgment of Christ in our place. As Eberhard Busch remarks, Calvin's motto in *Institutes* III.16.1 comes from 1 Corinthians 1:30, "Christ was made our righteousness" (which means that "we" are now the opposite of being guilty as charged).[10] So early on in book III of the *Institutes*, Calvin reasserts, "This then is true knowledge of Christ, if we receive him as he is offered by the Father: namely, clothed with his gospel." Yet of course Calvin has more to say, namely, about sanctification. This has led to some seeing the *unio cum Christo*, which is the actualization in time of the decree that predestined the elect, as the hinge of the diptych justification-sanctification.[11] Hence Calvin, in making union central, as that which stands between those two great moments of salvation, can be viewed as valuing "participation." (This move conveniently tends to ignore that justification remains forensic for Calvin, and that it is at least half of the overall story.)

The claim that justification means a divine, even trinitarian indwelling in the believer was of course far from being unknown in Reformation theology from the first moments of the disputes with Andreas Osiander on one side, and between Philipp Melanchthon and Calvin on the other. The delicious result of the parting of the ways through identification with the respective confessions, Lutheran, Reformed, and Catholic, as "confessionalization," was that, with the borders between traditions less open and well guarded, those within each tradition would turn to fall out among themselves. Obvious cases include the *De auxiliis* controversy in the Roman Catholic church in about 1600 and Arminius's teaching as a problem for the Reformed less than

---

9. Recent works include Billings, *Calvin, Participation, and the Gift*; Julie Canlis, *Calvin's Ladder: A Spiritual Theology of Ascent and Ascension* (Grand Rapids: Eerdmans, 2010); James K. A. Smith and James Olthuis, eds., *Radical Orthodoxy and the Reformed Tradition: Creation, Covenant, and Participation* (Grand Rapids: Baker Academic, 2005); and Hans Boersma, *Heavenly Participation* (Grand Rapids: Eerdmans, 2005).

10. E. Busch, *Gotteserkenntnis und Menschlichkeit: Einsichten in die Theologie Johannes Calvin* (Zurich: Theologischer Verlag Zürich, 2005), 45.

11. See recently, Richard Muller, *Calvin and the Reformed Tradition: On the Work of Christ and the Order of Salvation* (Grand Rapids: Baker Academic, 2012).

a decade later. In the Lutheranism of the mid-1570s, Tilemann Heshusius, under Osiander's influence, would dispute Johannes Wigand's interpretation of Galatians 2:19–20.[12]

> As he explored the concept of Christ's indwelling in the believer, Heshusius turned it into a trinitarian question. He first made it clear that the indwelling of God is not the same as his universal presence throughout the world nor is it the same as the relationship of Christ's human nature to his divine nature. The whole Godhead, not only the person of Christ, dwells in the hearts of believers, and the whole second person of the Trinity, not only his human nature or his divine nature, dwells within the Godhead. Luther had shown no interest in such a definition; he had focused on application of the text to the sinner.[13]

Furthermore, in the progress of Lutheran theology that followed, with a certain triumphalism to do with trinitarian indwelling, the note of *Anfechtungen* as part of Christian life was lost, and one might say, the note of a moral element. This did not seem to be a problem in Lutheranism officially, at least in the early days, for as Vainio in his recent study of Lutheran disputes on justification concludes concerning the architects of the Formula of Concord (1580), "Andreae and Wigand deny that Christ is the formal cause of justification, but describe justification as transformation into the likeness of Christ. Additionally, they admit that essential divine righteousness is present in faith, even though it does not have a justifying function."[14] This position, which keeps justification as basically forensic although with a dynamic and Christ-centered element, would win the day in 1580. However, Heshusius, along with Nikolaus Selnecker and Jacob Heerbrand, maintained that, even if the Trinity was to be left out of consideration, Christ was the form of the individual's faith. They did not articulate clearly the role of renovation, although the *presence of Christ* is considered the basis of justification. Andreae and Wigand's cause triumphed due to suspicion toward any notion of the indwelling of Christ's *essential* righteousness (as in Osiander's heresy) and a preference for *spiritual and moral* struggle on the disciple's way to Christ. Faith is not a given; it has to be struggled for. Yet today it seems more the case that the new perspective on Luther means that the minority position (that of Heshusius et

---

12. Gal. 2:20: ζῶ δὲ οὐκέτι ἐγώ, ζῇ δὲ ἐν ἐμοὶ Χριστός.
13. R. Kolb, "God's Select Vessel and Chosen Instrument: The Interpretation of Paul in Late Reformation Lutheran Theologians," in *Companion to Paul in the Reformation*, ed. Ward Holder (Leiden: Brill, 2009), 187–212, 194. Also see H. Ehmer, "Brenz and Paul," in Holder, *Companion to Paul*, 165–86.
14. Olli-Pekka Vainio, *Justification and Participation in Christ: The Development of Justification from Luther to the Formula of Concord* (Leiden: Brill, 2008), 225.

al.) of 1580 is now seeing its day. And that minority tradition represented by Osiander and Heshusius lived on healthily in Pietism. It has never gone away, for this "alternative tradition" found its way to Philipp Spener's definition of justification as rebirth, which in turn he thought of as no less than "die Wiederherstellung der ursprünglichen Gottebenbildlichkeit [the restoration of the original image of God]." This was because, by the time of the early eighteenth-century Pietists, *Rechtfertigung* preaching had led to a false sense of security among Lutheran Christians, just as the doctrine of election could sometimes make mediocre Presbyterians feel very smug. Therefore justification had to be redefined as rebirth, as being grasped by a divine reality, whether in a revivalist or home mission context.[15] This would continue up and through Friedrich Schleiermacher: there could be no justification before conversion.[16] August Hermann Francke had sounded a slightly different note when he held out the promise of participation as a far-off (eschatological) incentive to true repentance and crisis.[17] Yet even here the aspect of application was kept, though the aspect of the forensic was lost.

Almost two centuries later, Albrecht Ritschl's restating of Melanchthon's forensic teaching in terms of God's acting for the sake of his kingdom by pardoning sinners whose justification lies in knowing "deep down" that God is for them, despite what the law would strictly demand—Ritschl's restating might be considered a skeptical reaction to the bold claims of Pietism.[18] In contrast to Ritschl, the traditional justification doctrine is about God's showing himself to be righteous, or about God's being righteous in showing his own, rather than humans', faith in the goodness of the Creator being consistent and continuing. In Ritschl's account, faith supplies the wherewithal, the *locus standi* for humans to see things positively and say "Amen" to it, such that the

---

15. E. Lohse, "Theologie der Rechtfertigung im kritischen Disput," in *Göttingische gelehrte Anzeigen* 249 (1997): 66–81, 79: "Spener unterscheidet beide Begrife, Rechtfertigung und Wiedergeburt fallen nich etwa zusammen, sondern es wird faktsch der zweite Ausdruck *als umfassende Bezeichnung des gesamten Erneuerungsvorganges* angesehen."

16. See Falk Wagner, "Bekehrung. II, 1: Reformationszeit," *Theologische Realenzyklopädie* 5:459–69.

17. To be repeated by Tholuck's idea of "Höllenfahrt der Selbsterkenntnis" as the only way to the *Himmelfahrt der Gotteserkenntnis*, in *Dr. August Tholuck's Werke*, vol. 1 (Gotha: F. A. Perthes, 1862), 23.

18. For a good account, see A. McGrath, *Iustitia Dei: A History of the Christian Doctrine of Justification*, 3rd ed. (Cambridge: Cambridge University Press, 2005), 346–56; which draws on R. Schäfer, "Die Rechtfertigungslehre bei Ritschl und Kähler," *ZTK* 62 (1965): 66–85, which in turn argues for Ritschl's reliance (in Rechtfertigung und Versöhnung II, §14) on L. Diestel's account of "pardon" as something a priest does to a sinner: a declared righteousness, in his "Die Idee der Gerechtigkeit: vorzüglich im Alten Testament", *Jahrbuch für Deutsche Theologie* 5 (1860): 173–204.

doctrine can be claimed to be "applied theology." Faith as a means of seeing what already is the case goes back a long way in the Christian tradition. Haimo of Auxerre had commented on Galatians 1:16 that Christ was always in Paul, even as a Pharisaic sinner, since God fills all things. "But only later was Christ specifically revealed to Paul through faith."[19] Ritschl's view was that justification promoted an ethical responsibility inspired by Jesus, not by looking to him but rather by resting on the belief that there was gospel before law.[20] In so doing, the existential dimension of faith and its struggle was played down, as well as its Christocentrism. Against this type of liberal theology, an excessive Melanchthonian type of gospel, there has been a fierce reaction in modern theology.

The philosophy of personalism has also contributed to this new emphasis on the "real," such that Christian ontology becomes neither static nor coldly formal. In contemporary society, which by default works on first-name terms, the romance of Martin Buber's I–Thou has made its mark, and the metaphor of Bridegroom–bride for the Christ–church and even the divine–human relationship is taken very seriously in much Catholic theology.[21] Ever since Romanticism, the category of "relationship" goes beyond even private feeling and personal intention, since "connectedness to the whole" matters. It is quite opposed to the movement to view individual freedom and self-determination, such as the reception of the Reformation principle, a principle that found inspiration from that theme in Galatians, in, for example, Goethe's reflections around the time of the Luther Jubilee of 1817. The watchword of the Romantic movement, which can be seen as a backlash against that Enlightenment and Goethean doctrine of individualistic self-containment, was "connection," as seen in the respective theologies of Schleiermacher and Möhler.[22]

To come (almost) up to date: in the early 1960s a contribution to ecumenical personalism on the Lutheran side was made by the Luther scholar Wilfried Joest in an essay titled "Die Personalität des Glaubens."[23] Running through this

19. Ian C. Levy, *Galatians: A Medieval Commentary* (Grand Rapids: Eerdmans, 2011), 41.
20. "Der Glaube an die väterliche Vorsehung Gottes ist die christliche Weltanschauung in verkürzter Gestalt'" (A. Ritschl, *Unterricht in der christlichen Religion*, 6th ed., reprint of 3rd ed. [Tübingen: Mohr, 1903], §5). See O. H. Pesch and A. Peters, *Einführung in die Lehre von Gnade und Rechtfertigung* (Darmstadt: Wissenschaftliche Buchgesellschaft, 1981), 318.
21. Cf. Fergus Kerr, *Twentieth-Century Catholic Theologians: From Neoscholasticism to Nuptial Mysticism* (Malden, MA: Blackwell, 2007).
22. Friedrich Schleiermacher, *On Religion: Speeches to Its Cultured Despisers* (Cambridge: Cambridge University Press, 1996), esp. the second address. J. A. Möhler, *Unity in the Church or the Principle of Catholicism: Presented in the Spirit of the Church Fathers of the First Three Centuries*, trans. and ed. Peter C. Erb (Washington, DC: Catholic University of America Press, 1995).
23. W. Joest, "Die Personalität des Glaubens," *Kerygma und Dogma* 7 (1961): 36–53, 152–71.

essay, one of his concerns was to stress the maxim of loyalty or solidarity in the use of Galatians 6:10 ("household of faith"); again, on Galatians 5:22, he talks of *"pistos als Treue"* (faith as faithfulness) and mutual *Treu-sein*. Much of this sounds reassuring, even cozy. If one is simply following the history of ideas, the existentialist fashion would at some point give way to the structuralist by the end of the 1960s, and one finds this echoed in the reservations of one like Klaus Berger in his book *Ist Gott Person?*[24] Berger thinks that there must be a limit to personalism when it comes to God, for with the divine comes mystery, whereas personalism tends to think that all is fully disclosed. As for "the Person," the concept in the Bible is "extroverted," but in the sense that a person is anyone who can play their own role, unlike the modern concept, which is all about reflexivity, self-consciousness, and freedom of choice. For Berger, the Romantic or postmodern opposite side of the coin to modernity's view is "being in relationship," with frankness and intimacy: very different things from the *active* connotations of the biblical concept of "person."

Justification in Modern Theology (Twentieth and Twenty-First Centuries)

It might come as a surprise that Karl Barth did not include a section with the title "Justification" in the *Church Dogmatics* but only devotes to it a short discussion of a few pages, such that justification is hardly a major self-standing theme in the *Church Dogmatics* compared with that of reconciliation. Admittedly, as Bruce McCormack has argued, the topic *does* get treated in the doctrine of election in II/2, and in IV/1, where Barth devotes many pages to "the Judge judged in our place" and hence to justification[25] as something objective and outside of ourselves. It is worth considering that it was a book

24. Klaus Berger, *Ist Gott Person?* (Gütersloh: Gütersloher Verlag, 2004), 84: "Da der Personalismus tendenziell die Person in Beziehung auflöst, fehlt ihm der Sinn für das nicht kommunizierbare, verborgene Geheimnis jeder Identität." And on 109: "Jeder ist im Sinne der Bibel Person, der eine selbständige Rolle im sozialen Miteinander spielen kann. Dieser Personbegriff ist extrem extrovertiert und berücksichtigt alles das nicht, was als Bestandteil des neuzeitlichen Personbegriffs erst viel später in den Blick kommt. Diese späteren Elemente sind: Reflexivität, Selbstbewußtsein und Entscheidungsfreiheit."

25. Bruce L. McCormack, "Justitia Aliena: Karl Barth in Conversation with the Evangelical Doctrine of Imputed Righteousness," in *Justification in Perspective: Historical Developments and Contemporary Challenges*, ed. Bruce L. McCormack (Grand Rapids: Baker Academic, 2006), 167–96. Alister McGrath in his *Iustitia Dei* (Cambridge: Cambridge University Press, 1998), 363–70, argues that Barth's soteriology is dominated by his own version of a *decretum absolutum*, and by an Enlightenment liberal Protestant emphasis on knowledge, that one becomes no longer ignorant of the true situation—a view not much different from that of Karl Holl.

called *Justification*, by Hans Küng, subtitled *The Doctrine of Karl Barth and a Catholic Reflection* (1957), that put Barth's theology firmly on the ecumenical map in a positive sense. For Küng, justification is the heart of Barth's theology. According to Küng, Barth teaches that "it is a declaring righteous which without any reserve can be called a *making* righteous."[26] Hence, in justification there is a reality communicated to the creature that is not just forensic but also is a new being through a new relationship. This expansive concept of justification would be agreed to by the Roman Catholic–Anglican Malta Report of 1971, as Küng claims in a later preface to his *Justification* book.[27] However, in the Malta Report, on closer inspection, the word "relationship" is not mentioned, and the language is more reminiscent of a Käsemannian view of "the change of surroundings" that Christ brings rather than loaded with relational terms.

Indeed, in twenty-first-century theology we catch something of this concern for putting justification firmly in its place, namely, in fifth place in the scheme: Trinity–creation–salvation–history–justification, with each, like the famous Russian doll, fitting within the previous one. Hence John Webster can contend, "The theme of the gospel, however, is the eternal glory of the triune God, a glory that includes (though infinitely exceeds) the glorification of God's creatures." We must not allow "the order of knowing to overshape the order of being."[28] Justification is to be a servant rather than a master of the whole of the gospel: "The righteousness in Christ, like the original righteousness it secures, is gift, and so always *iustitia aliena*."[29] Now, on the traditional account, this alien righteousness is not something to be grafted on to our being, but is simply how God sees those *in Christ* and hence is nothing that would be imposed on them, such that the question of grace would not have to do with any quality or category within humans. In contrast, for Webster its alien character does not mean that it is wholly foreign to the creature, a fictional quality. "The double ontological rule of creaturely being is: what we are, we are *in God*; and what we are in God, *we are*."[30] Webster bases his understanding not so much on the preexisting image of God in human creatures but on the idea that creation, humans not least, exist *in* God. With this emphasis we are

---

26. Hans Küng, *Justification: The Doctrine of Karl Barth and a Catholic Reflection* (London: Burns & Oates, 1964), 69.
27. Ibid., 26: "Rather the righteousness of God actualized in the Christ event is conveyed to the sinner through the message of justification as an encompassing reality basic to the new life of the believer."
28. J. B. Webster, "Rector et iudex super omnia genera doctrinarum? The Place of the Doctrine of Justification," in *What Is Justification About? Reformed Contributions to an Ecumenical Theme*, ed. M. Weinrich and J. P. Burgess (Grand Rapids: Eerdmans, 2009), 35–56, esp. 46.
29. Ibid., 54.
30. Ibid.

in touching distance of the whole question of the extent to which creation can be said to be "graced," that in creation there was, and remains postlapsus, a *surnaturel*, a state of being in God, whatever any creature's attitude toward him or their *Lebenspraxis*. In spite of sin, there is no fall from supernatural to lowly natural, but a spiritual dignity is maintained, even while the way to God is occluded. And even when the new creation comes with Christ, the new humanity is not new in a heteronomous sense.

At the same time, to some degree the popularity of trinitarian theology in the last decade or so has also come at the expense of the theology of justification. The theology of the likes of Eberhard Jüngel,[31] when it tries to speak of "creative passivity" as the sole contribution humans can make, seems out of date. There is still this suspicion that Jüngel's anthropology drives his doctrine of God and not vice versa. In other words, the stated effect(s) of his doctrine—that we stop defining people by their achievements, that we admit honestly to a *Leistungsunfähigkeit* of faith, that we give more respect to the elderly in our churches exactly because they cannot *do* much—seem in reality to be the *causes* for holding to such a doctrine. Furthermore, this "anthropocentric" theology threatens to obscure not only the transcendence but also the energetic power of the trinitarian God in creation. With Jüngel's talk of "the death of God" as a meaningful *theologoumenon*, and with lines such as "the human can trust that God has become human and is human, in order that humanity can be human and can become ever more human"[32]—one might well wonder at the earthy pessimism of such a theology. It is hardly excessive, and it is modest and diffident to a fault.

One might care to compare a statement by Wolfhart Pannenberg that sounds similar but is significantly different from the position of Jüngel just described: "The focusing of salvation on the eschatological future of God stands in critical opposition to all achievement of human life in this world alone, for in striving for self-fulfillment in this world, we close ourselves off to God and his future."[33] Unlike Jüngel, who wants to be able to say that the battle is now over, the war is won, and believers as already justified can relax, for Pannenberg the journey is only just beginning. Justification and reconciliation stand as the proleptic stage on the way to full salvation, and the alternative to striving for worldly success is striving for spiritual success, with no rest until one's full eschatological justification. Now it does seem that this is what Paul had in

---

31. Not least in E. Jüngel, *Das Evangelium von der Rechtfertigung der Gottlosen als Zentrum des christlichen Glaubens: Eine theologische Studie in ökumenischer Absicht*, 2nd ed. (Tübingen: Mohr Siebeck, 1999).

32. E. Jüngel, *Unterwegs zur Sache* (Munich: Kaiser, 1972), 299.

33. W. Pannenberg, *Systematic Theology*, vol. 2 (Grand Rapids: Eerdmans, 1994), 399.

mind with his metaphors drawn from the world of athletic competition (1 Cor. 9:24–27; Phil. 3:13–14). For Barth too, as Webster has observed, "The human is understood by definition to be constituted by action and self-determination."[34] This is quite similar to how Albrecht Peters concludes his eponymous book. *Rechtfertigung* in modern Lutheranism is all about something to do with self-transcendence, so as to find one's place in the scheme of things: Lutherans are always involved in the world, and they are free people, the better to become servants or coworkers with God, although not cocreators.[35]

Yet for all his insistence on the importance of the theme, Jüngel wants to correct a misunderstanding. No Lutheran is claiming justification as a material principle, as the top doctrine, or even one that is *prima inter pares*. Yet justification can still play a role if it is understood as a hermeneutic for the Bible. Wilfried Härle, for example, sees it less as a doctrine and more as a criterion in proclamation or preaching.[36] But Jüngel wants more than a hermeneutic for the Bible; it is to be a hermeneutic for *doctrine*. In this regard, he criticizes the ecumenical Lutheran theologian Risto Saarinen for misunderstanding Martin Kähler's *Wissenschaft der christlichen Lehre*. It is not about reducing the content of Christian theology down to "justification," but about realizing that it is a hermeneutical principle through which other doctrines may be brought into proper focus: "Als Rechtfertigungslehre ist sie sachgemäße Christologie,"[37] making Christ's story present.[38] It might be equated with "the gospel," or perhaps as J. C. K. von Hofmann would have put it, with the *Thatbestand*, or in Reformed terms, with the covenant renewed.

Johann Fichte once complained that Paul's God is arbitrary, a God who made up salvation history as he went along. But as Jüngel comments, the New Testament covenant is prepared for and reinforced by the Old Testament, so it is not arbitrary; and the basic lines for the New Testament were set down a long time in advance, so that God remains true as part of his righteousness. This, one might say, is classically a Reformed emphasis and something that the NPP roughly favors. Yet a Reformed view of justification also presupposes the *believer* as sinner—which post-Enlightenment theology from John

---

34. J. B. Webster, "Justification, Analogy and Action: Barth and Luther in Jüngel's 'Anthropology,'" in *Barth's Moral Theology: Human Action in Barth's Thought* (New York: Continuum, 2004), 179–214, 202.

35. A. Peters, *Rechtfertigung*, HST 12 (Gütersloh: Mohn, 1984), 224: "Die Rechtfertigung und damit auch das Christusheil macht hierzu nur *den Rücken frei*; die vor uns liegende *Zukunft* scheint *in unsere Hände gegeben zu sein*."

36. W. Härle, *Dogmatik*, 3rd ed. (Berlin and New York: de Gruyter, 2000), 115: "In der Tat ist die Rechtfertigung nicht so sehr 'Lehre' als vielmehr Maßstab der Verkündigung."

37. Jüngel, *Evangelium von der Rechtfertigung*, 24.

38. "Iustus coram Deo; peccator vor dem Grund des eigenen Ich" (ibid., 184).

Wesley onward lamented as overly pessimistic if paid too much attention. For his part, Jüngel acknowledges Nikolaj Grundtvig's and Dietrich Bonhoeffer's reaction, that theology should not define humans by negative qualities. This can be acknowledged and taken into account if we realize that the logic of justification is that of recognizing that sin has already been forgiven, so it is not so pessimistic at all.[39] Sin is known only in its forgiveness. Justification turns one inside out. Recognition thus becomes a huge theme in Jüngel's *Rechtfertigung/Justification* book: the ruthless self-realization that seeks and responds to worldly recognition can be replaced by realizing how much God recognizes each of us. This is a Hegelian *topos*, of course, but here put to good use. Jüngel's perspective might seem to be a theology stuck in the early modern past, but it is none the worse for having such credentials.

On this account, faith is understood relationally in part because this can be seen as compensating for doubts concerning our worldview, our view of how things are, as well as our degree of certainty about the things of faith. Gerd Ebeling insisted that the former (faith) should not need reinforcement from the latter certainties about realities, including creedal ones.[40] But yet the two are linked;[41] assurance can come from seeing faith making sense in a life, which is not about doing works as such but about seeing change happen around one. Moreover, faith is something that responds not only to the offer of forgiveness but also to revelation and intellectual belief. Hence at the end of his book on faith, Martin Seils can write that the phenomenon of faith could in this way have its initial ground in the character of the Old Testament encounter with God, which can be understood as the history of a promise, since only a personally encountering God can be trusted for the duration.[42] Seils can then conclude that the category of "relationship" precedes that of substance.

In contrast and even opposition to this neo-Lutheran sobriety, trends in the interpretation of the Reformers reflect that, increasingly, theologians seem to want reality—if not objectivity then at least intersubjectivity—a grasping of something that is more real than what the realm of the senses can tell us. Sometimes this is described as *Surfeit*, for such *exaggeration* seems an understandable response to a poverty of spirit in our present age and church. One danger, however, is that it may play to acquisitive, consumerist, and

---

39. "Die Logik der Rechtfertigungslehre verlangt vielmehr, die Sünde *als bereits überwundene* zu erkennen" (ibid., 35).

40. G. Ebeling, *Wort und Glaube*, vol. 3 (Tübingen: Mohr Siebeck, 1975), 64–67.

41. M. Seils, *Glaube*, HST 13 (Gütersloh: Mohn, 1996), 538, makes reference to Paul Tillich's *Rechtfertigung und Zweifel* (Giessen: Töpelmann, 1924).

42. Seils, *Glaube*, 520: "Das Phänomen des Glaubens in dieser Weise seinen Grund zunächst einmal im *verheißungsgeschichtlichen Charakter* der alttestamentlichen Gottesbegegnung haben könnte"; 521: "Nur einem personhaft begegnenden Gott kann zeitübergreifend vertraut werden."

accumulative appetites, as well as being hyperbolic and rhetorical in a pejorative sense, analogous to the way in which academic referees are encouraged to accentuate the positive in written references for their protégés. In the work of Milbank and the like, the discourse of ontology outnarrates the mid-twentieth-century metaphysics of absence, sounded by Martin Heidegger and a school of timorous theologians in his wake.[43] Returning to the present issue: who wants to waste time with legal metaphors when sin, guilt, and despair are real enough? And so are love, joy, peace, and so forth. To "keep it real" is to keep it ontological. Even that most old-fashioned of terms, "imputation," if combined with "election," can come to mean something just as ontological as participation: it *really is*. The indicative renders the imperative possible. Or better, one just has to walk into the narrative, and one's imagination is reset for the ethical struggle ahead.

Back to Paul

To return to Paul and Galatians in view of the main lines of these developments, first, what can be said in favor of law court metaphors? For one thing, the idea that justification is related to the divine tribunal (Gal. 3:11: "Clearly no one who relies on the law is justified before God, because 'the righteous will live by faith'") reminds one that righteousness is eschatological: it is yet to be, and the idea of a tribunal is at least implicit. Hence, Peters can speak of a very otherworldly type of vindication, one completely different from that of psychological counseling and self-justification.[44] Second, justification in Galatians 3:10-13 also relates that status to the cross. Could "reconciliation" not do that? Perhaps, but if so, it would then contain "justification" within it, with the metaphor of "reconciliation" more "cultic" in its semantic range. It might be true that Paul in 2 Corinthians 5 is intending to say something about his ministry, and indeed the ambassador image seems to influence the choice of metaphor. But in 2 Corinthians 5:20-21 the basis of the reconciliation of the

---

43. John Milbank, *Theology and Social Theory: Beyond Secular Reason* (Cambridge, MA: Basil Blackwell, 1990), 380.
44. Peters, "Rechtfertigung," 281:
Beim neuzeitlichen Menschen entspricht dem unmäßigen Fordern an das Leben ein *Selbstmitleid nach innen*. Die amerikanische Seelsorgebewegung, aber auch der Widerstreit gegen sie, beides ist, verglichen mit Luthers Seelsorgepraxis, erschreckend humorlos. Es mangelt an Augenmaß sowie an Distanz zu sich selber. Die letzte Freiheit eines Christenmenschen bricht wohl nur dort auf, wo Gottes Anspruch unsere Augen über diese Welt emporhebt zu seinem Jüngsten Tag und Gottes Zuspruch uns ganz mit Christi fremder Gerechtigkeit umkleidet. Schließen wir diesen Gedankenkreis mit einigen Sätzen von Julius Schniewind: "Rechtfertigung heißt: im Jüngsten Gericht bestehen."

world to God is justification and vice versa: "God was . . . not counting their trespasses against them. . . . For our sake he made him to be sin who knew no sin, so that in him we might become the righteousness of God." There is language here that accords with that of justification.

Further, there is really no union with Christ until justification and reconciliation are in place, and the Holy Spirit creates that bond, although it is quite correct to emphasize that union is how believers come to *know* their status and receive the benefits of Christ. Michael Bird represents a broadly NPP (Mark II): "When discoursing on justification by faith, Paul immediately switches to participationist categories of 'seeking to be justified *in* Christ,' having been 'crucified *with* Christ,' and 'Christ lives *in* me' (Gal. 2:17, 19b–20). That is because justification, dying to the law, and living to God are realities that one apprehends only in union with Christ."[45] Well true, but a union's apprehending them does not mean grounding them, as seems the case with Calvin.

Also it seems that those who favor "the faith *of* Jesus Christ" appear to want to have their cake and eat it. If Christ exercises faith or faithfulness in which believers are to participate, how then is that very different from a representative role of a typological or federal sort, by which (as in the Westminster Catechism in 1647 and the Savoy Confession in 1653) Christ is the new Moses who gives both active and passive obedience by imputation to the believer? If we say that one participates in an actual or mystical way in Christ's righteousness, and that such participation is in no way idealist but very much has to do with sacraments, discipline, prayer, virtuous action, and so forth, what kind of righteousness is this? In its original form, justification was opposed to a (late medieval and then early modern) pietism that would put the objective work of Christ in the shade through a concentration on the work of the Spirit in the believer. This contemporary emphasis on participation among some streams of the NPP seems no better just because in speaking of church and sacraments one has a rhetoric that sounds less "individualistic." The divine presence associated with the church and the sacraments presupposes the life, death, and resurrection of Jesus; but these foundational soteriological realities are not like a ladder that, once climbed, can now be kicked away. To say that legal righteousness has been fulfilled does not mean that legal or moral categories are thereby nullified. It does not seem that once the cross has done its work, the legal (reality) is gone and "life" now takes over through resurrection. For according to Galatians 2:19–20, "Through the law I died to the law, so that I might live to God. I have been crucified with Christ; and it is no

---

45. Michael F. Bird, "Progressive Reformed," in *Justification: Five Views*, ed. James K. Beilby and Paul Rhodes Eddy (Downers Grove, IL: IVP Academic, 2011), 131–57, esp. 135.

longer I who live, but it is Christ who lives in me. And the life I now live in the flesh I live by faith in the Son of God, who loved me and gave himself for me" (NRSV). The last clause, "and gave himself for me," conveys the idea of payment or ransom still ringing out. In fact, the second sentence helps to explain the first. It is the faith of/in the Son of God that tells the reader what it means for Christ to live "in me." That is not to say that it is a fiction, but that it is not "reality" in a straightforward way. Is the Christian life one of moving on from justification at baptism into a new life from then onward? Is the metaphor of "the dying and rising life" really a pessimism that believers cannot afford? "You foolish Galatians! Who has bewitched you? It was before your eyes that Jesus Christ was publicly exhibited as crucified!" (Gal. 3:1 NRSV).

Finally, this will take the reader through the early verses of Galatians 3 to the idea of Christ as bearing the public curse and shame in 3:13. In other words, the law's power is ended, but the power is now taken up in and through the cross, a power that disdains the pretentious condescension of political authority. The vision of righteousness is external: categories of imputation do not seem to be required. Don Carson admits that Paul never uses *logizomai* to mean mutual imputation, yet then he adds, "But if one extends the discussion into the domain of constructive theology, and observes that the Pauline texts themselves (despite the critics' contentions) teach penal substitution, then 'imputation' is merely another way of saying the same thing."[46] But why then the need for imputation, participation, or something "ontological"? Christ has "already" borne the curse. Abraham's faith was in a God who would keep promise in the future. Abraham's trust in provision on Mount Moriah—that God will see to it—can be construed as faith toward liberation from a far-off place. His righteousness is external to him, and in flesh of his flesh, not on Moriah at that moment but at a distant point in time, beyond the realm of his imagination.

So all God needs to see on our side is faith as acceptance, not as a channel for imputation into an "account," or participation for that matter. It is not that faith is like a promissory note or an indulgence that can be cashed in for forgiveness. It already is counted: "Just as Abraham 'believed God, and it was reckoned to him as righteousness' so, you see, those who believe are the descendants of Abraham. And the scripture, foreseeing that God would justify the Gentiles by faith, declared the gospel beforehand to Abraham, saying, 'All the Gentiles shall be blessed in you'" (Gal. 3:6–8 NRSV).

Righteousness is not about "imputation" but about what God has done and is: in that sense, the πίστις may well be that of Jesus Christ as the new

---

46. D. Carson, quoted in ibid., 134n53.

Isaac-like reality of the Christian faith.⁴⁷ But a reality that comes toward us through the cross means a faith that has to do with Jesus the Messiah. Hence righteousness is something God does and is and sees in the mirror of faith held back to him. We do not "appropriate" justification, for we have no means by which to appropriate it, as Eduard Lohse has insisted,⁴⁸ and we do not reach out to get it. Rather, we simply regard it, or God, from a now close, yet worshipful distance.

---

47. W. Schenk, "Die Gerechtigkeit Gottes und der Glaube Christi," *TLZ* 97 (1972): 161–74, esp. 170, with reference to Gal. 3:22: "Vielmehr war πίστις an der Stelle objektiv als Glaubenbotschaft zu verstehen."

48. According to Lohse ("Theologie der Rechtfertigung"), righteousness is a divine attribute, and the *genitivum auctoris* (Fitzmyer and many others) is not to be preferred to the objective genitive: "righteousness which counts before God." Hence Lohse agrees with Schlatter on Rom. 10:3 that Paul's distinctive doctrine is that *faith* is the mode of appropriation of justification—something on the human side that has to be in place.

10

Can We Still Speak of "Justification by Faith"?

An In-House Debate with Apocalyptic Readings of Paul

BRUCE MCCORMACK

Introduction

The Joint Declaration on the Doctrine of Justification, signed by representatives of the Pontifical Council for Promoting Christian Unity and the Lutheran World Federation on Reformation Day 1999, was arguably the greatest ecumenical achievement of the twentieth century.[1] For the first time the Roman Catholic Church joined with a church of the Reformation to proclaim shared belief together—and shared belief not just on any doctrine but precisely on the doctrine that, in the sixteenth century, had been basic to all other doctrinal disputes: the doctrine of justification. To be sure, ratification of this agreement did not result in full communion; differences remained even with respect to justification. But the convergence achieved on certain "basic truths" with regard to justification enabled the two great churches to subsume remaining

---

1. The Lutheran World Federation and the Roman Catholic Church, *Joint Declaration on the Doctrine of Justification* (Grand Rapids and Cambridge, UK: Eerdmans, 2000), cited in this volume as *JDDJ* with relevant paragraph numbers, marked with §.

differences with respect to this doctrine beneath these truths, as differing forms of explication of them.[2]

This step also enabled both sides to acknowledge that the sixteenth-century condemnations issued publicly by each side against the other's teachings were not applicable to the dialogue-partner's confession *today*. This was a skillful move but one made in a spirit of charity and indeed wisdom. The traditional condemnations of sixteenth-century positions were not lifted *as such*; it was simply said that the Spirit had led both sides into a greater understanding of scriptural teaching and the authoritative teachings of their own traditions, with the result that the ways in which each upholds and explains its confession today takes a form that does not fall prey to condemnation. This conviction was expressed in the following words: "By appropriating insights of recent biblical studies and drawing upon modern investigations of the history of theology and dogma, the post-Vatican-II ecumenical dialogue has led to a notable convergence concerning justification."[3]

The Joint Declaration is the product of more than thirty years of dialogue. We are all aware that this same period saw revolutionary changes take place in Pauline studies. In *Paul and Palestinian Judaism*, E. P. Sanders sought to show that "justification by works" was a construct of sixteenth-century Protestant theologians and bore little resemblance to the "covenantal nomism" of the Judaism of Paul's time.[4] Richard Hays's field-changing dissertation argued that it was the faith *of* Jesus himself rather than faith *in* Jesus that was basic to the narrative substructure of Paul's theology, thereby shifting the locus of justification to Christology rather than the work of the Holy Spirit in believers.[5] The 1990s saw the emergence of a variety of new perspectives on Paul (NPP), chief among which were the contributions of Sanders, James D. G. Dunn, and N. T. Wright.[6] These

---

2. See Susan K. Wood, "Catholic Reception of the Joint Declaration on the Doctrine of Justification," in *Rereading Paul Together: Protestant and Catholic Perspectives on Justification*, ed. David Aune (Grand Rapids: Baker Academic, 2006), 47:
> The heart of the Joint Declaration on the Doctrine of Justification consists of seven affirmations of what Lutherans and Catholics confess together regarding justification. Each positive statement of common confession is followed by a paragraph clarifying the Catholic understanding and another clarifying the Lutheran understanding. These two paragraphs allow the differences within the two traditions to stand, but they are subsumed under a broader agreement. These differences do not destroy the consensus regarding basic truths. This document represents a differentiated consensus rather than uniformity in concept and expression.

3. *JDDJ*, §13.

4. E. P. Sanders, *Paul and Palestinian Judaism* (Philadelphia: Fortress, 1977).

5. See Richard Hays, *The Faith of Jesus Christ: The Narrative Substructure of Galatians 3:1–4:11*, 2nd ed. (Grand Rapids: Eerdmans, 2002).

6. E. P. Sanders, *Paul* (Oxford: Oxford University Press, 1992); James D. G. Dunn, "The New Perspective on Paul," in *Jesus, Paul, and the Law: Studies in Mark and Galatians* (Louisville: Westminster

were followed by apocalyptic readings of various kinds, promoted by J. Louis Martyn, Martinus de Boer, Beverly Gaventa, and Joel Marcus, among others. For the most part, this last-named development came too late in the process to have an impact on the Joint Declaration. But the earlier works were well known to biblical scholars participating in Lutheran-Catholic dialogue—and it is quite clear that these participants understood Paul differently.

David Aune has offered three possible reasons for the conspicuous gap between this new church teaching and the new perspectives. "First, the New Perspective originated as and has continued to remain a largely Anglo-American approach to Paul. . . . Second, the fields of systematic theology and biblical scholarship are separated by a wide gulf. . . . Third, the Lutheran-Catholic dialogue predates the advent of the new perspective by more than a decade and it [the NPP] is still being debated and tested in the academy."[7] Of these possible explanations, the second is almost devoid of significance (since biblical work from its beginning was foundational to discussions between dialogue members). The first does tell us something significant, that the variegated NPP has not been greeted in Europe with the kind of support it has found in North America and the United Kingdom. But the third is most important for my purposes here.

Revolutions in academic circles come and go. New readings excite the attention of many, in some cases giving rise to a new scholarly consensus. But just as quickly as it forms, a consensus among scholars can also quickly dissipate. The NPP are not everyone's cup of tea; nor, for that matter, are apocalyptic readings—though both enjoy sizable followings. If there is a consensus that stretches across these rather diverse groupings where Paul's doctrine of justification is concerned, it is this: the so-called Lutheran Paul constitutes a serious distortion of Paul's teaching.[8] But will even that consensus last? In my opin-

---

John Knox, 1990), 183–214; idem., *The Theology of Paul's Letter to the Galatians* (Cambridge: Cambridge University Press, 1993); idem., "Paul and Justification by Faith," in *The Road from Damascus: The Impact of Paul's Conversion on His Life, Thought, and Ministry*, ed. Richard N. Longenecker (Grand Rapids: Eerdmans, 1997), 85–101; N. T. Wright, *The Climax of the Covenant: Christ and the Law in Pauline Theology* (Minneapolis: Fortress, 1991); idem., *What St. Paul Really Said: Was Paul of Tarsus the Real Founder of Christianity?* (Grand Rapids: Eerdmans, 1997).

7. David Aune, "Recent Readings of Paul Relating to Justification By Faith," in Aune, ed., *Rereading Paul Together*, 242.

8. Some and perhaps many of the contributors to the changes just described did not engage in polemics against Luther. But Richard Hays, who contributed mightily to the emergence of an apocalyptic perspective with his work on the "faith of Christ" in Paul's theology, did make Luther a target. See Hays, *Faith of Jesus Christ*, 119–22. In any case, the impact of the work of the movement as a whole on the "Lutheran" Paul has been tremendous. So it does not really matter if a given NT scholar supportive of the just-mentioned trends made Luther a direct target of their work. The consequences for the central doctrine of the Reformation have been enormous.

ion, the participants in Lutheran-Catholic dialogue were right to take a long view where biblical studies are concerned and not get too excited over recent developments. And so, far from rejecting the Lutheran Paul, their agreement simply gave him a facelift; it introduced modifications based in part on later Lutheran interpretations of the doctrine of justification.

In any event, the gap between systematic theologians and biblical scholars is as nothing in comparison to the gap between church theologies and guild commitments. For those of us who understand ourselves to be "doctors of the church," the need to explain and (so far as possible) to defend church teaching cannot simply be subordinated to guild demands. Speaking for myself, I admit that the Reformation principle of *sola scriptura* (and the understanding of the relation of Scripture to tradition which it entails) has to incline me to take the question of what Paul really said with the utmost seriousness. But the task of establishing what Paul really said is one that, for me, must take place under the guidance of ecclesial authority—which, in the case of those belonging to Protestant churches, means "under the guidance of *Protestant* ecclesial authority" in the first instance. And this brings me back to the Joint Declaration.

The basic truths affirmed in the Joint Declaration constitute, one might say, a riff on the uniform teaching on the subject of justification found in the official teachings of the Protestant denominations—including the Presbyterian Church (USA), of which I am a member. And it is a riff that is gaining in prestige and what in we might call informal authority. It was adopted by the World Methodist Council in 2006. And it is being closely studied by member churches of the World Communion of Reformed Churches with a view toward adoption in 2017. So I have no other choice but to take the Joint Declaration seriously too, though I do so gladly. I have my objections to it, but thankfully those are confined (for the most part) to the differentiating elements, not to the "basic truths" confessed together by Lutherans and Catholics.

In this essay my central task is to explain some important elements in Galatians 2:16; 3:6–14; and 5:4–5. Close exegesis of these passages is not possible here; I confine myself to highlighting a few key exegetical decisions. And I do so with a view toward the role played by these decisions in understanding Paul's doctrine of justification and its place in his overall theology. My primary conversation partners will be Karl Barth (no surprise there) and two apocalyptic readers of Paul: J. Louis Martyn and Martinus de Boer. I have chosen to address the latter two because Martyn in particular has a self-conscious affinity with the theology of the early Karl Barth of the second edition of his Romans commentary (1922).⁹ But neither Martyn nor de Boer seems to appreciate the degree to which Barth's early apocalypticism was modified in his later work by being taken up into a judicial (or forensic) frame of reference—which, be it noted, places the later Barth's doctrine of justification within hailing distance of the Joint Declaration.¹⁰ In any event, I have chosen to limit my attention here to apocalyptic readings of Paul because they overlap in interesting ways on my own work on Barth.

In what follows, I begin with the exegetical issues touching upon justification in Galatians. Then in a second section I turn to Barth's contribution to a well-integrated doctrine of justification.

Galatians 2:16; 3:6–14; 5:4–5

Setting the Stage—with the Help of Louis Martyn

Translating a text is already an act of interpretation. How a particular text is received and understood by the exegete will often depend on decisions made with respect to textual elements found elsewhere in an epistle and even, perhaps, in other epistles written by the same author. To put it this way suggests that an overarching theology is being formed (or perhaps is fully formed) *even as* translation decisions are made with respect to a particular verse. The part is understood in the light of the whole, even as the whole is construed as the sum of its parts. There is absolutely nothing wrong with this in principle. We all do it to some degree or another, engaging in a movement from text to theology and a countermovement from theology to text—and both at the same time. But we do need to keep this twofold movement in mind, this dialectical to and fro, since our commentary on translations that we ourselves have devised is, at

---

9. Given that Richard Hays has testified to the influence of Karl Barth on his work, I could have chosen him instead. See Hays, *Faith of Jesus Christ*, xxiv–xxv. In my judgment, however, the apocalyptic readers of Paul stand closer to Barth's more central convictions than does Hays. After all, Hays thinks that "participation" (understood along the lines of the Eastern fathers) is more basic to Paul's theology than is "justification." Barth, early or late, would have had no sympathy with such a judgment. And it is one of the great virtues of the apocalyptic readers of Paul that they too have little patience with attempts to find the roots of a "divinization" theory in Paul. In sum, I have chosen to engage Martyn and de Boer because I thought they might be in a better position to understand what I am trying to do here.

10. These modifications cannot be explained simply as the consequence of a change of genre—a shift from the exegetical to the dogmatic task, since Barth sought at every stage of his dogmatic development to ground his dogmatic claims exegetically. Attention to the ecclesial context of Barth's dogmatics and the conception of ecclesial authority bearing on his exegetical work would be more fruitful—which brings us back to the Joint Declaration. Whatever else might be said of the Joint Declaration, it clearly was formulated under the guidance of a conception of ecclesial authority that the later Barth also broadly shared.

the same time, a commentary on our own theories and indeed on ourselves as exegetes. To keep this in mind can engender a healthy dose of self-criticism, which is all the more necessary when the translations we offer constitute a break with the history of translating the texts in question. A good case in point can be found in Martyn's much-discussed commentary on Galatians.

What Martyn does is to elaborate a fairly full depiction of Paul's overall theology of "rectification" early on in his commentary—already in relation to Galatians 1:4. Having put the "whole" in place, he then invites other exegetes into a conversation with him about the "parts." Can the relevant exegetical decisions in, say 2:16; 3:6–14; and 5:4–5 support and confirm this picture? Or are there elements that sit poorly with the picture and call it into question? As I say, I do not think this procedure is wrong. It is what exegetes often do when they are attentive to issues surrounding the coherence of the theology they find in biblical texts; they are doing theology even as they do exegesis.

Martyn introduces his understanding of Paul's theology of "rectification" (a word he prefers to "justification") already at Galatians 1:4. Two elements in this passage are of crucial importance for him. The first is "the present evil age." This is taken (quite reasonably, I think) as a bit of shorthand for "the powers that rule the present age." References to "the god of this age" (2 Cor. 4:4), "the rulers of this age" (1 Cor. 2:6–8), and "principalities and powers" (1 Cor. 15:24) are not infrequent in Paul's writings. Indeed, in 1 Corinthians 2:8 Paul says that it is the "rulers of this age" who put to death "the Lord of glory." The second element is found in the verb *exaireō*, "snatch from the grasp" (Gal. 1:4). For Martyn, both a sketch of the human plight and God's solution to it have already been announced. "The *root* problem lies not in our sins, but in the powers of the present evil age."[11] The solution is deliverance from the powers that hold the human race in thrall. Understandably at this point, Martyn takes a step back in his comments on the text to offer his initial discussion of Paul's theology of rectification.[12]

From the list of ten elements identified in this initial sketch, only two are missing that are foundational to Martyn's reconstruction as a whole (though the second is adumbrated). The first element is his translation of the phrase *pisteōs [Iēsou] Christou*, which appears six times in Paul's writings—twice in Galatians 2:16, once in 3:22, as well as in Romans 3:22 and 26 and Philippians 3:9. Martyn understands this phrase as a subjective genitive, the "faith *of* Christ" (rather than construing it as an objective genitive, "faith *in* Christ"),

---

11. J. Louis Martyn, "The Apocalyptic Gospel in Galatians," *Interpretation* (2000): 253.
12. J. Louis Martyn, *Galatians: A New Translation with Introduction and Commentary*, AB 33A (New York: Doubleday, 1997), 97–105.

so that Galatians 2:16 reads (in his translation): "Even we ourselves know, however, that a person is not rectified by observance of the Law, but rather by the faith of Jesus Christ [*dia pisteōs Iesou Christou*]. Thus, even we have placed our trust in Christ Jesus, in order that the source of our rectification might be the faith of Christ [*ek pisteōs Christou*] and not observance of the Law; for not a single person will be rectified by observance of the Law."[13] That this translation move is a relatively novel one is conceded. The Christian tradition had usually understood the crucial phrase as an objective genitive—"faith in Christ." And so the NRSV, for example, renders Galatians 2:16 this way: "Yet we know that a person is justified not by the works of the law but through faith *in* Jesus Christ. And we have come to believe in Christ Jesus, so that we might be justified by faith *in* Christ" (emphases added; cf. mg.). The decision made here by Martyn is decisive for his understanding of Paul's theology as a whole, and it is his picture of the whole (its power to explain this and other elements) that in turn justifies the decision made here.

The second decisive element has to do with Martyn's translation of the *dikaios* group in 2:16; 3:8 and 11 as "rectify" and "rectification"—words that Martyn prefers to the more traditional "justify" and "justification." "Rectification" stands closer to the "deliverance" mentioned in 1:4; as we shall see, it also submerges "justification" into "new creation" conceptuality: the creation of a new world through the destruction of the old one. In any case, "to rectify" means to set things right—which could have a legal meaning but in Martyn's hands does not. He discerns a meaning closer to liberation, the setting free of those who were imprisoned.

The "whole" of Paul's theology of "rectification"—in the light of which Martyn understands the parts—has the following contours:

First, God is the Subject who redeems. "Redemption" is described in terms of an invasion of enemy-held territory, a war of liberation. In this war, the decisive action is taken by God.

Second, God's opponents in this war are certain "anti-God powers." At this point it bears mentioning that, in spite of the antipathy of the Martyn school to Bultmann, they too engage in a bit of demythologizing at this point. For them, the anti-God powers are not "fallen angels" in the first instance (as they were for Paul). The anti-God powers are Sin (reified into a power that holds the human race in thrall) and the Law (insofar as it is made to be the tool of sin). Salvation is achieved through a war of liberation directed against these powers.

Third, the decisive event in this war is the crucifixion. Paul, Martyn says, "is concerned to offer an interpretation of Jesus' death that is oriented

---

13. Ibid., 5.

not toward personal guilt and forgiveness but rather toward corporate enslavement and liberation. Jesus's death was the powerful deed in God's apocalyptic war, the deed by which God has already freed us from the malevolent grasp of the present age."[14] How does the "faith of Christ" as the instrument of God's saving work relate to the event of the cross? The short answer is this: his death is itself faithful, though what that might mean is left somewhat vague.

Fourth, "the war is continued under the banner of co-crucifixion."[15] The eschatological Spirit makes those upon whom he is poured out to be "freedom fighters," who are caught up in the war of liberation. There is a bit of ambiguity here since it is not always clear when the war commenced or who brought it about. On the one hand, Martyn can say that "the invading Spirit has decisively commenced the war of liberation from the powers of the present evil age"[16] and "the Spirit of Christ has invaded the realm of Sin in order to commence the war of liberation."[17] On the other hand, he can also say that "Christ's advent has commenced the war that will lead to that victory. Thus, in an anticipatory but altogether real sense, Christ's advent is that victory"[18] and "the motif of cosmic warfare is focused above all on the cross. . . . There, in the thoroughly real event of Christ's crucifixion, God's war of liberation was commenced and decisively settled, making the cross the foundation of Paul's apocalyptic theology."[19] No doubt Martyn would say that there is no ambiguity here. The eschatological Spirit makes us to participate in Christ's victory; in this derivative sense only does the Spirit "commence" the war. But the ambiguity remains nonetheless because Martyn has no theological ontology at his disposal that would help him to explain the relation of Christ to his "freedom fighters," the relation of his activity to theirs. If he had one, the place to introduce it would have been in commenting on Galatians 2:19–20.[20] But no real light is shed there on the problem of "participation" even though the word is employed by Martyn himself.

Fifth, for Martyn the fundamental contrast in Paul's theology is not between "works of the law" and the faith of an individual, but between "works of the law" and the "faith of Christ." The contrast, then, is between an action of God and all human action—which means that not only have the "works

14. Ibid., 101.
15. Ibid., 102.
16. Ibid., 105; cf. Martyn, "Apocalyptic Gospel in Galatians," 258.
17. Martyn, "Apocalyptic Gospel in Galatians," 259.
18. Martyn, *Galatians*, 105.
19. Ibid., 101.
20. Ibid., 278–80.

of the law" been set aside as God's means for achieving rectification; so also is faith set aside, insofar as faith is something humans do. Paul's "gospel is not about human movement into blessedness (religion); it is about God's liberating invasion of the cosmos (theology)."[21] To be sure, humans do need to put their trust in Christ if they are to be "freedom fighters." But such trust contributes nothing to the victory already achieved by Christ's faith—and, in fact, Christ's faith is (in the enactment of a proclaimed promise) "causative"[22] of the faith of others.

Precisely at this point, however, a second ambiguity rears its head, one even more basic than the one already touched on. What is the relation of divine action to the human action of Christ expressed in his faithfulness unto death? How can what Jesus does be seen as what *God* does? Again, one needs a theological ontology to explain the relation of the divine to the human, of God to Christ. Martyn might well be forgiven for thinking that since Paul did not set forth an ontology, then it cannot be his task as an interpreter of Paul to provide one. But I hope the reader will understand the dilemma that this disciplinary restriction brings about. If New Testament scholars do not pause to consider the possibilities where theological ontology is concerned—that is, to ask whether Paul does not have an implicit ontology or perhaps even how systematic theologians might supplement Paul in order to make this theology more fully coherent—then they are left where Martyn himself winds up: with a rich battery of images and concepts. But images and concepts alone, no matter how rhetorically powerful, do not rise to the level of an adequate explanation. How is it that the "rectification" of the world is achieved by Christ's faithful death? How can the faithful death of a single human being achieve a military victory over the anti-God powers? That's my question—and really, it divides into two parts. First, what gives to Christ's death its *universal* significance? That's the ontological question. And second, *how does it work* in relation to the anti-God powers of Sin and the Law? Precisely *how* does Christ's faithful death effect deliverance from these powers? To raise this question is to make inquiry into the mechanism that would make sense of the military rhetoric employed.

Let me explain where matters stand with an example. Gregory of Nyssa's well-known ransom theory has a clearly defined mechanism for explaining how God's victory over the devil is accomplished. God enters into a bargain with the devil. An exchange takes place. God trades an innocent human for the sinners who are already in thrall to the devil. What happens is that the

---

21. Martyn, "Apocalyptic Gospel in Galatians," 255.
22. Martyn, *Galatians*, 276.

devil fails to recognize that Jesus is joined to the eternal Logos, in whom is Life itself. When the devil puts Jesus to death, he discovers too late that death cannot hold him. The life of God is in him in the form of the Logos, who raises Jesus from the dead. The way in which victory is achieved on Gregory's theory tells us something else of importance. What makes it "work" is its subordination to a divinization scheme in which the resurrection plays a pivotal role. Gregory's ransom theory, it turns out, is not a stand-alone item of belief. More on that later, when we turn to Barth. The point here is that Gregory is what we might call "proto-Cyrilline" in his Christology; he has an ontology in place that makes sense of God's victory over the devil. Martyn is not so fortunate. To be sure, his view does not involve a commercial exchange. His controlling metaphor is that of military conquest. Unlike Gregory, however, he lacks a theological ontology that would round out his attempted explanation and make it more complete.

One final issue before I turn to Galatians more directly. Martyn is certainly right in thinking that his association of "new creation" with the crucifixion rather than the resurrection is unexpected.[23] The thought that "new creation" would be inaugurated by the raising of Christ into a mode of embodied existence in which degeneration, decay, and death are no longer intrinsic is perfectly coherent. Less so is Martyn's attempt to make *the cross* the basis for "new creation." That liberation from the powers of Sin and the Law might well effect a change of lords over one's life is understandable, of course. But the life lived in the body would seem to remain unchanged by such an outcome. Part of the problem here is that Martyn does not seem to know what to do with the resurrection—a sizable problem on the face of it, since Paul says that Christ was "*raised* for our justification" (Rom. 4:25 NRSV). As a result of this deficit, Martyn makes the event of the cross do an awful lot of work. But that only raises new questions. Does Paul really limit "new creation" imagery to an exchange of lords that takes place "over our heads," so to speak? Is not the re-creation of the human (i.e., regeneration) an event that transforms human life from within? And is this transformation but a foretaste in time of the definitive change that will take place in human beings beyond the limits of history, in the general resurrection of the dead?

I turn then to Galatians. This time my interlocutor will be Martinus de Boer, whose recent Galatians commentary extends Martyn's perspective and provides an account of the Jewish literature that is thought to have influenced Paul's thinking.

---

23. Martyn, "Apocalyptic Gospel in Galatians," 259.

Paul's Doctrine of Justification

In his 1989 essay, Martinus de Boer first set forth a distinction between two forms of Jewish apocalyptic theology available to Paul as he formed his own understanding of justification.[24] De Boer called the two forms "cosmological apocalyptic" and "forensic apocalyptic." In a second essay published in 1998, de Boer argues that the first type understands the created world to have come under enslavement to demonic powers ("fallen angels") in the time of Noah. On this view there is, however, an elect remnant who patiently awaits God's invasion of this world to engage these forces and defeat them in a cosmic war. The key text for this cosmological pattern in Jewish apocalyptic theology is *1 Enoch*. The second type is a modification of the first. Here the emphasis on anti-God powers fades into the background, and the role played by the divine election gives way to a stress on the importance of free will and human decision:

> Sin is the willful rejection of the Creator God (the breaking of the first commandment), and death is punishment for this fundamental sin. God, however, has provided the law as a remedy for this situation, and a person's posture toward the law determines his or her ultimate destiny. At the last judgment, conceptualized not as a cosmic war but as a courtroom in which all humanity appears before the bar of the judge, God will reward with eternal life those who have acknowledged his claim and chosen the law and observed its commandments (the righteous), while he will punish with eternal death those who have not (the wicked).[25]

According to de Boer, we find elements of both patterns in Paul's writings, albeit in christologically modified forms. The cosmological pattern can be seen in Paul's talk of Satan as a diabolical power opposed to God as well as in allusions to the "rulers of this age."[26] In this case the modification is not obvious since de Boer does not call attention to it. It consists in the fact that de Boer himself has no interest in angelology. His interest lies in Paul's "personification" of Sin and Death "as oppressive cosmic powers."[27] Forensic thinking, however, comes to the fore in the focus on the fall of Adam and its consequences (i.e.,

---

24. See Martinus C. de Boer, "Paul and Apocalyptic Eschatology," in *Apocalyptic and the New Testament: Essays in Honor of J. Louis Martyn*, ed. Joel Markus and Marion L. Soards, JSNTSup 24 (Sheffield: Sheffield Academic Press, 1989), 169–90. For Martyn's acceptance of this distinction and its significance for interpreting Paul, see Martyn, *Galatians*, 97n51.

25. Martinus C. de Boer, "Paul and Apocalyptic Eschatology" in *The Encyclopedia of Apocalypticism*, ed. J. J. Collins, B. J. McGinn, and S. J. Stein, 3 vols. (New York: Continuum, 1998–2000), 1:359; derived from this *Encyclopedia* by the same scholars is *The Continuum History of Apocalypticism* (New York: Continuum, 2003).

26. De Boer, "Paul and Apocalyptic Eschatology," 1:361.

27. Ibid.

death as punishment). This perspective and the understanding of God as Judge is predominant, de Boer thinks, in Romans 1:1 through 5:11. Romans 5:12–21 is a transitional passage, after which cosmological categories become predominant in chapters 6–8.[28] Indeed, for de Boer, "motifs proper to cosmological apocalyptic eschatology circumscribe and, to a large extent, overtake forensic motifs."[29] Clearly the cosmological pattern is the more significant for de Boer's "Paul"—and this, even though Paul returns to the legal language of "condemnation" in Romans 8:1, precisely at the point at which he speaks of deliverance from the "power" of Sin, spoken of expansively in Romans 7. De Boer can come to this conclusion—and this point is crucial, I think—because he finds an irruption of the cosmological already in Romans 1–5, suggesting to his mind that Paul's use of the forensic in those chapters is something of a debater's ploy. Paul, on this reading, is actually giving voice to the position of his opponents (real or imagined) so as to be able to qualify and ultimately overcome that position. Evidence for this suggestion is found in 3:9 (where Paul says that both Jews and Greeks are "under the power of sin") and Romans 3:22 and 26 (where, as de Boer thinks, Paul makes the basis of justification to lie in "the faith of Christ"). What is clear in all of this is that construal of *pistis Christou* as a subjective genitive is doing a *lot* of heavy lifting here. Conceived as an objective genitive, there would be no obvious disruption of the forensic pattern, and one would be more naturally inclined to understand the forensic pattern as the more basic of the two, interpreting the work of Christ in Romans 3 in forensic terms (with the help of a cultic image in 3:25, *hilastērion*).[30] On this showing, use of the cosmological pattern in chapters 6–8 would be understood as drawing out some implications of the foregoing account for Christian life in this world and likewise for the future of the world itself. But de Boer clearly thinks otherwise.

As in Romans, so also in Galatians. Paul makes a start, de Boer thinks, with the forensic account of justification in 2:16 and again in chapter 3. But at the decisive points (where the "faith of Christ" is introduced in 2:16 and 3:22), Paul is setting forth a "'cosmological' redefinition of the forensic-eschatological understanding of justification."[31] This might seem to imply that Paul retains at least something of the forensic, and de Boer can speak in ways suggesting that this is so. He can say, for example, that justification *also* means forgiveness.

---

28. Ibid., 364–65.
29. Ibid., 365.
30. Strong support for this reading of Romans can be found in C. E. B. Cranfield, *A Critical and Exegetical Commentary on the Epistle to the Romans* (Edinburgh: T&T Clark, 1975).
31. Martinus C. de Boer, *Galatians: A Commentary* (Louisville: Westminster John Knox, 2011), 155.

He can say that it is not a matter of "approving the righteous (those who do right by observing the law)" but rather "of accepting sinners ('the ungodly' of Rom. 4:5 and 5:6), despite their sinfulness (Rom. 3:25; 4:6–8; 5:8)." Yet Paul's conception of justification entails more, de Boer says, than the acceptance of sinners. "Justification cannot mean only 'to accept' sinners but also 'to rectify' them, to make them righteous."[32]

Parenthetically, what emerges in this last-cited passage is a recrudescence of an old typological misrepresentation of the chief difference between sixteenth-century Protestant and Catholic views of justification in terms of a contrast between the imputation and the impartation of God's righteousness. I call this a "misrepresentation" because Protestants did not, at any rate in their best moments, play imputation off against impartation. Sixteenth-century Lutherans understood the divine declaration in justification as itself an *effective word*, a word with regenerative power, so that imputation was never without an accompanying impartation.[33] The real issue between Lutherans and Catholics had to do rather with the insistence of the former that the basis for justification is always and at every moment in the Christian life to be found in "alien" (*extra nos*) righteousness of Christ.

But it turns out that de Boer's Paul makes use of the forensic only in order to establish a point of rhetorical contact with the position he wishes to overcome. He has no independent interest in it.

> The justification language is . . . that of the new preachers, not that of Paul. . . . The Paul of Galatians prefers the language of deliverance (1:4), crucifixion with Christ (2:19; 6:14), redemption (3:13; 4:5), liberation (5:1), and walking by the Spirit (5:16). This language is much more important to his own theological understanding of Christ's death and resurrection than is the language of justification. In this passage (2:15–21), he focuses on justification because of its importance to the new preachers, so that he can show them . . . that works of the law are completely *irrelevant* for justification.[34]

What are we to say to all of this? It seems to me that the whole of de Boer's reading of Paul depends for its success on his construal of *pistis Christou* as a subjective genitive in 2:16 and 3:22. It is the copestone in his arch; without it, the arch crumbles. De Boer considers four arguments in favor of taking the contended phrase as an objective genitive and seven arguments in favor of taking

---

32. Ibid.
33. Melanchthon, *Apology* 4.72: "And because 'to be justified' means that out of unrighteous people righteous people are made or regenerated, it also means that they are pronounced or regarded as righteous. For Scripture speaks both ways."
34. De Boer, *Galatians*, 165.

it as a subjective genitive.[35] It is not possible to enter into each argument here. Suffice it to say that the central argument offered by de Boer in support of the objective genitive (i.e., the construal he rejects) is already a *distortion* of the traditional reading (at least in its leading Protestant forms)—so that the case is already prejudiced in favor of the subjective genitive before de Boer turns to the seven arguments he provides in favor of his preferred alternative. The argument in question is this: "If 'works of the law' refers to a human activity, *pistis Iēsou Christou* does as well; faith is the human response to God's act of grace."[36] The problem with this way of presenting the argument for the objective genitive is that it would never have occurred to Luther to think in this way. Faith is not, for Luther, a human work to be ranged alongside observance of the law. It is a gift of God's grace, effected by the Holy Spirit in a human individual who is passive in its reception. Even more important, the service that faith performs in the act of receiving has no significance in and of itself. The significance lies altogether in that which is received. As Luther puts it in his Galatians commentary, "Faith takes hold of Christ and has Him present, enclosing Him as the ring encloses the gem."[37] In and of itself, the clasp of a ring has little or no value; its value lies in the precious jewel it holds. And in the case of "laying hold" of Christ, the righteousness of Christ *in us* could never provide an adequate basis for justification (since sanctification is never complete in this life). Only *extra nos*—only in Christ himself—is righteousness full and complete and therefore an adequate basis for justification. So when de Boer says (in *support* of his preference for the subjective genitive) that "'Faith' functions as a metonym for Christ," it must be responded that "faith" functions in Luther's theology as a metonym too. In Luther's case, justification "by faith" means, in fuller expression, by the grace of God in Jesus Christ made effective in the human individual by the Spirit through the faith that the Spirit creates. "Justification by faith" is a shorthand; the phrase cannot be taken as the complete expression of what finally is a highly complex doctrine.

In any event, if the strongest weapon in the arsenal of arguments for the subjective genitive has to do with the contrast between divine activity and human activity, then the argument is in trouble, for it rests in part on a rather serious distortion of the ways in which the objective genitive was defended in the Reformation period.

Two other arguments not considered by de Boer can be added. The first is that Paul does indeed seem to understand the presence of faith in an individual

---

35. Ibid., 149–50.
36. Ibid., 149.
37. Martin Luther, *Lectures on Galatians 1535*, in LW 26:132.

as a "condition" of the person's salvation. However true it may be that this "condition" is one the Holy Spirit effects in the individual, this "condition" will always be found in the person who is being saved. Romans 10:9–10 declares: "If you confess with your lips that Jesus is Lord and believe in your heart that God raised Him from the dead, you will be saved. For one believes with the heart and so is justified, and one confesses with the mouth and so is saved" (NRSV). I also do not think that there can be any question but that it is the individual whom Paul has in view here.

This leads me to a second point. I think that the weight born by the subjective genitive in de Boer's theology of rectification is far too great for something quite so novel. The Christian tradition (both Protestant and Catholic) stands over against it in favor of the objective genitive. And the Joint Declaration establishes "faith in Christ" as basic to the shared understanding of justification. "Together we confess: By grace alone, in faith *in* Christ's saving work and not because of any merit on our part, we are accepted by God and receive the Holy Spirit, who renews our hearts while equipping and calling us to good works."[38] The Catholic exegete Joseph Fitzmyer, himself a participant in the drafting work leading up to the Joint Declaration, takes a very traditional line on the question. In relation to both Romans 3:22 and Philippians 3:9, he takes *dia pisteōs Iēsou Christou* to mean "through faith in Jesus Christ."[39] In addition to the position adopted in the Joint Declaration, every major translation of the Bible opts for the objective genitive (NRSV, RSV, NIV, ESV, NJB, NAB; yet NRSV and NIV offer the subjective genitive in mg.). What this amounts to, it seems to me, is an ecumenical obstacle far too great to overcome. At this point the subjective genitive is simply too controversial to obtain ecclesial standing. It is an interesting proposal but nothing more. Certainly I would not wish to rest my own case for an apocalyptic reading of Paul's theology on this slender reed.

But if the case for the subjective genitive is seen to be weak, then there remains no truly compelling reason to prefer "rectification" language over "justification" language as the translation of *dikaioutai, dikaiōthōmen,* and *dikaiōthēsetai* in Galatians 2:16. I am content to stay with the NRSV: "We know that a person is justified not by the works of the law but through faith

---

38. *JDDJ*, §15, emphasis added.
39. Joseph A. Fitzmyer, SJ, "Justification by Faith in Pauline Thought," in Aune, ed., *Rereading Paul Together*, 87. Given this translation, it is not surprising that Fitzmyer should affirm an understanding of justification lacking nothing that a traditionally minded Protestant might ask for: "When Paul speaks of Christ Jesus justifying the sinner, he means that because of the Christ-event the sinner stands before God's tribunal and hears a verdict of 'not guilty.' . . . The sinner is pronounced *dikaios* (Rom. 5:7) and stands before God's tribunal as 'righteous, acquitted.'" See ibid., 84.

in Jesus Christ." In my view, there is no irruption of the cosmological into Paul's forensic account of the saving significance of Christ's death in Romans 3:21–26. And the phrase "under the power of sin" in Romans 3:9 would then also rightly be seen as having to do with sin's power to condemn, to render one guilty and worthy of condemnation. And if that much is correct, then it also is not surprising for Paul to say that, in Christ's death, God was condemning sin in the flesh (Rom. 8:3).

Now none of what has been said thus far constitutes a straightforward victory for the Protestant doctrine of justification in its sixteenth-century forms. Nor does it require that we abandon apocalyptic readings altogether. By no means! In my opinion, a certain kind of apocalyptic thinking has the potential for enriching the traditional Protestant conception considerably. The one great impulse given to justification theology by the (in itself misguided) emphasis on the subjective genitive is how it honors the fact that Paul regards our justification as complete in Christ's death—and I add, in his resurrection. This is something that was not grasped in the sixteenth century. My own view is that what happens in the bestowal of faith on an individual does not add anything to the justification that is achieved in Christ, nor does it even make that work effective.[40] What happens as we believe is that we begin to live from and toward *the Christ in whom justification is already fully effective*. Christ became for us wisdom, righteousness, sanctification, and redemption, Paul says in 1 Corinthians 1:30. And so Martyn and de Boer are right to lay great emphasis upon a "turn of the ages" in Christ, the passing of the present age and the coming of "new creation." But rather than submerging justification into new creation (by redefining justification as rectification in order to bring it into line with the latter), what I think we find in Paul is the exact opposite: the divine verdict of "justification" pronounced in the raising of Christ from the dead (Rom. 4:25) is itself creative word.[41] Christ is raised to die no more. "New creation" is therefore a function of the resurrection. "Justification" is (dare I say?) the master term (encompassing both the death and resurrection of Christ), and "new creation" needs to be understood as derivative of it (just

---

40. The most basic question to be answered in Christian soteriology is this: is what Christ accomplishes the *reality* of reconciliation/redemption or merely the *possibility* of it—a possibility that is realized only at the point at which the Holy Spirit awakens us to faith in Christ? My own view—one that I share with apocalyptic interpreters of Paul—is that Christ accomplishes the reality of reconciliation/redemption. Hence, it is already effective for those who are elect and who are, therefore, present in Christ when he does what he does—*before* they are made to be aware of it.

41. Cf. Peter Stuhlmacher, *Revisiting Paul's Doctrine of Justification* (Downers Grove, IL: InterVarsity, 2001), 61: "The event of justification implies an act of *creation*. In justification God is active as the Creator 'who calls into existence things which do not exist' (Rom. 4:17)."

as God's turning toward us in mercy and grace are logically prior to the effects of that turning in us).

If, then, we cannot follow Martyn and de Boer in reading the "cosmological pattern" into the saving event itself, what are we to do? What is the *nature* of justification? What is its most fundamental meaning? And when does it take place? How are past and future related to the present?

The place to begin, in seeking answers to these questions, is with Christology. That Christ simply *is* our righteousness (1 Cor. 1:30) and that he was raised for our justification (Rom. 4:25) strongly suggest that the resurrection is an event of vindication and acceptance, the divine verdict pronounced on the sinless Jesus. No one would question that this acceptance is complete, full, and entire. But that then means that it is a verdict of "not guilty"—an *acquittal* in his case and precisely *not* the forgiveness of sins. Of what might Christ be forgiven? He was obedient to the point of death, and "therefore God also highly exalted him and gave him the name that is above every name, so that at the name of Jesus every knee should bend" (Phil. 2:9–10 NRSV). This Jesus stood in no need of forgiveness. He was acquitted at the bar of God's judgment. What we see in the resurrection, I think, is the irruption into time of the final judgment. The judgment that will be universally proclaimed at the end of time has already fallen upon Jesus.

But if acquittal is basic to the meaning of justification as applied to the One in whom we too are justified, then how can it be that the *ungodly* (Rom. 4:5) are justified? "Forgiveness" we could well understand. The traditional Protestant understanding of justification has been presented often enough in terms of a nonimputation of our own sins (i.e., God chooses not to hold them against us) and a positive imputation of Christ's (human) righteousness (i.e., God "credits" to us or "covers us" with the righteousness of Christ). And I have to admit that such a construction is not completely alien to Paul's thinking. He does have a place for it (see, e.g., Rom. 4:7). But the place he gives it, I suggest, is *provisional*. It is not yet the *final* judgment but is something like a holding action, an interim arrangement, until ungodliness has completely passed out of existence; until, that is to say, the "old Adam" is no more. The problem with the Protestant doctrine in its traditional form is not merely that it looks like a "legal fiction." That too is a problem, one not completely dealt with simply by making the divine declaration to be an "effective" (regenerating) word. But that is not the most basic problem. The most basic problem is that this view makes God seem arbitrary. God *chooses* not to impute our sins. God *chooses* to cover us with Christ's righteousness. If we ask *why* God does this, we would likely respond, "Because he has entered into a covenant of grace with the human race and is faithful to the promises made in that covenant." But why then does God enter into a covenant of this nature? Sooner or later, our "why" questions reach an end, a point at which no further reason for God's actions can be given. Heiko Oberman was not wrong, then, to seek the roots of the Protestant understanding of justification in medieval nominalism.[42] But if now we were to understand God's choices as limited to the *means* he selects for accomplishing an end that he has not chosen but is simply given in what God is (and in how God is what God is), then the specter of the arbitrary disappears. "Covering" as an interim arrangement is indeed a choice, but it is a choice that has no ultimacy. But then, if "forgiveness of sins" (and the "covering" that makes it possible) is only an interim arrangement, if it has no ultimate significance, then we must dig a bit deeper. It is precisely here, I think, that apocalyptic helps.

The final judgment that has fallen upon Jesus is not simply a judgment on him; it also is a judgment on us. That Christ's death is a faithful death is certainly true. But what is it that Christ's faithfulness leads him to do? It leads Jesus to die the death of a sinner. God "made him who knew no sin to be sin" (2 Cor. 5:21) so that he might "condemn sin in the flesh" (Rom. 8:3). The death of Jesus Christ is the death *of the sinner*, the complete and total destruction not only of sin but also of the sinner. In Christ, the sinner is no more. In us, the sinner continues to exist, of course, as (we might say) the ongoing effects of a socially mediated sinfulness that was already at work in the world before the sinner was put to death on the cross—which is why God sets up an interim arrangement. But the *being* of the sinner has already been destroyed; thus the existence that is now ours is impossible and has no future. God has already put the sinner out of the way: that is the apocalypse of the righteousness of God that has prevailed and will prevail in the final judgment.

So then, justification as the judgment of acquittal pronounced on the elect on the final day requires two things: (1) the death of the sinner in the crucifixion of Christ and (2) "new creation" in his resurrection. The crucifixion of Jesus and his resurrection must be seen *together* as providing the basis for God's just judgment of acquittal on the last day. Thus the situation of the (formerly) ungodly believer in time is framed by a twofold ultimacy. Behind her (or him) lies her death as sinner; before her lies her "new creation" in the general resurrection of the dead. In the interim, her trust in God's promise is "reckoned to her as righteousness." She is not yet what she will be; she is not yet the person who can *rightly* be pronounced acquitted. But God regards her

---

42. Heiko Augustinus Oberman, *The Harvest of Medieval Theology: Gabriel Biel and Late Medieval Nominalism* (Durham, NC: Labyrinth, 1983).

for even now as if she were because her end is already known to him. And since the "as if" here has no ultimacy, God's truthfulness cannot be questioned.

Seen in this light, several elements in Galatians 3:6–14 and 5:4–5 become more easily explained than would otherwise be the case. By his overall account of "rectification," de Boer was placed in the position of having to undermine (if not set aside) the analogy that Paul sets up in 3:6 between Abraham and the believer in Christ. "Abraham," de Boer says, "is not for Paul the model of believers in Christ."[43] But it seems, on the face of it, that this is precisely what Paul is saying (once one has decided the dispute over the objective and the subjective genitive on the side of the objective). As the NRSV puts it, "Just as Abraham 'believed God, and it was reckoned to him as righteousness,' so, you see, those who believe are descendants of Abraham" (3:6). The believer is surely "like" Abraham because she does what Abraham did: she believes a promise that is directed toward an as yet unrealized end. True, the end of all things has broken into time in the cross and resurrection of Christ. But the believer in the promise contained in the Christ event has not yet been re-created in such a way that she can no longer sin. Only the general resurrection of the dead can and will accomplish that. For now, she believes the promise and trusts the One who makes it—and this trusting belief is reckoned to her "as" the righteousness that will be hers when she has been completely remade.

This way of understanding justification also helps us understand Paul's reference to a "final justification" in Galatians 5:5. "For through the Spirit, by faith, we eagerly wait for the hope of righteousness" (NRSV). The "righteousness" of the believer lies behind her and before her—and it will not do to curtail either part of the frame that Paul places around the believing existence of the Christian in time.

Barth's Contribution to an Apocalyptic Understanding of Forensic Justification

The forensic framework of Reformation theology had two anchors: the twin doctrines of atonement and justification. Where the later Barth's relationship

---

43. De Boer, *Galatians*, 191. Cf. 190: "We must stress that Abraham provides *only* an analogy, and a rough one at that, for believers in Christ. It cannot be pressed too far, for obvious reasons. The 'believing' of Christians involves (1) trust in (2) Christ (*pisteuein* + *eis*), whereas the 'believing' of Abraham involves (1) giving credence to (2) God (*pisteuein* + dative). The 'believing' is thus not only different in kind from that of Abraham; it is also directed to Christ, not to God." The claim that the "believing" in question on each side of the analogy is "different in kind" would leave us with no analogy at all, and in any event, trusting and giving credence stand in a relation of reciprocity here, not opposition.

to these Reformation doctrines is concerned, the decisive questions are two: (1) In what ways did he see it necessary to modify the received doctrines? (2) What makes his later doctrine of justification "apocalyptic"? I have written extensively on the first of these problems and do not need to repeat that here.[44] A summary of the major points suffices. I take up the doctrine of atonement first since a discussion of the modifications introduced by Barth into that doctrine will help us to see not only his ongoing commitment to a genuinely *Protestant* conception but also how he was able to address the chief concerns of those who render *pistis Christou* as a subjective genitive—without committing himself to that rendering. I will then turn (very briefly) to Barth's treatment of justification and conclude with a few remarks on Barth's theological ontology.

Atonement

For Barth, the most significant question to be asked in Christian soteriology is this: is what Christ achieves the reality of reconciliation/redemption or merely its possibility, a possibility that is finally made effective only at the point at which the Holy Spirit awakens an individual to faith and obedience? Barth's answer is clear: what Christ accomplishes is the *reality* of reconciliation/redemption; all that belongs to human salvation (including, of course, justification) is already fully realized *and effectual* for all *in its accomplishment*.[45] It does not need to be "applied" or even "mediated" by the Holy Spirit—which means that the Spirit's work is not salvific in the strict sense. As the Spirit awakens an individual to faith in Christ, the Spirit enables her to *acknowledge* the reality and efficacy of Christ's work on her behalf and to make that acknowledgment basic to her lived existence in this world. Though her faith in Christ contributes nothing to making Christ's work effective for her, faith as acknowledgment will always be found in those who are finally redeemed.

Seen in this light, the "christological objectivism" that Richard Hays was aiming for with his recentering of justification in the event of Christ's faithfulness is secured by Barth in an even more thoroughgoing and self-consistent way. Hays, after all, still needed for those who come after Christ to be "incorporated" into Christ's faithfulness through baptism—which undermines the "already-efficacious" element in Barth's reading of Paul.[46] The Martyn school has a decided advantage over Hays at precisely this point in that their

---

44. See Bruce L. McCormack, "*Justitia Aliena*: Karl Barth in Conversation with the Evangelical Doctrine of Imputed Righteousness," in *Justification in Perspective: Historical Developments and Contemporary Challenges*, ed. Bruce L. McCormack (Grand Rapids: Baker Academic, 2006), 167–96.

45. Karl Barth, *Church Dogmatics* (CD), IV/2 (2000): 507.

46. Hays, *Faith of Jesus Christ*, xxix, xxxi.

"christological objectivism" is more complete than his—which brings them within hailing distance of even the later Barth. And yet important differences remain, differences that emerge most clearly into the light of day when Barth's thinking is understood in its historical development.

For the early Barth of the second edition of his commentary on Romans (1922), the work of Christ is subsumed largely into the category of revelation (*apocalypsis*). In that Jesus died a death to all human possibilities in his death on the cross and was raised by his Father, he revealed the true God—a God whose very being means the negation and reconstitution of all things.[47] This revelation is the turning of the ages; it is the proclamation that this world stands under the sign of death, that the "new world" is God's alone to bring. Revelation simply is reconciliation for Barth at this stage. The person who acknowledges God's self-revelation in Christ surrenders all that she has and is and lives in expectation of what God alone can and will do. Barth sets this constellation of ideas forth with the help of vivid images, many of which have been drawn from the sphere of military conquest. And so it should come as no surprise that at this stage of his development, Barth stood closest to the Martyn "school"—and its "members" can, with considerable legitimacy, lay claim to the early Barth's perspective on Paul as an anticipation of their own work. But it also has to be said that their weakness was his—and his long before it was theirs. Barth too had at that time no way to explain the relation of divine action to human action, and therefore no way to explain how one man's death could be the act of God that triumphs over sin, death, and the devil.

Without forgetting the lessons he had learned through his intensive engagement with Paul's Letter to the Romans, Barth began—just three years later—to lay the groundwork for a dogmatics.[48] For the first time he began to elaborate a doctrine of the incarnation and the rudiments of a doctrine of the Trinity. As he did so, he continued to wrestle with Paul. But he also listened to a host of other

---

47. Karl Barth, *Der Römerbrief, 1922* (Zurich: Theologischer Verlag Zürich, 1940), 72; ET, *The Epistle to the Romans* (Oxford: Oxford University Press, 1968), 97:

> At the high point, at the goal of His way, He is a purely negative magnitude; not a genius, not the bearer of manifest or hidden psychic powers, not a hero, a leader, a poet or thinker and precisely in this negation ("My God, my God, why have you abandoned me?"), precisely in that He *sacrifices* every brilliant, psychic, heroic, aesthetic, philosophical, every thinkable human possibility whatsoever to an impossible *more*, to an unintuitable *Other*, He is the One who fulfills to the uttermost those mounting human possibilities born witness to in the law and the prophets. *Therefore*, God exalted Him, *therein* is He recognized as the Christ, *thereby* He becomes the light of the last things which shines forth above everyone and everything. Truly we see in Him God's faithfulness in the depths of hell. The Messiah is the end of the human. There too, precisely there, God is faithful. The new day of the righteousness of God wants to dawn with the day of the "sublated" human. (my translation)

48. See Karl Barth, *The Göttingen Dogmatics*, vol. 1 (Grand Rapids: Eerdmans, 1990).

voices—above all, the voice of the Reformers, of whom he knew little when writing his commentary. His thinking about the atonement also experienced considerable development—*initially* (up through *Church Dogmatics* II/1) in the direction of penal substitution.[49] The final step forward was taken with his revision of the doctrine of election in *Church Dogmatics* II/2. Here for the first time he began to articulate the ontological conditions in God for the possibility that God makes himself the subject of the human experience of death in the event of the cross. And so, the stage was set for the emergence of the later Barth's understanding of the work of Christ in volume IV of the *Dogmatics*, an understanding that moved well beyond the older penal substitutionary theories of the Reformers. The later Barth's doctrine of the atonement constitutes a modification of Calvin's forensic understanding by means of what we might think of as an "apocalyptic supplement." For him, Christ not only bears the *guilt* of human sinfulness in his death; he also has himself been "made sin" (2 Cor. 5:21). The supplement offered by Barth has to do with his belief that what takes place in the cross is nothing less than the destruction of the sinner as such. The very being of sin is dealt with in Christ's death.[50] Such a view stands in close proximity to what de Boer describes as "forensic apocalypticism."[51]

The later Barth not only shares with this form of apocalyptic the thought that final judgment takes place in a courtroom setting; even more important, he also agrees that the judicial verdict rendered in the event of the cross is eschatological and therefore definitive and final. The one remaining difference between the later Barth and "forensic apocalyptic" lies in the fact that Barth thinks this has happened in the midst of time rather than bringing the curtain down on history as we know and experience it. What has taken place in the cross and resurrection of Christ is, for him, a turning of the ages; the old has passed away, new things have come. That much he had said before, of course. But now it is explained by means of a judicial understanding of the atonement, which has been deepened by being joined to a theological ontology that finds its root in the doctrine of election. We can best understand this if we look in two directions: first, how Christ is "made sin" for us, and second, how we are made to be "righteous."

First, then, how is Christ "made sin" for us? John Calvin answered, "Through the mechanism of imputation."[52] The guilt of human sin is "transferred" to

49. Barth, *CD* II/1:390–406.
50. Ibid., 253–54.
51. In saying this, I am obviously suggesting that, for Barth, "forensic apocalyptic" was not the position of Paul's opponents but of Paul himself.
52. See John Calvin, *Institutes* 2.16.5: "This is our acquittal: the guilt that held us liable for punishment has been transferred to the head of the Son of God." And 2.16.6: "'The Lord has

the God-human—probably at the point when Christ says in the garden, "Not my will, but yours be done." Barth's answer looks in a different direction. In his soteriology, the doctrine of election does all the heavy lifting that the idea of imputation had done for Calvin. The God-human does not need to have the guilt that accrues to the sins of the elect imputed to him; he already is "the sinner" by virtue of God's eternal choosing of himself in Christ to be the "reprobate" human. God chooses reprobation as his portion so that it will not be ours.[53] Thus Christ is "made sin" already in election. His embrace of the full consequences of human sinfulness (suffering, death, and perdition) is the concrete realization in time of what the God-human already *is* in pretemporal eternity—by way of anticipation. Moreover, Christ's embrace of the full consequences of sin is the medium by means of which God takes these human experiences up into himself in order there, in his own being as God, to bring an end to them. In putting it this way, I am suggesting that sin is not simply "paid for" but indeed destroyed.

Second, Barth's doctrine of election also provides the answer to problems surrounding "incorporation" into Christ's "story." Given that human beings are elected "in Christ," they do not have to be "engrafted" into him at a later point in time. They were already "in" Christ when he suffered, died, and was raised. The death that he dies to bring an end to the sinner is already our death *in that it takes place in him.* And the new creation effected by the verdict of the Father is already effective for them in advance of their own final resurrection.

In sum, Barth's treatment of the atoning work of Christ operates completely within the judicial frame of reference preferred by the Reformers. But the phrase "penal substitution" is not finally adequate to describe his view. Barth can certainly say that a "sentence" has been executed in Christ's death—and he does so frequently.[54] So he is still operating primarily within the constraints of courtroom imagery. But he understands the death of Christ as bringing an end to sin as such, as removing its ontological ground so that its ongoing existence in this world has been made an "impossible possibility"—a possibility still realized but that has no future. In pursuing this line of thought, he has deepened, clarified, and modified the Reformers' understanding of "penal substitution." He has also addressed the concerns of the *pistis Christou* crowd without following them in their rendering of that disputed phrase. Faith *in* Christ is still necessary if one is to live in acknowledgment of what has been accomplished in Christ. But faith does not make the work of Christ effective.

---

laid on him the iniquity of us all' [Isa. 53:6 NRSV]. That is, he who was about to cleanse the filth of those iniquities was covered with them by transferred imputation."

53. See Barth, *CD* II/2:122, 353.
54. See, e.g., Barth, *CD* IV/1:219, 221, 223.

Justification

The basic meaning of "justification" for Barth is what the Protestants in the later stages of the Reformation (after 1550) said it was, namely, *acquittal*, a verdict of innocence. But for him, unlike the Reformers, the verdict in question is pronounced in the resurrection of Jesus. We are already what we will be eschatologically, but we are this only *in Christ*. In him, we have died as sinners. In him, we have been raised and made new. No imputation of Christ's righteousness is necessary because we are the "new creation" in Christ's already-effective work. For Barth as for Paul, justification requires that the sinner be subjected to that death that is the penalty for sin and be re-created in Christ's resurrection. Basic to both is the divine judgment: a sentence of death in one direction and a verdict of innocence in the other. We might extend Barth's thinking just a bit further, and thereby bring even greater clarity into it, if we said that the divine verdict of innocence is itself an "effective word," a word that creates what it declares. To put it this way is to make God's justifying verdict the effective cause of new creation. And to say that much brings Barth very much into line with the insistence of the Reformers on the centrality of the doctrine.

Theological Ontology

Unlike the apocalyptic readers of Paul, Barth does have a theological ontology that grounds and makes sense of the moves he has made. In his view, election is an eternal act of God with ontological significance for both God and the human. First on the side of God: election is an eternal act of *self-determination* on the part of God that makes its content essential to him.[55] If this act of "making essential" is not to introduce a mutation into God's being already in pretemporal eternity, in God's turning toward the world in his electing grace, then the divine "essence" cannot be thought of as in any way preceding this act but rather as given and established in it. There is nothing behind this act, no empty space in which God is at rest in himself in an "undetermined" mode of existence.[56] God is not "at first" undetermined and "then" (subsequently) determined—for God is never without this determination for the covenant of grace. The eternal act of divine self-determination is the eternal life-act of God. God is never without this determination of his being, for it is proper to him.

---

55. On this point, see Barth, *CD* II/2:100: "In respect of the whole attitude and being of God *ad extra*, in His relationship with the order created by Him, can there be anything higher or more distinctive *and essential* in God than His electing?" (emphasis added).

56. Ibid.

Now if that justification of the ungodly that is the outworking of the covenant of grace is understood to be essential to God, then we will already have removed the fundamental objection that might rightly have been brought against the Protestant doctrine in its classical, sixteenth-century forms, the objection that it makes God "arbitrary." Given that God is never without the "determination" given in election, justification as the means by which the ends established in election are realized in time cannot be arbitrary. The ends of all God's activities are given in the very nature of God as self-giving love. No hint of arbitrariness remains.

But election is also basic to what it means to be truly "human." The true human, the real human, is Jesus Christ, crucified, risen, and exalted. No longer is it necessary to think of the divine verdict as something that happens over the heads of those men and women who are awakened to its reality and efficacy. It is something that happens to them in Christ.

Could this theological ontology be appropriated by those working with a soteriology of cosmic warfare to provide an answer to the unresolved question of the relation of divine action to the human action of Jesus's faithfulness? Perhaps. But there is a large obstacle in the way, for this ontology was generated while working within a judicial frame of reference. That something else—the military metaphors—could be made basic to Christian soteriology and still generate this theological ontology is doubtful.

Conclusion

What I have shown in this essay is that everything the defenders of the subjective genitive have tried to accomplish with their rendering of *pistis Christou* can be accomplished without it. And these aims can be accomplished without losing contact with the Reformation—or with the Joint Declaration for that matter. The Joint Declaration strikes the right note when it says, "We confess together that sinners are justified by faith in the saving action of God in Christ. . . . Whatever in the justified precedes or follows the free gift of faith is neither the basis of justification nor merits it."[57]

I conclude with an observation and a question. There can be no question but that significant progress has been made on the ecumenical front even as the Protestant churches, especially in North America, have drifted further and further and further away from their confessional moorings—which has certainly contributed to widening the gap between official teachings on the

---

57. *JDDJ*, §25.

one side and the content of the lived faith of theologians, ministers, and laity on the other. Our churches today are characterized by doctrinal fragmentation and even chaos. Confessing the faith together is becoming harder and harder to do. The question is posed: if we could correct Reformational teaching without contributing further to the doctrinal chaos in our churches, why wouldn't we do so? The later Barth has already provided us with a good example of how this might be done.

PART 2

Gospel

11

The Singularity of the Gospel Revisited

BEVERLY ROBERTS GAVENTA

Among recent developments in the study of Galatians, John Riches's history of interpretation warrants our sustained attention both for the information it gathers together and for Riches's own sagacious reflections. Particularly instructive are the concluding observations regarding the challenge posed by the end of the second chapter of the letter. Riches writes that interpreters are not only obliged to attend "to the sharp contrast which Paul makes between 'works of the Law' and faith in Christ as the means of securing 'righteousness'" but they must also attend to the "language of participation and mystical union which [Paul] uses to describe the relation between Christ and the believer in the last part of the chapter."[1] The challenge is not simply how to explicate each set of statements on its own, the first regarding the means of justification (or rectification),[2] and the second regarding Paul's death and life in Christ;

---

1. John Riches, *Galatians through the Centuries*, BBC (Oxford: Blackwell, 2008), 137. In context, Riches is criticizing E. P. Sanders for his treatment of both parts of the tension. He contends that Sanders "downplays" the discussion of justification and then declares Gal. 2:19–20 to be "beyond our comprehension." See also 106, where Riches observes that an interesting feature of the discussion of 2:11–21 is "the different weightings which the various commentators give to the two themes in this passage."

2. For the translation "rectify" and "rectification," see J. Louis Martyn, *Galatians*, AB 33A (New York: Doubleday, 1997), 249–50. F. Gerald Downing, although not endorsing the translation

the challenge includes that of accounting for these two sets of statements *in relationship to each other*.

This essay takes up that last challenge in particular, namely, how these two important moments in the argument of Galatians are to be understood in relationship to each other. I suggest that the movement from the beginning of this passage to its ending reflects my title, "the singularity of the gospel." The gospel's singularity has to do not only with its being single (as only one gospel) but also with its singular, all-encompassing action in the lives of human beings. The gospel claims all that a human is; the gospel becomes the locus of human identity; the gospel replaces the old cosmos. Both senses of the word "singularity" are required in order to appreciate the radical and radically troubling character of this letter.

A Single Gospel

Some years ago I adopted the phrase "the singularity of the gospel" from the important and often-overlooked work of John Schütz, *Paul and the Anatomy of Apostolic Authority*.[3] He employs it, as one might expect, for Paul's sharp remarks in Galatians 1:6–9. In a narrow lexical sense, the assertion that there is no other "gospel" is nonsensical, since there can be all sorts of good news. The contrast in verse 6, however, delimits Paul's use of the term. The Galatians are turning "*from* [ἀπό] the one who called you through the gift of Christ" and "*to* [εἰς] another gospel." Implicitly, then, the gospel is God's act of calling in the gift of Christ, which has already been explicated in 1:4: Christ "gave himself on behalf of our sins to rescue us from the present evil age." The gospel is not simply a good report of one sort or another but the *specific action* of God in Jesus Christ to rescue humanity.

If verse 6 implies that there *might* be another gospel, verse 7 adamantly denies it. ὃ οὐκ ἔστιν ἄλλο: there is no such thing as another gospel. And anyone who preaches this nonexistent gospel is anathema.

The contrast of verse 6 between "God who called you" and the nonexistent

---

"rectify," offers evidence that coheres with this translation: "Justification as Acquittal? A Critical Examination of Judicial Verdicts in Paul's Literary and Actual Contexts," *CBQ* 74 (2012): 298–318.

3. John Schütz, *Paul and the Anatomy of Apostolic Authority*, NTL (1975; Louisville: Westminster John Knox, 2007), 123. Wayne Meeks's introduction to the NTL edition helpfully situates Schütz's work in the landscape of NT scholarship (xiii–xxiv). My own earlier essay with much the same title as here ("The Singularity of the Gospel," in *Our Mother Saint Paul* [Louisville: Westminster John Knox, 2007], 101–11) was an exploration of the theology of Galatians focused on the "single" gospel and its exclusive claims but without attending to the dual sense of singularity taken up in the present essay.

"other" gospel preached by the "troublers" is reinforced throughout the remainder of Galatians 1. Paul is not a pleaser of human beings but a "slave of Christ" (v. 10). He did not receive the gospel through any human source or method but through ἀποκάλυψις Ἰησοῦ Χριστοῦ (1:11–12). When he was earlier zealous for "the traditions of my fathers," he was also trying to destroy God's own ἐκκλησία (1:13–14).[4] God's apocalyptic revelation to him required no supplement or modification in Jerusalem and received none (1:15–23). This reading is consistent with J. Louis Martyn's observations about the contrast between human and divine action.[5]

Such a contrast continues in the early lines of Galatians 2. When he went to Jerusalem again after fourteen years, it was not to submit "the truth of the gospel" for modification by other humans but to see it confirmed, as indeed it was (at least in Paul's account of events).

The harmonious understanding between Paul and the Jerusalem contingent vanishes from the text with the ὅτε δέ of 2:11, and it is at this point we learn why Paul has so relentlessly contrasted divine and human action, the "true" gospel with some "other" gospel that is simultaneously preached by some and impossible to imagine. In Antioch, under pressure from associates of James, Peter and other Jews, including even Barnabas, withdrew from table fellowship with gentiles. Paul characterizes this act as nothing less than failure to conform to "the truth of the gospel";[6] in verse 14 he recounts his challenge to Peter. But with verse 15, as is widely acknowledged, there is a subtle shift. Here Paul simultaneously addresses both Peter in Antioch and some other teachers in the Galatian churches.[7] These teachers insist that God rectifies human beings through the combination of law observance *and* Christ's faith-creating faithful death, so that gentiles must be circumcised and follow the law. Paul, by contrast, insists that God rectifies through Christ's faith-creating faithful death[8] and only through that single event.

---

4. As John M. G. Barclay notes, the only time God is referred to in Gal. 1:13–14 is in connection with God's church, "to which Paul was vehemently *opposed*" ("Paul's Story: Theology as Testimony," in *Narrative Dynamics in Paul: A Critical Assessment*, ed. Bruce W. Longenecker [Louisville: Westminster John Knox, 2002], 138).

5. Martyn, *Galatians*, 146–48, and often elsewhere.

6. The phrase "the truth of the gospel" appears only in Gal. 2:5, 14 and Col. 1:5, nowhere else in the NT.

7. For the term "the Teachers," see Martyn, *Galatians*, 117–26. As Martyn observes, this term is more neutral than "opponents" or even "agitators" and has the additional advantage of conveying their missional activity, which is not simply that of opposing Paul or stirring up opposition to Paul.

8. This paragraph of course leaps over vast interpretive problems, none of which can be addressed here. Among them is the highly contested question of how to translate the phrase πίστις Χριστοῦ. In this essay, I am employing neither the subjective "faith/faithfulness of Christ," nor

Galatians 2:16, then, gives us a glimpse of what this other gospel looks like, the one that does not exist but that some actually have proclaimed.[9] And the singular gospel that Paul preaches, which he refers to as the "truth of the gospel," is Christ-faith alone. The remainder of the letter explicates this single gospel, Christ-faith alone. The Galatians did not receive the Spirit by means of law-observance but through the message that elicited faith (3:1–5).[10] Both Abraham himself and those who are blessed with the promise to Abraham are those ἐκ πίστεως rather than law (3:6–9). Christ is the *single* offspring of Abraham (3:15). It is those who are in Christ Jesus who are the sons and daughters of God (3:26). Law observance is not merely *not required*; rather, gentile submission to Jewish law observance as though that were salvific completely negates the gift of Christ (5:1–5).[11] Repeatedly, then, Paul follows through with this insistence on the single gospel of Christ.

Singularity Reinterpreted

Although various students of Paul would describe this singular gospel in Galatians in different ways, the broad outlines of the previous paragraphs pertaining to the single gospel of Christ might not be too sharply contested. Yet the letter pushes further, introducing a second, more radical, and more disturbing sense in which Paul is advocating a singular gospel.

---

the objective "faith in Christ," but the admittedly cumbersome "faith-creating faithful death." This decision reflects a growing discomfort with the hard lines of the discussion as well as an increasing appreciation for the wisdom of Morna Hooker's earlier argument that the phrase occurs in contexts characterized by what she terms "participation" language ("Πίστις Χριστοῦ," NTS 35 [1989]: 321–42). Particularly in Rom. 3:26, the phrase becomes a shorthand expression for those who have been grasped by the gospel of Jesus Christ.

9. For a particularly insightful explication of the crucial 2:16, see the recent commentary of Martinus C. de Boer, *Galatians*, NTL (Louisville: Westminster John Knox, 2011), 141–56, as well as his essay "Paul's Use and Interpretation of a Justification Tradition in Galatians 2.15–21," *JSNT* 28 (2005): 89–216. De Boer contends that 2:16a is a statement susceptible to agreement by both sides, but with two entirely different meanings. The Teachers have insisted, "No human is made right from law observance *if not* also through the faith-creating faithful death of Jesus Christ." Paul, however, interprets the ἐὰν μή as the equivalent of the English "but." On de Boer's understanding, then, the remainder of v. 16 is Paul's interpretation of v. 16a, an interpretation that runs directly counter to that of the Teachers. For my argument, de Boer's reading is not crucial, but it does highlight the starkness of the contrast made here.

10. The phrase ἐξ ἀκοῆς πίστεως is notoriously difficult to translate. For the rendering offered here, see BDAG 36; Martyn, *Galatians*, 284–89; and de Boer, *Galatians*, 174–84. Crucial to the discussion is Rom. 10:16.

11. The severity of Paul's response is significant. This becomes clear when we imagine (as I did for solely heuristic purposes in "The Singularity of the Gospel," 104–6) the suggestion of a compromise between Paul and the Teachers.

The Singularity of the Gospel Revisited 191

Here we return to 2:16. As indicated earlier, and this also appears to be relatively noncontroversial, 2:16—or perhaps 2:15–18—provides us with the explanation for Paul's rigorous insistence in 1:6–9 that there is only one gospel and that the gospel cannot be interpreted as part of a larger complex of beliefs or traditions. In his view, what the other teachers have offered in the Galatian congregations is not simply incorrect; it actually amounts not only to a different but also to a false gospel. Paul's response is to insist that there is only one gospel and that gospel consists of God's making humanity right, delivering humanity from the grip of the present evil age, through the faithful death of Jesus Christ and only through the faithful death of Jesus Christ.

But if that is the answer to the question, if that is what Paul means by "only one gospel," then what is to be said about the final lines of Galatians 2? Verse 21 recapitulates verses 15–16, casting in first-person singular the claim that rectification comes through Jesus Christ and not through the law. But what is to be said of verses 19 and 20? Why are these statements needed, and what relationship do they bear to the lines that precede?[12] This is where Riches's comment mentioned at the outset has worked its way under my skin.

In my judgment, 2:19–20 are often minimized by restricting their sphere of reference either to the personal or to the mystical. This is the case not only in Schweitzer's interpretation of Paul's mysticism but also in other interpreters as well.[13] Lightfoot and Burton, for example, refer to these lines in "spiritual" terms.[14] Dunn sees these verses as reflecting the "very radical nature of the personal transformation effected by" Paul's conversion and uses the term "mystical," although with some caution.[15]

How would we go about doing justice to these verses, resisting the urge to underinterpret them? Taking them seriously begins with noticing the shift of linguistic register that takes place here. The language of sin(ners) and rectification saturates verses 15–18:

> We are Jews by nature and not gentile sinners.
> No human is rectified by law observance,
> so that we might be rectified out of the faithfulness of Christ.
> No flesh is rectified. . . .

---

12. See Scott Shauf's remarks on the scholarly tendency to treat 2:20 in isolation from its context, in "Galatians 2.20 in Context," *NTS* 52 (2006): 86–101, esp. 86–88.

13. Albert Schweitzer, *The Mysticism of Paul the Apostle*, trans. William Montgomery (New York: Seabury, 1931), esp. 3, 125, 225. See also Riches's discussion of 2:20 in the mystical tradition, in *Galatians through the Centuries*, 137–43.

14. J. B. Lightfoot, *The Epistle of St. Paul to the Galatians* (1890; Grand Rapids: Zondervan, 1957), 119; E. D. Burton, *The Epistle to the Galatians*, ICC (Edinburgh: T&T Clark, 1920), 136.

15. James D. G. Dunn, *The Epistle to the Galatians*, BNTC (London: A&C Black, 1993), 145.

> If we who seek to be rectified in Christ are found—we ourselves!—to
> be sinners,
> does that make Christ a servant of sin?
> Again I make myself a transgressor. . . .

By contrast, it is the language of life and death that dominates verses 19–20:

> I died to the law through the law, that I might live to God.
> I have been crucified with Christ.
> It is no longer I who live, but Christ lives in me.
> The life I now live in the flesh, I live in faith. . . .

With 2:21, rectification language returns, of course, but at present it is important to consider the content and significance of this linguistic shift.

Verse 19 opens with "For through the law I died to the law, so that I might live to God" (NRSV). Much discussion focuses on what specifically Paul has in view with the phrases "through the law" and "to the law." However this question is resolved, after verse 19a, νόμος is not mentioned again in verses 19–20.

Having said "I died that I might live," one might expect the next statement to be about that new life, to give some hint of its character. Paul will get to that point in 2:20bc, but first he asserts, "I have been crucified with Christ." In one sense, this statement repeats and reinforces the preceding line, but the differences between the two lines are also revealing. First, "I died" could simply mean that "I gave up my life" or "I died of natural causes" or even "the law put me to death" (given the "through the law" modifier attached to "I died"). With the claim that "I have been crucified together with Christ," no voluntary or natural interpretation is possible. To have been crucified is to have been killed, to have been killed with violence, and to have been killed by a hostile power.[16]

David Aune's important study of the Hellenistic philosophical "practice of death" (*commentatio mortis*) reinforces this contrast between the claim "I died" and the claim "I have been crucified."[17] Aune traces the commonplace among the moral philosophers, going back to Plato, that philosophers "study

---

16. It is difficult to agree with van Kooten's statement that Paul here is "imitating Christ" by metaphorically adopting "Christ's way of dying and living." At least as he describes the situation, Paul is acted upon ("crucified with Christ") rather than imitating (George H. van Kooten, *Paul's Anthropology in Context: The Image of God, Assimilation to God, and Tripartite Man in Ancient Judaism, Ancient Philosophy and Early Christianity*, WUNT 232 [Tübingen: Mohr Siebeck, 2008], 208).

17. David Aune, "Human Nature and Ethics in Hellenistic Philosophical Traditions and Paul: Some Issues and Problems," in *Paul in His Hellenistic Context*, ed. Troels Engberg-Pedersen (Minneapolis: Fortress, 1995), 291–312. A return to Martin Hengel's *Crucifixion in the Ancient*

nothing but dying and being dead" (*Phaedo* 64a). In that tradition, death becomes both a biological fact and also "a way of living . . . in which the self is transformed."[18] Aune suggests that Paul's use of death as a metaphor for Christian life derives, at least in part, from this theme in the philosophical tradition. He also notes, however, that Paul's introduction of crucifixion into these passages would be "shocking" in that tradition since crucifixion is never "referred to in a positive sense in connection with treatments of the *commentatio mortis* theme."[19] When Paul shifts to the claim that "I have been crucified together with Christ," he transgresses the philosophical commonplace.

Paul's introduction of the language of crucifixion is more than shocking to polite sensibilities, however; it takes us into the heart of his understanding of the gospel. The cross is both the historical event in which the human Jesus was put to death *and* the location of God's rescue of humanity from the "present evil age," the world as it is ruled by anti-God powers (1:4). For Paul to say that "I have been crucified with Christ" (2:19) is of a different order from affirming Jesus as Teacher, and it goes beyond even the confession that Jesus is Lord. It is to say, as Martinus C. de Boer observes, that one "is joined to or taken up into this all-embracing cosmic, apocalyptic event that spells the end of the old age, where malevolent powers hold sway over God's creation."[20]

Galatians 2:20 draws out the implications of verse 19, especially the implication of the perfect tense ("I have been crucified with Christ"). The result of that crucifixion is that "I" (ἐγώ) no longer live, but Christ lives "in me." Here is no sign that this death and life are the death and life of the nomistic self only (although that is included).[21] It is the whole of the ἐγώ that is gone.[22] Verse 20 could be said by anyone, Jew or gentile, and the remainder of the letter suggests that this is exactly what Paul wants his letter to achieve among the gentile Galatians—a recognition that they too no longer live except as

---

World and the Folly of the Message of the Cross (Philadelphia: Fortress, 1977) would only reinforce Aune's comment.

18. Aune, "Human Nature," 306.

19. Ibid., 310–11. Aune takes note of one passage in which Plato does use crucifixion metaphorically (*Phaedo* 83D), but the metaphor is used negatively rather than positively, as Paul uses it.

20. See de Boer, *Galatians*, 161. This verse (Gal. 2:19) is often connected with baptism, based on Rom. 6:4, but nothing in Gal. 2 suggests a connection with baptism, despite the later reference in 3:27.

21. Here I differ somewhat from de Boer, *Galatians*, 160.

22. Being in Christ, then, is "not some new piece of information, or some widening of the intellectual horizon, but a total reconstitution of the self. . . . Paul refers to the real and total demolition of the self, as previously constituted" (Barclay, "Paul's Story," 142–43). Douglas Campbell aptly observes that "since v. 17 Paul has been speaking of the execution of his own identity, and his immersion in Christ's" (*The Deliverance of God: An Apocalyptic Rereading of Justification in Paul* [Grand Rapids: Eerdmans, 2009], 848).

Christ lives in them.²³ In particular notice 4:19: "I am in labor with you again until Christ be formed in you."²⁴

There is still life in a human body, of course. Paul is not asserting a nonbodily existence or escape from history. This is far from a negation of human life, since actual fleshly life is here paralleled with life in the realm of faith:²⁵

> I live in flesh. . . . I live in faith.
> But this life in the flesh is life in the realm of πίστις,
>   life in the realm that belongs to God's Son,
>   "who loved me and who handed himself over on my behalf." (2:20)

Much more could be said on any of these points, but my concern at present is with the change in Paul's language and what it suggests. By moving to the language of "death" and "life," Paul has again shifted his discourse; the register of the argument changes. The canvas on which Paul depicts the gospel has enlarged from legal language to existential language. The question is no longer about making things right (rectifying or justifying) and how that is done; instead, it concerns death and life. Something more is at stake than justification, for Christ is not simply the one who justifies; now Christ is the one with whom "I" am crucified, the one who lives "in me." Here the gospel's singularity comes to expression in a form that is frightening: the gospel gives life by taking it away.

To be sure, in Galatians 3:11–12 (as later in Rom. 1:17), Paul will draw on Habakkuk 2:4 to associate life with being δίκαιος, so it could be objected that I have exaggerated the shift in 2:19–20. However, Paul has not yet made that association. More to the point, the language of dying and living in 2:19–20 differs from those places where Paul draws on Habakkuk 2:4 in that he does not there speak of dying and living in terms of being cocrucified or of dying to one's life.

To return to the question of how Galatians 2:19–20 relates to the language of rectification that precedes (and follows): Paul's *interpretation* of the singular character of justification transforms it. The singularity of the gospel is not simply the claim that there is only one interpretation of the gospel. The "truth of the gospel" is not only about rectification; rectification is necessary but not sufficient.²⁶ What the Galatians and the other teachers have failed to grasp,

---

23. On the general applicability of 2:20, see also Shauf, "Galatians 2.20," 98–99.
24. See Beverly Roberts Gaventa, "The Maternity of Paul," in *Our Mother Saint Paul*, 29–39.
25. John M. G. Barclay notes this parallel as well as the irony of Paul's usage of σάρξ, given the negative inflection that appears elsewhere in his letters (*Obeying the Truth: Paul's Ethics in Galatians* [Edinburgh: T&T Clark, 1988], 181).
26. Note E. P. Sanders, for whom "righteousness by faith and participation in Christ ultimately amount to the same thing. Paul sometimes speaks of righteousness as the preliminary juristic

from Paul's perspective, is that the gospel is singular in that it is all-consuming: there is no more ἐγώ. And the gospel is also all life-giving: "Christ lives in me." The living "I" now lives in the realm of πίστις, which comes from and is given by the Son of God. Paul is a paradigm, then, not only of the gospel of Jesus Christ and not of the law but also of the gospel that brings death and life, the gospel that gives life in a new place. That is, singularity involves the all-consuming character of the gospel. In an earlier essay on Galatians, I employed John Schütz's notion that Paul here writes a "biography of reversal," but now I find that a smallish way of describing Galatians 1–2.[27] It is not simply that Paul's life is "reversed" (that would be more accurate as a description of Acts 9 than of Gal. 1–2);[28] in some important sense, Paul's life is actually totalized by the gospel.

The Rest of the Letter: Singularity Radicalized

This reading of the singularity of the gospel in Galatians 1–2 finds confirmation and expansion elsewhere in the letter at two important junctures. Interestingly, in both instances it follows on the first kind of singularity, the claim that the gospel has to do with Christ or Christ-faith rather than with some combination of Christ and law.

First, let us examine the end of Galatians 3. In 3:2, Paul asks a rhetorical question ("How did you receive the Spirit?") that he proceeds in a sense to answer throughout the chapter. By the end of the chapter, the long discussion of Abraham, Abraham's seed, and the promise has yielded something of the culmination to the chapter: "All of you are sons and daughters of God through πίστις which is in Christ Jesus" (3:26). The implication of the entire preceding argument is that the Spirit is received through πίστις and not through law observance. So here again, as in Galatians 1–2, Paul is arguing for the first sense of singularity: there is only one gospel, and it has to do with belonging to the πίστις of Christ Jesus.

But in the lines that follow, similar to the ending of Galatians 2, the linguistic register changes again. For Paul, it is not enough to say that people are or

---

status which leads to life in Christ" (*Paul and Palestinian Judaism: A Comparison of Patterns of Religion* [Philadelphia: Fortress, 1977], 506). Although our positions are in some respects similar, I think Sanders here underinterprets what is being said in 2:19–20.

27. Beverly Roberts Gaventa, "The Apostle and the Gospel," in *Our Mother Saint Paul*, 90, citing Schütz, *Paul and the Anatomy of Apostolic Authority*, 133.

28. Beverly Roberts Gaventa, *The Acts of the Apostles*, ANTC (Nashville: Abingdon, 2003), 155. "Totalize" has acquired highly negative connotations, but lexically it seems to be the right word in that it has to do with taking something up into another totality.

become the children of God by virtue of πίστις. He goes on to say: "Whoever was baptized into Christ, you put on Christ. There is no more Jew nor Greek, there is no more slave nor free, there is no male and female. For you are all one in Christ Jesus. And if you belong to Christ, then you are Abraham's offspring, heirs according to the promise" (Gal. 3:27–29).

Numerous important questions arise from verses 28–29. At present, however, it suffices to observe simply that here Paul goes well beyond the claim that there is only one gospel, namely, the gospel of Christ's faith eliciting faithful death. He makes the further and more radical claim that this one gospel produces one humanity, a humanity that belongs to Christ, and a humanity in which the divisions that mark all humanity no longer exist.

J. Louis Martyn once referred to this verse in conversation as "everyone's favorite plaything," and it is easy to see how the text has been kicked around like a child's toy. Taken out of context, it becomes a manifesto for various liberation movements, or it becomes a disturbing call for a universalism that tramples over difference. Or it is domesticated with the claim that Paul is speaking in a limited sense of unity in the realm of faith without concern for the actual differences among humans.[29] But, of course, that minimizing reading of 3:28 is unimaginable in a Pauline context; in Paul's thinking, God's liberating action in sending Jesus Christ "to rescue us from the present evil age" (1:4) can scarcely be limited to some narrowly delimited "spiritual" sphere.[30] All the arenas, the distinctions, the statuses, the differentiations—they are all wiped away. Differences remain, but they are nondividing differences, differences subordinated to the gospel;[31] more than that, every source of human identity is taken up by and into the gospel.

At the end of the letter, Paul's discourse makes a shift yet again. In 6:11–14a, Paul holds against each other the act of circumcision and the cross of Christ. Those who would compel circumcision for gentile males act against the cross of Christ and for their own self-interest. Paul will boast only in the cross of

---

29. See Riches, *Galatians through the Centuries*, 204–13. Alongside the relatively recent concerns about the "sameness" of 3:28, the history of interpretation shows that many women have found in this passage a voice in support of their own insistence on full personhood; see Marion Ann Taylor and Agnes Choi, eds., *Handbook of Women Biblical Interpreters* (Grand Rapids: Baker Academic, 2012), esp. 48, 169, 406, 466, 548.

30. Paul's is not the only canonical voice at odds with the notion that the claims of God on human life can be limited to the "spiritual" realm. When Jesus utters, "Return to Caesar what belongs to Caesar and to God what belongs to God" (Luke 20:25; cf. Matt. 22:2; Mark 12:17), he not only sidesteps an attempt to "catch him out"; he also invites his auditors to recognize that there is nothing that does not belong to God's realm. Peter puts it directly in Acts 10:36, "He is Lord of all."

31. See the important essay of Susannah Ticciata, "The Nondivisive Difference of Election: A Reading of Romans 9–11," *JTI* 6 (2012): 257–78.

Jesus Christ. Here the first sense of singularity is, for the final time, at the fore: no compromise is offered, no accommodation is possible, between the gospel of the cross of Jesus Christ and the requirement of the law for circumcision. With verse 14b and verse 15, however, the radicalized singularity comes once again to the foreground:

> The cosmos has been crucified to me and I to the cosmos,
> because there is neither circumcision nor uncircumcision
>   but new creation.

The particular shift made here comes as a surprise. Throughout the letter, Paul has argued against circumcision for gentiles and thereby, one might think, for *uncircumcision*, but here he shifts the argument another step. Neither is anything. There is only new creation.[32]

In each of these three passages, which come at key points in the letter, Paul's comments go well beyond the initial claim that the singular gospel concerns Jesus Christ alone without any accompanying observance of the Mosaic law. God's deliverance of humanity from the present evil age reclaims and indeed re-creates humanity.

The Implications of the Gospel's Singularity

What does this larger and more radical notion of the gospel's singularity suggest for questions of human identity, whether couched as individual identity (as in 2:19–20) or couched in corporate terms of ethnicity or gender (as in 3:28)? This is a much-disputed question in Pauline scholarship. Where some early feminist treatments of Paul lifted up 3:28 as liberating and empowering, more recent work has criticized what it takes to be an implicit valuation of "sameness." On similar grounds, 3:28 is viewed as problematic to the extent that it undermines ethnic identity. It is clear that Paul knows there still *are* men and women; there still *are* Jews and Greeks; that there *are* human beings who are free and those who are enslaved. The force of the letter, however, is that these facts, these features of life in the flesh, are not for Paul what we would call "identities." They are not the places in which one finds self-understanding, not the areas that dictate worth or predict behavior or shape attitudes. The gospel's claim is exclusive.[33]

---

32. And see earlier Gal. 5:6.

33. The community "in Christ" is, as Bruce Longenecker (*The Triumph of Abraham's God: The Transformation of Identity in Galatians* [Edinburgh: T&T Clark, 1998]) describes it, a corporate body where plurality becomes unified. In that collective of human diversity, Paul

In our historical setting, that set of comments is disturbing, especially when we consider what they mean for interpreting the Mosaic law, Scripture, Israel, and Abraham. Paul is not saying that all these things (and they are not all the same)[34] are obliterated. He does say that he is "dead" to the law, but he does not announce himself dead to Scripture or to Abraham or to Israel. Scripture and Abraham and Israel have meaning, but they do so only as reinterpreted by the gospel.[35] Galatians 3:29 is especially revealing: it is because "you" belong to Christ that "you" are Abraham's children and heirs of the promise, not the other way around. The standard genealogical movement is here reversed.[36]

These brief comments are not intended to resolve the deeply complex scholarly debates regarding Galatians and questions of gender, ethnicity, and social standing. My purpose in identifying these particular implications is to suggest that the challenge of the letter is poorly understood if it is limited to matters of gender or ethnicity or social standing. It proves tempting to identify the controversies of Galatians as if they are confined to particular groups or issues and somehow removed or isolated from other groups or issues. But Paul's claims about the singularity of the gospel are not limited in their significance (whether construed "positively" or "negatively") to feminist interpreters or to students of ethnicity, and treating them as such only perpetuates a minimizing, reductive, domesticating interpretation of the letter. We have not genuinely wrestled with the radical character of the gospel until we reckon with this deeper "terror," and I use that word deliberately, the terror that Paul's understanding of the gospel means that the gospel is everything.

To put the matter succinctly: what is most deeply disturbing about Galatians has less to do with Marcion than with Barmen:[37] "We reject the false doctrine,

---

perceives God's eschatological power to be at work. The interconnectedness of diversity is unrealizable within the sphere of the present evil age from which Christ has delivered his people. Outside the sphere of God's power, plurality fragments into negative disassociation; within the sphere of God's power, plurality is brought within the positive context of interconnectedness and wholeness (67).

34. One of the serious exegetical pitfalls in reading Paul's Letters is that of extrapolating from individual critical remarks to global indictments. This happens, e.g., when Rom. 2:17–24, which introduces *the possibility* that there may be Jews who proudly claim their heritage and yet act contrary to that heritage, is read as a generalized description of Jewish "legalism" or "national pride."

35. I take this to be consistent with Barclay's comment: "Neither Paul, nor Israel, nor the church have any stories of significance before God except those that are fractured by the cross of Christ" ("Paul's Story," 146).

36. Standing outside the letter, reading it in the context of the canon, we of course see many continuities, but that is a different matter than attending to Paul's *presentation* of the gospel in relationship to what has preceded.

37. The Barmen Declaration was adopted by the Confessing Church in 1934 in opposition to Hitler's German church. It gives prominence to the sin of idolatry and to the lordship of

as though there were areas of our life in which we would not belong to Jesus Christ, but to other lords." Grappling with the singularity of the gospel places hearers of Paul's Letter to the Galatians in the presence of the God's whose claim over all of humanity knows no boundaries and permits no limits.

Christ, as featured in the brief quotation above. The full text is available online at http://www.sacred-texts.com/chr/barmen.htm.

12

Apocalyptic *Poiēsis* in Galatians

Paternity, Passion, and Participation

RICHARD B. HAYS

Apocalyptic *Poiēsis*

The Theological Keynote of Galatians: The "Grace and Peace" Salutation (Gal. 1:3-5)

Grace to you and peace from God our Father and from the Lord Jesus Christ, who gave himself for our sins, so that he might rescue us from the present evil age, in accordance with the will of our God and Father, to whom be the glory forever. (Gal. 1:3–5)

Thus runs the opening salutation of Paul's Letter to the Galatians. It is generally recognized that the openings of Paul's Epistles are not inconsequential; they are artfully composed to signal the chief themes and concerns of the letters that they introduce. Yet until rather recently, the apocalyptic opening lines of the Letter to the Galatians have rarely been given their full weight as a thematic key to the letter's message.

There are several possible reasons for the overlooking of verses 3–5.

Sometimes interpreters have zoomed in on Paul's forceful assertion in 1:1 of a divine authorization for his own apostleship—clearly a major topic in the first two chapters of the letter. Other times interpreters have found their attention arrested by Paul's abrupt Θαυμάζω in verse 6. In the absence of a preliminary thanksgiving paragraph, this expression of dismay plunges many interpreters immediately into attempting to reconstruct the historical problem in Galatia that evoked Paul's impassioned missive. Or again, Protestant theological exegesis has often thumbed its way quickly past the letter's opening to reach the juicy central section of the letter (Gal. 3–4), with its convoluted and challenging argument about law, faith, and justification—themes not mentioned in the first chapter. Or alternatively, some readers are drawn particularly to the hortatory and ethical "payoff" of the argument in chapters 5 and 6. Finally, partly because of the absence of "justification" language in the letter opening, and partly because of Paul's uncharacteristic use of the plural "sins" in the announcement that Christ "gave himself for our sins" (1:4), critics have often suggested that in 1:3–5 Paul is simply quoting a traditional formula that fails to express the distinctive substance of his own thought—or even stands in some tension with it.[1]

I suggest, however, that in Galatians, as in every other Pauline Epistle, the opening lines highlight precisely the themes that lie theologically at the heart of the letter. The salutation of Galatians allusively encapsulates the story of Jesus Christ, sent forth by God the Father into the world to rescue human beings from bondage to sin and death—that is, bondage to "the present evil age"—through his own self-giving death (and resurrection! [1:1]). It is *this* story that provides the narrative framework within which Paul proclaims his urgent message about the justification of gentiles and constructs his arguments against the requirement of circumcision for the Galatian believers.

During the past generation, a number of important developments in the study of Pauline theology have created the hermeneutical conditions necessary for a fresh reading of the letter that brings these themes into proper focus. First among these developments is a new attention to the *narrative* character of Paul's thought, as opposed to construals that approach the letters through a strictly conceptual/propositional filter.[2] But just as important for our present

---

1. J. Louis Martyn goes so far as to suggest that Paul cites the formula in order to "correct it by means of an additional clause" (*Galatians*, AB 33A [New York: Doubleday, 1997], 90). Cf. J. D. G. Dunn, *The Theology of Paul's Letter to the Galatians* (Cambridge: Cambridge University Press, 1993), 42–44.

2. My own work has played some role in this shift toward narrative. I also draw attention, however, to the contributions of N. T. Wright, James D. G. Dunn, Ben Witherington, Michael Gorman, and Douglas Campbell. For one significant survey and assessment of the narrative turn in Pauline interpretation, see B. W. Longenecker, ed., *Narrative Dynamics in Paul: A Critical*

concerns is the paradigm-challenging work of J. Louis Martyn, whose magisterial commentary on Galatians offers a comprehensive reading of Galatians as an *apocalyptic* proclamation of the gospel. Here is Martyn's vivid translation of Galatians 1:4: Jesus Christ "'gave up his very life for our sins,' so that he might snatch us out of the grasp of the present evil age."[3] From start to finish in his commentary, Martyn describes God's saving action through the imagery of invasion and battle, and he presses the case for reading Paul as an apocalyptic theologian. Martyn's work has become so widely influential for the current generation of Pauline scholarship that it now seems almost incredible to recall that just over thirty years ago, J. Christiaan Beker could describe Galatians as an anomalous contingent *exception* to Paul's otherwise coherent proclamation of a gospel centered on the eschatological cosmic triumph of God. Indeed, Beker saw Galatians as such a nonapocalyptic outlier that it threatened to undo his own advocacy of Paul as a thoroughgoing apocalyptic theologian.[4]

Martyn's provocative work has stimulated much debate, and Douglas Campbell's recent massive work *The Deliverance of God* has likewise pressed the case for reading Paul as a radical apocalyptic thinker.[5] In this essay, I shall not attempt to give a detailed review of the current vigorous debates about "apocalyptic" in Paul.[6] But I do want to offer a few broad observations about the contours of some key issues that have surfaced through Martyn's work and the various responses to it.

Marks of Apocalyptic Theology in Galatians

The major advocates of "apocalyptic" are using the term not chiefly to identify the historical sources of specific motifs in Galatians—and still less to identify the genre of the letter.[7] Instead, they are using "apocalyptic" as a

---

Assessment (Louisville and London: Westminster John Knox, 2002). Interestingly, this collection of essays on narrative in Paul contains only a few slight passing references to Gal. 1:3–4.

3. Martyn, *Galatians*, 81.

4. J. C. Beker, *Paul the Apostle: The Triumph of God in Life and Thought* (Philadelphia: Fortress, 1980), 58.

5. D. Campbell, *The Deliverance of God: An Apocalyptic Rereading of Justification in Paul* (Grand Rapids: Eerdmans, 2009).

6. For a critical perspective on the use of the category of "apocalyptic" to characterize Paul's thought, see, e.g., R. B. Matlock, *Unveiling the Apocalyptic Paul: Paul's Interpreters and the Rhetoric of Criticism*, JSNTSup 127 (Sheffield: Sheffield Academic Press, 1996); also N. T. Wright, "Paul in Current Anglophone Scholarship," *ExpTim* 123 (2012): 367–81, esp. 372–74. For interpretations that embrace the category of "apocalyptic," see, e.g., M. C. de Boer, "Paul, Theologian of God's Apocalypse," *Int* 56 (2002): 21–33; D. Harink, "Paul and Israel: An Apocalyptic Reading," *ProEccl* 16 (2007): 359–80; B. R. Gaventa, *Our Mother Saint Paul* (Louisville: Westminster John Knox, 2007).

7. As noted by L. E. Keck, "Paul and Apocalyptic Theology," *Int* 38 (1984): 229–41.

descriptor for a certain profile of *theological* claims and commitments. These theological tendencies in Paul are presumptively characterized as *analogous* to the underlying theological claims and commitments of Jewish apocalyptic thought. According to this reading, there is a family resemblance, a sort of theological DNA, that Galatians shares with Jewish apocalyptic texts, despite many evident surface differences. We may identify three salient characteristics of this apocalyptic DNA, as it is described by the scholars who champion the apocalyptic reading of Galatians.

1. The most fundamental of these underlying theological commitments is the insistence on *divine initiative and action* as the ground of salvation and hope, as opposed to any human religious practice or subjective disposition. This theological stance is elegantly expressed in Paul's rhetorically skillful self-correction in Galatians 4:9: "But now that you know God—or rather, now that *you have been known by God*" The grammatical correction signals the deep theological grammar of Paul's gospel. *God* is the primary agent, and human beings are the receivers of God's gracious action—just as in the letter opening, it is by God's gracious will that Jesus Christ gave himself to rescue us from the present evil age.

2. The reference to "the present evil age" highlights the second key apocalyptic perspective found in Galatians: a scheme of *two ages*. In the old age, humans were in bondage to sin and death. With the inbreaking of the new age, however, there is a "new creation" (6:15), a new era of freedom, righteousness, and life. As the expression "new creation" suggests, this new age comes about entirely through God's initiative, not from any human design or action. Everything is made new in Christ. To unpack what Paul means by speaking of "new creation" in Galatians 6, we may refer to his fuller exposition of this same image in 2 Corinthians 5:17: "If anyone is in Christ—new creation! The old things have passed away. Look! The new has come into being." Further, according to Martyn's reading, there is a radical *discontinuity* between the old age and the new. The death and resurrection of Jesus create a caesura in time and history; consequently, there can be no direct connection between the past and the present.

3. To some advocates of apocalyptic in Paul, this radical discontinuity between the ages suggests a third feature of Pauline apocalyptic thought: *a sharp break with Judaism, with "salvation history," and with Israel*—at least with Israel as defined in the past. Paul speaks of his "former life in Judaism" (1:13)[8] and can say that he has "died to the law" (2:19). He refers

---

8. On the interpretation of Paul's term Ἰουδαϊσμός, see now the valuable essay by Matthew Novenson, chap. 2 above.

to life under Torah as "slavery" (4:9, 25; 5:1) and warns the Galatians that if they undergo circumcision, they will be "cut off from Christ" (5:2-4). These radical disjunctions and apparent disavowals of Israel's sacred law allegedly make sense only in light of Paul's apocalyptic conviction that a new age has dawned, in which the Torah belongs to the past. During the old age, its function was to be a παιδαγωγός until Christ came, but now that in the fullness of time πίστις has arrived on the scene, the Torah is superseded and no longer valid (3:23-25).

It is this third aspect of the "apocalyptic" interpretation of Galatians that is most problematic—and at the same time most convergent with the Reformation's traditional law/gospel antithesis and its concomitant anti-Jewish readings of Paul. Even where contemporary "apocalyptic" interpreters are sensitive—as indeed J. Louis Martyn is[9]—to the theological dangers of such a position, they nonetheless tend to portray Paul as having broken decisively with Israel's history.

A Proposal: Reshaping the Hermeneutical Imagination

In the present essay, I argue that the first two features of the apocalyptic interpretation that I have described are on target as readings of Galatians: Paul does insist on the priority of divine initiative, and he does read present existence through the lens of a two-age schema, in which Jesus Christ has inaugurated a new creation. But I also suggest that the third tendency of many contemporary apocalyptic interpretations—the claim of radical discontinuity between present and past, between church and Israel—fails to describe with sufficient nuance either the way in which two-age thinking actually works in Jewish apocalyptic thought or the complex way in which Paul engages Israel's Scripture and tradition. I contend that Paul's understanding of the new age in Christ leads him not to a *rejection* of Israel's sacred history but to a *retrospective hermeneutical transformation* of Israel's story in light of the story of God's startling redemptive actions: God has sent his Son to rescue us and redeem the whole world, and God has sent forth the Spirit to confirm and continue God's transforming work in the community of God's people in Christ—a community that now embraces Jews and gentiles together without distinction. All this requires a dramatic rereading of Israel's story, but what is required is precisely a *rereading*, not a repudiation.[10]

9. See, e.g., J. L. Martyn, "Galatians, an Anti-Judaic Document?," in *Theological Issues in the Letters of Paul* (Nashville: Abingdon, 1997), 77-84.

10. On these themes, see R. B. Hays, *The Conversion of the Imagination: Paul as Interpreter of Israel's Scripture* (Grand Rapids: Eerdmans, 2005).

After all, as Paul strikingly claims in Galatians 3:8, Scripture *foresaw* that God, out of his own faithfulness to his promises, would justify the gentiles, and Scripture *preproclaimed the gospel to Abraham*. From this it follows that Paul's passionate engagement with scriptural interpretation in his Letter to the Galatians is not simply a reluctant concession to his opponents; rather, it is a necessary component of his own apostolic mission. Paul seeks to teach his gentile readers how to discover and interpret the complex hermeneutical relationship between Israel's story and the new creation in Christ.

Another way to put this point is to say that the dichotomy between apocalyptic and salvation history is false. Israel's sacred history is indeed a preparation for the gospel, but Paul does not understand that history as a simple linear progression toward triumphant fulfillment; rather, the story has to be reread retrospectively under the guidance of the Spirit in light of its fulfillment in Christ. However, God's "apocalyptic" act in Christ does not simply shatter and sweep away creation and covenant; rather, it hermeneutically reconfigures creation and covenant, under the guidance of the Spirit, in light of cross and resurrection.

All of this means that to understand "apocalyptic" in Paul, we must attend to *the gospel's imaginative remaking of the world*. To interpret the apocalyptic rhetoric and theology of Galatians, we must reflect on the *poetics* of the letter, the way in which Paul deploys language and imagery to reshape the symbolic world in which his readers live and move.

If we pick up Galatians and read through the Greek text from start to finish, we find ourselves immersed in a sea of images and sensibilities that may indeed be called apocalyptic, in the sense that they are revelatory of a world charged with spiritual conflict and spiritual power. There is no clearly defined dispensationalist scheme here, except for Paul's urgent conviction that when the time had fully come, God sent forth his Son, and everything changed. Reading this letter plunges us into a drama in which Paul, the zealous devotee of Jewish law who was persecuting the church and trying to destroy it, can suddenly receive what he calls "the apocalypse of Jesus Christ" and find himself seized by the commission to proclaim good news about Jesus Christ to the gentiles (1:11–16). Reading this letter plunges us into a drama in which God's Spirit is afoot in the world so palpably that Paul can impatiently ask his readers to recall just how they first received this Spirit that is now performing mighty works (δυνάμεις) in their midst (3:1–5). Reading this letter plunges us into a drama in which the powers of Spirit and Flesh are at war with each other (5:16–17), and the community now given life by the Spirit is called to stand fast and not submit to oppressive powers seeking to subjugate them again to slavery (4:8–11; 5:1).

This is not the world of the university classroom. It is more like the world of Martin Luther's hymn "Ein' feste Burg," particularly its third stanza:

> And though this world, with devils filled,
> should threaten to undo us,
> We will not fear, for God has willed
> his truth to triumph through us.[11]

Paul writes as a charismatic preacher; he writes as a strong poet. His arguments depend on rich narrative allusions, on metaphorical linkages, and even on fanciful allegorical interpretation. His logic is more associative than linear. And his rhetoric is aggressive and hyperbolic. Paul can say that his readers at one point would have torn out their own eyes for him (4:15); he can breathe the wish that the rival troublemaking preachers would castrate themselves (5:12); and he can declare metaphorically that he has been crucified along with Christ (2:19).

Apocalyptic Themes and Imagery: A Catalog

There may be value in offering a short catalog of some elements in Galatians in which we see Paul's *poiēsis* at work, shaping the apocalyptic imaginative matrix within which he wants his readers to see the world. Here is a selective list of some of the images and motifs that appear in the letter:[12]

1. God raised Jesus Christ from the dead (Gal. 1:1).
2. Christ died "to rescue us from the present evil age" (1:4; cf. 2:20).
3. Human beings may receive messages from angels, who may be either authentic messengers of God (3:19; 4:14) or deceptive and malevolent (1:8).
4. Paul received his gospel as a divine revelation (ἀποκάλυψις) (1:1, 11–12, 16), and God chose to reveal (ἀποκαλύψαι) his Son in and through Paul (1:16). Further, Paul's decision to go to Jerusalem was directed κατὰ ἀποκάλυψιν (2:2).

---

11. Martin Luther, "A Mighty Fortress Is Our God" ("Ein' feste Burg ist unser Gott"), hymn 110 in *The United Methodist Hymnal: Book of United Methodist Worship*, trans. Frederick H. Hedge, 1853 (Nashville: United Methodist Publishing House, 1989). Original German text:
Und wenn die Welt voll Teufel wär'
Und wollt' uns gar verschlingen,
So fürchten wir uns nicht so sehr,
Es soll uns doch gelingen.
12. For a similar list of "apocalyptic expressions" in Galatians—a shorter list, but with fuller interpretative comments—see Martyn, *Galatians*, 97–104.

5. The opponents of Paul's message are "false brothers" (2:4), who presumably stand under a curse (1:9). Those who are led astray from Paul's gospel are "bewitched" (3:1).
6. Paul has died to the law through being "crucified with Christ," and now Christ lives in him (2:19–20). Indeed, through Christ's death the whole world has been crucified, and Paul has been crucified to the world (6:14). He bears the *stigmata* of Christ on his body (6:17).
7. The Spirit is a power palpably active in the community and working miracles (3:5).
8. Scripture (ἡ γραφή) speaks in oracular fashion to predict future events (3:8–9; cf. 4:21–31).[13]
9. Israel, because of disobedience, stands under the curses of Deuteronomy 27–28 (Gal. 3:10).
10. Christ has redeemed "us" (Israel?) from the curse pronounced by the law through absorbing the curse in his death on a cross (3:13).
11. Paul's use of *Christos* to describe the agent of redemption and salvation strongly suggests that the term should be understood to refer to a Messiah figure (3:16).[14]
12. The phrase "sons of God" in 3:26 refers to the eschatological people of God, disclosed only at the end time (cf. Rom. 8:19).[15] Those who are sons and daughters of God have "put on Christ" and entered, at least proleptically, into an existence where the antinomies of the old age—the distinctions of race, class, and gender—are rendered insignificant (Gal. 3:26–28).
13. Paul says that both he and his readers were once enslaved under τὰ στοιχεῖα τοῦ κόσμου (4:3; cf. 4:8–9). But God has sent forth his Son to liberate his people and to send the Spirit upon them and make them "heirs" (4:4–7). As Rodrigo Morales has shown, this image of the giving of the Spirit was traditionally understood in Second Temple Judaism as a sign of the eschatological restoration of Israel.[16]

---

13. But these events are in the future from the perspective of the scriptural text, not from the perspective of Paul and his readers; one thing that sets Galatians apart from most apocalyptic literature is that it does not prophesy or speculate about events in future time.

14. On this, see N. T. Wright's essay for the St. Andrews conference, chap. 1 above. Note also the use of σπέρμα as recipient of the promises (3:16, 19), and its messianic sense in 2 Sam. 7:12–14a LXX. For a significant study reexamining the use of *Christos* as a messianic title in Paul, see M. V. Novenson, *Christ among the Messiahs: Christ Language in Paul and Messiah Language in Ancient Judaism* (Oxford: Oxford University Press, 2012).

15. See J. M. Scott, *Adoption as Sons of God: An Exegetical Investigation into the Background of* υἱοθεσία *in the Pauline Corpus*, WUNT 2/48 (Tübingen: Mohr Siebeck, 1992); S. G. Eastman, "Whose Apocalypse? The Identity of the Sons of God in Romans 8:19," *JBL* 121 (2002): 263–77.

16. R. Morales, *The Spirit and the Restoration of Israel*, WUNT 2/282 (Tübingen: Mohr Siebeck, 2010), esp. 41–77.

14. Paul depicts himself as being "in labor" with his converts until Christ is eschatologically formed in them (4:19).[17]
15. Paul's allegorical reading of the Sarah/Hagar story contrasts "the present Jerusalem" in slavery with the eschatological "Jerusalem above, which is free" (4:25–26).
16. The community now awaits "the hope of righteousness" (5:5). This should be understood as the community's earnest hope for eschatological fulfillment, as in Romans 8:18–25. But those who live by the flesh will not "inherit the kingdom of God"—another clear reference to future eschatological hope (Gal. 5:21). By contrast, those who "sow to the Spirit" will "reap eternal life" (6:8).
17. Several phrases point to Paul's expectation of an eschatological day of reckoning: those who trouble the Galatians will incur God's final judgment (5:7–10). The sowing/reaping imagery of 6:7–9 is a traditional set of metaphors for eschatological judgment.
18. The formerly salient distinction between circumcision and uncircumcision has been rendered meaningless by God's "new creation" (6:15). Those who live into this reality can be described as "the Israel of God," God's eschatological people (6:16).

More detailed exegesis would no doubt identify still more eschatological/apocalyptic ideas and images in the letter. But this list of some of the more obvious examples suffices to show how thoroughly Paul is seeking to reshape the imagination of his readers, seeking to narrate them into a symbolic world where God the Father, Jesus Christ the Son of God, and the Spirit are powerfully at work to bring a new world into being.

Shall we use the term "apocalyptic" to describe the imaginative *poiēsis* enacted in Paul's language? The question is really just a semantic quibble. This much is clear: the symbolic world created by Paul's imagery is one in which all the initiative in the rescue of God's people belongs to God. It is a world in which the death and resurrection of Jesus have decisively transformed the conditions of all human existence, so that the times before and after these events are qualitatively different from each other. Looking back at Israel's Scripture from the perspective of the new age, we can see that God had always scripted the story to prefigure God's action in Christ to justify the nations of the world and bring them into unity with Israel, but only in retrospect does this interpretation of Scripture become evident. The news of God's redemptive transformation of the world has been conveyed by divine revelation to

---

17. On the eschatological overtones of this labor/birthing imagery, see Gaventa, *Our Mother Saint Paul*, 29–39.

Paul. The world disclosed in this revelation is a world alive with superhuman powers, who are engaged in conflict and seeking to enslave or liberate human beings. Although God has decisively achieved the rescue of his people through the cross, the consummation of God's transforming righteousness remains a future hope. In this situation "the Israel of God" is summoned to walk under the guidance of the Spirit and resist the seduction of the powers of the old age, who seek to suck them back into slavery.

This is the story told—perhaps better, the picture drawn—by Paul's language in Galatians. It is a remarkable poetic performance, giving expression to the gospel with epic narrative sweep and linguistic power. Within the storied world that Paul portrays, I now want to focus on three motifs that may be illuminating for our ongoing theological reflection today. The three motifs are God as Father (*paternity*), Jesus's death as the pivotal liberating event (*passion*), and union with Christ (*participation*).

Major Motifs and Images in the Narrative World of Galatians

Paternity and Sonship: The Adoption of Gentiles into the Covenant People

In Galatians, Paul uses the word "Father" (πατήρ) only a few times to name God,[18] but the passages in which it does appear are fraught with theological significance. There are two key passages: 1:1–5 and 4:3–7.

First, in the letter's opening salutation, Paul names God as Father three times. He amplifies his usual greeting formula ("Grace to you and peace from God our Father") in two striking ways. He opens the letter by asserting first that his commission as an apostle comes "through Jesus Christ and God the Father," not from any human source (1:1). And then he expands the "grace and peace" formula by adding a phrase that describes Jesus's action of self-giving to rescue us from the present evil age as an action performed "in accordance with the will of our God and Father" (1:4). Thus, God the Father is portrayed here as the initiating source behind Jesus's saving action, as well as the one who commissions the dissemination of the gospel to the world through Paul's apostolic activity.

Second, the dramatic narrative passage in Galatians 4:3–7 even more clearly portrays God as the Sender,[19] the sovereign initiator of the saving event: in the fullness of time *God sent forth his Son* to redeem (i.e., emancipate) his people under the law, so that they might receive the status of sonship. Further, to those

---

18. The designation of God as Father appears in all thirteen letters of the extended Pauline corpus.
19. On this designation for God in Paul's master narrative structure, see R. B. Hays, *The Faith of Jesus Christ*, 2nd ed. (Grand Rapids: Eerdmans, 2002), 90–117.

who do receive this status, God sent the Spirit into their hearts, a Spirit who in turn enables them to cry out "Abba! Father!" Whether their cry is one of grateful praise or anguished petition is not clear in the context.[20]

In either case, this passage demonstrates that our interpretation of God's paternity must embrace not only the texts in which Paul refers directly to God as πατήρ but also the texts in which he refers to Jesus as "Son of God" and/or to God's people as "sons [and daughters] of God." Paternity and sonship are complementary images that require each other. Thus, alongside the two passages already noted, we should take particular note of 2:20, where "the Son of God" is described as the one "who loved me and gave himself for me." As a result of this self-donation of the Son, Paul has lost his independent existence and now lives "by the faithfulness of the Son of God."[21] In all three of these passages where Christ is designated as "Son of God," Paul is drawing attention to his self-sacrificial death and highlighting the redemptive effect of that death.[22] Furthermore, in a mysterious way, the Son's redemptive death effects υἱοθεσία, bringing his people into union with himself in such a way that they too become υἱοί (3:26; 4:6–7) and thereby become "heirs through God" (4:7).[23]

The theme of "inheritance" for the "sons of God" is of particular importance because it shows that Paul now thinks of his Galatian gentile readers as "heirs according to promise" (3:29), de facto participants in the covenant people Israel. It is the people Israel to whom the promise of an inheritance (κληρονομία) had long been given, starting with Abraham. This is precisely the focus of Paul's concern in the lengthy argument of 3:6–4:7.

Furthermore, it is the people Israel concerning whom God instructed Moses to say to Pharaoh, "Israel is my firstborn son" (Exod. 4:22). And Israel's filial tie to God is also invoked by the prophet Isaiah, who cries out, "You, O Lord, are our father; our Redeemer from of old is your name" (Isa. 63:16 NRSV). Or again, in Isaiah 64, the prophet pleads with God:

> Yet, O Lord, you are our Father;
>   we are the clay, and you are our potter;
>   we are all the work of your hand.
> Do not be exceedingly angry, O Lord,
>   and do not remember iniquity forever.
>   Now consider, we are all your people. (64:8–9 NRSV)

20. The parallel in Rom. 8:14–17 suggests the former.
21. On this interpretation, see Hays, *Faith of Jesus Christ*, 153–55.
22. The verb ἐξαγοράσῃ in 4:5 echoes ἐξηγόρασεν in 3:13, thus linking the Son's redemptive act to his cursed death on a cross.
23. On this theme, see Scott, *Adoption as Sons of God*.

And again, in the prophecy of Jeremiah, God answers Israel's prayers by reaffirming his paternal relation to the people who will ultimately return from exile:

> With weeping they shall come,
>> and with consolations I shall lead them back,
> I will let them walk by brooks of water,
>> in a straight path in which they shall not stumble;
> for I have become a Father to Israel,
>> and Ephraim is my firstborn. (31:9 NRSV)

In later Second Temple Judaism, these prophetic traditions about fatherhood and sonship are tied closely to the hope that God will restore Israel and that they will obediently keep the commandments of the Torah. For a clear example, see *Jubilees* 1.23–25:

> And I shall create for them a holy spirit, and I shall purify them so that they will not turn away from following me from that day and forever. And their souls will cleave to me and to all my commandments. And they will do my commandments. And I shall be a father to them, and they will be sons to me. And they will all be called "sons of the living God." And every angel and spirit will know and acknowledge that they are my sons and I am their father in uprightness and righteousness. And I shall love them.[24]

Thus, when Paul assures the Galatians that "you are all sons of God through the faithfulness of Jesus Christ" (3:26) and reminds them that the Spirit enables them to cry "Abba! Father!" and to claim the status of "heirs," he is saying in metaphorical language that they are now participants in "the Israel of God" (6:16), partakers in the covenant of promise, members of God's family whom he is bringing out of metaphorical exile. But their status of sonship is now granted and assured not because of their obedience to Torah, but because of Jesus Christ's faithful death for their sake, and their union with him through baptism. So God's covenant with Israel is not renounced but reconfigured.

These background intertexts show that the language of God's paternity and the sonship of those who belong to Christ is not meant to refer primarily to some sort of affective piety or individual experience of spiritual intimacy

---

24. *OTP* 2:54. For discussion of this passage, see Scott, *Adoption as Sons*, 107–9, 114, 178–80. For further relevant examples, both in the OT and in Second Temple Jewish texts, see the discussion in M. M. Thompson, *The Promise of the Father: Jesus and God in the New Testament* (Louisville: Westminster John Knox, 2000), 35–55. See also Morales, *Spirit and Restoration*, 43–48, 127–31.

with God; rather, when Paul tells the Galatians that they are "sons of God," this is *covenant* language that assures the Galatians of their participation in the covenant community of God's people.[25] Thus, any Christian theology that takes its bearings from Galatians needs to grapple with its apocalyptic emphasis on the fatherhood of God—made manifest through his redemptive action of creating a new eschatological covenant community, in which Jew and Greek, slave and free, male and female are all equally "sons of God."[26]

Passion: The Death of Jesus as Saving Event

As we have already noted, the keynote salutation in Galatians emphasizes that "the Lord Jesus Christ gave himself for our sins." This opening declaration alludes to the passion story of Jesus's death and places the cross at the heart of Paul's proclamation. The allusion is sounded again in 2:19b–20, this time with an explicit mention of Paul's cocrucifixion with "the Son of God who loved me and gave himself for me." This reference to the Son's loving death—the letter's only mention of "love" prior to the hortatory material in chapter 5—ensures that Paul's directives to the community to serve one another in love and to "fulfill the law of Christ" by bearing one another's burdens (5:13–14; 6:2) will be understood as admonitions to conform their lives to the self-giving pattern of Jesus Christ's death.[27] And the image of the cross is at last brought front and center at the beginning of chapter 3, as Paul, after the extended *narratio* of chapters 1 and 2, directly confronts the Galatians about their own faithless folly: "O foolish Galatians, who has bewitched you, before whose eyes Jesus Christ was portrayed [προεγράφη] as crucified [ἐσταυρωμένος]?" Paul here refers to the vivid *poiēsis* of his own preaching: in his initial proclamation to the Galatians, he vividly narrated the story of the passion of Jesus, his death on the cross, as an act of self-giving for the sake of all.[28]

---

25. After surveying the use of "Father" language for God in the OT and in Second Temple Judaism, Thompson observes, "It is this very notion of God as Father who gives his children an inheritance that is crucial to Paul's argument in Romans and Galatians. God the Father has, through the Spirit, made Jews and Gentiles together 'heirs of God and joint heirs with Christ' (Rom. 8:16–17; cf. Gal. 4:6)" (*Promise of the Father*, 116–17).

26. On this theme, see B. Byrne, *"Sons of God"—"Seed of Abraham": A Study of the Idea of Sonship of God of All Christians in Paul against the Jewish Background*, AnBib 83 (Rome: Biblical Institute Press, 1979); see esp. 189–90.

27. On this interpretation of "the law of Christ" in 6:2, see R. B. Hays, "Christology and Ethics in Galatians: The Law of Christ," *CBQ* 49 (1987): 268–90.

28. It is also possible that Paul's προεγράφη (3:1) alludes to his own physical scars, which in 6:17 he calls τὰ στίγματα τοῦ Ἰησοῦ, as a graphic visible portrayal of Christ's crucifixion. This is a possible secondary sense, but the meaning of προεγράφη as referring to vivid public narration is well established and should be taken as the primary sense of Paul's expression here. See the evidence cited by H. D. Betz, *Galatians: A Commentary on Paul's Letter to the Churches in*

The apostle continues to hammer home this theme insistently through the rest of the letter. For example, just a few sentences later, Paul explains that Christ accomplished his act of redemption by becoming a curse for us through being hanged on a tree (3:13). Because these texts so firmly bind the themes of redemption and rescue to the cross, at least two more subsequent passages also serve to remind the readers of Jesus's death:

> God sent forth his Son . . . in order that he might *redeem* those under the Law. (4:4–5)

> For freedom Christ has set us free. (5:1)

In addition to these references, I would also continue to commend strongly the interpretation of Paul's several references to the faithfulness of Jesus Christ (πίστις Ἰησοῦ Χριστοῦ; 2:16, 20; 3:22; 3:26) as metonymic allusions to the story of Jesus's faithful self-giving death on the cross.[29] If this reading is adopted, it adds even more weight to Paul's emphasis on the cross as the crux of his gospel.

In the final hortatory section of the epistle, Paul several more times refers to the cross as the heart of his proclamation. He alleges that to preach circumcision would be to avoid persecution for "the offense of the cross" (5:11; 6:12), and he declares his intention to boast in nothing other than "the cross of our Lord Jesus Christ" (6:14). These texts bear obvious links with Paul's more extended treatment of the foolishness of the *kērygma* of the cross in 1 Corinthians 1:18–2:5. But Galatians 6:14–15 extends the imagery of the cross into a remarkable apocalyptic dimension: through the cross of Christ, the *world* has been crucified, and Paul has been crucified to the world. It is this cataclysmic death of the old κόσμος through the cross that has cleared the way for "new creation" (6:15)—presumably brought into being through the resurrection of Jesus (1:1) and the work of the Spirit. The cross thus becomes the crucial pivotal event at the heart of the cosmic apocalyptic drama in which Paul sees himself and his churches living and acting. Thus any Christian theology that takes its bearings from Galatians will need to grapple with what we might call its apocalyptic *staurocentricity*.

Participation in Christ

Underlying both the paternity/sonship imagery and the imagery of the cross is a third closely related but distinguishable image: the motif of the believing

---

Galatia, Hermeneia (Philadelphia: Fortress, 1979), 131n39. See also B. S. Davis, "The Meaning of *Proegraphē* in the Context of Galatians 3.1," NTS 45 (1999): 194–212.

29. Hays, *Faith of Jesus Christ*. See esp. the "Introduction to the Second Edition," xxi–lii.

community's union with Christ. Why and how is the cross a saving event rather than a terrible cosmic tragedy? Why and how do former pagans become God's sons and receive the inheritance promised to Abraham? Paul's answer to both questions is the same: a mysterious union, a fusion of identities, has occurred, in such a way that Jesus has enacted our destiny in his death and resurrection, and we find ourselves caught up into him, incorporated into his life. Paul uses a variety of metaphors to characterize this union with Christ. Consider the following examples:

1. Paul has been crucified with Christ so that he no longer lives, but Christ lives in him. Or to put it a little differently, the life that he lives, he lives by the faithfulness of the Son of God (2:19–20).
2. Christ is the one messianic "seed" (σπέρμα) envisioned in God's promise to Abraham. Because he has received the promise (through his death and resurrection), we too receive it because we are "in" him and belong to him (3:16, 29).
3. In baptism we have been plunged into Christ, and we are now "clothed with Christ," so that we are all one in him (3:27–28).
4. Paul is a mother who is suffering the pangs of childbirth until Christ is fully formed in the Galatians (4:19).

The shorthand version of these metaphorical depictions is the simple formula "in Christ," which Paul uses repeatedly to characterize his own existence and the existence of his churches (Gal. 1:22; 2:4, 17; 3:14, 26, 28; 5:6). The second-order theological term that best describes the soteriological logic of all these passages—a term not used by Paul himself, but an apt summary of the force of these texts—is "participation in Christ." Gregory of Nyssa, in his reading of Paul, focuses clearly on this theme. His word for "participation" is μετουσία—a term that could usefully be adopted by Pauline scholarship today.[30]

This participatory soteriology is the dominant paradigm in Galatians for understanding the way in which Christ rescues his people.[31] In this respect, at

---

30. There is a particularly illuminating discussion of "participation" in Gregory of Nyssa's treatise *On Perfection*. For a brief discussion of the light shed on Paul by the comparison to Eastern patristic sources, see R. B. Hays, "What Is 'Real Participation in Christ'?" in *Redefining First-Century Jewish and Christian Identities: Essays in Honor of Ed Parish Sanders*, ed. F. E. Udoh et al. (Notre Dame, IN: University of Notre Dame Press, 2008), 336–51, esp. 347–49. For a study of participatory soteriology in Paul, see D. G. Powers, *Salvation through Participation: An Examination of the Notion of the Believers' Corporate Unity with Christ in Early Christian Soteriology*, CBET 29 (Louvain: Peeters, 2001). Yet Powers makes only slight use of patristic sources and does not cite Gregory of Nyssa at all.

31. The themes of participation in Christ and conformity to Christ have been particularly illuminated by Michael J. Gorman in two important studies: *Cruciformity: Paul's Narrative*

least with regard to Galatians, E. P. Sanders was right to contend that "the main theme of Paul's theology is found in his participationist language rather than in the theme of righteousness by faith."[32] Participation in Christ is certainly more foundational to the argument of Galatians than is any forensic conception of justification. Thus, any Christian theology that takes its bearings from Galatians must grapple with its apocalyptic vision of μετουσία: union with Christ as the means and meaning of salvation.

Paul's Apocalyptic *Poiēsis* as Theological Source and Stimulus

Reflections on the Theological Implications of Paternity, Passion, and Participation

What are the theological consequences and implications of the reading of Galatians offered in this essay? I have proposed that we should read the whole letter through the lens of 1:3–5. Paul's own introduction of his epistle frames his sharply critical pastoral response to the Galatian churches within a cosmic narrative about God's Son, Jesus Christ, who was sent forth by God the Father and gave himself up on the cross in order to rescue us from the present evil age. Consequently, if we are to take our theological bearings from Galatians, the church must work out all its teaching and all its moral and ecclesial practices within the world created through this decisive event and through the telling and retelling of this story.

The story is apocalyptic in the sense that it focuses resolutely on God's inbreaking action to end an age of slavery and bring into being a new age, indeed a new creation. But it is also very different from many other Jewish apocalyptic narratives—including Paul's own narratives in some of his other letters[33]—in that it lacks any specific speculations about future events,[34] and

---

Spirituality of the Cross (Grand Rapids: Eerdmans, 2001) and *Inhabiting the Cruciform God: Kenosis, Justification, and Theosis in Paul's Narrative Soteriology* (Grand Rapids: Eerdmans, 2009). Gorman's use of the term "theosis" in his more recent book has stirred controversy among some Protestant interpreters, but readers who attend carefully to his exposition of the term will see that he is using it in a sense that corresponds closely to the participatory and transformative soteriology found in Galatians and in Paul's other letters.

32. E. P. Sanders, *Paul and Palestinian Judaism: A Comparison of Patterns of Religion* (Philadelphia: Fortress, 1977), 552.

33. I am thinking here particularly of 1 Cor. 15:21–28, 50–57; 1 Thess. 4:13–18; and even Rom. 8:18–39.

34. The letter does gesture rather vaguely toward a future "hope of righteousness" (5:6) and God's ultimate judgment of human beings (5:7–10; 6:7–9), but these eschatological expectations are not presented as imminent, and they are given little specificity. Even the future hope of resurrection is not explicitly mentioned in Galatians.

it seems unconcerned with contemporary political events and powers. If we place Galatians and Daniel on the table alongside each other—or Galatians and Revelation—these differences stand out immediately in sharp relief. Thus, if Galatians is "apocalyptic," it is apocalyptic in its own particular transformative mode.

The hermeneutically transformative effect of this remarkable epistle is the product of Paul's *poiēsis*—his imaginative renarration of a symbolic world in which the gospel story reshapes everything. In this essay I have singled out three major motifs within that imaginative renarration. In conclusion I turn to a few brief suggestions about how each of these motifs might come into play in our theological reflection today.

1. *God the Father acts freely and graciously to rescue his people, in a totally unexpected way, to create a new covenant community of the "sons of God."* This new community is continuous with the covenant community of Israel reaching all the way back to Abraham yet at the same time is discontinuous in its surprising inclusion of gentiles as God's sons and daughters. The relation between continuity and discontinuity is worked out through scriptural exegesis that demonstrates how God's unexpected action was prefigured and promised in Israel's Scripture, whose true original sense is now at last disclosed through the apocalypse of Jesus Christ. This complex retrospective hermeneutical reconfiguration of "the Israel of God" complicates any attempt at simple judgment about whether Paul is or is not a supersessionist. A corollary of this point is that Pauline interpreters ought to quit lobbing the accusation of "supersessionism" at one another.[35]

2. *The cross is the decisive event that is the pivot point of the ages, ending the curse, ending humanity's slavery to the στοιχεῖα τοῦ κόσμου, and opening the way to the new creation.* It is remarkable that in Galatians, in contrast to his other letters, Paul pays relatively little attention to the resurrection of Jesus.[36] As we have seen, the resurrection of Jesus is foregrounded in the opening salutation; consequently, we know that Paul regards it as a key part of the gospel story. But in this particular letter, he makes it do remarkably little

---

35. For a particularly unfortunate example, see Douglas Harink's treatment of N. T. Wright in *Paul among the Postliberals: Pauline Theology beyond Christendom and Modernity* (Grand Rapids: Brazos, 2003), 151–207.

36. By contrast, see Daniel Kirk's helpful discussion of resurrection as a central theme in Romans: J. R. D. Kirk, *Unlocking Romans: Resurrection and the Justification of God* (Grand Rapids: Eerdmans, 2008). For an argument that the future resurrection of the dead plays an important *implicit* role in Galatians, see N. T. Wright, *The Resurrection of the Son of God* (Minneapolis: Fortress, 2003), 219–25: "Though Galatians does not mention the resurrection explicitly, there are many points at which it is so close to the surface that we can see it just below the waterline" (224).

specific critical work. To be sure, when he declares, "It is no longer I who live, but Christ lives in me" (2:20), it is the *risen* Christ who is portrayed as the active agent in Paul's new life. But in Galatians it is the death of Jesus on a cross that occupies most of Paul's attention and seems to fire his pastoral imagination.

The effect of this *staurocentric* narrative strategy is to highlight the radically transformative character of the gospel drama. To give one example, consider Galatians 2:21: "I do not nullify the grace of God. For if righteousness comes through the law, then Christ died for nothing." The very fact that such a drastic measure as the death of Jesus Christ was necessary demonstrates both the depth of the human predicament of bondage to death—which the law was powerless to rectify (3:21)—and at the same time the astonishing grace and love of God that conceived and executed such a costly rescue operation.

It is highly significant that God's means of carrying out this rescue is through the incarnation and self-giving death of Jesus, rather than through the violent conquest of enemies.[37] Paul formulates the logic of this position in his later Letter to Romans: "God proves his love for us in that while we were still sinners Christ died for us. . . . For if while we were enemies, we were reconciled to God through the death of his Son, much more surely, having been reconciled, will we be saved by his life" (5:8, 10 NRSV). Thus, as Michael Gorman rightly observes, for Paul the cross is the definitive sign of "God's nonviolent reconciliation."[38] This has wide-ranging implications that Christian theology and theological ethics must seek to address ever anew.

3. *In Galatians, human beings receive the benefits of God's saving action through incorporation in Christ.* The logic of salvation is *participatory.* For Christian theology, the ripple effects of this insight are extensive. It means, first of all, that the distinction between justification and sanctification is at best artificially heuristic and at worst positively misleading. One little phrase in Galatians indicates how closely these aspects of soteriology are bound together: in Galatians 2:17, Paul can speak of "seeking to be justified in Christ." Justification in fact means inclusion in the covenant community of God's people, and as we have seen, that inclusion takes place in and through union with Christ. So justification and sanctification should never be pried apart.

Of equal importance, Paul's emphasis on participation in Christ necessarily leads to a strong ecclesiology that is integral to Paul's soteriology. To be "in Christ" entails participation in the church, because "you are all one in Christ

---

37. That is one reason why Martyn's metaphor of Christ's action as an "invasion" is potentially misleading. See now the helpful essay of Susan G. Eastman, "Apocalypse and Incarnation: The Participatory Logic of Paul's Gospel," in *Apocalyptic and the Future of Theology*, ed. J. Davis and D. Harink (Eugene, OR: Wipf & Stock, 2012), 165–82.

38. Gorman, *Inhabiting the Cruciform God*, 129–60.

Jesus" (3:28). That is why the radical vision of Galatians 3:28 (neither Jew nor Greek, neither slave nor free, no "male and female") is not just a utopian social program. Instead, it is a normative vision of the new community that Jesus Christ has actually brought into being in the church. That is why Paul can complain that Cephas and his segregationist friends at Antioch were "not walking straight toward the truth of the gospel" (Gal. 2:14). The truth of the gospel is that there is one table where all the members of God's family, who all equally participate in Christ, share in the meal that embodies that communion. Any social arrangement that divides the one table into two is a denial of the new creation and a betrayal of our μετουσία in Christ.[39]

Reflections on the Style of Paul's Pastoral Theology

Of course, there are many significant theological themes in Galatians that I have not attempted to address here. For example, I have said too little about faith and about the role of the Spirit in the new creation.[40] But the three motifs I have identified offer at least a starting place for conversations about Paul's apocalyptic *poiēsis*. Yet I want to offer three concluding remarks not about the thematic substance of Paul's theology in Galatians, but about its *style*—the manner in which Paul writes as a pastoral theologian in this letter. I hazard the suggestion that each of these points might offer some useful instruction for theology in our time.

1. *Paul writes as a hermeneutical theologian.* Confronted with a fundamental challenge to his understanding of the gospel, his response is to return to a close and passionate reading of Israel's Scripture. Contrary to the once-influential view of Adolf von Harnack that Paul engaged in Old Testament interpretation only when forced to counter the views of judaizing opponents,[41] we should instead follow the much older and wiser opinion of Origen: Paul as "teacher of the gentiles" was deeply concerned about teaching his converts how to read Scripture.[42] In order to do this, he brought Israel's Scripture into a new generative conversation with the story of the death and resurrection of

---

39. For a prescient treatment of this theme, see N. A. Dahl, "The Doctrine of Justification: Its Social Function and Implications," in *Studies in Paul* (Minneapolis: Augsburg, 1977), 95–120.

40. If I were determined to keep my alliterative pattern going, I could add to my discussion of paternity, passion, and participation two additional sections on *pistis* and *pneuma*. But I forbear.

41. A. von Harnack, "Das Alte Testament in den Paulinischen Briefen und in den Paulinischen Gemeinden," *Sitzungsberichte der Preussischen Akademie der Wissenschaften: Philosophisch-historische Klasse* 12 (1928): 124–41; also as an offprint booklet (Berlin: de Gruyter, 1928).

42. Origen, in *Homilies on Exodus* 5.1, writes that the apostle Paul, "'teacher of the Gentiles,' taught the church which he had gathered from among the Gentiles, how to understand the books of the Law" (trans. amended); in Origen, *Origen: Homilies on Genesis and Exodus*, trans. Ronald E. Heine, FC 71 (Washington DC: Catholic University of America Press, 1982), 275.

Jesus Christ. In the case of Galatians, we see that this hermeneutical strategy produced reconfigured readings of the stories of Abraham, Sarah, and Hagar as well as surprising engagements with Deuteronomy and Habakkuk. We would do well to emulate this pastoral strategy; when facing challenges, we should constantly return to the study of Scripture.

2. *Paul is not afraid to think big.* Faced with a vexing controversy in his churches, he frames the problem in relation to a cosmic narrative of the gospel, a narrative of how, in the fullness of time, God the Father sent forth his Son. He does not appeal to custom or convention or to opinion polls. Instead, he retells the gospel story and thinks about the problem in radical terms. Surely that is one of the reasons why Galatians has perennially exercised such influence in the theological imagination of the church. Our knee-jerk tendency, by contrast, is to fiddle with adjustments and compromises, with procedural rules and refinements of recent political arrangements in the church. Paul might dare us to think bigger about fundamental questions.

3. *Paul is not afraid of polemic.* I offer this observation with some trepidation, because in some sectors of the church there is already all too great a readiness to adopt a polemical tone similar to Paul's brutally undiplomatic "O brainless Galatians, who has bewitched you?" (3:1). But I equally suspect that in other theological circles—and certainly in many approaches to pastoral care and preaching—the default tone has instead become one of unconditional, nonjudgmental inclusivity, a tone that greets any and all opinions and practices with tepid, suffocating tolerance. To the extent that this is an accurate diagnosis of a certain malaise in "mainstream" Protestantism, Galatians may come as a bracing blast of fresh air, with its uncompromising call: "Stand firm, and do not submit again to a yoke of slavery" (Gal. 5:1). Galatians reminds us that there are times when the truth of the gospel really is at stake, when we must not yield submission even for a moment to forces that would compromise or undermine the liberating message of Jesus Christ. The difficult task, of course, is to discern when those times are at hand, when we are confronting a *status confessionis*. We may receive help on such discernment if we return to Galatians again and again and reflect analogically on the powerful story it tells, a story of paternity, passion, and participation. And if we succeed in faithfully reading Galatians analogically as a word to the church in our time (as Luther did in his time), we too will be participating in the practice of apocalyptic *poiēsis*.

13

"Now and Above; Then and Now" (Gal. 4:21–31)

Platonizing and Apocalyptic Polarities in Paul's Eschatology

MICHAEL B. COVER

Introduction

A growing number of leading voices in the study of Galatians hold that Paul's method of scriptural exegesis in Galatians 4:21–31 is best categorized under the species of typology, but only qualifiedly under the genus of allegory.[1] While one cannot escape the word "allegory" in Galatians 4:24, in treatment after treatment one finds commentators hastily distancing themselves from its

---

I thank the Institute for Scholarship in the Liberal Arts, the Graduate School, and the Theology Department at the University of Notre Dame for their generous support of this paper.

1. See Richard B. Hays, *Echoes of Scripture in the Letters of Paul* (New Haven: Yale University Press, 1989), 105, 215n87; Susan Eastman, *Recovering Paul's Mother Tongue: Language and Theology in Galatians* (Grand Rapids: Eerdmans, 2007), 127n1; Jon Whitman, "From the Textual to the Temporal: Early Christian 'Allegory' and Early Romantic 'Symbol,'" *New Literary History* 22 (1991): 161–76, esp. 162: "By the late first century AD, however, *allegory* is implying not just a shift in language and thought, but [also] a transition in time."

literal sense.² Thus, while J. Louis Martyn notes that "for Paul, as for Philo, the two women in the Genesis story point beyond themselves," he quickly issues a caveat: "The two women are not timeless figures signifying timeless human qualities.... Allegory is here tempered fundamentally by typology."³ Martinus de Boer argues similarly: "Like Philo, [Paul] understands the text to say one thing... but to signify something other than that as well. *In contrast to Philo*, however, Paul discerns the deeper significance of the text to lie not in abstract ideas or the like but in the historical and eschatological realities of his own time and situation."⁴ One telltale thread that binds together the analyses of Martyn and de Boer is their agreement to read Paul "in contrast to Philo." Philo's timeless allegoresis (allegorical interpretation) stands in stark contrast to Paul's historicizing typology. Paul's use of the word "allegory" in Galatians 4:24 thus constitutes another potential warrant for "Galatians embarrassment," as Martyn has so aptly termed it.⁵

Of course, one can appreciate the rationale behind the preference for the term "typology." Like the Essene authors of the *Damascus Document*, who saw the fulfillment of prophetic promises taking place in their own ranks, Paul believed that he was living at the messianic turning of the ages (see 1 Cor. 10:11), a theme that is mostly absent from Philo's eschatology.⁶ However, as Frances Young pointed out some time ago, drawing a hard-and-fast line between allegory and typology often creates more problems than it solves; what is essential to both is a symbolic, even a sacramental, *mimēsis*.⁷

---

2. The unpopularity of the term "allegory" dates back to Romantic critics like Goethe, Schlegel, Schelling, and Coleridge, who considered the allegorical readings typical of early Christianity and Neoplatonism "rationalizations" that "violat[ed] the original integrity" of ancient texts. Much preferable was the tautegorical term "symbol." See Whitman, "From the Textual to the Temporal," 167–73,

3. J. Louis Martyn, *Galatians: A New Translation with Introduction and Commentary*, AB 33A (New York: Doubleday 1997), 436.

4. Martinus C. de Boer, *Galatians: A Commentary*, NTL (Louisville: Westminster John Knox, 2011), 296, emphasis added.

5. J. Louis Martyn, *Theological Issues in the Letters of Paul* (Edinburgh: T&T Clark, 1997), 111.

6. Philo does engage popular Jewish Messianism in *Rewards* 79–172, where the messianic era is assimilated to the Stoic/Roman "Golden Age," and again in a series of texts that link the Messiah and the *Logos*, such as *Confusion* 62. See Richard D. Hecht, "Philo and Messiah," in *Judaisms and Their Messiahs at the Turn of the Christian Era* (Cambridge: Cambridge University Press, 1987), 139–68.

7. Frances M. Young, *Biblical Exegesis and the Formation of Christian Culture* (1997; Peabody, MA: Hendrickson, 2002), 152: "'Typology' is a modern construct. Ancient exegetes did not distinguish between typology and allegory, and it is often difficult to make the distinction, the one shading into the other all too easily." Also 161: "Ultimately, typology and allegory contribute to *mimēsis*, or figural representation, both being so interwoven that a firm differentiation is very hard to make."

Similarly, Hans-Josef Klauck—drawing unlikely support from Leonhard Goppelt—has argued that it may actually be a methodological mistake to compare typology and allegory as parts of the same taxonomy: "Es geht bei der Typologie nicht um eine Methode, sondern um eine pneumatische Betrachtungsweise."[8] Finally, reading Paul primarily "in contrast to Philo" causes scholars to exaggerate the differences between their exegeses and unduly to overlook some illuminating common features, including typological exegesis in Philo.[9]

Counter to the prevailing trends, I read Galatians 4:21–31 not "in contrast to" but "in light of" Philo's allegorical practice and the related Hellenistic Jewish traditions found in the Epistle to the Hebrews. In doing so, I take a line still commonly held in contemporary German scholarship, which as a starting point grants Paul's use of an allegoresis similar to that found in Philo's commentaries on the Pentateuch.[10] This approach has the advantage of not presupposing a relationship between Paul and the Alexandrian corpora. Moreover, it allows the text of Galatians to speak in its full epistolary contingency, without being subjected first to a particular "typological" reading derived from Paul's method of arguing in 1 Corinthians 10:11.[11] I argue that Paul's allegory of Abraham's two sons and their two mothers *does* betray traces of a Hellenistic allegoresis that is very much concerned with the timeless, ethical figuration of the characters of Genesis 21:9–10.[12] Paul, it seems, was drawing on an exegetical tradition known to him from his advanced

---

8. Hans-Josef Klauck, *Allegorie und Allegorese in Synoptischen Gleichnistexten*, NTAbh 13 (Münster: Aschendorff, 1978), 124–25; Leonhard Goppelt, *Typos: Die typologische Deutung des Alten Testament im Neuen*, BFCT 2/43 (1939; Darmstadt: Wissenschaftliche Buchgessellschaft, 1973).

9. Klauck, *Allegorie*, 123n417, argues that Philo's allegoresis employs a kind of typology: "Angesichts der zahlreic hen Belege könnte man mit mehr Recht von einer philonischen Typologie sprechen, die aber nur ein Aspekt der philonischen Allegorese wäre." So, e.g., the Therepeutae in *The Contemplative Life* "fulfill" the type of Moses and Miriam's singing hymns at the Red Sea.

10. So Heinrich Schlier, *Der Brief and die Galater* (Göttingen: Vandenhoeck & Ruprecht, 1951), 155: "Doch handelt es nicht um reine Typologie"; Hans Dieter Betz, *Galatians: A Commentary on Paul's Letter to the Churches in Galatia*, Hermeneia (Philadelphia: Fortress, 1979), 241–43; Klauck, *Allegorie*, 118, 125: "Er soll uns nicht daran hindern, Allegorese zu nennen, was Allegorese ist"; Gerhard Sellin, "Hagar und Sara: Religionsgeschichtliche Hintergründe der Schriftallegorese Gal 4,21–31," in *Das Urchristentum in seiner literarischen Geschichte: Festschrift für Jürgen Becker zum 65. Geburtstag*, ed. Ulrich Mell and Ulrich B. Mülle, BZNW 100 (Berlin and New York: de Gruyter, 1999), 59–84.

11. Klauck, *Allegorie*, 121, like many others, succumbs to this homogenizing temptation.

12. Scholars are divided on the textual and contextual focus of Paul's allegory. While there is certainly some appeal to the broader context of the Abraham cycle, I think Paul primarily has Gen. 21:9–10 in view. For a midrashic analysis and narratological confirmation of this reading, see Michael B. Cover, "Lifting the Veil: 2 Corinthians 3:7–18 in Light of Jewish Homiletic and Commentary Traditions" (PhD diss., University of Notre Dame, 2013), 24–48.

Jewish education or the Hellenizing Antiochene prophetic circle to which he belonged.[13] By identifying rather than denying these Platonizing polarities in Paul's allegoresis, we are better able to witness how the "apocalyptic core" of Paul's gospel—even here in Galatians!—transforms Paul's engagement with Scripture and tradition.[14]

Allegoresis

There are two primary places where one can detect elements of timeless, Platonizing allegoresis in Paul's interpretation of Genesis 21:9–10.[15] These Platonizing nuances appear in Galatians 4:29, in the contrast between flesh and spirit, and in 4:26, in Paul's image of the heavenly Jerusalem.

Galatians 4:29: The Man of Flesh Persecuted the Man of Spirit

While Galatians 4:29 echoes key elements from 4:23, 28, the verse actually functions on quite a different interpretative plane. In 4:28 the phrase κατὰ Ἰσαὰκ ἐπαγγελίας recalls Paul's scriptural paraphrase in 4:23; both are literal. By contrast, 4:29 offers an interpretation of Paul's "text" (both the paraphrase and Gen. 21:9) that is allegorical.[16] One might object that the contrast between

---

13. For the theory that Gal. 4:21–31 draws on an Antiochene school exegesis, see Jürgen Becker, "Der Brief an die Galater," in *Die Briefe an die Galater, Epheser und Kolosser*, ed. J. Becker and U. Luz, NTD 8.1 (Göttingen: Vandenhoeck & Ruprecht, 1998), 9–103, esp. 70–74. For the postulation of a Jewish origin to the allegory, see Sellin, "Hagar und Sara," 61–62n3: "M.E. [*meines Erachtens*, "in my opinion"] ist sie aber weder antiochenisch-christlich noch frühpaulinisch, sondern *jüdisch*."
14. J. Christiaan Beker, *Paul the Apostle: The Triumph of God in Life and Thought* (Philadelphia: Fortress, 1980), x, who mentions that in Galatians "situational demands suppress the apocalyptic theme of the gospel." Cf. J. Louis Martyn, "A Review of *Paul the Apostle: The Triumph of God in Life and Thought*," in *Theological Issues*, 176–81; and Beker's acceptance of Martyn's critique in "Recasting Pauline Theology: The Coherence-Contingency Scheme as Interpretive Model," in *Pauline Theology*, vol. 1, *Thessalonians, Philippians, Galatians, Philemon*, ed. Jouette M. Bassler (1991; Atlanta: Society of Biblical Literature, 2002), 15–24, esp. 18.
15. "Platonizing" here includes Platonist appropriations of Stoic categories.
16. The allegorical dimension of κατὰ πνεῦμα is usually overlooked. Sellin, "Hagar und Sara," 61, appears to consider Gal. 4:28–29 an application and not part of "die eigentliche Allegorese V. 24–27" (65). However, Sellin also notes (64) that

in V. 23 ist κατὰ σάρκα freilich als Gegensatz zu δι' ἐπαγγελίας zunächst auf die natürliche Zeugung bzw. [*beziehungsweise*, "respectively"]. Geburt Ismaels bezogen. . . . In v. 29 steht dem κατὰ σάρκα jedoch das für Paulus geläufige κατὰ πνεῦμα gegenüber, das auch die am Fleische vollzogene sichtbare Beschneidung transzendiert. *So wird in der Scriftpräsentation V. 22–23 bereits die Basis für die folgende Allegorese gelegt.* (emphasis added)

In this latter characterization, Sellin seems to recognize Gal. 4:29 as an interpretation of Gal. 4:23 and as a part of the allegoresis (cf. 71). Klauck, *Allegorie*, 117–19, who also specifies "then and now" in Galatians 4:29ab points to a "typological" hermeneutic. Within the "then" clause of 4:29a, however, one finds at least two allegorical readings. First, Paul interprets Ishmael's "playing" (παίζειν) with Isaac as entailing persecution (διώκειν). Second, Paul has allegorized the literal polarity "according to the flesh" and "according to the promise" (4:23, 28), transferring their significance to the ethical plane. Ishmael and Isaac represent not merely two children, born biologically and supernaturally, but become figures of the person who is "born" carnally and of the person who is "born" spiritually. This shift is partially obscured by the fact that κατὰ σάρκα remains the same in both the literal and allegorical polarities. The δι' ἐπαγγελίας of 4:23, however, gives way to κατὰ πνεῦμα of 4:29 and shifts the ultimate significance of both phrases from the literal to the ethical.[17]

Some might object that κατὰ σάρκα here does not refer to some abstract Platonizing form of the carnal man, but to the particular judaizing Christian teachers of the Galatian crisis. Σάρξ, after all, is a polemic "cut" at these circumcising opponents. Such a polemic connotation in Paul's diction is undeniable. However, Paul does not say the "carnal" and the "spiritual" offspring exist only now (Gal. 4:29b), but also then (4:29a)—then, at the time when Ishmael and Isaac, who both were circumcised, were children. "Then" the fleshy and the spiritual man cannot have referred to Paul's immediate circumstances; rather, Paul's allegoresis of Ishmael and Isaac's births partakes in a much broader exegetical footprint, one that was common to the Judaism of Paul's day: the anthropological and eschatological contrast between flesh and spirit.[18] We find an illuminating parallel to Paul's usage in Philo of Alexandria's allegorical treatise *De gigantibus*.

De gigantibus is a treatise in Philo's *Allegorical Commentary*, which is dedicated to interpreting a mere four verses of Scripture, Genesis 6:1–4. Of particular interest are Philo's comments on Genesis 6:3: "My spirit will not

---

Gal. 4:24–27 as the allegoresis and 4:28–31 as a "praktische Anwendung," likewise, however, must explain the apparently violent implications of Gal. 4:30 by recourse to allegory: "Für das Verständnis der paulinischen Allegorese ist die Berücksichtigung der gegnerischen Front unerläßlich" (119).

17. In Gal. 3:14, God's promise to Abraham and the eschatological outpouring of the Holy Spirit are already associated with each other. Although Gal. 4:21–31 follows this passage in the letter, it nonetheless provides an independent exegetical basis for Paul's earlier reading of the promise, as a piece of technical exegesis with roots in the Jewish commentary tradition.

18. Of course, πνεῦμα in Gal. 4:29 refers first of all to God's Spirit. For both Philo and Paul, however, God's Spirit provides a ground for the proper functioning of the human spirit, and hence it has both anthropological and ethical implications. Thus Betz, *Galatians*, 278–79, appropriately characterizes Paul's flesh/spirit distinction as an "anthropological-soteriological theory" with roots in Hellenistic philosophical writers, "among them Hellenistic Judaism including Philo." See esp. Gal. 5:17 and Rom. 7.

abide with human beings forever, because they are flesh" (*Gig.* 19–54). The tension between spirit and flesh is already present in the primary biblical lemma, and Philo exploits it to good effect. The spirit is interpreted as "the pure knowledge in which every wise man naturally shares" (*Gig.* 22). This divine spirit cannot abide with most humans because of ignorance: "But the chief cause of ignorance is the flesh, and the tie that binds us so closely (οἰκείωσις) to the flesh" (*Gig.* 29). "One sort of men only does [the spirit] aid with its presence, even those who, having disrobed themselves of all created things and of the innermost veil and wrapping of mere opinion, with mind unhampered and naked will come to God" (*Gig.* 53).[19]

For Philo, as for Paul, σάρξ often expresses more than just physical matter; it represents a sphere of association and influence. Philo uses the philosophical word οἰκείωσις to demonstrate how σάρξ can appropriate things to itself (*Gig.* 29), much as relatives in a family are mutually affected by the actions of one another.[20] While Paul does not use this technical term, he does use the metaphor of indwelling (οἰκεῖν), which participates in the same semantic domain, with regard to his relation to both spirit and flesh as controlling principles.[21] That Paul and Philo use the spirit/flesh dichotomy with different nuances is certainly beyond dispute.[22] Rather than being *mere* contextual typology, however, Paul's allegory of the carnal man who persecutes the spiritual man in Galatians 4:29 draws on a broader Jewish exegetical tradition that relates certain pentateuchal characters to ethical types of behavior. This polarity undoubtedly becomes historicized in Paul's epistolary situation—but not before the allegorical shift has taken place.

---

19. All translations are based on F. H. Colson, LCL.

20. While Philo may draw the term οἰκείωσις from Stoic ethical vocabulary, his use of it is far from typical and, as such, his meaning must be determined from context. See Carlos Lévy, "Éthique de l'immanence, éthique de la trancendance: Le problème de l'*oikeiôsis* chez Philon," in *Philon d'Alexandrie et le langage de la philosophie*, Monothéismes et philosophie 1 (Turnhout: Brepols, 1998), 153–64.

21. See esp. Rom. 7:17–18; 8:9.

22. Neither is Paul's use identical to the use at Qumran. In at least one of the major Essene discourses on anthropological ethics, the primary polarity determining the individual is not the more Platonic polarity between flesh and S/spirit, but the ἀγών ("struggle") or (better) ריב ("strife") between *two spirits*, the spirit of truth and the spirit of deception: (1QS 3.18; 4.23: עד הנה יריבו רוחי אמת ועול בלבב גבר). Although flesh clearly provides a locus for the deceptive spirit's operation (4.20–21: להתם כול רוח עולה מתכמי בשרו), the primary polarity, in accord with the apocalyptic angelology of the *Community Rule*, is spiritual. This discontinuity between Paul and Qumran was already noted by W. D. Davies in his important article "Paul and the Dead Sea Scrolls: Flesh and Spirit," in *The Scrolls and the New Testament*, ed. Krister Stendahl (New York: Harper, 1957), 157–82, esp. 182: "The Scrolls and the Pauline Epistles share these terms [flesh, spirit], but it is not their sectarian connotation that is determinative of Pauline usage."

Galatians 4:26: Jerusalem Above

A second Platonizing polarity within Paul's Galatians allegory occurs in the beautiful, if perennially problematic, formulation of Galatians 4:26: "But the Jerusalem above is free, and she is our mother." Although Paul never mentions her by name, the allegory clearly refers to Abraham's wife, Sarah. The allegorical identification of Sarah as virtue or wisdom and the related notion of wisdom's spiritual motherhood are well-established traditions present in sources as diverse as Philo, the Synoptic Gospels, and the Catholic Epistles.[23] Less at ease in Paul's thought is the striking image of "Jerusalem above." Seemingly devoid of the apocalyptic dynamism that so often characterizes Paul's letters, Jerusalem above glistens in ethereal majesty, a city at peace and at rest. The image gives at least some justification to J. Christiaan Beker's famous if hyperbolic judgment that "the situational demands [of the Galatian crisis] suppress the apocalyptic theme of the gospel."[24]

Proponents of the typological reading of this pericope will be quick to note that the heavenly Jerusalem need not be a static image but rather signifies the heavenly and eschatologically descending Jerusalem of the Apocalypse of John (21:2). Paul, however, never says that the Jerusalem above is descending; to read this into Galatians 4:26 is to impose an external apocalyptic consistency onto his thought. Other traditions of Hellenistic Judaism relate a Platonized version of the heavenly city motif, which may be more germane to Galatians, such as that enshrined in Hebrews 11:13-16:

> All these died in faith, not having received the promises but seeing and greeting them from afar and confessing that they are strangers and pilgrims upon the earth [ἐπὶ τῆς γῆς]. For those who say these sorts of things reveal that they are seeking a fatherland [πατρίδα]. If they had recalled the land from which they set out, they would have had occasion to return; but now, they are yearning for a better country, that is, a heavenly one [ἐπουρανίου]. Therefore God is not ashamed to be called "their God"; for he has prepared a city [πόλιν] for them.

In Hebrews 11 this description of hope for a heavenly city (cf. Phil. 3:20) is sandwiched between two passages from the Abraham cycle. It immediately follows a description of the faith of Sarah, the barren woman (στεῖρα, Heb. 11:11; Isa. 54:1 LXX; Gal. 4:27), through whom numerous offspring were born (ἐγεννήθησαν, Heb. 11:12; see the same root at Gal. 4:23, 24, 29) to Abraham, who was as good as dead (νενεκρωμένου, Heb. 11:12; cf. Rom. 4:19). "All these" in Hebrews 11:13 probably refer to the heirs of Abraham's promise.

---

23. See Philo, *Cher.* 40–47; Luke 7:35; 1 Pet. 3:6; (cf. Matt. 11:19 par.).
24. See note 14 above.

Thus in Hebrews, as in Galatians, Sarah's spiritual children, who hope for a heavenly city, a heavenly Jerusalem, are identified with the pilgrim Christian community. The strong connection in Hebrews between the Abraham cycle and the heavenly city suggests that this, rather than the tradition represented in the *Syriac Apocalypse* (*2 Baruch* 4.1–6), represents the traditional spring of Paul's notion of "Jerusalem above" in Galatians 4:26.[25]

These two instances of abstract, timeless allegory—the carnal and the spiritual person (Gal. 4:29) and the heavenly Jerusalem (4:26)—are connected in the Platonic tradition through the adjective (ἐπ)ουράνιος.[26] The anonymous author of Hebrews uses that term to describe the heavenly Jerusalem in Hebrews 11:16. Similarly in Philo's ethical allegory, the spiritual man is linked with the first Adam of Genesis 1:27 and described as "heavenly."[27]

Apocalyptic

If the Platonizing-Jewish tradition of the heavenly person who is an exiled citizen of the heavenly city provides the context in which Paul's Galatians allegory was birthed, the thunderous clouds of apocalyptic are never far from the horizon. The apocalyptic dimension of the allegory makes itself felt most prominently in Paul's antithesis to "Jerusalem above," which is not the expected "Jerusalem below" (κάτω), but the more urgent and asymmetrical "Jerusalem now" (νῦν, Gal. 4:25; see the similar tension in Heb. 11:15–16). With this formulation, we are plunged back into the temporal polarity that seems to dominate the allegory

---

25. *Contra* Betz, *Galatians*, 246–47, who along with Schlier (*Der Briefan die Galater*), sees an "apocalyptic origin" to the tradition, followed by a kind of "Gnosticizing adaptation." It is important to note here that the spatial dimension of "Jerusalem above" is not thematized in *2 Bar.* 4.1–6; rather, its heavenly location is only implied through the explicit relational designation, the city "with me" (4.3, 6).

26. This connection in Galatians is conceptual rather than lexical, as (ἐπ)ουράνιος does not appear in Galatians. The word is Pauline, however, see, e.g., 1 Cor 15:40, 48. Harold W. Attridge, *The Epistle to the Hebrews: A Commentary on the Epistle to the Hebrews*, Hermeneia (Philadelphia: Fortress, 1989), 330, notes that "the imagery of the patriarchal confession was similar to what Greek tradition had long used to describe the fate of the soul in the world, an exile from its true heavenly home." While Philo's allegory "expand[s] the basic notion of earthly alienation," both he and the author of Hebrews clearly work from a "common Hellenistic Jewish interpretation."

27. A prime example of Philo's topological anthropology can be found in his *Allegorical Interpretation*, where he interprets the consecutive P and J accounts of creation. "There are two types of human beings," writes Philo, "the one a heavenly [οὐράνιος] human being, the other an earthly [γήϊνος] human being" (*Alleg. Interp.* 1.31). These humans represent two minds, Philo tells us, one created after the image of God (Gen. 1:27) and one molded from the earth (2:7). Only "the mind that was made after the image and original," however, "might be said to partake of the spirit (πνεῦμα)" (*Alleg. Interp.* 1.42).

in its final form, clearly thematized in the "then and now" of Galatians 4:29. Paul, it would seem, has taken a Platonizing exegesis and transformed but not effaced it in light of the apocalyptic urgency of his gospel to the gentiles.[28]

Thus κατὰ σάρκα comes more specifically to mean those fleshy people (gentile or Jew) who think Christians must be circumcised; κατὰ πνεῦμα, conversely, acquires an apocalyptic edge, signifying the people born through the eschatological outpouring of the Holy Spirit in baptism. Even "Jerusalem above," it seems, is transformed under the pressure of "Jerusalem now." The ἄνω (4:26) appears timeless at first blush; yet through the pressures of the Galatian crisis, it acquires an implicit temporal dimension and leaves the reader wondering whether to read it "Jerusalem above" or "Jerusalem hereafter/again." The Pauline ἄνω of 4:26 thus approaches but never completely attains the temporal dimension of the Johannine ἄνωθεν, when Jesus tells Nicodemus that participation in the kingdom, the kingdom of the spirit, which is at war with the flesh (John 3:6–8), depends on being born "again and from above" (3:3; cf. 3:13).

"Jerusalem above" thus bequeaths to Pauline eschatology a kind of messiness. On the one hand, contrary to any clear apocalyptic delineation between the two ages or the sequential account of salvation history found in Galatians 3:17–29, Jerusalem now and above exist, in the allegory, simultaneously.[29] On the other hand, Jerusalem above represents the holy city as both a present and a future transcendent reality. The relation between that future Jerusalem and "Jerusalem now," however, whether one understands the latter as a symbol of Mosaic Judaism or the Jerusalem church, remains finally underdetermined.[30]

---

28. Gregory E. Sterling, "Ontology versus Eschatology: Tensions between Author and Community in Hebrews," *SPhilo* 13 (2001): 190–211, esp. 209–10, reaches a similar conclusion about the confluence of Platonizing and apocalyptic elements in the Epistle to the Hebrews: "The introduction of Jesus Christ radically changed the static worldview presumed in these exegetical traditions by imposing an eschatological understanding of history." I prefer to think of the difference not in terms of eschatology versus ontology, but in terms of two different eschatological horizons, found in the apocalyptic and Platonizing strands of Judaism. David E. Aune, "Anthropological Duality in the Eschatology of 2 Corinthians 4:16–5:10," in *Paul beyond the Judaism/Hellenism Divide*, ed. T. Engberg-Pedersen (Minneapolis: Fortress, 2001), 215–39, has argued that Platonic and apocalyptic eschatologies are indeed combined by Paul in 2 Cor. 5.

29. So Whitman, "Textual to the Temporal," 163:

> Paul does not treat the two covenants in his allegory as two stages in a straightforward chronological succession. . . . Part of the tension in his approach to history comes from the fact that although for him the Redeemer has come with 'the fullness of the time' (*to plērōma tou kronou*, Gal. 4:4), time is not yet fully redeemed. "Old" and "new," like Ishmael and Isaac, remain nearly contemporaneous. Perhaps it is significant that in his allegory the "present Jerusalem" is contrasted not with the Jerusalem to come, but with "the Jerusalem above" (*anō Ierousalēm*, 4:26).

30. So Michael Wolter, "Das Israelproblem nach Gal 4,21–31 und Röm 9–11," *ZTK* 107 (2010): 1–30, esp. 9, argues that Paul's allegory in Galatians is not concerned with answering "the Israel-question as such."

In the contingency of his epistle, Paul chooses to emphasize the transcendence of Jerusalem as a present spiritual reality and its incompatibility with the visible Jerusalem of his day.

The importance of this messiness for the study of Pauline exegesis is likewise significant. It means that Paul does not simply "cast out" the Platonizing traditions of Hellenistic Judaism for temporal, apocalyptic ones, but draws the two traditions together. Platonizing ethical allegory thus becomes a co-laborer rather than a competitor with Paul's "core" apocalyptic hermeneutic in announcing the victory of God in space and time.

14

Christ in Paul's Narrative

Salvation History, Apocalyptic Invasion, and Supralapsarian Theology

EDWIN CHR. VAN DRIEL

What is the place of Christ in Paul's narrative? This question is central to the debate between a salvation-historical and an apocalyptic reading of Paul. On a salvation-historical reading, Christ is presented as only a chapter in a much more extended covenantal history of God and God's people—which seems inconsistent with what Beverly Roberts Gaventa calls "the singularity of the gospel."[1] On an apocalyptic reading, Christ's coming is understood as an apocalyptic invasion of God into this world—which seems to abrogate the previous salvific presence of God in and through Israel. In this essay I will analyze these different understandings of Paul's narrative, arguing that, in the end, both accounts are christologically deficient, ironically, in structurally similar ways. I then offer a third account as an alternative.

---

1. Beverly Roberts Gaventa, "The Singularity of the Gospel: A Reading of Galatians," in *Pauline Theology*, vol. 1, *Thessalonians, Philippians, Galatians, Philemon*, ed. Jouette M. Bassler (Minneapolis: Fortress, 1991), 147–59.

A Salvation-Historical Reading

For a salvation-historical reading of Paul, I turn to the work of N. T. Wright. In his writings, argues Wright, Paul "has in his head and heart, as a great many Second Temple Jews did, a grand story of creation and covenant, of God and his world and his people, which had been moving forward in a single narrative and which was continuing to do so."[2] This "single plan" is a salvific plan. In response to a world gone awry, a world described in Genesis 1–11, God "called Abraham so that through his family he, God, could rescue the world from its plight."[3] Call it, says Wright, "the reason God called Abraham" or "the Creator's purpose, through Israel, for the world."[4] Whereas "the whole world had been cursed through Adam and Eve, through the human pride that led to Babel, the Creator God would now bring blessing to that same whole world. That was the point of the covenant."[5] Alas, although Israel was supposed to be God's salvific answer to the problem of sin, in the course of its history Israel itself becomes part of the problem. As Paul concluded, says Wright, "the problem with the single-plan-through-Israel-for-the-world was the 'through Israel' bit: Israel had let its side down, had let God down, had not offered the 'obedience' which would have allowed the worldwide covenant plan to proceed. Israel, in short, had been faithless to God's commission."[6] It is in the context of this single plan, with its failed agency of Israel, Wright argues, that for Paul the meaning of Christ should be understood. "The task of the Messiah was to offer to God the 'obedience' which Israel should have offered but did not."[7] Since Israel had failed in its calling to become a blessing to all the nations, "what is needed ... is a faithful Israelite through whom the single plan can proceed after all."[8] The Messiah, the one "in whom God's people are summed up,"[9] offers what Israel was supposed to offer and thereby ushers in the long-awaited "beginning of the entire new creation."[10]

---

2. N. T. Wright, *Justification: God's Plan and Paul's Vision* (Downers Grove, IL: IVP Academic, 2009), 34.
3. Ibid., 94.
4. Ibid.
5. Ibid., 99.
6. Ibid., 104–5.
7. Ibid., 104.
8. Ibid., 105.
9. Ibid., 114.
10. Ibid., 106. The understanding of Israel embedded in this narrative, Israel as an agent in God's salvific response to sin, has been a constant in N. T. Wright's work, as in "The Paul of History and the Apostle of Faith," *TynBul* 29 (1978): 61–88, esp. 65–66; idem, *The Climax of the Covenant: Christ and the Law in Pauline Theology* (Edinburgh: T&T Clark, 1991), esp. 18–40; idem, *What Saint Paul Really Said* (Oxford: Lion; Grand Rapids: Eerdmans, 1997), 30–62; and idem, *Paul in Fresh Perspective* (Minneapolis: Fortress, 2005), 24–39.

The theological problem with this narration is that Christ becomes accidental to the "single plan" of salvation. The very thing Christ does could have been accomplished by another agent—Israel; in fact, it *should* have been accomplished by Israel, and it would have been done if Israel had not fallen into disobedience. But this means that, in the context of salvation, Jesus is really plan B, and this is not congruent to a robust christological account of salvation.[11] In the New Testament's account, salvation is intimately bound up with the person of Christ. For instance, as Paul puts it in Romans 8, our glorification and justification are embedded in our predestination, and the content of our predestination is that we are destined to be conformed to the image of Christ, "in order that he might be the firstborn within a large family" (Rom. 8:29–30 NRSV). If that is true, Christ is not accidental to salvation, as if although now salvation entails being conformed to the image of Christ, we could have been patterned after someone else. After all, predestination is the preorderly determination of one's eschatological goal. If to be justified rests in one's predestination, and if to be predestined is to be foreordained to conform to the image of Christ, and if the motivation of our being conformed to Christ's image is the desire to make Christ the firstborn within a larger family—then Christ is essential to salvation. A single-plan-through-Israel-for-the-world would not have accomplished that for which we are predestined to be: the family of Christ.

An Apocalyptic Reading

For an apocalyptic reading of Paul, I turn to the work of J. Louis Martyn.[12] Whereas on Wright's account salvation comes to us through time, Martyn's understanding of salvation is governed by the concept of space. For him, the incarnation does not embody the apex of a long history, but the invasion of an occupied territory. The image that shapes Martyn's interpretation is that of a twice-invaded world. He paints the picture of heaven and earth created in such a way that the earth part of it is permeable, subject to entry from heaven. The

---

11. Perhaps it would be better to speak of "plan C": the "single-plan-through-Israel-for-the-world" in response to a world gone awry is plan B; the "Messiah's offering the obedience that Israel should have offered but did not" is plan C.

12. See esp. J. Louis Martyn, "Events in Galatia," in *Pauline Theology*, 1:160–79; idem, *Galatians: A New Translation with Introduction and Commentary*, AB 33A (New York: Doubleday, 1997); idem, *Theological Issues in the Letters of Paul* (London: T&T Clark, 1997); idem, "The Apocalyptic Gospel in Galatians," *Int.* 54 (2000): 246–66; and idem, "World without End or Twice-Invaded World?," in *Shaking Heaven and Earth: Essays in Honor of Walter Brueggemann and Charles B. Cousar*, ed. Christine Roy Yoder et al. (Louisville: Westminster John Knox, 2005), 117–32.

first such incursion happened when sin entered the world. For Paul, Martyn argues, "sin" is not so much an individual affair caused by volitional choices but a matter of suprahuman powers that have invaded and enslaved God's creation.[13] This invasion leads to the establishment of what Paul calls "*this world*"—an entity in its own right, and with its own creator: "We would not be totally wrong to say—with the poetic language of tragedy—that Sin is virtually the *creator* of *this* world."[14] *This* world is what Paul also calls "the present evil age": a world "not under the immediate and exclusive hegemony either of God or of human beings" and therefore "the frightening, horrifying scene of genuine and profound disaster."[15]

This world was, however, invaded again when the earth was climactically and determinatively entered by God in the person of Christ. Paul calls this divine invasion apocalyptic (Gal. 1:12; 2:2), not in the sense of "God's unveiling something that was previously hidden, as though it had been eternally standing behind a curtain" and finally now in the present age was revealed, but rather as a violent divine apocalyptic incursion that brings *this* world, the cosmos as we know it, to an end.[16] In this context Martyn points out that, when Paul describes the result of Christ's coming, he does not speak of "a new age" but "a new creation."[17] By speaking of "a new creation," Paul signals that God's invasion was not "merely repairing *this* world" but rather, "in fundamental contrast to *this* world, God's new creation is *the* new."[18]

This new creation is established, Martyn holds, not in Christ's resurrection but in Christ's crucifixion. Even the resurrection does not leave the cross behind—as Martyn says, quoting Ernst Käsemann, "'The theology of the resurrection is a chapter in the theology of the cross, not the excelling of it.' Seen through resurrection lenses, the cross itself remains the event of God's weak power, the event in which power is, in fact, transfigured and thus fundamentally redefined."[19] The new creation is therefore fundamentally cruciform. The bodily shape of the new creation, says Martyn, is the church, and this church is "cross-bearing": it is "the community of those who . . . are conformed to the crucified one for the sake of others."[20]

For Martyn, understanding the incarnation as an invasion in enemy territory

---

13. Martyn, "World without End?," 121; *Galatians*, 95–97.
14. Martyn, "World without End?," 120.
15. Ibid., 122.
16. Martyn, *Galatians*, 99.
17. Martyn, "Apocalyptic Gospel in Galatians," 254.
18. Martyn, "World without End?," 126.
19. Ibid., 126, quoting from his teacher Ernst Käsemann's *Perspectives on Paul* (Fortress: Minneapolis, 1971), 59. Martyn's "theology of the cross" is strongly influenced by Käsemann.
20. Martyn, "World without End?," 128.

excludes any notion of a "linear *praeparatio evangelica*," a "salvific linearity prior to the advent of Christ."[21] An evangelical promise was given to Abraham, but, says Martyn with reference to Galatians 3:16, "the covenantal promise uttered by God to Abraham . . . remained in a sort of docetic state until the advent of the singular seed, Christ."[22] The relationship between Abraham and Christ is only punctiliar, not linear.

The theological problem with Martyn's reading is that it is christologically deficient in ways structurally analogous to the deficiency of Wright's salvation-historical account. On Wright's account, Christ is accidental with respect to salvation: Christ comes as the solution to Israel's failure. As such, Christ's coming is thus "plan B," accomplishing something that could and should have been accomplished through another agent. This cannot be said of Martyn's reading: the saving divine incursion that breaks the power of God's cosmic enemy is essentially bound up with the person of Christ. There is no suggestion that anyone but God could have brought this world to an end. However, the fact *that* God entered the world is nonetheless a response to a problem. It is not part of the original design of creation; it is solely contingent on a state of affairs that is an attack on God's design, not part of that design: the attack is sin's invading and enslaving God's creation. And if this is true, on Martyn's account Christ's coming is no less a "plan B" than on the reading offered by Wright.

That for Martyn the incarnation is indeed solely contingent on sin is underscored by his conceptualization of the eschaton. Martyn's account rightly suggests that Christ makes a twofold difference: he overcomes the power of sin, and he inaugurates an eschatological reality, the new creation. A theologically important question is how these two aspects of Christ's work relate. One could imagine an account that holds to a Christocentric eschatological consummation as the essential goal of God's creation. I propose such an account in the last pages of this essay. On such an understanding we are, as it were, created "for Christ" (Col. 1:16). Because Christ is central to all creation, he is also to be the one who, when creation is overcome by the powers of sin, draws creation back to God in reconciliation and redemption. This redemptive work of Christ is done for the sake of his eschatological work: we are redeemed so that we may be part of the new creation. The cross is thus a function of the eschatological difference Christ makes. And whereas Christ's redemptive work is accidental to God's relating to creation—after all, if no sin had invaded creation, no redemption would have been necessary—the eschatological is essential: for this we were created.

---

21. Martyn, "Events in Galatia," 174.
22. Ibid., 172; cf. Martyn, *Galatians*, 337–41.

However, on Martyn's account there is no sense of such a Christocentric eschatological future as the essential goal of creation. The cross is not a function of the eschaton, but the eschaton is a function of the cross: it is only in the cross that the new creation is being established, and this eschaton is cross-shaped. But the cross is, of course, contingent on sin—which means that on this account Christ's eschatological work is contingent on sin.

If the incarnation, in all its eschatological and redemptive aspects, is contingent on sin, Martyn no more than Wright can say, as Paul does in Romans 8, that we are predestined to be conformed to the image of Christ "in order that he might be the firstborn within a large family" (Rom. 8:29–30 NRSV). On Paul's account, our predestination and ensuing salvation are for the sake of *Christ*: we are predestined to be Christ's family. But on Martyn's account, Christ is there for the sake of *our* predestination and salvation.

Martyn's apocalyptic reading is certainly different from Wright's salvation-historical hermeneutic. Nonetheless, these accounts are theologically problematic in structurally the same way. Ironically, the very thing that makes Martyn resist salvation history makes him similarly christologically deficient. It is Martyn's understanding of Christ's coming as an apocalyptic invasion into this world that makes him resist a *praeparatio evangelica*, but it is also that very notion that makes him conceive of Christ's coming as a plan B.

A Supralapsarian Reading

For an alternative account, I take a page from the Letters to the Colossians and Ephesians. Often these are kept out of discussions about Paul because their Pauline authorship is in dispute, but since at least one of my conversation partners assumes the authenticity of these letters, I think that such an appeal is permissible and, as I will argue, actually helpful.[23] And even if these were not written by Paul, this would only discredit my proposal as a contribution to Pauline interpretation, not as a theological contribution to the debate about the issues at stake.

With respect to these letters, I draw attention to three points. First, both letters expound an understanding of the incarnation that could be called christologically *supralapsarian*: an understanding of the incarnation as not simply a response to human sin, but as also motivated by considerations that go deeper than the need to deal with the sin problem.[24] This is the clearest

---

23. N. T. Wright, *The Epistles of Paul to the Colossians and Philemon*, TNTC (Grand Rapids: Eerdmans, 1986), 31–34; cf. idem, *Justification*, 168.

24. Such supralapsarian Christology (from *supra*, "before," and *lapsus*, "fall") stands in opposition to an infralapsarian (*infra*, "after") Christology holding that the incarnation is

in the Colossians hymn that speaks of Jesus as the one who "is the image of the invisible God, the firstborn of all creation; for in him all things in heaven and on earth were created, things visible and invisible, whether thrones or dominions or rulers or powers—all things have been created through him and for him. He himself is before all things, and in him all things hold together" (Col. 1:15 NRSV). If Christ is "the firstborn of creation," and the one "for whom" all things have been created, then Christ is much more than one who is contingent on sin.[25] On the Colossians/Ephesians account, Christ does not enter a preexisting relationship between God and the world, but he is both this relationship's origin and source. It is also Christ and no one else who deals with the problem of sin. That itself is an expression of this preorderly priority of Christ: when the relationship between God and creation is undermined, it is also through Christ that God deals with the sin problem, "so that," as the hymn says, he who already was the firstborn of creation "might come to have first place in everything" (Col. 1:18 NRSV). All of this means that Christ is not accidental to the story of salvation, as in Wright's account, as if there first was salvation history, in which Israel fails, and then Jesus is introduced; it also means that Christ is not a stranger to the history preceding the incarnation, as in Martyn's account. Since everything is created by him and for him, he is this history's source and goal.

Second, both letters emphasize that the actual incarnation, the moment that Christ comes in the flesh, embodies the revelation of a mystery "that has been hidden throughout the ages and generations" (Col. 1:26 NRSV; Eph. 3:5), the content of which is "a plan for the fullness of time, to gather up all things in [Christ], things in heaven and on earth" (Eph. 1:9 NRSV). "Mystery" is apocalyptic language—not the same apocalyptic language as

---

contingent on sin. Wright and Martyn both hold an infralapsarian Christology. For an analysis and defense of supralapsarian Christology, see Edwin Chr. van Driel, *Incarnation Anyway: Arguments for Supralapsarian Christology* (Oxford and New York: Oxford University Press, 2008). For the sake of clarity, it may be helpful to point out that the terms "supralapsarian" and "infralapsarian" are used with respect to two theological loci: election and Christology. There is no direct correlation between one's position on the supralapsarian/infralapsarian debate with regard to these two loci. There have been theologians who were "supralapsarian" with regard to both (e.g., Karl Barth); there are also those who are supralapsarian with regard to election but infralapsarian with regard to Christology.

25. The meaning of each term used in the Colossians hymn to describe the relationship between Christ and creation is fraught with difficulties. The supralapsarian argument does not, however, hang on any particular exegesis as to what it means, for instance, to be "the image of the invisible God," "the firstborn of creation," or that "all things are created for him." While some readings of these concepts certainly strengthen the supralapsarian case more than others, all the argument hangs on the simple observation that if all things are created "for him" (Col. 1:16), then any christological account that makes the incarnation contingent on sin—and therewith contingent on creation—falls short of what Colossians says.

Paul uses in Galatians, but apocalyptic terminology nonetheless.[26] However, as it turns out, the content of this apocalyptic mystery is a plan of history: that all things are created so as, through the course of history, to be gathered together in Jesus Christ. According to Colossians/Ephesians, "a salvific history" and God's apocalyptic revelation are thus not opposites; they are in fact very tightly woven together.

Third, while the apocalyptic event of the incarnation reveals that everything is meant to be gathered into Christ, this gathering follows a particular pattern. Christ himself forges a new humanity, and Ephesians explains how this goes: "Now in Christ Jesus" the ones "who once were far off have been brought near." People who were "aliens from the commonwealth of Israel and strangers to the covenants of promise" are now being gathered to Israel so that those who once were strangers and aliens now are "citizens with the saints and also members of the household of God" (Eph. 2:13, 12, 19 NRSV). In other words, the gathering of all things has started with the gathering of Israel, the covenant with Abraham, and continues now with the goyim, the non-Jews, being gathered into this covenant as well. However, since the gathering activity of Christ is, according to these letters, not a response to sin but the (original) goal of creation, then the beginning of this gathering activity, the covenant with Israel, is also not in itself a response to sin, as Wright's salvation-history account has it, but has itself a supralapsarian character.[27]

---

26. See, e.g., Eduard Lohse, *Colossians and Philemon* (Philadelphia: Fortress, 1971), 74; and R. McL. Wilson, *A Critical and Exegetical Commentary on Colossians and Philemon* (London and New York: Continuum, 2005), 176.

27. Thus supralapsarian Christology implies a supralapsarian eschatology (the final goal of creation is essentially to form Christ as a large family [Rom. 8:29]), a supralapsarian understanding of Israel's election (the formation of this large family begins with the election of Israel), and a supralapsarian ecclesiology (the formation of the church itself is also not contingent on sin, but it is the community in which the final goal of creation already becomes visible). The latter of these lines up nicely with some of the ecclesiological comments in Wright's own work in which the newly defined "people of God" is called "an eschatological people," a people that will rule with Christ eschatologically. See esp. N. T. Wright, *Surprised by Hope: Rethinking Heaven, the Resurrection, and the Mission of the Church* (New York: Harper Collins, 2008); and idem, *After You Believe: Why Christian Character Matters* (New York: Harper Collins, 2010).

In response to the presentation of an earlier version of this essay at the "Galatians and Christian Theology Conference," N. T. Wright strongly rejected the notion that his is an infralapsarian Christology, referring to his 1980 publication *Evangelical Anglican Identity: The Connection between Bible, Gospel, and the Church* (reprinted in J. I. Packer and N. T. Wright, *Anglican Evangelical Identity: Yesterday and Today* [London: The Latimer Trust, 2008]). Indeed, there is a paragraph in that publication that is of supralapsarian character:

> This whole range of thought, reflected all through the gospels and summed up in such passages as Romans 5:12–21 and 8:1–30, 1 Corinthians 8:5–6 and 15:20–28, Ephesians 1:3–23, Philippians 2:5–11 and 3:2–21, Colossians 1:9–23, allows us to return to our starting-point and reflect on the eternal saving purposes of God. Within the confession

These three characteristics together shape a christological narrative that, theologically speaking, seems superior to both the salvation-historical and the apocalyptic alternative. It is a narrative that allows us to say, with the writer of the Letter to the Romans, that we are predestined to be conformed to the image of Christ "in order that he might be the firstborn within a large family" (Rom. 8:29–30). At the same time, it is an account that incorporates both the notions of the apocalyptic nature of the revelation and the salvific nature of history. If the Colossian and Ephesian letters are indeed some of Paul's later writings, Paul himself must have judged this account superior—after all, this is where he ended up. And even if these letters are by "Deutero-Paul," their theological superiority still stands. Therefore, when we do our own theological work, it is the third model that recommends itself for expansion.

---

that Jesus, the Messiah, is Lord, the church acknowledges him as the true sovereign over the universe, who takes the place intended for man from the beginning and thus, since humanity was made for him in the first place, takes at last his own rightful place, enters into his true inheritance, becomes manifest as the Lord of the World, which he was from the beginning. Here is the center of the Gospel. God made man to be Lord of the world so that his eternal Son, the Word through whom and for whom all things were made, should become manifest as Lord of the world by becoming true Man. (66–67)

Nevertheless, the problem is, first of all, that this single passage is preceded by several pages in which Wright gives his usual infralapsarian narrative of the gospel story:

In the context of the Old Testament, the call of Abraham is God's answer to the problem spelt out in Genesis 3–11. . . . But all through the Old Testament these truths are set out as paradoxes. God's covenant with Abraham, and with Moses, has not resulted in the salvation of the world, but has instead shown up Israel's own sin and failure. . . . Israel is unable to take her place as the key figure in God's worldwide saving plan. . . . God's rescue operation thus devolves onto Israel's representative. (90–91; cf. 92–95)

Also, Wright does not work out how the supralapsarian notion that follows may work as a corrective for the infralapsarian reading of things. Second, while the infralapsarian reading of the relationship between creation, Israel, and Christ becomes Wright's standard framework through which he reads the salvation-historical narrative (see note 10 above), this supralapsarian intuition is not repeated in Wright's later work.

15

"In the Fullness of Time" (Gal. 4:4)

Chronology and Theology in Galatians

TODD D. STILL

Introduction

In his magisterial commentary on Galatians, J. Louis Martyn maintains that the question the apostle Paul places at the center of the letter is "What time is it?"[1] Relatedly, Martyn reminds readers "that the matter of discerning the time lies at the heart of apocalyptic" and maintains that "in writing to the Galatians Paul addresses the issue of time in terms clearly apocalyptic."[2] For Martyn, "God's apocalyptic invasion of the cosmos in Christ . . . creates a radically new perception of time."[3]

An earlier version of this essay was published in the *Journal for the Study of Paul and His Letters* 2 (2012): 133–41, and appears here by the kind permission of Eisenbrauns.

   1. So J. Louis Martyn, *Galatians*, AB 33A (New York: Doubleday, 1997), 104, where he contends that Paul causes the question "What time is it?" "to be the crucial issue of the entire letter." According to Martyn (*Galatians*, 23), the other question that Paul is at pains to answer in Galatians is "In what cosmos do we actually live?" Cf. J. Louis Martyn, "Apocalyptic Antinomies in Paul's Letter to the Galatians," *NTS* 31 (1985): 410–24.

   2. Martyn, *Galatians*, 104.

   3. Ibid.

Martyn asks, "What time is it?" And Martyn answers:

> It is the time after the apocalypse of the faith of Christ, the time, therefore, of God's making things right by Christ's faith, the time of the presence of the Spirit of Christ, and thus the time in which the invading Spirit has decisively commenced the war of liberation from the powers of the present evil age.... If Paul is sure that Christ's parousia will bring the final victory of God over all his enemies (1 Corinthians 15), he is no less sure that Christ's advent has commenced the war that will lead to that victory.[4]

In Martyn's view, "Paul's apocalyptic perspective ... has, in fact, three foci: Christ's future coming, Christ's past advent (his death and resurrection), and the present war against the powers of evil, inaugurated by his Spirit and taking place between these two events."[5]

Whereas Martyn has emphasized the apocalyptic texture of Galatians and in doing so has drawn particular attention to the category of time, Richard B. Hays has alerted exegetes to the "narrative substructure" of the letter, that is, the narratival presuppositions regarding the story of Jesus Christ that undergird and shape the apostle's theological formulations and rhetorical expressions in Galatians.[6] In the words of Luke Timothy Johnson, Hays posits the following in his now thirty-plus-year-old volume *The Faith of Jesus Christ*, which Eerdmans subsequently issued in a second edition: "Unless we understand that Paul and his readers share a story and that Paul seeks both to allude to and to apply that story in ways that correct their misapprehensions and clarify the story's implications, we do not read him aright."[7]

Is it possible to combine narratival and apocalyptic readings of Paul in general and Galatians in particular? Even if it were possible, would it be advisable to do so? In response to these questions, Francis Watson might respond in Pauline parlance: μὴ γένοιτο. In the Bruce W. Longenecker–edited volume *Narrative Dynamics in Paul*, Watson concludes his essay by contending, "The only 'narrative substructure' in Paul is the scriptural narrative or narrative collection from which he draws in order to elucidate an essentially nonnarratable gospel."[8]

---

4. Ibid., 104–5.

5. Ibid., 105.

6. Richard B. Hays, *The Faith of Jesus Christ: The Narrative Substructure of Galatians 3:1–4:11*, 2nd ed. (Grand Rapids: Eerdmans, 2002).

7. Ibid., xv.

8. Francis Watson, "Is There a Story in These Texts?," in *Narrative Dynamics in Paul: A Critical Assessment*, ed. Bruce W. Longenecker (Louisville and London: Westminster John Knox, 2002), 231–39, esp. 239.

Watson's claim notwithstanding, in what follows I will follow trails blazed by Martyn as well as by Hays in examining aspects of (1) historical continuity/horizontal linearity and (2) apocalyptic discontinuity/vertical disruption in the apostle's fiery communiqué ταῖς ἐκκλησίαις τῆς Γαλατίας.[9] I begin by scouring the letter along temporal lines before turning to consider the timely/timeless story set forth in its weighty lines.

Time as More than Ticktock on the Clock

The concentration of time-related language in Galatians is arresting. It is surprising, therefore, that (to the best of my knowledge) no full-length study exists on this topic. To be sure, students of Pauline chronology have painstakingly treated Paul's mention of "three years," "fifteen days," and "fourteen years" in 1:18 and 2:1, respectively. Additionally, the apostle's contention in 3:17 that the law came 430 years after God's covenant with Abraham has occasioned no small amount of discussion. What is more, Paul's employment of χρόνος (4:1, 4), καιρός (4:10; 6:9, 10), αἰών/αἰώνιος (1:4, 5 [2x]; 6:8), and καινὴ κτίσις (6:15) has not been lost on interpreters of the letter. The same may be said of the apostle's mention of his former life in Judaism in 1:13–14 (cf. 1:23) and of the "days, months, seasons, and years" of which he speaks in 4:10 (cf. ὥρα ["hour"] in 2:5 and προθεσμία ["date"] in 4:2).

Albeit considerable, the following observations demonstrate that these texts are but the tip of the temporal iceberg in the apostle's Letter to the Galatians. In the first instance, let us note the concentration of adverbs of time in Galatians. Thus πάλιν ("again") appears nine times;[10] ὅτε ("when") and νῦν ("now") six times apiece;[11] οὐκέτι ("no longer") four times;[12] ἄρτι ("now"), ἔτι ("still"), ἔπειτα ("then"), and τότε ("when") three times each;[13] and ταχέως ("quickly," 1:6), πρότερος ("formerly," 4:13), and λοιπός (in the sense of "henceforth," 6:16) once. Less pervasive, though far from inconsequential, are the temporal participles found in 2:7 (ἰδόντες), 2:9 (γνόντες), and 3:3 (ἐναρξάμενοι);[14] and the verbs προεῖπον (to "say before") in 1:9 and 5:21; and προεῖδον (to "see before") in 3:8. Πρό ("before") also occurs as a preposition in 1:17; 2:12; and 3:23, as does μετά (meaning "after") in 1:18 and 3:17. Lastly, Paul employs

---

9. The words in quotations are from James D. G. Dunn, "The Narrative Approach to Paul: Whose Story?" in Longenecker, *Narrative Dynamics in Paul*, 217–30, esp. 222.
10. See Gal. 1:9, 17; 2:1, 18; 4:9 (2x), 19; 5:1, 3.
11. See ὅτε in Gal. 1:15; 2:11, 12, 14; 4:3, 4; and νῦν in 1:23; 2:20; 3:3; 4:9, 25, 29.
12. In Gal. 2:20; 3:18, 25; 4:7.
13. Note ἄρτι (Gal. 1:9, 10; 4:20); ἔτι (1:10; 5:11 [2x]); ἔπειτα (1:18, 21; 2:1); τότε (4:8, 29; 6:4).
14. Cf. the temporal nature of the perfect participle ἐνεστῶτος (from ἐνίστημι) in 1:4.

the preposition ἄχρι(ς) ("until") in 3:19 and 4:2 and the preposition μέχρις ("until") in 4:19.

What shall we say then about Paul's liberal employment of temporal terminology in Galatians? To begin, having "crunched the numbers," allow me to offer a few observations regarding the concentration and distribution of such language. Of the 149 verses in Galatians, terms pertaining to time occur in 51 verses—that is, in 34.23 percent of the verses that comprise the letter. Furthermore, at times there is more than one temporal element in a given verse (see, e.g., 1:4, 9, 10, 18; 2:1, 12; 4:2, 4, 9, 10, 19, 29). More specifically, timely terms occur in 50 percent of the verses comprising chapter 1 (12 of 24), 42.86 percent in chapter 2 (9 of 21), 24.14 percent in chapter 3 (7 of 29), 41.94 percent in chapter 4 (13 of 31), 15.38 percent in chapter 5 (4 of 26), and 33 percent in chapter 6 (6 of 18). Regarding the distribution of temporal language according to the broad, largely agreed-upon panels of the letter, it is as one might expect. In the so-called autobiographical section (chaps. 1–2), there are 21 references in 45 verses (46.66 percent); in the "doctrinal/theological/biblical" division (chaps. 3–4), 20 references in 60 verses (33 percent); and in the paraenetical/ethical part (chaps. 5–6), 10 references in 44 verses (22.73 percent).

At this point in the essay, you might be thinking, "There are three kinds of lies: lies, damned lies, and statistics." To be sure, statistics do not tell the whole story, but they can shape the plot. We will soon get to the rest of the story, but for now it is worth noting that the question Martyn believes drives Galatians—What time is it?—is more pervasive than he indicates and is broader ranging than his chosen interpretive framework of apocalypticism. Even as water is everywhere in "The Rime of the Ancient Mariner," time is everywhere in Paul's Letter to the Galatians.

How are we to read Galatians and the apostle's various references and appeals to time therein? Once again, Martyn is instructive. He maintains that Galatians is best read as a preachment, an announcement replete with antinomies, "more revelatory and performative than hortatory and persuasive, although it is both." Martyn remarks, "In short, Paul is concerned in letter form to repreach the gospel in place of its counterfeit."[15] Moreover, as John M. G. Barclay has recognized with special reference to Galatians: "In the preaching of the gospel, time becomes, as it were, concertinaed, and the past becomes existentially present. Without this constant present time, of gift and demand, the church becomes merely the bearer of a new tradition, playing out her part in a narrative whose turning point is long in the past. But for Paul the decisive event is always also now: Will Christ be formed in you?

---

15. Martyn, *Galatians*, 23.

(4:19)."[16] Along with ethnicity, social class, and gender (see Gal. 3:28), in the gospel Paul preaches in Galatians, time seems almost to collapse and to be relativized as Christ crucified is placarded afresh before the eyes of both the initial auditors and eventual readers of the letter (3:1).[17]

It Is Story Time

If time is warped in Galatians and if "in the Galatian context Paul's interest in time is dominated by his concern to affirm the *termination* of slavery under the law *after* Christ,"[18] it nonetheless seems to me that a certain sequence of events or episodes is present and significant. In his monograph *The Faith of Jesus Christ*, Hays remarks, "At least since Aristotle [see *Poetics* 1450B], people have been sagely observing that every story must have a beginning, a middle, and an end."[19] Hays then turns to note that the French semiotician A. J. Greimas incorporated this "conventional wisdom" when he posited that a "fundamental narrative structure is composed of three 'sequences'": the initial sequence, the topical sequence, and the final sequence. Hays explains these three sequences thus: "The initial and final sequences are called 'correlated sequences,' because they are related to one another in a very specific way: the final sequence represents the completion of a task that was somehow stymied in the initial sequence or the reestablishing of an order that was disrupted in the initial sequence. The 'topical' sequence is so called because it forms the center of attention ('topic') of the story. A single story may have several topical sequences (the more complex the story, the more of these are likely to appear)."[20]

Here, I apply Greimas's fundamental narratival model, as presented by Hays, to the apocalyptic story Paul spins in Galatians. I would like to do so in seven steps under three headings—the sequences set forth by Greimas. Unlike Hays, I will not seek to move beyond narrative sequences to narrative syntagmas. That being said, as Hays rightly observes, "The thing that matters is the message of the text, the story that it tells and interprets. Methodology

---

16. John M. G. Barclay, "Paul's Story: Theology as Testimony," in Longenecker, *Narrative Dynamics in Paul*, 133–56, esp. 146.
17. According to Barclay ("Paul's Story," 140), God's apocalypse of his Son in Paul enabled him to see "with utterly different eyes, from a perspective that radically relativises, if it does not wholly obliterate, all social and historical categories" (cf. 3:28; 6:15).
18. So Yon-Gyong Kwon, *Eschatology in Galatians: Rethinking Paul's Response to the Crisis in Galatia*, WUNT 2/183 (Tübingen: Mohr Siebeck, 2004), 128.
19. Hays, *Faith of Jesus Christ*, 84.
20. Ibid.

is a secondary and instrumental concern."[21] Similarly, Nils Dahl notes "that the really burning questions cannot be answered in principle but only through constant new encounter with the material."[22] Even as Paul wrote in large letters in concluding Galatians (6:11), in what follows I will necessarily employ rather broad brushstrokes in treating Galatians.

The Initial Sequence: The Time before Faith

Although Paul, of course, wrote Galatians subsequent to the revelation of faith/Christ in general and his proclamation of the gospel in Galatia in particular, in the course of his letter he will at times consider matters from the vantage point of "before faith came" (πρὸ τοῦ δὲ ἐλθεῖν τὴν πίστιν, 3:23). When he does so, the picture he paints is anything but pretty. Looking back over his spiritual shoulder, Paul sees the power and sinister effects of sin(s) (1:4; 3:22) and people enslaved to the στοιχεῖα τοῦ κόσμου (4:3), to the φύσει μὴ οὖσιν θεοῖς (4:8) (cf. 4:24, 25; 5:1).

Faith in God the Father (1:1, 3, 4; 4:6), who is one (ὁ δὲ θεὸς εἷς ἐστιν, 3:20), was not altogether absent in this epoch. Father Abraham evinced as much, and righteousness was resultantly credited to his account (3:6; cf. Gen. 15:6; Rom. 4:3). The promise that all the nations would be blessed in faithful Abraham (3:8; cf. Gen. 12:3) did not come to pass straightway, however. Instead, the law came into play, albeit 430 years after said promise (3:17). In the time between promise and fulfillment—both of which, Paul propounds, coalesce in Christ, τό σπέρμα (3:16)—the law held sway, serving as something of a spiritual holding card "until the offspring should come to whom the promise had been made" (3:19).

Although Paul forcefully insists that the law is by no means against the promises of God (3:21) and readily admits that before faith/Christ came, the law served the necessary, if negative, functions of restraining, imprisoning, and guarding (3:19, 23; cf. 5:23), it would be hard to confuse the *paidagōgos* with the promise in Galatians (3:24–25, 29; 4:28). Indeed, the abiding impression this interpreter gains from Galatians regarding the (works of the) law is its purported impotence. For instance, Paul contends that the law is unable to make alive (3:21), that righteousness does not come through the law, that no person is rectified before God by the works of the law (2:16, 21; 3:11, 21;

---

21. Ibid., xxvii. Hays continues by citing a comment made by Hans Frei (*The Identity of Jesus Christ: The Hermeneutical Bases of Dogmatic Theology* [Philadelphia: Fortress, 1975], xv): "The theoretical devices we use to make our reading more alert, appropriate, and intelligent ought to be designed to leave the story itself as unencumbered as possible."

22. Nils A. Dahl, "The Crucified Messiah," in *Jesus the Christ: The Historical Origins of Christological Doctrine*, ed. Donald H. Juel (Minneapolis: Fortress, 1991), 27–47, esp. 29.

cf. 5:4), and that spiritual inheritance does not come from the law (3:18). Additionally, Paul juxtaposes the works of the law with (the) faith(fulness) in (of) Christ (2:16), with the hearing of faith (3:2, 5), and with the Spirit (5:18). More ominous still, blending Deuteronomy 27:26 and 28:58–59 (cf. Deut. 30:10), Paul declares, "All who rely on the works of the law are under a curse" (3:10 NRSV). In moving from the initial sequence to the topical sequence, the plot thickens.

The Topical Sequence

THE TIME OF THE GOSPEL

Paul can perceive and speak of the present age as evil (1:4); he simultaneously recognizes that it was into the very sin-scarred cosmos of decay and death, bondage and travail, that "in the fullness of time God sent forth his Son, born of a woman, born under the law, to redeem those who were under the law, so that [they] might receive adoption as children" (4:4–5). This redemption, enabling the adoption of gentiles as well as Jews (3:8, 14), would prove to be quite costly.

Indeed, through the Lord Jesus Christ's cursed and yet faithful death on a tree (and his resurrection from the dead [1:1]), the law's curse was reversed, the Abrahamic blessing was extended to gentiles, and the eschatological promise of the Spirit was received in order that believers, now children and heirs, can cry "Abba! Father!" (3:13–14; 4:6–7). Christ's self-giving death for sin and transgression allows for and leads to liberty and life, to freedom from self-indulgence and freedom to loving service (1:4; 5:6, 13).

In a word, Christ's coming in the midst and fullness of time changed everything, for in and through his person and mission he has inaugurated a new creation (6:15; cf. 2 Cor. 5:17). Christ and his cross have become Paul's only boast; through the crucified Christ "the world was crucified to [Paul] and [Paul] to the world" (6:14). But it had not always been that way.

TIME AND THE APOSTLE

There was a time, Paul reminds the Galatians, when he was advancing in Judaism. So zealous was he for the ancestral customs that he was outstripping many of his Jewish contemporaries. So zealous was he for Yahweh and Torah that he was hell-bent on eradicating the church of God and the faith thereof (1:13–14, 22). He regarded it as a cancer on the body Jewish, whose removal was essential.

The time would come, however, when it pleased God, who, as with Jeremiah and the Isaianic Servant of old, "set [Paul] apart before he was born," to call him and to reveal his Son in him so that he might take the gospel to the gentiles (1:15–16). Disquiet and discord notwithstanding (2:1–14), preach the gospel to the gentiles he did, whether in Syria, Cilicia, or Galatia (see, e.g., 1:8, 21, 23).

The Apostle's Time in Galatia

When Paul first preached the gospel in Galatia, be it in the north or in the south, he was beset with a physical ailment (lit., "weakness of the flesh," 4:13). Nevertheless, those gentile people, who "formerly . . . did not know God" (4:8) yet would come to comprise the Galatian churches, received him as if he were "an angel of God," even "as Christ Jesus" himself (4:14). Not only did those Galatians to whom Paul writes enthusiastically embrace the apostle (4:15: "For I testify that, had it been possible, you would have torn out your eyes and given them to me" [NRSV]), they also appear to have eagerly and faithfully embraced the Christocentric, cruciform, grace-based, Spirit-inspired gospel that he preached (1:6; 2:5; 3:1–5).

The Apostle's Time Away from the Galatian Assemblies

Despite the kerygmatic and didactic labor of Paul and his fellow missioners (note, e.g., 1:9; 5:21; cf. 5:3; 6:6), after their departure certain rival teachers, whom Paul views as self-serving "agitators" and "troublemakers" (1:7; 4:17; 5:10, 12; 6:12), made their way to Galatia and took off from where Paul and his coworkers had left off. In so doing, they countered Paul's strong claim—that gentiles did not need to become law-observant in order to be part of the "household of faith," "the Israel of God" (6:10, 16)—and tacked on various "works of the law," not least circumcision (5:2–3; cf. 4:10). All the while, it appears that these Jewish-Christian teachers were committed to casting aspersions on both the apostle and his gospel (1:10; 5:11; 6:17).

For his part, Paul regards these latter ecclesial developments as nothing short of an unmitigated disaster; indeed, he thinks his converts are courting spiritual disaster. Doubtless, Paul is pulling out what little hair he is said to have (*Acts of Paul* 3.3). He fears that the Galatians have been bewitched (3:1) and that he has labored in vain (4:11; cf. 2:2; 3:4). The apostle is stunned and flummoxed that his *tekna* would turn so quickly and stupidly for another gospel, which is not a gospel at all (1:6–7a; 4:19). Such a turn, Paul figures, marks a return to paganism and its thralldom and a decided, fateful move away from the God "who called [them] in the grace of Christ" (1:6; 4:9).

Moving Back in Time

Since Paul is not able to be physically present with the Galatian congregations and "change [his] tone" (4:20), he crafts an impassioned letter encouraging these believers to dispense with their new teachers and to get back on spiritual track. To move forward, they first need to think backward. Paul likens the agitators' influence to leaven and insists that their "persuasion does not come from the one who calls [the Galatians]" (5:7–9 NRSV). Paul calls his converts, therefore, to recall that they began with the Spirit, not the flesh (3:3), and he admonishes them to walk by the Spirit and not carry out the desires of the flesh (5:16–23, 26). Indeed, "Those who belong to Christ Jesus have crucified the flesh with its passions and desires" (5:24 NRSV). Additionally, Paul enjoins the Galatian churches to concord, not discord; care, not conceit; discernment, not deceit; and well doing, not weariness (5:26–6:10).

The Final Sequence: The Time beyond Time

Paul's less-than-salutary wishes for his Jewish-Christian competitors (see esp. 1:9; 5:12) and his less-than-flattering depiction of his Galatian converts (see 3:1) should be, I contend, regarded as much more than apostolic saber rattling and muscle flexing. In terms of sequence, even as Paul is convinced that the initial sequence gives way to the topical one, he is no less persuaded that there will be, as it were, a final sequence. "For through the Spirit, by faith," Paul writes, "we [i.e., believers] eagerly wait for the hope of righteousness" (5:5 NRSV). Paul thinks and teaches that what one believes (or fails to believe) and how one behaves (or fails to behave) matters for both time and eternity.

Each person, Paul instructs, "will have to bear their own load" at the coming judgment (6:5). Those who cut themselves off from the grace of the crucified Christ and sow to the flesh—and bear the fruit thereof—will reap corruption and not inherit the kingdom of God, Paul says (5:3, 21; 6:8). Contrariwise, those who sow to the Spirit and manifest the Christomorphic character of the Spirit's fruit, having been more fully formed into the likeness and law of Christ (see 4:19; 5:14, 22–23; 6:2), will in due time—God's good time—reap a spiritual harvest (6:9). Until harvesttime, believers are to work for the good of all people, and especially for the faithful (6:8, 10).

Conclusion: Galatians as a Timely Call to Recall the Gospel Story

If the question that looms large in Galatians is "What time is it?," the answer the apostle offers in response is clear. It is high time the Galatian congregations, "upon whom the ends of the ages have come" (1 Cor. 10:11b), (re)turn to the true gospel that Paul has first proclaimed to them, which they have joyfully embraced. The apostle declares that the true, ever-new story of Jesus Christ's apocalypse, foreseen and proclaimed in Scripture (3:8), exposes the alternative narrative being offered by the teachers for what it is—passé and false. Paul is appalled that the Galatians, who have been baptized into and have put on Christ (3:27), would even contemplate, much less commit, to living in a BC-way in an AD-day.

In brief, Paul is banking the whole of his life and ministry on the truth and superiority of his story regarding the grace and gospel of Jesus Christ. This grace and gospel has arrested and grasped him to the extent that he lives his life by faith in/by the faithfulness of the Son of God, who loved him and gave himself for him (2:20). Paul's hope for the initial recipients of this letter is one and the same. One can imagine, and with good reason, that the apostle wants nothing less or else for contemporary believers who are willing to be addressed and redressed by Galatians.

16

Karl Barth and "The Fullness of Time"

Eternity and Divine Intent in the Epistle to the Galatians

DARREN O. SUMNER

One of Paul's aims in his Letter to the Galatians is to draw their attention to the history of God's covenant and the place of the Galatian converts in it. As Paul narrates it, this covenant unfolds in a sequence of historical moments: the promise to Abraham (Gal. 3:8), the giving of the law "430 years later" (3:17), the birth of Jesus (4:4–5), and finally the adoption of men and women in their baptism (3:25–27). The Galatians have a place in this history, and are thus charged to live in the recollection of it (1:6–9; 3:1–6). At the center of covenant history is the sending of God's own Son: "When the fullness of time had come, God sent forth his Son, born of a woman, born under the law, to redeem those who were under the law" (4:4–5a ESV). A theological reading of the letter finds this phrase "the fullness of time [τὸ πλήρωμα τοῦ χρόνου]" particularly provocative. In what follows I explore the theological nature of time as it relates to the covenant, expressed in Galatians in terms of the finitude of the law's authority over God's people.

Paul suggests that the time of the law ceases when God sends his Son into the world. But "the fullness of time" here has a more profound connection to the church's theological reflection on the covenant, particularly with respect to the doctrine of election. This time, I suggest, has reached its fulfillment not because the law has now finally accomplished its own task or because those who have been subject to the "pedagogy" of the law (cf. 3:24) have managed to learn something or to accomplish something. No, this moment was the time of fulfillment because God had predetermined it to be so from ages past—even before the law itself was given. And so in sending his Son, God is not changing his plan but enacting it, breaking into creation to bring the time of the law to an end. In classically trinitarian terms, this is the *mission* of the divine Son.[1]

Given a deliberately theological interpretation, then, Galatians 4:4 directs Christian reflection to election and Trinity—that is, to God's determination for relationship with creatures, and to the shape of that relationship. On these points it will be fruitful to consider both classical trinitarianism and the critical thought of one twentieth-century thinker, Karl Barth. As a Reformed theologian Barth was particularly preoccupied by questions of covenant relations, including the manner in which human temporality might relate to the eternity that is God's very being. Following the tradition, I suggest that what is taking place in a historical event—the birth of Jesus to a young woman in the city of David—is the accomplishment of what God intended from the first moment of the covenant. These two moments—the decision of God to send his Son, and its historical occurrence—are held together in Paul's letter by this phrase "the fullness of time." More than this, however, they indicate that the humanity of the incarnate Son has a part even in the eternal life of the triune God.

Creaturely Time and Expectation

It is common to the Christian tradition to say that God is eternal, not standing within the procession of linear time and not bound to a succession of stages.[2] Time itself is a creation, and so as the Creator God stands outside and above it. For Thomas Aquinas this is a consequence of confessing God as immutable and perfect in essence: time is the measurement of movement and change, and

---

1. In this essay much of what I am arguing for directly contradicts Thomas Aquinas in *Summa theologica*, trans. Fathers of the English Dominican Province, 2nd and rev. ed. (London: Burns, Oates, & Washbourne, [1921?]–1932), (hereafter: *ST*) I, q. 43, a. 2 ("Whether mission is eternal or only temporal?"). Not surprisingly, here Thomas uses Gal. 4:4 as his key proof text. It is beyond the scope of this essay, however, to engage Thomas's arguments point by point. In short, what I believe Thomas overlooks is the factor of *divine intent*: "mission" does not have a strictly temporal significance for God because, as I will argue below via Barth, (1) God is eternally present *to* the temporal moment of the Son's execution of his mission, and not apart from it; and (2) this decision is God's own self-commitment of his existence.

2. Cf. Augustine, *Confessions* 11; *City of God* 11.6; Thomas Aquinas, *ST* I, q.10.

eternity describes God's lack of these. Time, says Thomas, "is nothing but the numbering of movement by 'before' and 'after.'"[3] So far, so good. But in his description of time, Barth does not stop there. As the eternal One, God's relationship to time is not that of the Creator who merely reaches into his creation from without in order to effect revelation. God is rather the One who *enters into* time, not only acting within it as a venue but also committing to it his being as God—"[stepping] into the heart of the inevitable conflict between the faithfulness of God and the unfaithfulness of man," as Barth puts it.[4] This he calls "the time of revelation."

On Barth's account, then, time is multiform. God's own time is eternity—not an absence of time, but rather that which fully comprehends time but in turn is not exhausted by it. Nor is eternity an infinite quantity of time within which even God himself exists. Rather, "eternity is the simultaneity of beginning, middle and end," Barth says, and so it is *"pure duration."*[5] And eternity is not some *thing* that is other than God—for *all* that is not God is what we call creation. Therefore uncreated eternity is the divine essence itself.[6] God's eternity is his freedom from a temporal past that is also "no longer" and a future that is also "not yet."[7] The God who loves in freedom is therefore constant, without uncertainty or capriciousness in God's orientation toward creatures. It is this constancy that secures the covenant: the promise made in the past renders *certain* the fulfillment in the present and consummation in the future.

With this divine time, Barth contrasts the time of creatures, in which the past, present, and future are distinguished from one another and even opposed to one another.[8] Between time as God created it and time as we know it stands the fall. Time is a part of creation, and so it is not unaffected by sin. Our time is "lost time" and "fallen time,"[9] which stands in need of redemption. A third time is a much-needed intermediary, providing for an intersection between the real time of God and the lost time of creatures. This is the "time

---

3. *ST* I, q.10, a.1 *responsio*. See further *ST* I, q.10, a.1–2.
4. Karl Barth, *CD* (1956–75), II/2:397.
5. Barth, *CD* II/1:608; cf. Thomas Aquinas, *ST* I, q.10, a.2, r.4; *ST* I, q.10, a.4.
6. Barth, *CD* II/1:638–39: "Like every divine perfection it is the living God Himself.... Eternity is His essence. He, the living God, is eternity." Thomas agrees (*ST* I, q.10, a.2 *responsio*): "Nor is He eternal only; but He is His own eternity; whereas, no other being is its own duration, as no other is its own being. Now God is His own uniform being; and hence as He is His own essence, so He is His own eternity."
7. See Barth, *CD* II/1:608. "The Word of God is. It is never 'not yet' or 'no longer.' It is not exposed to any becoming or, therefore, to any passing away, or, therefore, to any change." Cf. *CD* I/2:52.
8. *CD* II/1:608.
9. *CD* I/2:47.

of revelation," where God not only "has time" for us but also "He Himself *is* time for us. For His revelation as Jesus Christ is really God Himself."[10] When we read in Galatians that God sent his Son, we should conclude neither that this Son is a creature nor that he is a second divine being emanating from the God and Father of Israel. More than the angel or the prophet who is sent to represent God, who even speaks with God's voice, the Son is the very presence of God in the world.

This third time is the time of Jesus Christ—God's own, self-revealing presence within the bounds of creation. Barth calls this *"fulfilled* time"—and now we see the immediate point of connection with Galatians 4:4. It is fulfilled because in Jesus Christ time itself "has discovered its origin and its aim."[11] To say that the Son is sent "in the fullness of time" is to say that *time itself exists for this moment*. God takes away our time that is broken by the fall and in its place gives us our real time, a time that is genuine. The covenant pattern to which Paul directs our attention makes this clear: the Old Testament is a time of expectation, where Israel through its prophets anticipates the coming fulfillment of God's promises—but where God himself remains hidden.[12] The law held men and women captive *until* the revelation of faith (3:23); it was our guardian *until* Christ came (3:24). "But now that faith has come, we are no longer under a guardian, for in Christ Jesus you are all sons of God, through faith" (3:25–26 ESV).[13] Indeed, Barth concludes, all the prophecies of the Old Testament are without content—"incomplete," even "defective"—apart from the coming of the kingdom in the man Jesus. And "so too it is with time in itself and as such." Without the fullness it finds in the time of Jesus Christ, time itself is without meaning.[14]

Paul's pointing the Galatians to their own history is what Barth identifies as the New Testament's time of *recollection*, where the church, through the witness of the apostles, testifies to the fulfillment of God's promises that has now taken place.[15] Expectation has a quality of vagueness or uncertainty, but recollection looks back to a particular, concrete time and event that is now

10. *CD* II/1:612, emphasis added.
11. *CD* I/2:69; cf. *CD* III/2:459.
12. *CD* I/2:70–101 (§14.2); cf. 84, 90.
13. The shift indicated by this coming is not "a gradual maturation, but rather of a punctiliar liberation, enacted by God in his own sovereign time," according to J. Louis Martyn. It is distinctively apocalyptic: God is not waiting for men and women to reach maturity under the tutelage of the law but is breaking in, closing "the enslaving parenthesis of the Law at the time chosen by him alone." See J. Louis Martyn, *Galatians: A New Translation with Introduction and Commentary*, AB 33A (New York: Doubleday, 1997), 389.
14. See Barth, *CD* III/2:461–62; *CD* IV/3:584.
15. *CD* I/2:101–21 (§14.3).

known.[16] It is to this witness, the gospel that they have heard, that Paul calls the Galatians to be faithful.

Between the two—the expectation that accompanies the promise of God and the recollection enabled by its fulfillment—stands the Christ event, the sending of God's Son to be born of a woman, born under law, to redeem those who were under the law. This "time of revelation" changes everything: the creature's orientation to God becomes that of an heir. *Now* the Spirit of Christ who is in you calls out, "Abba! Father!" (4:6). *Now*, through the cross of our Lord Jesus Christ, "the world has been crucified to me, and I to the world" (6:14 ESV). The "fullness of time" is the moment at which God's promise comes to pass: the pedagogy of the law is concluded, and the law gives way to faith.

Eternity and Nativity

There is a slight ambiguity in the way Paul uses the term *the fullness of time* in Galatians 4:4. Is this the time of the law or the time of the Son? If the former, is its fulfillment positive, in the sense that the objectives of the time leading up to Jesus's advent are complete? Or is it instead negative: struggle as it might to maintain a grip on men and women, its time is "up"? This is part of a much larger discussion about the purpose and the goodness of the law in Paul's theology. However we might navigate this question, though, what is important for my purposes is that the change is brought about by divine intent, in fulfillment of a plan already known to God from the beginning.

When, then, is this beginning? Paul offers us few clues in Galatians, since here his concern is with the covenant as it has played out in history—its execution and inevitable consummation. The closest Paul comes to suggesting an origin to the covenant is in 3:6—"Abraham believed God, and it was credited to him as righteousness," a citation of Genesis 15:6. The Abrahamic covenant is the oldest form of a covenant with the particular people who would become the nation of Israel, a covenant marked by the sign of circumcision (Gen. 17:10–14). But the covenant itself is indeed much older—or, we might say, God's *intention* to establish this covenant is much older. And here is where we must look away from Galatians to Ephesians 1, where we read that God chose us in Jesus Christ to be adopted sons and daughters "before the creation of the world" (Eph. 1:4–5). Based on this and other like statements in Scripture, it appears certain that this covenant has an eternal dimension. Insofar as its enactment is historical, and therefore temporal, its role in God's

---

16. "The form now has a content that corresponds to it exactly. The question has now achieved its precise answer" (*CD* I/2:104; cf. 111).

chosen means of relating to creatures is eternal—for its origin is in the will and the ways of an eternal God.

Barth himself took license to interpret the covenant addressed in Galatians by way of the protological activity of God spoken of in Ephesians. On two separate occasions in the *Church Dogmatics*, where Barth is considering the phrase "the fullness of time," he turns from Galatians 4:4 immediately to Ephesians 1:9–10.[17] Here we read that God set forth his will and purpose in Christ "as a plan for the fullness of time [τοῦ πληρώματος τῶν καιρῶν]" (Eph. 1:10). Indeed, Barth says, Jesus Christ *is* the "pleroma of the time"[18] because he is God's self-giving to creatures; he is the content and meaning that fills up the empty vessel, the ground of the only "real time."[19]

Now it is well known that Barth located election not within the dogmatic spheres of creation or reconciliation but within his doctrine of God. What implications might our reading of time and covenant in Galatians have for God's triune life? Three observations are in order. First, the end of the law and the sending of God's Son to be born is an event that rests on a free and eternal decision. God not only ordained this time but, because of the simultaneity in which God exists to all created moments, God is eternally present to this moment (and it is eternally present to him). Time, Barth suggests, is the "formal principle" of God's free activity outward (while "eternity is the principle of His freedom inwards").[20] It is the freedom of God that unites the divine missions and the divine processions, or God's temporal activity for creation and God's own eternity as One who exists as pure duration.[21]

Second, because the Son of God is not originated in being born of a woman but is before all time,[22] in his very person the Son is "God Himself in His turning

17. *CD* I/2:53; *CD* III/2:459.
18. *CD* I/2:55.
19. *CD* I/2:53.
20. *CD* II/1:609.
21. This much, at least, is consistent with Thomas when he grants that we may say that the mission "includes the eternal procession, with the addition of a temporal effect.... Hence the procession may be called a twin procession, eternal and temporal" (*ST* I, q.43, a.2, r.3).
22. Traditionally interpreters have pointed to Gal. 4:4 and the "sending forth" of the Son as indicating the preexistence of Christ—though modern criticism calls into question whether this conclusion is necessary. See, e.g., John Calvin, *Commentaries on the Epistles of Paul to the Galatians and Ephesians*, trans. William Pringle (Edinburgh: Thomas Clark, 1841), 98. James D. G. Dunn observes that God "sends forth" all sorts of agents (angels, Wisdom, plagues, human messengers, etc.) to do his will, and that does not mean they are eternally preexistent. See James D. G. Dunn, *Christology in the Making: A New Testament Inquiry into the Origins of the Doctrine of the Incarnation*, 2nd ed. (London: SCM, 1989), 38–44, esp. 39. Martyn agrees that preexistence is not a necessary conclusion, arguing that the important thing to Paul is not the incarnation of a preexistent Son but that "the Son's sending is an invasion of cosmic scope, reflecting the apocalyptic certainty that redemption has come from outside, changing the very

to the world." God "is identical with Jesus Christ," Barth says: "Eternity itself bears the name of Jesus Christ."[23] Jesus therefore has what the tradition called a *duplex nativitas*—a "double birth," one eternal and one temporal.[24] As the Son of God who is sent out from eternity, he is eternally generated by the Father. By this, the classical tradition has sought to secure not an atemporal origination (in the sense of a coming into being) but an eternal relation of Son to Father. He is, in the words of the creed, "begotten" and not made. But as Mary's son he also experienced a human birth, uniting himself with a human nature and subjecting himself to the full depths of temporality, in all its radical implications.

This is not to say, however, that this event—occurring in a historical moment—is new to God. God's self-relatedness as Father, Son, and Spirit already gives the being of God the character of an event,[25] and by virtue of divine election these mutual relations include the relation of the Son's history and the Son's eternity. In Barth's hands, then, the distinction between these two "nativities"—the eternal generation of the Son and Jesus's temporal birth—is qualified in an important sense: the Son's eternal existence is not a *lack* of time but a "fullness" of Jesus's divine-human history. The eternal moment in which God elects himself for the redemption of creatures is concretized in the historical event of Jesus's birth in Bethlehem.[26] Thus, Barth concludes, Jesus Christ is the eternity in which God is simultaneously present to creation's past, present, and future. And so what comes to be in time has, in a very real sense, *always been* for God—especially where God's own life is in question.

The *duplex nativitas* therefore has a significance far more profound than the tradition recognized: the birth of God's Son spoken of in Galatians 4:4 is a true *repetition* of his eternal generation, for it does not add to him anything that he did not previously possess.[27]

---

world in which human beings live, so that it can no longer be identified simply as 'the present evil age' (1:4)." See Martyn, *Galatians*, 407–8, esp. 408.

23. Barth, *CD* II/1:622, citing John 8:58; Eph. 1:4–6; 1 Pet. 1:18–21.

24. Barth cites Martin Luther: "God begat the same One from eternity whom [Mary] bore in time." Martin Luther, *Enarratio 53 cap. Essaiae prophetae* (1550), cited in *CD* I/2:139. The issue here is the identity of the man Jesus with the eternal Word of God, which the Council of Ephesus (431 CE) attempted to secure by calling Mary Θεοτόκος. On the double nativity, see also John of Damascus, *Exact Exposition of the Orthodox Faith* 3.7.12; and Thomas Aquinas, *ST* III, q.35, a.2–3 (cf. *ST* I, q.43, a.2, r.3).

25. On this point see Eberhard Jüngel, *God's Being Is in Becoming: The Trinitarian Being of God in the Theology of Karl Barth; A Paraphrase*, trans. John Webster (Edinburgh: T&T Clark, 2001), 42–43.

26. On this theme see further Bruce L. McCormack, "Karl Barth's Historicized Christology: Just How 'Chalcedonian' Is It?," in *Orthodox and Modern: Studies in the Theology of Karl Barth* (Grand Rapids: Baker Academic, 2008), 201–33.

27. This is not to say that Jesus brought his humanity with him from heaven. His humanity is taken from the Virgin Mary; Jesus "possesses" it even in his eternal generation because, as

Third, and finally, this double birth—the sending of God's Son that fulfills God's covenant intentions—is an act to which God has committed his own existence, according to Barth. God's gracious intentions toward creatures are eternal; thus the covenant has an eternal dimension. If this is the case, the "fullness of time" suggested by Paul is seen to be all the more profound: it is not simply a predetermined date for the birth of God's Son, but especially the historical actualization of God's relationship with creatures that God elected before time began—not *a* moment in covenant history but indeed *the* moment. The "fullness of time," in this sense, is the very fullness of creation itself. It is the original gospel, the grace of Christ in which men and women are called to live (Gal. 1:6).

Conclusions

God is eternal and triune. How then does God relate to a temporal creation? He does so by means of the covenant, which is fully realized in the sending of God's Son to redeem, that is, to fulfill the promise that came with the law. This relation is conditioned by the eternity that God is: for God the covenant is not past, present, and future, but eternally present in God's will and God's knowledge. This sending is God's own personal entrance into time, the repetition in time of who the Son is in eternity. The relationship that exists in the inner being of the Trinity "is repeated and reflected in God's eternal covenant with man as revealed and operative in time in the humanity of Jesus." In his being for humanity, then, the man Jesus "repeats and reflects the inner being or essence of God."[28] As the repetition of God himself, the humanity of Jesus is the *imago Dei*. And the Son, of course, is not alone in his procession: the Holy Spirit eternally proceeds from the Father and the Son.[29] In the same way, Paul follows the sending of the Son into time with the sending of his Spirit into the hearts of believers (Gal. 4:6).[30] We might therefore call Pentecost the repetition in time of the Holy Spirit's eternal procession. In this, its fulfillment,

---

God, he is eternally present to this historical event. The time-eternity dialectic therefore undoes all questioning about *when* the Son of God became human, which includes the vexing matter of the Son's divine immutability in the incarnation.

28. Barth, *CD* III/2:218–19. See also Jüngel, *God's Being Is in Becoming*, 120–21.

29. Considered as the effects of the grace that is their common cause, Thomas says, the missions of the Son and the Holy Spirit cannot be without each other "because neither takes place without sanctifying grace, nor is one person separated from the other" (*ST* I, q.43, a.5, r.3).

30. Martyn observes that the verb ἐξαποστέλλω, "to send out," appears in Paul's Letters only here in Gal. 4:4, 6. See Martyn, *Galatians*, 407. Charles B. Cousar is one who notes the trinitarian character of this divine work. See Charles B. Cousar, *Galatians*, Interpretation (Atlanta: John Knox, 1982), 97.

the covenant is seen to have a trinitarian shape—not as a *pactum* between Father and Son as discrete individuals, but as the activity of the One God's taking on a human existence, in his mode of being as Son, for the purpose of reconciliation.[31]

To complete the circle, one final observation is in order. If (1) in God's own life there is no before and after, no beginning, succession, and end; and if (2) the sending of God's Son into the world is the repetition of his generation in eternity; and if (3) this sending is to fulfill the covenant that God purposed before creation itself; and if (4) this covenant and its fulfillment signify God's self-commitment to creatures, then we conclude that the temporal existence of God—which is the humanity of the Son—has a reality even in the eternal life of God. This "humanity of God," as Barth called it, is grounded in the dialectic of promise and fulfillment. In sending his Son, God causes himself to correspond to the "time of revelation," so that in turn the lives of creatures are made to correspond to the image of the Son. We who were once slaves are now sons and daughters and heirs, because "God has sent the Spirit of his Son into our hearts."

---

31. Jüngel declares, "God's way into the far country is indeed the way of the *Son* of God; in that primal decision, in the unity of the *Spirit* between the *Father* who sends the Son upon this way, and the Son who is obedient, the Son was destined to be united with the man Jesus. Thus God's moved being will certainly have to be handled—most especially in the doctrine of the Trinity—as a being moved by *God*" (*God's Being Is in Becoming*, 15, emphasis in original).

17

"Heirs through God"

Galatians 4:4–7 and the Doctrine of the Trinity

SCOTT R. SWAIN

Introduction

Theological interpretation of Scripture is a human intellectual activity directed by and to the knowledge of the triune God. In contemplating the special object of its attention, theological interpretation gives special consideration to the biblical *sedes doctrinae* ("seats of doctrine") from which the doctrine of the Trinity emerges. While we focus our interpretive energies on these particular texts, we do not ignore the fact that the doctrine of the Trinity emerges most fully from "the antecedent logic of the Christian canon as a whole."[1] Nor do we (necessarily) set aside the historical and literary forms of the texts under consideration.[2] The contemplation of *sedes doctrinae* is not a flight from historical-literary particularity but to historical-literary particularity insofar

---

1. C. Kavin Rowe, "The Trinity in the Letters of St Paul and Hebrews," in *The Oxford Handbook of the Trinity*, ed. Gilles Emery and Matthew Levering (Oxford: Oxford University Press, 2011), 42. More fully on this point, see idem, "Biblical Pressure and Trinitarian Hermeneutics," *ProEccl* 11 (2002): 295–312.

2. Cf. the worries of Rowe, "Letters of St Paul," 43.

as such contemplation directs our thinking about particular doctrinal topics to the particular historical-literary "places"[3] where the prophets and apostles focus their attention on those topics. Because the mystery of the Trinity has been revealed in the Scriptures under a form suitable to Adam's race, theology is drawn to the concrete "situatedness" that characterizes the apostolic embassy. In his Letter to the Galatians, the apostle Paul does not speak in the tongue of angels; he speaks in Greek—and in one case, Aramaic. And this historical-literary form of the apostolic communiqué is not an obstacle to but an occasion for the Spirit's illuminating presence: *through* Paul's epistolary representation of Christ crucified, the Spirit awakens in human hearts the Son's own filial cry, "Abba! Father!" (Gal. 4:6; cf. 3:1–5). Attention to the biblical *sedes doctrinae* thus enables theology to remain "within the verbal atmosphere of the text,"[4] which is the atmosphere within which theology lives and moves and has its being.

The purpose of this essay is to contemplate the doctrine of the Trinity by considering one of its most venerable "seats of doctrine," Galatians 4:4–7. How shall we proceed? Eduard Schweizer concludes his masterful study of New Testament filial sending language with the assertion that a trinitarian theology is "already implied in the expression 'God sent his son.'"[5] Following Schweizer's observation, the major focus in what follows will be on the question of how Galatians 4:4–7 implies a trinitarian theology. Through an analysis of the grammar of divine agency exhibited in this text, I argue that Paul construes God's act of realizing his Son-making purpose through the missions of the Son and the Spirit as an act of God's immediate, natural agency. For Paul, saying that God acts through the Son and the Spirit is equivalent to saying that God acts "through God" (Gal. 4:7), and therefore that the distinction between God, his Son, and the Spirit of his Son is not a distinction *between* God and other (perhaps creaturely? angelic? semidivine?) agents but rather a distinction *within* God's own natural agency. After a discussion of how Galatians 4:4–7 implies a trinitarian theology, the concluding section of this essay briefly discusses the sort of trinitarian theology that our text implies, suggesting three elements that belong to a trinitarian theology of Galatians.

  3. Consider the double meaning of *locus* in classical Protestant divinity.
  4. R. R. Reno, "Biblical Theology and Exegesis," in *Out of Egypt: Biblical Theology and Biblical Interpretation*, ed. Craig Bartholomew, Mary Healy, Karl Möller, and Robin Parry (Grand Rapids: Zondervan), 396.
  5. Eduard Schweizer, "What Do We Really Mean When We Say: 'God Sent His Son . . .'?," in *Faith and History: Essays in Honor of Paul W. Meyer*, ed. John T. Carroll, Charles H. Cosgrove, and E. Elizabeth Johnson (Atlanta: Scholars Press, 1990), 312.

The Trinity in Galatians 4:4–7: How Is It There?

In recent discussion at least, the question of how Galatians 4 might imply a trinitarian theology is caught up with the question of whether Galatians 4 presupposes the Son's preexistence. Based on his analysis of early Jewish and Christian examples of divine sending language, James D. G. Dunn argues that our text does not presuppose the Son's preexistence.[6] Others, such as Richard B. Hays and Gordon D. Fee, argue that it does.[7] While I would not go as far as F. F. Bruce and claim that the question of preexistence is "irrelevant" to Paul's argument here,[8] I do not think that our text speaks to the issue of preexistence with the same directness of other Pauline texts (e.g., 1 Cor. 8:6; 2 Cor. 8:9; Phil. 2:6–7; etc.). Nor do I think that preexistence is the most pertinent issue to consider when reflecting on our text's trinitarian implications. Instead, I propose a different entryway into the trinitarian claim of Galatians 4:4–7, specifically by reflecting on the "grammar" of divine agency exhibited therein.[9] If, as Wittgenstein suggests, grammar tells us what kind of object a thing is, then the question before us is this: *what kind of action* is the act whereby God sends his Son and Spirit in order to realize his son-making purpose for Israel and the nations? In discerning Paul's answer to this question, I contend, we may best appreciate the trinitarian claim implied in this text.

The Twofold Mission of the Son and the Spirit as an Instance of Immediate Divine Agency

In Galatians 4:4–7, Paul describes the events whereby God's son Israel has been brought from a state of minority to a state of majority, and whereby gentile Christians, formerly enslaved to τὰ στοιχεῖα τοῦ κόσμου (4:3, 9), have been brought to share in Israel's filial status and privilege. According to Paul, these events have come to pass through the twofold mission of the Son and the Spirit, which, as the summary of his argument in verse 7 makes clear, is equivalent to saying that these events have come to pass διὰ θεοῦ ("through God") (4:7). What is the significance of describing events that occur through the Son and the Spirit as events that occur διὰ θεοῦ? In describing the twofold

---

6. James D. G. Dunn, *Christology in the Making: A New Testament Inquiry into the Origins of the Doctrine of the Incarnation*, 2nd ed. (Grand Rapids: Eerdmans, 1996), 38–44.

7. Richard B. Hays, *The Faith of Jesus Christ: The Narrative Substructure of Galatians 3:1–4:11*, 2nd ed. (Grand Rapids: Eerdmans, 2002), 96–111; Gordon D. Fee, *Pauline Christology: An Exegetical-Theological Study* (Peabody, MA: Hendrickson, 2007), 211–20.

8. F. F. Bruce, *The Epistle to the Galatians: A Commentary on the Greek Text* (Grand Rapids: Eerdmans, 1982), 195.

9. Similarly, Francis Watson, "The Triune Divine Identity: Reflections on Pauline God-Language, in Disagreement with J. D. G. Dunn," *JSNT* 80 (2000): 99–124.

mission of the Son and the Spirit in this way, Paul characterizes it as an instance of God's immediate action.

The contrast between God's immediate action (what God accomplishes by his own direct agency) and God's mediate action (what God accomplishes by the agency of another) runs throughout the Letter to the Galatians, representing one of Paul's "apocalyptic antinomies."[10] This contrast is what qualifies Paul's apostleship, which is "not from men nor through man but through Jesus Christ and God the Father" (οὐκ ἀπ' ἀνθρώπων οὐδὲ δι' ἀνθρώπου ἀλλὰ διὰ Ἰησοῦ Χριστοῦ καὶ θεοῦ πατρός) (1:1; see also 1:12). This contrast also seems to be one of the things that disqualify the Mosaic law from being the means of realizing God's promise to Abraham. Whereas God is one, the Mosaic law is mediatorial in nature, delivered "through angels by the hand of a mediator" (δι' ἀγγέλων ἐν χειρὶ μεσίτου) (3:19–20), and this mediatorial nature of the law (somehow) contradicts the unilateral nature of the divine action required to accomplish Israel's promised eschatological deliverance.[11] The unspoken premise in Paul's argument appears to be drawn from Israel's prophets: as the deliverance of the first exodus was accomplished "not by elder or by angel but by the Lord himself" (Isa. 63:9 LXX),[12] so too the deliverance of the second exodus must be accomplished not "by bow, or by sword, or by war, or by horses, or by horsemen," but "by the LORD their God" (Hosea 1:7 NRSV).

The aforementioned contrast between immediate and mediate divine agency is inscribed in the widely cited monotheistic formula "not by means of an angel, not by means of a messenger." As Terrance Callan observes, this formula emphasizes the superiority of direct, unmediated divine action over indirect, mediated divine action.[13] The formula in turn expresses a common monotheistic conviction that "God's redemptive activity is always direct and unilateral in nature, reflecting the oneness of his person."[14] In terms of the text before us, Paul's claim that God has acted redemptively "through God" seems to reflect this monotheistic conviction regarding the superiority of immediate

---

10. J. Louis Martyn, *Galatians: A New Translation with Introduction and Commentary*, AB 33A (New York: Doubleday, 1997), 94.

11. See further Richard N. Longenecker, *Galatians*, WBC 41 (Dallas: Word, 1990), esp. 142–43; and Alan F. Segal, "'Two Powers in Heaven' and Early Christian Trinitarian Thinking," in *The Trinity*, ed. Stephen T. Davis, Daniel Kendall, and Gerald O'Collins (Oxford: Oxford University Press, 1999), 83.

12. For the relevance of Isa. 63–64 to Gal. 4, see Rodrigo J. Morales, *The Spirit and the Restoration of Israel: New Exodus and New Creation Motifs in Galatians* (Tübingen: Mohr Siebeck, 2010), 26–28, 114–31.

13. Terrance Callan, "Pauline Midrash: The Exegetical Background of Gal 3:19b," *JBL* 99 (1980): esp. 555–59. See also Longenecker, *Galatians*, 139–43.

14. Longenecker, *Galatians*, 143. Similarly Hans Dieter Betz, *Galatians: A Commentary on Paul's Letter to the Churches in Galatia* (Philadelphia: Fortress, 1979), 172–73.

divine agency. What the law could not do—that is, bring to pass the redemptive realization of God's son-making purpose—God *himself* did through the missions of his Son and Spirit (cf. Rom. 8:3).

The immediate implication of this reading is obvious. By categorizing God's action through the Son and the Spirit as an instance of God's immediate saving action, Paul rules out the possibility of understanding the missions of the Son and the Spirit according to the pattern of creaturely emissaries, be they angels sent from heaven or prophets set apart from their mothers' wombs (cf. Gal. 1:15). The distinction between God, his Son, and the Spirit of his Son in carrying out God's redemptive purpose is not a distinction between God and other creaturely agents. It is rather a distinction within God's monotheistic agency.[15] In other words, God's singular saving agency is intrinsically threefold. We will return to this observation in due course.

The Twofold Mission of the Son and the Spirit as an Instance of Natural Divine Agency

Categorizing God's redemptive action through the Son and the Spirit as an instance of God's immediate action does not exhaust the Pauline grammar of divine agency exhibited in this text. To more fully appreciate the character of divine action in Galatians 4:4–7, we must analyze the more specifically metaphysical dimensions of the Pauline grammar.

Metaphysical analysis of New Testament witness to the Trinity is repugnant to many modern biblical scholars, even to some who are otherwise sympathetic to trinitarian readings of the biblical text. This attitude is commonly reflected in contrastive ways of summarizing biblical trinitarianism. For example, Schweizer asserts that the language of divine sending in the New Testament "describes God in the category of his acts (dynamically) and not in that of his 'divine nature' (substantially)."[16] Although such assertions are not uncommon in contemporary theology,[17] I believe that they are misleading and they unnecessarily hinder a historical understanding of Paul's theology of divine agency.

Returning to the broader argument of Galatians 3:1–4:7 will help us to appreciate the point. As we saw above, one thing that disqualifies the law of Moses from being the means of fulfilling God's promises to Abraham is its mediatorial nature. The law's mediatorial nature somehow stands in contrast

---

15. For a discussion of Jewish antecedents, see Schweizer, "What Do We Really Mean?," 300–301.
16. Ibid., 309.
17. For two recent examples, see A. Edward Siecienski, *The Filioque: History of a Doctrinal Controversy* (Oxford: Oxford University Press, 2010), 29; and Beverly Roberts Gaventa, "Pentecost and Trinity," *Int* 66 (2012): 12, 14.

to the fact that God is one (Gal. 3:19–20). Conversely, the immediate nature of God's redemptive action through the Son and the Spirit corresponds to the oneness of God's identity. The correspondence between God's identity and God's action provides a window into the oft-neglected metaphysical dimension of Paul's theology of divine agency.

Consider the correspondence between God's monotheistic being and God's monotheistic action in Galatians. As Hans Dieter Betz observes, "Paul's . . . soteriology conforms throughout to the principle of oneness." God's singular *identity* is reflected in God's singular *acts*, and also in the singular creaturely *effects* of those acts. Again following Betz, for Paul there is one God (3:20), one messianic offspring (3:16), one gospel (1:6–7), one messianic people of God (3:28), and one fruit of the Spirit (5:22).[18] To this list we might add that, for Paul, there is one common object of ecclesial petition, though this common object is addressed, quite remarkably, in different languages: αββα, ὁ πατήρ (Gal. 4:6; cf. Rom. 8:15; 15:6).

These are not the only correspondences worth noting. Just as God's monotheistic saving action *includes* a distinction between God, his Son, and the Spirit of his Son, so too the creaturely effect of God's monotheistic saving action reflects a triadic structure: the one God is addressed as Father, in and with the Son, by the indwelling power of the Spirit (Gal. 4:6).

What do these correspondences tell us about Paul's grammar of divine agency? Betz is probably right that these correspondences reflect the ancient rule, "Like is the friend of like."[19] This rule is certainly reflected in other New Testament texts (e.g., John 3:6; 1 Cor. 2:12–15). However, more can be said in explanation of the correspondences between God's (triune) identity, actions, and effects. One clue to the nature of these correspondences lies in the language Paul uses to describe God's agency in 4:7: διὰ θεοῦ. Though perhaps not as pronounced as it is in other Pauline texts (e.g., Rom. 11:36; 1 Cor. 8:6), this is the language of "instrumental causality," one of the metaphysical classifications of causality employed throughout the ancient world and in the apostolic writings (John 1:1–3; Rom. 11:36; 1 Cor. 1:30; 8:6; Eph. 4:6; Col .1:15–20; Heb. 1:2; 2:10).[20] Commenting on the notion of divine instrumental causality in relation to creation, Richard Bauckham states: "That God is not only the agent or efficient cause of creation ('from him are all things') and the final cause or goal of all things ('to him are all things'), but also the instrumental cause ('through him are all things') well expresses the typical Jewish monotheistic concern that God

---

18. Betz, *Galatians*, 173.
19. Ibid.
20. Robert M. Grant, "Causation and 'The Ancient World View,'" *JBL* 83 (1964): 34–40.

used no one else to carry out his work of creation, but accomplished it alone, solely by means of his own Word and/or his own Wisdom."[21] In keeping with my earlier argument, I suggest that Paul employs the language of instrumental causality in Galatians 4:7 in order to express the monotheistic concern that God used no one else to carry out his work of eschatological redemption, but accomplished it by himself alone, solely by means of his Son and his Spirit. In other words, the metaphysical language of instrumental causality is well suited to Paul's monotheistic concept of immediate divine agency.

Where does this get us? According to a widespread ancient conception of causality, certain *actions* and *effects* are exclusive to and indicative of certain *agents*. As noted above, for most Second Temple Jewish monotheists, the acts of creation and consummation belong exclusively to the agency of God: "They all were made through me alone, and through none other: by me also they shall be ended, and by none other" (*4 Ezra* 6.6). Some ancient thinkers explain the unique relation between an agent and that agent's characteristic actions and effects with the concept of a natural (or proper) power. On this understanding, a natural power is one that is intrinsic to a specific kind of agent and therefore that, when exercised, signifies the agent by its effect. Thus, for example, Philo argues: "As it is the property of fire to burn, and of snow to chill, so also it is the property of God to be creating."[22] Some such conception of divine natural power arguably lies behind the correspondences between God's triune identity, actions, and effects in Galatians 3:1–4:7. The triune act of redemption to which 4:4–7 attests is not only an instance of God's *immediate* saving agency; it is also an exhibition of God's *natural* saving power. "Salvation belongs to the LORD" (Ps. 3:8).

This interpretation is confirmed when we turn from Galatians 4:4–7 to the exasperated question that immediately follows in 4:8–9. There the apostle asks: "How can the gentile Christians of Galatia, who have come to know the true and living God through the gospel, embrace the law of Moses, effectively turning back to the elementary principles of the cosmos?" Paul's question presupposes the classical distinction between a true god, who is a god "by nature," and those who are falsely called gods "by human convention" (the λεγόμενοι θεοί of 1 Cor. 8:5).[23] Much could be said regarding the significance of Paul's

21. Richard Bauckham, *God Crucified: Monotheism and Christology in the New Testament* (Grand Rapids: Eerdmans, 1998), 39.

22. Philo, *Alleg. Interp.* 1.3 (*The Works of Philo Judæus*, trans. C. D. Yonge [London: George Bell & Sons, 1890], 1:53). See further Michel René Barnes, *The Power of God: Δύναμις in Gregory of Nyssa's Trinitarian Theology* (Washington, DC: Catholic University of America Press, 2001).

23. Thus Augustine. See Eric Plumer, *Augustine's Commentary on Galatians: Introduction, Text, Translation, and Notes* (Oxford: Oxford University Press, 2003), 183. More broadly on this

appeal to this distinction. For our present purposes, one observation is worth noting. In the present context, the mark that indicates the nondivine nature of the cosmic elements is their status as "weak and worthless" (4:9). What is notable about this? I believe this represents one of the strongest arguments Paul can muster against the mission of "the Teachers." The mission of these teachers begets children for slavery; Paul's mission begets children for freedom (see Gal. 4:21–31 and passim). And this because the Teachers' mission yokes its recipients to those "that by nature are not gods" (4:8), and who therefore are naturally impotent to deliver from slavery. However, the Pauline mission flows from the one who is God by nature: the one true and living God, who *is* Father, Son, and Spirit and who is therefore naturally potent to beget "children of the living God" (see Hosea 1:10). Adoption and its attending filial cry, we might say, are natural signs of divine paternity, filiation, and spiration. To paraphrase Romans 8:3 again:[24] What the law could not do, weakened as it was by the flesh, God did, sending his own proper (ἰδίου) Son (8:32), and the Spirit of his Son (Gal. 4:6), redemptively to beget children of God.

Conclusion: What Kind of Trinitarian Theology Does Galatians 4:4–7 Imply?

In the foregoing analysis of Paul's grammar of divine agency, I have argued that Galatians 4:4–7 implies a trinitarian theology insofar as it presents the twofold mission of the Son and the Spirit as an instance of God's immediate, natural agency. This is my answer, at least in part, to the question of how a doctrine of the Trinity is implied in this text. With this answer in place, I now briefly discuss the question of what doctrine of the Trinity this text implies. I offer three summary points.

First, as we have seen, the distinction between God, his Son, and the Spirit in God's Son-making activity is not a distinction between God and intermediary agents. It is rather a distinction within God's own immediate, natural agency. A trinitarian theology of Galatians follows from reflecting closely on the *kind* of distinction that is internal to God's monotheistic agency.

Second, Galatians 4:4–7 distinguishes the three agents internal to God's singular natural agency in two ways: by their named relations and by their various missions. In terms of the named relations: there is one who is named

---

distinction, see Walter Burkert, *Greek Religion*, trans. John Raffan (Cambridge, MA: Harvard University Press, 1985), chap. 7.

24. Romans 8:3 may be understood as an early Christian "commentary" on Gal. 4:4–7. See J. Louis Martyn, *Theological Issues in the Letters of Paul* (Edinburgh: T&T Clark, 1997), chap. 3.

"Father"; there is one who is named "his Son"; and there is another who is named "the Spirit of his Son." While these names are *intrinsic* to God's singular identity and action, they are also *irreducible* in relation to one another. The one name cannot be translated into another name. Indeed, each name entails an irreducible distinction from the others insofar as it signifies a "productive relation."[25] In the case of the present text: there is one who fathers and another who is fathered; there is one who breathes and another who is breathed.

In terms of their various missions: the three agents of God's singular agency are also distinguished insofar as there is one who sends, the Father; and there are two who are sent, the Son and the Spirit. Read within the context of the broader Pauline corpus, and the rest of the New Testament as well, we see that the various distinctions between sender and sendee correspond quite strictly to the named relations described above. The Father is sent by no one, but he sends forth his Son and the Spirit of his Son. The Son of the Father is sent by the Father; and the Son sends the Spirit. The Spirit of the Father and of the Son is sent by the Father and by the Son, though the Spirit himself sends no one. The "productive relations" that characterize the three in their irreducible distinctiveness are thus inflected in their missions.

Third, the gospel according to Galatians 4:4–7 is that the God who by nature is and acts as Father, Son, and Spirit acts not only in relation to himself but also in relation to us. If we are to grasp Paul's gospel of grace rightly, it is vital to observe the nature of God's triune action in relation to us. Note well: while Paul's Trinity is unreservedly a Trinity "for us," God's triune action toward us is not what constitutes God as Trinity. The named relations of Father, Son, and Spirit are the *presupposition* of the missions, not their *consequence*. The named relations indicate the *agents* of God's monotheistic saving action, not its *effects*. Following common apostolic pattern (see John 3:16–17; Rom. 8:3, 32), Paul's Letter to the Galatians complements the language of divine sending with the language of divine giving/self-giving: the sent Son is the one "who loved me and gave *himself* for me" (Gal. 2:20). Rather than being acts of divine self-constitution, the missions are thus portrayed as acts of divine self-*giving* that graciously *extend* the Son's natural and internal relation to the Father *to us* (4:5: ἵνα τὴν υἱοθεσίαν ἀπολάβωμεν), with the result that (4:6: Ὅτι δέ ἐστε υἱοί) the Spirit of the Son cries out from within the hearts of Jesus's redeemed and adopted siblings, "Abba! Father!"

---

25. As Thomas Aquinas observes: "Divine Scripture uses, in relation to God, names which signify procession," in *Summa theologiae*, trans. Fathers of the English Dominican Province, 5 vols. (New York: Benziger Bros., 1948), I, Q 27, art. 1, resp.

"By the work of adoption the likeness of natural sonship is communicated to men," Thomas Aquinas declares.[26] In so doing, God does not seek to supply his own wants but to communicate to us the abundance of his own intrinsic, natural, trinitarian perfection.[27] This is the gospel of grace. This, ultimately, is what it means to be made "heirs through God."

---

26. Ibid., III, Q 23, art. 1, *ad* 2; with Thomas Aquinas, *Commentary on Saint Paul's Epistle to the Galatians*, trans. Fabian Larcher (Albany, NY: Magi Books, 1966), chap. 4, lecture 2.
27. Thomas Aquinas, *Summa theologiae*, III, Q 23, art. 1, *ad* 2; and art. 2, *ad* 3.

PART 3

Ethics

18

Flesh and Spirit

Oliver O'Donovan

Thinking about flesh and spirit in Galatians involves, as a glance at the passages in question makes plain, examining 5:16–26, the one sustained treatment of this theme in the letter and its one passage of sustained moral catechesis. Yet we must also engage with the dramatic movement of the text as a whole. This drama is generated by two factors. There is interweaving of urgent pastoral warnings with high theological exposition, and there is kaleidoscopic sequence of conceptual oppositions, merging in and out of one another—law and faith, law and promise, slave and free—which come to a head in the opposition of "flesh" and "spirit," so that 5:16–26 forms a climax to the letter as a whole. That is one reason for selecting this opposition for special consideration. There is another: the opposition of flesh and spirit has proved to be a potent legacy to later Christian moral thought. It is central for patristic ethics, both orthodox and heretical, and remains vital in medieval and Reformation eras. That its interpretation evolves over the centuries should not prevent our marveling at its powers of endurance. When, with Thomas Cranmer on the First Sunday in Lent, we pray that we may "use such abstinence that, our flesh being subdued to the spirit, we may ever obey thy godly motions in righteousness and true holiness," we are near the end of a long tradition.[1] One might say

---

1. *Book of Common Prayer,* Collect for the First Sunday in Lent.

that all Christian moral thought relied on this opposition until the moral-philosophical innovations of the later seventeenth century, neoclassical in inspiration, banished it. To understand premodern Christian moral thought, it would seem, we need to explore this conceptual nexus, and there is no better place to start than the earliest text to give it thematic treatment, a text constantly made the object of later interpretative attention.

At once we confront a difficulty of method: the conceptual opposition of flesh and spirit is not a simple conjunction of two concepts, "flesh" and "spirit," but a complex. This makes it less open to conventional lexicographical inquiry. The difficulty is evident from a long note in Ernest deWitt Burton's 1922 International Critical Commentary (*Galatians*), headed "Πνεῦμα and Σάρξ." It is in fact two separate articles, one on πνεῦμα (*pneuma*), the other on σάρξ (*sarx*), each developing an elaborate semantic stemma. Only at the end, for some 10 percent of an article that runs well over five thousand words, do we find the two treated together.[2] Unsurprisingly, given the approach, Burton concludes that there is not one antithesis of flesh and spirit but several—a classic case of the philologist's lens bringing too close a focus and making the phenomenon disappear into its own surface. More recent scholarly fashions handle the problem not much better. A consensus, more than defensible in itself, that Paul's ethics arises from his doctrine of the Spirit, is taken to license an approach that swallows the opposition in a general account of the Spirit in Paul.[3] An opposite approach, giving primacy to a treatment of flesh, is that of J. Louis Martyn's Anchor Bible commentary, which devotes a whole excursus to a detailed account of what Paul's unnamed opponents taught, which turns out, again unsurprisingly, to have been entirely about flesh, with no reference to spirit.[4] We should perhaps clarify what the problem actually is. It is how a variety of self-standing observations—some about flesh, some about spirit, some about slavery, some about freedom, some about law, some about gospel—all find themselves drawn together into a powerful magnetic

---

2. Ernest deWitt Burton, *The Epistle to the Galatians* (Edinburgh: T&T Clark, 1921), 486–95.

3. The forging of the consensus is generally credited to Hermann Gunkel at the end of the nineteenth century. See Wolfgang Schrage, *The Ethics of the New Testament* (Edinburgh: T&T Clark, 1988), 178; and Siegfried Schulz, *Neutestamentliche Ethik* (Zurich: Theologischer Verlag Zürich, 1987), 350. For a recent example of the consensus, cf. Frank Matera, "Living in Newness of Life: Paul's Understanding of the Moral Life," in *Celebrating Paul*, ed. Peter Spitaler (Washington, DC: Catholic Biblical Association of America, 2011), 168: "Life in the Spirit—newness of life—is the essence of Pauline ethics." In case at some points these moralists' reflections on Paul might appear ungrateful to the work of NT exegesis, let it be said clearly that the very great importance of this understanding has still not been adequately appreciated by the scholarly community that professes Christian ethics as its business. On this failure see the remarks of Johannes Fischer, *Leben aus dem Geist* (Zurich: Theologischer Verlag Zürich, 1994), 11.

4. J. Louis Martyn, *Galatians*, 2nd ed. (New Haven: Yale University Press, 2010), 289–94.

field controlled by a dominant conceptual opposition that is more than the sum of its parts.

We must begin, then, from the texts in which flesh and spirit are set in explicit opposition to each other, and then take in the unpaired use of each term, which may or may not shed light on the opposition, in relation to those. So let us review the situation briefly. The first appearance in Galatians of flesh and spirit as a pair occurs at 3:3, a critical point in the argument of the letter, where Paul, having framed the beginning of Christian existence as crucifixion with Christ, asks how this existence is to be sustained through time on the same terms. Up to that point in the document, the dominant opposition has been between "the works of the law" and "the obedience of faith." The opposition of flesh and spirit is precipitated by an unpaired mention of "the spirit" in conversion and miracle (3:2). Until then, unpaired uses of "flesh" are various; from that point onward, the opposition takes over and governs the use of both its terms.

When we meet the pair for a second time in connection with the Hagar-Sarah allegory, the context is dominated by the opposition of servility and freedom. The third occurrence of the pair is the major section (5:16–26), to which we will return. The fourth (6:8), in the section of pastoral advice that brings the letter proper to a formal close at 6:10, comments on a demand that clergy should be properly paid. One thing is clear from this review: Paul understands "spirit" in this opposition as the Spirit of God at work in conversion, prayer, and patient waiting. There is no unpaired use of the word *spirit* that has any other sense.

So the flesh/spirit opposition in Galatians is in the service of a pneumatological conception of the moral life. The same can be said of the two other passages in the Pauline Letters with sustained reflection on flesh and spirit: 1 Corinthians 2–3, with its contrasts between πνευματικοί, σαρκικοί, and ψυχικοί (*pneumatikoi, sarkikoi, psychikoi*); and Romans 8, which resumes a number of themes from Galatians 4 and 5, as well as the passing use of the opposition in Philippians 3:3. If, however, we broaden our view to take in other New Testament uses of the flesh/spirit pair, we see that Paul is largely distinctive in this respect. Apparently unevidenced in pre-Christian literature, the antithetical pair was already an established element in early Christian discourse before Paul took it up.[5] The originating thought appears to be the

---

5. Of the four texts in the LXX that bring the words πνεῦμα and σάρξ into close association—Gen. 6:3; Num. 16:22; 27:16; and Joel 2:28—none offers a plausible anticipation of the NT contrast; Isa. 31:3 might do so if the contrast of בָּשָׂר (*bāśār*) and רוּחַ (*rûaḥ*) in the MT were reflected in the LXX. I am grateful to Michael Cover for pointing out Philo's *Gig.* 8, not a precise parallel but a contemporary reference suggestive of how the usage might arise. I have

transformation of human life by the resurrection of Christ: Romans 1:3–4; 1 Peter 3:18; and the formulaic hymn of 1 Timothy 3:16 deploy the antithesis in reference to the risen Christ himself. John 3:6, the sole instance outside Paul that makes reference to the divine Spirit/flesh opposition, speaks of the new birth of the baptized. To this central core certain more traditional and general observations have attached themselves. Popular anthropological observations that distinguish between intention and capacity, or mind and body, are reclothed in the language of flesh and spirit, as at Mark 14:38, to which we must add observations on the distinction between words and meaning, as at John 6:63. These more general observations can be observed at the very moment of attraction, as they are pulled into the field of the resurrection idea. So we meet a conventional contrast between physical absence and mental recollection at 1 Corinthians 5:3; and at Colossians 2:5 we find the same point made with the words *flesh* and *spirit*; meanwhile a hermeneutic distinction between the "letter" of a text and its "spirit," or meaning (2 Cor. 3:6), is rephrased at John 6:63 in terms of "flesh" and "spirit."[6]

These early Christian uses of the flesh/spirit pair are not forgotten as Paul develops his reflection on the distinctive nature of the Christian moral life, nor does it lose its capacity to organize a wider range of experience. The christological basis for the thought is present at the first great climax of the letter, Galatians 2:19–20, and is recalled in 5:24–25. Galatians 6:8, closely paralleled by Romans 15:27 and 1 Corinthians 9:11, develops the contrast in the direction of something like a secular-sacred distinction. But this broad cluster of ideas is now put to work for Paul's governing interest in the consistent extension of conversion experience into postconversion life. "Having begun in the Spirit, are you now made perfect in the flesh?" (Gal. 3:3) could be taken as the headline for the whole epistle. What is new in Paul's use of the pair is the insistence on *walking by* the Spirit and not by the flesh.[7]

We turn from these lengthy prolegomena to the key passage and begin from 5:17, posing a specific question: what is it, then, that Paul calls "flesh," this site of contrary desire opposed to the Spirit of God? The question has proved to be something of a *crux interpretum*. Late twentieth-century commentators

---

not found any further parallels from extrabiblical literature before the Christian era, though I remain open as to whether there may be any.

6. The use of the pair at 1 Cor. 5:5 to illuminate the logic of excommunication, though essentially anthropological, is so distinct from all the others and so heavy with questions of its own that it may safely be left to one side in a brief review.

7. We might say that the whole purpose of the letter was to prevent the kind of observation, supposedly an exposition of 5:8, which we find preserved in a fragment of Theodore of Mopsuestia (PG 66:909): τῆς χαρίτος Θεοῦ ἦν τὸ καλέσαι, τὸ δοῦναι τοῦ Πνεύματος τὴν χάριν, ὑποσχέσθαι τὰ μέλλοντα, τὸ μέντοι μένειν βεβαίους ἐπὶ τῆς πίστεως οὐκ ἦν ἐκείνου ἀλλ' ὑμέτερον.

have often been inclined to reach for models of a dualistic type. For Martyn, for example, flesh is a "cosmic power arrayed against God," an energy pitted against the Spirit in a conflict for which Martyn consistently invokes the language of apocalyptic war.[8] A similar view was taken by Siegfried Schulz, to whom a "cosmic dualism" seems indispensable to Paul's mature doctrine of the Spirit.[9] Human nature is thus seen as a battleground for superhuman forces. We do, of course, have occasional indications of what the New Testament church, and Paul himself, could imagine in the way of supernatural evil influence, but in these there is no hint of an association with flesh, and Galatians, anyway, contains no idea of diabolical agency.

How much less "metaphysical" are the explanations offered by patristic exegesis of the fourth and fifth centuries! One unchallengeable principle governs their reading, which is the status of bodily flesh, and of human nature in general, as the good creation of a good God. The flowering of exegetical activity around Galatians in the latter half of the fourth century may partly be due to the challenge of Manichaean readings, which could make use of the mutually opposed desires of 5:17. Catholic exegetes therefore set about *moralizing* the tension. So far from representing a titanic cosmic clash, the contrariety of impulse was the result of failure of human agency. As Augustine resonantly declared, "All this is us!"[10] The division of flesh and spirit is not cosmic, not a division of natures within the human being, but a division of ways that opens up before the agent. From this starting point their first step was anthropological: they turned to a fairly established Christian account of the human constitution, loosely Platonic in inspiration, in which soul and body, each with its function and scope, had to be ordered rightly, with the lower functions serving the higher.[11] This was congenial to Augustine because it encouraged his characteristic emphasis on inner moral struggle, a feature of human existence from which, as he came to insist, not even redeemed humankind could be exempt until the resurrection of the dead. At the same time it fended off imputations against bodily nature by locating the responsibility for moral weakness entirely in the soul's failure to direct the body appropriately. In his early *Commentary on Galatians*, Augustine read the words of 5:17, "They are opposed to each other so that you cannot do what you will," in the light

---

8. Martyn, *Galatians*, 493–94.

9. Schulz, *Neutestamentliche Ethik*, 348: "Vor allem sind Geist und Fleisch weltbeherrschende Mächte und Herrschaftsbereiche.... Ohne diesem kosmische Dualismus ist die spätpaulinische Geistlehre nicht zu verstehen."

10. Augustine, *Continence* 8.19.

11. We find good statements of it, also with a strong antidualist purpose, in Clement of Alexandria, *Strom.* 3.4.34 (PG 8:1137): Ἀλλὰ καὶ ἡ ὄρεξις οὐ τοῦ σώματός ἐστι, κἂν διὰ τὸ σῶμα γίνηται; 3.5.41 (PG 8:1144): ὁ δὲ σώφρων τὴν κυρίαν τοῦ σώματος ψυχὴν ἐλευθεροῖ τῶν παθῶν.

of Romans 7:23, which sets "the law in my members" at variance with "the law of my mind," a conjunction of texts that controlled his interpretation for some time.[12] For Augustine, Romans was the foundational Pauline text, assumed to have been written earlier than Galatians, and the seventh chapter its center of gravity.[13] The constituent elements of the human being were never at peace since the sin of Adam set them at variance.[14]

It is, perhaps, too easy to underrate this interpretation of the text in terms of inner functional disorder. This view had a strong appeal for the spiritual tradition of medieval and Reformation thought, and it found new echoes in the nineteenth century.[15] It can boast a straightforward explanation of the term *flesh* and a straightforward reading of the final phrase, ἵνα μὴ ἃ ἐὰν θέλητε ταῦτα ποιῆτε (*hina mē ha ean thelēte tauta poiēte*), "that you should not do whatever you wish," the rhetoric of which immediately invites comparison with Romans 7:15, οὐ γὰρ ὃ θέλω τοῦτο πράσσω, ἀλλ' ὃ μισῶ τοῦτο ποιῶ (*ou gar ho thelō touto prassō all ho misō touto poiō*), "for I do not do what I wish, but I do what I hate." It understood this final phrase to mean that we are hindered in forming an act of will and carrying it through by a divided purpose.[16] Yet this reading has one great weakness: it understates the radicality of the alternative Paul poses. Luther paraphrased Paul's intended meaning as follows: "When I exhort you to walk by the Spirit, . . . I do not demand that you should utterly put off the flesh, or kill it, but that you should bridle it and subdue it."[17] Is that credible? If we take Galatians 5:17 in sequence with what precedes and follows, we can conclude only that bringing the flesh into conformity with the Spirit cannot be done and should not be attempted. The end of verse 17 then reads differently: the will is not so much frustrated as superseded. Faced with the need to decide conclusively between two conflicting principles, our actions can no longer be guided by our successive acts of will. The ancient idea of the will is more passive and punctiliar, less active and less hypostatic than the modern, nearer an inclination than a determination. But our acts, Paul insists, express our irrevocable self-determinations, either

---

12. Augustine, *Exp. Gal.* 47. See Eric Plumer, trans., *Augustine's Commentary on Galatians* (New York and Oxford: Oxford University Press, 2003), 208n223.

13. See *C. Jul.* 3.61.

14. Cf. *Enarrat. Ps.* 143.5: "Ex peccato divisus es adversum te. Trahis concupiscentiae propaginem et traducem mortis."

15. Indeed, twentieth-century exegesis continued to read the passage in that way. Cf. L. H. Marshall, *The Challenge of New Testament Ethics* (London: Macmillan, 1947), 267–70; Birger Gerhardsson, *The Ethos of the Bible*, trans. S. Westerholm (London: Darton, Longman & Todd, 1982), 70.

16. Augustine, *Sermo* 30.4.

17. Martin Luther, *Commentary on Galatians*, in WA 40:85.

for flesh or for Spirit. Is 5:17, then, out of line with its context? It is very easy to overstate such a suggestion, conjuring up an opposition in which Paul's purpose in so expressing himself becomes unintelligible. Yet keeping well short of that point, we may still entertain a suspicion (it can be hardly more) that this saying, with its suggestion of balanced struggle between elements of the human constitution, quotes an expression of Christian piety that was not, on its own, as clear as Paul himself had become about the role of the Holy Spirit in the Christian life. In the surrounding passage, Paul differentiates the verbs and verbal nouns that are predicated of flesh and spirit: we "walk by" spirit but "satisfy the desire of" flesh; spirit has "fruit," flesh has "effects," and so on; the rhetoric of flesh is passive and mechanical; the rhetoric of spirit is active and purposeful.

So much, then, for the anthropological move, the first step in the moralization of the tension between flesh and spirit. Augustine's view of Galatians 5:17 underwent a slow but significant recalibration in his later writings. One telltale feature was the increasing role assigned to the soul, which emerged as a third element between flesh and spirit, representing the agent placed between the two, forced to make the decision. This meant hanging more loosely to the *grammatical* structure of Galatians 5:17, so that flesh and spirit were no longer the *subjects* of the contrary desires, but alternative horizons of practical decision in which we ourselves are the subjects. To say "the flesh lusts," Augustine thinks, is like saying "the eye sees"; *we* see through the eye; *we* lust through the flesh.[18] In the second place, as he reflected on the passage in the light of his trinitarian preoccupations, he became more conscious that the Spirit of God, so evidently present in 5:18, cannot be kept out of verse 17, so that what he had seen initially as an Adamic struggle of human flesh and human spirit now had to be understood, after Pentecost, to involve the divine Spirit alongside the human.[19]

There then followed a third and decisive development. When Augustine (somewhere around 418) took up the theme of the passions in book 14 of *The City of God*, he approached Galatians 5:17 not by way of Romans 7:23 but from Romans 8:4, "in us who walk not by the flesh but by the spirit."[20] The opposition of life *secundum carnem* and life *secundum spiritum* could not, he argued, be an opposition of the material and immaterial aspects of human nature. Only the first three of the fifteen vicious "works of the flesh" were sensuous; the remainder were sins of emotion and intellect. "Flesh" was to be

18. Augustine, *Gen. lit.* 10.12; cf. *Doctr. chr.* 1.24.
19. Augustine, *Sermo* 128.8.
20. Augustine, *The City of God* 14.2–4.

understood as a figurative expression on the rhetorical principle of the part for the whole; it refers to the human being as a totality. Support for this very characteristic move he found at 1 Corinthians 3:3, where the expressions σαρκικοί (*sarkikoi*) and κατὰ ἄνθρωπον (*kata anthrōpon*) are used apparently to explain each other. In reading 1 Corinthians 2–3 he also concluded that the distinction apparently made there between σαρκικοί and ψυχικοί was no distinction at all, but two names for the same people who live *secundum hominem,* which is to say, *as though* humankind were a self-sufficient end of its own endeavor, not called to lift its eyes to behold God. Yet human existence could not be fulfilled within the horizons of human nature, but only as it looked beyond them. Humankind could not *effectively* live on its own terms, *secundum hominem,* any more than angels could live *secundum angelum.* The decision lay between self-enclosure and transcendence. Thus Augustine restored the note of radical opposition to Paul's text. It was done, we notice, by setting the flesh and spirit at the *end* rather than at the *beginning* of the train of practical reason, treating them not as originating motives but as horizons of deliberation. In this way the agent is set one step back from the alternative, and so given space to consider and make a decision. The same logic emerges in a parallel but independent train of thought on the part of Augustine's contemporary John Chrysostom. The whole context of the flesh/spirit opposition, John insisted, was practical reason; the terms "flesh" and "spirit" must be understood accordingly to refer to "bad and good ways of thinking." So the flesh stands for "a kind of reasoning, which is earthly, superficial, and inconsiderate."[21]

This approach by way of practical reason sheds welcome light on two puzzling features in Paul's treatment of the flesh. In the first place it helps to explain the role of strife, on which Paul lays a strong emphasis in the later parts of the epistle. The theme emerges precisely at the end of our key section, at 5:26: "Let us not become vainly opinionated, challenging one another, rivaling one another." The vain opinion, the superficial and inconsiderate view, being as such partial and contestable rather than comprehensive and uniting, necessarily generates conflict. Second, it sheds light on the striking connection Paul makes between precisionist legal rigor and moral disorder, an association that counted for so much with the Protestant Reformers. "Flesh is understood for the righteousness and wisdom of the flesh," as Luther comments, "and for the judgment of reason."[22]

Yet there was one striking deficiency in the approach as it was made by Chrysostom and Augustine: it failed to recognize the *heilsgeschichtliche*

---

21. John Chrysostom, *In epistolam ad Galatas commentarius* (PG 61:671–72).
22. Luther, *Commentary on Galatians,* in WA 40:347.

character of the contrast. Augustine presents it in the context of the fall of Adam as a universal opposition of sin and obedience. But it is not Adam and Christ whom Paul contrasts in the historical proof of Galatians 4:21–31, through the allegory of Sarah and Hagar, but Moses and Christ. How then, we must ask, may we frame Paul's understanding of the radical moral alternative within the history of salvation? In what way is the history of salvation also a history of morality? We address this question through the weighty three verses (5:13–15) that lead into our section.

The declaration of 5:13, that the Galatians were called on the basis of freedom and should not let their freedom be an occasion for the flesh, is all of a piece with Paul's repeated insistence that the Christian life be sustained on the terms on which it was begun. The beginning conferred by the Spirit was freedom; the flesh, as we have been told, is servitude. A freedom that opens the door to flesh, then, abolishes itself. Two connected points about freedom are both familiar to later philosophy and theology. The first corresponds to a contrast often expressed by our contemporaries in terms of "negative freedom" and "positive freedom," freedom *from* some oppression and freedom *for* some fulfillment. Negative freedom is incompletely self-determining; in liberating us from some oppression, it does not complete itself by securing its position. That is why freedom is at risk of self-cancellation. We may so use it as to leave ourselves living as though we had never had it. A free *life* needs to be secured positively. The second point follows from this: freedom is secured positively only if the way out of our limitations leads to a moment of self-binding: an alternative service, *self*-determined and so not alienated, *fully* determined and so not merely revisiting an initial moment of liberation. The distinction we mark in English between "service" and "servitude," which is derived precisely from the point made by Paul here, was not available to him in Hellenistic Greek, so that the paradox in his double use of δουλεία (*douleia*) is sharp (4:24; 5:1).

But there is, for Paul, both a history and a sociology of freedom. He has already characterized the life of faith as "love" (5:6), which for him, here as always, means cooperative community, "bearing one another's burdens" (6:2).[23] Love is the service *of* freedom *to* freedom, an engagement in community for the freedom of each other. The pungent conclusion to these three verses (5:13–15), not to be separated off as a "parenthetic" throwaway,[24] focuses this point negatively: "But if you bite and gnaw at one another, take care you are

---

23. On this see Richard B. Hays, *The Moral Vision of the New Testament* (New York: HarperCollins, 1996), 33.
24. J. B. Lightfoot, *The Epistle to the Galatians* (London: Macmillan, 1869), 206.

not consumed by one another" (5:15). The quarrelsomeness that Paul detected in the Galatian defection is exactly the evidence of unfreedom he would expect; what makes freedom abolish itself is the idea that it is competitive, that my enlargement implies restriction for you.

But in offering love as the principle that gives freedom its positive form, Paul presents it as a *hermeneutic* principle, governing the application of the moral law. Love is not *a* principle on which we may act, one principle among others; it is not the most *important* of all principles; it is not even the *sole* principle. It is the architectonic structure of all principles, unifying the moral law and giving it coherence. But this is not just a *rational* claim; it also is a *historical* one. From the first appearance of the principle of love's primacy, with which we, like Paul, are familiar from the synoptic tradition of Jesus's teaching, it is understood as a climactic disclosure in the history of salvation. It is as the final and authoritative interpreter of the law of God given through Moses that Jesus propounds the law of love. John certainly sees it that way—"A new commandment I give you" (John 13:34)—and I believe it can be shown contextually that the synoptic evangelists do too. In saying that "the whole law is summed up in one word" (Gal. 5:14) and in referring to it as "the law of Christ" (6:2), Paul seems to intend a self-conscious reference to that climax of moral revelation. To be "under the law" is to remain in ignorance of the new hermeneutic authority conferred by the one whom God sent forth in the fullness of time to redeem those under the law and give them the status of sons (cf. 4:4–5).

That Paul's summary, unlike that of Jesus, is confined to neighbor-love, without mention of love of God, is explained quite simply from his context, which is how the law relates to the given structures of the world. In the course of his thinking and writing, Paul has acquired a repertoire of accounts trying to explain why the law was insufficient to evoke free and joyful obedience to God's will. In Romans 8 it was "weak because of the flesh." In 2 Corinthians 3 it was "veiled," concealing the blessing of God's glory. But in Galatians the law is bound up with what are elusively described as "worldly elements," στοιχεῖα τοῦ κόσμου (*stoicheia tou kosmou*) (Gal. 4:3, 9). On this puzzling expression, let us turn to the incisive summary of Jerome, the third great patristic commentator on Galatians:

> Not a few commentators think that these are angels, ruling the four elements of the world, earth, water, fire, and air.... Several there are who think it refers to the heaven and earth and all that is in them, since the sages of Greece and the nations of barbary—not to mention Romans, that bilge of all superstition—venerate sun, moon, seas, and the gods of forests and mountains. Others interpret

the "elements of the world" as the law of Moses and the prophets' oracles, the initial and early stages of our studies, as it were.[25]

If Jerome leans to the third of these, he does so without ruling out the second, not inappropriately, for it is in keeping with Paul's skill as a dialectician that this single phrase combines both cosmic determinism and pedagogical subjection.

These elements are certainly "of the world": "You watch days, months, times, and years," he says (4:10), displaying worldly reality across the spectrum of time like a fan. The world is presented through an infinite differentiation of kinds and relations, imposing themselves on practical reason as a succession of uncoordinated demands. It would be no world if it were not diverse, and yet that is our practical peril, reducing us to those who "watch" (παρατηρεῖσθε, *paratēreisthe*), the verb suggesting the paralysis that time and nature can induce. A moral law with multiple demands enslaves us. That is the truth of polytheism, explored long ago by the great poets of Greek antiquity, by Homer and the Attic tragedians: a world at odds with itself, its perpetual strife fought out across the field of our human actions, leaving us no scope for self-direction and responsibility. The ordering of worldly norms, a coherence that can authorize human agency, is essential to practical reason. Precisely that coherence is given us through the neighbor who is as ourself, in relation to whom every directive that the world can issue is ordered.

Yet Paul's leading simile of immaturity and adulthood also implies that these elements are pedagogical beginnings. Greek commentators were fond of observing that στοιχεῖα are letters of the alphabet learned by children, and learned, of course, in an age innocent of modern educational ideals, by rote. "So, as we have said," Jerome concludes, "the law of Moses and the prophets can be understood as the elements in that instruction by which syllables and vocabulary are fitted together and learned not for their own sake but in service of a higher end, that we may read a finished composition that invites our attention to its meaning and argument, not to the elements of its language."

Life lived as flesh, then, is both "elemental" and "elementary," reactive to a plurality of unconnected external demands and restricted to the disconnected building blocks of moral learning. To these disjointed elements, the Spirit supplies the missing meaning and coherence in the command of love, and therewith the authority to interpret and direct our lives accordingly. To decide for the Spirit against the flesh means taking up life as a moral privilege and task instead of merely reacting. The purpose of God that binds the

25. Jerome, *Commentarius in epistolam ad Galatas* (PL 26:371).

world together is clear, and in binding ourselves to that purpose we lay hold on positive freedom, knowing what we are doing and why, and ordering our lives consistently. Faith is the occasion of freedom, freedom takes form in love, and love grounds hope, for the meaning opened up to us is not merely an order of being but an order of time, too, and to live by the Spirit is to live in the light of promise, eschatologically.

Moral catechesis, we must suppose, was a feature of the Christian church since its inception, and such texts as the lists of fifteen vices in 5:19–21 and of nine virtues in 5:22–23 were, it is often assumed, typical of its style. For Paul, these lists are not an end in themselves. They display the contrast between life lived eschatologically and life lived elementally. This, I take Paul to say of the virtues, "is the kind of thing that lies beyond the scope of law." Paul does not relax his program of keeping the oppositions of this letter—law/faith, servility/freedom, flesh/spirit—consistently aligned.

Here I interject a doubt as to the universal Western tradition of translating the final phrase of 5:23, κατὰ τῶν τοιούτων οὐκ ἔστιν νόμος, as "against such things," a tradition going back to the Vetus Latina's *adversus*. This would imply that Paul is finally willing, on the basis of 5:13 and 6:2, to make a reconciliation between law and Spirit, aligning them together against the flesh. It is not impossible; some support for it may be found in 6:13, if we take that to mean that the law not kept by the circumcised is the law interpreted by love. Yet in the absence of any clear statement it is difficult, and especially difficult at the heart of this passage, which brings the series of oppositions to a climax. Interpreted in the Western manner, the phrase in 5:23 has the perplexing appearance of a non sequitur, suggesting that the virtues are not legally prohibited—and so appears gratuitous, even if read with a touch of irony. A simpler explanation is preferable. One is to hand: κατά + genitive may mean "over" in the metaphorical sense of "applying to" or "concerning," as is well documented from classical literature.[26] Though this sense is rare in the New Testament, John 19:11 is a clear parallel. John Chrysostom's comment on the verse (PG 61:674) acknowledges no relaxation of the opposition between law and Spirit, but reads the phrase to mean simply that the virtues are beyond the law's competence. "What, after all, would the law have to contribute to one who had all he needed at his disposal and had love as the most qualified teacher of philosophy? Good horsemen need no whip; the soul that practices virtue from the Spirit needs no legal advice. The law is entirely and decisively excluded, not because it is bad in itself, but because it is so inferior to the philosophy that is now given us."

26. LSJ, κατά A7.

Which brings us back, finally, to the word "flesh" itself. Among the idiomatic phrases involving σάρξ, we find κατὰ σάρκα, meaning "ordinarily" or "conventionally."[27] Life according to flesh may be thought of as the conventional life, governed by the perceptions of the unreflective understanding—"earthly, superficial, and inconsiderate," as Chrysostom described it—"earthly" in the sense of "materialistic," failing to reveal the meaning of things beyond the immediate communications of the senses. In Galatians one occurrence of σάρξ is close to this sense in Paul's handwritten postscript at 6:12, writing of those who "would make a good appearance in the flesh," a double entendre, to be sure, but referring in the first instance to the specious plausibility of the seducers' appeal. With this we may link the contrast between human tradition and direct revelation on which Paul insists at the beginning of the letter. "Flesh" is characterized at 5:24 by "passions," παθήματα, which are immediate emotional responses to stimuli. Flesh in opposition to Spirit, then, stands for instinctive reactions to successive and unconnected demands, not only of the body's needs but also of the emulative strife of society, the opaque symbolism of peremptory tradition, the chilling unknowns of nature, and the ominously threatening future.

In drawing our threads together, we shall make three observations of the greatest brevity on the implications of our theme for ethics at large. First, the conceptual opposition of flesh and Spirit is a way to frame the ethical questions; it is not itself a general law or a concrete demand. I know of no ground for denying the term *ethics*, in the fullest sense, to the intention and execution of Paul's thought in the argument of this letter, a claim that does not, of course, in the slightest affect its status as theology.[28] If one thinks the term serviceable, this element of the argument might be thought of as his "metaethics." Organizing concepts frame the categories that give shape to practical questions, and no moralist who knows his business will doubt for a moment that the large-scale moral landscape, or *ēthos*—to use a term that has enjoyed a recent revival of fashion—whether of Christianity or any other culture, takes its character from these.

Second, its purpose is to project across the field of moral life a narrative of liberation, a story of humankind that hinges on an event of death and

27. See BAGD σάρξ 5.
28. A fondness among NT scholars of the last generation for saying that Paul had no "systematic ethics" (J. L. Houlden, V. P. Furnish, e.g., and compare Siegfried Schulz *Neutestamentliche Ethik* [Zurich: Theologische Verlag, 1987] who consistently places the word *Ethik* within quotation marks) raises the question what their paradigm for a "systematic ethics" was. I can assume only that they were thinking of Spinoza's *Ethica more geometrico demonstrata*, an extravagance of Enlightenment speculation that has deservedly had no imitators.

resurrection. It projects it *across the field of moral life*, for "walking by the Spirit" is an enduring commitment to moral consistency through time, not a mere repetition of the pathos of a conversion moment. Yet across this consistent conduct Paul projects *the narrative of the new creation through the Son of God*, which stamps it with the character of postresurrection humanity, taken up into the friendship of God, awakened to the divine direction and guidance that inspires and liberates. Ethics was not given complete and entire in the created order, only to be worked out and applied in varying circumstances; instead, ethics had to come to fulfillment in history, not, as in the dreary historicism of modernity, through an immanent dynamics of progress, but through the saving intervention of God in his Son.

Third, life in the Spirit is known by the authority it commands to interpret moral law within a framework of mutual service, the love of neighbor as self. On the one hand, this liberated ethic is definitely not antinomian, and definitely not intuitive and antirational. It might perhaps be described as "transnomian" since the moral law acquires a new significance as a witness to the ultimate purposes of God to bless the human race. On the other hand, it is definitely not "autonomous"—in the sense that that word has generally acquired, as isolated and solitary self-responsibility. "I live, and yet not I." The masterful discernment to which the "son" is called belongs to a dialectical reason that constantly responds to the leading and questioning of the Spirit of God. Only those who exercise this spiritual hermeneutic can free themselves from reactive-defensive responses to moral order, whether subservient or rebellious, and begin to make sense of history, nature, and society in partnership with God, who created, restored, and will fulfill all things.

19

"Indicative and Imperative" as the Substructure of Paul's Theology-and-Ethics in Galatians?

A Discussion of Divine and Human Agency in Paul

Volker Rabens

Paul's Letter to the Galatians has been a source of theological and spiritual inspiration for many groups and individuals during the roughly two thousand years it has been around. Several passages of the epistle have become key texts to which students of Paul turn when they try to understand the mind of the apostle, particularly regarding his theology and ethics (e.g., Gal. 2:16 and 3:28 have provoked theological and ethical discussion, respectively). Galatians 5:25 is such a passage, and it relates to both Paul's theology and his ethics. The verse describes the new reality of Christian life, and it calls the believers in Galatia to live in accordance with this new dynamic state of affairs. It is striking that the Spirit plays a key role in both parts: "If we live by the Spirit, let us also walk by the Spirit" (5:25). In the first part of the verse, Paul appears to express positively what he then demands of believers in the second part—or at least he asks them to actively draw consequences from part one. This intriguing relationship of "is" and "ought" has become well known among exegetes and theologians as that of "indicative" and "imperative." Rudolf Bultmann's 1924 essay, "Das Problem der Ethik bei Paulus," has been particularly instrumental in this context. In his article Bultmann repeatedly refers to Galatians 5:25 as a prime example of what he conceived to be a key characteristic as well as fundamental problem of Paul's theology and ethics.[1]

This article critically engages with the much-debated relation of "is" and "ought" in Paul's theology-and-ethics, particularly as we find it in his Epistle to the Galatians. Are "indicative" and "imperative" helpful categories for understanding how Christian ethics should "work" according to Paul? And does the text of Galatians provide us with any answers in this direction, granted that the letter yields one of the prime texts upon which this concept of Paul's ethics has been built (i.e., 5:25)? To approach these questions, I start by entering a dialogue with the critics of the indicative-imperative model (part 1) and look at what they offer instead (part 2). Then I suggest a more dynamic model of the relationship of divine and human agency in Paul's theology-and-ethics, which will be demonstrated by a more detailed reading of Galatians (part 3).

Before we proceed, however, I briefly clarify that by using the designation "Paul's *ethics*," I do not intend to suggest that Paul's Epistles offer a systematic analysis of the grounds, motives, forms, or goals of Christian conduct. From a systematic perspective one would rather need to speak about Paul's "implicit ethics" (thus Ruben Zimmermann).[2] However, if one employs the term "ethics" in its everyday sense, it is certainly possible to speak of the "ethics" of Paul, because the apostle is obviously concerned for the practical conduct of Christ-believers, and this is inseparably related to the central themes of his preaching (hence the wording "theology-and-ethics"). The inquiry into the relationship of "indicative" and "imperative" looks at one aspect of the "enabling and grounds"[3] of Paul's ethics. Victor Furnish even thinks that this relationship of Paul's basic theological convictions and his ethical concerns, though "never raised to the level of critical examination by the apostle himself, never self-consciously formulated or presented by him, . . . is present, nonetheless, in the *dynamic of indicative and imperative which lies at the center of his thought*."[4]

---

1. R. Bultmann, "Das Problem der Ethik bei Paulus," ZNW 23 (1924): 123–40. Cf. the translations in idem, *The Old and the New Man in the Letters of Paul* (Richmond: John Knox, 1967), 7–32; and idem, "The Problem of Ethics in Paul," in *Understanding Paul's Ethics: Twentieth-Century Approaches,* ed. B. S. Rosner (Grand Rapids: Eerdmans, 1995), 195–216.

2. R. Zimmermann, "Jenseits von Indikativ und Imperativ: Zur 'impliziten Ethik' des Paulus am Beispiel des 1. Korintherbriefs," *TLZ* (2007): 260–84.

3. Cf. the definition of NT ethics by W. Schrage, *Ethik des Neuen Testaments*; GNT/NTD 4 (Göttingen: Vandenhoeck & Ruprecht, 1982), 9.

4. V. P. Furnish, *Theology and Ethics in Paul* (Nashville: Abingdon, 1968), 211, emphasis added.

Criticism of the Indicative-Imperative Model

It seems that both the inventors as well as some of the strongest critics of the terminology and concept of "indicative" and "imperative" are rooted in German scholarship.[5] Particularly at the Protestant faculty at the University of Mainz, the concept of "indicative" and "imperative" has been critically revisited. In 2009 Friedrich W. Horn and Ruben Zimmermann published the conference volume *Beyond Indicative and Imperative*.[6] While not all of the articles in the volume discard the indicative-imperative approach to ethics altogether, Ruben Zimmermann has done exactly this in a number of recent publications. He argues that there are good reasons to leave behind "indicative" and "imperative" and move ahead to a new model of "implicit ethics" that he has developed.[7] In this section, using the example of Galatians, I summarize and discuss the points critiquing the indicative-imperative approach to Paul's ethics that Zimmermann has collected in his essay "Jenseits von Indikativ und Imperativ."[8] In the course of this investigation, we will uncover various aspects of the relation of divine and human agency in Paul and discover that Zimmermann's criticism of the terminology of "indicative" and "imperative" is justified—whereas his criticism of the approach as such is not.

The Lack of Textual Evidence for the Model

Criticism 1: The indicative-imperative schema is a research construct that contradicts the actual structure of Paul's Epistles because they are not homogeneously divided into dogmatics and ethics.

Response: It is true that the structure of Paul's Letters cannot be split into

---

5. For the former, see already P. Wernle, *Der Christ und die Sünde bei Paulus* (Freiburg and Leipzig: Mohr Siebeck, 1897), 89, 105. On the latter, see Zimmermann, "Jenseits von Indikativ."

6. F. W. Horn and R. Zimmermann, eds., *Jenseits von Indikativ und Imperativ*, Kontexte und Normen neutestamentlicher Ethik/Contexts and Norms of New Testament Ethics 1, WUNT 1/238 (Tübingen: Mohr Siebeck, 2009).

7. Zimmermann, "Jenseits von Indikativ," passim; R. Zimmermann, "The 'Implicit Ethics' of New Testament Writings: A Draft on a New Methodology in Analysing New Testament Ethics," *Neot* 43 (2009): 398–422; idem, "Ethikbegründung bei Paulus: Die bleibende Attraktivität und Insuffizienz des Indikativ-Imperativ-Modells, in *Die Diskussion des Paulus in der Diskussion: Reflexionen im Anschluss an Michael Wolters Grundriss*, ed. J. Frey and B. Schließer (BThS 140, Neukirchen-Vluyn: Neukirchener Verlag, 2013), 237–55; idem, "Die Ethik der Kirche: Normen, Begründungen, Strukturen, Argumentation," in *Paulus Handbuch*, ed. F. W. Horn (Tübingen: Mohr Siebeck, 2013), 433–40; idem, "Pluralistische Ethikbegründung und Normenanalyse im Horizont einer 'impliziten Ethik' frühchristlicher Schriften," in *Ethische Normen des frühen Christentums: Gut—Leben—Leib—Tugend*, ed. F. W. Horn et al., WUNT 313(Tübingen: Mohr Siebeck, 2013), 3–28.

8. Zimmermann, "Jenseits von Indikativ," 264–65.

"indicative" and "imperative." This can be seen in Galatians. Despite some claims to the contrary, "ethics" is not restricted to the second part of the epistle. Rather, the entire epistle is aimed at establishing among the Galatians a religious-ethical life that is in accordance with the gospel of Christ. To give just one example of an imperative that is placed outside the so-called "ethical part"[9] of the letter (5:13–6:10): 4:12 starts a new subsection that is filled with grammatical imperatives and ethical argumentation (e.g., v. 12: "Become as I am, for I also have become as you are"). Also, the focal text of my present essay, 5:25, demonstrates that Paul can use "indicative" and "imperative" within the same part of one letter, even in the same sentence.

Nevertheless, while Zimmermann's criticism points to a functional limitation of the indicative-imperative approach, it certainly does not discredit its usefulness altogether, for those who believe that "indicative" and "imperative" are (one) characteristic of Paul's ethics usually do not derive this verdict (solely) from the formal structure of the Epistles, but from what they perceive as a substructure of the apostle's *thought* (which may, of course, in some cases express itself in the rhetorical structure of a letter, as we can see from the fact that one usually finds accumulations of ethical instructions in the second part of a Pauline epistle).

Criticism 2: The classification of certain content into the grammatical forms "indicative" and "imperative" cannot be demonstrated from the text. Paul can express the same content as a grammatical indicative as well as an imperative. For instance, the motif of "putting on Christ" is expressed in Galatians 3:27 as an indicative and in Romans 13:14 as an imperative.[10]

Response: That Paul can express the same content in statements of both "is" and "ought," points toward a complex relationship of divine and human agency in Paul (which will be discussed in greater detail in my response to criticism 5). However, it is the very strength of the indicative-imperative approach that it addresses this relationship.

Nonetheless, I agree that the grammatical terminology of "indicative" and "imperative" is confusing when applied to the ethics of Paul's Letters. For example, Galatians contains a fair amount of "implicit imperatives" that are not grammatical imperatives, such as 6:8: "If you sow to your own flesh, you will reap corruption from the flesh; but if you sow to the Spirit, you will reap

---

9. Thus, e.g., F. Mußner, *Der Galaterbrief*, HTKNT 9 (Freiburg im Breisgau: Herder, 2002), viii.

10. Further examples of indicatives and imperatives given by Zimmermann, "Jenseits von Indikativ," 164n40, include 1 Thess. 5:8 and Rom. 13:12 (armor) (here both instances are imperatives); 1 Cor. 5:7b and 5:7a, 8 (yeast); 1 Cor. 6:11 and 1 Thess. 4:3–4 (sanctification); 2 Cor. 5:18–19 and 5:20 (reconciliation with God); Rom. 6:2, 10 and 6:11–12 (freedom from sin).

eternal life from the Spirit" (NRSV). Paul's "implicit imperative" here is that the church should sow to the Spirit. Even in our key verse, the verb στοιχῶμεν (5:25b) is a (hortative) subjunctive and not a grammatical imperative. From the point of terminology, then, a solution to the justified critique from a linguistic perspective could be, in true Zimmermannian fashion (the central term of his approach is "implicit ethics"),[11] to speak of *Paul's (implicit) indicative* and *(implicit) imperative*. On this rendering, "(implicit) indicative and imperative" would encompass explicit, grammatical indicatives and imperatives (hence the parentheses around "implicit"), but also include other statements of "is" and "ought" in Paul's theology-and-ethics.[12]

Criticism 3: Nowhere in his epistles does Paul deduce the imperative from the indicative.

Response: It is a general problem of Paul's theology that he does not elucidate the specific details of how to relate "is" and "ought." Nevertheless, that Paul does not explicitly unravel the relationship between the (implicit) indicatives and imperatives in his letters does not prove that the two are either identical or otherwise totally unrelated in Paul's theology-and-ethics. Our key verse proves the opposite. Although 5:25 is cast in the form of a (chiastic)[13] conditional sentence, what is expressed in the protasis (which summarizes 5:1–24)[14] is assumed to be true (hence 5:25 NIV: "Since we live by the Spirit"). It is on this basis that the apodosis then makes an appeal.[15] This causal connection is hence well expressed by F. F. Bruce's words that "living by the Spirit is the root, walking by the Spirit is the fruit."[16]

Numerous further texts evidence the same reasoning (*Begründungsstruktur*).[17] For instance, see Philippians 2:12c–13: "Work out your own salvation with

---

11. Nonetheless, even in his own approach, Zimmermann searches for *imperatives* when trying to approach NT ethics from the perspective of moral language. See R. Zimmermann, "Ethics in the New Testament and Language: Basic Explorations and Eph 5:21–33 as Test Case," in *Moral Language in the New Testament: The Interrelatedness of Language and Ethics in Early Christian Writings*, ed. R. Zimmermann et al., Kontexte und Normen neutestamentlicher Ethik/Contexts and Norms of New Testament Ethics 2, WUNT 2/296 (Tübingen: Mohr Siebeck, 2010), esp. 30.

12. Alternatively, one could also put "indicative" and "imperative" in quotation marks in order to indicate that one is not merely concerned with grammatical indicatives and imperatives. See also the terminological suggestions in the conclusion to this first part of the article.

13. (A) If we live (B) by the Spirit, (B′) by the Spirit (A′) let us also walk. Cf., e.g., M. C. de Boer, *Galatians: A Commentary*, NTL (Louisville: Westminster John Knox, 2011), 371.

14. Cf. H. D. Betz, *Galatians: A Commentary on Paul's Letter to the Churches in Galatia*, Hermeneia (Philadelphia: Fortress, 1979), 293.

15. Cf. R. Y. K. Fung, *The Epistle to the Galatians*, NICNT (Grand Rapids: Eerdmans, 1988), 275.

16. F. F. Bruce, *The Epistle to the Galatians: A Commentary on the Greek Text*, NIGTC (Exeter: Paternoster; Grand Rapids: Eerdmans, 1982), 257.

17. E.g., 1 Cor. 5:7; Rom. 6:2, 6, 10–12; using conjunctions such as οὖν, ἵνα, and καθώς.

fear and trembling; for [γάρ] it is God who is at work in you, enabling you both to will and to work for his good pleasure" (NRSV). Here Paul explicitly deduces his imperative for human action from God's continuous activity of both motivating and enabling this very action.

The Lack of Functional Suitability of the Model

Criticism 4: Leading on from the last point, Zimmermann's first comment regarding the lack of functional suitability of the indicative-imperative schema criticizes that the model is rigid and inaccurate because it suggests some type of temporal or logical precedence of the indicative over the imperative.

Response: While Paul does not explicate the temporal or logical precedence of the (implicit) indicative over the (implicit) imperative whenever his writing relates to these issues, one can nonetheless attest an overall precedence of divine agency in Paul. For example, Galatians 4:4–5 gives evidence of both a temporal and a "logical" precedence of the (implicit) indicative: "But when the fullness of *time* had come, God sent his Son, born of a woman, born under the law, *in order to redeem* those who were under the law, so that we might *receive adoption* as children" (NRSV, emphasis added). Everything has started with God's act of redemption and adoption (cf. the salutation in 1:3–4).[18] In 4:9 Paul even explicitly corrects himself by stressing the priority of divine activity: "Now . . . that you have come to know God, or rather to be known by God" (NRSV; for further examples, see my response to criticism 5 below). Nevertheless, this precedence does not imply that the relationship of (implicit) indicatives and imperatives is necessarily rigid and would contradict the dynamics and variety of Paul's ethical reasoning. Rather, as will become clear below (in "A Relational Model"), it is possible to grasp a number of the key characteristics of Paul's thought on the relation of divine and human agency with the help of a dynamic model of (implicit) indicatives and imperatives in Galatians.

Criticism 5: The indicative-imperative schema introduces an artificial division into a matter that is presented as a unity by Paul.[19]

Response: This criticism seems to build on one particular model of divine and human agency in Paul (i.e., that both are presented by Paul as a unity). The indicative-imperative model is designed to address this important aspect of Paul's theology-and-ethics—namely, the respective roles attributed to

---

18. Cf. V. Rabens, "'Schon jetzt' und 'noch mehr': Gegenwart und Zukunft des Heils bei Paulus und in seinen Gemeinden," *JBTh* 28 (2013), part 1.

19. In this criticism, Zimmermann uses neither the terminology of "indicative and imperative" nor that of "divine and human" agency but remains as vague as possible: "führt eine künstliche Trennung ein, die *das von Paulus als Einheit Dargestellte* retrospektiv zergliedert" (Zimmermann, "Jenseits von Indikativ," 264), emphasis added.

divine and human agency. These two angles on Paul's theology-and-ethics are not identical, but they are intricately related: in Paul the (implicit) indicative sometimes designates the *result of divine agency*, that is, it describes the new state of affairs of the transformed believer (e.g., Gal. 6:14: "By the cross of our Lord Jesus Christ the world has been crucified to me, and I to the world"). And sometimes the (implicit) indicative expresses the (continuous) *divine agency itself* (e.g., Phil. 2:13: "It is God who is at work in you, enabling you both to will and to work for his good pleasure"; cf. 2 Cor. 5:5). With his implicit or explicit imperatives, however, Paul appeals to human agency—although in Paul, human agency is always dependent on God. The precise relationship of divine and human agency is, of course, a matter of much debate. Nonetheless, Zimmermann appears to criticize the appropriateness of this approach by assuming one particular model of the relation of divine and human agency: he claims that Paul presents them as a unity.

However, at least three types of correlation of divine and human activity in religious-ethical life can be conceptualized, as John Barclay points out in the volume *Divine and Human Agency in Paul*. The *first model* places divine and human agency in an essentially *competitive* relationship: the more that one is said to be effective, the less can be attributed to the other. Divine sovereignty and human freedom are thus mutually exclusive; human freedom must be understood as freedom from God. The *second model* presents divine and human agency as related to each other by *kinship* or unity. God and humanity are here within the same spectrum of being, and the agency of one is shared with the other, rather than standing in competition with each other. Human agency is bound up with that of God; the two are essentially identical when properly aligned. On this model, human freedom is not freedom from God, but it is exercised precisely by acting in accordance with God and willing what God has willed. The *third model* presents divine agency in terms of a *noncontrastive transcendence*. God's sovereignty does not limit or reduce human freedom; rather, God's sovereignty is precisely what grounds and enables human freedom. The more the human agent is operative, the more (not the less) may be attributed to God. However, human agency is not an empty shell for divine power or a threat to divine agency (as in model 1), nor is it ultimately identical to divine agency (model 2). Rather, created human agencies are founded in, and constituted by, the divine creative agency, all the while remaining distinct from God.[20]

20. J. M. G. Barclay, introduction to *Divine and Human Agency in Paul and His Cultural Environment*, ECC/LNTS 335, ed. J. M. G. Barclay and S. J. Gathercole (London: Continuum, 2006), 6–7.

Looking at these three models, it seems that Zimmermann is a proponent of model 2. However, the relation of divine and human agency and of (implicit) indicative and imperative in Paul appears to be more complex. On the one hand, we do find some "material" in Paul that is expressed *both* as (implicit) indicative *and* as (implicit) imperative, as we have seen in criticism 2. This may point toward the unity that Zimmermann appears to assume. However, even here it seems necessary to develop further subcategories: while Paul clearly stresses the divine "indicative" in salvation (e.g., Rom. 5:8–10, 15; 6:6–7; Gal. 1:3–4; 4:4–5; cf. Eph. 2:8–10), he can also at some points express the necessity of human agency in this regard by appealing to believers to fit their lives around the character and purpose of the divine agency and thus ensure the maximum possible match (e.g., Rom. 8:13; Gal. 6:8; Phil. 2:12c–13; cf. my response to criticism 7 below).[21] On the other hand, the "content" of (implicit) indicative and imperative is not always identical in Paul. For example, in Romans 8:13 Paul asks his audience to "put to death the deeds of the body"—a formulation that has no exact counterpart in Paul's positive statements of divine agency in the life of the church, although putting to death the deeds of the body is clearly based on divine agency (Rom. 8:3–4; cf. Gal. 5:24) and can be seen as its practical continuation (after all, it is *by the aid of the Spirit* [πνεύματι] that Paul's churches are to put to death the deeds of the body [Rom. 8:13]).[22]

In any case, Zimmermann would need to provide further support from Paul's Epistles for his assumption that the indicative-imperative model takes apart what Paul presents as a unity. The concept of (implicit) indicative and imperative merely gives a name to the entities that compose this "unity" in Paul. And whatever is meant by unity, it certainly should not be understood as the identity of divine and human action in Paul.

Criticism 6: The relation of *being able* and *being obliged* to act morally is not an issue at the heart of Pauline theology.

Response: Furnish's statement (quoted above) regarding Paul that "the dynamic of indicative and imperative ... lies at the center of his thought" is indeed exaggerated. Nonetheless, the fact that something is not at the center

---

21. Cf. J. M. G. Barclay, "Believers and the Last 'Judgment' in Paul: Rethinking Grace and Recompense," in *Eschatologie—Eschatology: The Sixth Durham-Tübingen Research Symposium; Eschatology in Old Testament, Ancient Judaism and Early Christianity (Tübingen, September, 2009)*, ed. H.-J. Eckstein et al., WUNT 1/272 (Tübingen: Mohr Siebeck, 2011), 204–8; V. Rabens, "Inclusion of and Demarcation from 'Outsiders': Mission and Ethics in Paul's Second Letter to the Corinthians," in *Sensitivity to Outsiders: Exploring the Dynamic Relationship between Mission and Ethics in the New Testament and Early Christianity*, ed. K. Kok et al., WUNT (Tübingen: Mohr Siebeck, 2014), parts 1 and 3.

22. Moreover, Paul's Epistles also evince imperatives that are not directly based on implicit indicatives (e.g., Gal. 5:15); cf. Zimmermann's criticism 8 below (and his overstated criticism 3).

of someone's thought does not mean that it does not play a role at all in that person's thinking. In Paul, the obligation of and the ability for moral action is an overt issue in one of the most central passages of theology: Romans 6–8. Paul's exposition of religious-ethical life in Galatians 5–6 evinces this concern too. For instance, in 5:17–18 Paul explicates both the apparent struggle and the potential inability to live according to the ethics of love proclaimed in the epistle (5:6, 13–14, 22). However, he also stresses the (implicit) indicative by pointing the Galatians to the fact that they are guided by the Spirit and hence free from "subjection to the law."

Thus, while the relation of divine and human agency may not be central in Paul, it clearly is a theme that Paul picks out in a number of his expositions. Zimmermann himself even thinks that Paul presupposes a clear relation between the two, as we will see in his next point of criticism (cf. criticism 5).

The Precarious Theological Assumptions of the Model

Criticism 7: The conception of "indicative" and "imperative" leads to insoluble problems regarding the validity of God's gift of salvation in the context of Paul's soteriology: if it has to be achieved or completed by human beings, then salvation is incomplete and limited.

Response: The complex relationship of "is" and "ought" that Zimmermann draws attention to is inherent in Paul's Letters. One can attempt to explain it by proclaiming the unity of "indicative" and "imperative," as Zimmermann appears to do in his criticisms 2 and 5 (cf. Barclay's category 2). Alternatively, one can stress divine action to the exclusion of human action (cf. Barclay's category 1), as Zimmermann appears to do here. In the end, Zimmermann does not disclose what his concept of the relation between divine and human action in Paul is. His own approach to ethics, which we will investigate in the next section, appears to leave divine agency out of the picture of Pauline ethics altogether.

The fact that there is a relation (or as some might say, an "underlying tension") in Paul's theology between "is" and "ought" does not discredit the model of "indicative" and "imperative," since it merely is giving a designation to this relation. As such, it does *not* suggest one particular model of that relation (or solution to the tension), as we can see from the two opposing models of "indicative" and "imperative" by Bultmann and Furnish.[23] However, we can observe the potentially "insoluble problems regarding the validity of God's gift of salvation" in Paul himself, as, for example, in Galatians 6:8. The apostle

---

23. Cf. the discussion in V. Rabens, *The Holy Spirit and Ethics in Paul: Transformation and Empowering for Religious-Ethical Life*, WUNT 2/283 (Tübingen: Mohr Siebeck, 2010), 273–82.

seems to say here, at least at face value, that only as the Galatians sow to the Spirit will they actually receive eternal life (cf. the example of Phil. 2:12c–13 and my discussion of criticism 5 above).

Critical Points from the Philosophy of Language and Morality

Criticism 8: "Indicative" and "imperative" are metaphors that cannot describe the details of Paul's moral reasoning with any precision. Rather, Paul's paraenesis evinces a variety of different linguistic forms and patterns of ethical reasoning, which ask for a more sophisticated method of analysis.

Response: The indicative-imperative model indeed focuses on (only) one particular aspect of Paul's ethics. However, this aspect of divine and human agency is related to other dimensions of Paul's theology (such as "identity and ethics").[24] To approach the interplay of these different dimensions of Paul's theology-and-ethics, we need to look at Paul's ethics from a wider perspective. Zimmermann provides a sophisticated method that has precisely this aim. It will be briefly introduced and discussed in the next section.

Conclusion: The indicative-imperative approach clearly points to an issue that is "under the surface" of Paul's theology—and sometimes even clearly "above the surface," as we have seen in a number of texts (focusing on Gal. 5:25). Of the critical points raised by Zimmermann, only the critique from the standpoint of linguistics holds ground: the terminology of "indicative" and "imperative" indeed has its primary reference in the realm of grammar. However, some scholars may still want to hold on to it[25] in the same way that Pauline scholarship has on the whole continued to use other debatable terminology, such as Paul's "ethics" or—though less common—his "mysticism."[26]

To indicate the terminological limitations of the indicative-imperative approach, I have suggested that we speak of "(implicit) indicatives" and "(implicit) imperatives," which encompass grammatical indicatives and imperatives, but also include other statements of "is" and "ought" in Paul's theology-and-ethics. They mark the "constitutive" and "appellative," or the "ascriptive" and

---

24. Cf. esp. D. G. Horrell, *Solidarity and Difference: A Contemporary Reading of Paul's Ethics* (London: T&T Clark, 2005).

25. E.g., M. Wolter, *Paulus: Ein Grundriss seiner Theologie* (Neukirchen: Neukirchener Verlag, 2011), 312–17.

26. E.g., H.-C. Meier, *Mystik bei Paulus: Zur Phänomenologie religiöser Erfahrung im Neuen Testament*, TANZ 26 (Tübingen: Francke, 1998). See the discussion in V. Rabens, "*Pneuma* and the Beholding of God: Reading Paul in the Context of Philonic Mystical Traditions," in *The Holy Spirit, Inspiration, and the Cultures of Antiquity: Multidisciplinary Perspectives*, ed. J. Frey and J. R. Levison, Ekstasis 5 (Berlin/New York: De Gruyter, 2014), 295–331.

"prescriptive" elements of Paul's theology-and-ethics,[27] *Gabe* and *Aufgabe* (gift and task), without suggesting one particular model of their relation (on the latter, see "A Relational Model" below).

An Alternative Approach to Paul's Ethics in Galatians

As the concept of (implicit) indicative and imperative targets only one aspect of Paul's theology-and-ethics, what could be a more comprehensive approach to the ethical dimension of Paul's thought, particularly as it is expressed in Galatians? Here too we turn to the most recent and sophisticated approach of those who have criticized the traditional indicative-imperative model—which is that of Zimmermann. With his model of "implicit ethics," Zimmermann aims to leave behind the focus of some scholars on a single, soteriological "indicative" in relation to a paraenetic "imperative" because Paul's Letters evidence a much broader set of reasons and grounds for ethical living.

Zimmermann provides us with eight avenues into Paul's implicit ethics, which are well illustrated by a diagram designed by Zimmermann.[28]

**Diagram 1
Zimmermann's Model of "Implicit Ethics"**

1. Linguistic Form
2. Norms and Values for Action
3. History of Traditions of Individual Norms
4. Priorities of Values
5. Ethical "Logic"/ Structure of Motives
6. The Moral Agent
7. The Resulting Ethos as Lived
8. Addressee/Field of Application

The "Implicit Ethics"

---

27. "Ascriptive" should not be understood along the lines of the German "Zuspruch" ("indicative") and "Anspruch" ("imperative"), because such a model of the (implicit) indicative seems to imply that the "indicative" of God's acting on human subjects boils down to mere words of encouragement. Cf. n. 45 below.

28. Zimmermann, "Ethics . . . and Language," 27.

Zimmermann has formulated a set of guiding questions to help us explore these eight aspects of ethics in general and Paul's ethics in Galatians in particular. Below I will list these questions[29] and indicate which aspect of Paul's ethics in Galatians they may help to elucidate.

1. Linguistic Form: Which linguistic form does the ethical statement take? Zimmermann rightly recognizes the complex difference between prescriptive and descriptive moral language. For instance, even narrative, metaphoric, and ironic texts can transport morality through their specific style.[30] Galatians 4:21–31 is an example of the former, although the narrative is already explicitly interwoven with an ethical argumentation. The linguistic form of ethics classically also involves the imperative mood. We have already looked at some grammatical imperatives in Galatians, to which we may add the central appeal in 5:1 (which builds on an "indicative").

2. Norms and Values for Action: Which leading norms and maxims of action are mentioned? Here we are looking for basic principles that put normative obligations on the behavior of individuals or groups. In Galatians, most fundamentally, this is "love" (5:6, 14; cf. criterion 4 below). We also find two norms that mark a spectrum: freedom (5:1; cf. 1:4; 2:4) and "being a slave for Christ" (1:10).

3. History of Traditions of Individual Norms/Moral Instances: In which traditional and contemporary context do these norms exist? Norms can be classified with regard to their tradition and religious history. In Galatians, for instance, Paul explicitly cites the Hebrew Scriptures in support of his ethical argumentation (3:10, 13; 4:22, 27). Also, the *Traditionsgeschichte* of ethical concepts from Hellenistic moral philosophy could be analyzed in this context (e.g., that of the central concept of ἐλευθερία, 2:4; 5:1, 13).[31]

4. Logic of Values: What inner relationship between different norms is produced? Which emphasis of norms and hierarchy of values can be recognized? This criterion investigates the hierarchy of values that is implicitly or explicitly presented in a text. In Galatians, such a hierarchy is clearly expressed in 5:6, 14 (love).

5. Ethical Argumentation/Structure of Motives: According to which internal structure of motives and according to which ethical argumentation does the

---

29. The list is taken from ibid., 24–26.
30. Zimmermann, "'Implicit Ethics,'" 405.
31. Cf., e.g., G. Dautzenberg, "Freiheit im hellenistischen Kontext," in *Der neue Mensch in Christus: Hellenistische Anthropologie und Ethik im Neuen Testament*, ed. J. Beutler, QD 190 (Freiburg im Breisgau: Herder, 2001), 57; T. Engberg-Pedersen, "A Stoic Concept of the Person in Paul? From Galatians 5:17 to Romans 7:14–25," in *Christian Body, Christian Self: Concepts of Early Christian Personhood*, ed. C. K. Rothschild et al. (Tübingen: Mohr Siebeck, 2011), 85–112.

ethical judgment take place? Ethical texts usually provide reasons (e.g., deontological or teleological arguments) why the addressees should live by them. For instance, when Paul demands a certain religious-ethical lifestyle from his audience in Galatia, he bases this request on their new, Spirit-worked identity and experience of adoption in their lives (4:1–11).

6. *The Carrier of Ethical Judgments: Who is the subject of ethical judgments? Which factors constitute the ethical subject?* Different factors influence an ethical subject in the process of decision making. These include reason and emotions. For example, Paul's argumentative structure in Galatians 4:12–20 appeals to both reason and emotion when he brings his personal relationship to the Galatians into play and asserts his moral authority over that of the agitators in Galatia.

7. *The Resulting Ethos as Lived: What concrete ethos corresponds to or contradicts the ethical argumentation?* It is heuristically helpful to differentiate the investigation of norms and motives for ethical action from their actual implementation, although Zimmermann acknowledges that it is impossible to separate them completely. With regard to Galatians, we can only speculate how Paul's ethical instructions were put into practice in the church. Nonetheless, the group ethos that Paul attempts to implement, for instance in 6:2, is clearly one of mutual support.

8. *Field of Application: What field of application of a norm is mentioned?* Paul often deals with concrete ethical questions facing his churches. In doing this he regularly differentiates between norms of action that are valid for him, for his assistants, for individual community members, for the community as a whole, or even for humanity in general. When looking at a specific epistle, we can therefore try to identify whether Paul applies his ethical teaching to a particular group within the congregation or to the congregation at large, or whether he is even setting up some universal ethical principle. In the case of Galatians, Paul addresses the entire church throughout—and in particular those who feel attracted to the "different gospel" and the Jewish customs that belong to it (e.g., 5:7–12), although he also formulates some more "universal" principles, as for example in 5:14, 19–24.

Zimmermann has provided us with a very helpful model for approaching the various aspects of Paul's implicit ethics beyond those relating to (implicit) indicative and imperative. Even our short survey has broadened our view of the different ethical issues that surface in Galatians. We can hence warmly recommend the model for further application to New Testament ethics (and to ethics in the wider fields of science and society for which it opens up avenues for dialogue). Nevertheless, from a practical point of view it might be useful to reduce the individual aspects to slightly fewer and more specific points. For instance, criteria 2 ("leading norms") and 4 ("emphasis of norms") could easily be subsumed under one point ("leading norms and their hierarchy"). More significantly, if this new approach is meant to go beyond and even replace the indicative-imperative schema, it seems that one important dimension of the "old model" is missing in the new approach: the aspect of *divine* and human agency. Zimmerman mentions the ethical subject at point 6, where he looks at human agency. However, one of the specifics of Jewish-Christian ethics, and of Paul's ethics in particular, is the role that is attributed to divine enabling.[32] In Paul's ethics human beings are transformed and empowered to live according to the ethical values set forth by the apostle and the ethical traditions that he endorses. For this reason I suggest that we add "divine agency" to Zimmermann's model, since this is one of the key aspects of Paul's ethics—also in Galatians. It comes to the fore, for instance, in 1:4 (cf. 3:23–29) and 2:19–20.

Diagram 2
"Implicit Ethics" Including "Divine Agency"

1. Linguistic Form
2. Norms and Values for Action
3. History of Traditions of Individual Norms
4. Priorities of Values
5. Ethical "Logic"/ Structure of Motives
6. The Moral Agent — Divine and Human Agency
7. The Resulting Ethos as Lived
8. Addressee/Field of Application

The "Implicit Ethics"

Zimmermann's model is designed to fathom the grounds and motivation (*Handlungsgrund*) of Paul's ethics. In this essay I am focusing on the enabling grounds (*Ermöglichungsgrund*) because this is the prime aspect of the indicative-imperative approach to Paul's ethics. In contrast to Zimmermann's model, the importance of this dimension of Paul's ethics is also recognized by another critic

---

32. For an example of Jewish ethics in this regard, see, e.g., V. Rabens, "Philo's Attractive Ethics on the 'Religious Market' of Ancient Alexandria," in *Religions and Trade: Religious Formation, Transformation and Cross-Cultural Exchange between East and West*, ed. P. Wick and V. Rabens, DHR 5 (Leiden: Brill, 2014), 341–50.

of the indicative-imperative schema, Udo Schnelle, for whom "transformation and participation" are the key to Paul's theology-and-ethics.[33] Schnelle's language and emphasis are useful, although the way in which he conceptualizes "transformation and participation" may be too static to be helpful for understanding the dynamics of Paul's ethics in Galatians, particularly in 5:25. Schnelle strongly emphasizes the "new being" from which the ethical life flows. For him, "Entsprechung zum neuen Sein" is the central thought of Paul's ethics. Believers need to live in correspondence with the new being.[34] However, in 5:25a Paul's emphasis is not on a new being—although other texts like 2:19–20 and 5:24 clearly presuppose such an ontic change. Rather, Paul speaks about "living by the Spirit" as the implicit indicative. This "living in the Spirit" is the *continuous* experience of divine agency that transforms and empowers the Galatians so that they can resist the flesh (5:16) and "walk by the Spirit" (5:25b). It has a relational dimension, as I will show in the next and final section.[35]

A Relational Model of Divine and Human Agency in Galatians

Applying Zimmermann's model of "implicit ethics" to Galatians has provided us with a broader and more nuanced picture of Paul's ethics in this epistle. However, the model does not provide any insights into the relation of divine and human agency (or into that of [implicit] indicative and imperative) in Paul. With regard to our test case, we are still left with questions: what is the relation of Galatians 5:25a to 5:25b? How does "walking in line with the Spirit" follow from "living in the Spirit"?

33. U. Schnelle, "Die Begründung und die Gestaltung der Ethik bei Paulus," in *Die bleibende Gegenwart des Evangeliums: Festschrift für Otto Merk zum 70. Geburtstag*, ed. R. Gebauer and M. Meiser, MTS 76 (Marburg: Elwert, 2003), 117; cf. idem, *Paulus: Leben und Denken* (Berlin and New York: de Gruyter, 2003), 630.

34. Schnelle, "Begründung . . . der Ethik," 122, 131.

35. In contrast to the supposed opposition of a substance-ontological *or* a relational concept of the work of the Spirit in Paul's ethics, I build on J. D. G. Dunn's insight that "the basic idea assumed by Paul was of a relationship in which God acts on behalf of his human partner, first in calling Israel into and then in sustaining Israel in its covenant with him. . . . The covenant God counts the covenant partner as still in partnership, despite the latter's continued failure. But the covenant partner could hardly fail to be transformed by a living relationship with the life-giving God" (J. D. G. Dunn, *The Theology of Paul the Apostle* [Edinburgh: T&T Clark, 1998], 344). Applying this insight to the debated ontological frameworks of ethical renewal (by the Spirit) leads us to appreciate that the dominance of the (covenant) relationship of God with his people in Paul's thinking rules out a "relational-as-opposed-to-ontological" approach to Paul's theology and anthropology. Paul's thinking rather encompasses both these aspects, and they are well captured by the concept of *transforming relationships*. Cf. Rabens, *Holy Spirit and Ethics*, vii, 143. See 123–24 on the definition of "relationship" in this context.

Gordon Fee writes that Paul does not provide any details on how "walking in the Spirit" works because the apostle could assume that his churches knew what he was talking about due to their fervent experience of the Spirit.[36] However, in this section I will show that it is possible to gain a deeper understanding of how, according to Galatians, ethical life can be empowered by the Spirit. We start by turning to the literary context of our key verse, since 5:25 is not the first description of the work of the Spirit in Galatians. A couple of lines earlier, Paul formulates his first explicit imperative that is related to the Spirit: "Walk by the Spirit, I say, and you will not gratify the desires of the flesh" (5:16). This command does not offer any further clues with regard to the question of how ethical life ("walking by the Spirit") is empowered, but it helps us to understand the content of what Paul is asking from the Galatians: walking by the Spirit means not gratifying the desires of the flesh. These desires are spelled out in detail in Paul's list of the works of the flesh (5:19–21), which is contrasted with the fruit of the Spirit (5:22–23). The question regarding the ethically transforming and empowering work of the Spirit in the believer (i.e., the "[implicit] indicative"), however, can be approached by turning to Galatians 3 and 4, for it is here that Paul first mentions the life-transforming activity of the Spirit.

In 3:1–5 Paul asks the Galatians if they have received the Spirit through the works of the law or through believing the gospel. His argumentation can be persuasive only if the Galatians can indeed recall their receiving the Spirit. That this memory is tied to a tangible experience comes explicitly to the fore through the way in which Paul connects in parallel "receiving the Spirit" (ἐξ ἔργων νόμου τὸ πνεῦμα ἐλάβετε ἢ ἐξ ἀκοῆς πίστεως [v. 2]) and "experiencing so much" (τοσαῦτα ἐπάθετε εἰκῇ [v. 4]). The Spirit-reception was, therefore, a "great experience." In the subsequent sentence it is listed together with powerful deeds brought about by God (cf. 1 Thess. 1:5–6). Galatians 3:1–5 thus shows that at the heart and at the start of the Christian life of the Galatians is the existential experience of the Spirit.

Galatians 4:1–7 then provides us with further details of the Spirit's empowering work: the Spirit draws people to God as their Father through crying "Abba! Father!" This relational work by the "Spirit of the Son" (which, like "abba," is family language) is placed within an ethical context. This is particularly evident from the way in which Paul continues his argument after 4:1–7. In the succeeding section (4:8–11) Paul explains to the Galatians that the filial relationship to God that they have come to experience through the Spirit is in

---

36. G. D. Fee, *God's Empowering Presence: The Holy Spirit in the Letters of Paul* (Peabody, MA: Hendrickson, 1994), 433.

stark contrast both to their former life in bondage (indicated by the opening ἀλλά; see also 3:23–27) and to their present inclination to return to this slavery (indicated by the rhetorical questions in 4:9). The issues at stake in the Galatian crisis were the identity of the Galatian Christians and their appropriate patterns of behavior.[37] Paul reacts to this insecurity by pointing them to their Christ-created and Spirit-sustained filial relationship with God, which is the reason why they no longer need the law as their identity marker and moral code, or as "guardians and trustees" (4:2) to look after their religious-ethical life. Since they have entered a relationship of filial intimacy with God (v. 6; cf. v. 9: knowing God and being known by God), the Galatians need not submit to the law[38] and thus return to being enslaved to the "weak and beggarly elements" (vv. 3, 9) by trying to perfect by the flesh what they had begun by the Spirit (3:3). Rather, through the transformation and empowering that derives from these intimate relationships,[39] they are enabled to live according to the values of the Spirit (cf. 5:16–25) and thus can demonstrate ongoing loyalty and public honor to their heavenly Father in the face of the agitators.

As I have shown elsewhere, the intimacy created by the Spirit of the Son between believers and their Father is not limited to the emulation of Jesus's prayer life (cf. Mark 14:36) but seems to extend more comprehensively to the imitation of the Son's religious-ethical life before God.[40] This gives further support to my argument that Galatians 4:4–6 (as well as further Pauline passages, esp. Rom. 5:5; 8:12–17; Eph. 3:16–19) demonstrates that the filial intimacy with God that believers come to experience through the Spirit of adoption as daughters and sons has become the fundamental formative force in the believers' lives and empowers them for religious-ethical living as it is demanded in 5:25b and the rest of the letter.

This thesis is further strengthened by a brief look at the parallel of Galatians 4:4–6 in Romans 8:12–17, for here Paul spells out the ethical aspect of the empowering through the relational work of the Spirit in more detail than in Galatians 4 and 5:25. Paul grounds his implicit imperative to put to death the deeds of the body "through the Spirit" (πνεύματι τὰς πράξεις τοῦ

---

37. Cf. J. M. G. Barclay, *Obeying the Truth: A Study of Paul's Ethics in Galatians*, SNTW (Edinburgh: T&T Clark, 1988), 73–74.

38. Cf. J. D. G. Dunn, *Romans 1–8*, WBC 38A (Dallas: Word, 1988), 460: Sonship, including adoptive sonship, "speaks of freedom and intimate mutual trust, where filial concern can be assumed to provide the motivation and direction for living, and conduct be guided by spontaneous love rather than by law." The Spirit provides all the necessary guidance in the fight against the flesh.

39. On the transforming and empowering character of intimate relationships in Paul, see Rabens, *Holy Spirit and Ethics*, esp. 133–38.

40. Ibid., 234–35. Cf. B. W. Longenecker, *The Triumph of Abraham's God: The Transformation of Identity in Galatians* (Edinburgh: T&T Clark, 1998), 62.

σώματος θανατοῦτε [Rom. 8:13]; cf. Gal. 5:25 πνεύματι καὶ στοιχῶμεν) in the experiential reality of the Spirit's leading (8:14), freeing from fear, enabling to cry "Abba!" (8:15), and bearing witness to one's being a child of God (8:16). This line of reasoning is indicated through the employment of the causative conjunction "because" (γάρ) at the beginning of both verses 14 and 15. Paul can describe the Spirit in verse 13 as an instrument (πνεύματι) for fighting temptations because the (implicit) indicatives of the Spirit's relational work in the following verses enable (and require) such ethical behavior. Thus we can see that the quality and character of these Spirit-wrought experiences of love and fellowship in the family of faith[41] function in both Romans 8 and Galatians 4–5 as empowerment as well as criteria for living as children of God.

Conclusion and Further Implications

It is not necessary to entirely give up the perspective on Pauline ethics that has come to be known as "indicative" and "imperative," as long as it is clear that this is merely *one aspect* of the substructure of Paul's theology-and-ethics. However, it is better to speak of "*(implicit)* indicative and imperative," because not all of Paul's language relating to divine enabling and human obligation is expressed with grammatical indicatives and imperatives. Moreover, with the help of Zimmermann's nuanced model of "implicit ethics," we have demonstrated that the "(implicit) indicative and imperative" approach to Paul's ethics in Galatians is only one (though important) aspect of the grounds for ethical life as it is presented in the epistle. Zimmermann's model, however, needs to be supplemented with the aspect of divine agency, which should be added to his category 6, "The Carrier of Ethical Judgments," currently focusing solely on human agency. The interplay of both agencies is reflected in, though not identical to, the concept of (implicit) indicative and imperative.

In Galatians we have discovered that the correlation between (implicit) indicative and imperative appears to be *more dynamic* than an approach that centers on the change of being of the believer. The relational approach that I have suggested reckons with the continuous transforming and empowering dynamic of the Spirit's drawing people closer to God and to one another. Applying this to Galatians 5:25, we can paraphrase Paul's words as saying, "Because we experience the transforming and empowering dynamic of the Spirit in our lives—by the Spirit's creation of filial intimacy with God and the

---

41. The movement from "you" to "we" is evident in Gal. 4:6: "Because *you* are children, God has sent the Spirit of his Son into *our* hearts, crying, 'Abba! Father!'" This shared experience existentially reinforces the corporate identity of the members of the community as children of God.

family of faith—we can and should orientate our lives toward precisely those values that are manifested among us through the expressions of life that the Spirit inspires." "Walking in the Spirit" thus means continuing in the gift of "life in the Spirit" that has already been given.

The results of this investigation of Paul's Letter to the Galatians have *further implications* for the broader theological debate regarding the relation of (implicit) indicative and imperative and of divine and human agency in Paul.[42] First of all, we need to emphasize that the transferal into the realm of influence of the Spirit has established new realities. The (implicit) indicative of "living in the Spirit" (Gal. 5:25a), or of the Spirit's being in the believer and the believer's being in the Spirit (Rom. 8:9), is not a state of affairs that would need to be "actualized" through the deeds of the believer.[43] There is an existential element in the Spirit-inspired Abba-cry of the believer (Rom. 8:15; Gal. 4:6); nevertheless, the existential encounter with God as one's Father is what gives rise to this cry as part of a continual filial relationship with God. What matters to Paul is therefore not just a new self-understanding as υἱοί τοῦ θεοῦ, but the ongoing experience of God's relating to believers as his sons and daughters through the Spirit. The experience of being part of God's family is part and parcel of this reality.

Therefore, one of the strengths of this model over against the line of scholarship that seems to collapse the "indicative" into the ethical "imperative" (as, e.g., Bultmann and those who have followed him)[44] is that it reckons with the reality of God's empowering presence—of a transcendent God who becomes immanent in his Spirit, but is not lost in the immanence of human relationships. Accordingly, the kind of relationality that is at the heart of Paul's Spirit-ethics in Galatians is one in which Spirit and believer do not fuse but remain independent subjects (cf. Barclay's category 3).

The new relational realities are established *by the Spirit*, not by the believer's ethical actions or feelings of being emotionally close to God. Nevertheless, while the precedence of the work of the Spirit in the ethical life of Christians needs to be maintained, the role of Paul's (implicit) ethical imperatives should not be undermined. The Spirit draws believers closer to God and to the faith community—both initially at conversion-initiation and continuously in the course of the Christian life. However, it is *the believer* who is transformed and empowered in the course of this process (cf. the continuation of human

---

42. These further implications are largely drawn from my study of the Pauline corpus in Rabens, *Holy Spirit and Ethics*; see esp. chap. 7.
43. *Pace* R. Bultmann, *Theology of the New Testament*, vol. 1 (London: SCM, 1952), 336.
44. E.g., K. Stalder, *Das Werk des Geistes in der Heiligung bei Paulus* (Zurich: Theologischer Verlag Zürich, 1962).

agency in Gal. 2:20c: "And the *life I now live* in the flesh I live by faith in the Son of God" [NRSV, emphasis added]). Accordingly, it is not the Spirit who lives ethically within the believer. Paul does not present the believer as needing, in the sense of a fusion, to "tune in" to the ethical conduct of the Spirit at the core of the person's being.[45] Rather, the Spirit enables ethical living by drawing believers into the loving and empowering presence of the divine and of the community of faith. The moral character and the ethical actions are that of the believer, but they are lived within these loving relationships and can to a large extent be regarded as an outflow of the continual experience of love (cf. Rom. 5:5; 15:30; Eph. 3:16–19). Nonetheless, it seems to be possible to resist the relational work of the Spirit. In other words, resisting the love of God and of Christ and defying the encouragement that can be experienced in the church (see 1 Cor. 12:7; Phil. 2:1–3; etc.) will mean missing out on the ethically transforming and empowering work of the Spirit.

Finally, it is now possible to reply to Fee's contention that Paul does not provide enough details for us to comprehend how one can practically do what Paul asks for, namely, to walk by the Spirit.[46] While it needs to be granted that Paul does not offer a psychological analysis of the conscious or subconscious cognitions of the individual in the process of change,[47] it nonetheless is possible to draw out a number of significant components of relational transformation and empowering. Most fundamentally, such a relational approach itself provides sufficient details about how change and empowering can happen. Psychological studies both cohere with this observation and offer further insights into the "mechanics" of how relationships transform and empower people.[48] As believers let the Spirit draw them into transforming and empowering re-

---

45. Cf. Barclay's apt summary in "'By the Grace of God I Am What I Am': Grace and Agency in Philo and Paul," in Barclay and Gathercole, eds., *Divine and Human Agency in Paul*, 156: "It appears that human agency is the *necessary expression* of the life of the Spirit, and certainly not its antithesis; the two are not mutually exclusive as if in some zero-sum calculation. And it is necessary not only because God's grace engages the will and action of the believer, but also because it is always possible to reject the grace of God." Barclay asks further how this human agency as reconstituted in Christ may be comprehended. He explains that "although in one sense we may speak properly of a 'dual agency,' in non-exclusive relation, this would be inadequately expressed as the co-operation or conjunction of two agents, or as the relationship of gift and response, if it is thereby forgotten that the 'response' continues to be activated by grace, and the believers' agency *embedded within* that of the Spirit."

46. Fee, *God's Empowering Presence*, 433.

47. Cf. A. Schweitzer, *The Mysticism of Paul the Apostle* (London: Black, 1953), 296–97.

48. See, e.g., R. A. Hinde, *Towards Understanding Relationships*, EMSP 18 (London: Academic Press, 1979), 4, 14, 273, 326; J. Bowlby, *A Secure Base: Parent-Child Attachment and Healthy Human Development* (New York: Basic Books, 1988), 119–36; H. LaFollette, *Personal Relationships: Love, Identity, and Morality* (Oxford: Blackwell, 1996), 89–90, 197–99, 207–9; P. R. Shaver and M. Mikulincer, "Attachment Theory, Individual Psychodynamics, and Relationship

lationships with God and the community of faith and then live according to the values set forth by Paul's gospel, the depth of their relationship to God and others will increase. Believers are thus further empowered as they put Paul's (implicit) ethical imperatives (which are, in fact, aimed at deepening their relationships to God and others) into practice. Human "walking by the Spirit" (Gal. 5:25b) is hence not only a continuation of "life in the Spirit" but also that which ensures a further unfolding of the divine gift of "life in the Spirit" (5:25a).

Functioning," in *The Cambridge Handbook of Personal Relationships*, ed. A. L. Vangelisti and D. Perlman (Cambridge: Cambridge University Press, 2006), 251–71.

20

Grace and the Countercultural Reckoning of Worth

Community Construction in Galatians 5–6

JOHN M. G. BARCLAY

There was a time when no one knew what to do with the paraenetic material in Galatians 5:13–6:10.[1] In recent decades a consensus has emerged that these notices, exhortations, and warnings are integral to the rest of the letter; the only question is *how*.[2] The connections have been traced in various ways, using tools from theology, sociology, rhetorical criticism, and the historical analysis of the Galatian crisis; different methods have converged in reintegrating this marginalized passage.[3] The fact that it featured so prominently in the St. Andrews conference is a sign, perhaps, that it is now fully recognized as a part of

---

1. For a survey of attempts up to the late 1980s, see J. M. G. Barclay, *Obeying the Truth: A Study of Paul's Ethics in Galatians* (Edinburgh: T&T Clark, 1988), 9–26.

2. Rightly pointed out by T. Wilson, *The Curse of the Law and the Crisis in Galatia*, WUNT 2/225 (Tübingen: Mohr Siebeck, 2007), 4; his survey of the *status quaestionis* is valuable (2–16).

3. See the survey by S. Schewe, *Die Galater zurückgewinnen: Paulinische Strategien in Galater 5 und 6* (Göttingen: Vandenhoeck & Ruprecht, 2005), 15–59. P. F. Esler's use of social-scientific tools (*Galatians* [London and New York: Routledge, 1998]) partly escapes her categorizations.

the whole. But the implication is that any reading of these verses depends on a reading of the rest of the letter—and vice versa. Returning to Galatians 5–6 after many years, I now offer a new reading of its focus and function, based on a fresh analysis of the letter as a whole. Approaching Galatians from the perspective of Paul's theology of "grace," I concentrate my focus on the most neglected passage in the letter, Galatians 6:1–6. Here I argue that this set of maxims is designed to protect the community from the destructive influence of their contest-culture, since the flourishing of a community free from the usual competition for honor is integral to the meaning of the good news. My argument amounts to the claim that social practice is, for Paul, the necessary expression of the Christ-gift, and that noncompetitive communities, ordered by a new calibration of worth, articulate and, in a certain sense, *define* the character of the Christ-event as an unconditioned gift.

The Christ-Gift and the Novel Reckoning of Worth

"I do not reject the grace of God" (2:21).[4] So Paul finishes the initial summary of his theology in this letter, and it is clear that the gift of God in Christ, or the self-gift of the Son (1:4; 2:20), forms the pivot on which the theology of this letter turns: if you are justified in the law, says Paul, you are disengaged from Christ, and you have fallen out of grace (5:4). Grace can be figured in many forms in antiquity (as today), but in the normal ancient configuration of grace, both human and divine, gifts or benefactions are properly given not to the unworthy but to the worthy. It is one thing to insist, as both Jews and non-Jews persistently did, that God is surpassingly generous and always takes the initiative in giving, since the divine Giver is never stingy or in debt. But it is quite another to hold that God gives gifts routinely, purposefully, or definitively without regard to worth. On the contrary, God's gifts/favors are given discriminately, since they represent the system of justice that upholds the cosmos: the good gift is given discerningly, to the fitting, the worthy, the people of value—indeed, they are *good* gifts only in being so given. Gifts thus typically express and reinforce a preexistent system of values: both gods and humans give gifts that uphold the standard reckonings of honor.

---

4. For a fuller attempt to articulate the points here summarized, see J. M. G. Barclay, "Paul, the Gift and the Battle over Gentile Circumcision: Revisiting the Logic of Galatians," *ABR* 58 (2010): 36–56. I offer a full-scale reading of Galatians along these lines in *Paul and the Gift* (Grand Rapids: Eerdmans, forthcoming). Parts of the following pages constitute extracts from that book. I am grateful to Eerdmans for permission to allow advance publication here.

Now Paul in Galatians announces the Christ-gift as that dangerous and unsettling phenomenon, the unconditioned gift. He has experienced this himself in his "calling in grace" (1:13–17). It was not because he was a good Jew (though he was) that he was called by divine favor; nor did his calling have regard to the fact that he had set himself violently against God's church. What he experienced in the revelation of Christ was the impact of a grace that had called him before he was born, unconditioned by his ethnicity, tradition, or advance in Judaism (1:11–17).[5] In the same way, sinful and idolatrous gentiles had been called by grace, without regard to their ethnicity, their moral behavior, or their intellectual achievements (Gal. 1:6; 4:8–9). Here and elsewhere Paul insists that the Christ-gift is given without regard to ethnic, social, or moral worth, disregarding normal construals of symbolic capital (cf. 1 Cor. 1:26–31; Phil. 3:2–11).

Galatians 3–4 relates this Christ-gift to the divine promise and the Mosaic Torah. Regarding the promise, Paul traces a continuity of divine intention all the way back to the promise to Abraham, finding echoes of the gospel in the Scriptures of Israel. But in regard to human history, the story is one of failure and disjunction, framed by human captivity to Sin, with an incompetent Torah playing only a temporary role. The purpose of that portrayal is to make clear, as was adumbrated already in 2:11–21, that the Christ-gift does not recognize or reward differentials in ethnicity or moral achievement: the true ancestry of Abraham is not by natural descent but by the incongruous operation of the promise (4:21–31). Since the Christ-gift was not given to Torah-observant Jews on the basis of their Torah-observance, it neither expresses nor supports their evaluation of the Torah as the moral order of the cosmos: it was given to Paul without regard to his Torah-excellence, and to gentiles without regard to their Torah-disobedience. In Christ, there is neither Jew nor Greek, slave nor free, male and female (3:28), not because these social/physiological conditions cease to exist, but because they cease to carry the symbolic value they enjoy outside of Christ; they are relativized not by a doctrine of equality but because those baptized into Christ are reconstituted by a gift that disregards all traditional differentials in worth.

The radical novelty of the unconditioned Christ-gift explains why Paul can declare himself dead to the ultimate authority of the Torah (2:19), why he disregards ethnic boundaries and Torah-restrictions in preaching to the gentiles (1:16), and why he insists that neither circumcision nor uncircumcision is worth anything (τι ἰσχύει), only faith working through love (5:6).[6] Crucified

---

5. See J. M. G. Barclay, "Paul's Story: Theology as Testimony," in *Narrative Dynamics in Paul*, ed. B. W. Longenecker (Louisville and London: Westminster John Knox, 2002), 133–56.

6. When ἰσχύει governs a direct accusative, as here, its sense is either legal (to validate something; cf. the intransitive in Heb. 9:17) or financial (to be worth something; e.g., Josephus,

to the world, he follows a different κανών, the allegiance to the Christ-event integral to the new creation (6:14–16). This takes place in the formation of communities that cross ethnic boundaries and discount regnant criteria of worth. It is no accident that the first and foundational discussion of "justification by faith" emerges in explication of the Antioch dispute, since Peter's behavior in withdrawing from meals with gentiles indicates a cataclysmic failure to enact the Christ-gift in social practice, "to walk in line with the truth of the good news" (2:14). By compelling gentiles to "judaize," Peter makes the Christ-gift conditioned by something outside and before itself. In this critical location of social practice, he betrays the gospel, which stands or falls with its revolutionary status as an unconditioned gift. Unless communities radically recalibrate their systems of worth, they fail to enact the good news: a failure here would nullify the gift.

Constructing Communities That Reflect the Gift

Galatians 5:13–6:10 sets out both to explain and to encourage the social expression of the good news. Freed in Christ from the prevailing norms of value, the Galatians are to submit to the authority of the Spirit, which is the presence of the Christ-gift in their hearts and in their midst. The prime expression of the "life" derived from the Spirit (5:25) is love (5:6, 13–14, 22), the social commitment to others that forms the foundation of community. The highest goal of existence "in Christ" is not self-knowledge or self-mastery for the sake of individual perfection, but a pattern of prosocial behavior represented by the fruit of the Spirit (5:22–23). Paul's cryptic reference to "the law of Christ," whether it gestures to a reconfigured Torah or to a Christ-determined regulative norm, indicates how their social life is now to be shaped by the newly paradigmatic Christ-event (2:20).[7] "Christ crucified" has shattered the believ-

---

Ant. 14.106; see BDAG, s.v. 4; LSJ, ἰσχύω III.2; MM, s.v.). J. L. Martyn is incorrect to find here connotations of power ("neither circumcision nor uncircumcision accomplishes anything"; see his *Galatians: A New Translation with Introduction and Commentary*, AB 33A [New York: Doubleday, 1997], 472–73), which are not applicable when the verb, as here in Gal. 5:6, has a direct object (τι). The connotation of "worth" is correctly identified by F. Mussner, *Der Galaterbrief*, HTKNT (Freiburg im Breisgau: Herder, 1974), 352, as already by Marius Victorinus (see S. A. Cooper, *Marius Victorinus' Commentary on Galatians: Introduction, Translation, and Notes* [Oxford: Oxford University Press, 2005], 330).

7. For full discussion, in debate with the major options, see Barclay, *Obeying the Truth*, 126–35. See further R. B. Hays, "Christology and Ethics in Galatians: The Law of Christ," *CBQ* 49 (1997): 268–90, taking the phrase to refer to the life pattern of Jesus, as paradigm for the community (cf. 2:20); cf. M. Winger, who insists that no legal instruction is here in view, only "the way Christ exercises his lordship over those called by him" ("The Law of Christ," *NTS* 46

ers' previous structures of allegiance; by recalibrating their values, it instills the mutuality of love as the essence of their new community.

Paul's appeal for mutual love is no bland generality: it specifically targets habits of intracommunal rivalry that were characteristic of ancient Mediterranean society. After setting a norm of mutual slavery in love (5:13), Paul issues a dire warning against its dysfunctional alternative: "If you bite and devour one another, watch out lest you be consumed by one another" (5:15). It is assumed that individuals will interact in one or another form of reciprocity: the only question is whether that interaction will be in mutual support or mutual destruction. In the following "works of the flesh" (5:19–21), the standard Jewish characterizations of the gentile world (sexual immorality, impurity, idolatry, magical practice, as in 5:19–20) are filled out with an extensive catalog of socially destructive behavior: "hostile acts, strife, jealousy, outbursts of anger, selfish actions, dissensions, factions, acts of envy, inebriated loutishness, and drinking parties" (5:20–21).[8] Although some such items appear often in ancient lists of "vices," including Paul's elsewhere (e.g., Rom. 1:29–31; 2 Cor. 12:20–21), commentators rightly note their heavy concentration here, as if the damage of social life was Paul's particular concern.[9] Matching this list, moreover, is an exhortation not to be vain, provoke one another, or envy one another (μὴ γινώμεθα κενόδοξοι, ἀλλήλους προκαλούμενοι, ἀλλήλοις φθονοῦντες [5:26]).

Recent commentators agree that the repetition of these warnings suggests actual or threatened disunity in Paul's churches, though it is unnecessary to account for their presence in this letter by speculative reconstruction of some specific local scenario.[10] Paul lived in a face-to-face society where self-advertisement, rivalry, and public competition were a perpetual cause of tension in everyday life. Part of the purpose of Galatians 5:13–6:10 is to present a vision of communal life where the destructive features of this agonistic culture can be both recognized and effectively repulsed. If so much hinges on the establishment of mutually constructive

---

[2000]: 537–46, esp. 544). For recent discussion, see Wilson, *Curse of the Law*, 100–104. The rarity of the phrase makes interpretation uncertain.

8. I include the last two items (μέθαι and κῶμοι) because it was often noted in Roman society that excessive drink was the cause of lasting damage to social relations. An earlier item, φαρμακεία ("magical practice") was also a cause of conflict, since "magic" was widely suspected of intent to cause harm.

9. See Barclay, *Obeying the Truth*, 153–54, with reference to the commentaries; cf. F. J. Matera, *Galatians*, SP 9 (Collegeville, MN: Liturgical Press, 1992), 210.

10. See Barclay, *Obeying the Truth*, 152–54, 156, 166–69; cf. R. Morales, *The Spirit and the Restoration of Israel: New Exodus and New Creation Motifs in Galatians*, WUNT 2/282 (Tübingen: Mohr Siebeck, 2010), 152–53; M. C. de Boer, *Galatians: A Commentary*, NTL (Louisville: Westminster John Knox, 2011), 360, 368. It is often suggested that these social malfunctions relate to the disturbance caused by the alternative missionaries (Gal. 5:12); 4:16–18 might hint at some such connection, but Paul does not develop the link.

communities, strong measures must be taken to counter the operations of "the flesh" that threaten to undermine this critical embodiment of the good news.

As recent research has emphasized, almost all social relations in Paul's Roman context were both ordered and threatened by the competition for honor.[11] In the absence of "objective" measures of quality, a person's worth was heavily dependent on his or her public reputation, a "dignity" energetically claimed and fiercely defended. The pursuit or defense of honor was, ancient commentators claimed, the chief motivating force for action: "By nature we yearn and hunger for honor, and once we have glimpsed, as it were, some part of its radiance, there is nothing we are not prepared to bear and suffer in order to secure it" (Cicero, *Tusc.* 2.24.58). The multiple criteria for honor—wealth, ancestry, age, education, legal status, physique, character, and virtuous action—made the quest for honor ubiquitous across the social scale; yet the very diversity of these marks of value ensured that strength in one dimension could be challenged by criticism of weakness in another.[12] And challenge was, indeed, the very essence of this culture. Honor was derived from comparison, from placing oneself (or being placed by others) higher on some hierarchical scale, in which one person's superiority means that another is comparatively demeaned. In this environment, every claim to honor was a real or potential provocation, and every challenge required an active riposte.[13] Honor was a precious but unstable commodity, requiring active promotion and persistent proof.[14] Precisely because glory needed to "shine," it was the object of perpetual surveillance. It was under the spotlight of communal attention that individuals would either display or damage their worth.[15]

---

11. The point was rightly stressed by P. F. Esler, "Group Boundaries and Intergroup Conflict in Galatians: A New Reading of Gal. 5:13–6:10," in *Ethnicity and the Bible*, ed. M. G. Brett (Leiden: Brill, 1996), 215–40; this followed the work of Malina and others (e.g., B. Malina, *The New Testament World: Insights from Cultural Anthropology*, rev. ed. [Louisville: Westminster John Knox, 1993]), who drew on the anthropology of Mediterranean culture (e.g., J. G. Peristiany, ed., *Honour and Shame: The Values of Mediterranean Society* [London: Weidenfeld & Nicolson, 1966]). Major studies of the honor dynamics specific to the Roman world of Paul's day include J. E. Lendon, *Empire of Honour: The Art of Government in the Roman World* (Oxford: Oxford University Press, 1997); and C. A. Barton, *Roman Honor: The Fire in the Bones* (Berkeley: University of California Press, 2001).

12. Although competition among the upper strata of society is most visible in our sources, there is good evidence that it was characteristic of all social levels in the Greco-Roman world; see Barton, *Roman Honor*, 11–13, 75.

13. Cf. Cicero, *Pro Sulla* 46: "You will compel me to give thought to my own dignity: no one ever brought the tiniest suspicion on me whom I did not overturn and wreck."

14. Cf. Barton, *Roman Honor*, 62: "The honor, the fullness of one's being in ancient Rome, was never safely or permanently earned."

15. On the importance of visibility, see Dio Chrysostom 31.22: "You could not get a single man out of a multitude to do what he deems a noble deed for himself alone, if no one else

Within strongly bonded communities, such honor contests could encourage great feats of heroism and even self-sacrifice.¹⁶ But with the slightest breakdown in mutual respect, the contest for honor becomes a socially destructive force, and Greek and Roman authors often note the danger that ambition will turn to arrogance, comparison to insult, and rivalry to aggression.¹⁷ The desire for honor provokes the strongest emotions—pride, envy, resentment—and can spawn the most destructive acts of insult and retaliation. As Carlin Barton comments, there is a tendency to "insistent inflation": "Every tiff is a tumult, every wrangle a war."¹⁸ In the modern world, the brazenness with which honor was advertised then and the ferocity with which it was attacked are liable to surprise only those whose honor is protected from competition. Paul's warning against vendettas (5:15) is neither empty nor unusual: the lust for honor could easily destroy a community.

Paul's strategy to counter these destructive forces of "the flesh" is double-pronged. On the one hand, the people reconstituted by the Christ-gift have discounted the value placed on forms of honor over which their contemporaries compete. Since ethnicity, status, or gender are no longer criteria of superior worth (Gal. 3:28), and since God pays no regard to the "face" (2:6) but distributes his grace without regard to worth, the normal grounds for competition have lost their significance. The assembly of believers forms a new community of opinion, constituted by the gift to the unworthy. Within this community there arises, of course, an alternative system of worth, a new form of "symbolic capital": here some are to be honored as teachers of the word (6:6) and others given responsibility as "spiritual people" (οἱ πνευματικοί, 6:1), insofar as they are attuned to the Spirit. But—and this is the second characteristic of Paul's social strategy—the hallmark of this alternative system of value is that it is directed specifically against rivalry: the greatest honor is for those who work *against* the competitive spirit of honor itself. Nearly all the characteristics cataloged as "the fruit of the Spirit" (5:22–23) are directed toward

---

shall know of it." Cf. Barton on the necessary glitter and audibility of honor (*Roman Honor*, 58–64). On the public acknowledgment of honor, see Lendon, *Empire of Honour*, 54: "Honour is a public thing; it is not a consequence of opinion merely, but of opinion publicly expressed."

16. For an analysis of such phenomena in the Roman Republic, in which the quest for honor, being more important than life itself, encouraged self-sacrifice for the public good, see Barton, *Roman Honor*, 29–88.

17. Sallust notes that whole cities are internally destroyed "when men will defeat other men by any means whatsoever, and when the defeated are bitterly intent on vengeance" (*Bell. Jug.* 42.4). Cf. Barton's analysis of "the bad contest" turned brutal, when "the rules of the game were arbitrary or unknown, where there were no limits to the scope or intensity of the contest, or where the contestants were too unequally matched" (*Roman Honor*, 89–90).

18. Barton, *Roman Honor*, 66.

the construction of community, from love downward. "Spirit-people" are so designated because they work with sensitivity to repair the community (6:1–2). What counts among believers, according to Paul, is precisely the antithesis to arrogance and competition.

The rubric that governs the ethos of this community is a formula of reciprocity as creative as it is paradoxical. The Galatian freedom will not become an opportunity for "the flesh" inasmuch as they are *"slaves to one another through love"* (διὰ τῆς ἀγάπης δουλεύετε ἀλλήλοις [5:13]). This is a remarkable expression since it adjusts an inherently hierarchical relationship (slavery) not by canceling it, in the name of "equality," but by making it reciprocal, a hierarchy that turns both ways. The simple but powerful word ἀλλήλοις turns a one-way relationship of power and superiority into a mutual relationship of reciprocal deference, where *each* seeks to promote the interests of the other. The same structure of relations is outlined in the matching phrase in 6:2: "Bear one another's burdens [Ἀλλήλων τὰ βάρη βαστάζετε], and you will fulfill the law of Christ." Burden-bearing, the work of slaves, is made a task for all, in relation to all. Submission to the interests of others is saved from becoming a charter for the crushing of the weak by being turned also into reverse, such that service and honor are continually exchanged. This reciprocity of relations, which does not eradicate but continually inverts a hierarchical order, is indeed a hallmark of Pauline social ethics, not only with respect to the church as a "body" (Rom. 12:3–8; 1 Cor. 12:12–31) but also in marriage (1 Cor. 7:3–4) and in the continual competition to be the first not to receive honor but to give it to others (Rom. 12:10).[19] This policy turns competition on its head. What matters is not to gain superiority but to cede it, and in ceding it to be honored in return. To this extent, Brigitte Kahl is right to point to Galatians 5–6 as evidence that Paul strongly resists the combative ethos ever present in Romanized culture—though Paul's policy is less the eradication of hierarchy than its continual inversion.[20]

Paul's redefinition of honor thus gives prestige to such traits that promote social cohesion and mutual construction. The finely crafted collection of maxims in Galatians 6:1–6 offers a good example of this social policy in practice.[21] After warning against the insidious tendency to provocation and envy (5:26),

---

19. On this remarkable policy of "reciprocal asymmetry," "making universalising egalitarianism pass through the reversibility of an inegalitarian rule," see A. Badiou, *Saint Paul: The Foundation of Universalism*, trans. R. Brassier (Stanford, CA: Stanford University Press, 2003), 98–106, esp. 104.

20. B. Kahl, *Galatians Reimagined: Reading with the Eyes of the Vanquished* (Minneapolis: Fortress, 2010), 261–71, redrafting the "combat squares" she considers typical of Roman imperialism.

21. For an earlier analysis of these maxims, see Barclay, *Obeying the Truth*, 155–70. Like many previous commentators, H. D. Betz, *Galatians: A Commentary on Paul's Letter to the*

Paul turns to the sort of occasion when a community is likely to splinter in the competitive quest for honor: when someone has transgressed a communal norm and is vulnerable to public disgrace, others naturally seize the opportunity for competitive advantage. Paul clearly recognizes this danger and counters it by appeal to the ethos of the Spirit (6:1). When someone has been overtaken (or found out) in such trespass, it is necessary for the community to act for the sake of its integrity. But the purpose is less judgment than restoration (καταρτίζετε τὸν τοιοῦτον), which is to be administered by those who are "spiritual" in a "spirit of gentleness" (ἐν πνεύματι πραΰτητος [6:1]), that is, without the opprobrium that brings irremediable dishonor for the offender. Meanwhile, the restorers must themselves guard against the temptation of pride, the tendency to honor themselves in comparison with others: "Look to yourself," says Paul (addressing each individual concerned), "lest you too be tempted" (6:1). "Gentleness" is thus allied to humility, the modesty that recognizes its own vulnerability and restrains the urge to advance a claim to superiority.

In 6:3–5 Paul presses further this demand for modesty, as a crucial preservative of community and a necessary antidote to the "hunger for honor."[22] His first move is to counter the tendency to an inflated self-opinion that he has already highlighted in the exhortation not to be κενόδοξοι (5:26): "If anyone thinks he is something, when he is nothing, he deceives himself" (6:3). This is not an assertion of universal worthlessness: if believers can say that "the Son of God loved me and gave himself for me" (2:20), who could have greater worth? Rather, Paul warns against the arrogance that delights in its own self-appraisal, or in a reputation granted by others that really counts for nothing; the echoes of Paul's comments on the Jerusalem pillars, ironically dubbed οἱ δοκοῦντες (2:6, 9), are loud. The social value of the moderate measure of oneself—the virtue of "shame" (*pudor*)—was well recognized in antiquity, though it was constantly threatened by the equal requirement to advertise one's virtues in an inflated form.[23] That tendency to display is directly countered in 6:4: "Let each person test his own work and then keep his boast to himself alone, and not direct it toward others" (καὶ τότε εἰς ἑαυτὸν μόνον τὸ καύχημα ἕξει καὶ οὐκ εἰς τὸν ἕτερον [6:4]).[24] The importance of self-scrutiny, the splitting of oneself

---

Churches in Galatia, Hermeneia (Philadelphia: Fortress, 1979), 291, considered these verses merely a loose collection of *sententiae*.

22. For a fine analysis of the coherence of these verses, showing how Paul's attention to the individual is for the sake of the harmony of the community, see D. W. Kuck, "'Each Will Bear His Own Burden': Paul's Creative Use of an Apocalyptic Motif," *NTS* 40 (1994): 289–97.

23. See Barton, *Roman Honor*, 210–15.

24. I continue to think that this is the best translation (see Barclay, *Obeying the Truth*, 160; supported by Martyn, *Galatians*, 550), despite some arguments still advanced to the contrary (de Boer, *Galatians*, 382–83, translating, "then he will have a boast in himself alone and not in

into both subject and object of scrutiny, is that this does *not* participate in the game of public self-advertisement, with its tendency to exaggeration and deceit. It is notable that Paul does not deny all grounds for "boasting" and thus all forms of honor. Believers take pride ("boast") in the cross, as the disavowal of every form of capital operative in "the world" (6:14–15), but they have grounds for honor in their "work," within the criteria of value established by the Christ-event: on the right basis and within the right limits, it is fine for honor to be offered and received (4:18).[25] But its public display is dangerous, especially when it becomes promotion by oneself: by telling the justly "proud" person to keep his or her boast to oneself, Paul effectively neuters a powerful impulse of his contest-culture.

The reason why the "boast" does *not* need to be broadcast is because its essential "audience" is not human but divine (cf. Rom. 2:29; 1 Cor. 4:1–5): the reminder that "each person will bear his own load" (6:5) is a gesture to the eschatological judgment, where the determinative arbiter of value will be God.[26] The fact that "each will bear his own load" does not prioritize the individual over the community. Paul has urged everyone to bear one another's burdens (6:2), and the purpose of this statement in 6:5 is to protect the community from the competitive boasting that threatens to unravel its bonds. That each is finally accountable before God removes from the community the necessity, or temptation, to adjudicate the value of one another; precisely because it is under responsibility to God, the community can be rid of envious comparisons and liberated for mutual construction in love.

That mutuality "in all good things" is given one further illustration, in the instruction to support those who "teach the word." Again, there is no need to invoke particular Galatian circumstances:[27] at this early stage of formation,

---

the other"; cf. J. Lambrecht, "Paul's Coherent Admonition in Galatians 6,1–6: Mutual Help and Individual Attentiveness," *Bib* 78 (1997): 33–56, esp. at 48–49; he discounts the excellent parallels in Rom. 4:2 and 2 Cor. 8:24.

25. See H. Hübner, *Law in Paul's Thought*, trans. J. Greig (Edinburgh: T&T Clark, 1994), 101–8: "Paul does recognise a genuine claim on the part of the Christian to 'glory' on the basis of his life's work" (108). The contrary argument of G. Klein ("Werkruhm und Christusruhm im Galaterbrief und die Frage nach einer Entwicklung des Paulus," in *Studien zum Text und zur Ethik des Neuen Testaments*, ed. W. Schrage, BZNW 47 [Berlin: de Gruyter, 1986], 196–211) is well critiqued by Lambrecht, "Paul's Coherent Admonition."

26. In context (cf. 5:10, 21; 6:7–8), the future tense is best taken in an eschatological sense (de Boer, *Galatians*, 383–84; *pace* Lambrecht, "Paul's Coherent Admonition," 50); the sense runs closely parallel to *4 Ezra* 7.105. Convincing arguments for this eschatological reading, with additional Pauline parallels, are supplied by Kuck, "Each Will Bear." As he notes, "The symbolic language of future judgement helps to resolve the tension between the desire for individual status and the need to sublimate that desire for the sake of the unity of the church" (296).

27. *Pace* Martyn, *Galatians*, 551–52, who posits a threat to the teachers whom Paul had installed in Galatian churches.

one of the few differentia between members of the community is that of those capable of offering instruction and those who receive it (cf. 1 Thess. 5:12–14). Paul frames this mutual relationship as a form of "sharing" (κοινωνείτω, 6:6; cf. 2:9–10), evoking not just a sharing of one another's goods but also a common sharing of divine benefits. The relationship of exchange between members does not take the form of self-authored gift and return, but arises from common dependence on the good news: within that context, the good things exchanged are "shared" benefits deriving from God (cf. 2 Cor. 8–9).[28] But it is crucially important for Paul that there *is* a pattern of exchange, that differing tasks are understood as mutuality in gift and receipt. This whole paragraph stands under the rubric of "bearing one another's burdens" (6:2), an ethos of mutually supportive relations that represents "the law of Christ." It is as they participate in long-lasting relationships of mutual enhancement that the community is created and enhanced, and it is the capacity of that community to flout the normal tendencies to aggressive competition that demonstrates what it means to live in accordance with the "new creation" (6:15–16).

Social Practice as the Definition and Realization of the Gift

The gift of God in Christ is articulated as an unconditioned gift in the creation of a community that neither mirrors nor endorses the regnant systems of value. Indeed, the incongruous gift is defined *as incongruous* in a community that marches to a distinct tune—and it is only in practice that that distinction can be recognized and achieved. By its strategic indifference to preconstituted evaluations of worth—ethnic, social, sexual, or other—the community declares and enacts its freedom. By its "crucifixion of the flesh" (5:24)—its break with the dispositions that stand contrary to the values of the Spirit—it demonstrates an alternative allegiance derived from an alternative source of "life." In resisting the tendencies to intracommunal rivalry, it affirms its special identity as a community beholden to "the law of Christ" (6:2).

Both sociology and theology thus point to the *necessity* of social practice as the realization of the Christ-gift. As Bourdieu would put it, to express and embody an alternative form of "capital"—in relative autonomy from other forms of capital, symbolic, social, or cultural—there has to be not an abstract idea but a community, one that accords and recognizes an alternative form of

---

28. On κοινωνέω in 6:6, see J. Hainz, *Koinonia: "Kirche" als Gemeinschaft bei Paulus* (Regensburg: Pustet, 1982), 62–89.

"wealth."[29] In theological terms, the new creation presses toward the formation and flourishing of a community in which the truth of God's self-giving in Christ is expressed in love, strongly resistant to the normal contest for honor. The relationship between "theology" and "social practice" is mutually constitutive: it is the Christ-event that gives meaning and shape to communal practice, while it is in social practice that the nature of the Christ-event is realized, or is not realized. If Paul's Galatian communities adopt Jewish circumcision as a condition of entry, or revert to the aggressive competition that bespeaks a "fleshly" code of honor, they would deny the truth of the unconditioned gift in Christ—indeed annul it altogether as a reality in Galatia. The truth of Paul's gospel must be both recognized and enacted—in fact, recognized in its enactment. It is only as communities are remolded in exclusive allegiance to "the law of Christ" that they may be said to affirm the baptismal confession "Jesus is Lord" (Rom. 10:9). Social practice is not, for Paul, an addition to belief, a sequel to a status realizable in other terms: it is the expression of belief in Christ, the enactment of a "life" that otherwise can make no claim to be "alive."

This dialectical relationship between the Christ-gift and social practice undermines the categorical distinction between "theology" and "ethics," without in the least reducing theology to ethics. Paul's good news is staked on the announcement of an event, the death and resurrection of Jesus as the gift of God. But the meaning of that event, and its quality as unconditioned gift, is discovered only in its social embodiment, in social experience and practice. If justification by faith means God's recognition of worth solely on the basis of the Christ-event, the continuation of ethnic distinctions at meals in Antioch is not just a communal malfunction, but indeed an outright denial of justification by faith. In this sense, justification *sola fide* cannot be "before and without works" (Luther), since it is in the practice of communities that, in the name of Christ, disregard other criteria of worth that the *sola fide* comes to necessary expression. Of course, such social practice does not create or elicit the gift, either past or present; it is so completely integral to the gift that without it the Christ-gift simply ceases to have existential reality.

---

29. P. Bourdieu, *Outline of a Theory of Practice*, trans. R. Nice (Cambridge: Cambridge University Press, 1977).

21

Paul's Exhortations in Galatians 5:16–25

From the Apostle's Techniques to His Theology

JEAN-NOËL ALETTI

In the Letter to the Galatians, difficult verses abound and thus provide numerous possibilities for study. I have chosen to present Galatians 5:16–25 because this passage provides the opportunity to address three controversial points: (1) Where does the exhortative section begin, in Galatians 5:1 or in 5:13? (2) What is the meaning of Galatians 5:17? (3) How is Paul's emphasis on the flesh/Spirit enmity in 5:16–25 to be explained? Since the meaning of the flesh/Spirit opposition depends mostly on the interpretation of Galatians 5:17, I will focus on this verse, the difficulties of which are well known, so much so that it has even been said that this verse is "one of the most difficult in the whole letter."[1] If, however, I am here taking up again the study of this verse in its context, it is less to present new interpretations than to state some of the important consequences that Paul's thought on justification has had on the exhortative part of the Letters to the Galatians and to the Romans.

---

1. J. M. G. Barclay, *Obeying the Truth. A Study of Paul's Ethics in Galatians*, SNTW (Edinburgh: T&T Clark, 1988), 112.

The Limits of the Exhortative Part of Galatians

For some exegetes, the exhortative section of Galatians begins in 5:1, but for others in 5:13. To determine with certainty its beginning, it is important to take into account the apostle's way of proceeding in this letter, a way that is customary for him. Indeed, paradoxically, in many of his argumentations Paul does not treat questions at the level at which they are asked. And this is the case in Galatians, in which the question confronting the communities of the region was clearly that of the circumcision of those believers coming from paganism. Paul does not give an immediate response by declaring loud and clear his rejection of circumcision; first he makes a long detour in order to show that his answer comes from the gospel.

This way of proceeding is found in the Pauline Letters more often than is thought. In 1 Corinthians 1, Paul says that he has heard about the disputes concerning the apostles, disputes ongoing between members of the community. But instead of responding immediately, he begins by recalling the cross's overthrow of the world's values in order to point out to the Christians of Corinth that they have remained attached to the values of the world and have not yet entered into those of the gospel, which are totally opposed to them. Only in 3:5–17 does he give his response—that the apostles are only servants of the gospel and that what is important is the status of the community. In short, *he makes a detour*, which is foundational, because he first returns to the decisive event of the cross and emphasizes above all that ecclesiological questions find their answer primarily in Christology. Elsewhere I have shown that this same way of proceeding is used in 1 Corinthians 8–10; 12–14; and 15.[2] This pattern confirms Paul's tendency to postpone the immediate responses; it also shows that in his responses the apostle is less concerned with his correspondents' reasons or motivations than with the consequences of their position. That is why it is often difficult to exactly reconstruct the situations or the difficulties confronting the Christians whom Paul is addressing.

From the sections of 1 Corinthians that have just been mentioned, one can draw an important methodological conclusion. In these arguments, the apostle responds to the communities' problems and questions only after making a more or less long and radical detour. This means that it is necessary to be careful not to believe too quickly that the communities' problems determine

---

2. J. N. Aletti, "La rhétorique paulinienne," in *Paul, une théologie en construction*, ed. A. Dettwiler, J. D. Kaestli, and D. Marguerat (Geneva: Labor & Fides, 2004), 47–66; repeated in idem, *New Approaches for Interpreting the Letters of Saint Paul: Collected Essays; Rhetoric, Soteriology, Christology and Ecclesiology* (Rome: Gregorian & Biblical Press, 2012), 11–35.

the rhetorical genre of the Pauline Letters,[3] because it is not the communities' problems that provide the criteria that determine the letters' rhetorical genre *but the way in which Paul treats them*. Thus, 1 Corinthians 14 could cause one to think that the genre of the entire section of 1 Corinthians 12–14 is deliberative—because what the apostle really wants is to lead his correspondents to *concrete decisions*. But by enlarging his response, which includes the eulogy of *agapē* (chap. 13), Paul is showing us that a concrete question can also be treated epideictically. He judges it to be less important to tell his correspondents what concrete decisions they must make than to give them the means to rectify their values and the false or superficial idea that they still have of the gospel.

Thus the apostle's tendency is to take a step back and not immediately respond to concrete questions but rather to carry the debate to a greater radicalness. This means that *Paul's discourse is much less contingent than has been said*, because, more than creating a casuistic work, he enlarges the questions by stating the fundamental and lasting relationships without which the questions (and the answers) would lose their pertinence.[4]

Let us return to Galatians, in which the way of proceeding is the same. If it is true that circumcision is the question confronted by the Christians of this region, the majority coming from pagan origins, Paul does not immediately enjoin them not to be circumcised. In Galatians 1–2, the question of circumcision appears only progressively.[5] Not until 5:2 does Paul declare to them, "If you receive circumcision, Christ will be of no advantage [*ōphelēsei*] to you."[6] The apostle has used the preceding chapters to remind them of the main point of the gospel by showing them that circumcision—in other words, their becoming subjects of the Mosaic law—has no part in the gospel, because circumcision can make them neither sons nor heirs. Since Galatians thus consists of a fundamental restating of the gospel and its consequences, one can see that Paul's goal is less to communicate moral instructions than the extraordinary power of the gospel.

In short, after the long, *distancing perspective*, which goes from Galatians

---

3. The three ancient rhetorical genres are the judiciary, the deliberative, and the epideictic.

4. Incidentally, this propensity to go to the root of the questions in order to deepen and universalize them resembles Hellenism's way of proceeding, as has been magnificently shown by J. de Romilly, *Pourquoi la Grèce?* (Paris: Editions de Fallois, 1992). Clearly, this observation neither denies nor forgets Paul's Jewish and scriptural background, but only highlights the influence that Greek culture and education had in the world at that time. On this subject, see the interesting work of M. Rastoin, *Tarse et Jérusalem: La double culture de l'apôtre Paul en Galates 3,6–4,7*, AnBib 152 (Rome: Pontificio Istituto Biblico, 2003).

5. The first mention of circumcision is found in Gal. 2:3.

6. The verb *opheilō* (as in 5:2) designates the goal of the deliberative genre, namely, the useful. This is what has caused some to interpret Galatians as belonging to this genre.

1:11 to 5:1 and treats the question at a deeper and more radical level, Paul returns to the concrete situation and expresses his disapproval of whoever is thinking about being circumcised or already has been. As for the unit 5:2–12, in which Paul gives an explicit opinion on circumcision, it proceeds in two subunits, verses 2–6 and 7–12. In the first, Paul takes up the situation in Galatia and the resolutions anticipated by the area's believers, along with their consequences (vv. 2–4); he then contrasts these plans with the situation in Christ (vv. 5–6). In the second subunit, he portrays the opponents and stigmatizes their influence on the Galatians: although he sees that all will end positively for them (those who will change their opinion), he nevertheless announces a rejection of the agitators. Paul's way of proceeding can thus be diagrammed:

the concrete problem	1:6–10			5:2–12
the distancing perspective		↘	1:11 to 5:1	↗

I have laid out Paul's way of proceeding in Galatians to show that the concrete problem was that of the circumcision of the gentile Christians and not questions concerning dietary and cultic regulations. Furthermore, it is the distancing perspective that has allowed him to radicalize the problem and to show that if the gentile Christians yield to the judaizers, the effects would be devastating.

The Composition of the Exhortations of Galatians 5:13–25

Thus the exhortative part of the letter goes from Galatians 5:13 to 6:10 and includes three units that are easily identifiable, thanks to their thematic changes and composition: 5:13–15;[7] 5:16–25; and 5:26–6:10. Some commentators connect 5:26 with 5:16–25, but others with 6:1–10. Because 6:1 is not syntactically linked to what precedes it and begins with an apostrophe ("Brothers"), the first reading seems to be preferred, but in Paul this apostrophe does not necessarily indicate the beginning of another rhetorical unit.[8] Moreover, 5:26 is introducing the themes that are developed in 6:1–10.

As for Galatians 5:16–25, its unity is easily noted, thanks to the opposition of the flesh/Spirit. If all commentators agree to recognize that these two terms alternate throughout this section, they are not in agreement on the passage's

---

7. A concentrically composed unit: A exhortation (5:13), B motivations (5:14), and A' resumption of the exhortation (5:15).

8. See, e.g., Rom. 1:13; 10:1; 1 Cor. 7:24; 14:20; Phil. 3:13; 1 Thess. 5:25.

composition. According to James D. G. Dunn, the section falls fairly naturally into an *A B C C′ B′ A′* pattern that runs from verse 16 to verse 24:[9]

A 16–17		{admonition} against flesh and its desires
B 18		led by Spirit, not under law
C 19–21		works of flesh
C′ 22–23a		fruit of Spirit …
B′ 23b		… law not against
A′ 24		{admonition} against flesh and its desires

It is possible to refine the composition in mainly semantic categories, as noted by Dunn, by first observing that, like the preceding verses (vv. 13–15) and like numerous exhortative units in the Pauline Letters, the overall composition is concentric:

a^1 = 5:16   *exhortation announcing the theme*
b = 5:17–24   *motivations or reasons*
a^2 = 5:25   *repetition of the exhortation*

The positive exhortation in verse 16a is immediately followed by its negative consequence (v. 16b), thereby portraying the two opposing powers, the Spirit (*c*) and the flesh (*d*), to which this unit is devoted:[10]

exhortation (pos.)	c	¹⁶ᵃ(But I say) walk by the Spirit
(neg.)	d	¹⁶ᵇand you will not gratify the desires of the flesh.

The exhortation's motivation (vv. 17–24) unfolds by continuing the flesh/Spirit contrast:[11]

motivations	d	¹⁷For the flesh desires against the Spirit, but the Spirit desires against the flesh, for those (powers) fight each other to prevent you from doing those (things) you would.
development of the motivations	c	¹⁸But if you are led by the Spirit, you are not under the law.

---

9. See James D. G. Dunn, *The Epistle to the Galatians*, BNTC (Peabody, MA: Hendrickson, 1993), 295.

10. The letters c/C designate the statements relating to flesh, and the letters d/D those relating to the Spirit. The lowercase letters designate short units, and the uppercase letters mark longer units.

11. Gal. 5:18–24 RSV, but my trans. in v. 17. See footnote 35 below.

the works of the flesh	D	¹⁹Now the works of the flesh are plain: fornication, impurity, licentiousness, ²⁰idolatry, sorcery, enmity, strife, jealousy, anger, selfishness, dissension, party spirit, ²¹envy, drunkenness, carousing, and the like. I warn you, as I warned you before, that those who do such things shall not inherit the kingdom of God.
the fruit of the Spirit	C	²²But the fruit of the Spirit is love, joy, peace, patience, kindness, goodness, faithfulness, ²³gentleness, self-control; against such there is no law.
conclusion		²⁴And those who belong to Christ Jesus have crucified the flesh with its passions and desires.

The motivation is thus deployed in two stages. In the first (vv. 17–18), Paul shows why it is important to allow oneself to be guided and led by the Spirit and not by the flesh: these two powers are opposed to each other, and one cannot associate them. In the second (vv. 19–23), the effects of each of these two powers are described, effects that clearly manifest the opposition stated in the first stage.

Galatians 5:17: Difficulties and Proposals

The overall arrangement does not pose a major problem, inasmuch as the flesh/Spirit contrast is obvious, as seen by Dunn:

(d)	v. 17	the flesh
(c)	v. 18	the Spirit
(D)	vv. 19–21	the flesh and its works
(C)	vv. 22–23	the Spirit and its fruits

The alternation, which is barely described, invites considering verse 17 as principally speaking of the flesh and its negative designs. Nevertheless, its syntactical construction can be interpreted in various ways and actually has been. The relationship of the four propositions in verse 17—

(a) ἡ γὰρ σὰρξ ἐπιθυμεῖ κατὰ[12] τοῦ πνεύματος

(b) τὸ δὲ πνεῦμα κατὰ τῆς σαρκός,

(c) ταῦτα γὰρ ἀλλήλοις ἀντίκειται,

(d) ἵνα μὴ ἃ ἐὰν θέλητε ταῦτα ποιῆτε

12. J. Louis Martyn, *Galatians: A New Translation with Introduction and Commentary*, AB 33A (New York: Doubleday, 1998), 493, rightly notes that only here (5:17) do we encounter the verb *epithymeō* with *kata* and the genitive; he asks if there could not be an influence of Aramaic syntax.

—raises important soteriological and anthropological questions. Three readings are possible: in the first two, (d) can be connected with (c), but in the third, (d) can also be related to (a), in which case (b) and (c) form an incidental clause. But even if (d) does depend on (c), two possible readings exist. In the first, the flesh/Spirit antagonism would result in the paralysis of the believer: "for[13] these [things][14] are opposed to one another *so that* [ἵνα][15] you cannot do the things that you would."[16] The verse has often been understood as describing a situation analogous to that in Romans 7:15 and 20.[17] In the second reading, far from causing the paralysis of the believer, the flesh/Spirit antagonism prompts the believer to discernment in order not to do everything that comes to mind, in other words, what is injurious and evil: "These things are opposed to one another in order to prevent you from doing whatever you would." The third reading, which has recently been proposed, makes (b) and (c) incidental clauses and connects (d) to (a): "For the flesh desires against the Spirit—and the Spirit desires against the flesh; for those fight each other[18]—to prevent you from doing those things

---

13. The Greek conjunction *gar* in 5:17a and 17c is each time explicative and not causal; cf. Alfio Marcello Buscemi, *Lettera ai Galati: Commentario esegetico*, Studium Biblicum Francescanum, Analecta 63 (Jerusalem: Franciscan Printing Press, 2004), 551.

14. The neuter demonstrative pronoun *tauta* in 5:17c clearly designates the flesh and the Spirit. As a consequence of their having different genders in Greek ("flesh" is feminine; "Spirit" is neuter), the pronoun must be neuter. This neuter pronoun does not allow us to conclude that Paul is making the flesh and the Spirit impersonal entities. With good reason, Buscemi (ibid., 552) opposes H. D. Betz, for whom "the neuter *tauta* (these things) identifies flesh and Spirit as impersonal forces acting within man and waging war against each other" (*Galatians: A Commentary on Paul's Letter to the Churches in Galatia*, Hermeneia [Philadelphia, Fortress 1979], 279). Undoubtedly, it would be better to translate it with "powers/ forces" rather than "things."

15. In that case, the ἵνα in 5:17 would be consecutive.

16. This last part of 5:17, "so that . . . ," is from KJV. According to Dunn (*Galatians*, 297), for the verse to make sense, it is necessary for the *hina* to be final (telic) and not consecutive. But "this fact forbids taking *ha ean thelēte* as referring to the things which one naturally, by the flesh, desires, and understanding the clause as an expression of the beneficent result of walking by the Spirit." He adds:

> The final clause is to be understood not as expressing the purpose of God . . . (for neither is the subject of the sentence a word referring to God, nor is the thought thus yielded a Pauline thought), nor of the flesh alone, nor of the Spirit alone, but as the purpose of both flesh and Spirit, in the sense that the flesh opposes the Spirit that men may not do what they will in accordance with the mind of the Spirit, and the Spirit opposes the flesh that they may not do what they will after the flesh. Does the man choose evil, the Spirit opposes him; does he choose good, the flesh hinders him.

17. For here and there one encounters a contrast between *wanting* and *doing* (in Greek, θέλητε/ποιῆτε), since Paul says that one cannot *do* what one *wants*—a reading generally qualified as Lutheran.

18. The verb ἀντίκειται is generally translated "are opposed." To avoid interpreting the opposition passively, I have preferred to use an active verb.

you would."[19] In this case, the verse is describing the negative designs of the flesh against the Spirit in order to prevent believers from doing the good they would like to do, and by using these incidental clauses, Paul adds that the Spirit does not remain passive: the Spirit's role is precisely to thwart the designs of the flesh.

An example of the first reading is found in Dunn's commentary,[20] for whom the verse is describing the situation of the Christian, in whom the Spirit's action exacerbates the human experience in general: "Where life previously could be lived on the level of the flesh with little or no self-questioning, now the presence of the Spirit brings with it a profound disease with the reduction of humanity to the level of animal appetites. It is important to recognize that Paul sees this as a Christian condition."[21] Dunn further comments about this situation: "There is no perfection for the Christian in this life; the desires of flesh as well as of Spirit characterize the ongoing process of salvation."[22] Whether the meaning given to the conjunction ἵνα is final or consecutive, the result of this struggle is the same: the flesh prevents the believer from doing what the Spirit prompts that one to do, and reciprocally, the Spirit prevents the same believer from following the solicitations of the flesh. Such a situation can be qualified as paralysis; still, according to Dunn (and others with him), it is analogous to what is described in Romans 7:14–25.

This being said, today commentators on the whole admit to a difference between Galatians 5:16–25 and Romans 7:7–25, the latter of which is not speaking about the Christian but the person without Christ. They are also convinced that the context of Galatians 5:17, in particular 5:24, is not describing believers paralyzed by an interior struggle because, if they allow themselves to be led by the Spirit, they are not yielding to the desires of the flesh: "And those who belong to Christ Jesus have crucified the flesh with its passions and desires."[23] Indeed, the passage's dynamic assumes that believers are able to be led by the Spirit and actually are. Otherwise the exhortation would no longer make sense: what would be the good of exhorting believers who were prevented from following the solicitations of the flesh as well as the promptings of the Spirit?

19. J. J. Kilgallen's reading; see "The Strivings of the Flesh . . . (Galatians 5,17)," *Bib* 80 (1999): 113–14.
20. The same reading is in Martyn, *Galatians*, 494, who furthermore notes that given 5:16, "one should have expected quite a different closure in this sentence: 'for the Flesh is actively inclined against the Spirit, and the Spirit against the Flesh.' These two powers constitute a pair of opposites at war with one another, and the result of this war, commenced by the Spirit, is that the Spirit is in the process of liberating you from the power of the Flesh."
21. Dunn, *Galatians*, 297.
22. Ibid.
23. Gal. 5:24 RSV.

However, because the immediate context of 5:17 assumes that believers are able to escape from the slavery of the flesh and are able to be guided by the Spirit, exegetes have been compelled to interpret this verse in a different way, as witnessed by the second and third readings. As seen above, in the second, the struggle between the flesh and the Spirit has a positive result: *preventing us from* doing *whatever* we want—in other words, *no matter what*, or even from wanting to satiate all our impulses.[24] The struggle between the flesh and the Spirit permits some options and excludes others. In short, this struggle prompts the believer to discern between what must be avoided (what is evil and thus harmful) and what must be preferred (what is good and thus profitable). If, in this case, the Greek relative pronoun ἅ is given a distributive meaning ("all those things that") or even a universal one ("absolutely all the things that"), it is nevertheless actually designating the evil orientations or impulses.

A passage from Plato's *Lysis*,[25] in which some expressions are close to those of Galatians 5:17, seems to favor this interpretation:

> Socrates—(207E) Do you consider that a man is happy when enslaved and restricted from doing the things he desires [ποιεῖν ὧν ἐπιθυμοῖ]?
>
> Lysis—Not I, on my word.
>
> Socrates—Then if your father and mother are fond of you, and desire to see you happy, it is perfectly plain that they are anxious to secure your happiness.
>
> Lysis—They must be, of course.
>
> Socrates—Hence they allow you to do what you want/like [ἐῶσιν ἄρα σε ἃ βούλει ποιεῖν], and never scold you, or hinder [διακωλύουσι] you from doing what you (could possibly) desire [ποιεῖν ὧν ἂν ἐπιθυμῇς]?
>
> Lysis—Yes, they do, Socrates. I assure you: they stop me from doing a great many things [μάλα γε πολλὰ κωλύουσιν].

In short, if one compares this passage from *Lysis* with Galatians 5:17, one could say that in the second reading the parents and the flesh/Spirit struggle have the same role, that of preventing the children/believers from expansively

---

24. In addition to Barclay, *Obeying the Truth*, 113, and the authors cited by Jan Lambrecht in "The Right Things You Want to Do," in his *Collected Studies on Pauline Literature and on the Book of Revelation* (Rome: Pontificio Istituto Biblico, 2001), see the commentary of A. Vanhoye, *Lettera ai Galati* (Milan: Paoline, 2000), 136.

25. Plato, *Lysis* 207E–208A. Cf. Rastoin, *Tarse et Jérusalem*, 234–43, in which is found a commentary on the passage and an interesting comparison with Gal. 4:1–2, because the ideas and words in common with *Lysis* and Gal. 3–4 are too numerous to speak of a coincidence.

desiring anything whatsoever and thus confusing true liberty with the absence of all constraint. In this case, Paul could have implicitly continued with the metaphor used in Galatians 4, once again reminding the Christians of Galatia that they have remained small children in need of a pedagogue that prevents them from doing all that they would like, from following all their desires, especially the most foolish and dangerous, in order that they may progressively experiment with what is true liberty, since, for the Socrates of *Lysis*, as for him, such is the role of the pedagogue.[26] Nevertheless, the comparison remains dubious, because it is the Spirit, and the Spirit alone, who prevents the believers from doing whatever might come to mind. In other words, more than the reciprocal flesh/Spirit enmity, it is the intervention and kind attention of the Spirit (and his alone) that prevents the believers from following all their impulses. One may also ask if in Galatians 5:17d the relative pronoun has all the extension—and the distributive meaning—given to it by the second reading: ("These things are opposed to one another in order to prevent you from doing whatever you would.") Indeed, when Paul wants to give the maximal (or distributive) extension to a relative pronoun, he precedes it with the adjective πᾶς, as in Colossians 3:17: πᾶν ὅ τι ἐὰν ποιῆτε ἐν λόγῳ ἢ ἐν ἔργῳ ("Whatever you do, in word or deed" [RSV]); or Galatians 3:10: ἐπικατάρατος πᾶς ὃς οὐκ ἐμμένει πᾶσιν τοῖς γεγραμμένοις ἐν τῷ βιβλίῳ τοῦ νόμου τοῦ ποιῆσαι αὐτά ("Cursed be every one who does not abide by all things written in the book of the law" [RSV]).[27] He also uses both the definite relative pronouns (ὅσος,[28] οἷος[29]) and the indefinites (ὅστις,[30] ὁποῖος[31]). But because none of these relative pronouns appears in Galatians 5:17, it is uncertain whether the simple ἅ should be translated by *whatever*.

Another possibility, a little different from the preceding one, understands the relative pronoun as referring to negative things: "the evil things that you want to do." The verse would then be saying that in the flesh/Spirit struggle, it is the Spirit that triumphs over the flesh and prevents us from executing the evil things to which the flesh impels us. Although in complete agreement with the immediate context, in which Paul assumes that the Christians are allowing themselves to be guided by the Spirit, this reading has been rightly rejected by

26. Plato's *Lysis* 208C and Gal. 3:24; 4:1–3.
27. Deut. 27:26 LXX reads: Ἐπικατάρατος πᾶς ἄνθρωπος, ὃς οὐκ ἐμμενεῖ . . . etc. See also Rom. 10:13.
28. In Paul's writings, 25x in total; in particular, 5x in Galatians (3:10, 27; 4:1, 6:12, 16). The neuter plural ὅσα is found in Rom. 3:19; 15:4; and Phil. 4:8 (6x).
29. Paul uses it 10x in total (but not in Galatians).
30. See, e.g., Gal. 5:10; Phil. 2:20; and Col. 3:17, which has just been mentioned.
31. See 1 Cor. 3:13; Gal. 2:6; 1 Thess 1:9. But he does not utilize ὁπόσος.

another exegete.[32] If Paul had wanted to indicate that the believers want to do evil, it would have been easy to add an ad hoc adjective.

Would it not be better, with others, to interpret this relative pronoun positively: "*the good things* that you would like to do"? Those, like Jan Lambrecht, for whom this is the meaning of the relative pronoun, invoke the positive denotation that the Greek verb θέλω has in Romans 7:14–20.[33] Even if the situation of the *egō* in Romans 7:7–25 and that of the believers in Galatians 5:16–24 is different, because the *egō* in Romans 7:7–25 is not a Christian, it is necessary to admit that Galatians 5:17 is not considering the good or evil desires of the Christian but the struggle between the flesh and the Spirit, which are the *only* active realities in this context.[34] Indeed, the flesh struggles against the Spirit (and not directly against the believers), and if it struggles against the Spirit, it is so that believers cannot be protected and, as a result, produce those evil works of the flesh enumerated in verses 19–21. Indeed, verse 17 supposes that believers want to be led by the Spirit since its meaning depends on that of the surrounding verses, especially verse 16 ("Walk by the Spirit") and verse 18a, a conditional proposition that takes up the line of thought and expresses an actual condition: "but if [= if it is true that] you are led by the Spirit." However, the objection made above on the negative denotation of the relative pronoun is also valid for a possible positive denotation insofar as one makes (d) depend on (c).

As to the relative pronoun ἅ, it can have a positive denotation if one follows the third reading, which connects verse 17d with 17a and makes the two intermediate lines (b and c) incidental clauses, as the following disposition indicates, in which the dashes indicate the limits of these incidental clauses:[35]

(a) For [γάρ] the flesh desires against the Spirit,

—(b) but [δέ] the Spirit desires against the flesh,

(c) for [γάρ] those [powers] fight each other,—

(d) to [ἵνα] prevent you from doing those (things) you would.

32. Barclay, *Obeying the Truth*, 114, who says this interpretation "has the great advantage of fitting the context well, supporting and illustrating the confident statement of 5:16. [But] its problems lie in accommodating the central clause ('These are opposed to each other') and *explaining why 'whatever you want' should be taken as 'what the flesh desires'*" (emphasis added).

33. Cf. Rom. 7:15, 16, 18, 19, 20. On this exact point, see J. Lambrecht, "The Right Things You Want to Do: A Note on Galatians 5:17d," *Bib* 79 (1998): 515–24.

34. On the difference of the perspective in Rom. 7 and Gal. 5:17, see, e.g., Betz, *Galatians*, 279–80.

35. See the articles of Kilgallen, "Strivings of the Flesh"; and of Otfried Hofius, "Widerstreit zwischen Fleisch und Geist? Erwägungen zu Gal. 5, 17," in *Exegetische Studien*, WUNT 223 (Tübingen: Mohr Siebeck, 2008): 161–72.

This way of seeing the relationships between the lines gives a positive meaning to the relative pronoun in (d).[36] The verse must then be understood thus: the flesh desires against the Spirit in order to prevent you from doing the good that you would like (and that the Spirit prompts you to do). The two central lines, the incidental clauses, have as their function supplying details to (a): the first (b), to indicate that the enmity is not one way, and the second (c), which is an *expolitio*,[37] to confirm that the flesh and the Spirit are really antagonistic powers and that this antagonism is not occasional but *structural*.

To this reading, one can raise the following objections.[38] First, this reading is very recent; indeed, over the centuries all readers have spontaneously connected (d) with (c). Equally, because of the δέ in (b), which denotes a contrast, it seems difficult to separate (b) from (a); as for (c), it seems to give the reason for both (a) and (b) and not only for (b). Nevertheless, the fact that this reading is recent does not invalidate its value, because several Pauline passages previously understood in erroneous ways have been revisited in recent decades and translated correctly.[39] As for the relationship that exists between the different lines, the close connection between the contrast of (a) and (b) is not destroyed by the incidental clause, but just the opposite, since the latter has as its primary function explaining and clarifying the enigmatic formulation that (a) makes of the flesh/Spirit relationship. Yet ultimately the third reading is to be preferred here not only because it makes clear sense of the argument but also because of the passage's rhetorical arrangement: since all of the other units of verses 17–23 deal, respectively, with only one of the agents, the flesh (D) or the Spirit (c/C), that of verse 17 (d) must deal with the flesh and its desires, so that line (a) is further explained in line (d); and means that in verse 17 the intermediary lines (b) and (c) are incidental clauses.

Notwithstanding the explanations provided above on the incidental clause (b) + (c), many readers connect (d) with (c) and stay with the second reading, and in the best of cases, the one proposed by Barclay and Albert Vanhoye. Nevertheless, let us add that in other passages of his letters—such as 1 Corinthians 14:2—Paul does not hesitate to insert parentheses that

---

36. Thus Hofius, "Widerstreit zwischen Fleisch und Geist?," 168 ; and it seems, Kilgallen, "Strivings of the Flesh," 113.

37. *Expolitio* is a figure that consists of repeating, in greater detail, the same thing or the same argument in equivalent terms.

38. A recent commentary has even declared that it was desperate, but without showing why; cf. J. P. Lémonon, *L'épître aux Galates*, Commentaire biblique: Nouveau Testament 9 (Paris: Cerf, 2008), 184, who follows the first reading instead.

39. I am thinking of Phil. 3:9 and Col. 1:24 in particular.

create semantic difficulties and oblige the reader to rely on his memory if he wants to recover the discourse's line of thought.[40] This could also be the case for Galatians 5:17. In fact, the third reading reduces the distance between "For the desires of the flesh are against the Spirit" and "to prevent you from doing what you would";[41] it does not prevent associating the final proposition with the first segment of the sentence. The adversative particle "but" (δέ) allows the existence of a parenthesis or incidental clause, whereas a καί ("the flesh desires against the Spirit *and* the Spirit against the flesh") would make it impossible.[42]

None of the readings of Galatians 5:17 that we have just presented are apodictically obvious. If here we have preferred the third to the other two, it is because it respects the passage's dynamic and the alternation of the flesh/Spirit presentations most excellently. Indeed, it permits recovering the final value of the ἵνα, which makes complete sense: if the flesh is opposed to the Spirit, it is really *so that* we do not do what we want. As articulated by the third reading, the verse takes into account the argumentation's dynamic: you who are led by the Spirit can finally do what you want, that is to say, *the good* you want. Far from emphasizing a defeat, Paul is indirectly highlighting the superiority of the Spirit. As for the incidental clauses, their function is also clear: Paul is reminding his readers that if the flesh struggles against the Spirit, the latter is there in order to respond to the attacks, because this is truly the Spirit's role.

At this point, it is not a bad idea to retrace the route taken so far because it clearly shows that different and even nonconfessional readings can have important theological consequences. The first reading highlights the imperfection and, at the worst, the ethical paralysis of believers; in the second, Paul is wanting to recall that liberty is not the equivalent of an absence of all constraint and that believers must resist their impulses; according to the third, by recognizing that the flesh struggles against the Spirit, the apostle is pointing out that the flesh has in the Spirit a lasting and effective antagonist. If each reading appeals to reasons that are nonconfessional, their way of understanding the status of works in Paul is clearly felt. Having stated my agreement with the choice of the third reading for Galatians 5:17, it remains for me to develop some of the components of the passage's exhortations.

---

40. In 1 Cor. 14:2, the explicative parenthesis, "for no one [*oudeis*] understands him," causes the reader to question who is the subject of the following verb ("He utters mysteries"), which clearly cannot be the *oudeis* of the parenthesis but "the one who speaks in tongues."

41. RSV for both lines.

42. Current translations unfortunately understand it as if there were a *kai* ("and").

The Exhortations of Galatians 5:13–15 and 16–25

The exegesis of Galatians 5:17 makes it possible to extricate several interesting points theologically:

- The flesh does not directly threaten the believer,[43] but it does directly take on the Spirit.
- It is the Spirit that the flesh opposes, in an attempt to keep the Spirit from guiding the believer in putting into action what (in other words, the good) the believer wants. And the incidental clauses of lines (b) and (c) opportunely recall that the Spirit, in response, is in no way passive.
- While recalling that the plan of the flesh is to render powerless the will and the liberty of believers and to prevent them from doing good, Paul implies, still in the incidental clause, that the Spirit is stronger than the flesh and is there precisely in order to defend believers continually and effectively. Thus verse 17 does not reflect a negative soteriology according to which believers cannot be freed from the mastery of the flesh.

The verses that follow clarify and confirm the statements of verse 17: the believers are left neither to their own forces nor enslaved to the flesh: they are able to allow themselves to be guided by the Spirit. Since this is so,[44] they have nothing to fear. This passage in Galatians 5:16–25 and Romans 8:1–17 are the only passages in Paul's Letters in which he develops the opposition of the flesh/Spirit, but without saying exactly what these terms entail, assuming that his readers know. Rather than clarifying what the vocabulary designates,[45] it is more important to determine the function of their opposition in these exhortations.

But first, a short examination of Galatians 5:18 is essential. Why does Paul say that if believers are led by the Spirit, they are not "under the νόμος" ("law"), whereas after the thoughts on the opposition of the flesh/Spirit and its implications, the reader expects Paul to declare that they are "beyond the reach of the *flesh*?" And what does the word νόμος designate? The Mosaic Law, without a doubt, because it is not the first time that Galatians has utilized the

---

43. There would have been a direct opposition if Paul were speaking of the (human) spirit of the believer; but as argued above, what guides the believer and works in the believer (*agapē*, kindness, etc.) can be only the divine Spirit.

44. Recall that the conditional proposition in Gal. 5:18a expresses an actual condition: "if you are led by the Spirit" is the equivalent of "*since* you are led by the Spirit."

45. Recall that in this passage the Greek word *pneuma* designates the Spirit of God, which has consistently been the case since its first occurrence in Gal. 3:2. Other occurrences are in 3:3 (the first opposition of the flesh/Spirit); 3:5, 14; 4:6, 29; 5:5, 16, 18, 22, 25; 6:1, 8, 18. An exception to this is 8:18.

expression "under the Law,"[46] and it has always designated the Mosaic Law.[47] If the affirmation in 5:18 is new, it has nevertheless been prepared for by the preceding argumentation, in which Paul says that believers are dead to the law (2:19); that they have not received the Spirit by practicing the law (3:2); and that God, by liberating them from the slavery of the law, has made them sons and daughters by the gift of the Spirit (4:4–5). The law and the Spirit are thus incompatible, just like the flesh and the Spirit. Verse 18 also implies that the one and only true guide for believers is the Spirit and not the law—which the Jews regard as a light for their steps, a sure guide toward salvation, and so forth.[48] Whoever has the Spirit for a guide is thus not submissive to the law. But why has the vocable "law" replaced "flesh" in verse 18? Because Paul is recalling and indirectly indicating to the Galatians that undergoing circumcision, and thus submitting to the law, would mean their falling back under the power of the flesh, against which the law remains powerless. In short, if they want to be "under the law," the Galatians will again be in the situation of subjection and enslavement (3:10–21; 4:5). As Dunn explains Paul, "To put oneself 'under the law,' in other words, was to look in the wrong direction for salvation. Worse still, to assume that only 'under the law' could salvation be found was to deny the reality of Gentile as Gentile having received the Spirit."[49]

One then understands why the theme of the law runs throughout the exhortations of Galatians 5:13–25: believers have been invited to fulfill the law (5:14), yet they must not become its subjects, because this would be falling back into slavery and allowing themselves to be subjected to the flesh (5:13). Actually, the law cannot judge and a fortiori condemn the fruit produced in believers by the Spirit (5:22–23). In short, in this rhetorical unit Paul wants to remind his readers of the *ethical* (and not only salvific, as in Gal. 1–4) stakes that a return to the law would have: concretely, it would mean a return to the slavery of the flesh. The opposition of flesh/Spirit in these exhortations thus refers indirectly but surely to the thought of Galatians 1–4 on justification. Paul's admonitions are not a question of specific exhortations touching on particular sectors of life, but of a radical attitude on which all concrete decisions depend. In this respect, we notice that in Galatians 5:16–25 there is a scarcity of verbs that have believers as their *active* subjects;[50] this obviously

---

46. The uppercase letter indicates that it is a question of the *Mosaic* Law and not any other type of law.

47. Cf. Gal. 3:23; 4:4, 5, 21.

48. Prov. 6:23; Isa. 51:4; Ps. 119:30 (118:30 LXX).

49. Dunn, *Galatians*, 300. For the apostle, "implicit here also is a clear distinction between being 'under the law' and 'fulfilling the law' (5:14)" (ibid.).

50. In 5:16 (exhortation), two verbs: "walk" and "do not gratify"; v. 17d, two verbs: "what you would," "prevent you from doing"; v. 25, "let us also walk."

shows that Paul wants to emphasize how ethical behavior is conditioned by one's salvific status: a doing by being.

If the background of Galatians 5:16–25 is actually constituted by the status of the believers, who are not "under the law" and thus are not slaves of the flesh, but are free, the passive in verse 18a ("if you are led [ἄγεσθε] by the Spirit") seems to denote a real determinism;[51] one also finds the same expression in Romans 8:14,[52] and one cannot see in it any heteronomy whatsoever. If in Galatians 5:16–25 Paul is minimizing the believers' behavior, it is only to highlight the power and efficacy of the Spirit on their behalf.

In regard to Galatians 3:10–14, recently I have shown that one cannot limit the problem of the law in Galatians to rules about Jewish festivals, food, and separation alone.[53] Therefore, there is no reason to be astonished that in 5:16–25, in which Paul is reminding the believers of Galatia of the stakes and the radicalness of the choice to be made—the flesh or the Spirit—there are no specific exhortations concerning these rules. As is his custom, Paul is radicalizing the questions and emphasizing the stakes that often have not been perceived by the churches he is addressing. This radicalization goes hand in hand with focusing on what is essential: that is why the exhortations in 5:16–25 place so much value on *agapē* and kindness toward other believers.[54] Though the lists of vices (5:19–21) and virtues (5:22–23) are encountered elsewhere in Paul,[55] here the vocables denoting *agapē* or attitudes associated with it are more numerous.[56] The reason for such an emphasis becomes clear when one recalls the statement of 5:15: "If you bite and devour one another, take heed

---

51. Cf. Prov. 18:2 LXX; 2 Tim. 3:6, in which the determinism is clear. For nonbiblical examples, see BDAG, ἄγω, §3.

52. Incidentally, Rom. 8:14 confirms the divine designation of the word *pneuma* in Gal. 5:16–25.

53. J. N. Aletti, "L'argumentation de Ga 3,10–14, une fois encore: Difficultés and propositions," *Bib* 92 (2001): 182–203; ET in Aletti, *New Approaches*, 237–60.

54. These exhortations do not say how to behave toward those on the outside, to those who are not members of the church. This does not mean that Paul is ignoring them, but since the question of circumcision is so urgent, he indirectly returns to it in the exhortations (Gal. 5:16–25 and 6:8) and explicitly in the epistolary *postscriptum* (6:12–16).

55. In the Pauline Letters, 2 Cor. 6:6–7a; Eph. 4:2–32; 5:9; Phil. 4:8; Col. 3:12; 1 Tim. 3:2–4, 8–10, 11–12; 4:12; 6:11, 18; 2 Tim. 2:22–25; 3:10; Titus 1:8; 2:2–10; but also elsewhere in the NT and nonbiblical literature. On the subject, see J. T. Fitzgerald, "Virtue/Vices Lists," in *Anchor Bible Dictionary*, ed. D. N. Freedman (New York: Doubleday, 1992), 6:875–76. For the list of vices in Paul, other than Gal. 5:19–21, see Rom. 1:29–31; 13:13; 1 Cor. 5:10–11; 6:9–10; 2 Cor. 12:20–21; Eph. 4:31; 5:3–5; Col. 3:5–8; 1 Tim. 1:9–10; 6:4–5; 2 Tim. 3:2–4; Titus 1:7; 3:3.

56. In the lists we find love (ἀγάπη) in 2 Cor. 6:6–7; Eph. 4:2; peace (εἰρήνη) only in Gal. 5; patience (μακροθυμία) in 2 Cor. 6:6; Eph. 4:2; Col. 3:12; kindness (χρηστότης) in 2 Cor. 6:6; Col. 3:12; goodness (ἀγαθωσύνη) in Eph. 5:9; meekness (πραΰτης) in Gal. 6:1; Eph. 4:2; Col. 3:12; 2 Tim. 2:25.

that you are not consumed by one another" (RSV). The condition of 5:15 is true, and one can assuredly conclude that the question of the circumcision of those believers coming from the gentile world had to have provoked large divisions in the local communities, so that what was at risk was the destruction or the disappearance of the church. Here the radical nature of the ethical exhortations is in service of the ecclesial life. This also explains why all, or almost all, the exhortations that go from Galatians 5:13 to 6:10 concern the ecclesial life and not the relationships of the believers to "those outside."[57] In short, after having led the believers in Galatia to the radicalness of the gospel (1:11 to 5:1), Paul is reminding them that the ethical and ecclesial stakes of the situation are no less decisive.[58]

Conclusions

After laying out the boundaries of the exhortative section of Galatians and showing that one cannot interpret Galatians 5:17 negatively as describing the ethical paralysis of the believers, we have found it possible to take into account the importance given to the opposition of flesh/Spirit that goes from 5:13 to 6:10. The radical nature of the ethical choices (the flesh or the Spirit) and their ecclesial consequences clearly indicate a posteriori the decisive importance of the argument of Galatians 1–4: what is at stake is quite simply the gospel!

In these exhortations the repeated mention of the term νόμος also shows that the law remains on the horizon of Paul's thought and confirms the radicalness of his position. Paul is not only criticizing the importance given to the *identity markers*, in other words, to the erroneous usage of the law; he is also placing the law beside the flesh and indicating that it cannot be a way of salvation.

---

57. The exhortation in Gal. 6:10b, "Let us do good to all men [πρὸς πάντας]" (RSV), is the only one to enlarge the ethical horizon.

58. Although the exhortations of Gal. 5:13–25 stress *agapē* and kindness toward the brothers, they are not however proposing Christ as a model of welcome and compassion; cf. Rom. 14:15; 15:7; Eph. 5:2, 25; Col. 3:13. This comes without a doubt from the importance given to the divine Spirit and to the effects of his presence in the believers in 5:22–23.

22

The Drama of Agency

Affective Augustinianism and Galatians

SIMEON ZAHL

The sequence in chapter 5 of Paul's Letter to the Galatians from verse 16 to verse 25 describes the priority and the power of the Holy Spirit in the Christian life, in light of a conflict between the Spirit and the flesh, and explains that when one or the other of these forces or approaches gains the upper hand, the result is radically divergent outcomes: the fruit of the Spirit on the one hand, and the works of the flesh on the other.

This sequence has been interpreted in various ways and in service of various agendas in the history of theology. In this essay I focus on one particular use to which this text has been put: as an important locus for discussions of the complex relationship between divine and human agency in Paul's thought in Galatians and beyond. Like so many topics in Paul, agency questions have been discussed many times, with real insight, and from many possible angles.[1] But I

In addition to many helpful comments from participants at the St. Andrews Galatians conference, I thank Wayne Coppins, David Lincicum, and Kyle Wells for their helpful input at various stages.

1. For excellent recent contributions, see the essays in John Barclay and Simon Gathercole, eds., *Divine and Human Agency in Paul and His Cultural Environment* (London: T&T Clark, 2007); as well as Kyle Wells, "Grace, Obedience, and the Hermeneutics of Agency: Paul and His Jewish Contemporaries on the Transformation of the Heart" (PhD diss., Durham University, 2009).

do believe there are a few more things that can be usefully said on the matter, especially in connection with this Galatians passage and with the Epistle to the Galatians more generally.

In service of this question, I draw attention to an old theological interpretation of this passage as having fundamentally to do with God's engagement with human affections, emotions, and desires. As we will see, this interpretation reintroduces a useful and neglected conceptual tool for understanding agency issues in Paul. But I also want to take the interpretation one step further, in conversation with certain themes in contemporary theology about the role of Christian practice and experience in the interpretation of scriptural texts, especially difficult ones. My concluding proposal is that understanding the deeply affective character of Galatians 5:16–25 grounds and supports an interpretive methodology that takes seriously Christian experience and practice as an aid to making sense both of this text in particular and of questions of divine and human agency in general.

"Affective Augustinianism" and Galatians 5:16–25

> [16]Live by the Spirit, and you will not gratify the desires of the flesh. [17]For what the flesh desires is opposed to the Spirit, and what the Spirit desires is opposed to the flesh; for these are opposed to each other, to prevent you from doing what you want. [18]But if you are led by the Spirit, you are not subject to the law. [19]Now the works of the flesh are obvious: fornication, impurity, licentiousness, [20]idolatry, sorcery, enmities, strife, jealousy, anger, quarrels, dissensions, factions, [21]envy, drunkenness, carousing, and things like these. I am warning you, as I warned you before: those who do such things will not inherit the kingdom of God.
>
> [22]By contrast, the fruit of the Spirit is love, joy, peace, patience, kindness, generosity, faithfulness, [23]gentleness, and self-control. There is no law against such things. [24]And those who belong to Christ Jesus have crucified the flesh with its passions and desires. [25]If we live by the Spirit, let us also be guided by the Spirit. (Gal. 5:16–25 NRSV, trans. alt. for v. 16)

Our passage brings together a remarkable array of theological and pastoral categories. First, there is the description of the whole of human ethical life in the simple, affective terms of a struggle between competing desires: those of the flesh and those of the Spirit (5:16–17). Here right desiring is seen to be in some sense more fundamental than right knowing, and as prior to and necessary for right doing. Then, second, there is the pneumatology of the passage, where the Spirit is understood as an enormously potent force in such matters, such that, according to verse 16, if you "live by the Spirit" you simply "will not gratify the desires of the flesh": such gratification just is not a possibility.[2] Third, there is the fact that this all somehow connects to a move away from the law in the Christian life, with the Spirit in some sense replacing the law or rendering it now unnecessary—as we see in verse 18: "If you are led by the Spirit, you are not subject to the law." Fourth, there is the description of the consequences of these alternative patterns of desire, the respective fruit of the Spirit and the works of the flesh, by means of which patterns the Galatians are meant to be able to interpret and assess their own particular experiences and behavior, as a community and as individuals. And finally, there is the curious combination of agencies behind all this in the passage: on the one hand, the Spirit as all-powerful ethical agent, whose presence renders the gratification of the flesh impossible; yet on the other hand the appeal and exhortation to the Galatians not only to live by the Spirit but also to be guided by the Spirit (5:25), as if such things are at least to some extent in their power.

There is a tradition in Christian theology that has viewed this particular set of categories and relationships as among the most useful and fundamental articulations in the New Testament of the outworkings of Christian soteriology. For lack of a better term, I will call this tradition "affective Augustinianism."[3] It stretches from key texts in middle-period Augustine, particularly from the early anti-Pelagian writings,[4] to Luther,[5] and reaches a high-water mark in the early writings of Luther's colleague Philipp Melanchthon.[6] This tradition

2. See note 23 below.
3. Although this term is my own, it is effectively a summary of a theological trajectory that Ashley Null has been describing in similar terms for years. See esp. Ashley Null, "Thomas Cranmer and Tudor Evangelicalism," in *The Emergence of Evangelicalism: Exploring Historical Continuities*, ed. Kenneth J. Stewart and Michael A. G. Haykin (Nottingham, UK: Apollos, 2008), 236; and idem., *Thomas Cranmer's Doctrine of Repentance: Renewing the Power to Love* (Oxford: Oxford University Press, 2000), 98–102, 130–31, 157–212.
4. Esp. relevant are Augustine's works *The Spirit and the Letter*, *The Grace of Christ and Original Sin*, and *On Nature and Grace*.
5. The high point of this tradition for Martin Luther is in the 1522 "Preface to Romans" (WA BI 7:3–26; for an ET of the slightly altered 1546 edition, see LW 35:365–80). It begins much earlier, however, starting with the 1515–16 *Lectures on Romans*, when Luther first begins citing Augustine's anti-Pelagian writings. For further references and commentary, see Simeon Zahl, "The Bondage of the Affections: Willing, Feeling, and Desiring in Luther's Theology, 1513–25," in *The Spirit, the Affections, and the Christian Tradition*, ed. Dale Coulter and Amos Yong (forthcoming).
6. This is the case above all in the 1521 first edition of Melanchthon's *Loci communes*, one of the most influential theological textbooks in early Reformation-era Europe. See esp. Karl-Heinz zur Mühlen, "Melanchthons Auffassung vom Affekt in den *Loci communes* von 1521," in *Humanismus und Reformation*, ed. Michael Bayer and Günther Wartenburg (Leipzig: Evangelische Verlagsanstalt 1996), 327–36; and Heinrich Bornkamm, "Melanchthons Menschenbild," in *Philipp Melanchthon: Forschungsbeiträge zur vierhundertsten Wiederkehr seines Todestages*, ed. Walter Elliger (Göttingen: Vandenhoeck & Ruprecht, 1961), 76–90.

also has a highly influential coda in the thought of English Reformer Thomas Cranmer and his seminal Book of Common Prayer.[7] The debt this tradition owes to Galatians 5:16–25 in particular is very large, explicit in many places and implicit in many more.[8]

The basic insight of "affective Augustinianism" is that the most powerful and central feature of human nature is not our rational capacities but our affective ones. Our emotions and affections—which these writers often call our "hearts"[9]—both are what ultimately serve to determine our actual behavior and are what God himself is most concerned with. As Melanchthon puts it in the 1521 edition of his classic theological summary, the *Loci communes*, "Since God judges hearts, the heart and its affections must be the highest and most powerful part of man."[10] In addition to our Galatians passage, this particular point draws especially on aspects of Jesus's teaching: the ethical prioritization of motive over outward behavior in the Sermon on the Mount (Matt. 5:21–22, 27–28); the statements about how it is what comes from within, from the heart, that makes a person unclean (Mark 7:17–23); and the statements about good and bad trees and their fruit (Matt. 7:16–20; 12:33–35; Luke 6:43–45).[11]

Ethics and good works matter greatly to this tradition, but they are relativized in comparison with inner dispositions and motivations. As Augustine puts it, commenting directly on Galatians 5:17: "That man" who "obliges himself to abstain from the work of sin" out of "fear of punishment which the law threatens, and not from any love for righteousness," "is [still] guilty"

---

7. See Null, *Thomas Cranmer*, 157–212.

8. See, e.g., Augustine, *On Nature and Grace*, chaps. 58, 61, 63, 66, and 67 (BWA, 559, 561, 563, 565–66); idem., *On the Spirit and the Letter*, chap. 59 (BWA, 511); Luther, "Explanation of Thesis 6" of the Heidelberg Disputation, WA 1:368 (LW 31:61); idem, *Assertio omnium articulorum*, in WA 7:103–4, 143, 147 (for an ET of the German version of the *Assertio*, see LW 32:19–20, 93); LC 1521, 40, 137–38; MB, 49, 131. See also the multiple references to "desires of the flesh" (a term that picks up Gal. 5:16 as well as Eph. 2:3; 2 Pet. 2:18; and 1 John 2:16) in Cranmer's homilies: Thomas Cranmer, *Miscellaneous Writings and Letters of Thomas Cranmer*, ed. John Edmund Cox for the Parker Society (Cambridge: The Parker Society, Cambridge University Press, 1846), 131, 139.

9. The term "heart," and its range of meaning theologically and biblically is an important and complex topic, not least in the writings of the "affective Augustinian" theologians in question. Here I am referring to the many instances when "the heart" is demonstrably used as a kind of affective shorthand, rather than to all uses of the term in their writings. For further analysis of this and related terms, see Zahl, "Bondage of the Affections."

10. Melanchthon, LC 1521, 15; MB, 29.

11. References to Matt. 7:17–18, in particular, are ubiquitous in Luther's writings. See, e.g., thesis 4 of the Disputation against Scholastic Theology, WA 1:224 (LW 31:9); "Explanation of Thesis 6" of the Heidelberg Disputation, WA 1:371 (LW 31:65–66); and WA 18:736 (ET, *The Bondage of the Will*, trans. J. I. Packer and O. R. Johnston [Grand Rapids: Fleming H. Revell, 1957], 243).

because he is not "yet free and removed from the desire of sinning."¹² What this means is that true ethical behavior is seen as impossible without the right affections, but at the same time such behavior becomes natural and inevitable once those affections are in place. Melanchthon puts it quite bluntly: "The Spirit of God cannot be in the human heart without fulfilling the Decalogue. The Decalogue is therefore observed by necessity."¹³

This tradition is also relatively skeptical about the powers of the human *ratio*, or rational faculty, not because we are incapable of knowing or determining what we ought to do but because that knowledge bears very little relation to whether we are actually able to do it. For these thinkers, Paul's concept of the "law" is then understood as closely connected to the *ratio*—because it too describes what should and must be done but is impotent to accomplish it. As Augustine puts it in *The Grace of Christ and Original Sin*, "It is not by law and teaching uttering their lessons from without, but by a secret, wonderful, and ineffable power operating within, that God works in men's hearts . . . good dispositions of the will."¹⁴ He makes effectively the same point in *The Spirit and the Letter*, explaining that it is not "by externally addressing to our faculties precepts of holiness" that "God assists us to work righteousness." Rather, "He gives His increase internally by 'shedding love abroad in our hearts by the Holy Ghost, which is given to us.'"¹⁵

Finally, this tradition understands this priority of the heart not just as a general or abstract prioritization of desiring over knowing or doing but also as a concrete emotional reality, ultimately rooted in love but also connected to joy, delight, and other affections. As Augustine puts it rather memorably, "One only loves, after all, what delights one."¹⁶

There is an excellent summary of this affective Augustinian theological approach in Martin Luther's 1522 "Preface to Romans":

> But [a right] heart is given only by God's Spirit, who fashions a man after the law, so that he acquires a desire for the law in his heart, doing nothing henceforth

---

12. Augustine, *On Nature and Grace*, chap. 67 (BWA, 566).
13. Melanchthon, *LC 1521*, 133; *MB*, 127.
14. Augustine, *The Grace of Christ and Original Sin*, chap. 25 (BWA, 601).
15. Augustine, *The Spirit and the Letter*, chap. 42 (BWA, 494).
16. *Serm.* 159 (on Rom. 7–8), in *The Works of Saint Augustine*, ed. Edmund Hill, vol. 3.5 (New Rochelle, NY: New City Press, 1992), 122. See also Luther on Gal. 5:14 (1519 version): "When this affection [i.e., love] has been set on the right course, the other parts no longer need any commandments; for everything flows out of this affection. [*Quo affectu in rectitudinem posito iam nullis praeceptis indigent alia membra. Omnia enim ex hoc affectu fluunt.*] As this is, so is everything; and without it all other things are foolish exertions" (WA 2:576; LW 27:349–50). For a discussion of Cranmer as following directly in this tradition, see Null, *Thomas Cranmer*, 180–81, 210–12, etc.

out of fear and compulsion but out of a willing heart.... How shall a work please God if it proceeds from a reluctant and resisting heart? To fulfill the law, however, is to do its works with pleasure and love, to live a godly and good life of one's own accord, without the compulsion of the law. This pleasure and love for the law is put into the heart by the Holy Spirit, as St. Paul says in [Romans] chapter 5[:5].[17]

Agency and the Affective Theology of Galatians 5

The usefulness of this tradition for understanding our Galatians passage is twofold.[18] First, it draws attention to the highly affective anthropology that is at work here. Desire and desiring in various forms[19] could not be more fundamental to what it means to be human beings before God than it is for Paul here. Furthermore, in this passage the chief consequences of God's work in Christian lives through the Spirit are the affections of love and joy—the first two fruits of the Spirit—as well as a series of further fruits that, with perhaps the exception of self-control, are also deeply affective and dispositional in nature: peace, patience, kindness, gentleness, and generosity. At times, biblical commentators seem to elide a bit too quickly over the concrete, emotional aspect of what is being described here to its meaning in some larger theological or salvation-historical context, such as the apocalyptic character of the Spirit's role.[20] Without undermining such meanings, the affective interpretation provides a helpful reminder at the same time of the day-to-day, almost mundane form the work of the Spirit takes in human realities of desiring, feeling, and loving others.

The second way the affective interpretive tradition is valuable for understanding this passage is in connection with the relationship between divine and human agency in Christian ethical life. Commentators on this passage consistently point out the difficulties Galatians 5 raises for understanding agency in Paul's

17. WA BI 7:4, 6; LW 35:367–68.
18. For a recent case showing the importance and value for NT studies of "effective history" and reception history of biblical texts, not least in the Christian theological tradition—perhaps not unlike the reception of Gal. 5:17–25 in Augustine, Luther, Melanchthon, and Cranmer being drawn on in this essay—see Markus Bockmuehl, *Seeing the Word: Refocusing New Testament Study* (Grand Rapids: Baker Academic, 2006), 64–68.
19. See *epithymian* in 5:16; *epithymei* and *thelēte* in 5:17.
20. See, e.g., J. Louis Martyn, *Galatians: A New Translation with Introduction and Commentary*, AB 33A (New York: Doubleday, 1997), 482–84 and 524–34, where the struggle between flesh and Spirit is immediately interpreted as an instance of and participation in a "cosmic," "apocalyptic war." This interpretation is quite helpful and plausible but also fails somewhat to bring out the simultaneously mundane and quotidian character of the fruit of the Spirit.

thought.²¹ The fundamental issue is how to make sense of verse 16, and to some degree of verse 18, in light of verse 25, and vice versa. There seems to be broad agreement, contra the NRSV translation, that verse 16 should be read "Live by the Spirit, and you will not gratify the desires of the flesh."²² The verse seems to speak of the effect of the Spirit in terms of what James D. G. Dunn calls "a deep-rooted passion or overmastering compulsion."²³ The guarantee of Christian ethical behavior in light of Paul's minimizing the role of the law is the active work of the Spirit as "a compelling inner force,"²⁴ stronger than the flesh, which transforms desires and produces love, joy, and other fruit. When the Spirit is properly present, the desires of the flesh simply are not gratified. In keeping with this picture, the metaphor of fruit is particularly apt for characterizing the priority of divine agency over human agency: Plants are in a key sense passive. They do not have wills or rational faculties. When they are granted fertile conditions by factors outside their control, like sunlight and water and good soil, they simply respond, naturally and organically, by producing fruit.²⁵

But then we have verse 25, with its exhortation to let ourselves be guided by the Spirit, as well as the exhortation to stand firm in freedom in 5:1—implying that it is perhaps possible not to do so. There is also the implication in 3:3 that it is possible for a person to begin with the Spirit but end with the flesh. And finally there is 6:7–10, with its warning and exhortation about sowing to the Spirit, not to the flesh. Each of these instances seems to open the door, at least to some small degree, for a contribution from human agency. In each of these cases, Paul apparently is appealing to the Galatians as agents to do

21. See, e.g., John M. G. Barclay, *Obeying the Truth: Paul's Ethics in Galatians* (Edinburgh: T&T Clark, 1988), 181–82; Martyn, *Galatians*, 531–32; and Jean-Noël Aletti in chap. 21 above.
22. James D. G. Dunn, *The Epistle to the Galatians*, BNTC (London: A&C Black, 1993), 297; Barclay, *Obeying the Truth*, 111; Hans Dieter Betz, *Galatians: A Commentary on Paul's Letter to the Churches in Galatia*, Hermeneia (Philadelphia: Fortress, 1979), 278; Martyn, *Galatians*, 492.
23. Dunn, *Galatians*, 300–301. Dunn is excellent on this feature of the Spirit and is probably the modern commentator most alert to desire and affect issues in this passage.
24. Ibid., 300.
25. The "affective Augustinian" tradition constantly draws on such plant metaphors in the Bible for making sense of the place of good works for Christians, precisely because of this combination of fecundity not being in the control of the plant, but the bearing of fruit at the same time being something that really does take place. In Luther, where appeal to plant imagery is particularly common, see, e.g., the references to Matt. 7:17–18 in note 11 above, and more generally the organic imagery in the preface to the 1531/35 *Lectures on Galatians* (WA 40:1.43b, 46b, 51b; LW 26:6, 8, 11). See also Melanchthon, *LC 1521*, 24, 86–87 (*MB*, 35, 88); and Cranmer, *Miscellaneous Writings*, 136, where he draws heavily on the tree imagery in Jer. 17:7–8. For more on this in connection with Luther and John's Gospel, see Simeon Zahl, "What Has the 'Lutheran' Paul to Do with John? Passive Righteousness and Abiding in the Vine," in *The Vocation of Theology Today: A Festschrift for David Ford*, ed. Tom Greggs, Rachel Muers, and Simeon Zahl (Eugene, OR: Cascade, 2013), 61–74.

one thing in relation to the Spirit rather than another, rather than simply to sit back and await the Spirit's action.

So which is it? Is the Spirit an "overmastering compulsion" that overrides human agency, or is it a power that waits at the door for us to let it in, and departs on command, according to human willing and decision making?[26] Is Dunn correct in saying that "following the Spirit (5:25) is no mere passive act of 'being led by the Spirit' (5:18), but requires also a resolute intention to 'walk by the Spirit' (5:16)"?[27]

One common approach to this problem is the one ultimately taken by Dunn, who acknowledges that both themes are present in Paul and that they are not easily resolved or synthesized. In light of this, his approach is to appeal to the rather weak category of "balance." As he puts it, for Paul "the balance between passive and active [is] deliberate."[28] The problem with appealing to "balance" or even "tension" like this is that it simply does not answer many of the actual pastoral-theological questions at stake in the divine-human agency problem. Agency issues are not just theoretical: different points of view on this subject carry very different consequences, for example, in the day-to-day work of Christian churches; historically speaking, it is as much these practical questions that have driven interest in the subject as philosophical or hermeneutical ones.

I refer to practical-theological questions like these: homiletically, should one primarily preach indicatives or imperatives? If both, then in what order, and how does this not simply come across as a kind of confusing doublespeak? And if the answer is simply that human and divine agency, passive and active, are to be kept in a general balance, are human beings, whom Christian theology understands to be in some sense in rebellion or prone to rebellion against God, not far more likely to turn to the side of the balance that gives them control rather than facing directly the uncomfortable possibility of their lack of agency in key areas? And what about when persons find themselves overmastered in some way by what they understand to be "the desires of the flesh"? Should someone seeking to help them appeal to their agency to fix the problem, as Paul at times seems to do? Or should they just express sympathy, then wait and pray for God to intervene? These are difficult questions, pastorally, and much depends on how they are answered. My point is just that the resort to interpreting agency issues in Paul simply in terms of "balance" or "tension" often fails to answer the actual theological questions at stake and proves difficult to apply in practice.

26. For an interpretation emphasizing the latter, see Gordon D. Fee, *God's Empowering Presence: The Holy Spirit in the Letters of Paul* (Grand Rapids: Baker Academic, 1994), 433–46.
27. James D. G. Dunn, *The Theology of Paul the Apostle* (London: T&T Clark, 1998), 110.
28. Ibid., 110; see also Dunn, *Galatians*, 300.

Fortunately, the affective interpretive tradition that I have described can come to our aid here because of two complementary insights that it has. The first is that human willing and human desiring and feeling are utterly intertwined. For this tradition, willing does not take place separately from feelings and desires; to a significant degree, our will is essentially whichever of our desires or affections is most powerful and compelling at the moment of action.[29] The second, related insight is that desires and affections are the part of conscious human experience least subject to our deliberate control. As agents, we cannot simply choose to feel joy or peace—these are not things that can be summoned on demand—and likewise we cannot choose not to feel grief, say, over the death of a loved one. It is simply in their nature that affections are remarkably resistant to conscious effort to alter them.[30]

What this means is that a category like desire in Galatians 5:17 is quite effective at describing a picture of agency that moves beyond a simple appeal to "balance," to an account in which human and divine actors are not simply competitors. To transform a desire, as the Spirit does, is not to run roughshod over a person's agency: it is rather to engage and attract and reconstitute the very core of their agency. Our desires are not some separate force or entity, distinct from our true selves: they are a fundamental part of who we are as agents. In other words, by employing language of the transformation of desire and affection, Paul is using categories that reveal divine and human agency not to be a zero-sum game. Only a force outside our conscious selves can effectively change our desires and dispositions:[31] thus it is divine agency through and through. But at the same time it really is *our* desires and dispositions, and thus our own human will, that are changing.[32]

This affective picture fits quite well with some of the more sophisticated

---

29. Melanchthon, *LC 1521*, 12–17; *MB*, 26–30. See also Luther on the insuperability of desire, anger, and fear, in WA 1:227 (LW 31:14) and WA 1:374 (LW 31:69), and Luther and Melanchthon's explicit conflations of the will (*voluntas*) and "the heart" (*cor*) at certain points: Luther in WA 4:308 (LW 11:418) and WA 1:366 (LW 31:59); Melanchthon in *Die Loci Communes Philipp Melanchthons in ihrer Urgestalt*, ed. G. L. Plitt and D. Th. Kolde, 3rd ed. (Leipzig: A. Deichert, 1900), 77. Augustine, too, at various points conflates willing with desire and love (see John M. Rist, *Augustine: Ancient Thought Baptized* [Cambridge: Cambridge University Press, 1994], 176–77, 188).

30. Contemporary psychology and neuroscience of emotion concur, broadly, with this picture: according to a recent overview of the literature, one of the three defining characteristics of emotions, in psychological terms, is that "they are less susceptible to our intentions than other psychological states." See Elaine Fox, *Emotion Science: Cognitive and Neuroscientific Approaches to Understanding Human Emotions* (Basingstoke, UK: Palgrave Macmillan, 2008), 25.

31. Augustine, *The Spirit and the Letter*, chap. 5 (*BWA*, 463–64) and chap. 42 (*BWA*, 494).

32. Relevant here is Phil. 2:13: "For it is God who is at work in you, enabling you both to will [*thelein*] and to work for his good pleasure" (NRSV).

recent accounts of agency in Paul. Kyle Wells[33] has recently written about what he calls the "reconstitution of human agency" in Christ, resulting in a "human competency" that is nevertheless founded solely on "divine initiative."[34] In Wells's view of Paul, "eschatological agents do not become less, but more fully human as God acts, and are constituted as agents precisely as they function as God's agency."[35] What I would simply add to this sort of account, building on Galatians 5:16–25 and also the affective Augustinian tradition, is that the most important particular form this takes in practice and in concrete situations is the transformation of affections and desires in the inner life of the believer. Affections language such as we find in Galatians 5 thus serves as an important grounding in concrete experiences and interpersonal contexts of broader soteriological and salvation-historical systems and concepts.

But a problem remains with the sort of picture painted by Wells, and indeed in the affective interpretive tradition. There is a basic optimism to these accounts of the Spirit as fundamentally reconstituting human agency, as actually transforming human desires and affections, that is in some ways difficult to reconcile with the continued role of the flesh and of sin in the church and in Christian lives. If the Spirit's power and effectiveness as ethically transformative agent is so clear, why does that transformation not take place as often or as potently as we might wish it would? Why are the church and those within it, on both global and local levels, still full of "works of the flesh" like "strife, jealousy, anger, quarrels, dissensions, [and] factions" (Gal. 5:20)?

One alternative answer, which I find highly uncompelling, is that of someone like Gordon Fee, who essentially views the flesh and the Spirit not as forces but as two "different ways of life"[36] or "perspective[s]"[37] between which Christian agents are free to choose, such that any continued works of the flesh are the consequence of competent agents deliberately choosing the wrong course. Unsurprisingly, Fee is forced in his interpretation to downplay the role of desire and affect in Galatians 5[38]—categories whose character is to be remarkably

---

33. See also John Barclay, "'By the Grace of God I Am What I Am': Grace and Agency in Philo and Paul," in Barclay and Gathercole, *Divine and Human Agency*, 140–57.

34. Wells, "Hermeneutics of Agency," 241.

35. Ibid., 244–45. Barclay seems to concur with Wells here: on the one hand, in his view, Paul "takes delight in the paradox of a scandalously profligate Giver, at the risk of falling into a hard and arbitrary predestinarianism"; on the other hand, in the Pauline view, "the work of the Spirit does not substitute for, but precisely energizes, the work of the believer" (Barclay, "Grace and Agency," 157).

36. Fee, *Empowering Presence*, 435.

37. Ibid., 432–35, throughout.

38. See ibid., 432n224.

resistant to the influence of conscious human agency—and he deliberately brackets and ignores the passive quality inherent in the fruit metaphor.[39]

If this sort of interpretation is so unpersuasive, perhaps once again we are left with some form of Dunn's "balance" and "tension," despite the problems already referred to with such accounts. Fortunately, there are two important further approaches to consider. The first, which in my view is to be taken very seriously, is simply to accept that the Spirit's decision to engage or withdraw, to transform desire or not to transform, to pour love into our hearts or not (Rom. 5:5), ultimately falls within the inscrutable freedom of God. This is a position of real power and theological weight, and, broadly speaking, this is where our "affective Augustinian" theologians go if pushed. But how does it connect to the energetic optimism and willingness to exhort that we find, at least at times, in Paul—the call to "walk by the Spirit" and not to fall back to the flesh?

Reading Galatians 5:16–25 "Dramatically"

There is still one further option, I think, and we find a clue to it in the practical character of our Galatians passage, with its descriptions of concrete affections and ethical behaviors and dispositions, its practical and empirical claim that the works of the flesh are "evident" or "manifest" (*phanera*, 5:19), and its use of categories that are unusually pragmatic, down-to-earth, and empirically recognizable like desire, joy, anger, love, and kindness.

Here we can take a cue from some recent developments in theology and pursue what could be called a "dramatic" approach to the interpretation of this passage. The category of "drama" has become increasingly central for a number of theologians—I think especially of Ben Quash and David Ford, but also of Kevin Vanhoozer and others[40]—and in various ways it clearly bears the marks of the postliberal, "Yale" theological tradition. At its best, "drama" is a theological category that brings together the sorts of insights one finds in two important schools of thought from the past century: (1) "narrative" theology, which emphasizes the importance of story and narrative for the communication of truth, not least in the Bible;[41] and (2) American pragmatism, the late

39. Ibid., 443–44.
40. Ben Quash, *Theology and the Drama of History* (Cambridge: Cambridge University Press, 2005); David Ford, *The Future of Christian Theology* (Oxford: Wiley-Blackwell, 2011), chaps. 2 and 3; Kevin Vanhoozer, *The Drama of Doctrine: A Canonical-Linguistic Approach to Christian Theology* (Louisville: Westminster John Knox, 2005).
41. For a representative set of essays, see Stanley Hauerwas and L. Gregory Jones, eds., *Why Narrative? Readings in Narrative Theology* (Eugene, OR: Wipf & Stock, 1997).

nineteenth- and early twentieth-century philosophical school associated with William James, Charles Peirce, and others.[42]

In his recent book *The Future of Christian Theology*, David Ford devotes two chapters to "drama," and he describes it like this:

> Drama, like life, unfolds over time. It can have plots and sub-plots; major and minor characters and events; clashes of people, ideas, and perspectives that may or may not be resolved. . . . [As a category] it is able to convey the dynamic particularity of human existence, with its physicality, surprises, initiatives, contingencies, necessities, tensions, and multi-leveled complexity. . . . Its core perspective is that of characters and events in interaction, irreducibly social. As it unfolds, drama invites us to become engaged, to inhabit its world.[43]

Then Ford explains what he sees as the result:

> The drama has to be followed, entered into, and meditated upon as it unfolds. Its purpose is not just to give factual knowledge (though some is given) or enable a new self-understanding (though [we would be] right in affirming that), but above all to enable the continuation of the drama in a life of faith that acts out the direction of Jesus: "As the Father has sent me, so I send you" (John 20:21).[44]

Part of the point Ford is making here is that Christian theology is not a static determining, in a vacuum, of the best formulations of doctrinal truths (though there is a place for that). Rather, theology is utterly and happily intertwined with actual life—with particular events, particular people, particular contexts, and a particular God. It unfolds over time, not so much in the sense that truth gets added to it or that new revelations are acquired as in the sense that the truth and God himself need to be engaged with and discovered anew by each person and each community in each generation and context. Above all—and here is in part my own gloss on it—the "dramatic" character of Christian theology and in turn of Christian life is determined and guaranteed pneumatologically. That is, Christian theology and life is "dramatic" in that we always ultimately have to do with a living God, a Holy Spirit who is still as active today as in first-century Galatia.

42. William James summarized his version of pragmatism like this: "Grant an idea or belief to be true. . . . What concrete difference will its being true make in any one's actual life? What experiences [may] be different from those which would obtain if the belief were false? How will the truth be realized? What, in short, is the truth's cash-value in experiential terms?" (William James, *Pragmatism: A New Name for Some Old Ways of Thinking*, ed. Fredson Bowers, The Works of William James [Cambridge, MA: Harvard University Press, 1975], 97).

43. Ford, *Future of Christian Theology*, 23.

44. Ibid., 30.

In my view, "dramatic" reading of a text has at least two qualities. First, it brings data from life and practice to bear as one useful tool in our quest to understand a text. Second, it takes seriously the fact that any reading of a text is taking place during a particular moment and particular place with particular readers and in light of particular issues and problems.[45]

As I have mentioned, we see this move toward the "dramatic," which means not least toward life experience, in Galatians 5:16–25. Especially in the descriptions of spiritual fruit and works of the flesh, Paul is describing feelings, dispositions, and events that tend to occur in human lives—that the Galatians can expect to happen in their lives—in order to give them some kind of map or guide or interpretive key with which to make sense of their own particular experiences. *The text actually expects and requires the Galatian readers to analyze their own lives and experiences and context in light of it, and to bring those experiences to bear in their understanding of the letter.* And if we view the text theologically, as Scripture, then to one degree or another it is also making the same request of readers today.[46]

So what is the upshot of all of this in light of the issues raised so far in this essay? It is that the place where divine and human agency issues are finally resolved, both in Paul and in the church, is *in practice*. The relationship between divine and human agency in Christians is just as live a practical-theological issue today as it ever was in the first century. Now, the argument is not that this sort of "dramatic" reading is easy. It is not that we can engage in a few quick moments of introspection and sort out, once and for all, what the Spirit does and what human agents are meant to be doing. Nevertheless, if theology is dramatic—if God's involvement in human lives is dramatic—then we should be able, at least very cautiously, to bring our own *particular* experiences, and those of our communities, and also those of our historical traditions,[47] into play as relevant factors for helping us to interpret Scripture in our particular lives and contexts.

To head off one or two objections, I am not saying that we should just take our own experiences and feelings and blithely read the text through them, in some naive eisegesis. Much of my own academic work to date has been on the

---

45. Without in any way wishing to exclude the latter or deny its value, in my view the category of "drama" has wider theological purchase when it is understood more generally, in the sense of a "dramatic" moment between two people or a "dramatic" political event, than when it is tied too closely or simply to language about theater and theatrical performance. In this respect Ford's approach is to be preferred to Vanhoozer's.

46. Important here also is the precedent in Gal. 3:2–4, where Paul explicitly appeals to the Galatians' experiences of the Spirit.

47. Such as the historical tradition of "affective Augustinianism," as it has been a resource for the interpretation outlined in this essay.

problem of self-deception as it relates to the issue of discerning the work of the Spirit in the world.[48] If there were space, there is much more that could be said here about the critical issue of self-deception in Christian experience of God. What I am advocating instead is something far more careful—namely, that the experiences of particular lives and communities can be genuinely useful, as one tool among others, for helping to interpret a text or a textual conundrum, *especially* when the text is already difficult, obscure, or difficult to square with other texts. This is a tool to be used with care, alongside and in light of the best tools of traditional biblical and historical scholarship.

Again, the theological justification for such a practice, especially for texts like this that explicitly describe aspects of the Christian life, is the belief that this God is a living God, and God's Spirit really is active in the world today.

Two Examples: The "Divided I" and Cranmer's Prayers

Let me conclude with two examples of what I might mean by reading Galatians 5 and the issues it raises "dramatically" or in light of practical experience. The first is perhaps a bit controversial, but at the very least it may get conversation going. It is that on the famous issue of whether there continues to be a conflict between flesh and Spirit in Christians, described in 5:17, or whether we should understand Paul as saying that that conflict is actually already decisively resolved for Christians in favor of the Spirit—this, of course, is also ultimately the great Romans 7 "divided I" question—we must take seriously the fact that *a huge number of Christians through the ages have reported experiences that match just such a conflict*. Augustine, Luther, Melanchthon, Calvin, Edwards, and many others all take this empirical observation for granted.[49] Gordon Fee censures J. B. Lightfoot—and Dunn, for that matter—for bringing in this sort of empirical argument to their commentaries on Romans 7 and

---

48. See Simeon Zahl, *Pneumatology and Theology of the Cross in the Preaching of Christoph Blumhardt: The Holy Spirit between Wittenberg and Azusa Street* (London: T&T Clark/Continuum, 2010), chaps. 2, 7, and 8; and idem, "The Spirit and the Cross: Engaging a Key Critique of Charismatic Pneumatology," in *The Holy Spirit in the World Today*, ed. Jane Williams (London: Alpha International, 2011), 111–29.

49. Augustine, *Serm.* 154 (on Rom. 7:14–25) in Hill, *Works of Saint Augustine*, vol. 5/5:68–78 (see also the reference to Gal. 5:16–18 in comparison with Rom. 7 in *Serm.* 151, in vol. 3/5:41); Melanchthon in *LC 1521*, 13, 16, 40 (*MB*, 27, 30, 48); Luther in WA 40.2:94–95 (LW 27:75) and WA 2:577 (LW 27:351); John Calvin on Rom. 7:15 (see also the whole of 7:14–25) in his 1539 *Commentary on Romans* and on Gal. 5:17 in the 1548 *Commentary on Galatians*; Jonathan Edwards, *The "Blank Bible,"* ed. Stephen Stein, The Works of Jonathan Edwards, vol. 24 (New Haven: Yale University Press, 2006), 1005–6; J. B. Lightfoot, *The Epistle to the Galatians*, rev. ed. (Cambridge: Macmillan, 1865), 200–201; Dunn, *Theology of Paul*, 476–77.

Galatians 5:17, finding it to be a kind of grasping at straws, unscholarly, and almost unseemly.⁵⁰ But from a theological perspective, Lightfoot and Dunn and others are simply taking seriously the idea that this God is real and alive today, and that the experiences of churches in the New Testament may relate in some small way to the experiences of churches today. Naturally, this sort of procedure can be done badly, and it is subject to a number of potential vulnerabilities, but the fact that a method or tool can be used badly does not mean it is a bad method or tool.

Of course, to say that it is possible for a Christian to experience what Paul is describing in Romans 7:14–25 and Galatians 5:17 is not necessarily to say that that conflict is the absolute sum total of Christian experience, or that it is the normative experience in all circumstances, or that it is even the only possible meaning of the passages in question. But since it is obviously possible for a Christian to experience this in practice—as, for example, Christopher Cook has shown memorably and persuasively in his book *Alcoholism, Addiction, and Christian Ethics*⁵¹—it seems very strange to say that Paul cannot possibly have meant that this is something a Christian can experience.

For a final example, we return to the great debates we have been discussing about the relationship between divine grace and human activity and agency in Paul. If you read Thomas Cranmer on these issues, including especially his well-known didactic homilies on faith, salvation, and good works, you will find the same poorly resolved dilemma we have been discussing. In the "Homily of Salvation," he writes, "These great and merciful benefits of GOD . . . move us to render our selves unto GOD wholly with all our will, hearts, might, and power, to serve him in all good deeds, obeying his commandments during our lives."⁵² This summary is preceded in the sermon, however, with a

50. Fee, *Empowering Presence*, 435n233.
51. Christopher C. H. Cook, *Alcoholism, Addiction, and Christian Ethics* (Cambridge: Cambridge University Press, 2006), 127–70. Cook makes a very strong case for the view that "Paul's theology of sin, and the subjective experience of the divided self described in Romans 7:14–25 . . . , would appear to be of a very similar nature to the subjective experiences of desire and compulsion which are associated with alcohol dependence" (145)—and alcoholism, of course, is no respecter of whether or not a person is a Christian. He is rightly careful to acknowledge the complexities and difficulties of identifying addiction straightforwardly with sin, while also making an inarguable case that ignoring the enormous similarities between the experience of addicts and the "divided I" descriptions in Paul is a theological mistake. On this, see also Gerhard Forde, *On Being a Theologian of the Cross: Reflections on Luther's Heidelberg Disputation, 1518* (Grand Rapids: Eerdmans, 1997), who employs the phenomenon of addiction as one way into understanding Luther's anthropology; and in a less academic key, John Z., *Grace in Addiction: The Good News of Alcoholics Anonymous for Everybody* (Charlottesville, VA: Mockingbird Ministries/CreateSpace Publishing, 2012).
52. Cranmer, *Miscellaneous Writings*, 134.

massive caveat: "[As Christians] our own imperfection is so great, through the corruption of original sin, that all is imperfect that is within us, faith, charity, hope, dread, thoughts, words, and works, and therefore not apt to merit or discern any part of our justification for us."[53] In other words, in his didactic writings, Cranmer articulates a classic "affective Augustinian" picture about the compelling power of the Spirit alone to transform hearts and desires for good works, and then simply tacks on a rather clumsy addendum emphasizing that in fact sin also continues to persist quite deeply in Christians.

But the story is quite different indeed when you look at how Cranmer deals with these themes in pastoral practice, in his famous liturgical book, the Anglican Book of Common Prayer. Consider the Prayer of Preparation, for use at the beginning of the Communion service. Alert listeners will recognize here and in the subsequent prayer the influence of our Galatians passage:

> ALMIGHTIE God, unto whom all hartes bee open, and all desyres knowen, and from whom no secretes are hid: clense the thoughtes of our hartes, by the inspiracion of thy holy spirite: that we may perfectly love thee, and worthely magnifie thy holy name: through Christ our Lorde. Amen.[54]

Equally relevant is the following collect, in the Cranmerian tradition, from the 1662 Book of Common Prayer:[55]

> O Almighty God, who alone canst order the unruly wills and affections of sinful men: Grant unto thy people, that they may love the thing which thou commandest, and desire that which thou dost promise; that so, among the sundry and manifold changes of the world, our hearts may surely there be fixed, where true joys are to be found; through Jesus Christ our Lord. Amen.

In these prayers we see the fundamental themes of Galatians 5:16–25: the centrality of desires, affections, and hearts, and the necessity of their transformation; God's Spirit appealed to as the sole agent capable of performing such a transformation; and ethical behavior, above all love for others, characterized affectively, and as fruit of the activity of the Spirit. The prayers also take for granted that Christians too, to some degree, continue to have "unruly wills and affections" and "hartes" that need to be "cleansed," though rather than dwelling on this, the prayers hope and ask for that situation to change.

---

53. Ibid., 143.
54. There are further echoes of Ps. 51:10 and 1 John 4:17–18 as well.
55. The deceptively humble title of this one is "The Collect for the Fourth Sunday after Easter." The opening clause about unruly wills and affections reflects a seventeenth-century revision, albeit one deeply in tune with Cranmer's own theology.

Furthermore, agency is complicated and multilayered here: primarily there is the admission in no uncertain terms that only God can perform the needed changes: dependence on God's Spirit here is absolute. But at the same time, a prayer is itself a kind of act of human agency: it does involve "doing something" as opposed to just sitting passively, doing nothing. And yet, the agency needed to pray this prayer is not some great act of moral assertion and obedience: it is actually extremely easy, as an agent, to pray a prayer that has been written for you in a church service that you have already decided to attend.[56] Altogether, what this means is that in significant ways the prayer matches the complexity of Paul's account of agency. But it also succeeds better than most academic accounts of the issue—such as the appeal to mere "balance" between passivity and activity, or overoptimistic accounts of the reconstitution of the ethical agent in the Spirit—and it does so by turning the problem of divine and human agency into a petitionary act. In other words, *Cranmer resolves the agency issue more effectively in his liturgy than in his didactic theology, and he does so by taking the affective Augustinian tradition here and making it into a prayer.*

Altogether, the collect and the prayer of preparation simply work. These are lovely, uncontroversial prayers that have been transmuted out of some of the most complex and fraught theological questions in the whole New Testament. If, as David Ford puts it, the Christian "drama . . . invites us to become engaged," then such prayers answer that invitation beautifully, and with real implications for theological reflection on issues of agency. In the prayer for God's Spirit to cleanse hearts and transform desires, the continued existence of the flesh and of "unruly wills and affections" is acknowledged and taken seriously, and the ball is, as it were, put back in God's court, to act according to his divine freedom. But this is not done in a resigned or hopeless or simply passive way: the prayer itself expresses already a desire, in the Spirit, for divine transformation, and a hope and confidence in God's own power and desire to do so. The prayer does not immediately resolve the problem of fleshly affection—the transformation asked for is still in the future, in the divine response—but it opens the individual and community praying to the reality of this possibility, in the Spirit. Furthermore, the simultaneously individual and communal character of liturgical prayer parallels the complexly individual and communal character of the work of the Spirit in Galatians. And the fact that these petitions are prayed repeatedly and regularly, from week to week and from

---

56. There are further complexities as well, e.g., in the role of affections, motivations, and internal states in the experience of public, liturgical prayer (e.g., issues of sincerity, boredom, or fervor), which themselves are connected in multilayered ways to divine and human agency issues.

year to year, means that one can continue to pray these prayers and others like them even as in certain ways they have already been answered and continue to be answered in new ways, as well as if and when they are not answered.

The praying of such prayers, *in practice*, which ask God to transform human desires by his Spirit, are little moments of ongoing theological "drama" in which one engages with the living God over a lifetime. In this drama they actually provide one legitimate and compelling answer, both theologically and practically, to the dilemma about human and divine agency as expressed in Galatians 5:16–25. After all, the true drama is now being played out not just in a biblical text or just in first-century Galatia but in the contemporary lives of real agents in the world, both human and divine.

23

Life in the Spirit and Life in Wisdom

Reading Galatians and James as a Dialogue

MARIAM J. KAMELL

There may be no two other epistles in the New Testament that have been so consistently contrasted to each other theologically as Galatians and James. Augustine noted the disparity between Paul's teaching in Galatians 2–3 and James 2:14–26 and suggested the following solution: "Seeing that the apostle Paul, in preaching that a man is justified by faith without works, is not rightly understood by those who received this statement such that they supposed they could be saved by faith when once they had believed in Christ, even if they were wickedly engaged and living in a criminal and disgraceful manner, . . . [James 2:14–26] explains in what way the precise meaning of the apostle Paul is to be understood."[1] Luther described James as one who "wanted to guard against those who relied on faith without works, but was unequal to the task,"[2] and this perspective remains dominant. More recently, Martin Hengel viewed the Epistle of James as paraenesis written to disguise an intentional

---

1. Augustine, *Eighty-Three Different Questions* 76: "*Locus iste huius epistulae eundem sensum Pauli apostoli, quomodo sit intellegendus, exponit.*"
2. Martin Luther, *Word and Sacrament I*, ed. E. Theodore Bachmann, in LW 35 (1960): 397.

anti-Pauline polemic, to attack Paul's behavior and mission and to counter the "gefährlichen Tendenzen seiner Theologie."[3]

Unfortunately, the majority of the scholarship regarding the relationship between James and Paul tends to focus either on the purportedly stormy relationship between James and Paul as read in Galatians 2, or on their different views of law and Abraham in Galatians 3 and James 2.[4] By implication, the conclusions have largely remained binary: either the two engaged in a power conflict in the early church, or James was a clumsy corrector of Paul's message of a law-free salvation. The question of the theology of sanctification as presented in these two epistles is generally framed only by contrasting Galatians 2–3 with James 1–2, as witnessed to by Augustine, Luther, and Hengel above.

In chapters 5–6 of Galatians, however, where Paul discusses life in the Spirit, one might gain an impression of theological congruence between James and Paul. Peter Davids, for instance, notes the similarities between Paul's "fruit of the Spirit" (Gal. 5:22–23) and James's characteristics of wisdom (3:13–18),[5] while Gordon Fee emphasizes Paul's consistent stress on the necessity of *doing good* in the Spirit (Gal. 5–6), which parallels James's call for a faith that works (1:22–25; 2:14–26; 3:13).[6] Examining how Paul and James describe the faithful life may move us forward in developing a biblical theology of sanctification that is thoroughly integrated with soteriology in both epistles. This essay seeks to highlight a number of parallels that arise between Galatians 5:13–6:10 and the Epistle of James, and then concludes with some thoughts on how these similarities may affect how we read Galatians and do biblical theology.

Paul and the Galatian Freedom

Frank Matera observes that the majority of articles on Galatians focus on chapters 1–4 and theorizes that "one of the reasons Galatians 5–6 has played such a minor role ... has to do with the assumption—sometimes hidden, at other times overt—that Paul's theological arguments are confined to chapters 1–4 while the material of 5–6 is primarily ethical and exhortative" and therefore

---

3. M. Hengel, "Der Jakobusbrief als antipaulinische Polemik," in *Tradition and Interpretation in the New Testament*, ed. Gerald F. Hawthorne and Otto Betz (Grand Rapids: Eerdmans, 1987), 265.

4. Cf. Joachim Jeremias, "Paul and James," *ExpTim* 66 (1955): 368–71; see also Richard Longenecker, "The 'Faith of Abraham' Theme in Paul, James and Hebrews: A Study in the Circumstantial Nature of New Testament Teaching," *JETS* 20 (1977): 203–12; Ryan Jenkins, "Faith and Works in Paul and James," *BSac* 159 (2002): 62–78.

5. Peter H. Davids, *James* (Peabody, MA: Hendrickson, 1989), 20.

6. Gordon D. Fee, *God's Empowering Presence* (Peabody, MA: Hendrickson, 1994), 877.

not part of "Paul's fundamental argument."[7] In contrast, Matera argues that it is precisely in these final chapters that Paul's argument against circumcision comes to its culmination. Chapters 5–6 of Galatians are not simply a paraenetic parenthesis but are theologically essential to understanding Paul's argument in the epistle, for 5:1–6:10 describe "not ordinary ethical conduct but behavior which characterizes those led by the Spirit,"[8] and this behavior results from being *in Christ* (cf. Gal. 5:24–25). These people provide a direct contrast to those who urge obedience to the law. Paul's call to walk in the Spirit in 5:16 and 25 is thus what Fee calls an "argument by way of exhortation."[9] As such, the paraenesis serves as the theological outworking of the truth Paul has been arguing: the *only* way one can live a godly life is by the Spirit, which does *not* come through returning to Torah, as the legalists propose (see Gal. 3; 4:21–26; 5:18). Paul is very clear in 5:1 and 13 that freedom in Christ is exactly that, *a freedom* that does not bring with it regulations dividing the community (cf. the controversy of 2:12–21 and the celebration of 3:23–29, culminating in the argument of 5:1–6). If freedom comes through Christ and is evidenced by life in the Spirit, then the law as embodied by circumcision or separate table fellowship cannot bring about life and, in fact, enslaves.

But what does this freedom look like? First, it is freedom *for service in love* to one another (5:6, 13–14). This is a crucial distinction in an age in which "freedom" has been equated with license to live as we please.[10] Rather than freedom as "an opportunity for self-indulgence"[11] (5:13) or for gratifying "the desires of the flesh" (5:16), this freedom is *from* a focus on the self and its desires *to* service of one another ("through love become slaves to one another," διὰ τῆς ἀγάπης δουλεύετε ἀλλήλοις [5:13]). Paul sets this up as a contrast of freedoms in order to show the true freedom of life in the Spirit, in stark distinction to life controlled by one's desires. Galatians 5:17 clearly pits the two as opposing paths, with the caution that this opposition from the flesh is "to prevent you from doing what you want" (5:17). To illustrate this warning, Paul then

---

7. Frank J. Matera, "The Culmination of Paul's Argument to the Galatians: Gal. 5:1–6:17," *JSNT* 32 (1988): 79. For Matera, Gal. 5:16–24 provides the alternate, theological reading of reality, life in the Spirit, in contrast to life under the law, and it is this alternate reality that provides the contrast: one is either under the law *or* led by the Spirit.

8. Matera, "Culmination of Paul's Argument," 86.

9. Gordon D. Fee, "Freedom and the Life of Obedience (Galatians 5:1–6:18)," *RevExp* 91 (1994): 213n4.

10. Cf. Richard Bauckham, *God and the Crisis of Freedom: Biblical and Contemporary Perspectives* (Louisville: Westminster John Knox, 2002), 25. Bauckham warns against a selfish freedom that is interested only in one's own desires, cautioning, "Liberation worthy of the name requires people who have been freed to live for others."

11. Unless otherwise noted, all biblical quotations in this essay are from the NRSV.

gives a list of the "works" of the flesh, to which the "antidote"[12] is the Spirit and *its* way of being. Life in the Spirit leads to a very specific and clear way of living, which the list in 5:22–23 illustrates. And for Paul this changed life is not optional. Indeed, he warns that those who continue to live according to the desires of the flesh "will not inherit the kingdom of God" (5:21; cf. 1 Cor. 6:9–10; 15:50). This is no mere ethical exhortation; how those "in Christ" *live* is inherent to Paul's soteriology. Those who persist in living according to either Torah—in terms of its outward markers of circumcision and separated table fellowship, not in terms of its rightful and necessary fulfillment in neighbor-love—or the desires of the flesh reveal that they are not "in Christ." And so Paul concludes, "Let us not become conceited, competing against one another, envying one another" (5:26). Conceited, vain competition stands in vivid contrast to the Spirit's freedom for service for the other.

To summarize the contrast between these two ways of living, Paul begs them to live as guided by the Spirit (5:18), having crucified "the flesh with its passions and desires" (5:24), which is necessary to "inherit the kingdom" (5:21). Galatians 5:1–6:10, therefore, is the continuation of Paul's fundamental argument throughout Galatians: the locus of salvation is in Christ and his Spirit, not in the external Torah regulations or libertine freedom.[13] The ethics of this section are in no way secondary for Paul's argument. Rather, surprisingly, Paul reserves his harshest language for this section because *how one lives* expresses the new reality in Christ. The circumcision faction may have agreed that salvation came through grace, by the work of Christ on the cross, but they still sought to supplement and thereby subvert that grace with mandatory Torah regulations. Likewise, those who took freedom to mean unrestrained liberty revealed a fundamental misunderstanding of their new identity in Christ.

Reading Galatians 5:13–6:10 with the Epistle of James

There are a number of parallels in language and theme between Galatians 5–6 and the Epistle of James that, when read in relationship to one another, could make for a richer understanding of sanctification and its relationship to soteriology. James 1 is crucial, therefore, not only for understanding the epistle but also for a dialogue with Galatians, for it describes the gracious birth of God's people by his will and God's generous giving of wisdom and the implanted word, which will train and empower people in how they ought to live.

---

12. Fee, "Freedom and the Life of Obedience," 202.
13. Matera, "Culmination of Paul's Argument," 88.

The key to James is the presupposition of a new birth by God's will, which is the fulfillment of his new-covenant promise to Jeremiah, the implanted word with the power to save their souls (James 1:21).[14] This lies behind the ethical exhortations: since they have received this rebirth, they will act accordingly because it empowers them to live free of the cycle of sin and death.[15] As for Paul, so also with James, living out their freedom in service to one another in community is paramount (James 1:26–27; chap. 2; 4:1–12). For both Paul and James, Christianity—life in the Spirit—is worked out together.[16]

On the opposite side of life in the Spirit, there are also parallels of language regarding desire and its (negative) role in the life of the redeemed. In Galatians, the only three uses of "desire" occur in passages in which the desires of the flesh are explicitly opposed to the desires of the Spirit,[17] concluding with the assertion that "those who belong to Christ Jesus *have crucified* the flesh with its passions and desires"[18] (5:24, emphasis added). Our natural desires oppose those of the Spirit. Gordon Fee summarizes Paul's perspective thus: "Although the flesh is still about, and stands in mortal opposition to the Spirit, Christ's death has brought about our death—both to Torah (2:19) and to the flesh (5:24)."[19] For James, two of his three uses of "desire" language occur in a similar setting. In 1:14–15, James depicts the life cycle of desire (ἐπιθυμία), sin, and death, a life cycle that is fundamentally and even eschatologically opposed to the life that comes through the rebirth given by God in 1:12 and 18. Desire is the path that leads to death, while endurance leads to "the crown of life" (1:12).

James's other two uses of "desire" language come in 4:1–3, where ἐπιθυμέω is paired with ἡδονή ("pleasure, desire"). Here James describes the life in community that requires immediate repentance and humility. In a grammatically challenging section, he posits that the audience's internal conflicts stem from their own unbounded desires. Much like the description of the false "wisdom" in 3:15–16, here conflict, envy, greed, and destruction characterize those who live as driven by their desires. Likewise for Paul, a congregation

---

14. Jason A. Whitlark, "ἔμφυτος λόγος: A New Covenant Motif in the Letter of James," *HBT* 32 (2010): 144–65; Mariam J. Kamell, "Incarnating Jeremiah's Promised New Covenant in the 'Law' of James: A Short Study," *EQ* 83 (2011): 19–28. See, e.g., *Barn.* 9.9, which speaks of the "implanted gift of his covenant [τὴν ἔμφυτον δωρεὰν τῆς διαθήκης αὐτοῦ]."
15. Mariam J. Kamell, "The Implications of Grace for the Ethics of James," *Bib* 92 (2011): 274–87; cf. Richard Bauckham, *James* (London: Routledge, 1999), 141; Douglas J. Moo, *The Letter of James* (Grand Rapids: Eerdmans, 2000), 32.
16. Cf. James Riley Strange, *The Moral World of James* (New York: Peter Lang, 2010), 21.
17. See ἐπιθυμία in Gal. 5:16, 24 and ἐπιθυμέω in 5:17.
18. Emphasis added.
19. Fee, "Freedom and the Life of Obedience," 205.

controlled by the flesh leads to his warning in Galatians 5:15 that "if . . . you bite and devour one another, take care that you are not consumed by one another," a warning where the apodosis is the certain outcome of the protasis.[20] Paul's list of the works of the flesh includes "enmities, strife, jealousy, anger, quarrels, dissensions, factions, [and] envy" (5:20–21). Many of the terms in this sin list are paralleled in James 3:13–4:12 as he describes the character of those living by false, earthly "wisdom." Selfish desires are tied to the *old* life, which, according to both Paul and James, is bound by the law of the flesh and destined for death. To live as controlled by desires, characterized by competition and strife, should be a serious warning sign. Wisdom, for James, frees the individual and community from the control of self-centered desire, just as the Spirit does for Paul.

In contrast to a life driven by cravings, James and Paul agree that Jesus's summative law guides the Christian life. Paul, in Galatians 5:14, affirms, "For the whole law is summed up in a single commandment, 'You shall love your neighbor as yourself.'" For Paul, keeping this law immediately prevents a person from falling into the sins characterizing the flesh, for those are the result of selfish desires for self-gratification. In contrast, the law of Christ is all-encompassing, a complete transformation of perspective to the *other*'s good. Galatians 5:14 and Romans 13:9 are the only two times Paul reiterates this law, which first appears in Leviticus 19:18 and occurs in each Synoptic Gospel (Matt. 22:35–40; Mark 12:28–34; Luke 10:25–28). James 2:8 is the only *other* place in the Epistles where this law appears. Given their history of interpretation, it is intriguing that Romans, Galatians, and James are the only three epistles wherein this summative law appears. Paul, in his supposedly most doctrinal arguments, concludes at the same point that James does. James says not a word about circumcision or food laws, the major issues in Galatians, but for him, as for Paul, the faith "of our glorious Lord Jesus Christ" (2:1) is summed up in neighbor-love. External regulations that divide the community are necessarily ruled out, because love of the neighbor (as defined by Jesus in the parable of the good Samaritan in Luke 10:29–37) epitomizes the community of the redeemed.[21]

---

20. Ronald Y. K. Fung, *The Epistle to the Galatians* (Grand Rapids: Eerdmans, 1988), 248: "Whatever its cause, such conduct—as of a pack of wild animals 'biting and devouring' one another (NIV)—is the opposite of 'serving one another through love' and can only lead to the disastrous end of mutual annihilation." Or more recently, Martinus C. de Boer, *Galatians: A Commentary* (Louisville: Westminster John Knox, 2011), 351: "Paul describes the world outside the church as determined by 'the Flesh,' a world from which mutual love is absent. It is a world in which biting and tearing at one another inevitably leads to mutual consumption, bringing death and destruction."

21. See Miroslav Volf, *Exclusion and Embrace: A Theological Exploration of Identity, Otherness, and Reconciliation* (Nashville: Abingdon, 1996), 44–50, for his discussion of the

For both Paul and James, there are other discernible marks of those who are living according to the gift of God. For Paul, that gift is the Spirit, which bears καρπός ("fruit, harvest" [Gal. 5:22–23]). For James, that gift is the wisdom "from above" (3:17), which bears its own καρπός of righteousness (3:18). Peter Davids suggests a type of "wisdom pneumatology" in his commentary on James,[22] and this proposal has merit in that throughout the New Testament the Spirit takes on much of the prior function of Wisdom (as characterized in Proverbs and subsequent Wisdom literature) in revealing God and empowering righteous living.[23] Intriguingly, while James's list in 3:17 seems driven by euphony as a mnemonic device, 2:8 spells out *love* as the dominant characteristic of those living by the "royal law," and 1:2 begins the epistle with the words "consider it nothing but joy" (Πᾶσαν χαρὰν ἡγήσασθε), where the only way to gain this perspective is to ask God for his wisdom (1:5). So for James, although ἀγάπη ("love") and χάρις ("grace, joy") do not appear on his list of the fruit of wisdom in 3:17, they are intimately tied to the life of wisdom and of crucial importance in the epistle. Likewise, the themes of "endurance" and "faithfulness" dominate the Epistle of James.[24] One can create a startlingly uniform picture of what these two seemingly disparate epistles picture as the life of those in Christ: what Paul lists, James spells out.

There is one more minor parallel to Galatians 5. Twice in his epistle, James speaks of those who will receive something that has been promised to those loving God. In 1:12, those who endure will receive the crown of life, and in 2:5 the poor who are rich in faith will receive the kingdom. In both

---

universality and particularity of the elect community as reinterpreted by Paul in Gal. 3–4: "The 'One' in whom Paul seeks to locate the unity of all humanity is *not disincarnate transcendence, but the crucified and resurrected Jesus Christ*. The 'principle' of unity has a *name*, and the name designates a person with a *body that has suffered on the cross*. . . . The crucified Messiah creates unity by giving his own self" (47, emphasis original).

22. Davids, *James*, 19–20, who follows the proposal of J. A. Kirk, "The Meaning of Wisdom in James: Examination of a Hypothesis," NTS 16 (1970): 24–38.

23. Cf. Mariam J. Kamell, "Wisdom in James: An Examination and Comparison of the Roles of Wisdom and the Holy Spirit" (MA thesis, Denver Seminary, 2003). William Baker, "Searching for the Spirit in the Epistle of James: Is 'Wisdom' Equivalent?," *TynBul* 59 (2008): 293–315, questions a full equation of the two while acknowledging overlap. However, Fee, *God's Empowering Presence*, 813, argues that the Spirit is "the new covenant *replacement* of Torah," a particularly intriguing statement given the equation that had happened between Wisdom and Torah in texts such as Sir. 1:26; 15:1–4; 24:1–34.

24. R. T. Kendall, *Justification by Works: How Works Vindicate True Faith* (Carlisle, UK: Paternoster, 2001), 9, argues that the central thesis of the epistle is James 1:4 and that "the theme *patience* underlies all that the writer says. He wants to produce patience in us, which will in turn provide us with the kind of Christian life that reflects the special grace of God." He also points out that this theme dominates the close of the epistle in chap. 5.

verses the emphasis rests on the faithful character of the one who promised the inheritance.[25] This is remarkably close to the notion of "inheriting the kingdom," a term that has significant soteriological emphasis in the Gospels and that throughout the Pauline corpus can serve as a warning against returning to the law or living unrighteously, *for those who do so will not inherit it* (Rom. 4:13; 1 Cor. 6:9–10; Eph. 5:5). In Galatians, the warning in 5:21 is straightforward: those who live according to the desires of the flesh will not inherit the kingdom, for they reveal themselves not to be in Christ or of the Spirit. In James 2:5, the context of the inheritance language is similarly double-edged: James's audience *has failed* to appreciate the ones to whom God's promise stands, and so they themselves risk judgment. The kingdom, according to James, is promised to those loving God; but those loving God will also love the poor.

In Galatians 6 the parallels continue. For instance, in 6:1, as Paul draws toward his conclusion, he calls his audience to "restore" (καταρτίζετε) the one "detected in a transgression" (προλημφθῇ ἄνθρωπος ἔν τινι παραπτώματι); similarly, the Epistle of James concludes with the exhortation in 5:19–20 to "bring back" (ἐπιστρέψῃ) the fellow believer who "wanders from the truth" (πλανηθῇ ἀπὸ τῆς ἀληθείας), also known as "the sinner" (ἁμαρτωλόν). This kind of comparison, while not strong on its own, continues the emphasis on living the Christian life in community: love of neighbor entails assuming responsibility for those who stray. The members of the body are to watch out for one another and help one another stay on track, restoring and strengthening one another.

There are several more general, conceptual parallels. For instance, one of James's major themes is the danger of self-deception, against which there are three explicit warnings in 1:13–27 (esp. 1:16, 22, 26), along with several illustrative warnings (1:13–15, 19–20, 23–24). Self-deception about one's state has dangerous soteriological implications.[26] James 1:9–11 addresses the perspective that people ought to have: the humble celebrate their elevation, while the already-elevated should be aware of the transience of their position. In language reminiscent of James 1:9–11, Paul also warns against self-deception in Galatians 6:3, cautioning, "If those who are nothing think they are something, they deceive themselves." The temptation is to misunderstand one's true status before God, becoming boastful and unwarrantedly arrogant. Paul in Galatians 6:2–4 seeks to balance a humility that is willing to bear another

---

25. So also Chris A. Vlachos, *Exegetical Guide to the Greek New Testament: James* (Nashville: Broadman & Holman, 2013), 40, 73.

26. Dan G. McCartney, "Self-Deception in James," *CTR* 8 (2011): 31–43.

person's burdens with the humility that is able to evaluate one's own work honestly before boasting. James puts it more baldly: "Humble yourselves before the Lord, and he will exalt you" (4:10). For James, the call is always to become one of the humble.

Both authors also warn of a certain foundational reality, a principle commonly depicted in Wisdom literature: one reaps what one sows. These two texts, Galatians 6:7–9 and James 1:12–16, are worth seeing in parallel, since they are essentially the same argument in reverse order:

Galatians 6:7–9	James 1:12–16
[7b]God is not mocked, for you reap whatever you sow. [8]If you sow to your own flesh, you will reap corruption from the flesh; but if you sow to the Spirit, you will reap eternal life from the Spirit.	[13]No one, when tempted, should say, "I am being tempted by God"; for God cannot be tempted by evil and he himself tempts no one. [14]But one is tempted by one's own desire, being lured and enticed by it; [15]then, when that desire has conceived, it gives birth to sin, and that sin, when it is fully grown, gives birth to death.
[9]*So let us not grow weary in doing what is right, for we will reap at harvest-time, if we do not give up.*	[12]*Blessed is anyone who endures temptation. Such a one has stood the test and will receive the crown of life that the Lord has promised to those who love him.*
[7a]Do not be deceived [Μὴ πλανᾶσθε].	[16]*Do not be deceived* [Μὴ πλανᾶσθε], my beloved.

Here in transposed order (with some added emphasis), both Paul and James warn their audiences against being deceived in their thinking (Gal. 6:7; James 1:16). In the center of these passages, both authors depict the reality of sowing what one reaps (flesh → corruption, Gal. 6:8; desire → death, James 1:13–15), and both spell out the crucial need for endurance all the way to the end (Gal. 6:9; James 1:12). Without enduring in the good, the harvest and the crown of life will remain elusive.

Ultimately, both authors want their audiences to take seriously their changed reality as members of a new creation, for then they will themselves to live no longer according to rules of the flesh and its desires, but empowered by wisdom and the Spirit. And so Paul can conclude in Galatians 6:15: "For neither circumcision nor uncircumcision is anything; but a new creation is everything [ἀλλὰ καινὴ κτίσις]!" And James, in contrast to the life cycle of desire leading to death, can celebrate in 1:18: "In fulfillment of his own purpose he gave us birth by the word of truth, so that we would become a kind of first fruits of his creatures [ἀπαρχήν τινα τῶν αὐτοῦ κτισμάτων]." Paul and James agree on the identity of their audience: they are the first fruits of a triumphal new creation, and this identity should characterize the audience members, shaping them in their new existence in Christ.

Conclusions

Both James and Paul make clear that they are not writing mere ethical niceties; their paraenesis provides pictures of who will receive the kingdom. For both authors, the beginning point is always grace, which cannot be compromised either by returning to Torah regulations or by following a different law than the implanted law of freedom. For both Paul and James, there is an empowering agent without which it is impossible to live righteously. Paul emphasizes the role of the Spirit in empowering, while for James it is wisdom that empowers. To live according to any other control is to guarantee failure, because the only other alternatives are being controlled by the flesh and its desire or by the Torah, neither of which has the power to save and therefore are simply means of death. The Spirit is given by God as a response to faith, not to works (Gal. 3:1–5), just as wisdom is given by God as a response to faith because one lacks it (James 1:5–8). In both cases, the empowering agent cannot be earned, only given. Once one has the Spirit or wisdom, the problem for both authors becomes people's tendency to slide into other, easier ways of control: a return to selfish desire or Torah obedience, both of which allow an element of self-promotion. In contrast to self-promotion, the law of neighbor-love is highlighted, whereby the new law is summed up by focus on the other. For both, then, the sin lists entail various types of self-indulgence that lead to strife, while the virtue lists are characteristics that create harmonious community. And the picture ends with echoes of Jesus's teaching on inheritance: no one inherits the kingdom except those who live according to life in the kingdom, who live by the power of wisdom and the Spirit.

Finally, this sort of reading has impact for biblical theology: given the unfolding of these texts, any doctrine of soteriology that does not incorporate sanctification as an essential part runs the risk of becoming unbalanced. Luther's concern to avoid linking justification with works led him to introduce the last two chapters of Galatians in his commentary as "all kinds of admonitions and precepts" that came "*after* [Paul] had taught faith and instructed the conscience."[27] He conceived of these injunctions not as of soteriological import but as an addendum to prevent Christians from being seen as "enemies of decency and of public peace."[28] In contrast, the more recent interpretations by Matera and Fee argue that chapters 5–6 of Galatians actually form the climax of Paul's argument and help one to develop a Pauline soteriology that is much more coherent and comprehensive for the entirety of his writings.

---

27. Martin Luther, *A Commentary on St. Paul's Epistle to the Galatians*, trans. Theodore Graebner (Grand Rapids: Zondervan, 1965), text on 5:1–13 and 5:13, emphasis added.
28. Ibid.

This exercise may also point to a common teaching core in the early church that has not been sufficiently explored: if these close parallels exist between Galatians and James, it may well be possible to show this coherence across other such diverse texts. Comparing the role of the Spirit in Galatians 5 and the wisdom ideology of James may further help to bridge the perceived divide between Paul and James.

Contributors

Jean-Noël Aletti
Pontifical Biblical Institute, Rome

John M. G. Barclay
Durham University

Michael B. Cover
University of Notre Dame PhD, then at Valparaiso University

Edwin Chr. van Driel
Pittsburgh Theological Seminary

Mark W. Elliott
St. Mary's College, School of Divinity
University of St. Andrews

Javier A. Garcia
PhD candidate, Cambridge University

Beverly Roberts Gaventa
Baylor University

Timothy G. Gombis
Grand Rapids Theological Seminary

Scott Hafemann
St. Mary's College, School of Divinity
University of St. Andrews

Richard B. Hays
The Divinity School
Duke University

Mariam J. Kamell
Regent College, Vancouver

Bruce McCormack
Princeton Theological Seminary

Matthew V. Novenson
School of Divinity
University of Edinburgh

Oliver O'Donovan
New College
University of Edinburgh

Karla Pollmann
University of Kent (Canterbury)

Volker Rabens
Friedrich-Schiller-Universität Jena, Germany
Theological Faculty of North-West University, South Africa

Thomas Söding
Ruhr-Universität Bochum

Todd D. Still
Truett Seminary
Baylor University

Darren O. Sumner
Fuller Seminary Northwest

Scott R. Swain
Reformed Theological Seminary-Orlando

Timothy Wengert
Retired, The Lutheran Theological Seminary at Philadelphia

N. T. Wright
St. Mary's College, School of Divinity
University of St. Andrews

Simeon Zahl
St. John's College
University of Oxford

Subject Index

Abraham
  apocalyptic and, 177
  faith and, 97–100, 105–10, 124
  imputation and, 157–58
  the Messiah and, 10–14, 19–20, 125–26
acquittal, justification as, 182
actualization, ecumenism and, 67–70
addiction, ethics and, 349
ad fontes, principle of, 49–50
adoption, gospel as, 210–12
affective Augustinianism, 336–52
Against Latomus (Luther), 139–40
agency
  apocalyptic and, 203, 216
  ethics and, 275–77, 290–93, 298–304, 340–52
  the Trinity and, 259–66
ages, apocalyptic, 203–4, 216–17, 239–48
alcoholism, ethics and, 349
allegory, 55–56, 220–29
Ambrosiaster, 41, 44–47
anthropology
  biblical interpretation and, 49, 58
  Christology and, 141–42
  ethics and, 275–78, 340
  the gospel and, 195–96, 197–99

participation and, 213–15, 217–18
antinomies, apocalyptic. *See* apocalyptic writing; law, the
apocalyptic writing
  allegory and, 227–29
  Christology and, 232–35, 236–37
  hermeneutics and, 204–6, 209–13
  justification and, 10–11, 163–83
  marks of, 202–4, 206–9, 215–18
  participation and, 213–15
  time and, 239–48
apostle, vocation of, 64–65
appellative ethics, 294–95
applied theology, 149
arbitrary, justification as, 175–76, 183
argumentation, ethics and, 296–97
argumentum, 92–96
asceticism, 49, 58
ascriptive ethics, 294–95
assumptions, ethical, 293–94
atonement, 174n40, 178–81
Augustine, 41, 53–54, 56–58, 60, 71–72
Augustinianism, affective, 336–52
authority, ethics and, 297

authorization, paraphrase as, 104–5

balance, ethical, 342–43
baptism, 56–57, 66, 71, 178
Barmen Declaration, 198–99
Barth, Karl, 150–51, 177–83, 249–57
Biblical Foundations of the Doctrine of Justification, 78–79
birth, double, 255–56
blessings, 103, 105–9
boasting, 314–15
Budapest Anonymous, 41
Bultmann, Rudolf, 75

Calvin, John, 146
canon, the, 49, 50, 59
Carmen adversus Marcionitas, 41, 58–60
catechesis, 281–82
Christology
  apocalyptic and, 167–68
  curse and, 51–52, 103, 112–15
  faith and, 44, 125–28, 158
  incorporation and, 14–23
  justification and, 3–23, 135–42, 143–45, 175–77, 182–83
  the law and, 123–24
  narrative and, 4–7, 9–11, 230–38

objective, 178–79
preexistence and, 260
sonship and, 21–22, 67, 210–12, 216
time and, 252–56
the Trinity and, 260–65
Christ Present in Faith (Mannermaa), 132–42
church, the. *See* ecclesiology
Church Dogmatics (Barth), 150–51
circumcision, justification and, 66
City of God (Augustine), 60
co-crucifixion, 122n10, 166
comfort, gospel as, 112, 115
commentaries, early church, 40–61
Communion, Holy, 66
community, ethics and, 306–17, 355–57, 360. *See also* ecclesiology
confessionalization, 146–47
consolation, gospel as, 112, 115
constitutive ethics, 294–95
convention, flesh as, 282–83
cosmological apocalyptic, 169–71
council, apostolic, 65–66
Cranmer, Thomas, 349–52
creation
  apocalyptic and, 168, 174–75, 176–77, 179, 203
  Christology and, 216–17, 233, 236
  community and, 317
  the gospel and, 197
  the Spirit and, 283–84, 361
  time and, 250–56
  the Trinity and, 263–64
cross, the
  apocalyptic and, 165–66, 174–77, 179–80, 212–13, 216–17
  creation and, 233
  eschatology and, 235
  flesh, spirit and, 283–84
  as gospel, 191–95, 196–97
  incarnation and, 135–36, 137–39, 140
  justification and, 155–58, 167–68

culture, ethics and, 306–17
curse/cursed
  Christ as, 51–52, 103, 112–15
  law as, 83–87, 100–103, 108
Cyprian, 56–57

de Boer, Martinus C., 169–77
De gigantibus (Philo), 224–25
deification, 132–42. *See also* participation
desire, ethics and, 336–52, 357–58
despair, gospel and, 112, 115
detour, Pauline, 319–21
dimensions, ecumenical, 64–70
discernment, believer's, 324
distancing perspective, Pauline, 319–21
divided I, 348–49
divine agency. *See* agency
divinization. *See* participation
docetism, 49, 59
doctrine, seats of, 258–59
double birth, 255–56
drama, agency and, 345–48, 351–52
duplex nativitas, 255–56

ecclesiology
  ecumenism and, 81
  ethics and, 306–17, 355–57, 360
  justification and, 40–61, 67, 69–72
  the Messiah and, 18–23
  participation and, 217–18
ecumenism, 62–81, 159–62, 171
election, 181, 183, 254
emotion, ethics and, 336–52, 357–58
enthymeme, 97
eschatology, 125–28, 129–31, 234–35, 247
eternity, 250–56
ethics
  agency and, 275–77, 290–93, 298–304, 340–52
  desire and, 336–52, 357–58
  ecclesiology and, 306–17, 355–57, 360
  exegesis and, 287–90, 294–95

flesh, spirit and, 271–84, 318, 336–52
interdisciplinary studies and, xi–xii
soteriology and, 293–94, 362
the Spirit and, 299–304, 336–52, 355–63
ethnicity, grace and, 309
Eucharist, the, 66
example, Christ as, 68–69, 106–7
exchange, happy, 136
exegesis
  apocalyptic and, 204–6, 218–19
  ethics and, 287–90, 294–95
  harmonization and, 112–13
  Reformation, 92–96, 103–5, 117–31
  translation and, 47–56, 163–65, 166–67, 170, 171–73
  the Trinity and, 258–59
  See also Scripture
exodus narrative, 10–11
expectation, time and, 252–53

faith
  Abraham and, 97–100, 105–10
  apocalyptic and, 164–65, 166–67, 170, 171–75, 181
  as co-crucifixion, 122n10, 166
  ecumenism and, 79
  as gospel, 189–90
  imputation and, 111–12
  justification and, 44, 47, 56–58, 67–69, 118–20
  the law and, 87–89, 100–103, 109–10
  the Messiah and, 123–24, 125–28, 143–45
  modern theology and, 150–55
  participation and, 132–42, 156–58
  passive, 129–31
  reason and, 110–11
  the Reformers and, 145–50
  righteousness and, 95–96
  time and, 244–45
family, seed as, 16–17

Subject Index

Father, the, 209–12, 216
favor, gift and, 139–40
favor Dei, 98
Finnish School, 132–42
flesh
  allegory and, 223–25, 228
  spirit and, 271–84, 318, 321–34, 336–52
forensic apocalyptic, 169–71, 180
Formula of Concord, 133, 134, 140
freedom, Christian, 66–67, 278–80, 291, 301, 355–56
fruits, spiritual, 340–41, 359
functionality, ethical, 290–93

genres, rhetorical, 320n3
gentiles, 84, 210–12
gift, favor and, 139–40
gospel, the, xi, 118–19, 135–37, 187–99, 245
government, 72
grace, God's, 98, 102–3, 139–40, 306–17

Hagar, 55–56
happy exchange, 136
harmonization, 112–13
Harnack, Adolf von, 74–75
hebraica veritas, 49, 50. *See also* canon, the
Hebrew Bible, 49–52
heresy, 49, 54–55
heretical imperative, the, 35
hermeneutics. *See* exegesis
history, salvation
  apocalyptic and, 203–4, 205
  Christology and, 231–32, 237
  ethics and, 278–80
  time and, 249, 252–53
honor, competition for, 311–16
honorific, *Christos* as, 3–4
humility, virtue of, 360–61

I, divided, 348–49
identity, human, 197–99, 213–15. *See also* anthropology
imitation of Christ, 68–69, 106–7
immediate agency, divine, 260–62, 265. *See also* agency

imperative, the, 287–99
implicit ethics, 295–99
implicit imperatives, Pauline, 288–89
imputation
  faith and, 111–12, 157–58
  incarnation and, 138–39
  of righteousness, 171
  sin and, 175, 180–81
incarnation
  Christology and, 4, 21–22, 135–42, 233–37
  justification and, 113–15
  Marcionism and, 59
incorporation, 14–23. *See also* participation
indicative, the, 287–99
individual, the, 68–69, 70, 71–72
indulgences, 102
inheritance, Israel's, 210–12
initiative. *See* agency
interpretation, biblical. *See* exegesis
is, ought and. *See* indicative, the
Isaac, 223–25
Isaac the Jew, 45
Ishmael, 223–25
Israel
  apocalyptic and, 203–4, 210–12, 216
  of God, 37–38
  the Messiah and, 4–7, 20–21
  salvation history and, 231–32, 237
iustitia formalis, 111, 120, 130

James, the Epistle of, 353–54
Jerome, 41, 47–56
Jerusalem, 4, 226–29
Jesus. *See* Christology
Joest, Wilfried, 149–50
Joint Declaration on the Doctrine of Justification, 75–76, 159–62
Judaism
  apocalyptic and, 203–4
  the early church and, 43, 45, 48, 50
  grace and, 309

  justification and, 66–67, 71, 82–90
  the Messiah and, 3–23, 143–45
  translation of, 24–39
judgment, ethical, 297
Jüngel, Eberhard, 152–54
justification
  apocalyptic and, 163–83
  the cross and, 191–92, 194
  the early church and, 40–61
  ecumenism and, 62–81, 159–62, 171
  the Finnish School and, 132–42
  Judaism and, 24–39, 143–45
  the law and, 82–90, 143–45, 155–58
  modern theology and, xi, 150–55, 160–62
  participation and, 14–23, 71–81, 217–18
  the Reformers and, 91–116, 117–31, 145–50
  See also law, the

kingdom, the, 359–60

Laato, Timo, 139–40
land, promise of, 13
law, the
  apocalyptic and, 165, 166–67, 169, 203–4
  court metaphors and, 155
  the cross and, 192, 196–97
  as curse, 83–87, 100–103, 108
  the early church and, 46–47, 54
  ethics and, 282, 331–34, 337, 339
  faith and, 94–96, 109–10
  gospel and, 189–90
  grace and, 308–9
  justification and, 66–67, 72, 82–90, 118–23, 135–37
  love and, 107, 280
  the Messiah and, 125–28, 143–45
  the Spirit and, 300–301, 355, 358, 359, 362
  time and, 244–45
  the Trinity and, 261
  See also justification

Subject Index

Lectures on Galatians 1535 (Luther), 134–42
liberty. *See* freedom, Christian
limitations, ecumenical, 63–64
linguistic form, 287–90, 296
literary criticism, 47–56
lived ethics, 297
logic, 97–100, 296. *See also* reason
Lord's Supper, the, 66
love, Christian
  ethics and, 279–80, 284, 310–16
  faith and, 130–31
  justification and, 69–70
  the law and, 107, 358, 359
  See also service, Christian
Luther, Martin, 73, 91–116, 117–31, 145–46
LXX. *See* Septuagint, the (LXX)
Lysis (Plato), 326–27

Maccabean Revolt, 34–35
Mannermaa, Tuomo, 132–42
Marcionism, 58–60
Martyn, J. Louis, 163–68, 234–35, 239–40
Mason, Steve, 28–33
mediate agency, divine, 260–62, 265. *See also* agency
Messiah, the, 3–4. *See also* Christology
mission, 67, 69, 70–71, 80
modus loquendi theologicus, 97
monasticism, exegesis and, 103–4
monotheism, 262–66
motive, ethics and, 296–97, 336–52

narrative, Pauline, 201, 219, 243–47
narratives, messianic, 4–7, 9–11
narrative theology, 345
nativity, time and, 253–56
natural agency, divine, 262–66. *See also* agency
new creation. *See* ages, apocalyptic; creation
new perspective on Paul (NPP), xi, 76–81, 129, 160–62

New Yale School. *See* new perspective on Paul (NPP)
norms, ethical, 296
NPP. *See* new perspective on Paul (NPP)

obedience, faith and, 88–89
objectivism, christological, 178–79
ontology, theological, 182–83
Osiander, Andreas, 140–41
ought, is and. *See* imperative, the

paralysis, believer's, 324–26
paraphrase, 104–5
participation
  apocalyptic and, 163n9, 213–15, 217–18
  the cross and, 122n10, 166
  the Finnish School and, 132–42
  justification and, 14–23, 62–81, 144–50, 156–57
  the law and, 85n5, 122–23
passion, the. *See* cross, the
paternity. *See* Father, the
patience, Christian, 359n24
Paul, the apostle, xi, 245–47, 286
Pelagianism, 71–72
Pelagius, 41
penal substitution, atonement as, 180–82
people of God, 18. *See also* ecclesiology
personalism, philosophy of, 149–50
perspective, distancing, 319–21
Peter, the apostle, 49–55, 57–58, 66–67, 189
Philo, 221–22, 224–25
philology, 47–56. *See also* literary criticism
Pietism, 148–49
Platonization, allegorical, 223–27
poetics, Pauline, 205–9, 215–18
polemic, Pauline, 219
political, the Messiah as, 4, 23
polytheism, 281

practice of death, Hellenistic, 192–93
pragmatism, American, 345–46
prayer, 71, 349–52
preexistence, Christ's, 260
prescriptive ethics, 294–95
promises, God's, 100

ransom, atonement as, 167–68
reason, 80, 97–100, 110–11, 278–79, 339
reconciliation, 71
rectification, justification as, 164–65, 167, 173–74. *See also* righteousness
Reformation, the, 145–50
relationship, category of, 149–50
remembrance, 64–67
resurrection, the
  apocalyptic and, 168, 174–75, 176–77, 179, 216–17
  ethics and, 274, 283–84
  the Messiah and, 19–20
revelation, atonement and, 179. *See also* apocalyptic writing
righteousness
  faith and, 95–96, 111–12, 120, 130
  justification and, 114–15, 118–19, 171
  types of, 136–37
Ritschl, Albrecht, 148–49
rivalry, social, 311–16
Romanticism, 149–50

salutation, Pauline, 200–202, 209
salvation. *See* soteriology
salvation history. *See* history, salvation
sanctification, ethics and, 362
Sarah, 55–56, 60, 226–27
Scripture
  apocalyptic and, 204–6, 218–19
  ethics and, 294–95
  justification and, 47–56, 59, 79–80, 82–90
  See also exegesis

Second Vatican Council, 75
sedes doctrinae, 258–59
seed, family as, 16–17
self-deception, 360–61
Septuagint, the (LXX), 49, 50–51
service, Christian
 ecumenism and, 80
 ethics and, 279–80, 284, 310–16
 justification and, 69–70
 the Spirit and, 355–56
 See also love, Christian
shame, virtue of, 314
sharing, community and, 315–16
simul iustus et peccator, 112, 146
sin
 apocalyptic and, 165, 169, 176, 180–81, 212–13
 Christology and, 234–35
 creation and, 232–33
 inward, 102–3
 the law and, 84–87
 righteousness and, 112, 146
situational ethics, 297
society. *See* community, ethics and
sola fide, 44, 47
Son of God. *See* Christology
soteriology
 apocalyptic and, 212–13, 217–18
 atonement and, 174n40, 178–81
 ethics and, 293–94, 356, 362
 the Messiah and, 18–23
 salvation history and, 231–32
soul, the, 277
sperma, 16–17
Spirit, the
 allegory and, 223–25
 the early church and, 43–44, 47
 ethics and, 299–304, 312–16, 336–52, 355–63
 faith and, 126–28
 flesh and, 271–84, 318, 321–34
 justification and, 67, 178
 the Trinity and, 260–65
style, Pauline, 218–19
subjective genitive, 164–65, 170, 171–74, 183
supersessionism, 216
supralapsarian Christology, 235–38
syllogisms, Pauline, 97–100. *See also* reason

Teachers, the, 189n7, 190n9
Ten Commandments, 130–31. *See also* law, the
theosis, 132–42. *See also* participation
Thomas Aquinas, 72
time, fullness of, 239–57
Torah. *See* law, the

tradition, ethics and, 296
transgression, 84–87
translation, 163–65, 166–67, 170, 171–73, 189n8
Trent, Council of, 73–74
Trinity, the, 42–44, 59, 151–52, 258–67
typology, allegory and, 220–23

unconditional, grace, 308–9
unio cum Christo, 146
union. *See* participation
unity, Christian, 81. *See also* ecclesiology
universal ethics, 297

values, ethical, 296
Vatican II. *See* Second Vatican Council
Victorinus, Marius, 41, 42–44
vita passiva, 129–31
von Harnack, Adolf, 74–75
Vulgate, the, 50

Webster, John, 151–52
will, human. *See* agency
wisdom, gift of, 359
Word, the, 137
word count, *Christos* and, 7–9
works, 100–101, 118–22, 130–31. *See also* law, the
world, the, 280–81
Wright, N. T., 234–35, 237n27

Zimmermann, Ruben, 287–99

Scripture Index

Old Testament

Genesis
1–11 231
1:27 226n27, 227
2:7 226n27
3–11 238n27
6:1–4 224
6:3 273n5
12 10, 99
12:2–3 19n51
12:3 16, 244
13:15 16n44
15 10, 12, 13n38, 15, 16, 99
15:4 12
15:5 12
15:6 124, 125, 244, 253
15:16 14n39
16 55–56, 60
16:10–12 56
16:21 58
17 56, 66
17:8 16n44
17:10–14 253
17:20 56
18:18 16n43, 19n51
21:9 223
21:9–10 222, 223
22 99
22:17–18 125
22:18 19n51
24:7 16n44
26:4 19n51
28:14 19n51
49:10 4n6

Exodus
3:6 13n38
3:13–15 13n38
3:16–22 13n38
4:22 15n41, 210

Leviticus
18:5 88–89, 101, 119n4, 127
19:18 63, 358

Numbers
16:22 273n5
24:17 4n6
27:16 273n5

Deuteronomy
6:4–5 128, 128n19
21:22f 145
21:23 51
26 5
27–28 207
27–30 6, 86n6
27:15–26 83, 85, 86n6
27:26 51, 83, 85–87, 100, 101, 119n4, 121, 122, 126, 245, 327n27
28–30 86n6
28:58–59 245
30:10 245

2 Samuel
7:4–17 4n6
7:12–14a 207n14

Ezra
9 6

Nehemiah
9 6
9:29 89

Esther
8:17 31

Psalms
2 4n6, 6n14, 10, 13, 21n59
3:8 264
8 4n6
19:5 63
51:10 350n54
72 6n14, 13
89 6n14
105 6
106 6
110 4n6
118:30 332n48
119:30 332n48
143:2 80

Proverbs
6:23 332n48
18:2 333n51

Isaiah
11:1–10 4n6
31:3 273n5
40–55 11
51:4 332n48
53:6 181n52
53:12 103
54:1 55, 226
63:9 261
63:16 210
64 210
64:8–9 210

Jeremiah
17:7–8 341n25
31:9 211
31:34 125

Ezekiel
20:11 88–89
20:13 88
20:21 88

Daniel
2 6
7 6
9 6, 11

Hosea
1:7 261
1:10 265

Joel
2:28 273n5

Habakkuk
2:4 87, 101, 119n4, 123n13, 194

Old Testament Apocrypha

1 Maccabees
2 6

2 Maccabees
2:21 32, 34
4:13 32n45, 34
8:1 32, 34
14:38 32, 34

4 Maccabees
4:26 32

Sirach
1:26 359n23
15:1–4 359n23
24:1–34 359n23

New Testament

Matthew
1 7n17
5:21–22 338
5:27–28 338
7:16–20 338
7:17–18 338n11, 341n25
9:6 44
11:19 226n23
12:33–35 338
19:17 109
22:2 196n29
22:35–40 358

Mark
7:17–23 338
12:17 196n29
12:28–34 358
14:36 301
14:38 274

Luke
1 7n17
6:43–45 338
7:35 226n23
10:25–28 358
10:29–37 358
20:25n30 196n29
24:25–27 7n17
24:44–46 7n17

John
1:1–3 263
1:29 113n82
3:3 228
3:6 263, 274
3:6–8 228
3:13 228
3:16–17 266
6:63 274
8:58 255n23
13:15 107
13:34 280
19:11 282
20:21 346

Acts
6:14 35n57
7 7n17
9 195
9:1–22 64
10:28 84n3
10:36 196n29
26:24 100
28:17 35n57

Romans
1–5 170
1:1 170
1:3–4 22n62, 274
1:13 321n8
1:16–17 65, 70
1:17 123n13, 194
1:18–3:20 70
1:18–25 80
1:29–31 310, 333n55
1:32 128n19
2:12–29 89n11
2:17 77
2:17–24 198n34
2:23 77
2:26 128n19
2:29 315
3 15
3:9 170, 174
3:19 327n28
3:21–8:38 70
3:21–22 124n13
3:21–26 174
3:22 164, 170, 173
3:25 170, 171
3:26 164, 170
3:27 77
3:29 17
3:29–30 80
4 13, 97, 105
4:2 77
4:3 244
4:4 47
4:5 171, 175
4:6–8 171
4:7 175
4:13 360
4:17 174n41
4:19 226
4:25 168, 174, 175
5:1 65
5:1–11 70
5:5 301, 304, 340, 345
5:6 171
5:6–9 21n60
5:7 173n39
5:8 21n60, 171
5:8–10 292
5:11 170
5:12 45
5:12–21 170, 237n27
5:15 292
5:16 128n19
5:18 128n19
6 15
6–8 170, 293
6:1–11 71
6:2 288n10, 289n17
6:4 193n19
6:6 289n17
6:6–7 292
6:10 288n10
6:10–12 289n17
6:11–12 288n10
6:13 71
6:16 71
6:18–19 71
7 70, 170, 224n18, 328n34, 348
7:7–25 325, 328
7:14–20 328
7:14–25 325, 348n48, 349
7:15 324, 328n33, 348n48
7:16 328n33
7:17–18 225n21
7:18 328n33
7:19 328n33
7:20 328n33
7:23 276, 277
7:24 70, 73
7:25a 70

8 10, 13, 273, 302
8:1 170
8:1–17 331
8:1–30 237n27
8:3 21, 174, 176, 262, 265, 266
8:3–4 292
8:4 128n19, 277
8:9 225n21, 303
8:9–11 5n13, 21n57
8:12–17 301
8:13 292, 302
8:14 333, 333n52
8:14–17 210n20
8:14–30 71
8:15 263, 303
8:16–17 212n25
8:17–25 10n30
8:18–25 208
8:18–39 215n33
8:19 207
8:22 77
8:29 68, 237n27
8:29–30 232, 235, 238
8:31–32 21n61
8:32 265, 266
8:35 21n61
8:37 21n61
8:39 21n61
9 7
9–11 22n62, 37, 38n65
9:4–5 36
9:5 22n62
9:6 38
9:14–29 38
9:27 38
9:31 38
9:31–32 39
10 7
10:1 321n8
10:3 39
10:4 22n62
10:5 89nn10–11
10:9 317
10:9–10 173
10:12 22n62
10:13 327n27
10:16–17 127n18
10:18 63
10:19 38
10:21 38
11:2 38
11:7 38
11:20–31 71
11:25 38
11:25–32 38
11:26 38

11:36 263
12:3–8 67, 313
12:10 313
13:9 358
13:12 288n10
13:13 333n55
13:14 288
14:1–15:13 71
14:15 334n58
14:17 65
15:4 327n28
15:6 263
15:7 334n58
15:27 274
15:30 304

1 Corinthians

1 319
1:18–2:5 213
1:26–31 308
1:30 146, 174, 175, 263
2–3 273, 278
2:6–8 164
2:8 164
2:12–15 263
2:14 44
2:16 68n14
3:3 278
3:5–17 319
3:9–17 64
3:13 327n31
4:1–5 315
4:14–15 68
4:16 68
5:3 274
5:5 274n6
5:7 288n10, 289n17
5:8 288n10
5:10–11 333n55
6:5 315
6:9–10 333n55, 356, 360
6:11 288n10
7:3–4 313
7:24 321n8
8–10 319
8:5 264
8:5–6 237n27
8:6 260, 263
9:11 274
9:24–27 153
10:11 221, 222
10:11b 247
10:18 38
11:1 68
12–14 319

12:7 304
12:12–27 67
12:12–31 313
13 320
14 320
14:2 329, 330n40
14:20 321n8
15 319
15:1–11 68
15:9 64
15:20–28 237n27
15:21–28 215n33
15:24 164
15:40 227n26
15:48 227n26
15:50 356
15:50–57 215n33

2 Corinthians

3 280
3:6 44, 274
3:7 38
3:13 38
4:4 164
4:16–5:10 228n28
5 155
5:5 291
5:17 67, 203, 245
5:18 80
5:18–19 288n10
5:20 288n10
5:20–21 155–56
5:21 103, 113n82, 176, 180
6:6 333n56
6:6–7 333n56
6:6–7a 333n55
8–9 316
8:9 260
12:20–21 310, 333n55

Galatians

1 45n20, 212
1–2 88, 195, 320
1–4 332, 334, 354–55
1:1 8n19, 201, 206, 209, 213, 244, 245, 261
1:1–4 123
1:1–5 209
1:2 233
1:3 8n23, 244
1:3–4 290, 292
1:3–5 200–201, 215
1:4 7n18, 79, 125, 164, 165, 171, 188, 193, 196, 201, 202, 206, 209, 241, 242, 244, 245, 255n22, 296, 298, 307
1:6 8n20, 23, 63, 188–89, 201, 241, 246, 256, 308
1:6–7 263
1:6–7a 246
1:6–9 188, 191, 249
1:6–10 321
1:7 8n20, 63, 188, 246
1:8 8n20, 63, 206, 246
1:9 8n20, 63, 207, 241, 242, 246, 247
1:10 189, 241nn12–13, 242, 246, 296
1:11 8n20, 43, 321, 334
1:11–12 189, 206
1:11–16 205
1:11–17 308
1:11–5:1 321
1:12 261
1:13 27, 203
1:13–14 25, 27, 30, 32, 36, 38, 39, 189, 189n4, 241, 245
1:13–16 64
1:13–17 308
1:13–2:16 64
1:14b 197
1:15 197, 241n11, 262
1:15–16 25, 246
1:15–23 189
1:16 8n20, 8n22, 65, 88, 206, 308
1:16–2:14 88
1:17 241
1:18 241, 242
1:19 8n23
1:21 64, 241n13, 246
1:22 17n49, 214, 245
1:23 8n20, 241, 246
2 17, 21, 22, 30, 42n7, 67, 189, 191, 212
2–3 121, 353–54
2–4 125n14
2:1 241, 242
2:1–10 63, 65
2:1–14 246
2:2 8n20, 206, 233, 246
2:3 66, 320
2:4 63, 207, 214, 296
2:5 8n20, 63, 189n6, 241, 246
2:5–18 191
2:6 54, 312, 314, 327n31

2:6–7 66
2:7 8n20, 241
2:7–8 38
2:8 37
2:9 63, 66, 77, 241, 314
2:9–10 316
2:10 44n16
2:11 66, 189, 241n11
2:11–13 52
2:11–14 48, 52–55, 57, 66, 84
2:11–21 187n1, 308
2:12 66, 85, 124, 241, 242
2:12–21 355
2:14 8n20, 25, 30, 32, 38, 126, 189, 189n6, 218, 241n11, 309
2:15 7n18, 42n7, 124, 124n14, 189
2:15–16 37, 66, 83, 125n14, 143, 191
2:15–18 191–92
2:15–21 20, 83–85, 171
2:15–3:29 124
2:15–5:12 67
2:16 8n19, 52n51, 63, 69, 79–80, 121, 122, 123, 123n13, 124, 124n14, 125, 125n14, 162, 163–68, 170, 171, 173, 190, 191, 213, 244, 245, 285
2:16–21 125, 127n18
2:17 7n18, 8n19, 84, 156, 214, 217
2:18 84, 86, 241n10
2:19 58, 86, 110, 122, 171, 192, 193, 203, 206, 308, 332, 357
2:19a 192
2:19–20 18, 65, 68, 70, 125, 147, 156–57, 166, 187n1, 191, 192, 194, 197, 207, 214, 274, 298, 299
2:19b–20 156, 212
2:19–21 84, 85
2:20 8n22, 21, 58, 88, 124n13, 127, 128, 193, 194, 206, 210, 213, 217, 241nn11–12, 248, 266, 307, 309, 314
2:20bc 192
2:20c 304

2:21 8n19, 47, 122, 123, 126, 191, 192, 217, 244, 307
3 10, 11, 14, 123n13, 170, 195, 212, 300, 355
3–4 201, 308, 326n25, 359n21
3:1 8n19, 57n65, 67, 69, 157, 207, 219, 243, 246, 247
3:1–4 44
3:1–5 11n31, 104, 128, 190, 205, 246, 259, 300, 362
3:1–6 128, 249
3:1–18 49
3:1–4:7 262, 264
3:2 69, 122, 123, 124, 127, 127n18, 195, 245, 273, 300, 331n45, 332
3:2–4 347n46
3:3 96, 119n4, 127, 241, 247, 273, 274, 301, 331n45, 341
3:4 246, 300
3:5 97, 122, 123, 124, 127, 127n18, 207, 245, 331n45
3:5–6 126
3:5–7 97–98
3:6 8n19, 11, 12, 47, 97, 109, 124, 125, 127n17, 177, 244, 253
3:6–7 98–99
3:6–8 157
3:6–9 12, 190
3:6–14 11n31, 12, 96–116, 117–31, 162, 163–68, 177
3:6–4:7 11, 210
3:7 83, 124, 125, 125n14
3:7–9 124
3:7–10 83
3:8 8n19, 16n43, 127n17, 165, 205, 241, 244, 245, 247, 249
3:8–9 207
3:9 83, 99, 105, 124, 125, 125n14
3:10 51, 82, 83, 85, 87, 100, 109, 120, 121, 125n14, 126, 128, 128n20, 130, 207, 245, 296, 327, 327n28
3:10a 86, 122
3:10b 122
3:10–11 119n4
3:10–13 155
3:10–14 11, 82–90, 107, 119, 333
3:10–21 332
3:11 8n19, 87, 101, 155, 165, 244
3:11b 87
3:11–12 82, 87–89, 194
3:11–13 122
3:12 46, 88, 101, 119n4, 123, 123n13, 124, 125, 144
3:12b 127
3:13 86, 115, 125, 128, 128n20, 171, 207, 210n22, 213, 296
3:13–14 51, 83, 101, 102, 112, 245
3:14 8n20, 124, 126, 127, 214, 224n17, 245, 331n45
3:15 12, 46, 190
3:15–18 104
3:15–20 124
3:15–22 11n31, 12
3:16 4, 8n20, 12, 16–17, 19, 123n12, 125, 126, 207, 207n14, 214, 234, 244, 263
3:16–22 12n36, 15, 16
3:17 8n20, 124, 241, 244, 249
3:17–22 17n47
3:17–29 228
3:18 8n20, 10, 126, 241n12, 245
3:19 8n20, 206, 207n14, 242, 244
3:19–20 12n35, 17, 261, 263
3:19–25 66, 80
3:19–5:12 49
3:20 42, 244, 263
3:21 8nn19–20, 217, 244
3:21–22 123
3:21–25 124
3:22 7n18, 8n20, 12, 13, 17, 44, 47, 124, 125, 125n15, 164, 170, 171, 213, 244
3:22–29 125

3:23 124, 241, 244, 252, 332n47
3:23–25 204
3:23–26 125n15
3:23–27 301
3:23–29 11n31, 13, 298, 355
3:23–4:7 11n31
3:24 8n19, 13, 66, 124, 250, 252, 327n26
3:24–25 244
3:24–27 15
3:24–29 14, 19
3:25 13, 15, 124, 241n12
3:25–26 252
3:25–27 249
3:25–29 124
3:26 15, 190, 195, 207, 210, 211, 213, 214
3:26–28 207
3:26–29 67
3:27 15, 193n19, 248, 288, 327n28
3:27–28 214
3:27–29 196
3:28 15, 81, 196, 196n29, 197, 214, 218, 243, 263, 285, 308, 312
3:28b 15
3:28–29 196
3:29 8n20, 10, 12, 15, 18n49, 20, 124, 126, 198, 210, 214, 244
4 10, 11, 14, 43, 260, 273, 300, 301, 327
4–5 302
4:1 8n23, 241, 327n28
4:1–2 326n25
4:1–3 327n26
4:1–7 10, 11n31, 12n36, 13, 15nn40–41, 126, 300
4:1–11 297
4:2 241, 242, 301
4:3 207, 241n11, 244, 260, 280, 301
4:3–7 209
4:4 8nn22–23, 14, 21, 43, 49, 228n29, 239–48, 250, 252, 253, 254, 255, 332n47
4:4–5 213, 245, 249, 280, 290, 292, 332
4:4–5a 249
4:4–6 128, 301

4:4–7 207, 258–67
4:5 128, 171, 210n22, 266
4:5 332, 332n47
4:6 8n22, 21n57, 47, 69, 128, 212n25, 244, 253, 257, 259, 263, 265, 266, 301, 303, 331n45
4:6–7 210, 245
4:7 10, 69, 210, 241n12, 259, 260, 263, 264
4:8 241n13, 244, 246, 265
4:8–9 207, 264, 308
4:8–11 11n31, 13, 205, 300
4:9 22n63, 69, 80, 203, 204, 241nn10–11, 242, 246, 260, 265, 280, 290, 301
4:10 241, 242, 246, 281
4:11 246
4:12 68, 288
4:12–20 297
4:13 8n20, 241, 246
4:13–14 69, 80
4:14 68, 206, 246
4:15 206, 246
4:17 246
4:18 315
4:19 21, 68, 194, 208, 214, 241n10, 242, 243, 246, 247
4:20 241n12, 246
4:21 88, 126, 332n47
4:21–26 355
4:21–31 55–56, 58–59, 60, 80, 126, 128, 207, 220–29, 265, 279, 296, 308
4:21–5:1 15n40
4:22 296
4:22–31 47
4:23 8n20, 124, 126, 223, 224, 226
4:24 126, 220–21, 226, 244, 279
4:24a 55
4:24–27 224n16
4:25 204, 227, 241n11, 244
4:25–26 208
4:26 47, 223, 226–27, 228
4:27 55, 226, 296

4:28 8n20, 126, 223, 224, 244
4:28–29 125n14, 126, 223n16
4:28–31 224n16
4:29 126, 223, 224, 224n18, 225, 226, 227, 228, 241n11, 241n13, 242, 331n45
4:29a 224
4:29ab 224
4:29b 224
4:30 224n16
5 129, 201, 273, 333n56, 340–45, 348, 359, 363
5–6 293, 313, 354–55, 356, 362
5:1 80, 171, 204, 205, 213, 219, 241n10, 244, 279, 296, 318, 319, 321, 334, 341, 355
5:1–5 190
5:1–6 17n49, 355
5:1–24 289
5:1–6:10 355, 356
5:1–6:17 355n7
5:2 18n49, 320
5:2–3 246
5:2–4 204, 321
5:2–6 321
5:2–7 21n54
5:2–12 38, 321
5:3 241n10, 246, 247
5:4 8n19, 69, 121, 128, 245, 307
5:4–5 126, 162, 163–68, 177
5:5 8n19, 47, 128, 208, 247, 331n45
5:5–6 127, 321
5:6 18n49, 69, 85, 89, 122n10, 124, 127, 128, 130, 197n32, 214, 215n34, 245, 279, 293, 296, 308, 309, 355
5:6a 128
5:7–9 247
5:7–10 208, 215n34
5:7–12 297, 321
5:8 82, 217, 274n7
5:10 8n23, 38, 217, 246, 315n26, 327n30
5:11 8n19, 213, 241n13, 246

5:12 206, 246, 247
5:13 245, 279, 282, 296, 310, 313, 318, 319, 321, 332, 334, 355
5:13–14 212, 293, 309, 355
5:13–15 279, 321, 322, 331–34
5:13–25 321–23, 332, 334n58
5:13–26 49
5:13–6:10 288, 306, 309, 310, 334, 354, 356–61
5:14 63, 127, 128, 247, 280, 296, 297, 332, 332n49, 358
5:14–16 127
5:15 280, 310, 312, 333, 334, 358
5:16 128, 171, 299, 300, 325n20, 328, 331n45, 332n50, 336, 338n8, 341, 342, 355, 357n17
5:16–17 205, 336
5:16–18 348n48
5:16–23 247
5:16–24 322, 328, 355n7
5:16–25 301, 318, 321, 325, 331–34, 336–40, 344, 345–48, 350, 352
5:16–26 128, 271, 273
5:17 46, 49, 224n18, 274, 275, 276–77, 318, 323–30, 331, 334, 338, 340n19, 343, 348–49, 355, 357n17
5:17d 332n50
5:17–18 293, 323
5:17–23 329
5:17–24 322
5:17–25 340n18
5:18 128, 245, 331, 331n45, 332, 337, 341, 355, 356
5:18a 328, 333
5:19 128, 345
5:19–20 310
5:19–21 282, 300, 310, 328, 333, 333n55
5:19–23 323
5:19–24 297

5:20 344
5:20–21 310, 358
5:21 128, 208, 241, 246, 247, 315n26, 355n7, 356, 360
5:22 150, 263, 293, 309, 331n45
5:22–23 49, 247, 282, 300, 309, 312–13, 332, 333, 334n58, 354, 355n7, 359
5:23 128, 244, 282
5:24 8n19, 18n49, 124, 247, 283, 292, 299, 316, 325, 356, 357, 357n17
5:24–25 127, 274, 355
5:25 285–86, 288, 289, 294, 299, 300, 301, 302, 305, 309, 331n45, 332n50, 337, 341, 342, 355
5:25a 303
5:26 247, 278, 310, 313, 314, 321, 356
5:26–6:10 247, 321
6 201, 203, 360
6:1 312, 314, 321, 331n45, 333n56, 360
6:1–2 313
6:1–6 307, 313
6:1–10 321
6:2 212, 247, 279, 280, 282, 297, 313, 315, 316
6:2–4 360
6:3 224–25, 314, 360
6:3–5 314
6:4 241n13, 314
6:5 247
6:6 69, 246, 312, 316
6:7 361
6:7–8 315n26
6:7–9 208, 215n34, 361
6:7–10 341
6:8 208, 241, 247, 273, 274, 288, 292, 331n45, 333n54, 361
6:9 69, 241, 247, 361
6:10 63, 150, 241, 246, 247, 273, 321, 334
6:10b 334n57
6:11 244
6:11–14a 196
6:11–16 21n54
6:12 8n19, 213, 246, 283, 327n28

6:12–13 37n64
6:12–16 333n54
6:13 88, 282
6:14 8n19, 8n23, 171, 207, 213, 245, 253, 291
6:14–15 127, 213, 315
6:14–16 309
6:15 38, 64, 67, 85, 124, 127n17, 203, 208, 213, 243n17, 245, 361
6:15–16 86, 316
6:16 37, 38n65, 64, 89, 208, 211, 241, 246, 327n28
6:17 207, 246
6:18 8n23, 331n45
8:14 302
8:15 302
8:16 302
8:18 331n45

Ephesians

1:3–23 237n27
1:4–5 253
1:4–6 255n23
1:9 236
1:9–10 254
1:10 254
2:3 338n8
2:8–10 292
2:12 237
2:13 237
2:19 237
3:5 236
3:16–19 301, 304
4:2 333n56
4:2–32 333n55
4:6 263
4:31 333n55
5:2 334n58
5:3–5 333n55
5:5 360
5:9 333nn55–56
5:21–33 289
5:25 334n58

Philippians

2:1–3 304
2:5–11 237n27
2:6–7 260
2:7 68
2:9–10 175
2:12c–13 289, 292, 294

2:13 291, 343n32
2:20 327n30
2:22 68
3:2–11 308
3:2–21 237n27
3:3 273
3:5 38
3:5–6 36
3:8 65, 69
3:9 123n13, 164, 173, 329n39
3:13 321n8
3:13–14 153
3:15 56
3:20 80, 226
4:8 327n28, 333n55

Colossians

1:5 189n6
1:9–23 237n27
1:15 236
1:15–20 263
1:16 234, 236n25
1:18 236
1:24 329n39
1:26 236
2:5 274
3:5–8 333n55
3:12 333nn55–56
3:13 334n58
3:17 327, 327n30

1 Thessalonians

1:5–6 300
1:6–7 68
1:9 38n68, 327n31
2:7 68

2:11 68
2:13 127n18
4:3–4 288n10
4:13–18 215n33
5:8 288n10
5:12–14 316
5:25 321n8

1 Timothy

1:9 100n30
1:9–10 333n55
3:2–4 333n55
3:8–10 333n55
3:11–12 333n55
3:16 274
4:12 333n55
6:4–5 333n55
6:11 333n55
6:18 333n55

2 Timothy

2:22–25 333n55
2:25 333n56
3:2–4 333n55
3:6 333n51
3:10 333n55

Titus

1:7 333n55
1:8 333n55
2:2–10 333n55
3:3 333n55

Philemon

10 68

Hebrews

1:2 263
2:10 263
11 7n17
11:11 226
11:12 226
11:13 226
11:13–16 226
11:15–16 227
11:16 227

James

1 356
1:2 359
1:4 359n24
1:5 359
1:5–8 362
1:9–11 360
1:12 357, 359, 361
1:12–16 361
1:13–15 360, 361
1:13–27 360
1:14–15 357
1:16 360, 361
1:18 357, 361
1:19–20 360
1:21 357
1:22 360
1:22–25 354
1:23–24 360
1:26 360
1:26–27 357
2 357
2:1 358
2:5 359, 360
2:8 358, 359
2:14–26 353, 354

2:21–25 7n17
3:13 354
3:13–18 354
3:13–4:12 358
3:15–16 357
3:17 359
3:18 359
4:1–3 357
4:1–12 357
4:10 361
5 359n24
5:10–11 7n17
5:17–18 7n17
5:19–20 360

1 Peter

1:18–21 255n23
3:6 226n23
3:18 274

2 Peter

2:18 338n8

1 John

2:16 338n8
4:17–18 350n54

Revelation

21:2 226

Author Index

Aletti, Jean-Noël, xii, 318–34
Alexander Polyhistor, 31n41
Althaus, Paul, 77n43
Ambrosiaster, 41, 44–47, 58
Amir, Yehoshua, 33n50, 34n52
Anderson, Hugh G., 75n33
Aratus, 55
Aristotle, 110, 111
Arius, 113n84
Arminius, Jacobus, 146–47
Attridge, Harold W., 227n26
Augustine, 27, 41, 53–54, 55, 56–58, 59, 60, 71–72, 94, 98n20, 107n58, 250n2, 264n23, 275, 277, 337, 338–39, 343n31, 348, 353
Aune, David E., 161, 192–93, 228n28

Badiou, A., 313n19
Baker, William, 359n23
Barclay, John M. G., x, 23n66, 27n15, 30n37, 189n4, 193n22, 194n25, 198n35, 243nn16–17, 291, 301n37, 303, 304n45, 306–17, 318n1, 326n24, 328n32, 329, 335n1, 341n21, 344n33
Barth, Karl, 27, 150–51, 153, 162–63, 177–83, 249–57
Barton, C. A., 311nn11–12, 311nn14–18, 314n23
Bassler, Jouette M., 223n14
Bauckham, Richard, 263, 355n10, 357n15

Baur, Ferdinand Christian, 65n7
Bayer, Oswald, 129–31, 137n31
Becker, Jürgen, 223n13
Beker, J. Christiaan, 202, 223n14, 226
Benz, Ernst, 42n8
Berger, Klaus, 150
Berger, Peter L., 35
Berkowitz, Beth A., 28n25
Betz, Hans Dieter, 27, 87n8, 212n28, 222n10, 227n25, 263, 289n14, 313n21, 324n14, 328n34
Beutel, A., 145n7
Bickerman, Elias, 35n55
Biel, Gabriel, 100n30, 102
Bieringer, Reimund, 24
Billings, J. Todd, 145n6, 146n9
Bird, Michael F., 156
Blank, Josef, 75n32
Boer, Martinus C. de, 127n18, 161, 162–63, 169–77, 190n9, 193, 202n6, 221, 310n10, 314n24, 315n26, 358n20
Boersma, Hans, 146n9
Bonhoeffer, Dietrich, 154
Bordieu, P., 316–17
Bornkamm, Günther, 9n27
Bornkamm, Heinrich, 337n6
Bornkamm, Karin, 91n1
Bowden, John, 30n35
Bowlby, J., 304n48
Boyarin, Daniel, 28n25, 32n46
Braaten, Carl E., 122n11
Bray, Gerald, 45

Brecht, Martin, 110n71
Bruce, F. F., 260, 289
Brueggemann, Walter, 13n37
Buber, Martin, 149
Budapest Anonymous, 41
Bultmann, Rudolf, 27, 65n7, 75, 121, 286, 293, 303n43
Burchard, Christoph, 69n15
Burkert, Walter, 265n23
Burton, Ernest deWitt, 191, 272
Busch, Eberhard, 146
Bussières, Marie-Pierre, 45, 46n29, 47
Byrne, B., 212n26

Cain, Andrew, 47n33, 48n35, 48n37, 49n39, 52nn48–51
Calduch-Benages, N., 6n16
Callan, Terrance, 261
Calvin, John, 145, 146, 156, 180–81, 254n22, 348
Cameron, John, 50n44
Campbell, Douglas, 129, 193n22, 201n2, 202
Caneday, Ardel B., 123n13, 124n14, 125nn15–16, 127n17
Canlis, Julie, 146n9
Carson, Donald A., 64n3, 157
Casey, Thomas G., 24
Chester, A., 5n12, 8n26
Choi, Agnes, 196n29
Chrysostom, John, 54, 278, 282–83
Cicero, 110, 311
Clement of Alexandria, 275n11

377

Cohen, Shaye J. D., 26n11, 29, 31n42, 32n46, 34n52
Collins, John J., 5n12
Cook, Christopher, 349
Cooper, Stephen, 43, 44n14, 58n66
Cousar, Charles B., 257n30
Cover, Michael B., x, 220–29, 273n5
Cranfield, C. E. B., 121n7
Cranmer, Thomas, 271, 338, 348–52
Cullmann, Oscar, 9n27
Cyprian, 56–57

Dahl, Nils A., 9n27, 18n50, 218n39, 244
Das, A. A., 144n1
Dassmann, Ernst, 71n17
Dautzenberg, G., 296n31
Davids, Peter, 354, 359
Davies, W. D., 13n37, 24n2, 225n22
Davis, B. S., 213n28
de Boer, Martinus C., 127n18, 161, 162–63, 169–77, 190n9, 193, 202n6, 221, 310n10, 314n24, 315n26, 358n20
Deissmann, Adolf, 5n8, 11n32, 21n55
Del Riccio, Roberto, 73n26
de Romilly, J., 320n4
Diestel, L., 148n18
Donaldson, Terence L., 30n35
Downing, Gerald, 187n2
Dunn, James D. G., 11n32, 66n10, 76n40, 122n8, 144, 160, 191, 201n2, 241n9, 254n22, 260, 299n35, 301n38, 322–25, 332, 341–42, 345, 348–49

Eastman, Susan Grove, 38, 64n6, 207n15, 220n1
Ebeling, Gerhard, 73n24, 91, 137, 154
Edwards, Jonathan, 348
Edwards, Mark U., 104n45
Ehmer, H., 147n13
Eisenbaum, Pamela, 30n36
Elliott, Mark W., x, xi, 40–61, 143–58
Engberg-Pederson, T., 296n31
Epimenides, 55

Erasmus of Rotterdam, 93–96, 98, 105nn46–47, 110n71, 112, 116
Erdt, Werner, 44n15
Esler, P. F., 306n3, 311n11
Eusebius, 5n9, 31n41

Fee, Gordon D., 260, 300, 304n46, 342n26, 344–45, 348–49, 354, 355, 356n12, 357, 359n23, 362
Feldman, Louis H., 31n40
Fichte, Johann, 153
Finan, Thomas, 60n73
Fischer, Johannes, 272n3
Fitzgerald, J. T., 333n55
Fitzmyer, Joseph, 173
Fladerer, Ludwig, 71n18
Ford, David, 345, 346, 351
Forde, Gerhard O., 134n15, 349n51
Forsberg, Juhani, 91n1
Fox, Elaine, 343n30
Francke, August Hermann, 148
Fredriksen, Paula, 27n16, 38n68
Frerichs, E., 4n3
Fung, Ronald Y. K., 289n15, 358n20
Furnish, Victor, 286, 293
Fürst, Alfons, 54

Gadamer, Hans Georg, 117–18
Gager, John G., 5n12, 30n36
Garcia, Javier A., xi, 132–42
Gaston, Lloyd, 5n12, 30n36
Gathercole, Simon J., 144, 335n1
Gaventa, Beverly Roberts, x, 21n56, 68n13, 161, 187–99, 202n6, 208n17, 230n1, 262n17
Gazda, E. K., 23n65
Geerlings, Wilhelm, 41, 46
Gerhardsson, Birger, 276n15
Goethe, Johann Wolfgang von, 149
Gombis, Timothy G., x, 82–90
Goppelt, Leonhard, 222
Gorman, Michael J., 21n58, 122n10, 201n2, 214–15n31, 217n38
Grane, Leif, 97
Grant, Robert M., 263
Green, W. S., 4n3
Gregg, Robert, 113n84

Gregory of Nyssa, 167–68, 214
Greimas, A. J., 243
Groh, Dennis, 113n84
Grundtvig, Nikolaj, 154
Gryson, Roger, 48n34
Gualandri, Isabella, 59n70
Gunkel, Hermann, 272n3

Hadot, Pierre, 42
Hafemann, Scott J., x, xi, 117–31
Hagen, Kenneth, 103–4
Hägglund, Bengt, 140
Haimo of Auxerre, 149
Hainz, J., 316n28
Hammer, P. L., 9n27
Hardin, Justin K., 23n66
Harink, Douglas, 202n6, 216n35
Härle, Wilfried, 153
Harnack, Adolf von, 26n14, 74–75, 218
Hart, Trevor, 58n69
Hauerwas, Stanley, 345n41
Hays, Richard B., 84n3, 160, 161n8, 163n9, 178–79, 200–219, 220n1
Hays, Robert B., 200–219, 240–41, 243–44, 260, 279n23, 309n7
Hecht, Richard D., 221n6
Heckel, Ulrich, 25
Heerbrand, Jacob, 147
Heidegger, Martin, 155
Hengel, Martin, 5n11, 20n52, 25, 26n11, 30n35, 144, 145, 192n17, 353–54
Hennings, Ralph, 54n55
Henten, Jan Willem van, 32n48, 34n52
Heshusius, Tilemann, 147–48
Hilary of Poitiers, 44, 47n30
Himmelfarb, Martha, 34n53
Hinde, R. A., 304n48
Hofius, Otfried, 328n35, 329n36
Hofmann, J. C. K. von, 153
Holl, Karl, 150n25
Hooker, Morna, 190n8
Horbury, W., 22n64
Horn, Friedrich W., 287
Horrell, D. G, 294n24
Hübner, Hans, 30n35, 73n25, 315n25
Hultgren, Arland J., 36n59
Hume, David, 80n46

Hunsinger, George, 145
Hunter, David, 47n31
Hurd, John C., 63n2

Ignatius of Antioch, 26

James, William, 346
Jenkins, Ryan, 354n4
Jenson, Robert W., 122n11, 134n10
Jeremias, Joachim, 354n4
Jerome, 41, 45n20, 46, 47–56, 94, 96, 99, 101–2, 103, 116, 281
Joest, Wilfried, 149–50
Johnson, Luke Timothy, 240
Jones, L. Gregory, 345n41
Josephus, 5, 6n15, 31n41, 308n6
Jüngel, Eberhard, 152–54, 255n24, 256n28, 257n31
Justinian, 110

Kahl, Brigitte, 23n66, 313
Kähler, Martin, 153
Kamell, Mariam J., xii, 353–63
Käsemann, Ernst, 233
Keck, L. E., 202n6
Kendall, R. T., 359n24
Kerr, Fergus, 149n21
Kilgallen, J. J., 325n19, 328n35, 329n36
Kirk, J. R. Daniel, 216n36
Klauck, Hans Josef, 222, 223n16
Klein, G., 315n25
Kolb, R., 147n13
Kooten, George H. van, 192n16
Korsch, Dietrich, 145
Kramer, W. G., 8n26
Krostenko, Brian A., 31n40
Kuck, D. W., 314n22, 315n26
Küng, Hans, 151
Kwon, Yon-Gyong, 243n18

Laato, Timo, 25, 133n8, 139–41
LaFollette, H., 304n48
Lambrecht, Jan, 315n24, 315n26, 328
Lehmann, Karl, 75n34, 76n35
Lémonon, J. P., 329n38
Lendon, J. E., 311n11
Levine, Lee I., 33n50
Lévy, Carlos, 225n20
Levy, Ian C., 149n19
Liesen, J., 6n16

Lietzmann, Hans, 33n51, 36
Lightfoot, J. B., 191, 279n24, 348–49
Lohse, Eduard, 148n15, 158, 237n26
Longenecker, Bruce W., 87n7, 197n33, 201n2, 240, 261n11, 301n40
Longenecker, Richard, 354n4
Lüdemann, Gerd, 24, 65n8
Lunn-Rockliffe, Sophie, 45
Luther, Martin, 27, 73–74, 91–116, 117–31, 132–42, 206, 276, 278, 337, 339–40, 343n29, 348, 353, 362

Macaskill, Grant, 58n69
MacDonald, Nathan, 58n69
Malina, B., 311n11
Mannermaa, Tuomo, 123n11, 132–42, 145
Marcion of Sinope, 26, 51n47, 52, 56, 59–60
Marcus, Joel, 161
Marmorstein, A., 33n50
Marshall, L. H., 276n15
Martin, Thomas, 40n1
Martyn, J. Louis, 27–28, 84n4, 122n10, 161, 162–68, 178–79, 187n2, 189, 196, 201n1, 202, 203, 204, 217n37, 221, 223n14, 232–35, 239–41, 242, 252n13, 254n22, 257n30, 261n10, 265n24, 272, 275, 309n6, 314n24, 315n27, 323n12, 325n20
Mason, Steve, 28–33, 36
Matera, Frank, 272n3, 354–55, 356n13, 362
Matlock, R. B., 202n6
Mattes, Mark C., 133n9, 134, 136n25
McCartney, Dan G., 360n26
McCormack, Bruce L., ix, 135n16, 150, 159–84, 255n24
McEvoy, James, 60n73
McGrath, Alister, 148n18, 150n25
McInroy, Mark J., 141n54
Meeks, Wayne, 188n3
Meier, H.-C., 294n26
Meiser, Martin, 40n1, 49n40, 58n67

Melanchthon, Philipp, 92n2, 98, 106–7, 146, 148, 337–38, 339, 341n25, 343n29, 348
Menander, 55
Mikkonen, Juha, 91n1
Mikulincer, M., 304n48
Milbank, John, 155
Miller, David M., 28n25
Milton, John, 58n69
Möhler, J. A., 149
Moll, Sebastian, 59n70
Moo, Douglas J., 357n15
Morales, Rodrigo J., 207, 211n24, 261n12, 310n10
Mühlen, Karl Heinz zur, 337n6
Muller, Richard, 146n11
Mussner, F., 309n6

Neusner, Jacob, 4n3
Ng, D. Y., 23n65
Niebuhr, Karl-Wilhelm, 65n9
Nongbri, Brent, 29n32
Novenson, Matthew V., x, 3–4, 24–39, 123n12, 203n8, 207n14
Null, Ashley, 337n3, 338n7

Oberman, Heiko, 176
O'Brien, Peter T., 64n3
O'Donovan, Oliver, ix
Oepke, Albrecht, 9n27
Olthuis, James, 146n9
Origen, 40n1, 44, 48, 54, 218n42
Osiander, Andreas, 140–41, 146–47, 148

Pannenberg, Wolfhart, 76n35, 152
Pavese, Settimana Agostiniana, 71n18, 72n20
Peirce, Charles, 346
Pelagius, 41
Pesch, Otto Hermann, 72n21, 74n27, 149n20
Peters, Albrecht, 74n27, 149n20, 153, 155
Peterson, Erik, 75
Petzold, Klaus, 103n43
Philo of Alexandria, 55, 221, 224–25, 226n23, 227, 264, 273n5
Plato, 192–93, 326–27
Plumer, Eric, 27n16, 40n1, 57
Plutarch, 31

Pollefeyt, Didier, 24
Pollmann, Ines, 25
Pollmann, Karla, x, xi, 40–61
Porphyry, 53, 54, 55
Powers, D. G., 214n30

Quash, Ben, 345

Rabens, Volker, x, 67n12, 285–305
Raspanti, Giacomo, 43, 47n31, 48–50
Rastoin, M., 320n4
Ratzinger, Joseph, 71, 72n19
Rebenich, Stefan, 51n45
Reno, R. R., 259n4
Riccio, Roberto Del, 73n26
Riches, John, 26n11, 62n1, 187–88, 191, 196n29
Rieger, Reinhold, 73n23
Ritschl, Albrecht, 148–49
Robinson, H. Wheeler, 19
Romilly, J. de, 320n4
Rowe, C. Kavin, 258nn1–2

Saarinen, Risto, 153
Sallust, 312n17
Sanders, Ed P., xi, 20, 24n2, 38n66, 76n39, 118n3, 129n21, 144, 160, 194n26, 215
Schäfer, Rolf, 98n19, 148n18
Schatkin, M. A., 48n34
Scheck, Thomas, 43
Schewe, S., 306n3
Schleiermacher, Friedrich, 148, 149
Schlier, Heinrich, 75, 222n10, 227n25
Schnelle, Udo, 299
Schrage, W., 286n3
Schreiner, Tom, 122n9
Schremer, Adiel, 28n25
Schrenk, Gottlob, 38n67
Schulz, Siegfried, 275
Schulz-Flügel, Eva, 43, 44
Schumacher, William W., 138–39, 141–42
Schütz, John, 188, 195
Schwartz, Seth, 28n25
Schweitzer, Albert, 144, 191, 304n47

Schweizer, Eduard, 259, 262n15
Scott, James M., 86n6, 207n15, 210n23
Segal, Alan F., 25n10, 261n11
Seifrid, Mark A., 64n3
Seils, Martin, 154
Sellin, Gerhard, 223n13, 223n16
Selnecker, Nikolaus, 147
Sextus Empiricus, 31n44
Shaver, P. R., 304n48
Siecienski, A. Edward, 262n17
Smith, James K. A., 146n9
Söding, Thomas, ix, 62–81
Souter, Alexander, 44–46
Spencer, Philipp, 148
Stalder, K., 303n44
Stanley, Christopher D., 10n29, 17n48
Stefani, Massimo, 44n13
Steinmetz, David C., 112n80
Stendahl, Krister, 36n61, 76n38, 118n3, 145
Sterling, Gregory E., 228n28
Still, Todd D., x, 239–48
Stolle, Volker, 91n1
Stowers, Stanley K., 30n36
Strange, James Riley, 357n16
Strüder, Christof, 68n14
Stuhlmacher, Peter, 77n41, 174n41
Stumme, Wayne, 145n8
Sumner, Darren O., 249–57
Swain, Scott R., 258–67

Taylor, Justin, 24
Taylor, Marion Ann, 196n29
Tertullian, 26–27, 59
Theodore of Mopsuestia, 274n7
Tholuck, August, 148n17
Thomas Aquinas, 100n30, 250–51, 254n21, 255n24, 266n25
Thompson, M. M., 211n24
Ticciata, Susannah, 196n31
Trueman, Carl R., 133n7, 136n24
Twomey, Vincent, 60n73

Vainio, Olli-Pekka, 133n4, 147
van Driel, Edwin Chr., 230–38
van Henten, Jan Willem, 32n48, 34n52
Vanhoozer, Kevin, 345

Vanhoye, Albert, 329
van Kooten, George H., 192n16
Victorinus, Marius, 41, 42–44, 48, 57–58, 309n6
Visser, Arnoud S. Q., 73n22
Vlachos, Chris A., 360n25
Volf, Mirslav, 358n21
von Harnack, Adolf, 26n14, 74–75, 218
von Hofmann, J. C. K., 153
Vorholt, Robert, 64n5

Wagner, Falk, 148n16
Watson, Francis, 144n2, 240–41, 260n9
Watson, Philip, 110n73
Webster, John B., 151–52, 153
Wedderburn, Alexander J. M., 19n51
Wells, Kyle, 335n1, 344
Wengert, Timothy J., x, xi, 91–116, 117–18, 119n4, 121, 140–41
Wernle, P., 287n5
Wesley, John, 153–54
Whitlark, Jason A., 357n14
Whitman, Jon, 220n1, 221n2, 228n29
Wigand, Johannes, 147
Wiles, Maurice, 57
Wilk, Florian, 77n42
Williams, Margaret H., 33n50
Williams, Megan Hale, 51n46
Willitts, Joel, 88n9
Wilson, R. McL., 237n26
Wilson, T. A., 128n20, 306n2, 310n7
Winger, M., 309n7
Witherington, Ben, 201n2
Wolter, Michael, 228n30, 294n25
Wood, Susan K., 160n2
Wright, N. T., x, 3–23, 86n6, 87n7, 89n10, 123n12, 160, 201n2, 202n6, 207n14, 216n36, 231–35, 237n27

Young, Frances M., 221

Zahl, Simeon, xi, 137, 335–52
Zetterholm, M., 5n8
Zimmermann, Ruben, 286–99, 302